From the Library
of Julie Wright

Presented to

_____

By

_____

Date

_____

Bible Pathway

The Best Of

Compiled from

Bible Pathway

Dr. John A. Hash

Associate Editors
Barney E. Bell, Benjamin Wallace

THRU THE BIBLE IN ONE YEAR READING 15 MINUTES A DAY

Bible Pathway is a Christ-centered through-the-Bible devotional commentary, and not a theological exposition.

The devotional thought reveals how each day's Bible reading relates to our personal relationship with God, our fellow man, as well as our own spiritual needs.

Its goal is to encourage worldwide reading of "all scripture" as essential to one's spiritual life and growth (see II Timothy 3:16-17).

Bible Pathway adheres to the authenticity and authority of a God-inspired Bible as the foundation of Christianity.

Recommended by leaders in all major denominations, and educators throughout the world.

More than 77 million copies have gone into 186 nations in more than 26 languages since 1974.

The world's most-widely-read through-the-Bible devotional commentary.

Bible Pathway Ministries
P.O. Box 1515
Murfreesboro TN 37133-1515

CONTENTS

Preface

The strength of our spiritual life and our ability to please the Lord will be in exact proportion to the time we set aside to read through the Bible. No one's education is complete without comprehensive knowledge of all the Holy Scripture. And no Christian worker is qualified or fully effective without a basic knowledge of the purpose and application of each book of the Bible.

We are all dependent upon the Holy Spirit to reveal His will as we read His Word. But the Holy Spirit will not reveal what we refuse or neglect to read. And there are no shortcuts to spiritual maturity. Furthermore, the Creator has allotted just one lifetime with a dual responsibility:

1. **To prepare ourselves to be the person God wants us to be.**
2. **To accomplish the purposes for which He created us.**

Think how tragic it would be to fall short of fulfilling God's perfect will ... wasting our few short years achieving material, social, and financial goals for self-gratification – but failing to achieve the purpose for which He created us -- like the steward who buried his talent. He did not waste it like the prodigal son but he eventually heard the master say: *"You wicked and slothful servant ... cast the unprofitable servant into outer darkness ... into everlasting punishment"* [Matthew 25:24-46]. We all have just one life to live. Everyone has just 24 hours in each day. No one has more or less. As stewards of our lives, we are accountable for how we invest our time.

All the world is programmed to feed, strengthen, and enhance the "old nature." But there is only one guide for our "new nature" – the Word of God.

The Best of Bible Pathway is designed to benefit all who desire a better understanding of the Word of God, whether a first-time reader, teacher, or minister. We would emphasize, however, that the devotional commentary is not a substitute for reading the Bible. To do that would be to miss the purpose of *Bible Pathway*. Our prayer is that each reader will devote a minimum of 15 minutes a day, beginning with Genesis, and reading through the entire Bible – at least once each year.

We urge that, as you read through the Bible, you read for the sake of learning truth for your own personal life. All else will follow in its rightful order. *"Let us hear the conclusion of the whole matter: Fear God, and keep his commandments: for this is the whole duty of man"* [Ecclesiastes 12:13].

Introduction

Our Lord Jesus Christ taught that He is the focal point of all Scripture from Genesis to Revelation. After His resurrection, Christ revealed to His disciples the vital importance of Old Testament Scripture: *"Beginning at Moses and all the prophets, he expounded unto them in all the scriptures the things concerning himself"* [Luke 24:27]. And in verses 44-45, He said: *"All things must be fulfilled, which were written in the law of Moses, and in the prophets, and in the psalms, concerning me. Then opened he their understanding, that they might understand the scriptures."* If Jesus is correct, reading the Old Testament is to read about Him and to understand Him more fully. It also provides clarification of the New Testament.

We, too, need our eyes of understanding open to see Christ in the Old Testament and to have the same regard for Old Testament Scripture He had.

Jesus Christ set the example of how important the Old Testament was to Him and should be to us. His emphasis started in the GOSPEL OF MATTHEW with the first recorded words of our Lord following His baptism. After 40 days of fasting, He was tempted of the devil who said: *"If you be the Son of God, command that these stones be made bread."* And Jesus answered and said: *"It is written, Man shall not live by bread alone* [physical necessities], *but by every word that proceeds out of the mouth of God"* [spiritual necessities] [Matthew 4:3-4; compare Deuteronomy 8:3]. By quoting this Old Testament Scripture, our Lord revealed the "Key to Victory" over satanic deceptions. We can have that same victory over Satan, but we need to become familiar with *"every word that proceeds out of the mouth of God."*

Our Lord compared the necessity of eating food for our physical well-being to the necessity of *"every word"* -- all the Scripture -- for our spiritual well-being. When we eat physical food, it is assimilated into our bodies and becomes our very life. Without it, we would soon perish; with it we are strengthened throughout our whole body and no longer able to separate the two. This principle is true with the Scriptures. As we read them, they become much more than just "head knowledge" that provide dos and don'ts; they become our way of life.

Jesus quoted from the Book of Deuteronomy more than any other book. Perhaps it was because Deuteronomy proclaims how vital knowing His Word is to enjoy the best in life, and how disobedience always results in disappointments, sorrows, and suffering.

1

Only the Creator could know what is best, and the God of perfect love appeals to His children: *"O that there were such an heart in them, that they would fear me, and* <u>*keep all my commandments always*</u>*, that it might be well with them, and with their children . . . And these words, which I command you this day, shall be in your heart: And you shall teach them diligently unto your children, and shall talk of them when you sit in your house, and when you walk by the way, and when you lie down, and when you rise up . . . And the Lord commanded us to do all these statutes, to fear the Lord our God, for our good always"* [Deuteronomy 5:29,33; 6:6-7,24].

Jesus made some startling remarks in His Sermon on the Mount when He said: *"Think not that I am come to destroy the law, or the prophets: I am not come to destroy, but to fulfill. For verily I say unto you, Till heaven and earth pass, one jot or one tittle shall in no wise pass from the law, till all be fulfilled. Whosoever therefore shall break one of these least commandments, and shall teach men so, he shall be called the least in the kingdom of heaven: but whosoever shall do and teach them, the same shall be called great in the kingdom of heaven. For I say unto you, That except your righteousness shall exceed the righteousness of the scribes and Pharisees, you shall in no case enter into the kingdom of heaven"* [Matthew 5:17-20].

Some have assumed since Christ was the proclaimer of grace and the dispenser of mercy, the friend of publicans and sinners, He set aside the law since *"we are saved by grace . . . not of works"* [Ephesians 2:8-9].

It is true that all the wonderful promises are far more acceptable and popular today than the Words of Jesus that demand obedience. We fear there are a great many professing Christians who believe that since we are saved by grace, we can break the law with little consequence, and therefore, have license to *"sin, that grace may abound"* [Romans 6:1].

We need to take a serious look at what He said and address the following questions:

What is the meaning of the word "the law"?

The Jewish law was three-fold: Ceremonial, judicial, and moral. The ceremonial law included ordinances to be observed in the worship of God. The judicial law described the ordinances for government of the Jewish nation and the punishment of offenders. The moral law was given and applied not only to Jews but to all mankind.

1. Christ was the fulfillment of the ceremonial ordinances since they were the type and "shadow" of Himself.

2. Christ fulfilled all the law -- restoring its true meaning.

2

3. He perfectly obeyed all the law demanded -- by being the "sacrifice once and for all" and enduring the death on the cross that was due every sinner.

4. He also came to fulfill the moral law in His believers as foretold: *"I will give them one heart, and I will put a new spirit within you; and I will take the stony heart out of their flesh, and will give them an heart of flesh: That they may walk in my statutes, and keep my ordinances, and do them: and they shall be my people, and I will be their God"* [Ezekiel 11:19-20]. He has given to His disciples the Holy Spirit who imparts to believers a love for the law and a desire to obey it. This is confirmed in Romans 3:31: *"Do we then make void the law through faith? God forbid: yea, we establish the law." "That the righteousness of the law might be fulfilled in us, who walk not after the flesh, but after the Spirit"* [8:4].

What did Jesus mean by: *"Unless your righteousness shall exceed the righteousness of the scribes and the Pharisees"* [Matthew 5:20]?

The scribes were the doctors of the law, the teachers, the interpreters, and the Pharisees were known for their legalistic practice of the law. *"The righteousness of the scribes and the Pharisees"* was an external one consisting of meticulous external observances of portions of the Law with equal or greater importance placed upon traditions. That is why Jesus, in denouncing them, said: *"You have omitted the weightier matters of the law, judgment, mercy, and faith: these you should have done"* -- teaching the importance of keeping the moral law [23:23].

Whether it was Phariseeism in Jesus' day or Christendom in our day -- the world over is a religion satisfied with practicing external performances. Millions have been deluded into thinking their external conduct is good enough to insure Heaven as their home. They worship -- not in Spirit and Truth and not with a desire to please and glorify Christ -- but merely to satisfy their social interests. Seldom do we hear anything today about repentance, obedience, or inward holiness. The righteousness which will bring men to Heaven is not only imputed but also imparted righteousness. Justification and sanctification are as inseparable as two sides of one coin. *"For this you know, that no whoremonger, nor unclean person, nor covetous man, who is an idolater, has any inheritance in the kingdom of Christ. Let no man deceive you with vain words: for because of these things comes the wrath of God upon the children of disobedience"* [Ephesians 5:5-6].

Imputed righteousness can be recognized in no other way than by inward righteousness which is its effect in one's life. God requires *"truth in the inward parts"* [Psalm 51:6]. The righteousness that Christ demands results from a reverence for His authority and a true desire to please Him. It can only proceed from a heart that is reconciled to God *"because the carnal mind is enmity against God: for it is not subject to the law of God, neither indeed can be"* [Romans 8:7].

We become partakers of His righteousness at the new birth, when His nature is imparted to us producing *"a delight in the law of God"* [7:22] as a result of being made a *"partaker of the divine nature"* [II Peter 1:4]. It must have been a real shock for His crowd of scribes and Pharisees to learn that they would not qualify to be citizens of His kingdom.

It was ignorance of the Scripture which permitted Phariseeism to flourish, and it is ignorance of God's Word today that has made an "easy believism gospel" so popular in Christendom today.

"By their fruits you shall know them" [Matthew 7:20].

When the Lord was tempted or challenged by the Pharisees, scribes, or Sadducees, he quoted the Old Testament Scriptures. When they asked: *"Why do your disciples transgress the tradition of the elders?"*; our Lord's reply was: *"Why do you also transgress the commandment of God by your tradition?"* He concludes by saying: *"In vain they do worship me, teaching for doctrines the commandments of men"* [15:2-3,9].

Jesus preceded the Parable of the Sower and the Seed in the GOSPEL OF MARK saying: *"Whosoever shall <u>do the will of God</u>, the same is my brother, and my sister, and mother"* [3:35]. Then He illustrated this truth by saying His Word is like seed that is sown. Some seed falls by the wayside -- symbolic of the majority who have a total disregard for the Word of God. Some is sown in shallow ground -- with an immediate response but never taken seriously. Some seed falls among thorns -- in good soil and well received -- but the cares of the world, although not evil in themselves, continue to grow and crowd out the Word; and it becomes unproductive. Some seed falls in good soil -- *"do the will of God"*; and some produces thirty -- sixty -- one hundred-fold [see Mark 4:3-20]. It is a fact you can't do something you don't know, and you can't know the Scriptures that you haven't read.

Again when the Sadducees tempted Him, He said: *"You do therefore err, because you <u>know not the scriptures</u>, neither the power of God"* [12:24]. The word *"err"* means "you have wandered out of the way." They had deceived themselves -- assuming that they knew the will of God and that God would be just as satisfied with what pleased them.

The importance of God's Word is also brought to our attention in the GOSPEL OF LUKE when Jesus said: *"Why call me Lord, Lord and do not the things which I say"* [6:46]. Again, when told His mother and broth-

4

ers wanted to see Him: *"He answered and said unto them, My mother and my brethren are these which hear the word of God, and do it"* [8:21].

On another occasion, when a woman in the crowd to which He was speaking said: *"Blessed is the womb that bare you, and the paps which you have sucked"*; Jesus replied: *"Yea rather, blessed are they that hear the word of God, and keep it"* [11:27-28]. Surely *"the Word of God,"* which Jesus refers to here, is the Old Testament Scriptures.

The opening chapter of the GOSPEL OF JOHN reveals Christ as the Word in Genesis and continues through the Book of Revelation: *"In the beginning was the Word, and the Word was with God, and the Word was God.... And the Word was made flesh, and dwelt among us"* [1:1,14].

Therefore, in every book from Genesis to Revelation, we need to see, within the written Word, Him who is the Living Word. Our great objective in reading all the Bible should be to know Christ, to become more like Him and more fully controlled by the Holy Spirit.

As in Matthew, Mark, and Luke, the Holy Spirit in John reveals how our Lord, in answering His critics, continues to focus attention on the authority and value of the Old Testament when He says: *"Search the scriptures; for . . . they testify of me . . . had you believed Moses, you would have believed me: for he wrote of me. But if you believe not his writings, how shall you believe my words?"* [John 5:39,46-47].

To make it unmistakably clear to would-be followers of today, that possessing eternal life is far more than merely "making a decision," He said to those who believed on Him: *"If you continue in my word, then are you my disciples indeed. And you shall know the truth, and the truth shall make you free"* [8:30-32] -- free from sin; from guilt and condemnation; and free from fear of what others may think, say, or do.

Again and again, Jesus emphasizes the necessity of knowing and living the Word of God. Jesus said: *"If you love me, you will keep my commandments.... He that has my commandments, and keeps them, he it is that loves me: and he that loves me shall be loved of my Father, and I will love him . . . If a man loves me, he will keep my words . . . He that loves me not keeps not my sayings"* [14:15,21,23-24].

When we love someone, we want to do what they like to do, go where they like to go, talk about what they like to talk about; and we wouldn't want to offend or disappoint them. If we love someone, we want to be worthy of their love. *"He that says, I know him, and keeps not his commandments, is a liar, and the truth is not in him"* [I John 2:4].

To give His true followers assurance that they could fully understand all His commandments, Jesus said: *"The Comforter, which is the*

Holy Spirit . . . he shall teach you all things" [John 14:26]. Again, He warns: "If you keep my commandments, you shall abide in my love; even as I have kept my Father's commandments, and abide in his love . . . You are my friends, if you do whatsoever I command you" [15:10,14]. But, my friend, if we are not concerned enough about knowing His will to read His Word, then how can the Holy Spirit teach us "all things"?

Bringing our lives into submission to His will, as recorded in the Scriptures, is the condition upon which Christ said that our prayers will be answered. "If you abide in me, and my words abide in you, you shall ask what you will, and it shall be done unto you" [15:7]. This was uppermost in the heart of Christ as He prayed: "Sanctify them through your truth: your word is truth. As you have sent me into the world, even so have I also sent them into the world. And for their sakes I sanctify myself, that they also might be sanctified through the truth" [17:17-19]. On the other hand, "He that turns away his ear from hearing the law, even his prayer shall be an abomination [revolting, disgusting, loathsome]" [Proverbs 28:9]. Why insult God, believing that He wants to hear what we have to say if we're not concerned to read all of what He has to say?

Let us, therefore, come to the Scriptures reverently, praying that "the God of our Lord Jesus Christ, the Father of glory, may give unto you the spirit of wisdom and revelation in the knowledge of him: The eyes of your understanding being enlightened; that you may know what is the hope of his calling, and what the riches of the glory of his inheritance in the saints, And what is the exceeding greatness of his power to us-ward who believe, according to the working of his mighty power" [Ephesians 1:17-19]. And let the dominating motive in all our reading of God's Word be: "That [we] might walk worthy of the Lord unto all pleasing, being fruitful in every good work, and increasing in the knowledge of God" [Colossians 1:10].

We should be so thankful that He has provided "a lamp for our feet, and a light for our path" [Psalm 119:105]. If we were to walk on the darkest night along the most dangerous path, we would not need a great beam of light to lighten all the area around us. We would only need sufficient light to guide us step-by-step for a safe journey. The Bible does not need to reveal everything in the universe -- only that which is necessary to provide a safe journey through this sin-darkened world. He has not left us in the dark, and, as we continue reading through His Word, we shall always know our next step. We truly need to praise Him.

The only book that records the activities of the first church following the day of Pentecost is the BOOK OF ACTS. In Acts we continue to see the high estimation that His apostles and followers placed upon the Word of God, for it is mentioned more than 30 times in 28 chapters. Beginning with the first converts, it is recorded: *"Then they that gladly received His word were baptized"* [2:41].

As we continue through Acts, the Holy Spirit records: *"Many of them which heard the word believed"*; and, following this, *"Lord, behold their threatenings: and grant unto your servants, that with all boldness they may speak your word . . . And they were all filled with the Holy Ghost, and they spake the word of God with boldness"* [4:4,29,31].

As we read further, Philip was led to an Ethiopian official, who was reading from the Book of Isaiah in the Old Testament. Philip said to him: *"Do you understand what you read?"* And the official replied: *"How can I, except some man should guide me?"* Philip did not guide him by saying: "There is no longer a need to read the Old Testament since the day of Pentecost. Now, we need to hear what Peter and Paul have to say." But Philip did guide him to see Christ in the Old Testament, *"and began at the same scripture and preached unto him Jesus"* [8:30-31,35].

Again the Holy Spirit focuses our attention on the eternal power and importance of the Old Testament Scriptures as Peter spoke to Cornelius and the others who were gathered for that occasion: *"To him give all the prophets witness"*; and when the Holy Spirit brought conviction upon the listeners, we read: *"The Holy Ghost fell on all them which heard the word"* [10:43-44]. What *"word"* could it be? Certainly not the New Testament. It is evident that the New Testament believers were reading, teaching, and preaching from the Old Testament Scriptures.

The concerned believers in Berea *"were more noble than those in Thessalonica, in that they received the word with all readiness of mind, and searched the scriptures daily, whether those things were so"* [17:11]. They did not search the New Testament; it wasn't written yet. We, too, need to be *"more noble."*

The Book of Acts covers about 30 years of church history with a glorious, victorious conclusion: *"So mightily grew the word of God and prevailed"* [19:20].

In the BOOK OF ROMANS, the Holy Spirit speaks through Paul saying: *"I had not known sin, but by the law: for I had not known lust, except the law had said, You shall not covet. . . . the law is holy, and the commandment holy, and just, and good. . . . we know that the law is spiritual"* [7:7,12,14] -- and it becomes our guideline that we might know how we measure up to God's standard of righteousness.

Paul said: *"I delight in the law of God after the inward man"* [7:22]. The indwelling Holy Spirit leads all believers to delight in the law of

7

God: *"That the righteousness of the law might be fulfilled in us, who walk not after the flesh, but after the Spirit . . . . For if you live after the flesh, you shall die"* [8:4,13].

In Paul's first letter to the CORINTHIANS, we discover that: *"The world by wisdom knew not God"* [1:21]. In fact: *"The wisdom of this world is foolishness with God"* [3:19]. All the wisdom of the world with all its science, technology, and intelligentsia is foolishness with God and void of understanding what life is all about.

To achieve the ultimate performance of what manufacturers intend from the equipment they have produced, a manual of instructions is included. And the more complicated the equipment, the more information is provided that the user may achieve its maximum capability.

Our Father has provided just one "manual of instruction" for His children to live by, and it is very detailed. The Bible is absolutely complete and perfect to meet every need and every possible decision for our best interest. *"The law of the Lord is perfect, converting the soul: the testimony of the Lord is sure, making wise the simple. The statutes of the Lord are right, rejoicing the heart: the commandment of the Lord is pure, enlightening the eyes. The fear of the Lord is clean, enduring for ever: the judgments of the Lord are true and righteous altogether. More to be desired are they than gold, yea, than much fine gold: sweeter also than honey and the honeycomb. Moreover by them is your servant warned: and in keeping of them there is great reward"* [Psalm 19:7-11]. What a thrilling incentive for you and me to: *"Study to show ourselves approved unto God, workmen that need not to be ashamed"* [II Timothy 2:15].

Once our eyes are opened to the need for God to have priority in our lives, we enter into a warfare of numerous interruptions and distractions, both from others and even from our own minds.

The enemy in the battle to keep us from reading through the Scriptures is not some other human being, but *"against the rulers of the darkness of this world"* [Ephesians 6:12] -- motivated by Satan.

In the letter to the EPHESIANS, we discover that God has provided an invincible armor to assure our success over sin, self, and Satan.

"Take on the whole armor of God, that you may be able to stand against the wiles of the devil" [6:11]. We discovered that the "key" to victory over Satan when Jesus defeated the devil was the skillful use of the Word of God [Deuteronomy 8:3; Matthew 4:4]. Now we see that five parts of *"the whole armor of God"* covering all the vital areas of life, from head to foot, have to do directly with reading God's Word.

The first part is our *"loins girt about with truth"* [Ephesians 6:14].

Jesus prayed: *"Sanctify them through your truth: your word is truth"* [John 17:17].

The second part is *"having on the breastplate of righteousness"* which His Word alone reveals and makes possible *"being made free from sin you become the servants of righteousness"* [Romans 6:18].

The third part is *"your feet shod with the preparation of the gospel of peace"* [Ephesians 6:15] which involves the prayerful reading of the Word of God to know Him who is our peace.

The fourth part is *"the shield of faith"* [6:16]. Our faith is not increased because we prayed longer or louder, but *"faith comes by hearing, and hearing by the word of God"* [Romans 10:17].

And the fifth part is *"the helmet of salvation"* [6:17]. There is no part of the body which does not require the armor of God. But the most vital of all is the helmet that protects the mind -- the strategic battleground of Satan's attacks. There is a "war" aimed at the mind to defeat every Christian. Paul warned the Corinthian church: *"I fear . . . as the serpent beguiled Eve . . . so your minds should be corrupted"* [II Corinthians 11:3]. The mind by nature is: *"a reprobate mind"* [Romans 1:28]; *"a blinded mind"* [II Corinthians 3:14]; *"causing men to walk in the fleshly mind"* [Colossians 2:18]; and *"enmity against God: for it is not subject to the law of God, neither indeed can it be"* [Romans 8:7]. Our Lord has made it possible for us to be *"more than conquerors"* [Romans 8:31].

"The weapons of our warfare are not carnal, but mighty through God to the pulling down of strongholds; Casting down imaginations, and every high thing that exalts itself against the knowledge of God, and bringing into captivity <u>every thought</u> to the obedience of Christ" [II Corinthians 10:4-5; compare Galatians 5:19-21; Ephesians 5:5-17]. It is our "reasonable" responsibility *"not to be conformed to this world: but to be transformed by the renewing of our mind"* [Romans 12:1-2].

Since our victory over Satan is dependent upon knowing the Scriptures, Satan uses every deception possible to divert our attention from reading the Bible. He poses as a *"roaring lion"* as well as *"an angel of light"* with numerous deceptions.

The Bible is being replaced today not only by the higher critics who deny the authority of the Scriptures, but also by some who *"exalt themselves"* above the knowledge of God with "supernatural revelations" that become substitutes for reading the Word of God. There are wounded and wrecked lives because of false revelations that replace God's Word. We are facing an alarming increase in alternatives for Scripture that pose grave dangers -- including psychiatry, psychology, crystal balls, astrology, palm reading -- the list is growing. And deceptions will increase as we near the end of this age.

At conversion we receive the mind of Christ [I Corinthians 2:16]. We, too, must crucify the lusts of the flesh, deny ourselves, and follow Him. Just as Joshua was *"given"* the land of Canaan, he still had to fight for every foot of it. His gift was dependent upon his faith to advance and defeat the enemy -- not by his wisdom, but by keeping *"all that is written therein"* [Joshua 1:3,8]. This warfare to control the mind was no imaginary thing to the Apostle Paul who said: *"I buffet my body daily lest I myself be a castaway"* [I Corinthians 9:27]. It is essential, but not enough, to renounce all evil thoughts that seek to invade our minds. That vacuum must be replaced by: *"Whatsoever things are honest...just...pure...lovely ...of good report; if there be any virtue, and if there be any praise, think on these things"* [Philippians 4:8].

Finally, we are to use our chief weapon -- *"the sword of the Spirit, which is the word of God"* [Ephesians 6:17]. The Lord Jesus knew the Scripture perfectly. And when the devil tempted Him after 40 days of fasting, on each occasion the Lord quoted from Old Testament Scriptures to overcome him [Matthew 4:4,7,10]. Christ was wielding *"the sword of the Spirit"* [Ephesians 6:17] to defeat Satan. It was true for Him, and it can be true for us.

And when we take *"the sword"* as we are commanded to do, we must face the question, "Just how big is our sword?" We're not talking about just holding the Bible, but how much of *"the sword"* are we familiar with -- does it include all the Bible, Genesis through Revelation?

We need to begin where God begins in Genesis and continue to read through all the Scripture in the order in which the Bible was arranged. We should give God credit for being as wise as the average author, who would expect us to read his book from its beginning to the end in order that we might fully understand what he had in mind.

All the great men of God in the Bible are known for their allegiance to the Word of God. Consider Joshua, who was miraculously successful in the conquest of all of Canaan -- even when ten powerful kings united their armies in an effort to maintain control of the Northern Territory. What was the secret of his success? God made it clear: *"This book of the law shall not depart out of your mouth; but you shall meditate therein day and night, that you may observe to do according to all that is written therein: for then you shall make your way prosperous, and then you shall have good success"* [Joshua 1:8]. His obedience is confirmed as the reason for his miraculous conquest of

10

Canaan. *"As the Lord commanded Moses . . . so did Joshua; he left nothing undone of all that the Lord commanded Moses."* This is followed by: *"And the land rested from war"* [11:15,23].

Job was a giant for God, for *"there was none like him . . . a perfect and an upright man, one that feared God"* [Job 1:8]. The key to his victory over sorrow, rejection, financial collapse, and extreme physical suffering can be seen in his response to his critics: *"I have esteemed his words . . . more necessary than my daily food"* [23:12].

Who wants to be a loser? Hosea gives us a sure plan for failure. It's easy. You don't have to deny that the Bible is the infallible Word of God -- just don't read it. As Hosea observed the decline of the once-great nation of Israel which had rejected the Scripture as its guide through life, God inspired him to write: *"My people are destroyed for lack of knowledge: because you have rejected knowledge, I will also reject you"* [Hosea 4:6]. The chosen people could have continued as the most powerful and respected nation of the world. And for our benefit, God recorded, through the prophet Jeremiah, the reason for their failure: *"My people have committed two evils; they have forsaken me the fountain of living waters, and hewed them out cisterns, broken cisterns, that can hold no water"* [Jeremiah 2:13].

Doesn't it seem strange we spend so many years of our life studying to be successful for the few short 70 years of this life? We insist on 8 years of grade school, 4 additional years of high school, 4 more years of college; and, if we expect to be skilled in some profession, we must add another 4 years of study – all for the brief life of 70 years. And yet we give so little time to the study of God's Word, in preparation for all eternity.

When Paul wrote his second letter to TIMOTHY, we read: *"I call to remembrance the unfeigned faith that is in you"* [1:5]. But how did it come about? He leaves no room for doubt: *"From a child you have known the holy scriptures, which are able to make you wise unto salvation through faith which is in Christ Jesus"* [3:15]. Paul commended Timothy for his great faith -- a result of knowing the Old Testament that was *"able to make him wise unto salvation."* But *"salvation"* is just the beginning. The Holy Spirit continues to unfold the great purpose of God's redeeming love as Paul continues to write: *"All scripture [Old Testament] is given by inspiration of God, and is profitable for doctrine, for reproof, for correction, for instruction in righteousness . . . That the man of God may be . . . throughly furnished"* -- meaning fully equipped, complete, prepared to be the person God wants us to be in order to accomplish the purposes for which He created us [3:16-17]. If the Bible isn't sufficient for all life's needs, then God is truly less than God.

His final message to Timothy was: *"Preach the word; in season, out of season; For the time will come when they will not endure sound doctrine; but after their own lusts shall they heap to themselves teachers, having itching ears; And they shall turn away their ears from the truth, and shall be turned unto fables"* [4:2-4]. There are a million books [fables] with "all the answers" competing with God for our time. The Bible was written for our profit [3:16]. Most other books were written for the publisher's profit. It is an awesome thought that whatever book we choose to read for that time, we have chosen not to read what God has written.

Jesus said: *"You shall know the truth"* [John 8:32]. But how ... and from whom ... 20th century best-selling popular authors? Or from the one who said: *"I am The Truth"* [14:6]. A good test concerning our reading list is: Does the book encourage me to read God's Word or does the book imply that its author has all the answers?

And that leads us to what is the real reason that many Christians do not read through the Bible. Some read a little here or there -- perhaps from the Psalms -- for personal satisfaction; while others decide on a subject and treat the Bible as a source book. For example, to know more about the Holy Spirit, they'll just read verses on the Holy Spirit, or whatever appeals to them most at the time. Is it a spirit of self-sufficiency? The Holy Spirit led the great prophet Jeremiah to write: *"O Lord, I know that it is not within man to direct his own ways"* [Jeremiah 10:23]; and the writer of Proverbs was led to record: *"Lean not unto your own understanding. But in all your ways acknowledge him, and he shall direct your paths"* [Proverbs 3:5-6]. The only way we can acknowledge Him in the true meaning of the word is to read His Word to hear what He has to say, and then to conform our lives according to what His Word leads us to do.

In the letter to the COLOSSIANS, we are again directed by the Holy Spirit: *"Let the word of Christ dwell in you richly in all wisdom; teaching and admonishing one another in psalms and hymns and spiritual songs, singing with grace in your hearts to the Lord"* [3:16]. Now what is the *"word of Christ"*? Does this mean only the words in red ink in Matthew, Mark, Luke, and John as found in some 20th century Bibles? Doesn't the *"word of Christ"* begin in Genesis 1, as recorded in John 1:1: *"In the beginning was the Word"*; and end with Revelation 22?

In the final message of Christ, in the BOOK OF REVELATION, it is written: *"Blessed is he that reads, and they that hear the words of this prophecy, and keep those things which are written therein"* [1:3]. Our Lord's closing thoughts -- and oh, how we ought to continually keep His thoughts before us: ***"Blessed are they that do his commandments, that*** *they may have right to the tree of life, and may enter in through the gates into the city. For without are dogs, and sorcerers, and whoremongers, and murderers, and idolaters, and whosoever loves and makes a lie"* [22:14-15]. And then His last warning: *"For I testify unto every man that hears the words of the prophecy of this book, If any man shall add unto these things, God shall add unto him the plagues that are written in this book: And if any man shall take away from the words of the book of this prophecy, God shall take away his part out of the book of life, and out of the holy city, and from the things which are written in this book"* [22:18-19].

"God's Holy Word has surely been
Inspired of God and not of men;

No power or eloquence of men
Could ere conceive God's wondrous plan.

Withstanding all the tests of time,
It stands unchanged, unique, sublime;

Proving to every tongue and race,
God's wisdom, mercy, love and grace.

So hammer on, ye hostile hands
Your hammers break, God's anvil stands."

M.E.H.

Paul's First Missionary Journey

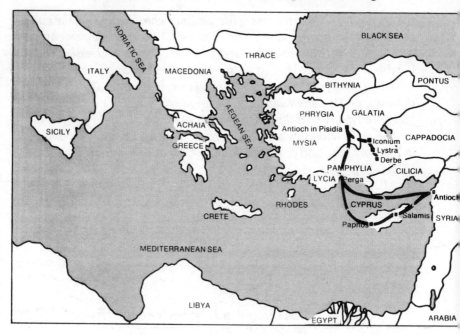

Paul's Second Missionary Journey

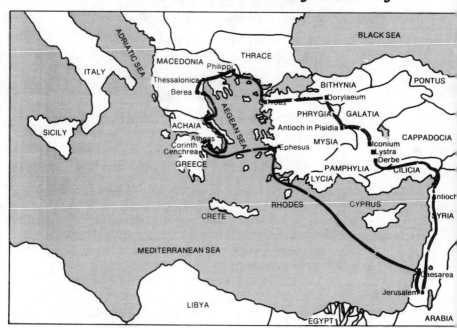

14

Paul's Third Missionary Journey

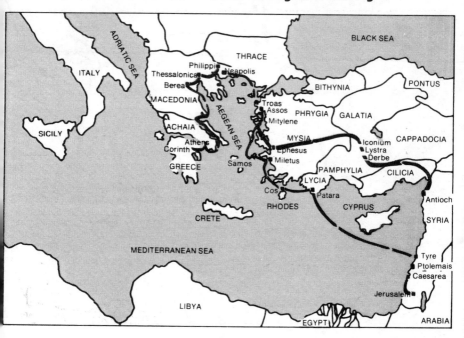

Paul's Journey to Rome

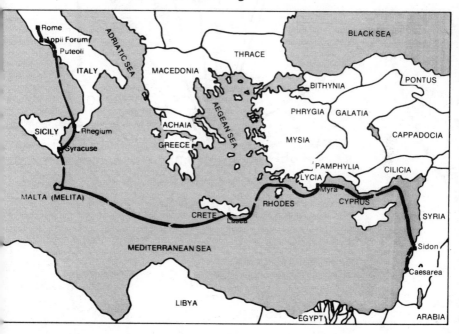

15

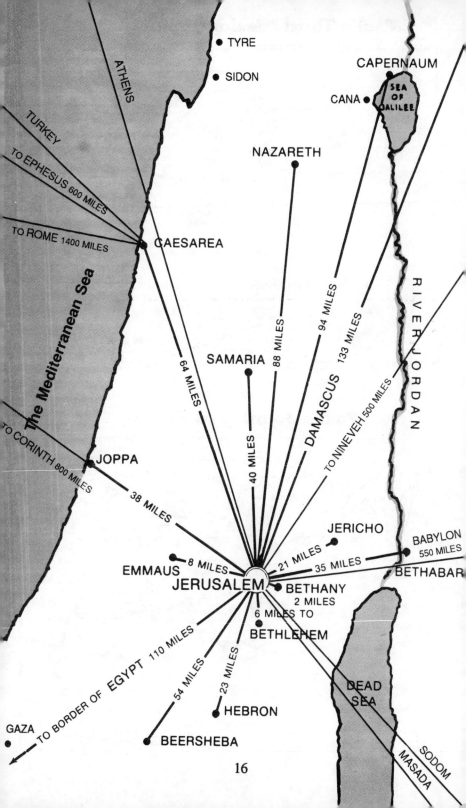

TYRE

SIDON

CAPERNAUM

CANA

SEA
OF
GALILEE

ATHENS

TURKEY

TO EPHESUS 600 MILES

TO ROME 1400 MILES

CAESAREA

NAZARETH

The Mediterranean Sea

94 MILES

133 MILES

R
I
V
E
R

J
O
R
D
A
N

64 MILES

SAMARIA

88 MILES

DAMASCUS

TO NINEVEH 500 MILES

40 MILES

TO CORINTH 800 MILES

JOPPA

38 MILES

JERICHO

21 MILES

35 MILES

BABYLON
550 MILES

EMMAUS

8 MILES

JERUSALEM

BETHANY
2 MILES

BETHABAR

6 MILES TO

BETHLEHEM

TO BORDER OF EGYPT 110 MILES

54 MILES

23 MILES

DEAD
SEA

GAZA

HEBRON

BEERSHEBA

SODOM

MASADA

16

JANUARY

1	Genesis 1–3	
2	Genesis 4–6	
3	Genesis 7–9	
4	Genesis 10–12	
5	Genesis 13–15	
6	Genesis 16–18	
7	Genesis 19–21	
8	Genesis 22–24	
9	Genesis 25–27	
10	Genesis 28–30	
11	Genesis 31–33	
12	Genesis 34–36	
13	Genesis 37–39	
14	Genesis 40–42	
15	Genesis 43–45	
16	Genesis 46–48	
17	Gen. 49–Ex. 1	
18	Exodus 2–4	
19	Exodus 5–7	
20	Exodus 8–10	
21	Exodus 11–13	
22	Exodus 14–16	
23	Exodus 17–19	
24	Exodus 20–22	
25	Exodus 23–25	
26	Exodus 26–28	
27	Exodus 29–31	
28	Exodus 32–34	
29	Exodus 35–37	
30	Exodus 38–39	
31	Exodus 40	

FEBRUARY

1	Leviticus 1–3	
2	Leviticus 4–6	
3	Leviticus 7–8	
4	Leviticus 9–10	
5	Leviticus 11–13	
6	Leviticus 14–15	
7	Leviticus 16–18	
8	Leviticus 19–21	
9	Leviticus 22–23	
10	Leviticus 24–25	
11	Leviticus 26–27	
12	Numbers 1–2	
13	Numbers 3–4	
14	Numbers 5–6	
15	Numbers 7	
16	Numbers 8–9	
17	Numbers 10–11	
18	Numbers 12–13	
19	Numbers 14–15	
20	Numbers 16–18	
21	Numbers 19–20	
22	Numbers 21–22	
23	Numbers 23–25	
24	Numbers 26–27	
25	Numbers 28–29	
26	Numbers 30–31	
27	Numbers 32–33	
28	Numbers 34–35	
29	Numbers 36	

MARCH

1	Deut. 1–2	
2	Deut. 3–4	
3	Deut. 5–7	
4	Deut. 8–10	
5	Deut. 11–13	
6	Deut. 14–16	
7	Deut. 17–20	
8	Deut. 21–23	
9	Deut. 24–27	
10	Deut. 28	
11	Deut. 29–31	
12	Deut. 32–34	
13	Joshua 1–3	
14	Joshua 4–6	
15	Joshua 7–8	
16	Joshua 9–10	
17	Joshua 11–13	
18	Joshua 14–16	
19	Joshua 17–19	
20	Joshua 20–21	
21	Joshua 22–24	
22	Judges 1–2	
23	Judges 3–5	
24	Judges 6–7	
25	Judges 8–9	
26	Judges 10–11	
27	Judges 12–14	
28	Judges 15–17	
29	Judges 18–19	
30	Judges 20–21	
31	Ruth 1–4	

APRIL

1	I Samuel 1–3	
2	I Samuel 4–7	
3	I Samuel 8–11	
4	I Samuel 12–14:23	
5	I Samuel 14:24–16	
6	I Samuel 17–18	
7	I Samuel 19–21	
8	I Samuel 22–24	
9	I Samuel 25–27	
10	I Samuel 28–31	
11	II Samuel 1–2	
12	II Samuel 3–5	
13	II Samuel 6–9	
14	II Samuel 10–12	
15	II Samuel 13–14	
16	II Samuel 15–16	
17	II Samuel 17–18	
18	II Samuel 19–20	
19	II Samuel 21–22	
20	II Samuel 23–24	
21	I Kings 1–2:25	
22	I Kings 2:26–4	
23	I Kings 5–7	
24	I Kings 8	
25	I Kings 9–11	
26	I Kings 12–13	
27	I Kings 14–15	
28	I Kings 16–18	
29	I Kings 19–20	
30	I Kings 21–22	

MAY

1	II Kings 1–3	
2	II Kings 4–5	
3	II Kings 6–8	
4	II Kings 9–10	
5	II Kings 11–13	
6	II Kings 14–15	
7	II Kings 16–17	
8	II Kings 18–20	
9	II Kings 21–23:20	
10	II Kings 23:21–25	
11	I Chron. 1–2	
12	I Chron. 3–5	
13	I Chron. 6–7	
14	I Chron. 8–10	
15	I Chron. 11–13	
16	I Chron. 14–16	
17	I Chron. 17–20	
18	I Chron. 21–23	
19	I Chron. 24–26	
20	I Chron. 27–29	
21	II Chron. 1–3	
22	II Chron. 4–6	
23	II Chron. 7–9	
24	II Chron. 10–13	
25	II Chron. 14–17	
26	II Chron. 18–20	
27	II Chron. 21–24	
28	II Chron. 25–27	
29	II Chron. 28–30	
30	II Chron. 31–33	
31	II Chron. 34–36	

JUNE

1	Ezra 1–2	
2	Ezra 3–5	
3	Ezra 6–7	
4	Ezra 8–9	
5	Ezra 10	
6	Nehemiah 1–3	
7	Nehemiah 4–6	
8	Nehemiah 7–8	
9	Nehemiah 9–10	
10	Nehemiah 11–12	
11	Nehemiah 13	
12	Esther 1–3	
13	Esther 4–7	
14	Esther 8–10	
15	Job 1–4	
16	Job 5–8	
17	Job 9–12	
18	Job 13–16	
19	Job 17–20	
20	Job 21–24	
21	Job 25–29	
22	Job 30–33	
23	Job 34–37	
24	Job 38–40	
25	Job 41–42	
26	Psalms 1–9	
27	Psalms 10–17	
28	Psalms 18–22	
29	Psalms 23–30	
30	Psalms 31–35	

JULY

		Check this coupon as you read each day.
1	Psalms 36–39	
2	Psalms 40–45	
3	Psalms 46–51	
4	Psalms 52–59	
5	Psalms 60–66	
6	Psalms 67–71	
7	Psalms 72–77	
8	Psalms 78–80	
9	Psalms 81–87	
10	Psalms 88–91	
11	Psalms 92–100	
12	Psalms 101–105	
13	Psalms 106–107	
14	Psalms 108–118	
15	Psalm 119	
16	Psalms 120–131	
17	Psalms 132–138	
18	Psalms 139–143	
19	Psalms 144–150	
20	Proverbs 1–3	
21	Proverbs 4–7	
22	Proverbs 8–11	
23	Proverbs 12–15	
24	Proverbs 16–19	
25	Proverbs 20–22	
26	Proverbs 23–26	
27	Proverbs 27–31	
28	Eccles. 1–4	
29	Eccles. 5–8	
30	Eccles. 9–12	
31	Song of Sol. 1–8	

AUGUST

		Check this coupon as you read each day.
1	Isaiah 1–4	
2	Isaiah 5–9	
3	Isaiah 10–14	
4	Isaiah 15–21	
5	Isaiah 22–26	
6	Isaiah 27–31	
7	Isaiah 32–37	
8	Isaiah 38–42	
9	Isaiah 43–46	
10	Isaiah 47–51	
11	Isaiah 52–57	
12	Isaiah 58–63	
13	Isaiah 64–66	
14	Jeremiah 1–3	
15	Jeremiah 4–6	
16	Jeremiah 7–10	
17	Jeremiah 11–14	
18	Jeremiah 15–18	
19	Jeremiah 19–22	
20	Jeremiah 23–25	
21	Jeremiah 26–28	
22	Jeremiah 29–31	
23	Jeremiah 32–33	
24	Jeremiah 34–36	
25	Jeremiah 37–40	
26	Jeremiah 41–44	
27	Jeremiah 45–48	
28	Jeremiah 49–50	
29	Jeremiah 51–52	
30	Lam. 1–2	
31	Lam. 3–5	

SEPTEMBER

		Check this coupon as you read each day.
1	Ezekiel 1–4	
2	Ezekiel 5–9	
3	Ezekiel 10–13	
4	Ezekiel 14–16	
5	Ezekiel 17–19	
6	Ezekiel 20–21	
7	Ezekiel 22–24	
8	Ezekiel 25–28	
9	Ezekiel 29–32	
10	Ezekiel 33–36	
11	Ezekiel 37–39	
12	Ezekiel 40–42	
13	Ezekiel 43–45	
14	Ezekiel 46–48	
15	Daniel 1–3	
16	Daniel 4–6	
17	Daniel 7–9	
18	Daniel 10–12	
19	Hosea 1–6	
20	Hosea 7–14	
21	Joel 1–3	
22	Amos 1–5	
23	Amos 6–9	
	Obadiah 1	
24	Jonah 1–4	
25	Micah 1–7	
26	Nahum 1–3	
	Habakkuk 1–3	
27	Zephaniah 1–3	
	Haggai 1–2	
28	Zech. 1–7	
29	Zech. 8–14	
30	Malachi 1–4	

OCTOBER

		Check this coupon as you read each day.
1	Matthew 1–4	
2	Matthew 5–6	
3	Matthew 7–9	
4	Matthew 10–11	
5	Matthew 12	
6	Matthew 13–14	
7	Matthew 15–17	
8	Matthew 18–20	
9	Matthew 21–22	
10	Matthew 23–24	
11	Matthew 25–26	
12	Matthew 27–28	
13	Mark 1–3	
14	Mark 4–5	
15	Mark 6–7	
16	Mark 8–9	
17	Mark 10–11	
18	Mark 12–13	
19	Mark 14–16	
20	Luke 1	
21	Luke 2–3	
22	Luke 4–5	
23	Luke 6–7	
24	Luke 8–9	
25	Luke 10–11	
26	Luke 12–13	
27	Luke 14–16	
28	Luke 17–18	
29	Luke 19–20	
30	Luke 21–22	
31	Luke 23–24	

NOVEMBER

		Check this coupon as you read each day.
1	John 1–3	
2	John 4–5	
3	John 6–8	
4	John 9–10	
5	John 11–12	
6	John 13–16	
7	John 17–18	
8	John 19–21	
9	Acts 1–3	
10	Acts 4–6	
11	Acts 7–8	
12	Acts 9–10	
13	Acts 11–13	
14	Acts 14–16	
15	Acts 17–19	
16	Acts 20–22	
17	Acts 23–25	
18	Acts 26–28	
19	Romans 1–3	
20	Romans 4–7	
21	Romans 8–10	
22	Romans 11–13	
23	Romans 14–16	
24	I Cor. 1–4	
25	I Cor. 5–9	
26	I Cor. 10–13	
27	I Cor. 14–16	
28	II Cor. 1–4	
29	II Cor. 5–8	
30	II Cor. 9–13	

DECEMBER

		Check this coupon as you read each day.
1	Galatians 1–3	
2	Galatians 4–6	
3	Ephesians 1–3	
4	Ephesians 4–6	
5	Philippians 1–4	
6	Colossians 1–4	
7	I Thess. 1–5	
8	II Thess. 1–3	
9	I Timothy 1–6	
10	II Timothy 1–4	
11	Titus 1–3	
	Philemon 1	
12	Hebrews 1–4	
13	Hebrews 5–7	
14	Hebrews 8–10	
15	Hebrews 11–13	
16	James 1–5	
17	I Peter 1–2	
18	I Peter 3–5	
19	II Peter 1–3	
20	I John 1–3	
21	I John 4–5	
22	II John 1	
	III John 1	
	Jude 1	
23	Revelation 1–2	
24	Revelation 3–5	
25	Revelation 6–8	
26	Revelation 9–11	
27	Revelation 12–13	
28	Revelation 14–16	
29	Revelation 17–18	
30	Revelation 19–20	
31	Revelation 21–22	

GENESIS

The book of Genesis reveals God as the supreme Creator of the universe who is absolutely sovereign over everything (chapter 1; compare Colossians 1:16). He created all things by the power of His Word—just by speaking it into being. His Word is just as powerful today (Hebrews 4:12). God reveals His will to us through His Word. In order to accomplish His whole will, we must read His whole Word. The book of Genesis helps to show the importance of reading all the Bible in order to allow God to accomplish His will for our lives.

Chapters 1—11 record the first 2,000 years* of man's history. During that time, four major events took place: the creation of all things, the sin of Adam and Eve, the great Flood, and the building of the tower of Babel.

Genesis reveals man as God's creation which has a body, a soul, and a spirit (compare I Thessalonians 5:23). He was created with a free will and given the choice to say yes or no to temptation.

Man was created in God's image for fellowship with Him. But, in disobedience to the expressed will of their Creator, Adam and Eve chose to sin. Their sin broke their relationship with God, and death began to reign over all mankind (Romans 5:12-14).

The rebellion of Adam and Eve resulted in the tragic fall. Sin continued to fill the hearts and minds of people with hate, murder, and violence. Eventually, God in judgment brought a great Flood upon the world and reduced mankind to one family—that of godly Noah. But again, sin prevailed, and the people decided to build the huge tower of Babel in defiance of God (Genesis 11:1-9).

Chapters 12—50 of Genesis cover about 300 years* and center around four men—Abraham, Isaac, Jacob, and Joseph. Through these men, we see God's love and ability to protect and provide for His people who are obedient to His Word.

Christ declared Genesis to be vital to one's faith in Him, saying: *If you had believed Moses, you would have believed Me because he wrote about Me* (see John 5:46).

The importance and reliability of Genesis is apparent in that it is quoted more than 60 times in the New Testament and is confirmed by Christ. Note His references to creation in Matthew 19:4-6 (compare Genesis 2:21-24); to Noah in Matthew 24:37-38 (compare Genesis 6:5,13; 17:6-23); to Abraham in Matthew 3:9 (compare Genesis 17:1-16); and to Sodom and Gomorrah in Matthew 10:15 (compare Genesis 19:24-25).

*NOTE: *These are approximate time periods to give the reader a general idea of events in relation to time intervals.*

Highlights: Creation of all things; creation of Adam and Eve; temptation by the serpent; Adam and Eve rebel against God and forfeit the Garden of Eden.

Verse for Today: *"Now the serpent was more subtil than any beast of the field which the Lord God had made. And he said unto the woman, Yea, hath God said, Ye shall not eat of every tree of the garden?"* (Genesis 3:1).

God placed Adam and Eve in a perfect environment and provided their every need. He said they could eat from all the trees but one. Eating the fruit from this one tree was forbidden in order to test their loyalty and obedience to Him.

In the early days of history, Satan sought to overthrow God's authority over the human race. His chief purpose was to separate man from his Creator and to inspire confidence in self. The Bible clearly sets forth some of Satan's methods which he still uses today.

Satan first caused Eve to question the Word of God, asking, *Can it really be that God has said you shall not eat of every tree in the garden? . . . God knows that when you eat the fruit from this tree you will be like Him, knowing what is good and what is evil* (see Genesis 3:1,5). Satan implied that God was holding back something good from them, raising a doubt as to whether He cared for their best interest.

Once Eve questioned the goodness of God in providing what was best, Satan had won a major victory. His next move was to undermine her reliance upon the truth of God's Word by contradicting it: *You shall not die.* Questioning God easily leads to contradicting His Word. Satan then appealed to Eve's natural desires and worked through her to get Adam to sin (3:4-6).

Satan led them to believe that they were capable of deciding what was best for themselves. They believed his lie rather than the Word of God. Adam and Eve chose to disobey God, and sin entered the world. With sin came all the evil, misery, suffering, and sorrow that is in the world today. As a result of sin, mankind became self-seeking, self-centered, and self-willed.

It is our responsibility to serve, obey, and glorify our Creator. But, like Adam and Eve, many people refuse to accept the fact that we are not independent creatures—free to do things our own way without regard for God's Word—for we are His creation. We can and should—for our best interest—choose God's way.

Satan often appears as an "angel of light" and deceives many by quoting a verse of Scripture that, by itself, sounds reasonable. But reading all the Bible is the only safeguard against making wrong decisions.

When Adam sinned, sin entered the entire human race. His sin spread death throughout all the world, so everyone began to grow old and die, for all sinned (see Romans 5:12).

Thought for Today: Eternal destiny is determined by choice, not chance.

Christ Revealed: As Creator (Genesis 1:1). See John 1:1-4; Col. 1:15-17; Heb. 11:3. As the seed of woman (Gen. 3:15). See Isa. 7:14; 9:6-7; Gal. 4:4.

Word Study: 1:6 **firmament** means the expanse of the sky surrounding the earth.

NOTE: *Definitions may not agree with present-day usage as given in your dictionary; we attempt to explain the thought expressed in the original language.*

Prayer Needs: Country: Spain—39 million—in southwestern Europe • Limited religious freedom • 94% Roman Catholic; .5% Protestant.

JANUARY 2: Read Genesis 4 — 6

Highlights: Sacrifices of Cain and Abel; Cain murders Abel; genealogy from Adam to Noah; universal corruption because of sin; Noah builds the ark.

Verses for Today: *"And the Lord said, My spirit shall not always strive with man. . . . And God saw that the wickedness of man was great in the earth, and that every imagination of the thoughts of his heart was only evil continually"* (Genesis 6:3,5).

A fter Adam's sin, God showed His mercy and grace by providing a covering for sin. He also told of the coming Savior who would defeat Satan, the source of sin (see Genesis 3:15; Hebrews 10:12-14).

As time passed, mankind became more and more evil. Although God was *grieved at heart* at the rebellion of mankind (see Genesis 6:6), He did not leave them to their own destruction—He gave many warnings to keep them from going to hell.

God raised up great men of faith, such as Enoch, and preachers of righteousness, such as Noah (Hebrews 11:5,7). Added to this, God's own Holy Spirit spoke to the consciences of men (Genesis 6:3). But the people continued to ignore His message.

The Spirit of God moves in the heart of every person, convicting of sin and seeking to turn him to God. The allotted time for each of us is sufficient to accept God's message of love and receive Christ as Savior and Lord. Continual rejection of God's mercy causes a person to become so hardened that he may no longer hear the voice of the Holy Spirit.

The striving of God's Spirit eventually comes to an end—not because God is no longer willing to help, but because of the hardheartedness of those who refuse to yield their wills to His will.

Today, if you will hear His voice, do not harden your hearts (see Hebrews 3:7-8).

Thought for Today: Either you will yield to Satan's influence and become hardened to the things of God, or you will yield to God's Spirit and become more like Christ.

Christ Revealed: Through Abel's blood sacrifice (Genesis 4:4-7). Christ is the Lamb of God. (See John 1:29; Heb. 9:22; 11:4.) Man's best achievements can never take the place of Christ's atonement.

Word Studies: 4:5 **wroth** means exceedingly angry; 4:8 **slew** means killed; 4:22 **artificer** means craftsman; 6:9 **perfect** means righteous; 6:14 **shalt pitch it** means cover it inside and out.

Prayer Needs: Country: Thailand—54 million—in Southeast Asia • Limited freedom of religion, Buddhism is the state religion • 92% Buddhist; 4% Muslim; 2% Chinese folk-religionist; 1% Christian.

JANUARY 3: Read Genesis 7 — 9

Highlights: Noah enters the ark; the great Flood; the rainbow, the sign of God's covenant; Noah's prophecy concerning his three sons.

Verse for Today: *"And Noah builded an altar unto the Lord . . . and offered burnt offerings on the altar"* (Genesis 8:20).

T he first thing Noah did after he left the ark was to build an altar, where he offered a sacrifice and worshiped God.

By faith Noah, when warned by God about things not yet seen, in holy fear prepared an ark to save his household. Through this action of faith, he condemned the unbelief of the rest of the world and became the possessor of the righteousness that results from faith (see Hebrews 11:7).

Offering a sacrifice on the altar was an open confession of Noah's faith, as well as his gratitude for God's saving grace. It was an acknowledgement that he was undeserving of mercy and that someone, or something apart from himself, must become his substitute for the penalty of sin.

The altar-sacrifice is symbolic of Christ, the only sacrifice which God accepts as the full and complete atonement for our sins.

It is this revelation that creates within the child of God a desire to worship Him for who He is, as well as for what He has done—paid the price for our sins. Such a revelation of God's grace should cause us to humble ourselves before Him and accept His ways. We can thank Him for everything He allows to come into our lives, as well as everything He chooses to take away from us.

There is nothing you can do that will save you—it is God's gift of grace. It is not by your own works; it is a gift from God. So it is impossible for anyone to boast about deserving it (see Ephesians 2:8-9).

Thought for Today: It is not *things* that we need, but *Christ*.

Christ Revealed: Through the ark (Genesis 7:1,7). See Acts 4:12; I Pet. 3:20. Christ, our Ark of safety, protects the believer from the water of judgment.

Word Study: 8:1 **assuaged** means lowered.

Prayer Needs: Country: West Germany—61 million—in north-central Europe • Religious freedom • 46% Protestant; 43% Roman Catholic; 2% Muslim.

JANUARY 4: Read Genesis 10 — 12

Highlights: Descendants of Noah's sons; tower of Babel; origin of languages; ancestry of Abram; God's call to Abram; God's covenant with Abram; his journeys to Canaan and to Egypt.

Verse for Today: *"Say, I pray thee, thou art my sister: that it may be well with me for thy sake; and my soul shall live because of thee"* (Genesis 12:13).

G od spoke to Abram, saying, *Leave your country and your relatives and go to a land that I will show you* (see Genesis 12:1). Abram expected God's blessings in the Promised Land, but instead, he faced severe famine. This caused him to go down to Egypt.

In Egypt the weakness in Abram's faith was once again exposed through his agreement to deception with Sarai. Fearing that someone might kill him in order to have his beautiful wife, Abram and Sarai had agreed—before they entered Egypt—that if anyone asked who Sarai was, they would say she was his sister (12:10-13).

God could not bless Abram until he gave up his reliance on human wisdom and his selfish reasoning. He reasoned with Sarai that, *my life will be spared because of you*. This reasoning expressed a lack of faith in God's ability to protect him and exposed a greater concern for his own well-being than for Sarai's chastity.

Abram had a threefold weakness that God exposed—an unwarranted fear of man, a foolish reliance on his own schemes, and a sinful desire to please himself at the expense of the happiness and welfare of others.

In Abram's act of self-preservation, he was rebuked by the unbelieving Pharaoh. Surely Abram had to feel that he had dishonored God, but these trials were necessary to perfect his faith.

The experience of Abram should teach us to take God at His Word and, in simple faith, to depend wholly upon Him.

Direct my life according to Your Word; and let no sin rule over me (see Psalm 119:133).

Thought for Today: Christians who commit foolish acts of unbelief leave themselves open to Satan's destructive power.

Christ Revealed: As the Seed of Abraham (Genesis 12:3; 18:18). See Matt. 1:1; Acts. 3:25-26; Gal. 3:16. Abram was a type of Christ who leads the way to a better land (John 14:2-4; Heb. 11:8-10).

Word Study: 11:3 **slime** means an asphalt pitch.

Prayer Needs: Country: Sierra Leone—4 million—in western Africa • Increasing restriction on Christian work in some areas • 50% belief in river spirits, medicine men, and witchcraft; 39% Muslim; 7% Protestant; 2% Roman Catholic.

JANUARY 5: Read Genesis 13 — 15

Highlights: Abram and Lot separate; Abram moves to Hebron; Abram rescues Lot; Melchizedek blesses Abram; God's covenant with Abram.

Verse for Today: *"And the Lord said unto Abram, after that Lot was separated from him, Lift up now thine eyes, and look from the place where thou art northward, and southward, and eastward, and westward"* (Genesis 13:14).

G od had promised to give Abram all the land of Canaan (Genesis 12:7). Yet, Abram generously waived his rights and surrendered his claim to the land in an attempt to end the strife that had developed between his herdsmen and Lot's herdsmen.

Lot exposed his greediness when he chose all the well-watered plains at the expense of losing daily fellowship with Abram, the father of the faithful.

What a contrast between Abram and Lot! Lot lifted up his eyes to see material gain, but Abram lifted up his eyes to see a faithful God.

Lot, who chose this world's gain, soon lost it. But Abram was willing to give up the best land in order to maintain peace with his fellowman. Abram's desire was to please the Lord, and in doing so, he received eternal riches and rewards.

God is able to compensate Christians for the loss of any material wealth and companionship which we give up for His sake.

Set your heart first on the kingdom of God, and His righteousness—His way of doing and being right—and then all things shall be given to you (see Matthew 6:33).

Thought for Today: Our relationship with God can grow dearer as we trust Him

21

during times of trials, sufferings, and problems.

Christ Portrayed: By the high priest, Melchizedek (Genesis 14:18-20). See Heb. 4:15-16; 5:5-10; 7:1-4. Christ is our High Priest today, interceding in prayer for us.

Prayer Needs: Country: New Zealand—3 million—two large islands southeast of Australia • Religious freedom • 51% Protestant; 16% Roman Catholic; 3% cults.

JANUARY 6: Read Genesis 16 — 18

Highlights: Birth of Ishmael; Abram's name changed to Abraham; covenant of circumcision; Sarai's name changed to Sarah; a son promised to Abraham and Sarah; Abraham's intercession for Sodom.

Verses for Today: *"And Abraham drew near, and said, Wilt thou also destroy the righteous with the wicked? . . . Shall not the Judge of all the earth do right?"* (Genesis 18:23,25).

When the angels left Abraham's tent on their way to destroy Sodom, he prayed earnestly to God (Genesis 18:22-33). The angels had told of God's coming judgment upon the wicked city of Sodom—the city in which his nephew Lot lived.

The prayer of Abraham, the first long prayer recorded in Scripture, is also the first example of intercessory prayer—praying for others.

It would have been an example of forgiving love had Abraham prayed for Lot to be spared, but to plead for a wicked city where he had no personal interest at stake—for lost souls in whom he had nothing personal to gain—brings to light the compassion and mercy of this man of faith.

Six times Abraham offered his intercessory prayer, and each time God's gracious answer gave him encouragement to continue asking.

Sodom was not spared in answer to Abraham's prayer. But God went even further than his prayers and saved Lot's family, which doubtless consisted of all the righteous who were in the city.

Here is an example to teach us to pray for the unsaved. Guilty, lost souls have been spared in answer to the prayers of God's people.

The greatest need today is for intercessors. Few are ever saved until someone begins to pray for them by name. Check your prayer list. Are you praying for the lost by name today? Just remember, *whatever you ask in prayer, you will receive if you have faith* (see Matthew 21:22).

Thought for Today: We can intercede for others with the assurance that God will be just and fair—regardless of the way He chooses to answer our prayers.

Christ Revealed: As the Seed of Isaac (Genesis 17:19). Christ was a descendant of Isaac (Luke 3:34; Heb. 11:18).

Word Study: 17:1 **be thou perfect** means be wholeheartedly sincere.

Prayer Needs: Country: Yugoslavia—23 million—on the Balkan Peninsula • Virtually no freedom to preach the gospel • 40% Eastern Orthodox; 31% Roman Catholic; 10% Muslim; 1% Protestant.

JANUARY 7: Read Genesis 19 — 21

Highlights: Sodom and Gomorrah destroyed; Lot and his daughters; Abraham's lie to Abimelech; the birth of Isaac; Hagar and Ishmael sent away; the agreement between Abraham and Abimelech.

Verses for Today: *"Then the Lord rained upon Sodom and upon Gomorrah brimstone and fire from the Lord out of heaven. . . . But his [Lot's] wife looked back from behind him, and she became a pillar of salt"* (Genesis 19:24,26).

I t does not appear that the inhabitants of Sodom had any warning of their sudden destruction. Lot's sons-in-law, who scoffed at Lot's warning, were typical of the people in Sodom whose hearts were hardened beyond repentance.

Lot's wife had known Abraham for many years. Through him, she had learned of the one true God and His guidance. Added to this, angels had come to her home and urged her to leave the city. She had taken steps toward salvation, but she was destroyed with the wicked because her heart still longed for the things she was leaving behind.

God's dealing with Lot's wife shows us how He regards sin—how so few people escape the corruption that is in the world and are saved.

Many want just one more look, one more act of sin, one more object of self-satisfaction. But Christ said to follow Him and added that *anyone who lets himself be distracted from the work He planned for him is not fit for the kingdom of God* (see Luke 9:62).

To emphasize this fact, Jesus reminded them of what happened to Lot's wife. Then He added: *Whoever tries to save his own life will lose it; but whoever loses his life will save it* (see Luke 17:33).

Just as the people of Sodom were destroyed by fire and brimstone because of their wickedness, there will be a final judgment of eternal fire where all the unsaved will be cast—a place of eternal torment, with weeping and wailing and gnashing of teeth.

These, then, will be sent off to eternal punishment, but the righteous will have eternal life (see Matthew 25:46).

Thought for Today: Sin seeks to attract, control, and eventually destroy the soul.

Christ Portrayed: By Isaac, the promised son (Genesis 21:12)—in contrast to Ishmael, the son of a bondwoman (Gal. 4:22-31). Life in Christ sets us free from the bondage of the Law.

Word Study: 20:6 **suffer** means permit.

Prayer Needs: Country: Denmark—5 million—in northern Europe • Religious freedom • 92% Protestant; 1% Muslim; .5% Roman Catholic; .5% cults; .1% Jewish.

JANUARY 8: Read Genesis 22 — 24

Highlights: Abraham's willingness to offer Isaac; God's covenant renewed; Sarah's death; providential arrangement of Rebekah's marriage to Isaac.

Verses for Today: *"And he said, O Lord God of my master Abraham, I pray thee, send me good speed this day, and show kindness unto my master Abraham. . . . And let it come to pass, that the damsel to whom I shall say, Let down thy pitcher, I pray thee, that I may drink; and she shall say, Drink, and I will give thy camels drink also: let the same be she that thou hast appointed for thy servant Isaac . . . "* (Genesis 24:12,14).

A braham was determined that his son, Isaac, would not marry a woman from the families of Canaan. So he sent his most trusted servant (presumably Eliezer) on a 500-mile journey to choose a wife for Isaac in Mesopotamia, the land of Abraham's origin.

Eliezer undertook his mission with every desire to satisfy his master as well as Almighty God. In reverent humility, Eliezer interceded in prayer on behalf of Isaac and Abraham, asking God to lead him to the woman He wanted Isaac to marry. When the young woman, Rebekah, came to the well, she did not know that God had led her to be the answer to Eliezer's prayer. Little do we realize how God is working out the answers to our prayers through the ordinary activities of our lives.

Eliezer of Damascus had the qualifications of an intercessor; he had nothing to gain for himself. His only desire was to fulfill God's perfect will and to bring blessings to others.

God is seeking men and women who will intercede in prayer, making any sacrifice necessary in order to reach lost souls—to please the Master. *The earnest (heartfelt, continued) prayer of a righteous man can bring powerful results* (see James 5:16).

Thought for Today: God answers the prayer of faith when our desire is to please Him.

Christ Revealed: Through Isaac's willingness to be offered (Genesis 22:7-10; compare John 10:11-18).

Prayer Needs: Country: Cameroon—10 million—in west-central Africa • Pressure on Christians from authorities and Muslims • 28% Roman Catholic; 23% Muslim; 18% animism, divination, and animal sacrifices; 14% Protestant.

JANUARY 9: Read Genesis 25 — 27

Highlights: Abraham's marriage to Keturah; his death; birth of Jacob and Esau; Esau sells his birthright; Isaac and Abimelech; Isaac blesses Jacob.

Verse for Today: *"And Esau said, Behold, I am at the point to die: and what profit shall this birthright do to me?"* (Genesis 25:32).

A s the firstborn son, Esau was entitled to the family birthright, giving him the privilege of being the leader of the tribe and serving as priest. But this worldly minded man placed no importance on his spiritual responsibilities. Consequently, he sold his birthright for one meal, thus exposing his lack of concern for the covenant promise which God had given to his grandfather, Abraham.

Two different ways of life are evident in the lives of these two brothers: while Esau was living to satisfy present desires, Jacob had an intense desire to please God. As a result, Jacob not only became a great man of faith, but he also obtained the privilege of being an ancestor of Christ, the Messiah.

Even though some of Jacob's actions may seem questionable, he did believe in the promises of God. As we read the history of Jacob, it may seem that he did not deserve to become Israel—one of the great spiritual leaders of the people of God—but no child of God ever deserves or earns a right to God's blessings. It is only because of God's mercy and His great love that anyone receives His blessings.

We should never criticize the questionable actions of another Christian. We have no way of knowing his heart and how much he desires to please the Lord. He may

24

be another Jacob whom God will use to accomplish His purposes.

Who are you to judge someone else's servant? It is his own master who will decide whether he succeeds or fails. And he will succeed, because the Lord is able to make him succeed (see Romans 14:4).

Thought for Today: We must not judge by mere appearances.

Christ Revealed: As the spiritual Seed (Genesis 26:4). All believers in Christ are the children of promise (John 1:12-13; I John 3:9).

Word Studies: 25:8 **gave up the ghost** means died; 25:29 **pottage** means lentil stew; **faint** means tired; 27:31 **savory meat** means tasty food.

Prayer Needs: Country: Bhutan—2 million—in the eastern Himalayas of central Asia • Public worship, evangelism, and proselytization by any religion other than the state religion of Buddhism are illegal • 70% Buddhist; 24% Hindu; 5% Muslim; .1% Christian.

JANUARY 10: Read Genesis 28 — 30

Highlights: Abrahamic Covenant confirmed upon Jacob; vision of Jacob's ladder; journey to Haran; Jacob's marriages to Leah and to Rachel.

Verse for Today: *"And, behold, I am with thee, and will keep thee in all places whither thou goest, and will bring thee again into this land; for I will not leave thee . . . "* (Genesis 28:15)

J acob feared that Esau would kill him as he threatened to do. So Jacob left his home in Beersheba and went to live 500 miles away in Padan-aram, the land of his mother's family.

Stopping near Bethel along the way, God gave this lonely man the comforting promise that He was with him.

Following the miraculous revelation of God's never-failing presence, Jacob left Bethel and journeyed on to Padan-aram. There at the well where the shepherds had gathered to water their sheep, he met Rachel, the daughter of Laban, his mother's brother. God had brought him to this place to meet the woman who was to be his wife.

It was no accident or chance happening that Jacob stopped at the exact well where Rachel watered her father's flocks, or that she came by at that very hour. Unknown to either Jacob or Rachel, God had worked out all the details in advance.

The way before us may seem long and wearisome, and there may be much to distress us. But if we live to please the God of Jacob, we will have the assurance that He is protecting and directing each step of our way.

For this great God is our God forever and ever. He will be our guide until we die (see Psalm 48:14).

Thought for Today: There are no chance happenings or accidents in the lives of those who have placed their faith in the God of Jacob.

Christ Revealed: As the Lord whose unseen presence protects (Genesis 28:13-16).

Word Study: 29:17 **tender** means weak.

Prayer Needs: Country: Trinidad and Tobago—1 million—two islands seven miles off the coast of Venezuela • Religious freedom • 34% Protestant; 29% Roman Catholic; 25% Hindu; 7% Muslim.

JANUARY 11: Read Genesis 31 — 33

Highlights: Jacob's wealth causes jealousy; Jacob flees; covenant between Laban and Jacob; Jacob wrestles; his name changed to Israel; reunion and peace between Jacob and Esau.

Verse for Today: *"I am the God of Bethel ... where thou vowedst a vow unto me: now arise, get thee out from this land, and return unto the land of thy kindred"* (Genesis 31:13).

J acob's life was filled with many fears and disappointments, but his greatest fear had haunted him for 20 years. At last, he was forced to face his brother, who had vowed to kill him.

Although Jacob had gone to great expense and made many plans in preparing to face Esau, he finally realized that his only hope rested in God—not his own efforts (see Genesis 32:24-30).

Like Jacob, many Christians have struggles in the energy of the flesh—scheming, planning, striving—in an effort to accomplish spiritual victories. But God's mercy leads us to see that the victorious Christian life is nothing short of living in the power of the Holy Spirit.

But God has brought you into union with Christ Jesus, and revealed to us the divine plan of salvation. By Him we are put right with God; we have become God's holy people and are set free from the eternal penalty for sin (see I Corinthians 1:30).

Thought for Today: We can depend on God to supply us with the answer that satisfies—Christ.

Christ Revealed: As the Angel of God who guides (Genesis 31:11-13). The Angel speaks not merely in the name of God, but as God, leaving no doubt that He is the Lord.

Word Studies: 31:34 **camel's furniture** means camel's saddle; 31:36 **chode** means contended; 32:10 **bands** means companies; 32:15 **kine** means cows; 33:2 **hindermost** means last.

Prayer Needs: Country: Wales—3 million—in western Britain • Religious freedom • 82% Protestant; 18% Roman Catholic.

JANUARY 12: Read Genesis 34 — 36

Highlights: Dinah disgraced; Jacob's return to Bethel; Abrahamic Covenant renewed with Jacob; descendants of Esau.

Verse for Today: *"And God appeared unto Jacob again, when he came out of Padan-aram, and blessed him"* (Genesis 35:9).

A t least 10 years had passed since Jacob left Padan-aram and began his 500-mile journey back to Bethel, the place where God had promised to bless him. He was off to a good start; however, he was sidetracked along the way by the beautiful valleys of Succoth. There he built a home and settled down near Shechem, where his family became associated with their heathen neighbors.

Jacob had also failed to destroy the idol which his favorite wife, Rachel, had taken from her father. Jacob's failure to separate his family from ungodly influences and his other compromises resulted in the disgrace of his daughter Dinah and the cruel crimes of his sons. Not until then did he exert his parental authority and insist that his family get rid of all idols (Genesis 35:2,4), purify themselves, leave their home near Shechem, and journey to Bethel.

Just as Jacob had to leave Succoth, each of us must separate ourselves from the things that keep us from fulfilling God's will for our lives. Failure to separate ourselves from the world—its lusts and desires—always ends in disaster. That is the real reason why God has warned us to *stop loving this evil world and all that it offers; for when we love these things, we show that we do not really love God, for all worldly desires—the craze for sex, the ambition to buy everything that appeals to us, and the pride that comes from wealth and importance—are not from God. They are from this evil world. And this world is fading away, and these evil, forbidden things will go with it; but whoever keeps doing the will of God will live forever* (see I John 2:15-17).

Thought for Today: We can praise God for His mercy in providing an opportunity to commit ourselves afresh to Him!

Christ Revealed: As God Almighty (Genesis 35:11). Jesus said, *Before Abraham was born, I am* (see John 8:58).

Prayer Needs: Country: Zimbabwe (formerly Rhodesia)—9 million—in south-central Africa • Limited religious freedom • 43% Protestant; 38% animism, mediums, and spirit-possession cults; 16% Catholic.

JANUARY 13: Read Genesis 37 — 39

Highlights: Joseph's dreams; Joseph sold into slavery; Judah and Tamar; the deceit of Potiphar's wife; Joseph imprisoned.

Verses for Today: *"And Joseph's master took him, and put him into the prison, a place where the king's prisoners were bound: and he was there in the prison. But the Lord was with Joseph, and showed him mercy, and gave him favor in the sight of the keeper of the prison"* (Genesis 39:20-21).

A s a teenager, Joseph was misunderstood by his family and friends, cruelly hated, betrayed, sold by his brothers as a slave, and then taken to Egypt by some Ishmaelite traders.

In Egypt Joseph was once again sold in the slave market. There he was cast into prison—not because of sin, but because of his high moral integrity. As a homesick prisoner, Joseph remained shut up for many years. During that time his feet were injured by the cruel treatment he received there (Psalm 105:17-18). Without a doubt, his faith was tested. Although he was innocent, in the eyes of men he suffered as one who was a guilty criminal, having to bear shame and physical cruelty.

But God had not forgotten Joseph. In His time, God brought Joseph to the favorable attention of Pharaoh, who soon made him a top official in the land of Egypt. This was God's plan for Joseph from the beginning. Joseph was put in a position where God could use him to supply the needs of His people. God always tests our loyalty to Him by bringing circumstances into our lives that we cannot understand. This is His means of perfecting our patience as well as our faith in Him.

Yes, we know that all things go on working together for the good of those who keep on loving God, those who are called in accordance with His purpose (see Romans 8:28).

Thought for Today: As *"the Lord was with Joseph,"* He will be with those who love Him and remain faithful to Him.

Christ Portrayed: By Joseph, who was lifted from the pit and eventually became a world ruler (Genesis 37:28). Joseph, a type of Christ, was rejected by his own brothers, cast into a pit, sold to Gentiles, and imprisoned while waiting for the fulfillment of prophecy (dreams) that he would rule.

Word Study: 38:28 **travailed** means was giving birth.

Prayer Needs: Country: Swaziland—700,000—in southern Africa • Religious freedom • 67% Protestant; 19% animism, spirit-possession cults, and divination; 11% Roman Catholic; 2% Baha'i.

JANUARY 14: Read Genesis 40 — 42

Highlights: Dreams interpreted by Joseph; Joseph made ruler of Egypt; his brothers buy corn (grain) and bow down to him.

Verses for Today: *"And Pharaoh said unto Joseph, Forasmuch as God hath showed thee all this . . . thou shalt be over my house. . . . And he made him to ride in the second chariot which he had; and they cried before him, Bow the knee: and he made him ruler over all the land of Egypt"* (Genesis 41:39-40,43).

S atan had used Potiphar's wife to cause Joseph to be put into prison (chapter 39), but God was behind the scenes, guiding and protecting His servant until He was ready for Joseph to be exalted.

It was no accident that Pharaoh had a dream. Nor was it an accident that Pharaoh's butler remembered how Joseph had interpreted his dream two years earlier. God's time had come for Joseph to be released from prison and given a position of high honor and responsibility.

After Joseph interpreted Pharaoh's dream, Pharaoh made him ruler over the land of Egypt—second only to Pharaoh himself. What a marvelous change took place in Joseph's circumstances—from shame to glory, from prison to palace, from slave to exalted ruler! This was his reward for faithfulness to the Lord.

In many ways, Joseph's life parallelled the life of our Lord. He was dearly loved by his father, he suffered cruel treatment at the hands of those who should have loved him, he was wrongly accused and sentenced, and in God's time, he was highly exalted.

Have you ever bowed before this highly exalted One, the Lord Jesus Christ? He lovingly extends His invitation, *Come to Me.* He is able and willing to forgive every sin. In fact, *anyone who calls out to the Lord will be saved* (see Romans 10:13).

Thought for Today: Even when our situation seems hopeless, God can—in His time—deliver us.

Christ Revealed: Through the interpretation of Pharaoh's dream by Joseph. Christ is the true interpreter of all the circumstances of life (Genesis 41:16-36; compare Matt. 13:18-43).

Word Studies: 41:2 **kine** means cows; 42:34 **shall traffic** means do business.

Prayer Needs: Country: Algeria—23 million—in North Africa • Authorities have virtually ended all open mission work • 99% Muslim; .9% Christian.

JANUARY 15: Read Genesis 43 — 45

Highlights: Jacob's sons return to Egypt for food; Joseph makes himself known to his brothers; Jacob convinced that Joseph is a ruler in Egypt.

Verse for Today: *"And Joseph said unto his brethren, Come near to me, I pray you . . . "* (Genesis 45:4).

D uring the great famine, Jacob sent his sons to Egypt to buy food. As they stood before the great ruler of Egypt, asking for grain to carry back to their father, they were not aware that the ruler was Joseph, the brother whom they had sold into slavery about 20 years earlier.

After questioning them about their family, Joseph had them put into prison for three days—not for revenge, but to give them time to think. Joseph had not revealed his identity to them, but God caused them to realize that they were in prison because of their sin in selling Joseph.

Joseph wept secretly as he heard them confess how evil they had been in selling their brother (Genesis 42:21-23). He fully forgave them, and fellowship was restored.

Then Joseph invited his brothers to come near him (45:4). There was no barrier to be broken down, no aloofness—just sweet fellowship and peace.

This is the way the Holy Spirit works in the heart of a lost sinner. He brings him to the place where he no longer tries to defend himself but confesses that he is a sinner and asks for mercy and forgiveness. Then Christ will reveal Himself, even as Joseph revealed himself to his brothers.

Each Christian *has been chosen by God, who has given us this new kind of life. Because of His deep love and concern for us, we should practice tenderhearted mercy and kindness to others. We need not worry about making a good impression on them, but we should be ready to suffer quietly and patiently* (see Colossians 3:12).

Thought for Today: There is no peace with God until sin has been confessed and forsaken.

Christ Revealed: Through Joseph's dealings with his brothers as Christ deals with us—in such a way as to bring about a recognition of God's mercy and forgiving love, as well as His sovereignty over the affairs of life (Genesis 45:5-8,15).

Word Studies: 43:30 **bowels** means the heart; 45:6 **earing** means plowing; 45:24 **see that ye fall not out by the way** means do not quarrel.

Prayer Needs: Country: Bahrain—464,000—11 islands in the Persian Gulf near Saudi Arabia • No evangelical work is allowed among the Bahraini people • 95% Muslim; 4% Christian.

JANUARY 16: Read Genesis 46 — 48

Highlights: Jacob's vision at Beersheba; journey to Egypt; Joseph and the famine; best land given to Jacob; Joseph's sons blessed.

Verse for Today: *"And he blessed Joseph . . . "* (Genesis 48:15).

E arly in life, Joseph had set his heart on pleasing the Lord. God not only richly blessed him as a result of his faithfulness, but before his father Jacob died,

Jacob was led by God to bestow a covenant blessing upon Joseph that carried down through his descendants for many generations.

Oh, that Christians today would realize the rich rewards that God bestows upon all who abandon worldly attractions and set their hearts on pleasing Him! But there are alluring voices sounding everywhere, demanding attention and seeking to draw Christians away from the Word of God. Far too often, the desire to satisfy self overrules one's desire to please God.

God's greatest blessings are bestowed upon steadfast followers—those who see the importance of faithfully serving the Lord, even when it interferes with what they personally would like to do.

We are set free from the self-centered life as we read and submit to God's Word and choose His will.

Since future victory is sure, continue to remain firm and unmovable. Faithfully devote yourselves to working for the Lord. Work without limit, for you know that nothing you do for the Lord is ever wasted (see I Corinthians 15:58).

Thought for Today: Have you set your heart on pleasing the Lord or self?

Christ Portrayed: By Joseph, who was on the throne to sustain life and give provisions (Genesis 47:15). Jesus said, *For the Bread of God is He who comes down from Heaven and gives life to the world* (see John 6:33).

Word Studies: 46:4 **shall put his hand upon thine eyes** means will be with you when you die; 47:13 **sore** means severe.

Prayer Needs: Country: Western Samoa—175,000—in the South Pacific • Religious freedom • 68% Protestant; 21% Roman Catholic; 9% cults; 2% Baha'i.

EXODUS

The book of Exodus is a continuation of the history of the descendants of the 12 sons of Jacob. The last chapters of Genesis tell how Jacob and his family went to live in Egypt during the time Joseph was serving as a high official under Pharaoh. At that time, Jacob's family consisted of 70 people. Because of Joseph, Pharaoh gave the Israelites the land of Goshen, the most productive land in Egypt.

After Joseph's death, the prestige that the Israelites once enjoyed in Egypt gradually disappeared.

In the first chapter of Exodus—which means "the way out" or "departure" (see Hebrews 11:22)—just two short verses cover the many years between Joseph's death and the time of Moses (1:6-7).

Chapters 1 — 11 cover the period when the Israelites were slaves to the Egyptians and were forced to endure much suffering. God directed Moses to pronounce a series of nine plagues upon Egypt; then He sent the death angel throughout the unbelieving nation.

Chapters 12 — 13 deal with the Israelites' miraculous deliverance from Egypt. It was made possible by their obedience as they, by faith, applied the blood and ate the Passover lamb.

At the time they were delivered from slavery, there probably were about

600,000 Israelite men, plus women, children, and the "mixed multitude" (12:37-38). The total number has been estimated at more than two million people.

Chapters 14 — 18 provide an account of the journey of the Israelites from the Red Sea to Mount Sinai, which took about 50 days.

Chapters 19 — 40 take place at Mount Sinai where God gave them the Ten Commandments and detailed instructions for constructing the Tabernacle and offering sacrifices.

The Tabernacle portrayed the life and purpose of Christ. From the time the priest entered the gate of the fenced enclosure of the Tabernacle court until he entered the holy place, each procedure was symbolic of Christ and the development of the believer's relationship with the Lord.

About 430 years passed from the time God gave the Abrahamic Covenant to the giving of the Law on Mount Sinai (Galatians 3:16-17).

The book of Exodus reveals God's protection and provision for His people in the midst of our greatest difficulties.

JANUARY 17: Read Genesis 49 — Exodus 1

Highlights: Jacob's prophecies concerning his twelve sons; Judah to be an ancestor of the Messiah; deaths of Jacob and Joseph; Hebrew people oppressed in Egypt.

Verse for Today: *"Joseph is a fruitful bough ... whose branches run over the wall"* (Genesis 49:22).

When Jacob called his sons together and foretold God's blessing upon them, he emphasized the abuse which Joseph had suffered: *"The archers have sorely grieved him, and shot at him"* (Genesis 49:23; see also 40:15; Psalm 105:17-18).

Joseph's difficulties began with his spiritual insight and God-given dreams. However, God was preparing him to become the man He could use to protect and provide for His people in Egypt.

Perhaps the first and most vital step toward fulfilling God's will is being convinced of His overruling hand in all circumstances.

It is easy to manifest the characteristics of a spirit-filled life—love, joy, and peace—to those we love. But when we allow Christ to rule our hearts, we can go beyond our feelings of ill will, jealousy, and resentment toward those we feel have wronged us and love the unlovely.

In ourselves, we do not have the ability to cope with our unstable and unpredictable emotions. But we can rest in the assurance that what we cannot do in ourselves, Christ can accomplish through us.

"For if ye forgive men their trespasses, your heavenly Father will also forgive you: but if ye forgive not men their trespasses, neither will your Father forgive your trespasses" (Matthew 6:14-15).

Thought for Today: It is always the responsibility of the innocent person to be forgiving.

Christ Revealed: As the Messiah who would come through the tribe of Judah. *"The scepter [right to rule] shall not depart from Judah ... until Shiloh [Rest or Peace*

31

Giver] come" (Genesis 49:10; compare Luke 3:33). Jesus is the Prince of Peace who said, " . . . *I will give you rest"* (Matt. 11:28).

Word Studies: Genesis 49:6 **in their self-will they digged down a wall** means in their angry rage they destroyed the princes; 49:26 **progenitors** means ancestors; Exodus 1:10 **when there falleth out any war** means if war breaks out; 1:13 **serve with rigor** means work under cruel circumstances.

Prayer Needs: Country: Nauru (formerly Pleasant Island)—9,000—in the central Pacific just south of the equator • Religious freedom • 57% Protestant; 24% Roman Catholic; 10% Buddhist and Chinese folk-religionist.

JANUARY 18: Read Exodus 2 — 4

Highlights: Early life of Moses; his flight into Midian; the burning bush; his commission to free the nation of Israel; his return to Egypt.

Verse for Today: *"Now therefore go, and I will be with thy mouth, and teach thee what thou shalt say"* (Exodus 4:12).

W hen God spoke to Moses about leading the Israelites to freedom, Moses began making excuses. He was afraid to go alone, even when God said He would be with him. He could not be persuaded until the Lord permitted Aaron to be the spokesman.

Although Aaron's eloquence added nothing in the way of spiritual power, Moses was willing to go when God assured him that Aaron, a mere human like himself, would go with him.

Oh, how prone we are to trust something or someone other than the living God! We may step out boldly when we are supported by other people—even though they are mere humans, like ourselves. Christians should boldly act upon God's Word, knowing that His Spirit indwells every believer (John 14:17).

Many Christians have failed to obey the Lord, giving the excuse that they are inadequately prepared to have an effective ministry. But all the schooling in the world is useless unless the Lord is guiding the Christian and teaching him what to say. It is the Spirit of God anointing *what* we say—not *how* we say it—that really matters. *For what this world considers to be wisdom is nonsense in God's sight* (see I Corinthians 3:19).

Thought for Today: God is more concerned with willingness than He is with eloquence.

Christ Revealed: As the *"I AM THAT I AM"* who commissioned Moses (see Exodus 3:13-14; compare John 8:58; Heb. 13:8).

Word Studies: 2:1 **took to wife** means married; 3:22 **borrow** means ask.

Prayer Needs: Country: Costa Rica—3 million—in Central America • Religious freedom is increasing • 90% Roman Catholic; 6% Protestant.

JANUARY 19: Read Exodus 5 — 7

Highlights: Moses' demands to Pharaoh; Aaron to speak for Moses; Moses' rod turned into a snake; the plague of blood.

Verse for Today: *"Then the Lord said unto Moses, Now shalt thou see what I will* *do to Pharaoh: for with a strong hand shall he let them go, and with a strong hand shall he drive them out of his land"* (Exodus 6:1).

A lthough Moses had just blamed God for the added suffering which had come upon the Hebrew slaves, the Lord did not answer Moses' impatient, faultfinding questions. He merely reaffirmed His purpose to free His people..

Pharaoh had defiantly refused to let the Israelites leave Egypt (Exodus 5:2), but the God of creation declared that Pharaoh *would* let them go. In fact, God said that Pharaoh himself would drive them out of the land.

There was no need for Moses' faith to be shaken or for him to become discouraged over the criticism of the people. The added burdens and sufferings they experienced after Moses told Pharaoh to let God's people leave Egypt need not have depressed Moses. God had given His Word, and He would keep His promise.

No matter how much someone may criticize, threaten, or even persecute us, he cannot thwart the purposes of God: *There is no wisdom, no insight, no plan that can succeed against the Lord* (see Proverbs 21:30). God has assured us that His Word will accomplish what He intends for it to accomplish (Isaiah 55:11).

Whenever the evil one casts his fiery darts of suffering, disappointments, or opposition, just remember: *The Spirit who is in you is more powerful than the spirit in those who belong to the world* (see I John 4:4).

Thought for Today: We defeat ourselves when we become fearful about the difficulties that confront us.

Christ Revealed: As the Redeemer from the bondage of sin. *"I will bring you out . . . I will redeem you"* (Exodus 6:6). *"Christ hath redeemed us from the curse of the law . . . "* (Galatians 3:13; see also I Peter 1:18-25).

Word Studies: 5:18 **tale** means number; 5:19 **minish** means diminish; 7:22 **enchantments** means magic; tricks.

Prayer Needs: **Country:** San Marino—23,000—inside north-central Italy • Religious freedom • 95% Roman Catholic; 5% atheist.

JANUARY 20: Read Exodus 8 — 10

Highlights: Plagues of frogs, lice, flies, death of cattle, boils, hail, locusts, and darkness.

Verse for Today: *"And Pharaoh said, I will let you go, that ye may sacrifice to the Lord your God in the wilderness; only ye shall not go very far away: entreat for me"* (Exodus 8:28).

E gypt was the most powerful kingdom on earth at the time the Israelites were in bondage. Her idols and gods were considered equally powerful. Consequently, when Moses requested that the Israelites be permitted to worship the one true God, it was an insult to Pharaoh, who was considered one of the gods of Egypt.

Pharaoh did not refuse Moses' request to let the people worship Jehovah God, but he disagreed with the way they should worship. He wanted them to compromise what God had told them to do.

By studying Pharaoh's three efforts to cause Moses to compromise the Word of God, we can see why so many people experience spiritual defeat:

First, *" . . . sacrifice to your God in the land"* (Genesis 8:25). Worship your God, but do not leave Egypt; be one of us. This is typical of how a Christian is tempted to become involved in worldly activities and fail to live a separated life. There are many people who consent to worship God but who never intend to forsake their sins.

Second, " . . . *ye shall not go very far . . .* " (8:28). Just be lukewarm; don't get too involved in serving the Lord. Lukewarm Christians want to worship in their own way, avoid any service for Christ that conflicts with their own desires, and cooperate with the world.

Third, " . . . *Go . . . only let your flocks and your herds be stayed . . .* " (10:24). Keep your Christian testimony and your work separate. Entangle yourself with the world in your business associations.

Satan seeks to deceive us into believing that it is enough just to worship God. Yet, our worship is unacceptable to God unless it is according to His Word.

"He that saith, I know him, and keepeth not his commandments, is a liar, and the truth is not in him" (I John 2:4).

Thought for Today: In seeking worldly advantages, it's easy to lose sight of God's will.

Christ Revealed: As a Light to His people. " . . . *there was a thick darkness in all the land of Egypt . . . but all the children of Israel had light in their dwellings"* (Exodus 10:22-23). Jesus said, *"I am the light of the world: he that followeth me shall not walk in darkness . . ."* (John 8:12). " . . . *the Lord will lighten my darkness"* (II Samuel 22:29).

Word Studies: 9:3 **murrain** means plague; pestilence; 9:10 **blains** means blisters.

Prayer Needs: Country: El Salvador—5 million—in Central America • Churches outside the state religion (Catholicism) are free to operate, though sometimes with official obstruction • 96% Roman Catholic; 3% Protestant.

JANUARY 21:   Read Exodus 11 — 13

Highlights: Death of the firstborn; the Passover; the Exodus; pillar of cloud and pillar of fire.

Verses for Today: *"For I will pass through the land of Egypt this night, and will smite all the first-born in the land of Egypt . . . and when I see the blood, I will pass over you . . . "* (Exodus 12:12-13).

Many of the Israelites probably were skeptical of the peculiar method of deliverance from Egypt. But their only hope of escape from the death angel was to kill a lamb and apply the blood to the lintel and the two side posts of their doors.

Some could have protested, expressing their distaste for the sight of blood above and around their doors. The "more enlightened" could have paid guards in an effort to protect their homes from intruders. But deliverance from the death angel could not be bought. No amount of gold could take the place of the blood. Nor was there a family so good that they did not need the blood of a lamb applied as God had said. God had only one plan, and His divine command had to be obeyed.

Just as the blood of the Passover lamb was the only possible means of saving the life of the firstborn, so the blood of Christ is the only means by which sinful man can receive eternal life. One may hope that as long as he is sincere, some other means will satisfy God, but he will still be eternally lost.

34

Through the eternal Spirit, Christ offered Himself as a perfect sacrifice to God. His blood will purify our consciences from dead works so that we may serve the living God (see Hebrews 9:14).

Thought for Today: Our assurance of eternal life is only through a personal acceptance of Jesus Christ as our Lord and Savior.

Christ Revealed: Through the sacrifice of lambs without blemish. Not one of the lamb's bones was to be broken (Exodus 12:5,46). We were redeemed *"with the precious blood of Christ, as of a lamb without blemish and without spot"* (I Peter 1:19). It was foretold of Christ: *"He keepeth all his bones: not one of them is broken"* (Psalm 34:20; compare John 19:36).

Prayer Needs: Country: Brazil—147 million—in South America • Religious freedom • 87% Roman Catholic; 7% Protestant; 4% various forms of spiritism.

JANUARY 22: Read Exodus 14 — 16

Highlights: Crossing the Red Sea; song of Moses; the waters of Marah; murmurings; manna and quail.

Verse for Today: *"Then sang Moses and the children of Israel this song unto the Lord . . . for he hath triumphed gloriously"* (Exodus 15:1).

S oon after the Israelites left Egypt, Pharaoh decided to bring them back. God miraculously parted the Red Sea, and all the Israelites escaped to the other side. But Pharaoh's army was drowned when they attempted to cross.

The Israelites sang praises to God for the wondrous deliverance from Pharaoh and his armies (Exodus 15:1-19). They did not praise Moses, their great leader; nor did they attribute their victory to their own wisdom, strength, or good fortune. They recognized that this was the hand of God; and they praised Him for His power, holiness, glory, mercy, and supremacy.

This song of Moses and the Lamb will continue in Heaven for all eternity. It is the first song mentioned in the Scriptures and is mentioned again in the last book of the Bible (Revelation 15:3).

Combining judgment and grace, destruction and deliverance, this song sets forth God's final victory over all enemies—a victory that will be celebrated by all Christians in Heaven.

Jesus said that *everyone who wins the victory will receive His blessings; He will be their God, and they will be His people* (see Revelation 21:7).

Thought for Today: How sweet will be the heavenly song when all the enemies of the soul are forever defeated!

Christ Revealed: Through the bread (manna) from Heaven (Exodus 16:15). Jesus said, *"I am the living bread which came down from heaven . . . "* (John 6:51; see also 6:35,41,48).

Word Studies: 15:25 **proved them** means put them to the test; 16:16 **according to his eating** means according to the size of his family; 16:18 **did mete it** means measured it; 16:23 **seethe** means boil; 16:36 **an ephah** contains about one bushel.

Prayer Needs: Country: Guam—125,000—in the western Pacific, the most southerly of the Marianas • Religious freedom • 79% Roman Catholic; 17% Protestant.

JANUARY 23: Read Exodus 17 — 19

Highlights: Thirst causes murmuring against Moses; water from the rock; Amalek defeated; Jethro's advice accepted; God speaks on Mount Sinai.

Verse for Today: *"And the people thirsted there for water ... and said, Wherefore is this that thou hast brought us up out of Egypt, to kill us and our children and our cattle with thirst?"* (Exodus 17:3).

F rom the time the Israelites left Egypt to the time they reached the border of the Promised Land, they were so concerned with satisfying their immediate needs that they always found fault and murmured when they faced problems. *They even spoke against God Himself* (see Psalm 78:17). Consequently, that generation never experienced the satisfaction of fulfilling God's purpose—conquering the Promised Land.

Every thought of unbelief in the wisdom and goodness of God is evidence of a self-centered person who believes that he—not God—knows best and should control the affairs of his life.

At times, it may seem that God has not met our needs, but praising the Lord during times of testing always honors God and is the key to victory and receiving blessings from Him. (See I Thessalonians 5:18.) He always knows what is best.

The Christian's faith is not based on favorable circumstances, but in a person— the Lord Jesus Christ. *God has promised to supply your every need according to His riches in glory by Christ Jesus* (see Philippians 4:19).

Thought for Today: Peace fills the heart when our desire is "Whatever pleases You, Lord, pleases me."

Christ Revealed: As the Rock and the Water that came forth (Exodus 17:6). *" ...for they drank of that spiritual Rock that followed them: and that Rock was Christ"* (I Cor. 10:4).

Word Studies: 17:13 **discomfited** means weakened; disabled; 19:15 **against** means by; 19:18 **altogether on a smoke** means covered with smoke.

Prayer Needs: Country: Papua New Guinea—4 million—in the southwestern Pacific • Growing pressure to limit activities of missions and churches • 64% Protestant; 33% Roman Catholic; 2% ancestor worship, belief in spirits, and witchcraft.

JANUARY 24: Read Exodus 20 — 22

Highlights: Ten Commandments and other laws and regulations given.

Verses for Today: *"And God spake all these words, saying ... Thou shalt have no other gods before me"* (Exodus 20:1,3).

T he Ten Commandments were *"written with the finger of God"* (Exodus 31:18). These commandments reveal the absolute perfection of God's holy nature, but they also reveal the terrible sinfulness of mankind.

If God had given or commanded less than that which is perfect, He would have been compromising—which He cannot do. But there is no way, humanly speaking, for a person to keep the Law perfectly—whereby the mind, body, and spirit will all be in total agreement and obedience to the Law—because *the natural mind is not capable of obeying God's Law* (see Romans 8:7). No one—except Christ Himself—has ever been able to live without sinning.

This only points out how far mankind fell when Adam sinned and how true the Scripture is that says, *All have sinned, and come short (far shorter than we can understand) of God's glorious ideal* (see Romans 3:23).

Everyone has the characteristics of the fallen nature—*there is none that seeks God's will* (see Romans 3:11). By accepting Christ as our Savior, we receive His nature, for *"the Spirit of God"* indwells us (8:9). Then our spirit agrees with the Lord that His Word is good, right, holy, and just; and our inward desire is to do what He has commanded. (See I John 4:5-6.)

For what the Law could not do, ineffective as it was through the flesh (the entire nature of man without the Holy Spirit), God did: sending His own Son in the likeness of sinful flesh and as an offering for sin, He condemned sin in the flesh, in order that the requirement of the Law might be fulfilled in us, who do not walk according to the flesh, but according to the Spirit (see Romans 8:3-4).

Thought for Today: Are you truly seeking God's will as you read His Word?

Christ Revealed: Christ's nature and character are revealed through the Ten Commandments (Exodus 20:1-17). He was perfect and without sin (Heb. 4:15). Christ gave us a New Commandment—*"That ye love one another; as I have loved you, that ye also love one another"* (John 13:34).

Word Studies: 20:13 **kill** means murder; 21:14 **guile** means trickery; 21:29 **push** means gore; 22:18 **witch** means sorceress; 22:25 **usury** means interest on money loaned; 22:30 **dam** means mother.

Prayer Needs: Country: North Korea—22 million—in northeastern Asia • Violent oppression against Christianity • 39% Buddhism, Confucianism, and other Korean religions; 40% no religious belief; 1% Christian.

JANUARY 25: Read Exodus 23 — 25

Highlights: Laws instituted; three feasts which must be kept; angel promised for a guide; instructions for Tabernacle furnishings.

Verse for Today: *"And he said unto Moses, Come up unto the Lord, thou, and Aaron, Nadab, and Abihu, and seventy of the elders of Israel; and worship ye afar off"* (Exodus 24:1).

T hese men were summoned into the very presence of God Himself. Never before in history had Jehovah—the God of creation—met with any group of men. Because God is absolutely holy and man is defiled by sin, they had to worship Him from a distance. To do otherwise would mean instant death. Yet, they seemed at ease, for they ate and drank in His presence (Exodus 24:11).

Notice what made it possible for them to be able to eat and drink in His presence. Moses had arisen early, built an altar, offered burnt offerings, and sacrificed peace offerings of oxen to the Lord (24:4-5). This was in obedience to what the Lord had said to Moses (20:24). The shedding of blood made it possible for the people to have a new relationship with God.

It was after the blood was applied that Moses, Aaron, Nadab, Abihu, and 70 of the leaders of Israel went up the mountain and feasted in the presence of the God of Israel (24:8-10).

These events point out the importance of the blood of Christ and the wonderful privileges it obtains for all who have acknowledged themselves as lost sinners and received Christ as their Savior. *Christ died for the sins of all us guilty sinners, although He Himself was innocent of any sin at any time, that He might bring us safely home to God* (see I Peter 3:18).

Thought for Today: Because of Christ's sacrificial death on the cross, each of us has the privilege of being in His presence through prayer and hearing Him speak to us as we read His Word.

Christ Portrayed: By the servant who voluntarily bound himself to his master, although he was free to do whatever he wished (Exodus 21:5-6). Here we see Christ's devotion to the Father. *"I delight to do thy will, O my God . . . "* (Psa. 40:8).

Prayer Needs: Country: Italy—57 million—in southern Europe • Religious freedom • 81% Roman Catholic; .4% Protestant; .1% Eastern Orthodox.

JANUARY 26: Read Exodus 26 — 28

Highlights: Directions given for constructing the Tabernacle, court, furniture, and enclosure; plans for the altar; Aaron's priestly garments; plans for the ephod.

Verse for Today: *"And thou shalt rear up the tabernacle according to the fashion thereof which was showed thee in the mount"* (Exodus 26:30).

T he purpose of the Tabernacle was to provide a place where God could reveal Himself to His people and dwell among them. The Tabernacle was a rectangular structure 30 cubits (about 45 feet) long and 10 cubits (about 15 feet) wide. It was protected by an enclosure that measured 50 cubits (75 feet) wide and 100 cubits (150 feet) long.

There was only one entrance to this enclosure (Exodus 27:16). It portrayed our Lord as the only way to God's presence. Jesus said, *I am the door; if any man comes in through Me, he will be saved* (see John 10:9).

After passing through the entrance into the fenced enclosure, the worshiper approached the brazen altar, known as the altar of burnt offering.

The sacrifice offered upon the brazen altar was a type of Christ's death (see Hebrews 13:10-12). Just as the ram was wholly burned upon the altar, Christ was wholly dedicated to God, willing to die on the cross for our sins. Our wonderful Lord was both *the Lamb of God, who takes away our sin* (see John 1:29), and our High Priest. *As our High Priest, he is in Heaven at the place of greatest honor with God Himself* (see Hebrews 8:1).

Thought for Today: God no longer lives in a Tabernacle; He dwells within the heart of every believer.

Christ Revealed: Through the brazen (bronze) altar, where the sacrifice was burned (Exodus 27:1-8). Christ is *the* Sacrifice (Ephesians 1:7).

Word Studies: 26:17 **tenons** are projections for dovetail joints; 27:5 **compass** means top edge; rim; ledge; 27:6 **staves** means poles for carrying; 27:10 **fillets** means support cords or bands connecting the posts; 28:4 **mitre** means turban; 28:8 **curious girdle** means interlaced belt; 28:11 **ouches** means settings of a gem; 28:14 **wreathen** means braided; 28:17 **carbuncle** may be a garnet or emerald; 28:19 **ligure** was possible jacinth or amber.

Prayer Needs: Country: Brunei—250,000—on the northern coast of Borneo • Limited religious freedom • 66% Muslim; 19% Chinese religions; 6% animist; 4% Protestant; 4% Roman Catholic.

JANUARY 27: Read Exodus 29 — 31

Highlights: The rules and sacrifices for consecrating the priests; continual burnt offering; altar of incense; the ransom of souls; the holy anointing oil; sabbath regulations; Moses receives two tables of stone.

Verse for Today: *"This shall be a continual burnt offering throughout your generations at the door of the tabernacle of the congregation before the Lord: where I will meet you, to speak there unto thee"* (Exodus 29:42).

W hen the Israelite worshiper brought an acceptable sacrifice to the brazen altar to offer a burnt offering, the priest killed the animal and prepared the sacrifice on behalf of the worshiper. The *"continual burnt offering"* provided a way for the Israelite to be reconciled to a holy God.

The purpose of the burnt offering is found in the words: *"I will meet you, to speak there unto thee."* The Lord wants to meet and speak with His people.

Some people assume that as long as their outward conduct is good, God is pleased with them. But mere obedience to the Law does not soften and warm the heart, for the letter of the Law leads to death. It is the indwelling Spirit of God that gives life (see II Corinthians 3:6).

When we acknowledge our sinful, lost condition and turn to Christ—the One who became an acceptable offering for our sins—our hearts will be filled with His presence and the Bible will become more than "dos and don'ts." It is the indwelling Holy Spirit that enables a Christian to worship God acceptably (see John 4:23-24).

Thought for Today: The power of victorious Christian living is experienced through prayer and hearing what God has to say as we read His Word.

Christ Revealed: Through the laver, Christ is revealed as both the container and the dispenser of *"living water"* (Exodus 30:18; John 4:10; compare I Cor. 10:4; Heb. 10:22).

Word Studies: 29:22 **caul** means appendage or lobe on the liver; 29:24 **wave them** means present them with a waving motion; 30:25 **apothecary** means perfumer.

Prayer Needs: Country: Tuvalu (formerly Ellice Islands)—8,000—nine islands in the southwestern Pacific • Religious freedom • 92% Protestant; 5% Baha'i; 2% Roman Catholic.

JANUARY 28: Read Exodus 32 — 34

Highlights: Moses delayed on Mount Sinai; Aaron's golden calf; its destruction; death of 3,000 Israelites; Law renewed; God's covenant; three feasts.

Verse for Today: *"And the Lord said unto Moses, I have seen this people, and, behold, it is a stiff-necked people"* (Exodus 32:9).

W hile Moses was on Mount Sinai waiting for the Lord's direction as to how they were to worship the Holy God, the Israelites were at the foot of the mountain proclaiming *"a feast to the Lord."* They offered burnt offerings and made a golden calf as an object of worship (Exodus 32:5-10).

The golden calf stands as a symbol of human intellect, which devises a system of worship apart from divine direction. It bears out the fact that when people turn from the Lord and ignore His Word, they will worship the works of their own hands (compare Acts 7:41; Romans 1:21,23).

True worship takes place only when we are living and worshiping in obedience to His Word.

Jesus said, *Why do you call me "Lord" and do not practice what I tell you?* (see Luke 6:46).

Thought for Today: There is no substitute for obedience!

Christ Revealed: As the One who is ever-present. *"My presence shall go with thee, and I will give thee rest"* (Exodus 33:14; compare Matt. 11:28; 28:20).

Word Studies: 32:12 **mischief** means evil intent; 32:20 **strawed it** means scattered it; 33:22 **clift** means cleft.

Prayer Needs: Country: Vatican City—800—in Rome, Italy • Religious freedom • Approximately 100% Roman Catholic.

JANUARY 29: Read Exodus 35 — 37

Highlights: Freewill offerings for the Tabernacle; construction of the Tabernacle; the ark; mercy seat; table of showbread; candlestick (lampstand); altar of incense.

Verse for Today: *"The candlestick also for the light, and his furniture, and his lamps, with the oil for the light"* (Exodus 35:14).

A fter the priest had washed his hands and feet at the laver, he proceeded toward the Tabernacle and entered the only door to the Holy Place.

On the left was the seven-branched golden candlestick that provided the only source of light in the Holy Place. Without this light from the golden candlestick, the room would have been in total darkness. The golden candlestick represents Christ, who is the Light of the world and who bestows light to make Himself known through His Word. (See John 8:12.)

On the right was the table of showbread with its 12 loaves sprinkled with incense. They were eaten by the priests only in the Holy Place. None could be removed and eaten elsewhere. Its name "showbread" suggests more than bodily nourishment. It indicates seeking God—gaining spiritual insight that is not obtainable in any other way. Beyond our ability to explain, the Holy Spirit enlightens, empowers, and then transforms the lives of those who prayerfully continue to "eat" the Bread of life.

I am the living bread that came down from Heaven. If anyone eats of this bread, he will live forever (see John 6:51).

Thought for Today: Christ is the Bread of life, the Sustainer of each individual believer.

Christ Revealed: Through the "candlestick" (lampstand) (Exodus 35:14). Christ is *the Light of the world* (see John 9:5; compare Luke 1:78-79).

Word Studies: 35:11 **his** means its; 35:32 **curious** means artistic.

Prayer Needs: Country: Cambodia—7 million—in Southeast Asia • Churches have suffered under Communism • 88% Buddhist; 3% animism and spirit worship; 2% Muslim; .6% Christian.

JANUARY 30: Read Exodus 38 — 39

Highlights: Altar of burnt offering; the Tabernacle courtyard; the priest's garments.

Verse for Today: *"Thus was all the work of the tabernacle of the tent of the congregation finished: and the children of Israel did according to all that the Lord commanded Moses . . . "*(Exodus 39:32).

A bsolutely nothing about the Tabernacle was left to human planning, for God had an exact design for the Tabernacle—His holy dwelling place.

God had walked with Adam in the Garden of Eden; He had spoken to Abraham; He had given His Law to Moses; but the Tabernacle in the wilderness was God's first dwelling place on earth.

Later, God the Son came to earth to dwell among His people, and *the Word was made a human being, and lived (tabernacled) among us* (see John 1:14).

After Jesus ascended into Heaven, the precious Holy Spirit of God came to indwell all who accept Christ—the Son of God—as Savior: *Your body is a temple of the Holy Spirit* (see I Corinthians 6:19).

We are God's *dwelling place*—tabernacle, or holy temple—*being built together as a place where God lives through His Spirit* (see Ephesians 2:21-22). Therefore, no true child of God can plead ignorance to the fact that God wants him to live a different kind of life from the way the world lives. The life He would have us live is more than keeping the Ten Commandments, and is never the result of human wisdom. It is made possible by the indwelling Holy Spirit who enlightens our understanding as we read the Word of God.

" . . . the Spirit of truth . . . will guide you into all truth . . . " (John 16:13).

Thought for Today: Before making any decision, prayerfully consider: "Will it glorify God?"

Christ Revealed: Through the golden altar and the incense—representing prayers going up to Heaven—we see Christ praying for us (Exodus 39:38; see also John 17:9).

Word Studies: 38:17 **chapiters of silver** means tops with silver; 39:23 **habergeon** means breastplate; coat of mail (the opening in the linen robe is being compared to the opening in a coat of mail); **band** means a woven binding to keep it from tearing.

Prayer Needs: Country: Jordan—3 million—in southwestern Asia • Considerable tolerance of the few Christians in Jordan • 93% Muslim; 5% Christian.

JANUARY 31: Read Exodus 40

Highlights: Tabernacle completed and erected; furnishings arranged; consecration of Aaron and his sons; the glory of the Lord filling the Tabernacle.

Verses for Today: *" . . . set up the tabernacle. . . . And thou shalt put therein the ark of the testimony . . . "* (Exodus 40:2-3).

T he Ark of the Testimony was about four feet long, two feet wide, and two feet high (Exodus 25:10; 37:1-5). It was made of wood and overlaid with gold, both within and without, so that nothing but the gold was seen. It was the visible symbol of God's presence.

The Ark typified the Lord Jesus Christ. The wood and the gold represented the two natures of our Lord—the human and the divine. The two tables of stone preserved inside the Ark pictured Christ as the Living Word. (See 25:21-22; 31:18; Deuteronomy 10:1-2; compare John 1:1-2.)

Also within the Ark was a golden pot of manna—food which the Lord gave to Israel for their journey to the Promised Land after their release from bondage. It foreshadowed Christ as the Bread of life—the food of His faithful people.

In addition, the Ark held Aaron's rod that budded (Numbers 17)—a symbol of the resurrection of Jesus Christ.

After leaving Mount Sinai, the Ark of the Testimony went before the Israelites (Numbers 10:33)—a type of Christ as the leader of His pilgrim people. When they reached the Jordan River, the Ark of the Lord's presence entered, dividing the waters for Israel to pass over on dry ground. This symbolizes our Lord Jesus Christ making possible the impossible to be *"more than conquerors"* (Romans 8:37).

The Ark of the Testimony led the way as Israel marched around the walls of Jericho. This teaches us that strongholds of Satan will fall when the people of God are faithful to His Word.

The man who has received My commands and obeys them is the one who loves Me. My Father loves whoever loves Me; I too will love him and make Myself real to him (see John 14:21).

Thought for Today: Is Jesus truly Lord and Master of your life, or is He Lord in name only, because you insist on pleasing yourself?

Christ Portrayed: By the high priest (Exodus 40:13). *"But Christ being come a high priest . . . now to appear in the presence of God for us"* (see Heb. 9:7-24).

Word Studies: 40:8 **hanging** means veil; 40:10 **sanctify** means set apart for God; **most holy** means exclusively for God; 40:11 **his foot** means its stand.

Prayer Needs: Country: Dominican Republic—7 million—in the West Indies, occupying the eastern two-thirds of the island of Hispaniola • Religious freedom • 96% Roman Catholic (one-half of which are spiritists); 2% Protestant; 1% Afro-American spiritist.

PRAYERS/CONVERSATIONS WITH GOD

LEVITICUS_____

The book of Leviticus contains instructions to teach the Israelites how to live holy lives. *Be holy, because I am holy* is a key statement for the entire book (see 11:44-45). Laws are given not only for worship and religious ceremonies, but also to regulate all of life.

The sacrificial system of worship made it possible for God's people to draw near to Him. In Leviticus, He is no longer speaking from Mt. Sinai, but from the mercy seat within the Holy of Holies in the Tabernacle. From there He gives instructions for the five sacrificial offerings (chapters 1—7).

All the sacrifices represent different aspects of Christ, the Lamb of God, giving Himself as a sacrifice for lost sinners.

Chapters 8—10 tell of the ordination of Aaron and his sons. Chapters 11—15 give regulations for holy living. Chapter 16 is devoted to the Day of Atonement.

The book of Leviticus reveals that our enjoyment of God's presence is based upon our trust in Him and our obedience to His Word. Obedience brings us into harmony with His holy nature, thereby imparting His peace.

The word "peace" is mentioned more times in Leviticus than in any other book of the Bible.

The word "holy" does not occur even once in Genesis, but it appears about 90 times in the book of Leviticus.

The events in the book of Leviticus possibly took place in just one month, beginning with God speaking from the erected Tabernacle (Exodus 40:1-2; Numbers 1:1), and ending after He gave the five feasts and the laws on holiness and worship (chapters 17—27).

FEBRUARY 1: Leviticus 1 — 3

Highlights: Burnt offering; meat (meal) offering; peace offering.

Verse for Today: *"And he shall offer of the sacrifice of the peace offering an offering made by fire unto the Lord . . . "* (Leviticus 3:3).

The peace offering was the last one to be offered because there could be no peace or fellowship with God until all the regulations of the sin and trespass offerings had first been obeyed.

The peace offering was a "sweet savor offering"—giving to God that which satisfied Him. Bread that was offered as part of the sacrifice had to be made without yeast (leaven), for yeast was symbolic of corruption. The absence of leaven in the offering represented the removal of sin.

This offering naturally follows the other sacrifice as an offering of completeness, expressing restored fellowship between God and man.

The peace offering was distinctly different from the burnt offering and the meal offering in that it was always shared with others. As the priest, the worshiper, and his family and friends ate this meal, they were conscious of the presence of God and were grateful for His ability to protect His people and supply their needs. It was always a joyful occasion of thankfulness for God's blessings.

Many Christians never experience the full meaning of the peace offering. They have been delivered from the power of sin (see Romans 6:22; Jude 1:24) and have *peace with God*—and perhaps have desired to present their bodies a living sacrifice, as represented in the burnt offering—but they know little of the *peace of God* which goes beyond human understanding (Philippians 4:7). The peace of God is the result of making peace and maintaining peace with others. Ill will, jealousy, envy, and hatred for others destroys the peace of God.

We can ask for nothing greater than having the God of peace ruling our hearts! *Let the peace of God, which comes from Christ, be always present in your hearts and lives, for this is your responsibility and privilege as members of His body. And always be thankful* (see Colossians 3:15).

Thought for Today: As we yield our lives to the God of peace, we experience the peace of God.

Christ Revealed: Through the grain (meal) offering which was made without leaven (symbolic of sin) (Leviticus 2:11). Christ was without sin (Heb. 4:15).

Word Studies: 1:6 **flay** means skin; 1:9 **sweet savor** means pleasing odor; 2:1 **meat offering** means meal offering or cakes of such flour; 2:3 **a thing most holy** means only to be used as God directs; 2:9 **memorial** means remembrance-offering; 2:12 **oblation** means offering; 3:3 **inwards** means internal organs; 3:4 **flanks** means loins; **caul** means lobe of the liver; 3:9 **hard by** means near.

Prayer Needs: **Country:** Mauritania—2 million—in western Africa • An Islamic state with no open mission work allowed• 99+% Muslim; .5% Roman Catholic; about 170 Protestants—there are no known native Mauritanian believers.

FEBRUARY 2: Read Leviticus 4 — 6

Highlights: Sin offering; trespass offering; further directions about offerings.

Verse for Today: *"And he shall bring the bullock unto the door of the tabernacle of the congregation before the Lord; and shall lay his hand upon the bullock's head, and kill the bullock before the Lord"* (Leviticus 4:4).

T he sin offering was the first sacrifice presented to God. Each person was required to bring his own animal to offer upon the altar before the Tabernacle.

With other offerings, the Israelite came as a worshiper; but when offering a sin or trespass offering, he came confessing himself a sinner. The offerer placed his hands upon the head of the animal as an act of passing his sins to the innocent animal. The animal was then put to death instead of the sinner. The priest sprinkled the blood before the Lord, and the worshiper's sins were covered (but his sins were not removed until Christ died on the cross—Hebrews 10:9-14).

The sin offering was a testimony not only to the fact that the worshiper was a sinner, but that God had provided a way for him to be acceptable to God.

When Jesus shed His blood on the cross for the sins of mankind, there was no longer any need for animal sacrifices. *"For he hath made him to be sin for us, who knew no sin; that we might be made the righteousness of God in Him"* (II Corinthians 5:21).

The Lord Jesus Christ not only presented Himself as a sacrifice to God, but He also fulfilled the position of the priest, becoming our great High Priest who *"ever liveth to make intercession"* for us (Hebrews 7:25). Thus, He became both the sacrifice for our sins and the mediator between God and man. (See Hebrews 2:17; 4:15.)

"If we confess our sins, he is faithful and just to forgive us our sins, and to cleanse us from all unrighteousness" (I John 1:9).

Thought for Today: Christ, who is in the presence of God, intercedes on our behalf when we pray.

Christ Revealed: Through the body of the young bull which was burned outside the camp (Leviticus 4:12). This pictures Jesus as He suffered *outside the gate* (see Heb. 13:11-12).

Word Studies: 4:20 **an atonement** means a reconciliation; 5:2 **unclean** means ceremonially defiled; 5:4 **swear** means make a vow; 5:11 **an ephah** contains about one bushel; 6:5 **appertaineth** means belongs; 6:10 **breeches** means undergarments; 6:22 **wholly burnt** means entirely given to the Lord; 6:28 **sodden** means boiled.

Prayer Needs: Country: Uganda—16 million—in eastern Africa • Religious freedom • 51% Roman Catholic; 30% Protestant; 10% animist; 7% Muslim.

FEBRUARY 3: Read Leviticus 7 — 8

Highlights: Trespass offering; peace offering; wave offering; the consecration of Aaron and his sons for the priesthood.

Verse for Today: *"In the place where they kill the burnt offering shall they kill the trespass offering: and the blood thereof shall he sprinkle round about upon the altar"* (Leviticus 7:2).

T he trespass offering was offered for specific acts of wrongdoing, either against God or man. But the offender was just as guilty before God for trespasses committed in ignorance, since ignorance is due to willful neglect of His Word. (See Leviticus 5:15—6:7.)

The trespass offering was actually a part of the sin offering. God demanded that all who had committed a trespass bring an offering, restore what he had taken, and also give an additional 20% to the one he had wronged.

No part of these trespass offerings was eaten by the offerer, such as with the peace offering. The sacrificer came as one unworthy, and the purpose of his offering was to restore peace with God.

Our Lord has provided mankind with His Word—the Bible. It sets forth the moral and spiritual principles necessary to maintain harmony with both God and man. All who neglect to read the Bible, or having read it, refuse to live according to its revelation, will face the judgment of God. *"For if we sin willfully after that we have received the knowledge of the truth, there remaineth no more sacrifice for sins"* (Hebrews 10:26).

Thought for Today: How foolish to depend on one's conscience for guidance without having enlightenment from God's Word!

Christ Portrayed: By Moses consecrating the priests who presented themselves for the work (Leviticus 8:23-24). Christ is the One who sets the believer apart for service as the believer presents himself to Christ (Romans 12:1).

Word Studies: 8:3 **unto the door** means at the doorway; 8:8 **Urim, Thummim** were unknown objects worn by the high priest; 8:13 **bonnets** means headpieces; 8:22 **consecration** means an act of dedication; 8:35 **keep the charge of the Lord** means perform what the Lord has charged.

Prayer Needs: Country: Finland—5 million—in northern Europe • Religious freedom • 91% Protestant; 1% Eastern Orthodox; 1% Roman Catholic.

FEBRUARY 4: Read Leviticus 9 — 10

Highlights: First offerings of Aaron; sin and deaths of Nadab and Abihu; restrictions for the priesthood.

Verses for Today: *"... the glory of the Lord appeared unto all the people. And there came a fire out from before the Lord, and consumed upon the altar the burnt offering and the fat: which when all the people saw, they shouted, and fell on their faces"* (Leviticus 9:23-24).

T he Israelites were required by the Law to offer sin and trespass offerings. They also offered a public burnt offering sacrifice each morning and evening. But a burnt offering could also be brought by one who felt the need of humbly coming before the Lord in deep gratitude for His mercy, confessing any offenses and failings which were not specifically mentioned in the Law. But most of all, it signified his dedication and consecration to God.

The burnt offering sacrifice could be a young bull, ram, goat, or sheep. The very poor could bring a pair of turtledoves or two young pigeons (see Luke 2:24), having assurance that their offerings would be just as acceptable to God as the costly gifts of their more prosperous neighbors.

But whatever was chosen for the offering, it was to be the most excellent of its kind—*"a male without blemish"* (Leviticus 22:19). It would have been highly offensive to God to offer anything that was lame, blind, diseased, or in any other way imperfect. This offering was a type of our perfect Savior—the Lamb of God who was *"without blemish and without spot"* (I Peter 1:19). But this offering was also designed to teach us that we, too, are to offer our best unto God—the best of our time, talents, and possessions.

Too many people think that they can meet their needs first, and then consider what they will give to God from what—if anything—is left. This might agree with worldly economics, but it is spiritually unsound. No person is too poor to give.

We cannot shirk our responsibilities to serve and to give by rationalizing that someone else will do it or can do it better.

"Every man according as he purposeth in his heart, so let him give; not grudgingly, or of necessity: for God loveth a cheerful giver" (II Corinthians 9:7).

Thought for Today: Each of us is unique in God's plan; no one else can fill our place.

Christ Revealed: Through the sacrifice of a lamb without defect (Leviticus 9:3). Peter likened Jesus to an unblemished lamb (I Pet. 1:19; see also John 1:29).

Word Studies: 10:10 **unholy** means unacceptable; 10:13 **thy due** means your share; 10:19 **befallen** means happened to.

Prayer Needs: Country: Greenland—54,000—northeast of Canada • Religious freedom • 98% Protestant; .1% Roman Catholic.

FEBRUARY 5: Read Leviticus 11 — 13

Highlights: Animals that may be eaten; the cleansing (purification) of women after childbirth; signs and regulations concerning leprosy.

Verses for Today: *"And the leper in whom the plague is, his clothes shall be rent, and his head bare, and he shall put a covering upon his upper lip, and shall cry, Unclean, unclean. All the days wherein the plague shall be in him he shall be defiled; he is unclean: he shall dwell alone; without the camp shall his habitation be"* (Leviticus 13:45-46).

T he word "leper" struck terror in the heart of an Israelite for two reasons. First, the person who had leprosy became an outcast from society. He was forced to leave his home—his family, friends, and place of worship—and live outside the camp. When anyone went near him, the leper had to cry out, "Unclean, unclean." But perhaps the most horrifying reason leprosy was so feared was that there was no known cure for it.

Leprosy is symbolic of the horribleness of sin. Sin destroys the joy of life and, if it continues, will eventually lead to the ruin of both body and soul. The leper's being separated from the place of sacrifice and worship illustrates how sin separates us from the presence of God. (See II Thessalonians 1:8-9.)

Don't blame God for the wickedness and miseries all around us; blame Satan, the one who brought all sin and death into the world. Christ is the revelation of our loving Father who desires to impart eternal life and cleansing from sin.

"The thief cometh not but for to steal, and to kill, and to destroy: I am come that they might have life, and that they might have it more abundantly" (John 10:10).

Thought for Today: When Christ forgives our sins, He cleanses our hearts.

Christ Revealed: Through the clean food of the believer (Leviticus 11:47). Our Lord is the Bread of life (John 6:35), supplies living water (4:14), and His Father's will was His meat (food) (4:34).

Word Studies: 11:10 **abomination** means unfit to use; 11:19 **lapwing** is an unclean bird; 11:35 **ranges for pots** means hearth; 13:3 **plague in the skin of the flesh** means infection; 13:39 **freckled spot** means scaly white spot; 13:48 **warp or woof** means the yarn prepared to be woven or knitted; 13:51 **fretting** means spreading.

Prayer Needs: Country: Uruguay—3 million—on the southeastern coast of South America • Religious freedom • 60% Catholic; 2% Protestant; 2% Jewish; .7% Eastern Orthodox.

FEBRUARY 6: Read Leviticus 14 — 15

Highlights: Purification after having skin diseases; signs of leprosy; the uncleanness of men and women; sacrifice for cleansing.

Verse for Today: *"And the priest shall offer the burnt offering and the meat offering upon the altar: and the priest shall make an atonement for him, and he shall be clean"* (Leviticus 14:20).

T he Hebrew word used here for "meat Offering" means meal offering. It consisted of fine flour, oil, and frankincense (Leviticus 2:1). The priest took a handful of the meal offering and burned it on the altar.

The grain of wheat represents Christ in His human perfections. Just as the grain in the meal offering had to be ground into flour before it could be used, Jesus was broken by His death on the cross to become the Bread of life for His people.

A meal offering made with leaven (yeast) was not acceptable to God. Yeast is symbolic of the moral impurity and evil that corrupts human hearts. What a lesson for those who are expecting God's blessings without removing the moral impurities from their lives!

Don't you realize that if even one person is allowed to go on sinning, soon all will be affected? So let us leave entirely behind us the cancerous old life with all its hatreds and wickedness. Let us feast instead upon the pure Word of God and live in sincerity and truth (see I Corinthians 5:7-8).

Thought for Today: For us to be an expression of the meal offering, the leaven of sin and self-will must be removed from our lives.

Christ Portrayed: By the priest who made atonement for the leper (Leviticus 14:20). Christ made atonement for our sin (Rom. 5:11).

Prayer Needs: Country: Guinea—7 million—on the Atlantic coast of western Africa • Freedom for nationals, but strict limitations on missionaries • 71% Muslim; 28% animist; 1% Christian.

FEBRUARY 7: Read Leviticus 16 — 18

Highlights: Day of Atonement; the scapegoat; the eating of blood forbidden; immorality forbidden.

Verses for Today: *"And he shall take a censer full of burning coals of fire from off the altar before the Lord, and his hands full of sweet incense beaten small, and bring it within the veil: and he shall put the incense upon the fire before the Lord, that the cloud of the incense may cover the mercy seat that is upon the testimony, that he die not"* (Leviticus 16:12-13).

T he altar of incense that was *"before the Lord"* in the Holy Place was much smaller than the brazen altar in the outer court where the sacrifices were offered. It was covered with gold and was placed just in front of the curtain that led to the Holy of Holies. The high priest offered incense on it morning and evening, symbolizing the offering of prayer to God "without ceasing."

When the priest went in to light the lamps in the evening, and again when he trimmed the lamps in the morning, he burned incense on this golden altar, using live coals from the altar of burnt offering. This signified that all acceptable prayer has its foundations in the redeeming love of a forgiving God.

The incense ascending toward Heaven was symbolic of the desires of the heart of the worshiper reaching upward to God. It gives meaning to the Scripture, *"Pray without ceasing"* (I Thessalonians 5:17) and reveals the power that praying Christians have with God. God will, and does, answer prayer.

Only as we read God's Word can we know how to pray and what to ask for— what pleases the Father. What a privilege—and a responsibility—we have to offer acceptable prayers to God day and night—praying for those things which the Holy Spirit has laid upon our hearts.

"And all things, whatsoever ye shall ask in prayer, believing, ye shall receive" (Matthew 21:22).

Thought for Today: We have the privilege of communicating with God through prayer and Bible reading. Have you communicated with Him today?

Christ Revealed: Through the two goats used on the Day of Atonement (Leviticus 16:8). The slaying of the first goat typifies that our peace with God was restored by the blood of Christ. The second goat represents the precious mercy of God in forever removing from His sight the sins of His people—*"as far as the east is from the west"* (Psa. 103:12; compare Heb. 10:17).

Word Studies: 16:4 **mitre** means turban; 16:8 **scapegoat** means goat of removal; 16:19 **hallow it** means dedicate it only for God; 16:21 **a fit man** means a man appointed to do it; 16:31 **afflict your souls** means humble yourselves; 17:4 **cut off** means executed or excommunicated; 17:14 **the blood of it is for the life thereof** means its blood sustains its life; 18:3 **ordinances** means laws.

Prayer Needs: Country: Saudi Arabia—15 million—on the Arabian Peninsula in southwestern Asia • Christian worship services for foreign personnel are tolerated, but those who seek to convert Muslims to Christianity face persecution • 99% Muslim; 1% Christian.

FEBRUARY 8: Read Leviticus 19 — 21

Highlights: Laws of holiness for the people and priests; penalties for immorality; rules for priests.

Verses for Today: *"And the soul that turneth after such as have familiar spirits, and after wizards . . .[I] will cut him off from among his people. . . . If a man also lie with mankind, as he lieth with a woman . . . they shall surely be put to death . . . "* (Leviticus 20:6,13).

I f God's people were to receive His blessings, they had to enforce the death penalty upon anyone who was convicted of worshiping false gods or associating with familiar spirits (through spirit-mediums), or anyone who participated in homosexuality or other sexual perversions.

Millions of people have rejected Christ and His Word; consequently, they are confused. And, in an effort to find the answers to their fears, they are turning to astrology, fortune-tellers, palm readers, and spirit mediums. These counterfeit guides have caused millions of people to be deceived.

In addition, Christ foretold that the immorality which existed in Sodom during the time of Lot would become prominent just before His return. (See Luke 17:28-32.)

It is a serious offense against God to participate in these sins. It is equally serious to question the wisdom of God for imposing the death sentence as punishment for committing these sins.

The works of the flesh are very evident—adultery, fornication, uncleanness, lasciviousness, idolatry, witchcraft . . . and such like. Those who participate in such things will not inherit the kingdom of God (see Galatians 5:19,21).

Thought for Today: God alone is the final authority on how we should live.

Christ Revealed: As the source of true guidance, in contrast to evil guidance through spiritualist mediums (Leviticus 20:6-8).

Word Studies: 19:16 **blood** means life; 19:19 **gender** means breed; 19:23 **uncircumcised** means forbidden; 19:26 **enchantment** means magic; sorcery; **observe times** means astrology; 19:27 **round the corners** means shave, as the pagans do; 19:28 **print any marks upon you** means tatoo yourself; 19:32 **the hoary head** means the aged; 19:35 **meteyard** means measures of length; 20:2 **sojourn** means stay temporarily; 21:4 **chief man** means husband or master of the house.

Prayer Needs: Country: Morocco—23 million—on the northwestern coast of Africa • Government is hostile to Christians and missions • 99+% Muslim; .5% Christian.

FEBRUARY 9: Read Leviticus 22 — 23

Highlights: Separation of the priests; the holiness of the offerings; the appointed feasts.

Verses for Today: *"Speak unto Aaron and to his sons.... Whosoever ... goeth unto the holy things ... having his uncleanness upon him, that soul shall be cut off from my presence ..."* (Leviticus 22:2-3).

I f a priest was defiled, he could not perform his priestly functions or partake of the priestly food until he was cleansed (Leviticus 22:4-6).

The animals that were offered to God were to be without blemish—symbolic of our sinless Savior. Likewise, the priests were to be washed and consecrated. This symbolized their separation from worldly things that would keep them from a right relationship with God.

Just as the priest was only temporarily disqualified from serving the Lord or offering sacrifices, so the Christian should be quick to change wrong attitudes in order to worship the Lord acceptably.

Any gift or service—regardless of how great it may be—is unacceptable if it is given with the intent of self-glory or expectation of praise from others. This is also true if the giver is harboring a spirit of hatred or jealousy in his heart. These attitudes make a believer "unclean"—unfit to worship or offer praise to the Lord.

"...first be reconciled to thy brother, and then come and offer thy gift" (Matthew 5:24).

Thought for Today: The Christian who serves the Lord acceptably will have a desire to be clean in body and in spirit.

Christ Revealed: Leviticus 23—in the seven great religious feasts: Passover, Feast of Unleavened Bread, Feast of First Fruits, Feast of Pentecost, Feast of Trumpets, Day of Atonement, Feast of Tabernacles (Booths)—all typical of Christ.

Word Studies: 22:22 **a wen** means a running sore; 22:23 **any thing superfluous** means a growth (deformity); 22:27 **dam** means mother.

Prayer Needs: Country: Sudan—24 million—at the eastern end of the Sahara Desert • Limited religious freedom • 74% Muslim; 15% king worship, ancestral spirit worship, and spirit-possession cults; 5% Roman Catholic; 3% Protestant.

FEBRUARY 10: Read Leviticus 24 — 25

Highlights: The lamps; showbread; punishment for blasphemy; sabbath years; year of jubilee.

Verses for Today: " . . . *bake twelve cakes thereof. . . . And thou shalt set them in two rows . . . upon the pure table before the Lord. And thou shalt put pure frankincense upon each row, that it may be on the bread for a memorial, even an offering made by fire unto the Lord*" (Leviticus 24:5-7).

The 12 loaves on the table in the Holy Place were called "showbread." The table of showbread was never to be without bread, for God had said, *"Thou shalt set upon the table showbread before me always"* (Exodus 25:30).

Pure frankincense was put on each of the two rows of bread, showing how closely the bread and the altar of incense were united. The offering of incense was symbolic of prayer. Putting incense on the bread implied that the bread did not become acceptable food for the priests until God's blessing rested upon it. After this was done, the bread became holy and acceptable to God.

Just as the priests ate of the showbread, we are to partake of the spiritual food through reading the Word of God. But it must be accompanied by prayer. Through prayer and the Word, the Holy Spirit gives us strength—a power that we could not otherwise have. The power of the Word, released by believing prayer, is able to transform our lives into the image of God's Son.

" . . . *our sufficiency is of God; who also hath made us able ministers . . . not of the letter, but of the spirit: for the letter killeth, but the spirit giveth life*" (II Corinthians 3:5-6).

Thought for Today: Faith grows as we allow God's Word to work in our lives daily.

Christ Portrayed: By the kinsman-redeemer (Leviticus 25:47-55). Christ is our Redeemer (Isa. 60:16).

Word Studies: 24:6 **pure table** means table of pure gold; 25:30 **shall not go out** means shall not be returned to the original owner; 25:34 **field of the suburbs** means pasturelands; 25:36 **usury** means interest; 25:47 **wax** means becomes; **the stock of the stranger's family** means a member of the foreigner's family.

Prayer Needs: **Country:** American Samoa—38,000—six small islands between Hawaii and New Zealand • Religious freedom • 64% Protestant; 17% Roman Catholic; 13% cults.

FEBRUARY 11: Read Leviticus 26 — 27

Highlights: Idolatry; blessings of obedience; penalties for disobedience; laws concerning dedications.

Verse for Today: *"Ye shall make you no idols nor graven image, neither rear you up a standing image, neither shall ye set up any image of stone in your land, to bow down unto it: for I am the Lord your God"* (Leviticus 26:1).

All the nations surrounding ancient Israel were idolatrous nations. The Israelites, on entering the Promised Land, were commanded to destroy all idols (Exodus 23:24; 34:13; Numbers 33:52; Deuteronomy 7:5). The purpose of their existence was to manifest the love and sustaining power of the living God.

Perhaps the most subtle deceptive form of idolatry in this affluent society is the accumulation (or the desire for the accumulation) of material things. For example, covetousness of material things is idol worship.

"For the love of money is the root of all evil: which while some coveted after, they

51

erred from the faith, and pierced themselves through with many sorrows. But thou, O man of God, flee these things ... " (I Timothy 6:10-11). Paul counted it a privilege to suffer the loss of all things *"That I might know him ... and the fellowship of his sufferings ... "* (Philippians 3:10). Barnabas, *"Having land, sold it, and brought the money, and laid it at the apostles' feet"* (Acts 4:37). A spiritual principle is revealed in these men so greatly used of God. They followed the example of The Master who was not obsessed with possessing worldly wealth.

"Hath not God chosen the poor of this world rich in faith" (James 2:5).

Thought for Today: We have no need to grasp after material things. God still sustains His people.

Christ Revealed: As the One who will dwell among us (Leviticus 26:11). Our hope of glory is Christ in us (Col. 1:27).

Word Studies: 26:13 **bondmen** means slaves; 26:16 **consumption** may mean tuberculosis; **burning ague** means fever; 26:25 **avenge the quarrel** means execute punishment; 26:30 **images** means altars for heathen worship; 26:31 **will not smell the savor of your sweet odors** means will take no delight in your offerings; 27:2 **a singular vow** means a special personal commitment.

Prayer Needs: Country: Philippines—62 million—in Southeast Asia • Some religious persecution • 64% Roman Catholic; 11% Protestant; 8% indigenous Catholic; 8% Muslim; 7% cults.

NUMBERS

The book of Numbers gets its name from the census taken during Israel's wandering in the wilderness (chapters 1 and 26).

Just a few weeks elapsed from the time the Tabernacle was erected in the last chapter of Exodus to the time of the census in the first chapter of Numbers. (See Exodus 40:17; Numbers 1:1-2.) During that time, the instructions in the book of Leviticus were given.

Numbers covers the period of Israel's history from the second year after the Exodus from Egypt to the fortieth year. (Compare Numbers 1:1; Deuteronomy 1:3.) During this time, the people of Israel were registered (numbered) twice. (An earlier census was taken of males, 20 and older—Exodus 30:11-16; 38:25-26.)

While they were in the wilderness of Sinai, instructions were given for the care of the Tabernacle, for the Passover, and for camping and marching (Numbers 1:1—10:10).

From the wilderness of Sinai, they traveled to the plains of Moab on the eastern border of the land that God had promised to give them (10:11—21:35).

With the exception of Joshua, Caleb, and Moses, the people accepted the discouraging report of the 10 spies and refused to believe they could conquer the Promised Land. Because of their sin of unbelief and rebellion, they wandered in the wilderness for 38 years.

This was a period of transition, during which the old generation died (except Joshua and Caleb), and the new generation grew up.

The second census in the book of Numbers was of the new generation (26:1-65). It took place in the plains of Moab in the fortieth year after they left Egypt. Prior to traveling to Moab, the new generation had assembled at Kadesh for a new commitment to enter the Promised Land. After their arrival at Moab, they were given instructions for the conquest and occupation of Canaan (26:52—36:13).

FEBRUARY 12: Read Numbers 1 — 2

Highlights: Moses' first numbering (census) of the Israelites; appointment of the Levites; arrangement of the camps; leaders of the tribes.

Verse for Today: *"As the Lord commanded Moses, so he numbered them in the wilderness of Sinai"* (Numbers 1:19).

T he people were numbered three times in the wilderness. Nine months earlier they were numbered for the purpose of collecting atonement-money from every male of 20 years old and upward. (Compare Exodus 30:11-16 with 38:25-26.) Thirty-eight years later the new generation was numbered before entering the Promised Land.

The purpose of this numbering was to organize an army. God had promised to give the children of Israel the land of Canaan, but not without many battles. Innumerable enemies had to be conquered before they could enter the Promised Land.

This numbering was exactly one month after the setting up of the tabernacle (Exodus 40:2,17) and about 11 months from the time of their arrival in the desert of Sinai. Nearly a whole year had elapsed. (Compare Exodus 19:1 and Numbers 1:1 and 10:11.)

With so great a destiny as the Promised Land, why the delay? What was the meaning of the aimless and futile wandering for 38 years? In His foreknowledge, God had to first prepare the new generation for the promised inheritance. Then too, time was needed for the older generation of slaves who had complained and rebelled, to die in the wilderness (Numbers 14:26-35).

In this we have an illustration of God's dealings with His people today. There are times in the Christian's life when the years pass, opportunities come and go, and life hastens on toward its close, but so little progress seems to be made in transforming our character, so little eternal work accomplished. Are the wasted years evidence that much in us of the old nature is not yet buried?

The fruitless years of the past need not be in vain. Let us recognize our "desert experiences" as the means of dying to unbelief and as the Divine design to prepare us for spiritual service.

"Know ye not, that to whom ye yield yourselves servants to obey, his servants ye are to whom ye obey; whether of sin unto death, or of obedience unto righteousness?" (Romans 6:16).

Thought for Today: In all our circumstances we should remember that God is preparing His own (His people) for the promised inheritance.

Christ Portrayed: By Moses as he led the people (Numbers 1:54). Jesus said, *"I am the good shepherd, and know my sheep . . . "* (John 10:14).

Word Studies: 1:2 **Take ye the sum** means take a census; **by their polls** means individually; one by one; 1:18 **pedigrees** means ancestry; 2:2 **ensign** means banner; **far off about** means round about; on every side.

Prayer Needs: Country: Argentina—31 million—in southern South America • Still much religious intolerance • 87% Roman Catholic; 5% Protestant; 2% Jewish.

FEBRUARY 13: Read Numbers 3 — 4

Highlights: Census and duties of the Levites: the Kohathites, Gershonites, and Merarites.

Verses for Today: *"As for the sons of Merari . . . this is the charge of their burden . . . "* (Numbers 4:29,31).

The Tabernacle and all its furnishings, including the furniture, skins, hangings, cords, boards, posts, and metal sockets, may have weighed several tons. Yet, just the three families of the Levite tribe—the Kohathites, the Gershonites, and the Merarites—were appointed to transport the Tabernacle and its furnishings throughout the wilderness journey.

The Kohathites were only responsible for the few items of furniture. The Gershonites were in charge of the hanging curtains, the coverings of the Tabernacle, and the instruments of the service. But the Merarites had to carry all the pillars, boards, bars, sockets, and the heavier parts of the Tabernacle. Therefore, four wagons and eight oxen were given to them (see Numbers 7:8).

Although there were fewer Merarites, their burden was much, much heavier than that of either the Kohathites or Gershonites.

The Gershonites and Kohathites probably felt fortunate that their assignments were not so burdensome. But the Lord is looking for workers, like the family of Merari, who don't complain because their job seems heavier or less desirable than that of others.

The completion of any worthwhile project is usually dependent upon a few who count it a privilege to do the Lord's work.

"And I will very gladly spend and be spent for you" (II Corinthians 12:15).

Thought for Today: How much we are permitted to accomplish for the Lord is determined by our willingness—not by our own strength.

Christ Portrayed: By Aaron, the high priest, who was served by the Levites (Numbers 3:6). We serve Christ, our great High Priest (John 12:26; Heb. 4:14).

Word Studies: 3:12 **matrix** means womb; 3:31 **charge** means responsibility; 3:50 **shekel** is a weight of silver equal to about four days' wages; 4:14 **fleshhooks** means large forks; 4:48 **fourscore** means 80.

Prayer Needs: Country: Botswana—1 million—in southern Africa • Limited religious freedom because of local chiefs • 49% animist; 21% Protestant; 4% Roman Catholic.

FEBRUARY 14: Read Numbers 5 — 6

Highlights: Laws concerning cleansing, recompense, jealousy; the Nazarite vow; the threefold blessing of the Lord.

Verses for Today: *"The Lord bless thee, and keep thee: the Lord make his face* *shine upon thee, and be gracious unto thee: the Lord lift up his countenance upon thee, and give thee peace"* (Numbers 6:24-26).

C hapter five revealed laws regarding people who didn't measure up—who *"trespass against the Lord"* (Numbers 5:6), but chapter six is given for the few who desired to go beyond what was required and be wholly committed to Him. This was the purpose of the Nazarite vow. The vow could be any set period of time, from a month to a lifetime. Among the life-long Nazarites were Samuel, Samson, and John the Baptist.

The Nazarite abstained from eating or drinking anything prepared from the vine, *"from the kernels even to the husks"* (6:4). This revealed his willingness to deny every physical satisfaction. Although grapes and raisins were good food, the Nazarite was more concerned about pleasing the Lord than in indulging in the pleasures of life.

The *"consecration of his God is upon his head"* (6:7) was a testimony that the Nazarite had surrendered his strength wholly unto the Lord. His hair was a symbol of strength which came from God, therefore Samson did not cut his hair. Samson had said, *"If I be shaven, then my strength will go from me."* It was when *"the hair of his head began to grow again"* that his strength returned and *"the dead which he slew at his death were more than they which he slew in his life"* (Judges 16:17-31).

A Nazarite would not approach a dead body, not even if it were the closest member of his family, for fear of defiling his vow and missing the priceless privilege of hearing the Lord say, *"The Lord bless thee, and keep thee: the Lord make his face shine upon thee, and be gracious unto thee: the Lord lift up his countenance upon thee, and give thee peace."*

The disciple, like the Nazarite, who will go beyond what he thinks is necessary to "just be a Christian," will gladly release his hold on all he holds dear—if it pleases the Father.

"For though I be free from all men, yet have I made myself servant unto all, that I might gain the more" (I Corinthians 9:19).

Thought for Today: Is there anything you are not willing to deny yourself if it would allow you to better please the Lord.

Christ Revealed: As the One who blesses us and keeps us (Numbers 6:24-26; compare Jude 1:24-25).

Word Studies: 5:7 **recompense** means make restitution; pay back; 5:8 **kinsman** means a relative; 5:12 **go aside** means becomes unfaithful; 5:13 **be kept close** means it is undetected; **taken with the manner** means caught in the act; 6:3 **moist** means fresh; undried; 6:4 **vine tree** means grapevine; 6:6 **come at** means go near; 6:9 **by him** means near him; 6:10 **turtles** means turtledoves; 6:11 **by** means through contact with.

Prayer Needs: Country: Senegal—7 million—in western Africa • Religious freedom • 92% Muslim; 4% animism and ancestor worship; 3% Roman Catholic; .1% Protestant.

FEBRUARY 15: Read Numbers 7

Highlight: The princes' offerings for the dedication of the altar.

Verses for Today: *"The princes of Israel ... brought their offering before the Lord ... "* (Numbers 7:2-3).

The princes (leaders) of the tribes could not participate in the duties of the Tabernacle; but through their offerings, they were able to assist the Levites in their God-appointed responsibilities. Since the leaders could not hold the position of prominence, as the Levites did, they could have shown contempt or a spirit of jealousy, and given little or nothing to help them. But instead, they willingly brought generous, sacrificial gifts to supply the needs of the Levites—*to every man according to the work he had to do* (see Numbers 7:5).

Since the offerings from each of the princes were exactly the same, it may seem monotonous to read all the details that were given for each one. But the repetition reveals the significance God places on every sacrifice given to support His ministry. Our individual offerings may seem small and unimportant to us, but God gives equal notice to every gift that is given from the heart, regardless of its size.

As a Christian, by faith, gives to the Lord's work, both his desire to give and his ability to give increase.

"Give, and it shall be given unto you; good measure, pressed down, and shaken together, and running over, shall men give into your bosom. For with the same measure that ye mete withal it shall be measured to you again" (Luke 6:38).

Thought for Today: God records every act of service done in His name—even "a cup of water."

Christ Revealed: Through the offerings of the leaders (Numbers 7). Each one is carefully noted, just as Christ noticed the widow's offering (Mark 12:41-44).

Word Studies: 7:13 **charger** means large dish or platter; 7:21 **bullock** means young bull.

Prayer Needs: Country: Indonesia—180 million—five large and 13,662 lesser islands in Southeast Asia • Growing pressure from Muslim leaders to limit advances of Christianity by not renewing many of the missionaries' permits to stay in the country •44% Muslim; 35% Islamic mixtures; 10% Protestant; 4% animist; 4% Roman Catholic; 2% Hindu; 1% Buddhist .

FEBRUARY 16: Read Numbers 8 — 9

Highlights: Aaron lighting the lamps; cleansing of the Levites; observance of the Passover; the guiding cloud over the Tabernacle.

Verse for Today: *"And Moses spake unto the children of Israel, that they should keep the passover"* (Numbers 9:4).

The Passover Feast and the Feast of Unleavened Bread were considered the most important of all feasts. The Passover served as a memorial of the Israelites' deliverance from Egypt by the blood that satisfied God and protected them from death. Even so, Christ is our Passover Lamb who was sacrificed for us (see I Corinthians 5:7).

The Feast of Unleavened Bread was celebrated on the second day of the eight-day Passover Feast. It foreshadowed Christ, the Bread of life. God's redeemed people have received eternal life through Christ (see John 6:47-48; I John 5:11). Through His Word, we continue to be strengthened and sustained throughout life's journey.

But God proved His love for us by the fact that while we were still sinners, Christ died for us. Much more, then, now we have been pronounced righteous by virtue of the shedding of His blood; it is far more certain that through Him we shall be saved from God's anger (see Romans 5:8-9).

Thought for Today: Christ's resurrection is the assurance of victory over death for all who are saved.

Christ Revealed: The Passover serves as a beautiful illustration of the redemption Christ accomplished at Calvary (Numbers 9:2; compare John 1:29; I Cor. 5:7).

Word Study: 8:14 **mine** means for God's special purpose.

Prayer Needs: Country: Guadeloupe—336,000—in the Leeward Islands of the West Indies • Religious freedom • 94% Roman Catholic; 2% Protestant.

FEBRUARY 17: Read Numbers 10 — 11

Highlights: The Israelites leave Sinai; complaint of the people; fire from the Lord; complaint of Moses; the 70 elders; the Lord sends quails.

Verses for Today: *"And when the people complained, it displeased the Lord. . . . And the mixed multitude that was among them fell a lusting: and the children of Israel also wept again, and said, Who shall give us flesh to eat? We remember the fish, which we did eat in Egypt freely . . . But now . . . there is nothing at all, beside this manna . . . "* (Numbers 11:1,4-6).

The Israelites were always complaining about something. It would appear the *"mixed multitude"* originated the complaints that spread throughout all the people. They failed to see that every problem, every disappointment, and every difficulty was an opportunity to trust God to supply their every need (Philippians 4:19).

Thankfulness and praise should have been their reaction; but instead, they complained that manna was *"nothing at all"* compared to the variety of food they had enjoyed in Egypt.

So God gave them their demands, but it resulted not only in leanness in their souls—a lack of spiritual depth—but also in years of trouble (Psalm 106:15).

God often allows His people to face trials and disappointments to test our faith in Him as the All-Sufficient One.

We will discover satisfaction and pleasure as we praise the Lord each day (I Thessalonians 5:18). To complain about adverse circumstances shows a failure to recognize that our present circumstances are *"his good pleasure"* (Philippians 2:13).

Thought for Today: God is at work within each Christian, giving him a desire to obey the Lord.

Christ Revealed: The two trumpets were made of silver (Numbers 10:2). Silver in the Bible stands for truth. Christ is *"the way, the truth, and the life"* (John 14:6).

Word Studies: 10:21 **the other** means the Gershonites and the Merarites; **against they came** means before the Kohathites arrived; 10:25 **which was the rearward** means acting as the rear guard; 11:5 **freely** means without cost; 11:6 **our soul is dried away** means we are disappointed and discouraged; 11:10 **kindled greatly** means stirred up intensely; 11:15 **out of hand** means at once; 11:20 **loathsome** means nauseating; disgusting; 11:23 **Is the Lord's hand waxed short?** means is the Lord's power limited?; 11:30 **gat him** means returned; 11:32 **homer** means about 10 bushels.

Prayer Needs: Country: Mexico—82 million—in North America • Limited religious freedom in some areas of the country • 88% Roman Catholic; 4% Protestant; .1% Eastern Orthodox.

FEBRUARY 18: Read Numbers 12 — 13

Highlights: Miriam and Aaron speak against Moses; Miriam stricken with leprosy; Moses' prayer for Miriam's healing; 12 spies sent to Canaan; their report.

Verses for Today: "... *We came unto the land whither thou sentest us, and surely it floweth with milk and honey.... We be not able to gò up against the people; for they are stronger than we*" (Numbers 13:27,31).

T welve leaders of Israel were chosen to explore the land of Canaan (see Numbers 13:3,17). *So the men went north and explored the land ... and came to Hebron* (13:21-22).

It was in Hebron that God had promised Abraham the land of Canaan hundreds of years earlier (see Genesis 13:14-17). But 10 of the spies failed to believe God's promise; they could see only the high walls and the giants.

Joshua and Caleb spoke in faith when they said, *The Lord is with us. Do not be afraid* (see Numbers 14:9). But the people refused to trust God and exercise faith in Him. They wanted to decide if the enemy was too powerful to defeat before they attempted to act upon the Word of God.

Depending upon human reasoning and physical strength before committing oneself to the Lord's work reveals a lack of faith in God's ability to fulfill His promises.

Many become frightened at the giants of difficulties, but no one can prevent God's will from being accomplished. Even the weakest Christian who will trust in God's strength can accomplish what the Lord wants him to do (see Philippians 4:13). Unbelief in God's sufficiency keeps many from experiencing the fulfillment of His abundant promises.

Without faith, man cannot please God, for those who draw near to God must believe that God exists and that He rewards those who seek Him (see Hebrews 11:6).

Thought for Today: Spiritual accomplishments are never obtained without a battle.

Christ Portrayed: By Moses the servant (Numbers 12:8). Christ is the Servant chosen by God (Matt. 12:18).

Word Studies: 12:8 **apparently** means clearly; **in dark speeches** means in obscure language.

Prayer Needs: Country: Chad—5 million—in north-central Africa • Limited religious freedom • 35% Muslim; 31% animist; 11% Protestant; 5% Roman Catholic.

FEBRUARY 19: Read Numbers 14 — 15

Highlights: The people rebel against the Lord; Moses intercedes; God's punishment of Israel; death of the 10 spies; laws concerning offerings.

Verse for Today: "*Wherefore hath the Lord brought us unto this land, to fall by the sword ... ?* " (Numbers 14:3).

I t seems strange indeed that the people who had been miraculously delivered from the death angel and from Egyptian slavery would say, *We should choose a leader and go back to Egypt* (see Numbers 14:4).

Little did they realize how their tenth act of rebellion marked the transition of the nation from *pilgrims* being led by God during the first two years to *wanderers* in the desert for the next 38 years. During this time, they made no further progress toward the Promised Land.

When God pronounced judgment upon their unbelief, they confessed, *"We have sinned."* Then they actually attempted to enter the Promised Land without God's direction (see 14:40-45).

All too many Christians are just as determined as the Israelites to guide their own lives. They refuse to submit to God's Word and consequently know nothing about letting Him direct their lives.

It is so important that we *trust in the Lord with all our hearts instead of depending on our own understanding. As we seek His will in all things, He will guide us* (see Proverbs 3:5-6).

Thought for Today: Rebellion against God leads to eternal death.

Christ Revealed: As God's glory (Numbers 14:22). Jesus Christ is the radiance of God's glory (Heb. 1:3).

Word Studies: 14:11 **signs** means miracles; 15:22 **erred** means unintentionally sinned; 15:30 **presumptuously** means openly; defiantly; 15:34 **in ward** means in custody; jail; 15:39 **a whoring** means playing the harlot; following after desires against God's will.

Prayer Needs: Country: Liberia—2 million—in West Africa • Religious freedom • 41% ancestor worship and witchcraft; 21% Muslim; 13% Protestant; 2% Roman Catholic.

FEBRUARY 20: Read Numbers 16 — 18

Highlights: Korah's rebellion; ravages of the plague; Aaron's rod; provision for the priests and Levites; gift ("heave") offering.

Verses for Today: " . . . *two hundred and fifty princes of the assembly, famous in the congregation, men of renown . . . gathered themselves together against Moses* . . . " (Numbers 16:2-3).

K orah, Moses' cousin, gained the confidence of the majority of the nation's leaders and led them in opposing Moses' leadership. They believed they should have a voice in making the decisions for the nation—that the majority should rule.

Even though Korah and his followers may have been sincere, God had placed Moses in the position of leadership. Therefore, they were opposing God—not Moses.

There is a tendency to magnify the natural weaknesses and inabilities of God's leaders. But those with spiritual insight recognize that God is the One who places His leaders in positions of authority—regardless of their shortcomings. And He is able to accomplish His work through them. Besides, what may appear to be shortcomings may actually be traits or abilities God has given them—and weaknesses are a means by which God shows His strength.

Rather than criticize those who are in authority over us, God desires that we pray for and encourage them.

Some people pour out abuse on things they do not understand. . . . How terrible for them! They follow Cain's path. For a profit they have rushed headlong into the errors of Balaam; they have rebelled as did Korah and perished. . . . These persons are grumblers, always dissatisfied with life. Their lives are guided by their evil passions and they flatter men for the sake of what they can get from them (Jude 1:10-11,16).

Thought for Today: It is impossible to have a right attitude toward God while maintaining a wrong attitude toward your parents, spiritual leaders, or other delegated authorities.

Christ Revealed: Through the first ripe fruits (Numbers 18:13; compare Lev. 23:9-14). *Christ has been raised from the dead, the firstfruits of those who are asleep in death* (see I Cor. 15:20). Christ's resurrection is a promise of the resurrection to come (John 11:25-26).

Word Studies: 16:6 **censers** means incense burners; 17:10 **quite take away** means put an end to it; 18:17 **savor** means satisfying aroma.

Prayer Needs: Country: Netherlands Antilles—182,000—a Dutch-speaking territory in the Caribbean area • Religious freedom • 80% Roman Catholic; 8% Protestant.

FEBRUARY 21: Read Numbers 19 — 20

Highlights: The red heifer sacrifice; Miriam's death; water from the rock; Edom refuses passage to Israel; Aaron's death.

Verses for Today: *"And the Lord spake unto Moses, saying, . . . speak ye unto the rock. . . . And Moses lifted up his hand, and with his rod he smote the rock twice: and the water came out abundantly . . . "* (Numbers 20:7-8,11).

On one occasion during the first year of Israel's journey in the wilderness, God commanded Moses to strike the rock, and an abundance of water came out (Exodus 17:1-6).

To the Israelites, the water that gushed out of the rock was just plain water, but the New Testament reveals its spiritual significance: *They continued to drink from the supernatural Rock that went with them; and that Rock was Christ Himself* (see I Corinthians 10:4).

The first striking of the rock was in obedience to God's Word. It was symbolic of Christ, who was stricken by God for our sins (Isaiah 53:4-5).

But on this occasion, about 40 years later, God told Moses to *speak* to the rock (Numbers 20:8). Instead, he *struck* the rock twice, implying that one sacrifice was not enough and thereby contradicting God's Word that says, " . . . *he died unto sin once"* (Romans 6:10).

Moses could not comprehend the magnitude of his disobedience at the time he struck the rock twice. But his failure to enter the Promised Land because of disobedience emphasizes to us the importance of obeying God's Word.

Jesus said that *if we continue to keep His commands, we will remain in His love, just as He kept His Father's commands and remained in His love* (see John 15:10).

Thought for Today: Immediate obedience to God's will is a sure way to express our faith.

60

Christ Revealed: Through the rock that was struck (Numbers 20:8-11). Christ, our Rock who was struck once through His death on the cross, does not need to be struck again (see I Cor. 10:4; Rom. 6:10).

Word Studies: 19:18 **hyssop** means an aromatic plant; 20:12 **sanctify me** means hold Me in reverential honor; 20:14 **travail** means painful trouble; adversity.

Prayer Needs: Country: Burundi—5 million—in east-central Africa • May be losing religious freedom • 51% Roman Catholic; 12% animist; 11% Protestant; 1% Muslim.

FEBRUARY 22: Read Numbers 21 — 22

Highlights: The Canaanites attack the Israelites; the poisonous snakes; the Israelites conquer the Amorites; Balak and Balaam.

Verses for Today: *"And the Lord sent fiery serpents among the people . . . And Moses made a serpent of brass, and put it upon a pole, and it came to pass, that if a serpent had bitten any man, when he beheld the serpent of brass, he lived"* (Numbers 21:6,9).

A spirit of contempt prevailed in the camp of Israel as they bitterly *"spake against God, and against Moses"* (Numbers 21:5). Consequently, His marvelous protection from the desert dangers was withdrawn. Until this time, there was no record that anyone had been bitten by a serpent. (Note Deuteronomy 8:15.) Their need for the Lord's protection was renewed when thousands of Israelites were bitten by fiery serpents and died.

In the conversation that Jesus held with Nicodemus, He referred to this historic event. Nicodemus could not understand how to be born again. So the Lord used the same means to show Nicodemus how to be saved as He does anyone today—He pointed him to His Word.

The brazen serpent was made to resemble the poisonous serpents. If they believed the promise of God's Word and looked to the brazen serpent, they were healed. So God sent *"his own Son in the likeness of sinful flesh, and for sin, condemned sin in the flesh"* (Romans 8:3, compare II Corinthians 5:21).

Mankind was poisoned by *"that old serpent, called the Devil"* (Revelation 12:9) and his painful bite torments his victims unto death. *" . . . and sin, when it is finished, bringeth forth death"* (James 1:15).

This world is like the camp of Israel. Sin has brought eternal death, but salvation is within the reach of all. The dying Israelites did not deserve to be healed but if they believed in God's provision and *"beheld the serpent of brass"* they lived.

"And as Moses lifted up the serpent in the wilderness, even so must the Son of man be lifted up: That whosoever believeth in him should not perish, but have eternal life" (John 3:14-15).

Thought for Today: The way to eternal life can still be found only in the Bible.

Christ Portrayed: By Moses the intercessor (Numbers 21:7). *Christ always lives to make incession for us* (see Heb. 7:25).

Word Studies: 21:5 **loatheth** means detest; 22:3 **sore** means exceedingly; 22:4 **lick up** means consume; devour; 22:5 **over against me** means in front of; opposite; 22:6 **wot** means know; 22:7 **rewards of divination** means payment for his predictions; 22:30 **wont** means accustomed; in the habit of.

Prayer Needs: Country: Mainland China—1,064 million—in eastern Asia • Very

61

limited religious freedom • 18% folk-religionist; 6% Buddhist; 2% Muslim; number of Christians unknown but growing.

FEBRUARY 23: Read Numbers 23 — 25

Highlights: The prophecies of Balaam; happiness of Israel foretold; Israel's sin in worshiping with the Moabites; plague stopped because of Phinehas' intercession.

Verse for Today: " . . . *Let me die the death of the righteous, and let my last end be like his!*" (Numbers 23:10).

T he Israelite nation had peaceably passed the borders of Balak's Moabite kingdom, but they were still in the plains of Moab, preparing to enter the Promised Land.

King Balak and the Moabites were distressed because the Israelites were near their borders. They had heard that the Israelites had overcome the powerful Egyptian empire and the nearby Amorites, and they were fearful—thinking the Israelites were a threat to their future safety. Therefore, Balak offered rewards of honor and great wealth in an attempt to hire the prophet Balaam to curse the Israelites.

At first, Balaam refused, saying, *How can I curse those whom God has not cursed* (see Numbers 23:8). But Balaam's covetous desire for wealth soon caused him to compromise what he knew was God's will.

In spite of God's warning, Balaam attempted to pronounce a curse on the Israelites. But each time he opened his mouth to curse the Israelites, he spoke words of blessing from God. Humiliated, but determined to gain the riches and fame which Balak offered him, Balaam went to the Midianites with a plan to lead the Israelites to sin against God. In this way, he hoped God would judge Israel and he would gain favor with Balak.

Balaam is typical of many people who know the right Scriptures and long to *"die the death of the righteous,"* but are unwilling to live the life of the righteous.

The Bible strongly warns us to beware of those who *"hold the doctrine of Balaam, who taught Balak to cast a stumbling block before the children of Israel . . . to commit fornication"* (Revelation 2:14; see also Jude 1:11). *They have forsaken the right way and have gone astray, having followed the way of Balaam the son of Beor, who set his heart on dishonest gain* (see II Peter 2:15).

Thought for Today: Those who deceive God's people are, in reality, opposing God Himself.

Christ Revealed: As the Star and Scepter (Numbers 24:17). Christ is coming to reign in great glory, not only over Israel, but over all men (Rev. 19:15-16).

Word Studies: 23:22 **unicorn** means wild ox; 25:3 **kindled** means aroused; 25:18 **wiles** means treacherous deceit (compare Eph. 6:11).

Prayer Needs: Country: Ecuador—10 million—in South America, crossed by the equator • Religious freedom • 91% Roman Catholic; 3% Protestant.

FEBRUARY 24: Read Numbers 26 — 27

Highlights: Second numbering (census) of the Israelites; law of inheritance; Joshua to succeed Moses.

Verses for Today: *"And Moses did as the Lord commanded him: and he took Joshua ... and gave him a charge, as the Lord commanded ... "* (Numbers 27:22-23).

M oses' usefulness to God as a great leader is revealed by the often-repeated words, *"And Moses did as the Lord commanded him."* Furthermore, it was said, *There has never been a prophet in Israel like Moses; whom the Lord spoke with face to face* (see Deuteronomy 34:10).

Moses had prayed that God would allow him to see the fertile land on the other side of the Jordan River (Deuteronomy 3:25), but God told him he could not enter the Promised Land.

Only one recorded sin kept Moses from the land of promise, but Moses represented the Law that could not allow one exception. God is perfect and holy, and justice demands that whoever keeps the whole Law, yet makes only one mistake is guilty of breaking it all (James 2:10).

Many people are deceived in thinking that if they try to keep the Ten Commandments, God will be satisfied and they will go to Heaven. But all have sinned many times and deserve to go to hell. That is why Christ said, *No one can come to the Father except through Me* (see John 14:6).

"And be found in him, not having mine own righteousness, which is of the law, but that which is through the faith of Christ, the righteousness which is of God by faith" (Philippians 3:9).

Thought for Today: Although your external conduct may be as perfect as Moses' was, unless you accept Christ as your Savior, you cannot be saved (see John 1:12).

Christ Portrayed: By the man who would lead the people like a shepherd (Numbers 27:17). Jesus said, *"I am the good shepherd"* (John 10:11).

Word Study: 27:19 **give him a charge** means commission him as your successor.

Prayer Needs: Country: Congo—2 million—in west-central Africa • Limited religious freedom but government hostility seems to have lessened • 41% Roman Catholic; 20% fetishism and belief in ancestral spirits; 17% Protestant; 9% cults.

FEBRUARY 25: Read Numbers 28 — 29

Highlight: The offerings.

Verse for Today: *"And on the fifteenth day of the seventh month ... ye shall keep a feast unto the Lord seven days"* (Numbers 29:12).

T he Feast of Ingathering (Feast of Tabernacles or Booths) was the last of the annual festivals under the old covenant. It marked the conclusion of the Jewish sacred year (Numbers 29:12-40) and the completion of harvest. There were far more sacrifices offered during this feast than during any other feast. On the first day, 13 bullocks were offered. Then each day, one less bullock was sacrificed. A total of 70 bullocks, 14 rams, 98 lambs, and 7 goats were sacrificed. In addition, there were daily burnt offerings and meal offerings. All these sacrifices were a means of offering praise and thanksgiving to God for the abundant harvest. The prolonged, detailed account of the offerings reveals how important it is that we give praise to the Lord.

"That we should be to the praise of his glory ... " (Ephesians 1:12).

Thought for Today: Acceptable praise is not primarily praising Him for what He gives us, but for who He is.

Christ Revealed: Through the peace offerings—sometimes called fellowship offerings (Numbers 29:39). We have peace (and fellowship) with God through our Lord Jesus Christ (see Romans 5:1).

Word Studies: 28:18 **servile** means laborious; 29:3 **three tenth deals** means about 1/3 bushel; 29:7 **ye shall afflict your souls** means you shall have a day of solemn fasting, personal soul searching, prayer, and repentance of all known sin.

Prayer Needs: Country: Suriname—390,000—on the northeastern coast of South America • Very limited religious freedom • 27% Hindu; 22% Roman Catholic; 20% Protestant; 20% Muslim; 6% witchcraft and spirit worship.

FEBRUARY 26: Read Numbers 30 — 31

Highlights: Law concerning vows; Midianites conquered; division of booty.

Verse for Today: *"And Moses spake unto the people, saying, Arm some of yourselves unto the war, and let them go against the Midianites, and avenge the Lord of Midian"* (Numbers 31:3).

T hrough the influence of Balaam, the Midianites caused Israel to sin. Twenty-four thousand Israelite men died because of their idolatrous and immoral sins. But the day came when God gave the command to *"avenge the Lord of Midian."*

Then Moses sent Phinehas, the priest, and a thousand men from each tribe to battle. They took with them the silver trumpets. Israel's confidence rested in the promise of God: *"If ye go to war . . . blow an alarm with the trumpets; and ye shall be saved from your enemies"* (Numbers 10:9). God gave Israel an overwhelming victory without the loss of a single Israelite. *"And they slew the kings of Midian . . . Balaam also the son of Beor they slew with the sword"* (31:8).

The same Balaam who once said, *" . . . I cannot go beyond the word of the Lord my God . . . "* (22:18) died as he had lived—in fellowship with the heathen Midianites.

"Mortify . . . evil concupiscence, and covetousness . . . for which things' sake the wrath of God cometh on the children of disobedience" (Colossians 3:5-6).

Thought for Today: Spiritual laws are absolute! If we choose to live in sin, we die in sin.

Christ Revealed: As the ruling One who will righteously judge the wicked (Numbers: 31:1-12; compare II Thessalonians 1:7-9).

Word Studies: 30:5 **disallow** means refuses to allow; 31:29 **for a heave offering** means to be presented as a sacrifice; 31:38 **beeves** means cattle; 31:39 **tribute** means an assessment; taxes; 31:50 **tablets** means necklaces or gold beads.

Prayer Needs: Country: South Korea—42 million—in northeastern Asia • Religious freedom • 33% Buddhist; 24% Protestant; 22% Confucianism and other eastern religions; 4% Roman Catholic.

FEBRUARY 27: Read Numbers 32 — 33

Highlights: Reuben, Gad, and half the tribe of Manasseh settle east of the Jordan;

a summary of the wilderness journeys; Canaanites to be expelled.

Verses for Today: *"And Moses said unto the children of Gad and to the children of Reuben, . . . wherefore discourage ye the heart of the children of Israel from going over into the land which the Lord hath given them?"* (Numbers 32:6-7).

D own through the years, God's people looked forward to the fulfillment of His promise to Abraham that his descendants would inherit the land of Canaan. When the time arrived for these privileged people to enter the Promised Land, the tribes of Reuben, Gad, and half the tribe of Manasseh said, *Do not take us across the Jordan* (see Numbers 32:5,33).

They evidently believed they would have greater opportunity for material success in the beautiful fertile plains and valleys they had won from the Amorites than in the land God had chosen for them. But they were the first of the Israelites to be defeated by enemy nations (I Chronicles 5:25-26).

God's direction for our lives seldom seems to be what we expect, but the spiritually-minded are not as concerned in obtaining their desires as they are in being in God's perfect will. Many have suffered defeat because they chose their way instead of God's way.

An unsaved person does not accept the things the Holy Spirit teaches because spiritual truth can be understood only through spiritual insight (see I Corinthians 2:14).

Thought for Today: It is impossible to gain God's best when our hearts are set on the things of the world.

Christ Revealed: Through the Promised Land—filled with abundance, as well as protection, for those who live in harmony with His Word.

Word Studies: 32:39 **dispossessed** means drove out; 33:52 **pictures** means carved idols.

Prayer Needs: Country: Ivory Coast—11 million—in western Africa • Religious freedom • 40% animist; 25% Muslim; 10% Roman Catholic; 5% Protestant.

FEBRUARY 28: Read Numbers 34 — 36

Highlights: The boundaries of Canaan; dividing the land; inheritance of the Levites; laws of inheritance; laws concerning murder.

Verse for Today: *"These are the commandments and the judgments, which the Lord commanded by the hand of Moses unto the children of Israel in the plains of Moab by Jordan near Jericho"* (Numbers 36:13).

T he *"commandments and the judgments"* (Numbers 27—36) reveal the importance of God's Word in instructing His people to live a holy life pleasing to the Lord.

The new generation of Israelites was *"near Jericho,"* about to take possession of the Promised Land. But before they did, Moses reviewed the happenings of the past 40 years in the light of the commandments of the Lord. He reminded them of the reason their fathers had not been allowed to enter Canaan. Moses emphasized the importance of having God Himself guide them if they were to possess the Promised Land.

Many Christians are making the same mistake today. Because of their fault-finding—a witness to their unbelief in the guidance of God—they fail to receive His blessings. What a blight grumbling is to the Christian life!

"Take heed, brethren, lest there be in any of you an evil heart of unbelief, in departing from the living God" (Hebrews 3:12).

Thought for Today: Oh, what a curse faultfinders are to the Church!

Christ Revealed: As the Christians' "city of refuge" (Numbers 35). In Him we are protected from the judgment of God and the curse of the Law. (See Phil. 3:9; Heb. 6:18.)

Prayer Needs: Country: Tanzania—23 million—in eastern Africa • Government pressure on churches to help implement Marxist policy • 33% Muslim; 19% Roman Catholic; 19% animist; 15% Protestant.

PRAYERS IN THIS MONTH'S READING

DEUTERONOMY

The book of Deuteronomy is the fifth and final book of Moses and means "second law." It was given by Moses, the mediator-representative of God, to the new generation of Israelites—those who were either unborn or under 20 years of age at the time of the Exodus (with the exception of Joshua and Caleb).

This book starts with a review of Israel's history from the first year after they came out of Egypt to the close of the 40 years of wandering in the wilderness (chapters 1—4). In the third month after the Israelites' Exodus from Egypt, they arrived at Mt. Sinai (Exodus 19:1). There they received the Ten Commandments and other laws and also built the Tabernacle. After one year, they were guided to Kadesh-barnea, where they appointed 12 spies to survey Canaan—the land of promise. (Compare Numbers 13; Deuteronomy 1:19-28.) Ten of the spies convinced the people that they could not enter the Promised Land because the Canaanites were too powerful to overcome. Consequently, the adult generation, with the exception of Joshua and Caleb, died in the wilderness.

Before the new generation could enter the Promised Land, Moses reminded them of the meaning of God's covenant and called for them to commit themselves to a personal covenant relationship with God.

Obedience is the central message of Deuteronomy. Some form of the words "obey" and "do" occurs an average of five times in each chapter. In fact, except for the larger book of Jeremiah, the word "obey" occurs more times in Deuteronomy than in any other book of the Bible.

Most of Deuteronomy deals with Israel's obligation to obey God's Word (chapters 5—26).

Jehovah chose the Israelites because He loved them and was keeping the promise He had made to their ancestors. By choosing the fewest and most helpless of all people, God let the world see that it was not brilliance, power, or goodness on the part of the Israelites that brought them Jehovah's blessings and prosperity. Rather, it was the mercy of a mighty God who rules the affairs of earth and is able to bless those who walk in harmony with His laws.

Through Moses, God revealed His perfect, holy nature and His great love for His people. He urged them: *Set your hearts . . . to obeying all the words of this law. These teachings are not empty words; they are your very life* (see 32:46-47). Moses spoke of the nation of Israel and Jehovah's love for them, spanning the time from past to future (4:37; 7:8,13; 23:5). Four chapters (27—30) cover a prophetic revelation of Israel's future.

Deuteronomy ends with the song of Moses, his final blessings on Israel, and his death and burial (chapters 31—34). In Moses' final commission to Joshua, he said: *You are the one who will lead these people to occupy the land that the Lord promised to their ancestors* (see 31:7).

This book also speaks to us, revealing the principles of receiving abundant blessings from God. It tells how we cheat ourselves when we live in disobedience to Him.

Jesus quoted from the book of Deuteronomy more than any other book of the Old Testament. This book is referred to more than 80 times in the New Testament.

MARCH 1: Read Deuteronomy 1 — 2

Highlights: The command to leave Horeb; the appointment of leaders; failure to enter the Promised Land because of unbelief; wanderings in the wilderness; Israelites defeat Sihon.

Verse for Today: *"On this side Jordan, in the land of Moab, began Moses to declare this law . . . "* (Deuteronomy 1:5).

The adult generation of Israelites that left Egypt had not recognized that the hardships of the desert were not accidental nor caused by poor leadership; they were the plan of God. Their wilderness journey should have caused them to exercise faith in His power—not only to provide their needs but also to guide them into the Promised Land. But instead, they complained and murmured. As a result of their sin of unbelief, they could not possess the land. They wandered in the wilderness for 38 more years—perhaps on the plains of Moab, just outside the border of the Promised Land.

After the older generation died (except Joshua and Caleb), Moses began to "declare" the original message God had given the Israelites 40 years earlier on Mt. Sinai. "To declare this law" meant more than merely repeating the Law; it meant "to dig in"—to go deeply into God's Word and search for new meaning. A new revelation of God's love for His people was given and repeated four times (see Deuteronomy 4:37; 7:7-8; 10:15; 23:5). This added assurance of God's love was to strengthen the new generation's faith in Him to lead them into the Promised Land.

Likewise for the Christian, the desire and effort to "dig in"—to go deeply into God's Word—will reveal the never-ending love of God and strengthen one's faith to trust Him for whatever lies ahead.

"Blessed are they that do his commandments, that they may have right to the tree of life" (Revelation 22:14).

Thought for Today: The Lord and His Word become more precious each day when we read the Bible with a desire to obey its truth.

Christ Portrayed: By Moses, who spoke to the children of Israel according to all that the Lord had commanded him (Deuteronomy 1:3). Jesus very faithfully told others everything God told Him to say (John 8:28).

Word Studies: 1:12 **bear your cumbrance** means endure your problems; 1:17 **respect persons** means show partiality; **cause** means case; dispute; 1:19 **wilderness** means desert; 1:42 **smitten** means defeated; 2:9 **Distress not** means do not fight with; 2:14 **were wasted out** means had died; **host** means camp.

Prayer Needs: Country: Lebanon—3 million—in the Middle East • Limited religious freedom • 67% Muslim; 19% Roman Catholic; 10% Eastern Orthodox; 1% Protestant.

MARCH 2: Read Deuteronomy 3 — 4

Highlights: Defeat of Og, king of Bashan; division of the land; Moses' prayer to enter Canaan; his view of the Promised Land; his plea for national obedience; warning against idolatry; cities of refuge.

Verse for Today: *"Ye shall not fear them: for the Lord your God he shall fight for you"* (Deuteronomy 3:22).

B efore the people of Israel crossed the Jordan River, they traveled northward to the fertile region east of the Sea of Galilee. There they faced the powerful king of Bashan who controlled a vast territory.

The Lord had encouraged them through Moses, saying, *"Ye shall not fear them: for the Lord your God . . . shall fight for you."*

To trust the Lord when we are faced with overwhelming problems is not natural for anyone. This faith *"cometh by hearing, and hearing by the word of God"*

(Romans 10:17). As we read and meditate upon His Word—and act upon it—our faith is increased.

As we read the Bible with a willing heart to obey it, the Holy Spirit makes the Word *"quick and powerful"*—meaning life-giving and active—so that Bible truths become a living reality in our lives.

God's people often face seemingly impossible situations. But the Lord has provided the Christian with His Word, which is the *"sword of the Spirit"* and the *"shield of faith."* God protects and preserves us from the *"fiery darts"* of Satan which are aimed at defeating His purpose. (See Ephesians 6:16-18.)

"Now unto him that is able to keep you from falling . . . be glory and majesty, dominion and power, both now and ever. Amen" (Jude 1:24-25).

Thought for Today: It is our faith in God—not our strength or wisdom—that leads to victory.

Christ Portrayed: By Joshua, who led the Israelites into the land God gave them as an inheritance (Deuteronomy 3:28). Through Jesus we receive forgiveness of sin and an inheritance of His abundance and blessings—both here and in eternity (Acts 26:18).

Word Studies: 3:28 **charge** means command; 4:12 **similitude** means form; 4:34 **assayed** means ever attempted; tried.

Prayer Needs: Country: Ethiopia—47 million—in eastern Africa • Enemies of Christianity hostile toward the Church • 41% Eastern Orthodox; 35% Muslim; 10% Protestant; 10% animist; .7% Roman Catholic.

MARCH 3: Read Deuteronomy 5 — 7

Highlights: The Ten Commandments; teaching God's Law to children; warnings against disobedience; blessings of obedience; command to destroy evil nations.

Verses for Today: *"Hear, O Israel: The Lord our God is one Lord: and thou shalt love the Lord thy God with all thine heart . . . "* (Deuteronomy 6:4-5).

The Israelites believed that what Moses had spoken was the Word of God. But for them to believe with all their hearts meant they not only would have to obey God, but also their actions would have to be motivated from the heart. This commandment was not only repeated many times, but reemphasized by Jesus as the great commandment (Deuteronomy 10:12; 11:1,13,22; Matthew 22:37).

Jesus also revealed that our love for God should go even further and include not only *"all thy heart . . . all thy soul . . . all thy strength"* but also *"all thy mind"* (Luke 10:27; Mark 12:30). This means that our innermost thoughts should reflect our love for Him.

It is possible to have bitter thoughts while doing kind deeds—to say loving words while having wrong attitudes and motives. Our relationship with God and with others goes much deeper than word or deed; it goes to the very heart of our thoughts, for they reveal what we really are.

"Casting down imaginations, and every high thing that exalteth itself against the knowledge of God, and bringing into captivity every thought to the obedience of Christ" (II Corinthians 10:5).

Thought for Today: When we have a desire to obey God's Word, it becomes more precious to us every day.

Christ Revealed: Through the land flowing with milk and honey (Deuteronomy 6:3). The land pictures our resting in Christ (see Heb. 3:18).

Word Studies: 5:17 **kill** means murder; 6:22 **sore** means grievous; 7:13 **fruit of thy womb** means your children; **kine** means cattle; 7:25 **graven images** means idols; objects of worship.

Prayer Needs: Country: Ghana—14 million—in western Africa • The government gives freedom to churches and missionaries that do not get involved in politics • 31% belief in spirits and witches; 22% Protestant; 17% Muslim; 11% Roman Catholic.

MARCH 4: Read Deuteronomy 8 — 10

Highlights: Warning against forgetting the Lord; judgment upon ungodly nations; the golden calf; second tables of stone; God's requirements for Israel.

Verse for Today: *"And he humbled thee, and suffered thee to hunger, and fed thee with manna . . . that he might make thee know that man doth not live by bread only, but by every word that proceedeth out of the mouth of the Lord doth man live"* (Deuteronomy 8:3).

O ur Lord quoted this verse when He was in the wilderness being tempted by Satan (see Matthew 4). His victory over Satan is an example of the power of God's Word to overcome the enemy. In each of His three testings, Christ overcame Satan by quoting passages of Scripture from Deuteronomy (compare 8:3 with Matthew 4:4; 6:16 with Matthew 4:7; and 6:13 with Matthew 4:10).

The 38 years of desert wanderings permitted the older generation of Israelites to die and taught the new generation not to trust in their abilities, but to daily depend upon God.

Christians today need day-by-day strength. Christ, the Living Word, is the Bread of life—our source of spiritual nourishment. Neglecting the Word of God results in spiritual malnutrition.

" . . . It is written, Man shall not live by bread alone, but by every word that proceedeth out of the mouth of God" (Matthew 4:4).

Thought for Today: No one who knows God's Word should doubt that satisfaction in life is dependent upon one's loving obedience to Him.

Christ Revealed: Through the acacia ("shittim") wood (Deuteronomy 10:3). Acacia wood, a desert growth, is symbolic of Christ in His human form as a *root out of dry ground* (see Isa. 53:2).

Word Studies: 8:16 **prove** means test, so that your trust in Him would grow; **at thy latter end** means in the end; in the future; 10:16 **stiffnecked** means stubborn and hardened.

Prayer Needs: Country: Rwanda—7 million—in central Africa • Religious freedom • 40% Roman Catholic; 21% Protestant; 14% belief in false gods, spirit-possession cults, and ancestor worship; 9% Muslim.

MARCH 5: Read Deuteronomy 11 — 13

Highlights: Israel to love and obey God; blessing for obedience; curse for disobedience; God to choose place of worship; idolatrous cities to be destroyed.

A fter the 40 years of wandering in the wilderness and the dreadful history of disobedience, the new generation was about to enter Canaan. Throughout their history, Israel was reminded that obedience to God's Word was the only way they could be assured of His presence. Furthermore, they were taught that obedience was the key to enjoying God's blessings.

At Sinai, God had directed Moses to tell the people, *" . . . If ye will obey my voice indeed, and keep my covenant, then ye shall be a peculiar treasure unto me above all people . . . "* (Exodus 19:5). The importance of obedience was emphasized 19 times in the instructions concerning the building of the Tabernacle. (See Exodus 38—40.) Also, as Moses stood in sight of the Promised Land, he said, *"I set before you this day a blessing and a curse; A blessing, if ye obey . . . and a curse, if ye will not obey . . . "* (Deuteronomy 11:26-28).

Yes, *"a blessing if ye obey"* is also the key to our enjoying abundant life in Him. Under the covenant of grace, the Christian has already received God's greatest blessing in Christ. Let's not be so concerned about praying for blessings as we are in praying to be obedient to His Word; then, God will take care of the continued blessings.

"And he that keepeth his commandments dwelleth in him, and he in him. . . . " (I John 3:24).

Thought for Today: It is the obedient ones who enjoy God's presence.

Christ Revealed: Through the burnt offerings, which typified Christ's offering of Himself unto death (Deuteronomy 12:6; Heb. 10:5-7).

Word Studies: 11:6 **all the substance** means all their belongings and every living thing that was with them; 11:14 **first rain and the latter rain** means autumn rain and spring rain; 11:21 **fathers** means ancestors; forefathers; 11:30 **the champaign** means desert plains; **plains** means oaks; 12:15 **gates** means towns; **whatsoever thy soul lusteth after** means as much as you desire; 13:5 **thrust thee** means draw you away.

Prayer Needs: Country: Syria—11 million—in southwestern Asia • Limited religious freedom for Christians • 90% Muslim; 4% Eastern Orthodox; 2% Roman Catholic; .25% Protestant.

MARCH 6: Read Deuteronomy 14 — 16

Highlights: Clean and unclean food; the law of the tithe; the year of release; three feasts that must be observed.

Verses for Today: *"Beware that there be not a thought in thy wicked heart . . . and thou givest him nought; and he cry unto the Lord against thee. . . . For the poor shall never cease out of the land: therefore I command thee, saying, Thou shalt open thine hand wide unto thy brother, to thy poor, and to thy needy . . . "* (Deuteronomy 15:9,11).

G iving to the poor was recognition that all the Israelites' possessions actually belonged to the Lord. They were merely stewards of God's love, distributing to the less fortunate.

When we give to someone who needs our help, we are loaning to the Lord. He

71

gives His Word as security: *"He that hath pity upon the poor lendeth unto the Lord; and that which he hath given will he pay him again"* (Proverbs 19:17).

God has always identified Himself with the poor and the helpless. Giving a cup of cold water in His name is the same as giving to the Lord: *I was hungry, and you gave me food; I was thirsty, and you gave me drink; I was a stranger, and you took me in; naked, and you clothed me* . . . (see Matthew 25:35-36). The sufferings of distressed people touch the heart of God—our hearts should be touched too.

"But whoso hath this world's good, and seeth his brother have need, and shutteth up his bowels of compassion from him, how dwelleth the love of God in him?" (I John 3:17).

Thought for Today: The Christian does not give because of the law but because of love.

Christ Revealed: Through the year of release, which typifies Christ's forgiveness of our sins (Deuteronomy 15:1). This should teach us to forgive others, even as He has forgiven us.

Word Studies: 14:2 **a peculiar people unto himself** means people living to please God; 14:7 **cloven** means split in two; 14:21 **seethe** means boil; 15:14 **floor** means threshing floor; 16:19 **wrest judgment** means pervert justice; **a gift** means a bribe.

Prayer Needs: Country: Grenada—85,000—the southernmost of the Windward Islands • Religious freedom • 61% Roman Catholic; 31% Protestant.

MARCH 7: Read Deuteronomy 17 — 20

Highlights: Laws concerning idolaters and obedience to authority; warning to kings; offerings for priests and Levites; prophecy concerning Christ; cities of refuge; laws concerning witnesses and war.

Verses for Today: *"I will raise them up a Prophet from among their brethren, like unto thee, and will put my words in his mouth; and he shall speak unto them all that I shall command him. And it shall come to pass, that whosoever will not hearken unto my words which he shall speak in my name, I will require it of him"* (Deuteronomy 18:18-19).

Moses interceded for Israel in prayer to God and delivered them from His judgment (Deuteronomy 9:25-26). But Jesus is the Mediator of a better covenant established upon better promises (Hebrews 8:6). Although cursed by the law and condemned by conscience, any lost sinner who will *"call on the name of the Lord"* will receive forgiveness (Acts 2:21).

Moses was a prophet who received and proclaimed the will of God to his people, yet he was powerless to change the hearts of his followers. But Christ is the manifestation of God's character and indwells the life of every believer.

Moses was a faithful servant who for 40 years served his people, but he could not control them. However, Christ has the sovereign right *"as a son over his own house"* (Hebrews 3:6) to be Master in His house—not merely an honored guest while we retain the keys and the control. No! The keys belong to Him, and He must have control. He dwells within *"his own house,"* as a life within a life, permeating and transforming our whole being. He should rule *"over his own house,"* fulfilling His ownership and maintaining His possessions.

"For the law made nothing perfect, but the bringing in of a better hope did; by the which we draw nigh unto God. . . . Wherefore he is able also to save them to the uttermost that come unto God by him, seeing he ever liveth to make intercession for them" (Hebrews 7:19,25).

Thought for Today: Christ intercedes for all (His house) who come to the Father through Him.

Christ Revealed: Through the Old Testament sacrifices which were without blemish or defect (Deuteronomy 17:1). Christ was perfectly pure from all sin and all appearance of evil (I Pet. 1:19).

Word Studies: 17:1 **evilfavoredness** means defect; flaw; 17:3 **the host of heaven** means the stars; 17:11 **thou shalt not decline** means you shall not turn aside, you must fulfill all that is commanded; 18:3 **maw** means stomach; 18:10 **pass through the fire** means burning children alive as a sacrifice, a common practice wherever there was worship of Baal or Molech; **witch** means one supposed to exercise supernatural powers by evil spirits; 18:13 **perfect** means blameless and sincere; 19:5 **fetcheth a stroke** means swings; **helve** means handle; **lighteth** means strikes; 19:11 **lie in wait** means plan to deliberately murder; 19:18 **inquisition** means inquiry; 20:11 **tributaries** means involuntary servants; forced laborers.

Prayer Needs: Country: St. Kitts-Nevis—55,000—in the Leeward Islands of the West Indies • Religious freedom • 74% Protestant; 7% Roman Catholic.

MARCH 8: Read Deuteronomy 21 — 23

Highlights: Laws and responsibilities concerning unsolved murder, governing children, marriage, enemies, separation, and integrity.

Verse for Today: *"Thou shalt not sow thy vineyard with divers seeds: lest the fruit . . . be defiled"* (Deuteronomy 22:9).

G od had chosen Israel to be *"an holy people"* who belonged wholly to Him. He established laws, such as not sowing *"divers seeds,"* that may appear to the casual observer to be unnecessary restraints. But these laws were to protect the Israelites from being corrupted by the surrounding nations that would destroy their desire to fulfill His plan.

The same principle is true in the New Testament, where Christians are warned: *"Wherefore come out from among them, and be ye separate, saith the Lord, and touch not the unclean thing . . . "* (II Corinthians 6:17). Again, the Word declares: *"Be ye not unequally yoked together with unbelievers . . . "* (6:14), and *" . . . a friend of the world is the enemy of God"* (James 4:4). God asked, *"Can two walk together, except they be agreed?"* (Amos 3:3).

A single-hearted love for God is the secret to victorious Christian living, for *"no man can serve two masters"* (Matthew 6:24). There is room for only one lord in our lives, and we must decide who that lord will be.

The child of God is not *of* the world, but is *in* the world as a *witness* against its evil influences. We should live as ones who possess the *"light of the world."* (Note John 1:4-5 and Matthew 5:14-16.)

"Be not ye therefore partakers with them. For ye were sometimes darkness, but now are ye light in the Lord: walk as children of light" (Ephesians 5:7-8).

73

Thought for Today: Covetousness for material things has cheated many from fulfilling the will of God.

Christ Revealed: Christ died on the cross in our place, submitting to the penalty of death imposed by the Law for our sins (Deuteronomy 21:23). In the evening He was taken down from the cross, a token that now the Law was satisfied (John 19:31; Gal. 3:13).

Word Studies: 21:4 **rough valley** means valley with running water; **eared** means plowed; **strike off** means break; 21:5 **stroke** means assault; 21:12 **pare** means cut; 21:13 **bewail** means mourn; 21:15 **hated** means unloved; 22:3 **ass** means donkey; 22:6 **dam** means mother; 22:8 **battlement** means railing or wall; 22:9 **diverse seeds** means more than one kind of seed; 22:12 **fringes** means tassels; 22:18 **chastise** means rebuke and whip; 22:19 **amerce** means fine; 22:25 **force** means rape; 22:30 **discover his father's skirt** means commit adultery with his father's wife; 23:19 **upon usury** means with interest; 23:25 **corn** means grain field; **ears** means grain.

Prayer Needs: Country: Bulgaria—9 million—in southeastern Europe • Severe limitations and control of all religious groups • 62% Eastern Orthodox; 10% Muslim; .75% Catholic; .5% Protestant.

MARCH 9: Read Deuteronomy 24 — 27

Highlights: Laws for relationships with others; the offering of tithes; blessings at Mount Gerizim and curses at Mount Ebal.

Verses for Today: *"Thou shalt not have in thine house divers measures. . . . But thou shalt have a perfect and just weight . . . that thy days may be lengthened. . . . For all . . . that do unrighteously, are an abomination unto the Lord thy God"* (Deuteronomy 25:14-16).

T he Israelites were taught that all business transactions should reflect the integrity and justice of God. Many laws were given to show the seriousness of unfair dealings between a buyer and a seller.

It is of utmost importance in our relationships with others not to take advantage of them or misrepresent the facts in our business dealings. If we are to manifest a true Christian spirit, we will conduct our business transactions in a way that conforms to the character of our heavenly Father. One of the most cruel business dealings is for a person to refuse to pay what he owes another.

"Therefore all things whatsoever ye would that men should do to you, do ye even so to them: for this is the law and the prophets" (Matthew 7:12).

Thought for Today: Honesty really is the best policy.

Christ Revealed: Through the deliverance of the Israelites from Egypt and Pharaoh (Deuteronomy 26:8). Jesus left His home in Heaven to deliver us from Satan and his control.

Word Studies: 24:10 **to fetch his pledge** means to secure collateral; 24:11 **abroad** means outside; 24:12 **not sleep with his pledge** means not keep it overnight; 25:8 **stand to it** means still refuses; 25:18 **smote the hindmost of thee** means struck down those who were weary and lagging behind; 26:5 **Syrian** means wandering Aramean; 26:17 **avouched** means openly declared; 27:16 **setteth light** means dishonors; 27:17 **removeth his neighbor's landmark** means move the boundary landmark between his land and his neighbor's to enlarge his own property.

Prayer Needs: **Country:** Gibraltar—29,000—on the southern coast of Spain • Religious freedom • 72% Roman Catholic; 9% Muslim; 8% Protestant; 2% Jewish; 1% Hindu.

MARCH 10: Read Deuteronomy 28

Highlights: Blessings of obedience; consequences of disobedience.

Verses for Today: *" ... if thou shalt hearken diligently unto the voice of the Lord thy God.... The Lord shall open unto thee his good treasure ... "* (Deuteronomy 28:2,12).

T he Israelites' enjoyment of *"his good treasure"* was inseparably linked with willing obedience to God's Word. This is an inflexible spiritual principle.

God bestows *"his good treasure"* of blessings on all who desire to be alone with Him in reading His Word. This means more than reading the Scriptures for knowledge. Our entire attention during the time we read His Word should be given to desiring to know His will—that we *"might walk worthy of the Lord unto all pleasing, being fruitful in every good work, and increasing in the knowledge of God"* (Colossians 1:10). Too often desiring to please Him is regarded as something incidental.

Obeying merely to fulfill our responsibility does not qualify us to receive *"his good treasure."* But when we delight in His ways, we experience the greatest satisfaction.

"Open thou mine eyes, that I may behold wondrous things out of thy law" (Psalm 119:18).

Thought for Today: Our true enjoyment of life is in direct relation to our desire to obey God's Word.

Christ Revealed: As the One from whom our blessings come (Deuteronomy 28:1-2).

Word Studies: 28:5 **store** means kneading trough or bowl; 28:20 **vexation** means confusion; 28:26 **fray away** means frighten away; 28:27 **botch** means boils; **emerods** means tumors; 28:28 **madness** means mental disorder; 28:53 **fruit** means offspring; children; **straitness** means terrible, distressing confinement.

Prayer Needs: **Country:** Panama—2 million—in southern Central America • Limited religious freedom • 78% Roman Catholic; 12% Protestant; 5% Muslim; .1% Eastern Orthodox.

MARCH 11: Read Deuteronomy 29 — 31

Highlights: Moses' appeal for obedience and warning against disobedience; Joshua commissioned as Moses' successor; Moses' last counsel and his warnings.

Verses for Today: *" ... I have set before you life and death ... therefore choose life ... that thou mayest love the Lord thy God, and that thou mayest obey his voice, and that thou mayest cleave unto him: for he is thy life ... "* (Deuteronomy 30:19-20).

M oses concluded the covenant blessings and curses with an appeal to *"choose life"*—to love the Lord, obey Him, and remain loyal to Him. A determination and choice rest within each individual.

75

Moses had an intense desire for the people's welfare. He described two possible courses of life—one of which every person must take; a third option does not exist.

The first option is life: a right heart relationship—to *"love the Lord."* The alternative is spiritual death—a constant warfare with God—the road to eternal destruction—*"Ye shall surely perish"* (Deuteronomy 8:19).

We are created to worship something or someone. If we do not worship God, our love and devotion will be turned to material securities, power, wealth, social or physical ambitions. The final outcome is eternal death.

We gradually bring ourselves to hear only what we wish to hear. The majority, like the Israelites, have made themselves deaf to God's voice—*"And worship other gods"* (see 8:19).

"Life" is more than physical existence and "death" is not equivalent to non-existence. But *"eternal life"* has been provided through faith in Jesus Christ. (See Galatians 3:26-27 and Ephesians 2:8-9.) God not only assures His blessings of love throughout this life, but our being with Him throughout eternity.

The unbeliever is in a state of "eternal death"—and soon "eternal punishment" (Matthew 25:46; John 3:36). How strange that between such alternatives there should be a moment's hesitation.

"God hath given to us eternal life, and this life is in his Son. He that hath the Son hath life." (I John 5:12).

Thought for Today: Christ came that we might have life, and have it in abundance.

Christ Revealed: As Life. Jesus is the Resurrection and the Life (Deuteronomy 30:15; John 11:25).

Word Studies: 29:7 **smote** means defeated; 29:19 **bless himself** means will boast, flatter, and congratulate himself; 30:4 **unto the outmost parts of heaven** means to the most distant lands under Heaven; 30:18 **denounce** means strongly declare; 31:10 **solemnity** means set time.

Prayer Needs: Country: St. Helena—8,500—in the southern Atlantic about 1,200 miles west of Angola, Africa • Religious freedom • 95% Protestant; 3% cults; .75% Roman Catholic.

MARCH 12: Read Deuteronomy 32 — 34

Highlights: The song of Moses; Moses permitted to see the Promised Land; Moses blesses the 12 tribes; death of Moses; Joshua succeeds Moses.

Verse for Today: *" . . . my speech shall distil as the dew, as the small rain under the tender herb . . . "* (Deuteronomy 32:2).

L ike dew in the darkness, God's Word refreshes and provides growth in those who *"thirst after righteousness"* (Matthew 5:6).

Who hears the dew fall or sees the formation of water take place? Dew comes unobserved to refresh the grass in dry seasons, descending gently and softly during the night. And in the morning, the earth is refreshed and prepared for the heat of the day.

The heat of the sun and the dew of the night may seem far apart and even opposed to each other. But, unaided by human hands, God has arranged for them to work together to produce the harvest.

Only living things benefit from the dew. It does nothing for stones, but it refreshes plants that have been wilted by the afternoon sun.

Although we are not aware of any great change, God's Word is doing its work in the heart of every sincere Bible reader. We are usually unaware of this gentle, refreshing growth. Daily meditation on His Word will refresh and sustain, as unnoticed and gentle as the dew that appears in the morning following the darkest night.

Happy are those who hunger and thirst after God's will, for they will be fully satisfied (see Matthew 5:6).

Thought for Today: Nothing compares to fresh insight gained through hearing or reading God's Word.

Christ Revealed: *"For their rock is not as our Rock..."* (Deuteronomy 32:31). Christ was *"that spiritual Rock that followed them"* (I Cor. 10:4).

Word Studies: 32:6 **requite** means repay; 32:33 **dragons** means serpents; 32:44 **Hoshea** means Joshua; 33:17 **unicorns** means wild oxen; **push** means gore; butt.

Prayer Needs: Country: Andorra—48,000—in the eastern Pyrenees between France and Spain • Religious freedom • 88% Roman Catholic; .2% Protestant.

JOSHUA _____

The five books of Moses (Genesis—Deuteronomy) record about 500 years of Israel's history—from the time of Abraham to the end of the 40 years of wandering in the desert.

The book of Joshua is a continuation of the book of Deuteronomy. It begins with God's commission to Joshua after the death of Moses and covers the first 25 to 50 years of Israel's history in Canaan.

The Promised Land was a place of conquest and conflict. Very few battles took place during the wilderness years; but as soon as they entered Canaan, the Israelites, by faith, were to fight for possession of the land. Victory was assured because *"the Lord God of Israel"* fought for them (Joshua 10:42).

After conquering the land, the Israelites began to occupy Canaan. Each tribe was assigned its territory. Israel's entrance and settlement in the land are evidence of God's faithfulness in keeping His covenant promise to Abraham, as well as to Joshua (see 1:1-6; 21:43-45).

The book of Joshua ends with the conclusion of Joshua's ministry.

The land of Canaan is symbolic of the spiritual victory that can be enjoyed here on earth by every believer—a rest from fear and failure.

Just as Joshua was given the responsibility of leading the various tribes to victory, so Christ, the Captain of our salvation, gives victory to those who act on the promises of God. Through faith, we win the victory over the "giants" in our lives—jealousy, greed, hatred, lust, and other works of the flesh (see I John 5:4).

MARCH 13: Read Joshua 1 — 3

Highlights: Joshua given the position of leadership; spies sent to Jericho; pledge between the spies and Rahab; crossing the Jordan River.

Verses for Today: *"I will not fail thee, nor forsake thee. . . . Be strong and of a good courage; be not afraid, neither be thou dismayed: for the Lord thy God is with thee whithersoever thou goest"* (Joshua 1:5,9).

J oshua was born in Egyptian slavery, but during the desert trials God used him as a co-worker with Moses. His faith in God almost caused him to be stoned to death by the former generation when he urged them to advance into Canaan. (See Numbers 14:6-10.)

To be "brought out" of Egypt was one thing, but it was altogether another thing to *"go over this Jordan"* (Joshua 1:2) and thus become committed to the struggles against the power of the Canaanites with their chariots of iron and their armies of giants. To do this was to commit themselves to a course which had been condemned by 10 out of 12 spies who reported on the land 40 years earlier. The crossing of *"this Jordan"* was a major step of faith which the former generation had refused to take. To the natural eye, it was a risk of losing everything—even their very lives.

Christians face a similar choice of faith—whether or not there will be a once-and-for-all abandonment of self to the will of God, so that He is truly first in one's life.

It is one thing to take Christ as Savior from one's sins, but it is another thing to take Him as Master of one's will and life. It is one thing to be brought out of Egypt—a type of the unregenerate life—and to join God's redeemed and live by faith; but it is another thing to cross over Jordan and *"present your bodies a living sacrifice . . . and be not conformed to this world . . . "* (Romans 12:1-2).

When the Lord is leading the way, we will conquer the *"giants in Canaan"* in our lives. Victory is assured. Whether it's overcoming a Pharaoh, a Red Sea, the wilderness, or other "giants" in one's life, such as fear, lust, jealousy, envy—His grace is sufficient.

"And they overcame him by the blood of the Lamb, and by the word of their testimony; and they loved not their lives unto the death" (Revelation 12:11).

Thought for Today: Our victories in life depend upon whether or not we desire to do His will as revealed in His Word.

Christ Revealed: Through the scarlet line in the window that saved Rahab and her household—symbolic of the blood of Christ. (See Joshua 2:21; Heb. 11:31; James 2:25; compare I John 1:7.)

Word Studies: 1:4 **Great Sea** means Mediterranean Sea; 1:11 **victuals** means provisions of food; 2:20 **quit** means guiltless; free.

Prayer Needs: Country: Mali—9 million—in West Africa • Religious freedom despite Muslim majority • 81% Muslim; 17% animism and spirit worship; 2% Christian.

MARCH 14: Read Joshua 4 — 6

Highlights: The memorial of 12 stones; circumcision renewed; Passover at Gilgal; manna ceases; Jericho besieged and destroyed.

Verse for Today: *"At that time the Lord said unto Joshua, Make thee sharp knives,* *and circumcise again the children of Israel the second time"* (Joshua 5:2)

When the estimated two million Israelites crossed the Jordan River, the Canaanite inhabitants were gripped with terror (Joshua 2:9). This may have seemed like the perfect time to rush into battle and claim the land God had promised them. But they were not yet in a right covenant relationship with God to take possession of the Promised Land.

During the 40 years of wilderness wanderings, the Israelites had ignored the practice of circumcision, a symbol of their covenant relationship with God (see Jeremiah 9:25-26).

Before assuming leadership as God's appointed leader of His covenant people, it was vitally important that Moses' own son be circumcised (compare Exodus 4:24-26 and Genesis 17:7-14).

In keeping with God's covenant with Abraham the new generation had to submit to the humbling rite of circumcision. Their obedience ensured them of God's continued protection and direction.

We may assume that God is in a hurry for us to do something for Him, but it is vital that we first humble ourselves in willing submission to His Word.

Through our union with Christ, we once received not a hand-performed circumcision but one performed by Christ, in stripping us of our lower nature, for we were buried with Him in baptism and raised to life with Him through our faith in the power of God, who raised Him from the dead (see Colossians 2:11-12).

Thought for Today: God's delays are always more profitable than our haste.

Christ Revealed: As the Captain of the host of the Lord (Joshua 5:14).

Word Studies: 4:1 **were clean passed over** means had finished crossing; 4:9 **unto this day** means when this book was written; 5:1 **by the sea** means along the Mediterranean Sea; 5:11 **old corn** means ripe grain; produce; **unleavened cakes** means bread made without yeast; **parched corn** means roasted grain; 6:9 **rearward (rereward)** means rear guard; 6:18 **accursed** means devoted to God—the irrevocable giving over of things or persons to the Lord, often by totally destroying them; 6:23 **kindred** means other relatives; 6:26 **adjured them** means gave them a most solemn oath—as if repeating it seven times.

Prayer Needs: Country: Qatar—316,000—in southwestern Asia • Muslim conversion to Christ is forbidden, but expatriate Christians are allowed to meet informally • 92% Muslim; 4% Protestant; 2% Roman Catholic; 1% Hindu; .5% Eastern Orthodox.

MARCH 15: Read Joshua 7 — 8

Highlights: Sin of Achan; Israelites flee at Ai; Ai destroyed; Law recorded at Mount Ebal.

Verse for Today: *"So there went up thither of the people about three thousand men: and they fled before the men of Ai"* (Joshua 7:4).

The Israelites had seen the Lord roll back the waters of the Jordan River and overthrow the mighty walled city of Jericho. But in their battle at Ai, a much weaker city, they suffered humiliation and defeat. Thirty-six Israelites were killed in battle.

Joshua had not sought counsel from the Lord before going to battle with Ai;

instead, he accepted the advice of his spies (Joshua 7:2-4) and made his own decision. But Jehovah Himself was their Captain, their Commander-in-Chief. He alone could issue orders that would result in success (5:13-15). This is confirmed by the fact that, nine times in the first six chapters of the book of Joshua, the Bible records how the Lord directed Joshua. (Note Joshua 1:1; 3:7; 4:1,8,10,15; 5:2,15; 6:2.) Then in Joshua 7:2-5, Joshua and his committee (not the Lord) unanimously decided what action was to be taken, and it resulted in failure.

Instructions had been given as to where Joshua was to get direction from God: *"And he shall stand before Eleazar the priest, who shall ask counsel for him ... "* (Numbers 27:21).

It is true that Joshua was ignorant of the sin of Achan, which brought defeat at Ai. But Joshua should have asked counsel of the Lord *before* going to battle instead of *after* the death of 36 people (see Joshua 7:5-11).

God's people are never in greater danger of supposing they no longer need to pray for guidance than when the Lord has just answered prayer or greatly blessed them.

"Be careful [anxious] for nothing; but in every thing by prayer and supplication with thanksgiving let your requests be made known unto God" (Philippians 4:6).

Thought for Today: The most honored of God's servants fail when they fail to pray!

Christ Revealed: Through the uncut stones of the altar (Joshua 8:31). Daniel saw Christ as a stone which was not cut by human hands (Dan. 2:34).

Word Studies: 7:5 **in the going down** means on the hillside; 7:6 **put dust upon their heads** means mourned; 7:11 **dissembled** means lied; 7:19 **give, I pray thee, glory to the Lord** means I solemnly charge you to confess the truth, which honors God; 7:26 **Achor** means trouble; 8:14 **wist not** means did not know.

Prayer Needs: Country: Solomon Islands—300,000—in the southwestern Pacific • Religious freedom • 66% Protestant; 17% Roman Catholic; 4% spirit worship, ancestor worship, and sorcery; 3% cargo cults.

MARCH 16: Read Joshua 9 — 10

Highlights: Deceit of the Gibeonites; their servitude to the Israelites; defeat of the Amorites; sun and moon stand still.

Verses for Today: *"Then spake Joshua to the Lord in the day when the Lord delivered up the Amorites before the children of Israel, and he said in the sight of Israel, Sun, stand thou still upon Gibeon; and thou, Moon, in the valley of Ajalon. And the sun stood still, and the moon stayed, until the people had avenged themselves upon their enemies ... "* (Joshua 10:12-13).

S ome people believe the main purpose of the miracle in prolonging daylight *"about a whole day"* (Joshua 10:13) was to dishonor the Canaanites' sun-god Baal and their moon goddess Ashtoreth. But it was also a confirmation of the Lord's promise to Joshua that He would *"magnify thee in the sight of all Israel, that they may know that, as I was with Moses, so I will be with thee"* (3:7).

Books have been written to explain how the miracle was performed, but they are of little consequence. The process of stopping the rotation of the earth and preventing all the adverse reactions would be as easy for God to accomplish as it was for Him to bring life back into the body of Lazarus, who had been dead for several days. (See John 11:38-44.) Which of these miracles was most miraculous?

There should be no doubt of Joshua's long day for the believer who looks forward to that longer eternal day when the sun and moon will no longer exist and we shall be with the Lord forever. (See Revelation 22:5.)

"For whether is easier, to say, Thy sins be forgiven thee; or to say, Arise, and walk?" (Matthew 9:5).

Thought for Today: Any of our accomplishments that are worthwhile are the result of God's working through us.

Christ Revealed: As the One through whom we have victory (Joshua 10:25; compare I Cor. 15:57; II Cor. 2:14).

Word Studies: 9:5 **clouted** means patched; 9:6 **league** means peace treaty; 10:10 **discomfited them** means caused them to panic, thus creating confusion (compare Psalm 18:14); 10:40 **springs** means ravines; gulches.

Prayer Needs: Country: Benin (formerly Dahomey)—5 million—in western Africa • Some hostility toward Christians • 59% animism and voodoo; 17% Muslim; 16% Roman Catholic; 3% Protestant.

MARCH 17: Read Joshua 11 — 13

Highlights: Defeat of many kings within Canaan; much land still to be possessed; inheritance of Reuben, Gad, and half the tribe of Manasseh on the east side of the Jordan River.

Verse for Today: *" . . . there remaineth yet very much land to be possessed"* (Joshua 13:1).

The communication between God and Joshua closes with the dividing of the remainder of the land of Canaan.

Many years had passed since Israel crossed over Jordan into the Promised Land; yet, the Amorites, Jebuzites, and Hittites were still in possession of Canaan. At this time, the nation of Israel was living for the most part in the mountainous regions. The cities in the valleys had not yet been conquered, but by faith Joshua divided the remaining land and claimed it according to the promise of God. Without hesitation, Joshua said, *"Judah, this portion belongs to you; Asher, this is yours; Simeon . . . "* and on and on.

Joshua was virtually warning Israel not to be satisfied with past victories—that if all the land of promise was to be possessed, it must be taken without compromise.

The older generation that first entered and defeated many nations within Canaan should have led the way for final conquest. Often Christians, once useful in the Lord's service, become inactive and satisfied with past achievements when years of experience and spiritual discernment could enable them to render the Church a more valuable service than ever.

History and Scripture alike join in saying to every one, *"Whatsoever thy hand findeth to do, do it with thy might"* (Ecclesiastes 9:10). The young are prone to presume they have plenty of time; the aged often feel they have done their share.

The Lord never promised His children an easy time in serving Him or told them to look forward to retirement. In fact, Christ has said, *"The night cometh, when no man can work"* (John 9:4).

Only one life 'twill soon be past; Only what's done for Christ will last.

"Wherefore he saith, Awake thou that sleepest, and arise from the dead, and Christ shall give thee light" (Ephesians 5:14).

Thought for Today: Make the most of each opportunity to bring glory to the Lord.

Christ Portrayed: By Moses, the servant of the Lord (Joshua 12:6). Jesus was the servant of God (Matt. 12:18).

Word Studies: 11:9 **houghed** means crippled; 11:13 **in their strength** means on their mounds (tells); 12:4 **coast** means territory; 13:22 **soothsayer** means fortune-teller.

Prayer Needs: Country: Tonga—99,000—in the southwestern Pacific • Religious freedom • 55% Protestant; 22% Mormon; 14% Roman Catholic.

MARCH 18: Read Joshua 14 — 16

Highlights: Promised Land divided among the tribes; Caleb inherits Hebron; territories allotted to Judah, Ephraim, and half the tribe of Manasseh on the west side of Jordan.

Verse for Today: *"And they drove not out the Canaanites that dwelt in Gezer: but the Canaanites dwell among the Ephraimites unto this day, and serve under tribute"* (Joshua 16:10).

W hy did the Ephraimites fail to defeat the Canaanites in Gezer? Was it because of cowardice, inability, or something far more serious? We have no record that the tribe of Ephraim even attempted to claim that territory. The fact remains, they disobeyed the Lord's command. This is the inevitable result of unbelief.

Ephraim's unbelief gave way to a spirit of compromise. Instead of the Canaanites being defeated, they *"dwell among the Ephraimites unto this day, and serve under tribute."*

The tribe of Ephraim was powerful enough to dominate the Canaanites, so they had no excuse for allowing the idol-worshiping Canaanites to live among them. Apparently their financial gain was more important to them than being obedient to God. It is no surprise that they eventually followed the ways of their heathen neighbors and became idolaters.

Many complain and give up when their circumstances seem difficult or not in their best interest. But God always honors the faith of those who rely upon His Word.

"But now I have written unto you not to keep company, if any man that is called a brother be a fornicator, or covetous, or an idolater, or a railer, or a drunkard, or an extortioner . . ." (I Corinthians 5:11).

Thought for Today: Since we are greatly influenced by those with whom we associate, we need to choose friends who will lead us closer to the Lord.

Christ Portrayed: By Caleb, who fully followed the Lord (Joshua 14:14). Our Savior said, *Behold, I have come . . . to do Thy will, O God* (see Heb. 10:7).

Word Studies: 14:9 **sware** means promised; 15:3 **fetched a compass** means turned about.

Prayer Needs: Country: Chile—13 million—on the southwestern coast of South America • Religious freedom • 63% Roman Catholic; 23% Protestant.

MARCH 19: Read Joshua 17 — 19

Highlights: Inheritance of Manasseh; sons of Joseph receive more land; Tabernacle set up at Shiloh; remainder of the land divided.

Verse for Today: *"And there remained among the children of Israel seven tribes, which had not yet received their inheritance"* (Joshua 18:12).

T he Israelites had crossed the Jordan River, destroyed Jericho, and finally, after seven years of war, had control of the Promised Land. But all the Canaanites had not been conquered. Joshua asked, *How long are you going to wait before you go in and take the land that the Lord, the God of your ancestors, has given you?* (see Joshua 18:3).

What was true of the tribes of Israel is true of Christians today. A general indifference to obeying all of God's Word prevails. We must *"press toward the mark"* (Philippians 3:14). This means denying self and often sacrificing pleasure that would otherwise keep us from doing what He has told us to do.

Christians should not be satisfied with past victories and accomplishments; we should continually be doing God's will. This can only be accomplished as we understand His will and read His Word. This involves more than just reading the Bible and enjoying new truths; transforming power is the result of a sincere desire to obey Him.

Fight the good fight of faith; take hold of eternal life to which you are called (see I Timothy 6:12).

Thought for Today: To postpone doing God's will robs us of our usefulness and often causes us to become a stumbling block to others.

Christ Revealed: Through Shiloh. *"The children of Israel assembled together at Shiloh, and set up the tabernacle"* (Joshua 18:1). Shiloh was the dwelling place of God's presence and was prophetic of our coming Lord, as foretold in Genesis 49:10—*"until Shiloh come."*

Word Studies: 17:13 **tribute** means forced labor; 18:6 **describe** means diagram; survey; give a written description.

Prayer Needs: Country: Dominica—94,000—in the British West Indies • Religious freedom • 75% Roman Catholic; 12% Protestant.

MARCH 20: Read Joshua 20 — 21

Highlights: Six cities of refuge appointed; 48 cities given to the Levites; the Israelites possess the land.

Verses for Today: *" ... Appoint out for you cities of refuge, whereof I spake unto you by the hand of Moses: that the slayer that killeth any person unawares and unwittingly may flee thither: and they shall be your refuge from the avenger of blood"* (Joshua 20:2-3).

C ities of refuge were established to protect those who accidentally killed someone; but the original command God gave was still in force: *"Whoso sheddeth* man's blood, by man shall his blood be shed: for in the image of God made he man" (Genesis 9:6).

However, there was a definite distinction made between the person who intentionally murdered someone and the one who accidentally killed another. Instead of a person being put to death for accidentally killing another, he could flee to one of the cities which God had appointed for shelter and protection.

Murder is a crime against God because man was created *"in the image of God."* Because of this, it is written, " . . . *the land cannot be cleansed of the blood that is shed therein, but by the blood of him that shed it"* (Numbers 35:33). Therefore, it was of utmost importance for the welfare of the nation that anyone who purposely killed another *"be surely put to death"* (Exodus 21:12). A nation that persistently ignores this fact will face God's judgment.

Thoughtlessly slandering others is often as deadly as carelessly killing another. How vital it is that we flee to Jesus—our refuge—and ask for His mercy and forgiveness!

"Whosoever hateth his brother is a murderer: and ye know that no murderer hath eternal life abiding in him" (I John 3:15).

Thought for Today: Gossip often creates barriers that keep us from being the blessing we should be.

Christ Portrayed: By Eleazar, the chief priest (Joshua 21:1). Christ is our High Priest (Heb. 3:1).

Word Studies: 21:2 **suburbs** means pasturelands; 21:32 **refuge** means protection.

Prayer Needs: **Country:** Mongolia—2 million—in east-central Asia • Christianity is strongly suppressed • 29% shamanist; 2% Buddhist; 2% Muslim; .2% Christian.

MARCH 21: Read Joshua 22 — 24

Highlights: Two and one-half tribes sent home; controversy over the altar of testimony; Joshua's final reminder of God's goodness to the Israelites; the altar of witness; Joshua's death.

Verse for Today: *"And the children of Reuben and the children of Gad and the half tribe of Manasseh returned, and departed from the children of Israel out of Shiloh, which is in the land of Canaan, to go unto the country of Gilead . . . "* (Joshua 22:9).

The people of the tribes of Reuben, Gad, and the half-tribe of Manasseh asked to live on the east side of Jordan, where they could take advantage of the rich grazing land of Gilead. Moses consented to their decision if they would first help the other tribes conquer the Promised Land.

These two-and-one-half tribes united with the other tribes in bringing about great victory. Then, after seven years of conquest, they returned to their rich grazing land on the other side of the Jordan River.

Living outside the God-protected Promised Land, they were the first tribes to sink into idolatry and were eventually destroyed by the Assyrians. (See I Chronicles 5:26.)

God has a definite plan for each of us. He may permit us to go our own way, as He did the two-and-one-half tribes; but when we do, we are in danger of being trapped by worldliness, defeated by compromise, and ensnared by the devil. Some have decided that the conflict is too great, the war too long; and they settle for less than God's best.

"Know ye not that they which run in a race run all, but one receiveth the prize? So run, that ye may obtain" (I Corinthians 9:24).

Thought for Today: God's Word may not satisfy our fleshly desires, but we can be confident that He alone knows what is best for His children.

Christ Revealed: Through the peace offering (Joshua 22:27). Our Lord offered Himself to God as our means of peace with the Father (Rom. 5:1).

Word Studies: 22:10 **to see to** means that was very impressive in appearance; 22:29 **meat offerings** means cereal grain offerings made with fine flour (or unleavened bread), oil, and a portion of incense; 23:1 **waxed old** means grew old; 23:8 **cleave** means remain faithful; 24:7 **covered** means drowned.

Prayer Needs: **Country:** Guinea-Bissau (formerly Portuguese Guinea)—930,000—on the western coast of Africa • Religious freedom • 51% animist; 42% Muslim; 6% Roman Catholic; .7% Protestant

JUDGES

The book of Judges covers between 300 and 400 years of Israel's history—from the beginning of the period of the judges until Samuel the prophet.

After Joshua's death, *"there arose another generation after them, which knew not the Lord. . . . they forsook the Lord, and served Baal and Ashtaroth"* (2:10,13). This marked the turning point in the conquest and control of the Promised Land and showed the national condition after Joshua's death (chapters 1—2).

Civil wars broke out as self-interest weakened national unity (12:1-6; 20). Their independent spirit was summarized by the words, *Everyone did whatever he wanted to do* (see 17:6; compare 18:1-28; 21:25).

To avoid war, the Israelites compromised with the Canaanites and thus failed to fully obey God's command to drive out the Canaanites (Joshua 17:18). Soon the Israelites were participating in Canaanite idol worship. Because of this, the Lord withdrew His protection, and the Israelites were attacked by invading nations. But each time the children of Israel prayed, God raised up a judge—a deliverer (Judges 3—16).

The book of Judges centers on six particular times when *"the children of Israel did evil in the sight of the Lord."* Although 12 judges are mentioned, the book focuses on the 5 judges God raised up when the Israelites prayed, and around Abimelech's violent rule.

The death of Samson marked the close of the long period of the judges. What follows in the remaining chapters is not a continuation of Israel's history, but an illustration of the moral and spiritual level within the Promised Land (chapters 17—21).

The book of Judges is more than a record of battles between the Israelites and their enemies. It is a "book of wars" where God was contending with sin in the hearts of His people. The main purpose of the book is to reveal what inevitably results when man rejects God as his King and becomes his own judge.

MARCH 22: Read Judges 1 — 2

Highlights: Judah chosen to lead the wars against the Canaanites; Israel's failure to drive out the Canaanites; the Israelites rebuked by an angel; death of Joshua; Israel's apostasy.

Verses for Today: *"And an angel of the Lord came up from Gilgal to Bochim, and said, I made you to go up out of Egypt, and have brought you unto the land which I sware unto your fathers; and I said, I will never break my covenant with you. And ye shall make no league with the inhabitants of this land; ye shall throw down their altars; but ye have not obeyed my voice: why have ye done this?"* (Judges 2:1-2).

T he deliverance from Egypt, the miracles of the wilderness, and the long period of discipline in the desert were all designed to prepare Israel for their full inheritance in Canaan. But following the death of Joshua, the tribes all settled within their territories, defeating but not destroying the Canaanites. *"And it came to pass when Israel was strong, that they put the Canaanites to tribute, and did not utterly drive them out"* (Judges 1:28). Instead of fully obeying the Lord, they thought it was wiser to make slaves of them and collect taxes.

God is either Lord of all or not Lord at all, so it is no surprise to read that soon Israel was worshiping idols. And in the midst of this crisis, the Lord Himself appeared saying, *Why have you done this?*

"The people lifted up their voice, and wept" (Judges 2:4). Furthermore, they offered sacrifices to the Lord, but did not defeat the enemy or destroy their idols. No amount of tears or sacrifice can substitute for full obedience.

" . . . who without respect of persons judgeth according to every man's work, pass the time of your sojourning here in fear" (I Peter 1:17).

Thought for Today: Many of our heartaches can be avoided if we obey God's Word.

Christ Revealed: By *"an angel of the Lord."* "Angel" means messenger sent from Heaven with a message of God's love. Perhaps this is the Lord Himself who had caused them to *"go up out of Egypt"* (Judges 2:1).

Word Studies: 1:15 **nether** means lower; 1:23 **descry** means spy out; 2:5 **Bochim** means weepers.

Prayer Needs: Country: Mozambique—15 million—on the eastern coast of Africa • Christians are harassed and churches have been closed by the government • 60% worship of false gods, ancestral spirits, and some witchcraft; 13% Roman Catholic; 13% Muslim; 6% Protestant.

MARCH 23: Read Judges 3 — 5

Highlights: Deliverances through Othniel, Ehud, and Shamgar; victories of Deborah and Barak; song of Deborah and Barak.

Verse for Today: *" . . . And Deborah said unto Barak, Up; for this is the day in* *which the Lord hath delivered Sisera into thine hand . . . "* (Judges 4:14).

B ecause *"they did evil,"* the Lord delivered the Israelites into the hand of Jabin, king of Canaan. During the next 20 years of captivity, there is no record of anyone in Israel praying to the Lord for deliverance.

Deborah was God's messenger to bring His Word of deliverance to His people and free them from oppression. Through her spiritual leadership, God brought peace to the land for 40 years (Judges 5:31).

It is God's Word and intercessory prayer that enables us to be victorious. *"He sent his word, and healed them, and delivered them from their destructions"* (Psalm 107:20).

The Lord is seeking Christians today who will intercede in prayer on behalf of others.

"And he saw that there was no man, and wondered that there was no intercessor . . . " (Isaiah 59:16).

Thought for Today: Afflictions become blessings when they cause us to turn to Him.

Christ Portrayed: By Othniel, a deliverer upon whom the Spirit of the Lord rested (Judges 3:9-11). The Spirit of God was also upon Christ, our Deliverer (see Matt. 3:16; Rom. 11:26).

Word Studies: 3:4 **prove** means test; 3:7 **served Baalim and the groves** means worshiped the idols of Baal and Asherah; 3:16 **dagger** means sword; **gird** means fasten; 3:22 **haft** means handle; 3:29 **lusty** means strong or vigorous; 3:30 **fourscore** means 80.

Prayer Needs: Country: Puerto Rico—4 million—smallest island of the Greater Antilles • Religious freedom • 66% Roman Catholic; 27% Protestant.

MARCH 24: Read Judges 6 — 7

Highlights: The Midianites oppress the Israelites for seven years; call of Gideon to deliver Israel from the Midianites; Gideon's fleece; his army reduced to 300; his victory.

Verse for Today: *"And the Lord looked upon him [Gideon], and said, Go in this thy might, and thou shalt save Israel from the hand of the Midianites: have not I sent thee?"* (Judges 6:14).

G ideon, a God-fearing man from the half-tribe of Manasseh, where Baal worship was popular, was called by God to *"go in this thy might"* against an invading army of 135,000 Midianite soldiers. Just what was *"this thy might"*? Surely God was not speaking of Gideon's tribe, for it was the smallest of all; nor could it be his family, for it was the poorest. Gideon's strength—*"this thy might"*—rested in one thing—*"I sent thee."*

But before he could deliver them from the Midianites, the altar of Baal had to be destroyed and the worship of Jehovah restored.

After Gideon had accomplished that task, he issued a call to the tribes of Israel to defend their country. Out of many thousands who volunteered to go to war, God instructed Gideon to reduce his forces to 300 men. This way, God alone could receive the praise and honor for the victory.

Like Gideon's 300, the number of men and women who are dedicated enough to accomplish God's will AT ANY COST is amazingly small. The believer's strength to win the battle comes from the Lord.

"For the weapons of our warfare are not carnal, but mighty through God to the pulling down of strongholds" (II Corinthians 10:4).

Thought for Today: God can use the weakest, smallest, or the least likely in men's eyes to perform His work.

Christ Revealed: As the angel of the Lord (Judges 6:11). This expression usually implies the presence of Deity, thought by many to be the Second Person of the Trinity.

Word Study: 6:24 **Jehovah-shalom** means the Lord is peace.

Prayer Needs: Country: Fiji—728,000—in the southwestern Pacific • Religious freedom • 41% Hindu; 40% Protestant; 9% Roman Catholic; 8% Muslim.

MARCH 25: Read Judges 8 — 9

Highlights: Ephraim's complaint; kings of Midian slain; Gideon's ephod; his death; reign and death of Abimelech.

Verse for Today: *"And Gideon made an ephod thereof, and put it in his city, even in Ophrah: and all Israel went thither a whoring after it: which thing became a snare unto Gideon, and to his house"* (Judges 8:27).

G ideon's great faith shines as a star on the pages of Scripture (Hebrews 11:32). At the angel's command, he destroyed the altar of Baal at his own father's house (Judges 6:28-29). With implicit obedience, he reduced his army to 300 men to fight the vast armies of Midian *"without number, as the sand by the seaside for multitude"* (7:12). Furthermore, when Gideon was urged by all, *"Rule thou over us . . . "* he immediately rejected the tempting proposal saying, *"The Lord shall rule over you"* (8:22-23).

Yet *"Gideon made an ephod."*

The ark, containing the commandments—the dwelling place of God—was in Shiloh, the God-appointed center for Israel's worship; and the high priest alone was commissioned to wear the ephod. But Shiloh was located in the tribe of Ephraim who had shown themselves hostile to Gideon.

Perhaps this godly man of faith thought that since there existed so much hypocrisy in Shiloh, he was justified in making the ephod (priestly garment—Exodus 28:6-12) and in establishing his own worship center. Though his intentions were good, the act was wrong; and he lost the battle of greatest importance.

He attempted to accomplish a right thing in a wrong way. Not even a godly Gideon—no, not even Moses—was permitted to alter the Word of God.

"For they being ignorant of God's righteousness, and going about to establish their own righteousness, have not submitted themselves unto the righteousness of God" (Romans 10:3).

Thought for Today: Only if God blesses your efforts will anything of eternal value result.

Christ Portrayed: By Gideon, who delivered the Israelites from Midian (Judges 8:22). The Lord Jesus has delivered us out of the hands of our spiritual enemies, and it is fitting that He should rule over us.

Word Studies: 8:1 **chide** means quarrel; 8:3 **abated** means cooled off; 9:14 **bramble** means thorn bush.

Prayer Needs: Country: France—56 million—in western Europe • Religious freedom • 74% Roman Catholic; 5% Muslim; 2% Protestant; 1% Jewish.

MARCH 26: Read Judges 10 — 11

Highlights: Tola judges Israel; Jair judges Israel; Jephthah chosen to lead Israel; his vow; victory over the Ammonites.

Verses for Today: *"And Gilead's wife bare him sons; and his wife's sons grew up, and they thrust out Jephthah, and said unto him, Thou shalt not inherit in our father's house; for thou art the son of a strange woman. . . . And it came to pass in process of time, that the children of Ammon made war against Israel. And it was so, that when the children of Ammon made war against Israel, the elders of Gilead went to fetch Jephthah out of the land of Tob"* (Judges 11:2,4-5).

E veryone does not begin life with the same advantages. Some are born of parents with great wealth and influential friends. But a far greater number of people are born among the poor who must work long hours for the necessities of life; still others are born under the shadow of reproach and have to face strong prejudice.

And so it was with Jephthah who was rejected by his own brethren. Because he was an illegitimate child, he was forced into exile for 18 years. Jepthah did not use this as an excuse to hate those who rejected him or blame God and turn to idols. But he allowed this rejection to deepen his faith and trust in God.

Had Jephthah become bitter and resentful because "everyone" was against him, he would never have risen in life to be a judge in Israel and have his name associated in the same verse with Samuel and David as heroes of faith (Hebrews 11:32).

All who are used of God will experience a time of preparation when it may seem that one's efforts result in disappointments. Accept with gratitude everything that God allows through friends or enemies—through failures or humiliations—as a means to see yourself as nothing and to see your need of full dependence upon Him. Then will come the time of fulfillment when your faith will be rewarded.

"Humble yourselves therefore under the mighty hand of God, that he may exalt you in due time" (I Peter 5:6).

Thought for Today: Recognize that God allows trials to build your faith in Him.

Christ Portrayed: By Jephthah's only child as she submitted to her father's will (Judges 11:34-40; compare Matt. 26:39).

Word Studies: 11:37 **fellows** means female companions; 11:40 **lament** means commemorate.

Prayer Needs: Country: Hong Kong—6 million—at the mouth of the Canton River in China • Religious freedom • 66% Buddhist and other Chinese religions; 7% Protestant; 5% Roman Catholic .

MARCH 27: Read Judges 12 — 14

Highlights: Jephthah's victory over the Ephraimites; Israel judged by Jephthah, Ibzan, Elon, and Abdon; Israel delivered to the Philistines; birth of Samson;

Samson and the girl from Timnath; feast and riddle.

Verses for Today: *"And the woman bare a son, and called his name Samson: and the child grew, and the Lord blessed him. And the spirit of the Lord began to move him at times . . ."* (Judges 13:24-25).

E ach time the children of Israel *"cried unto the Lord,"* God prepared a deliverer. But this time, there was no national prayer for deliverance, although they had been slaves of the Philistines for 40 years.

Israel had forsaken Jehovah, but God in mercy *"began to move"* upon Samson, who could have delivered them. But the people had not prayed for deliverance, and therefore remained powerless under the control of the Philistines.

Samson was more concerned over pleasing himself than he was in pleasing God. This was evident when he insisted on having a Canaanite wife, saying, *"Get her for me; for she pleaseth me well"* (Judges 14:1-3). The three women in Samson's life represent the attractions of the pleasure-loving world which rob the Christian of his power with God.

"Ye ask, and receive not, because ye ask amiss, that ye may consume it upon your lusts" (James 4:3).

Thought for Today: Many lives are empty because God is not asked to fill them.

Christ Portrayed: By Jephthah, who showed a loving spirit to the nation that rejected him (Judges 12:1-3; compare Matt. 18:15).

Word Studies: 12:14 **nephews** means grandsons or other descendants; 13:5 **Nazarite** means separated to God (see Numbers 6:2-21 for Nazarite vow); 13:6 **terrible** means awesome; 13:18 **secret** means wonderful.

Prayer Needs: **Country:** Bangladesh (formerly East Pakistan)—107 million—in southern Asia • Present religious freedom may become limited • 87% Muslim; 12% Hindu; .4% Christian.

MARCH 28: Read Judges 15 — 17

Highlights: Samson loses his wife; 1,000 Philistines slain; Samson and Delilah; Samson avenged in his death; Micah's idols.

Verse for Today: *" . . . every man did that which was right in his own eyes"* (Judges 17:6).

T he Israelites were set apart as a holy nation under the leadership of God. But they soon ignored the laws given on Mt. Sinai by their true King and no longer looked to Him for daily direction.

Samson was a typical example of Israel's condition. What was wrong with him was wrong with the nation. It is recorded in the book of Judges that everyone *"did that which was right in his own eyes"* (see "Introduction to Judges"). They were not concerned with knowing or doing God's will.

The same deceptive reasoning is popular today. Many conform to external standards of doing whatever they want to do, supposing that it doesn't matter what one believes as long as he is sincere; but when Christ rules our lives, our chief concern will be, "What would Jesus have me do?"

Now flee from youthful lusts and pursue righteousness, faith, love, and peace with those who call on the Lord from a pure heart (see II Timothy 2:22).

Thought for Today: The person who lives to satisfy self cannot fulfill God's purposes for his life.

Christ Revealed: In the strength of Samson. *"I have been a Nazarite unto God"* (Judges 16:17). A Christian's spiritual strength is his faith in Christ and his consecration to God (see I Pet. 1:5).

Word Studies: 15:4 **firebrands** means torches of flax on fire; 16:7 **green withes** means small new ropes; 16:11 **fast** means securely; 16:21 **did grind** means worked as a grinder at the mill; 16:25 **make us sport** means entertain us; 16:26 **Suffer me** means Allow me; 17:4 **founder** means silversmith.

Prayer Needs: Country: Lesotho—2 million—within the east-central part of the Republic of South Africa • Limited religious freedom • 43% Roman Catholic; 30% Protestant; 6% ancestor worship, divination, and spirit-possession cults.

MARCH 29: Read Judges 18 — 19

Highlights: Danites take Micah's idols and priest; Danites attack Laish; moral decline; a Levite's concubine slain.

Verse for Today: *" . . . the tribe of the Danites sought them an inheritance to dwell in . . . "* (Judges 18:1).

T he tribe of Dan numbered more than 64,000 men, but they had not succeeded in driving the Amorites from their territory (see Numbers 26:42-43). In fact, the Amorites forced the Danites into the mountains (Judges 1:34).

The Danites' failure to claim their inheritance was a faith failure. Perhaps they thought they were too weak . . . or perhaps they just didn't want to put forth the effort.

They became dissatisfied with the territory God had allotted to them and moved north. As a result, their spiritual condition continued to decline.

Likewise, our failure to claim God's promises causes us to be dissatisfied with the blessings we have. This results in further spiritual decline.

" . . . be not slothful, but followers of them who through faith and patience inherit the promises" (Hebrews 6:12).

Thought for Today: Worldly compromise is a silent witness of unconcern about what God has to say.

Christ Portrayed: *"In those days there was no king in Israel"* (Judges 18:1). Christ was the rejected King of Israel (John 19:14-15).

Word Studies: 18:12 **Mahanehdan** means Camp of Dan; 18:15 **thitherward** means in that direction; 18:21 **carriage** means baggage; 19:11 **Jebus** means Jerusalem; 19:17 **wayfaring** means traveling; 19:19 **provender** means fodder; food.

Prayer Needs: Country: Singapore—3 million—in Southeast Asia • Religious freedom • 54% Chinese religions; 17% Muslim; 5% Protestant; 4% Roman Catholic.

MARCH 30: Read Judges 20 — 21

Highlights: War against the Benjamites; their defeat; wives for remaining Benjamites.

Verse for Today: *"In those days there was no king in Israel: every man did that which was right in his own eyes"* (Judges 21:25).

B ecause the Israelites failed to recognize God as King, they were constantly defeated by the Canaanites, whom God had intended for them to drive out.

God was Israel's true King (see I Samuel 12:12); but four times in the book of Judges, these or similar heartbreaking words were recorded: *"In those days there was no king in Israel, but every man did that which was right in his own eyes"* (see 17:6; 18:1; 19:1; 21:25).

When everyone does that which is right in his own eyes, there will be lawlessness, immorality, and deception by false teaching. When God's Word is ignored, as by the tribe of Dan (Judges 18), man is without a true guide.

Man was created with a desire to worship God. But unless he worships God according to His Word, he will turn to some form of false worship.

"Holding faith, and a good conscience; which some having put away concerning faith have made shipwreck" (I Timothy 1:19).

Thought for Today: Man was not created to be master of his own will.

Christ Revealed: As our Deliverer (Judges 20:26,28). As we pray and seek the Lord's will, He delivers us from all evil forces (see I Cor. 10:13).

Word Studies: 20:5 **forced** means raped; 20:6 **lewdness** means immoral, lustful conduct; 20:10 **folly** means wicked conduct; 20:29 **set liers** means set an ambush; 20:34 **sore** means fierce; 20:45 **gleaned** means cruelly maltreated and abused; 21:6 **repented them** means had compassion for them; 21:10 **valiantest** means bravest.

Prayer Needs: **Country:** Macao—438,000—on a small peninsula on the southern coast of China • Religious freedom • 66% Chinese religions; 11% Roman Catholic; 1% Protestant.

RUTH

The events in the book of Ruth occurred sometime during the period of the judges. The purpose of the book is to reveal how the mercy and providential care of God extend far beyond man's limited faith.

God used even the unbelief of Elimelech to bring Ruth, the Gentile Moabitess, to Bethlehem. There she married Boaz, a Bethlehemite from the tribe of Judah. Their union was blessed by a son named Obed. Ruth and Boaz became the great-grandparents of David (4:16-17; I Chronicles 2:12-15).

Little could the gracious and godly Boaz realize what would be accomplished when he accepted his responsiblity as a *"near kinsman"* (Ruth 3:11-12; compare Leviticus 25:23-25). Through the marriage of Boaz and Ruth, God united both Jew and Gentile in the ancestry of David, the greatest king of Israel, and in the genealogy of our Lord, the Messiah (Matthew 1:5-6; Luke 3:31-32).

MARCH 31: Read Ruth 1 — 4

Highlights: Elimelech and Naomi move from Bethlehem to Moab; return of Naomi and Ruth to Bethlehem; Ruth working in Boaz's field; marriage of Boaz and Ruth; genealogy of David.

Verse for Today: " . . . *why then call ye me Naomi, seeing the Lord hath testified against me, and the Almighty hath afflicted me?*" (Ruth 1:21).

B ecause of a famine, Elimelech took his wife, Naomi, and their two sons and left Bethlehem (which means "house of bread"). They crossed the Jordan River and sojourned in the land of Moab, the place of God's curse (see Numbers 24:17; Amos 2:1-3).

What they thought would be an escape from starvation by a temporary "sojourn" became a permanent dwelling place, for they remained there about 10 years (see Ruth 1:1-4). During that time, both of their sons married women of Moab.

Eventually Elimelech (whose name means "my God is King") and his sons died and were buried there. God was no longer King of this family that failed to trust Him for "bread" in Bethlehem. Naomi, whose name means "pleasant" was left empty. She felt she no longer had anything worth living for.

News that *"the Lord had visited his people in giving them bread"* caused Naomi to return to Bethlehem, taking Ruth with her (see Ruth 1:6). Naomi expressed her deep sorrow, saying, *"Call me not Naomi, call me Mara"* (meaning "bitter"—1:20). She confessed, *"I went out full, and the Lord hath brought me home again empty . . . "* (1:21).

The thrilling conclusion is that God used Naomi to bring the Gentile Moabitess, Ruth, to Boaz, which brought the Gentiles into the ancestry of the Messiah.

This story should give the most despondent, defeated person encouragement and hope.

"Nay, in all these things we are more than conquerors through him that loved us" (Romans 8:37).

Thought for Today: Out of our most bitter experiences, God can perfect His will.

Christ Revealed: Through Bethlehem, which means "house of bread." Jesus, the Bread of life, satisfies the spiritual hunger of all who come to Him.

Word Studies: 1:17 **the Lord do so to me, and more also** means may the Lord's worst punishment come upon me; 2:1 **kinsman** means relative. The people of Israel were to preserve their family heritage from the time of Joshua to the birth of Christ; therefore, the Law declared that if a man died, leaving a widow and no sons, a near relative (kinsman) must marry her, preserve the ancestry, and pay whatever was necessary to restore her late husband's inheritance. Naomi's case was even worse, for she was widowed, she had no living sons, and she was too old to bear children. Aged Boaz accepted the responsibility of kinsman by marrying Ruth and purchasing the property of her first husband's father, a near relative (2:20-21; 4:13-14); 2:2 **glean** means gather grain that was left by the reapers; **corn** means grain; 2:3 **her hap was to light** means she happened to come; 2:8 **fast by** means close by; 2:15 **reproach her not** means don't shame or insult her; 3:4 **mark** means notice; 3:18 **fall** means turn out; 4:1 **the gate** means the meeting place to transact legal or official business; 4:4 **advertise** means to inform; 4:5 **thou must also buy it of Ruth** means in order to redeem property, you must take Ruth as your wife.

Prayer Needs: Country: Sweden—8 million—in northern Europe • Religious freedom • 66% Protestant; 2% Roman Catholic; .7% Eastern Orthodox .

PRAYERS IN THIS MONTH'S READING

I SAMUEL

The book of I Samuel is a continuation of the book of Judges and covers Israel's history from the time of Eli (chapters 1—5) to the death of King Saul (chapter 31). It records Israel's transition from the period of the judges to the monarchy. During that period of time, the Israelites were often oppressed by the Philistines.

Both Samuel the prophet and Samson the judge lived during this corrupt, backslidden era. Samuel's life of great faith and loyalty to God stands in contrast to Samson's. The moral weakness of Samson's life typifies the spiritual condition of Israel during the period of the judges.

Through Samuel, the tribes were united as a kingdom (chapters 5—8). But as Israel gained strength and Samuel grew old, the nation demanded a king to rule over them (8:5; compare Acts 13:21).

Samuel knew that if the people chose a man to rule them, they would place their faith in him and no longer depend on God for leadership. Therefore, he was strongly opposed to their request. Then, because of their continued demands, God instructed Samuel to anoint Saul as king of Israel (8:22; 10:1; see also chapters 9—15).

Saul's 40-year reign is best expressed by his own words, *I have been a fool* (see 26:21). Because of his disobedience and pride, *"the spirit of the Lord departed from Saul"* (16:14), and God commanded Samuel to anoint David as king.

Not only was David a man after God's own heart, but he was also a mighty warrior (13:14; 18:7; compare Acts 13:22). While he was still a young man, he killed a bear and a lion, and defeated Goliath, a giant from the Philistine army.

As David became more and more popular in the eyes of the people, King Saul became more and more jealous. Because of this jealousy, Saul made a vicious attempt to murder David, who was then forced to live in exile until the time of Saul's death in the tragic battle on Mt. Gilboa (chapters 16—31).

The book of I Samuel points out that faithfulness to God brings success, while disobedience brings disaster (see 2:30).

APRIL 1: Read I Samuel 1 — 3

Highlights: Hannah's prayer for a child; her vow to God; birth of Samuel; Hannah's prayer; Eli's wicked sons; God's warning to Eli; the Lord calls Samuel.

Verse for Today: *" . . . And the word of the Lord was precious in those days; there was no open vision"* (I Samuel 3:1).

S amuel and the two sons of Eli grew up together in Shiloh, performing their duties in the Tabernacle. Because Eli was slack in disciplining his children, Hophni and Phinehas were indifferent to God's Word (I Samuel 3:12-13.) But Samuel grew in favor with the Lord (2:26) and was careful to do His will (3:9-10).

The ark of the covenant and the Tabernacle, which represented God's Word and His presence among them, had been at Shiloh since Joshua placed them there hundreds of years earlier. But general indifference to God's will prevailed. Consequently, *"the word of the Lord was precious"*—meaning, there was seldom a prophetic revelation. The sins of Eli and his sons are brought to our attention as the reason for this spiritual blindness. It is said, *"There was no open vision"*—meaning, little was known of the will of God.

The reason the Word of the Lord was not clearly understood is the same reason it is not clearly understood today. We cannot understand God's Word or His will if we do not read the Bible with a desire to know and then do His will. And we cannot keep His commandments if we are not concerned about knowing what they are.

In the hectic pace of twentieth-century America, countless thousands of *words* fill our minds every day from newspapers, magazines, books, television, and radio. There is a serious neglect of setting aside time to read the Bible—the only written *Word* from God to mankind.

We must *let Christ's teaching remain as a rich treasure in our hearts in all wisdom* (see Colossians 3:16).

Thought for Today: Sin can keep you from the Word, or the Word can keep you from sin.

Christ Revealed: Through Samuel's miraculous birth (compare I Samuel 1:5 and 1:11,20). Jesus' birth was even more miraculous because He was born to a virgin (Luke 1:27,31).

Word Studies: 1:4 **offered** means sacrificed; 1:5 **worthy** means double; 1:6 **provoked her sore** means troubled her greatly; 1:10 **sore** means with a sorrowful heart; 1:16 **Count not thine handmaid for a daughter of Belial** means "Do not think I am such a wicked woman"; 1:24 **ephah** is a measure containing about one bushel; 2:1 **horn** means strength; 2:3 **weighed** means judged; 2:12 **sons of Belial** means wicked, worthless men; 2:13 **in seething** means boiling; 2:15 **sodden** means boiled; 2:29 **Wherefore kick ye** means "Why are you dissatisfied?" 2:31 **cut off thine arm** means reduce your strength; 2:33 **consume** means blind; 3:19 **did let none of his words fall to the ground** means the Lord was with him and made everything come true that Samuel foretold; and the people recognized that what he said came from God.

Prayer Needs: Country: England—57 million—in the British Isles • Religious freedom • 48% Protestant; 9% Roman Catholic.

APRIL 2: Read I Samuel 4 — 7

Highlights: Israel's defeat by the Philistines; ark of God taken; Eli's death; the Philistines plagued because of the ark; the ark returned; Samuel rules Israel.

Verse for Today: *"And Samuel spake unto all the house of Israel, saying, If ye do return unto the Lord with all your hearts, . . . serve him only: and he will deliver you out of the hand of the Philistines"* (I Samuel 7:3).

T wenty years had passed since the Philistines had defeated Israel. When Israel was again threatened by war with the Philistines, Samuel appealed to the people to put away their idols and serve the Lord only.

After Samuel offered a sacrifice and prayed, God intervened. The Philistines were so badly defeated that they did not attack Israel again during Samuel's lifetime (I Samuel 7:7-13).

One's confession of faith may be as bold as the "great shout" that accompanied Phinehas and Hophni when they brought the ark into Israel's camp before they were slain (4:5). But the triumphant faith of Samuel is experienced by those who worship the Lord only.

"Then saith Jesus unto him, Get thee hence, Satan: for it is written, Thou shalt worship the Lord thy God, and him only shalt thou serve" (Matthew 4:10).

Thought for Today: Serving the Lord acceptably requires single-hearted love for Him.

Christ Revealed: Through the rock called Ebenezer, which means "the stone of help" (I Samuel 7:12). Jesus is the Rock of our salvation; our help comes from Him (Psa. 18:2; 121:2).

Word Studies: 4:12 **with earth upon his head** means a sign of grief; 4:13 **his heart trembled** means he was very concerned; 4:18 **judged** means governed or ruled; 5:6 **emerods** means hemorrhoids or tumors; 6:2 **diviners** means fortune-tellers; 6:7 **kine** means cows; 6:8 **coffer** means box; 6:14 **clave** means split; 7:10 **discomfited them** means caused them to panic, thus creating confusion (compare Psalm 18:14).

Prayer Needs: Country: Hungary—11 million—in east-central Europe • 61% Roman Catholic; 24% Protestant.

APRIL 3: Read I Samuel 8 — 11

Highlights: Samuel's evil sons; the Israelites' request for a king; Saul chosen to be their king; the Ammonites' defeat by Saul; Saul confirmed as king.

Verse for Today: *"And ye have this day rejected your God, who himself saved you out of all your adversities and your tribulations; and ye have said unto him, Nay, but set a king over us . . . "* (I Samuel 10:19).

S amuel and the judges who ruled the nation of Israel desired to please God— their invisible King. These judges were chosen by God and received direction from Him. However, Israel openly rejected Him as King and persistently asked to have a king such as other nations.

The Lord knew what was best for the Israelites, but the nation insisted—*"Nay; but we will have a king over us . . .[to] go out before us, and fight our battles"* (I Samuel 8:19-20). This decision represented rebellion against God.

Samuel called a national assembly at Mizpeh and again warned the people of their serious mistake in demanding a king. Saul *looked* like a king and the people were satisfied with his external appearance, but he was a symbol of the spiritual weakness of the nation.

Desiring to be like the majority has caused many to ignore the Bible and seek counsel from others. God leaves the choice to us to accept or reject His leadership.

"He that rejecteth me, and receiveth not my words, hath one that judgeth him: the word that I have spoken, the same shall judge him in the last day" (John 12:48).

Thought for Today: Unless we confess and forsake our sins, we will face eternal consequences.

Christ Revealed: Through the favored food set before Saul (I Samuel 9:24). The shoulder denotes strength; the breast which went with it denotes affection. Christ is our food who imparts strength to all who choose Him. (See John 6:51,56.)

Word Studies: 8:3 **lucre** means money; 8:12 **ear** means plow; 9:26 **spring** means dawn.

Prayer Needs: Country: Ireland—4 million—on the second largest of the British Isles · Religious freedom · 93% Roman Catholic; 4% Protestant; .1% Eastern Orthodox.

APRIL 4: Read I Samuel 12 — 14:23

Highlights: Samuel's farewell speech; war with Philistines; priest's office usurped by Saul; defeat of Philistines.

Verses for Today: *"Only fear the Lord, and serve him in truth with all your heart. . . . And Saul said, Bring hither a burnt offering to me, and peace offerings. . . . And*

97

Samuel said to Saul . . . thou hast not kept the commandment of the Lord thy God . . . " (I Samuel 12:24; 13:9,13).

Saul had been commanded to wait until Samuel returned, who alone was qualified to offer sacrifices. But his failure to wait until Samuel arrived at the *"appointed"* time (I Samuel 13:8) revealed Saul's lack of submission to God's Word.

Saul did not seem as concerned about God having authority over him as he did with God making him successful in the eyes of the people. This was more than poor judgment on the part of Israel's first king; it revealed the self-will of his heart.

Saul tried to justify his impatience and self-will as an act of worship when he made the peace offering himself. Because the enemy could attack at any hour, and many of his soldiers were deserting, he did not wait for Samuel the prophet. By violating *one* spiritual principle (waiting on God) and performing *another* (offering sacrifices), he assumed he could bring victory to Israel. But the faith that God honors comes as a result of surrendering one's life to doing all His will; this makes our service or sacrifice acceptable.

"Then said I, Lo, I come (in the volume of the book it is written of me) to do thy will, O God" (Hebrews 10:7).

Thought for Today: Obedience to God's Word is better than sacrifice.

Christ Portrayed: By Samuel the intercessor (I Samuel 12:23). Right now Jesus Christ is interceding for believers (Heb. 7:25).

Word Studies: 13:20 **share, coulter, and mattock** are agricultural tools, possibly a plow blade, a hoe, and a pickax; 14:16 **melted away** means scattered in all directions.

Prayer Needs: **Country:** St. Vincent and the Grenadines—131,000—in the Lesser Antilles of the eastern Caribbean • Religious freedom • 50% Protestant; 17% Roman Catholic; 2% spiritist.

APRIL 5: Read I Samuel 14:24 — 16

Highlights: Saul's curse; Saul commanded to destroy the Amalekites; his disobedience; Saul rejected as king; David anointed king; David in Saul's service.

Verses for Today: *"And Samuel said, How can I go? if Saul hear it, he will kill me. . . . the Lord seeth not as man seeth; for man looketh on the outward appearance, but the Lord looketh on the heart"* (I Samuel 16:2,7).

Israel was suffering from the misrule of a king who would not be ruled by God, and God purposed to use Samuel to bring about a change.

Those who are instruments of God sometimes shrink from the work which He calls them to do. Samuel asked, *"How can I go?"*

God's methods of making His servants instruments of good to others are often perplexing and sometimes painful.

When Moses was called to stand before Pharaoh, he excused himself as not qualified (Exodus 4:14). Yet, in his case, as in that of Samuel, the cause of reluctance was the same—a momentary failure of full confidence in God, a prominent characteristic of both these godly men.

A striking contrast is recorded when Jonah was entrusted with a dangerous mission. There is no record that he made known his fears to God. He took counsel with no one but himself, and the result was disaster. Unlike Jonah, neither Moses nor Samuel attempted to *"flee from the presence of the Lord"* (Jonah 1:3). But they made known their fears to the Lord and their reasons for doubting God's commission. The result in both cases was the same—their faith was strengthened to accomplish God's purpose.

Then, too, we can be encouraged to know that Elijah, who called down fire from heaven, *"was a man subject to like passions as we are, and he prayed . . . "* (James 5:17).

God's most honored servants in all the ages have had their hours of fear. Failure is not the result of fear, but it is the consequence of looking within ourselves rather than to Him for our answers.

"Let us therefore come boldly unto the throne of grace, that we may obtain mercy, and find grace to help in time of need" (Hebrews 4:16).

Thought for Today: When God gives you a task to do, remember that He is with you.

Christ Revealed: Through David's name (I Samuel 16:13), which means "beloved." David is a type of the Beloved Son (Mark 1:11).

Word Studies: 14:24 **adjured** means solemnly commanded; put them under oath; 15:29 **repent** means change His mind; 15:32 **delicately** means with a cheerful attitude.

Prayer Needs: Country: Cook Islands—18,000—several islands in the South Pacific, between Tonga and Tahiti • Religious freedom • 70% Protestant; 11% Roman Catholic; 6% cults; 1% Baha'i.

APRIL 6: Read I Samuel 17 — 18

Highlights: David and Goliath; Jonathan's loyalty to David; Saul's jealous attempts to kill David; David's marriage to Michal.

Verses for Today: *" . . . Saul hath slain his thousands, and David his ten thousands. . . . And Saul eyed David from that day forward. . . . David behaved himself wisely in all his ways; and the Lord was with him"* (I Samuel 18:7,9,14).

D avid became very popular with the people after his victory over Goliath, the Philistine. But his victory was too much for the pride-filled King Saul. As it became evident to Saul that another man was gradually gaining the influence and honor which was once exclusively his own, he became obsessed with a jealous spirit.

Self-centered Saul ruled Israel with one thought in mind: "How will this affect me?"

There are many people like Saul who are anxious to serve God if it brings recognition to themselves.

Success often leads to a sense of self-sufficiency. Many people speak of what "they" accomplish and do not give God the praise for what was done. God gives us the privilege to choose His ways or ours. If we are too self-willed to yield to Him, we are left on our own like Saul—destitute in the hour of crisis.

"Pride goeth before destruction, and a haughty spirit before a fall" (Proverbs 16:18).

Thought for Today: True success in life comes from humbly knowing and obeying God's Word, not in seeking popularity or the praise of others.

Christ Portrayed: By Jonathan (I Samuel 18:3-4), whose love for David is an illustration of the love the Lord Jesus has shown to us.

Word Studies: 17:4 **six cubits and a span** means nine feet, nine inches; 17:6 **greaves of brass** means bronze shin armor; **target of brass** means bronze shield; 17:22 **carriage** means baggage; 17:40 **a scrip** means his wallet; 17:53 **spoiled their tents** means looted their camp; 17:56 **stripling** means youth; 18:9 **eyed** means viewed with suspicion and malice.

Prayer Needs: Country: The Gambia—760,000—in West Africa • Religious freedom • 87% Muslim; 10% animism and ancestral spirit worship; 2% Roman Catholic; .7% Protestant.

APRIL 7: Read I Samuel 19 — 21

Highlights: Saul's attempt to kill David; Jonathan's friendship and covenant with David; David's flight to Nob, then to Gath.

Verse for Today: *"And Saul spake to Jonathan his son, and to all his servants, that they should kill David"* (I Samuel 19:1).

F ollowing David's victory over Goliath, he became very popular with the people. As David gained prestige in the nation, King Saul became obsessed with jealousy. He set out to destroy David at any cost.

Saul eventually confessed that David was chosen by God (I Samuel 24:20). But, blinded by self-interest, Saul was driven from one desperate act to another. Ultimately, his obsession to destroy David ended in his suicide after he was wounded in battle (see 31:3-6).

Like Saul, many have brought about their own downfall while attempting to destroy another. When we are controlled by pride, we no longer recognize God's sovereign right to arrange the affairs of earth and to rule the heart of every person.

"But he giveth more grace. Wherefore he saith, God resisteth the proud, but giveth grace unto the humble" (James 4:6).

Thought for Today: To some people, wordly popularity and power appear as a dazzling, giant prize to be gained at any price.

Christ Portrayed: By David (I Samuel 19:2), who was rejected by Saul. *Christ came to His own, but they refused to receive Him* (see John 1:11).

Word Studies: 19:13 **image** means household idol; 20:26 **not clean** means ceremonially unfit; 20:33 **javelin** means spear; 20:40 **artillery** means small armor; weapons; 21:4 **hallowed bread** means bread set aside for use in worship; 21:13 **mad** means insane.

Prayer Needs: Country: Anguilla—7,000—part of the British West Indies • Religious freedom • 97% Protestant; 2% Roman Catholic.

APRIL 8: Read I Samuel 22 — 24

Highlights: David's escape to Adullam and Mizpeh; the slaughter of the priests of Nob; Philistines defeated by David; his further flight from Saul; Saul's life spared by David.

Verse for Today: *" . . . I will not put forth mine hand against my lord; for he is the Lord's anointed"* (I Samuel 24:10).

S aul made a great mistake when he said that God had delivered David into his hand (see I Samuel 23:7). This shows how man can be deceived in his interpretation of providential events, especially when he is not living in subjection to God.

Such a misinterpretation of circumstances is more than poor judgment. Saul was so determined to have his own way that he gave no thought to the wishes of a sovereign God.

When David knew that Saul was planning to kill him, he did not know which way to turn. The friends he had once trusted turned against him. The way seemed more uncertain each day, but he continued to pray for guidance (23:10-12).

At times, because of our circumstances, we may think that God does not care; but, like David, we can be confident in the unchanging, eternal Word of God. Our all-wise heavenly Father often allows us to experience times of deep distress in order to develop in us a greater faith in Him. He does care, and He stands ready to answer our call for help when we are in submission to Him.

Every Christian can overcome the temptations of the world. This victory is possible through faith (see I John 5:4).

Thought for Today: We can praise God because the victory is the Lord's and He shares it with us.

Christ Revealed: In David's refusal to take the kingdom by force before the appointed time set by God (I Samuel 24:10-13). Christ refused to become King of Israel by force, even though the people wanted to make Him an earthly king before the appointed time (John 6:15).

Word Studies: 22:4 **hold** means stronghold; 22:17 **footmen** means guards; 23:16 **strengthened his hand** means encouraged him; 24:4 **privily** means secretly; 24:7 **stayed** means restrained.

Prayer Needs: Country: St. Lucia—152,000—in the eastern Caribbean • Religious freedom • 83% Roman Catholic; 13% Protestant; 2% spirit worship.

APRIL 9: Read I Samuel 25 — 27

Highlights: Death of Samuel; David and Nabal; David's marriage to Abigail; David's further refusal to slay Saul; Saul's confession of sin; David's flight to Gath.

Verses for Today: *"Then said Abishai to David, God hath delivered thine enemy into thine hand this day: now therefore let me smite him, I pray thee, with the spear. . . . And David said to Abishai, Destroy him not: for who can stretch forth his hand against the Lord's anointed, and be guiltless?"* (I Samuel 26:8-9).

D avid had an opportunity to remove the only person blocking him from becoming king over Israel. In fact, his men strongly urged him to do so (I Samuel 24:4). On another occasion, Abishai insisted, *God has delivered your enemy into your hands this day; now therefore let me kill him.*

But David refused to harm King Saul; he knew Saul was the Lord's anointed (I Samuel 24:6) and was willing to wait until the Lord Himself removed Saul from the throne.

Although the prophet Samuel had anointed David as king several years earlier, David's willingness to wait proved his submission to God's authority. Through many years of patiently waiting for God's perfect timing, the Lord had prepared

David to receive the kingdom in a spirit of grateful dependence on Him.

And still today, God's people are prepared for His service as they put the Lord's will above their own desires.

Each of us should pray, *Lord, I am trusting in You. Save me from the shame of defeat; don't let my enemies triumph over me! No one whose hope is in You will ever be put to shame* (see Psalm 25:2-3).

Thought for Today: Decisions made without a regard for God's will can never receive His blessings.

Christ Revealed: Through Abigail's efforts to make peace between David and Nabal (I Samuel 25:21-28). God was in Christ reconciling the world to Himself (II Cor. 5:19).

Word Studies: 25:3 **churlish** means cruel; hardhearted; stubborn; 25:21 **requited** means repaid; 25:28 **a sure house** means an established family, such as a lasting dynasty; 25:29 **bound in the bundle of life** means protected to live—an oriental phrase expressing the perfect security of David's life from all the assaults of his enemies, under the protecting shield of God, who had destined him for high things; 26:11 **bolster** means pillow; 27:10 **road** means raid; 27:11 **so will be his manner** means was his policy.

Prayer Needs: **Country:** Cyprus—684,000—in the Middle East • No open evangelism or conversions to Christ • 75% Greek Orthodox; 19% Muslim; 1% Protestant; 1% Roman Catholic.

APRIL 10: Read I Samuel 28 — 31

Highlights: War between the Philistines and the Israelites; Saul's counsel from the medium (fortune-teller) at Endor; David dismissed by the Philistines; his defeat of the Amalekites; deaths of Saul and his sons.

Verse for Today: *"Then said Saul unto his servants, Seek me a woman that hath a familiar spirit, that I may go to her, and inquire of her . . ."* (I Samuel 28:7).

G od had given Saul the unique position of being the first king to reign over His people. But he forfeited this privilege because of his continual disobedience.

Eventually, Saul turned to a witch for advice. His ride to Endor through the long, dark night proved futile for the once-powerful king who had lived to please himself.

Those who reject the truth of God easily become victims of false prophets, fortune-tellers, astrologers, and the like. (See Matthew 24:24; I John 4:1.) To these dupes God shall send *"strong delusion, that they should believe a lie"* (II Thessalonians 2:11).

Thinking it is a *fun thing* that will do no harm, many Christians read astrology columns and go to palm readers or fortune-tellers. But participating in activities that border on dealing with "spirits" is not only contrary to God's Word, but it leaves that person open to satanic forces.

"Idolatry, witchcraft . . . seditions, heresies . . . they which do such things shall not inherit the kingdom of God" (Galatians 5:20-21).

Thought for Today: When man rejects the light of God's Word, he leaves himself open to spiritual deception.

Christ Revealed: Through the Urim (I Samuel 28:6), which was used to determine

102

God's will. Today Christ speaks to us through His Spirit and His Word.

Word Studies: 28:7 **hath a familiar spirit** means is a fortune-teller; a spiritualist medium; 28:14 **mantle** means robe; 29:3 **fell unto me** means came over to my side; deserted to me; 31:2 **followed hard upon** means overtook.

Prayer Needs: Country: Angola—8 million—in west-central Africa • Christianity is gradually being driven underground • 70% Roman Catholic; 22% Protestant; 8% belief in ancestor spirits, witches, and medicine men.

II SAMUEL _____

The book of II Samuel covers the 40-year period of Israel's history during David's reign.

Immediately after the death of King Saul, David inquired of the Lord and was directed to go to Hebron, where he reigned as king over the tribe of Judah (chapters 1—4).

Abner, leader of Saul's army, was responsible for Israel's decision to make Ishbosheth, Saul's son, their king. After Ishbosheth's assassination, all the tribes of Israel went to Hebron and anointed David as their leader, their shepherd-king (5:3; compare I Chronicles 12:18).

David then captured the city of Jebus, changed its name to Jerusalem, and made it the capital of the united kingdom of Judah and Israel (chapters 5—7).

During Saul's 40-year reign, very little emphasis was placed on the ark of the covenant. After David became king, he brought the ark to Jerusalem, thus recognizing Jehovah as the supreme Ruler of the united kingdom.

David fought a series of successful wars and conquered the enemies of Israel—the Ammonites, Philistines, Syrians, Moabites, Edomites, and Amalekites. His victories extended the borders of the Promised Land from the Mediterranean Sea to the Euphrates River (chapters 8—10).

David's sin (chapters 11—12) occurred in the middle of his 40-year reign. It marked the tragic division between his great success (chapters 1—10) and the many tragedies in his family and nation (chapters 13—24).

APRIL 11: Read II Samuel 1 — 2

Highlights: David mourns the deaths of Saul and Jonathan; David made king of Judah at Hebron; Ishbosheth made king of Israel; war between Israel and Judah.

Verse for Today: " . . . *David inquired of the Lord* . . . " (II Samuel 2:1).

S aul and David had many similarities: both were anointed king of Israel; both reigned about 40 years; both had the loyal support of Samuel, the prophet of God. But there was a marked difference which made Saul a miserable failure and David a successful king.

Saul was a self-willed man who made decisions without waiting for God's direction. David never lost sight of his need to pray and wait upon the Lord to fulfill

His promises at *His* appointed time. Even after Saul was dead, David made no effort to seize control of the nation. Instead, he *"inquired of the Lord."*

One of David's greatest desires was to worship the Lord in the Temple at Jerusalem. With this in mind, we can better appreciate his patience in waiting for God's appointed time (see Psalm 27:4).

So often we tend to get ahead of the Lord in our eagerness to have something. But there is a peaceful rest for those who wait patiently for the Lord's timing. *"Rest in the Lord, and wait patiently for him . . . those that wait upon the Lord, they shall inherit the earth"* (Psalm 37:7,9).

Thought for Today: God always knows the best time to answer prayer.

Christ Revealed: In David's noble poem (II Samuel 1:17-27). David forgot all his injuries and considered only the pleasant things. Here David typifies Christ, who loved us even when we were dead in trespasses and sins.

Word Studies: 1:2 **rent** means torn; 1:18 **use** means song; 2:6 **requite** means repay; 2:14 **play before us** means stage a contest; 2:32 **sepulcher** means grave.

Prayer Needs: Country: Israel—5 million—in the Middle East • Witnessing to Jews about Christ the Messiah is actively discouraged • 88% Jewish; 8% Muslim; 2% Christian.

APRIL 12: Read II Samuel 3 — 5

Highlights: Abner deserts Ishbosheth to join David; Abner murdered by Joab; Ishbosheth murdered; David made king of Israel; capture of Jebus (Jerusalem); the defeat of the Philistines.

Verse for Today: *"So all the elders of Israel came to the king to Hebron . . . and they anointed David king over Israel"* (II Samuel 5:3).

W hile David was still a youth, he was anointed king over Israel. Years later, after King Saul's death, David was welcomed as king over the tribe of Judah. It was not until seven and one-half years later that all the other tribes of Israel acknowledged their need for the Lord's leadership and asked David to be their king.

David faced many hardships and difficulties throughout his lifetime—especially during the years Saul was seeking to kill him. Eventually, David cried out in despair, saying, *"I shall now perish one day by the hand of Saul"* (I Samuel 27:1).

Through these seemingly hopeless experiences, God was preparing him to be His faithful shepherd-ruler—*"a captain over Israel"* (II Samuel 5:2). David learned of the absolute care of the Great Shepherd for His children and could say of the Lord, *"He is my refuge and my fortress: my God; in him will I trust"* (Psalm 91:2).

In some Christians, there is no clear image of Christlikeness. Even after many years, they still are not living by the principle of dying to self.

Few are willing to accept and endure the Lord's discipline because they do not recognize the hand of God in their difficulties. They only see people or problems opposing them and cry out as David did, *"I shall now perish."*

The greatest obstacle to being used of God is self. Only when we are willing to die to self can we be an expression of His life.

"For we which live are always delivered unto death for Jesus' sake, that the life also of Jesus might be made manifest in our mortal flesh" (II Corinthians 4:11).

Thought for Today: As we grow spiritually, we lose confidence in self—in our own abilities—and develop a confidence in the Lord's wisdom to sustain and guide us.

Christ Portrayed: By David, the anointed king of Israel (II Samuel 5:3). Christ is God's Anointed. "Christ" means *Messiah*, "Anointed One" (Psa. 2:2; John 1:41).

Word Studies: 3:1 **waxed** means grew; 3:12 **league** means covenant; 3:31 **bier** means coffin; 5:8 **getteth up to the gutter** means gets through the water tunnel and manages to enter the city; 5:23 **fetch a compass** means circle around behind them.

Prayer Needs: Country: Northern Ireland—2 million—on the second largest of the British Isles • Religious freedom • 63% Protestant; 36% Roman Catholic.

APRIL 13: Read II Samuel 6 — 9

Highlights: Ark taken to Jerusalem; Michal's criticism of David; God's promise to David; David's prayer; his victories; his kindness to Mephibosheth.

Verse for Today: *"And thine house and thy kingdom shall be established for ever before thee: thy throne shall be established for ever"* (II Samuel 7:16).

D avid was the greatest king ever to rule the nation of Israel. He was not made great for his own sake, but to fulfill God's covenant promise, *Your kingdom shall be established forever.*

God's covenant with David was a guarantee that He would one day send a perfectly righteous king—the Messiah. This was fulfilled in Jesus Christ, the descendant of David (see Matthew 1:1).

The angel of the Lord had appeared to Mary (a descendant of David), saying, *"He shall be great, and shall be called the Son of the Highest: and the Lord God shall give unto him the throne of his father David"* (Luke 1:32).

When a person accepts Christ as Savior and Lord, Christ begins His reign in that life.

Christ is Lord of lords and King of kings; and those who are with Him are His called, and chosen, and faithful followers (see Revelation 17:14).

Thought for Today: The mind cannot imagine all the wonders prepared for those who accept Christ as Lord and Savior.

Christ Revealed: Through David's kindness to Mephibosheth (II Samuel 9:7). This gives us a picture of salvation by God's grace in Christ. Grace comes to the helpless, those sold into bondage to sin (see Rom. 7:14).

Word Studies: 6:8 **a breach** means a great calamity; 7:8 **sheepcote** means pasture; 7:12 **seed** means offspring; descendants; 7:23 **terrible** means full of wonder; awesome; 8:13 **being** means slaying.

Prayer Needs: Country: Guatemala—9 million—in Central America • Religious freedom • 93% Roman Catholic; 5% Protestant.

APRIL 14: Read II Samuel 10 — 12

Highlights: Hanun's abuse of David's messengers; defeat of the Ammonites and Syrians; David and Bathsheba; David's command for Uriah to be killed in battle; Nathan's parable and rebuke of David; David's repentance; birth of Solomon; the capture of Rabbah.

Verses for Today: " ... *at the time when kings go forth to battle ... David tarried still in Jerusalem. And it came to pass in an eveningtide, that David arose from off his bed, and walked upon the roof of the king's house: and from the roof he saw a woman washing herself ... "* (II Samuel 11:1-2).

D avid was a man of exceptional character—a man after God's own heart (I Samuel 13:14). But on this occasion, he yielded to the lust of the flesh instead of turning from temptation.

When David inquired about the beautiful woman he saw bathing, he learned that she was the wife of one of his very best soldiers who was away in battle. Instead of turning from the lust that was in his heart, he dishonored the God-ordained family relationship of Uriah and Bathsheba and stole his neighbor's wife. In an attempt to cover up one evil, David committed other sins.

Perhaps Bathsheba could have prevented this wickedness and all the sorrows that followed if she had resisted and said, as Tamar did, *No, do not force me; for no such thing ought to be done in Israel* (see II Samuel 13:12).

From the moment David first lusted after this woman until their marriage, there seemingly was not one adverse circumstance to interfere with his plan—except that it *"displeased the Lord"* (II Samuel 11:27).

When David confessed his sin, God forgave him. But the prophet Nathan foretold that the bitter consequences of his sin—suffering, incest, murder, rebellion, and civil war—would continue throughout David's lifetime (II Samuel 12:10-12).

David learned firsthand that God does not show partiality. His former reputation as a man after God's heart was greatly marred, and many others fell into sin because of his bad example.

Then when lust has conceived, it results in sin: and sin, when it is finished, results in death (see James 1:15).

Thought for Today: Sin seldom ends with one act alone; one sin usually leads to another.

Christ Revealed: In the prophet's giving Solomon the name Jedidiah, which means "beloved of the Lord" (II Samuel 12:25). Christ was greatly loved by the Father (John 17:24).

Word Study: 12:30 a **talent** equals about 75 pounds.

APRIL 15: Read II Samuel 13 — 14

Highlights: Amnon's sin against Tamar; Absalom's revenge; his flight; Joab arranges for Absalom's return.

Verse for Today: *"But Absalom fled.... And David mourned for his son every day"* (II Samuel 13:37).

A fter David's great sin became publicly known, it appears that he was filled with remorse. He was no longer seen in public, and his palace became his hiding place.

Sin always produces side effects—often with evil consequences which go far beyond all calculation or expectation. David had lived a godly life up to that time, but his older sons did not follow his good example; instead, they followed his sinful ways.

His oldest son, Amnon, cruelly raped his half-sister Tamar, but David did not punish his son as the Law required. Then Absalom, motivated by a selfish ambition to become king and by hatred toward Amnon for raping his sister, welcomed the opportunity to carry out justice. Eventually, he murdered his half-brother Amnon, who was heir to the throne.

The crimes of David's two sons must have caused him to recall memories of two similar sins he had committed—adultery and murder.

The consequences of sin cannot be avoided, postponed, or ignored by anyone—whether king or peasant. Sin always brings immeasurable, unending suffering and sorrow.

Encourage one another day after day, while there is still time, so that none of you will be hardened by sin's deceiving ways (see Hebrews 3:13).

Thought for Today: All who compromise their Christian convictions for self-satisfaction leave themselves open to the attacks of Satan.

Christ Revealed: Through David's restoration of Absalom (II Samuel 14:33). If an earthly father's compassion reconciles him to his estranged son, how much more will our loving Heavenly Father reconcile us to Himself when we confess our sin.

Word Studies: 13:3 **subtil** means crafty; 13:25 **chargeable** means a burden; 14:2 **feign** means pretend; 14:4 **did obeisance** means showed respect; 14:7 **quench my coal which is left** means destroy the last of my family; 14:26 **polled his head** means cut his hair.

Prayer Needs: Country: Netherlands—15 million—in northwestern Europe • Religious freedom • 39% Roman Catholic; 29% Protestant; 2% Muslim.

APRIL 16: Read II Samuel 15 — 16

Highlights: Absalom's popularity and conspiracy against David; David's flight from Jerusalem; Ziba's deceit; Shimei's cursing of David; Absalom's entrance into Jerusalem.

Verses for Today: *"And there came a messenger to David, saying, The hearts of the men of Israel are after Absalom. And David said unto all his servants that were with him at Jerusalem, Arise, and let us flee; for we shall not else escape from Absalom: make speed to depart, lest he . . . smite the city with the edge of the sword"* (II Samuel 15:13-14).

One of the most pitiful passages in the Bible is of King David having to escape from his son, Absalom. Heartbroken, the aged king is described as barefoot, his head covered, running across the rough hills leading to the Mount of Olives.

Shimei, one of Saul's relatives, followed David as he fled from Jerusalem, cursing him and throwing stones at him. He accused David of being responsible for Saul's death and *"all the blood of the house of Saul"* (II Samuel 16:8). This accusation was not true, and Abishai asked David for permission to kill Shimei. David refused, saying, *" . . . let him curse, because the Lord hath said unto him, Curse David"* (16:10).

David felt he had lost the throne because of his sin and therefore deserved the humiliation and insults from Saul's relative.

Too often we retaliate, fight back, or seek revenge, and do not see the hand of God in our sufferings. But once we see this truth and yield to Him, we discover His perfect will. The highest privilege Christians can have is to yield our will to His ways. May God teach us the precious privilege of accepting and loving His ways!

"For as the heavens are higher than the earth, so are my ways higher than your ways, and my thoughts than your thoughts" (Isaiah 55:9).

Thought for Today: God is our strength in times of trouble.

Christ Revealed: Through David as he rebuked his people when they wanted to execute his enemies (II Samuel 16:10-11; compare I Sam. 26:8-9; Luke 9:54-56).

Word Studies: 15:27 **seer** means prophet; 15:28 **certify me** means give me a full report on what is happening.

Prayer Needs: **Country:** Paraguay—5 million—in southern South America • Religious freedom • 96% Roman Catholic; 2% Protestant.

APRIL 17: Read II Samuel 17 — 18

Highlights: Advice of Ahithophel and Hushai; Ahithophel's suicide; Absalom's defeat and murder by Joab; David's mourning over Absalom's death.

Verse for Today: *" . . . O my son Absalom, my son, my son Absalom! would God I had died for thee, O Absalom, my son, my son!"* (II Samuel 18:33).

The majority of Israel's leaders and many of the people joined Absalom in an attempt to overthrow King David. Absalom was then declared king and entered Jerusalem without resistance.

Up to this point, all his plans had been successful. But Absalom was determined to pursue and execute his father David. However, in the ensuing battle, Absalom was defeated, and 20,000 men died (II Samuel 18:7).

There were many who had once stayed by Absalom; but now, with his hair caught in the limbs of the oak tree, he didn't have a friend to help him escape. Everyone rushed past, intent on saving his own life.

Absalom's rebellion against David is typical of those who *take their stand against the Lord and against His Anointed One* (see Psalm 2:2). But the wicked are successful only until God's purposes have been fulfilled. God permitted an insignificant branch of a tree to hold Absalom by his hair until he was killed by Joab.

Many people have died an untimely death after having taken an open stand against one of God's leaders. It is so important that we pray for those in authority instead of taking matters into our own hands without having direction from God.

Let everyone submit himself to those in authority over him. God has put people in authority for a definite purpose in carrying out His will (see Romans 13:1).

Thought for Today: No one can defeat God's purposes.

Christ Revealed: Through Mahanaim, a city of refuge where David went when he was fleeing from Absalom (II Samuel 17:27). Christ is our refuge (Heb. 6:18).

Word Studies: 17:8 **chafed** means angered; **whelps** means cubs; 17:17 **wench** means maidservant; 17:25 **host** means army; 17:28 **pulse** means peas and beans; 18:3 **succor** means assist.

Prayer Needs: **Country:** Madagascar—11 million—an island in the Indian Ocean off

108

the coast of Mozambique • Increasingly anti-Christian • 43% witchcraft, ancestor worship, and some astrology; 21% Protestant; 21% Roman Catholic; 2% Muslim.

APRIL 18: Read II Samuel 19 — 20

Highlights: Joab's rebuke of David; David's return to Jerusalem; Sheba's revolt against David; Sheba's death.

Verse for Today: *"So every man of Israel went up from after David, and followed Sheba the son of Bichri: but the men of Judah clave unto their king, from Jordan even to Jerusalem"* (II Samuel 20:2).

T he general discontent of Israel gave Sheba, an ambitious leader, the opportunity to start a civil war. The years of suffering, rebellion, murder, and civil war during David's reign were directly related to his sin with Bathsheba. Little could David realize, when he held the beautiful Bathsheba for one night of enjoyment, that his sin would bring so much suffering!

Although the Lord forgave David's sin (II Samuel 12:13), its consequences continued to plague him throughout his reign. Year after year, with each tragedy, he must have cried out, "Why did I do it? How could I have done it?" These are some of the most pathetic questions men and women can ask themselves. The pleasures of sin always come at a price much higher than expected!

Let us count everything as worthless in comparison to the priceless privilege of knowing our Lord and, for His sake, be willing to put aside all else (see Philippians 3:8).

Thought for Today: Satan finds it easy to influence the life that is unguarded by daily prayer and reading God's Word.

Christ Portrayed: By David, who wished to be invited back as king (II Samuel 19:11). Our Lord Jesus wants to be invited into the hearts of all mankind. He won't force His will on us; He only comes by invitation.

Word Studies: 19:3 **by stealth** means secretly; 20:18 **wont to speak** means said.

Prayer Needs: **Country:** Zaire—32 million—in south-central Africa • Limited religious freedom • 42% Roman Catholic; 28% Protestant; 12% magical practices, ancestor worship, and witchcraft; 1% Muslim.

APRIL 19: Read II Samuel 21 — 22

Highlights: Famine; seven members of Saul's family put to death; David's victories; song of thanksgiving.

Verse for Today: *"Then there was a famine in the days of David three years . . . "* (II Samuel 21:1).

D avid prayed, asking God why there was a famine in the land. God told him it was because Saul had broken the covenant Joshua had made with the Gibeonites more than 400 years earlier (Joshua 9:16-27).

This incident in the life of David shows how sacred God considers a vow, even though it was made to an unbelieving Canaanite nation.

God has clearly stated, *"When thou shalt vow a vow unto the Lord thy God, thou shalt not slack to pay it: for the Lord thy God will surely require it of thee . . . "*

(Deuteronomy 23:21; see also Numbers 30:2).

The three years of famine that resulted from a broken vow reveal the seriousness of keeping one's word.

Can people depend upon what you say, or are your vows meaningless? Do you say only what others want to hear? Far too many Christians have good intentions, but they allow circumstances to sway their convictions; consequently, their word is unreliable.

"That which is gone out of thy lips thou shalt keep and perform . . . " (Deuteronomy 23:23).

Thought for Today: When you make a promise, God expects you to keep your word.

Christ Revealed: As the One we call upon for salvation (II Samuel 22:4). *There is salvation in no one except Christ; for there is no other name under Heaven that has been given among men, by which we can be saved* (see Acts 4:12).

Prayer Needs: Country: Belize—168,000—on the eastern coast of Central America • Religious freedom • 54% Roman Catholic; 26% Protestant.

APRIL 20: Read II Samuel 23 — 24

Highlights: David's last words; his famous soldiers; his sin in taking a military census; the three-day plague; David's sacrifice.

Verse for Today: *"And David's heart smote him after that he had numbered the people. And David said unto the Lord, I have sinned greatly in that I have done . . . "* (II Samuel 24:10).

S atan, the author of pride, prompted David to take a census to determine how many men were available for his army (see I Chronicles 21:1). Although the counting of the people may have seemed quite harmless, *"the anger of the Lord was kindled against Israel"* (II Samuel 24:1). Even Joab recognized that David's purpose in taking the census was to enhance his own prestige (see I Chronicles 21:3).

There was never to be a numbering of the people or a census taken without making an atonement offering. The atonement offering was necessary not only to protect the Israelites against a plague (Exodus 30:12), but also to remind them of how easily man can become a victim of his own success and lose his dependence upon the mercy of God.

God always has a definite plan for His people. Sometimes when He gives special talents or abilities, here is a tendency to become proud of our accomplishments and no longer depend on Him. We must always give Him the glory and praise for anything worthwhile.

You are worthy, our Lord and our God, to receive glory, honor, and power. For you created all things; and by Your will they were given existence and life (see Revelation 4:11).

Thought for Today: When the Lord says, *I will send you,* we can rest assured He will provide everything necessary for the appointed task.

Christ Revealed: Through the altar of sacrifice which David built (II Samuel 24: 25). Christ is our sacrifice. It is only through Him that we can receive favor with God and escape His wrath for our sins.

110

Word Studies: 23:30 **brooks** means valleys; 24:10 **heart smote** means conscience bothered.

Prayer Needs: Country: Honduras—5 million—in Central America • Religious freedom • 86% Roman Catholic; 10% Protestant.

I KINGS _____

The book of I Kings is a continuation of Israel's history from the book of II Samuel and covers about 120 years. The opening chapters cover the death of David and the crowning of Solomon (1—2:12). The balance of the first 11 chapters is devoted to the 40-year reign of Solomon (2:13—11).

Under Solomon's reign, Israel enjoyed her most prominent years of fame. Kings all over the world heard of his wisdom and sent people to listen to him (4:34).

At the beginning of his reign, Solomon expressed a desire to honor God. But his many foreign wives, his wealth, and his great fame all influenced him away from God.

Solomon not only had the privilege of building the Temple, but also of fully knowing God's will, for God appeared to him at least twice. In addition, God had spoken to him in an unmistakable way. (Compare 3:5-14; 9:2-9; 11:9-13.) Still, there was no genuine repentance.

Although Solomon inherited a powerful united kingdom that was growing in wealth and world superiority, he brought about its division, as pronounced by the Lord: *Because you have not observed My covenant but have disobeyed My commands, I will surely take the kingdom away from you* (see 11:11).

Not only did the nation continue to decline spiritually, but the people also became bitter under the heavy burden of paying the excessive taxes that were necessary to maintain Solomon's government and his luxurious lifestyle.

After Solomon's death, the 10 tribes, commonly called Israel or the Northern Kingdom, immediately rejected Solomon's son, Rehoboam, and appointed Jeroboam as their king.

Jeroboam is best remembered as the king who led Israel into the sin of worshiping the golden calves (22:52; II Kings 10:29).

The Southern Kingdom of Judah consisted of the tribes of Judah and Benjamin, and the majority of the Levites.

The capital of Israel was Samaria; the capital of Judah was Jerusalem. The divided kingdoms are covered in chapters 12—16.

The final chapters (17—22) focus primarily on the prophet Elijah and on Israel's most wicked king, Ahab.

The book of I Kings shows how the rise and decline of the Hebrew kingdoms were in direct relation to the people's obedience to or rejection of God's will.

111

APRIL 21: Read I Kings 1 — 2:25

Highlights: Abishag's ministry to David; Adonijah's plot; Solomon anointed king; David's last instructions to Solomon; David's death; Adonijah put to death.

Verse for Today: *"And keep the charge of the Lord thy God, to walk in his ways, to keep his statutes, and his commandments . . . that thou mayest prosper . . . "* (I Kings 2:3).

D avid's last words to Solomon revealed his greatest desire for his son—that he would live to please the Lord. David said nothing to Solomon about gaining fame for his kingdom. But he stressed the importance of keeping God's commandments so that he might please God. David's concern was not that Solomon gain material wealth, but that he prosper spiritually by living in harmony with God's Word.

Material blessings are incidental and may or may not be obtained by those who "prosper" from God's point of view. Stephen and Paul did not "prosper" in the eyes of the world, but their true prosperity cannot be measured.

The truly "blessed" man is protected against a fruitless life of failure because *he delights in the law of the Lord, meditating on the Word of God day and night. He prospers in whatever he does* (see Psalm 1:2-3).

Through the Scriptures, we can discover the unique revelation of God's will—one of the greatest gifts that can be bestowed upon man. What a privilege we have to prayerfully read the Bible each day!

Whoever accepts My commandments and obeys them is the one who loves Me. And whoever loves Me will be loved by My Father, and I will love him and will make Myself real to him (see John 14:21).

Thought for Today: Our day-by-day happiness should not be dependent upon material prosperity.

Christ Portrayed: By Solomon, whose life was threatened by those who feared he would be king (I Kings 1:11-12; compare Matt. 2:13-18).

Word Studies: 1:2 **cherish** means attend; be of service to; 1:40 **pipes** means flutes; 2:6 **hoar** means gray; 2:17 **say thee nay** means refuse to grant your request.

Prayer Needs: Country: Sao Tome and Principe—114,000—two larger and several smaller islands in the Gulf of Guinea, 125 miles off the western coast of Africa • Religious freedom is fairly new • 83% Roman Catholic; 3% Protestant; 2% animist.

APRIL 22: Read I Kings 2:26 — 4

Highlights: Abiathar banished from the priesthood; Joab put to death; Shimei killed; Solomon's marriage to Pharaoh's daughter; Solomon's dream; his wise ruling; his officials, daily provisions, and wisdom.

Verses for Today: *"And Solomon made affinity with Pharaoh king of Egypt, and took Pharaoh's daughter. . . . And Solomon loved the Lord . . . only he sacrificed and burnt incense in high places"* (I Kings 3:1,3).

A t the beginning of his reign, Solomon loved the Lord and followed the teachings of his father David. But it soon became evident that Solomon did not take seriously his sacred responsibility to obey the laws of God (I Kings 2:3). His alliance with Pharaoh was the first association between Israel and Egypt since the time of the Exodus 480 years earlier (see 6:1).

Solomon's marriage to Pharaoh's daughter may have been politically motivated to prevent future wars with Egypt and to increase his prestige among the surrounding nations (see I Kings 9:16). But this association paved the way for other alliances that eventually separated Solomon from the blessings of God.

Instead of loving the Lord with all his heart (Deuteronomy 6:5), he offered sacrifices and burned incense on the high places. The thousand burnt offerings to the Lord (I Kings 3:4) could not compensate for his compromises.

Worldly associations, compromise, and powerlessness are inseparably linked.

We must not team up with unbelievers; for what common interest is there between righteousness and unrighteousness or between light and darkness? What accord is there between Christ and Satan, between a believer and an unbeliever? (see II Corinthians 6:14-15).

Thought for Today: It is impossible to obtain God's best while trying to gain the best of both worlds.

Christ Portrayed: By Solomon, a type of Christ in whom are hidden all the treasures of wisdom and knowledge (I Kings 3:12; see also Col. 2:3).

Word Studies: 2:44 **which thine heart is privy to** means which you acknowledge or admit in your heart; 3:1 **made affinity** means formed a marriage alliance; 4:28 **dromedaries** are running camels, but used here, can also mean swift steeds and mules; **charge** means responsibility.

Prayer Needs: Country: India—800 million—in southern Asia • Religious freedom, but increasing harassment and persecution of Christians by religious radicals • 78% Hindu; 12% Muslim; 4% Christian; 2% Sikhs.

APRIL 23: Read I Kings 5 — 7

Highlights: Solomon's Temple and palace built; furnishings of the Temple.

Verses for Today: *"And it came to pass in the four hundred and eightieth year after the children of Israel were come out of the land of Egypt, in the fourth year of Solomon's reign over Israel . . . he began to build the house of the Lord. . . . and in the eleventh year . . . was the house finished . . . "* (I Kings 6:1,38).

No other building in the world compared with Solomon's Temple. The most costly materials and treasures were lavished upon it. But the world observed only the external beauty of the Temple; its true glory was inside. The Shekinah glory—the presence of God—dwelled within the Holy of Holies. The world could only hear about this glory; they could never experience it.

This is also true of the Christian, who is a temple of God. God's glory dwells within each believer. The miracle of the new birth and the indwelling Holy Spirit make the difference between the Christian and the unsaved, who cannot share in His glory.

God's presence is experienced by those who honor Him. Just think! The God of Heaven lives within every Christian.

And through union with Him, we are continuously being built into a dwelling place for God through the Spirit (see Ephesians 2:22).

113

Thought for Today: Christ is the great Victor who lives in our hearts, and we must willingly cooperate with Him.

Christ Revealed: Through the Temple (I Kings 6). Christ is the true Temple (John 2:21). God Himself prepared Christ (Hebrews 10:5). Through Him all have access to God.

Word Studies: 5:4 **occurrent** means activity; 5:13 **levy** means forced labor; 6:2 **a cubit** equals about 18 inches (therefore the Temple was 90 feet long, 30 feet wide, and 45 feet high); 6:5 **oracle** means Holy of Holies; 7:9 **coping** means top; 7:14 **cunning** means skilled; 7:26 **hand-breadth** means about 3 inches; **two thousand baths** means 17,000 gallons; 7:30 **undersetters** means supports; 7:33 **axletrees** means axles; **naves** means hubs; **felloes** means rims; 7:50 **censers** means incense burners.

Prayer Needs: Country: Sri Lanka (formerly Ceylon)—17 million—an island in the Indian Ocean off the southeastern tip of India • Religious freedom officially, but Buddhism is actively promoted by the government • 67% Buddhist; 15% Hindu; 8% Roman Catholic; 7% Muslim; .75% Protestant.

APRIL 24: Read I Kings 8

Highlights: Ark brought into the Temple and dedicated; Solomon's prayer; his sacrifice.

Verses for Today: *"What prayer and supplication soever be made by any man ...Then hear ... and forgive ... and give to every man according to his ways, whose heart thou knowest ... "* (I Kings 8:38-39).

A t the dedication of the Temple, King Solomon knelt before God, stretching his hands toward Heaven, and prayed one of the longest prayers recorded in the Bible.

Solomon proclaimed, *"Lord God of Israel, there is no God like thee, in heaven above, or on earth beneath ... "* (I Kings 8:23). Not only did he recognize God as the one true God, but he reaffirmed before the people that receiving God's blessings was dependent upon their returning to the Lord *"with all their heart"* (8:48). Yet, *"Solomon did evil ...and went not fully after the Lord ... "* (11:6). Eventually, pride and his love for power, luxury, and physical satisfaction brought God's judgment upon him. (See 11:1,3,9,11.) What a difference the outcome would have been if Solomon had lived the truths he expressed in prayer! The Lord knows whether our prayers are mere passing emotion or if they are truly an expression of our innermost desire to please Him. The emphasis we place on the things of this world—wealth, fame, and other physical attractions, will eventually reveal the depth of our sincerity and loyalty to God.

"For all that is in the world, the lust of the flesh, and the lust of the eyes, and the pride of life, is not of the Father, but is of the world" (I John 2:16).

Thought for Today: One who knows the truth, but does not live it, deceives himself.

Christ Revealed: In Solomon's dedicatory prayer as a type of Christ's high priestly prayer (I Kings 8:22-54; John 17).

Word Study: 8:64 **hallow** means set aside for holy use.

Prayer Needs: Country: French Polynesia—186,000—in the south-central Pacific
• Religious freedom, but Christianity opposed because of animistic beliefs • 45% Protestant; 39% Roman Catholic; 8% cults.

APRIL 25: Read I Kings 9 — 11

Highlights: God's covenant with Solomon; Solomon's other activities; the queen of Sheba's visit; Solomon's riches and fame; his wives and idolatry; his rebuke by God; his enemies; his death.

Verses for Today: *"And he said to Jeroboam, Take thee ten pieces: for thus saith the Lord, the God of Israel, Behold, I will rend the kingdom out of the hand of Solomon, and will give ten tribes to thee . . . Because . . . they have forsaken me, and have worshiped Ashtoreth . . . "* (I Kings 11:31,33).

T he discontent of the Ephraimites continued to grow as Solomon's popularity diminished. Jeroboam, who at one time was highly honored in Solomon's administration, became a spokesman for his tribe, the Ephraimites, and instigated a rebellion (I Kings 11:26).

The prophet Ahijah had announced to Jeroboam that he would rule over 10 tribes of Israel. God had promised to leave one tribe to the house of David and, strange as it may seem, only that one tribe remained faithful to the City of God and the temple worship. Furthermore, God had promised Joseph while he was in Egypt that kings would proceed from him (see Genesis 49; Deuteronomy 33), and this was re-markably fulfilled when Jeroboam, an Ephraimite, became king.

Solomon was unsuccessful in his attempt to kill Jeroboam. Rehoboam later declared war against Jeroboam's new kingdom and also made every effort to prevent the fulfillment of God's Word to Jeroboam. But the great God of Truth always keeps His Word.

"Heaven and earth shall pass away: but my words shall not pass away" (Luke 21:33).

Thought for Today: God is able to to fulfill what He has promised, regardless of adverse circumstances.

Christ Portrayed: By King Solomon, who became greater than all the kings of the earth (I Kings 10:23-25). Christ will reign as KING OF KINGS AND LORD OF LORDS (Rev. 19:16).

Word Studies: 9:22 **bondmen** means slaves; 9:24 **Millo** means a rampart; a mound of earth raised as a fortification or citadel; 10:2 **train** means company of followers; 10:5 **there was no more spirit in her** means she was overwhelmed; 10:21 **nothing accounted of** means not considered valuable; 10:24 **sought** means consulted; 11:1 **strange** means foreign; 11:5 **abomination** means detestable idol; 11:10 **commanded** means warned; 11:27 **repaired** means closed; 11:28 **charge** means forced labor; 11:31 **rend** means tear.

Prayer Needs: Country: Burma—39 million—in Southeast Asia • Limited religious freedom • 87% Buddhist; 5% Protestant; 4% Muslim; 3% spirit worship, Hindu, and other Asian religions; 1% Roman Catholic.

115

Highlights: Rehoboam made king; the revolt of the 10 tribes; idolatry of Jeroboam and the nation of Israel; Jeroboam's rebuke; death of the disobedient prophet.

Verse for Today: *"And when the prophet that brought him back from the way heard thereof, he said, It is the man of God, who was disobedient unto the word of the Lord: therefore the Lord hath delivered him unto the lion, which hath torn him, and slain him, according to the word of the Lord, which he spake unto him"* (I Kings 13:26).

J eroboam successfully led a revolt that divided the kingdom and gained the support of the 10 northern tribes. The tribe of Judah, as well as the tribe of Benjamin and most of the Levites, remained faithful to the worship of God in Jerusalem.

Jeroboam feared that if the people from the 10 tribes continued to worship in Jerusalem, they might desire to reunite the kingdom; therefore, he set up two worship centers—one in Dan and the other in Bethel.

Three tragedies are presented in these chapters. First, King Jeroboam was more concerned about his control over a nation than he was about God's control over himself and the nation. Second, although the old prophet knew the will of God, he lied. He influenced the young prophet not to complete what God had called him to do. The third tragedy was the young prophet's untimely death. He had God's message and the courage to preach it, and he had refused all the king's bribes. He had stood fearlessly in the center of a crowd, proclaiming the judgment of God upon disobedience. Neither the pleasures of a luxurious meal nor the prospect of comfortable lodging after the fatigue of a long journey could persuade him to turn from doing what God had commanded.

But when the young prophet accepted the warm reception of the aged, backslidden prophet, it resulted in death. This judgment seems severe, but it was necessary because he, too, disobeyed God.

It is not difficult to recognize obvious sins—such as theft, murder, or adultery—and reject them. But Christians often miss God's best by becoming involved in something that, in itself, may not seem sinful. But we must be aware of the suggestions or activities of "friends" that would keep us from accomplishing God's purposes.

It is of utmost importance that we guard against loving things or people more than we love the Lord.

We must not love the world or anything the world has to offer—what people see and want and are so proud of. None of this comes from the Father, but is of the world (see I John 2:15).

Thought for Today: Those who please God are obedient to His Word.

Christ Revealed: Through the *"man of God"* who spoke the Word of God (I Kings 13:1-5). He is a type of Christ, who *is* the Word of God (John 1:1,14; Rev. 19:13).

Word Studies: 12:32 **high places** means pagan shrines; 13:6 **Entreat** means pray to; 13:32 **cried** means preached.

Prayer Needs: Country: Faeroe Islands—47,000—a group of islands in the Atlantic Ocean, north of Scotland • Religious freedom • 99% Protestant; .1% Roman Catholic.

APRIL 27: Read I Kings 14 — 15

Highlights: Ahijah's prophecy; reign and death of Rehoboam; wicked reign of Abijam in Judah; Asa's good reign in Judah; evil reigns of Nadab and Baasha in Israel.

Verses for Today: "... *Shishak king of Egypt came up against Jerusalem: And he took away the treasures of the house of the Lord ... and he took away all the shields of gold ... "* (I Kings 14:25-26).

G od Himself was the strength of Jerusalem, but He withdrew His presence when idol worship continued to be practiced. Therefore, the kingdom of Judah was easily overrun by Shishak, king of Egypt.

When Rehoboam's position as king was established and he had become strong, he and all his people abandoned the Law of the Lord (II Chronicles 12:1). Therefore, God permitted Shishak to invade Jerusalem and carry away immense wealth, including the golden shields—the symbol of God's protection.

Not wanting to be embarassed by the absence of the golden shields, Rehoboam made shields of brass (bronze) and continued his ceremonies as though nothing had happened. He had substituted cheap metal for gold. They were similar in appearance, but the cheap shields could not symbolize the precious, priceless power of God to protect them.

Pity the poor soul that gives the appearance of worshiping God, but does not worship Him from the heart in obedience to His Word. His worship is worthless.

Jesus said, *Not everyone who calls Me, "Lord, Lord," will enter the kingdom of Heaven—only those who are obedient to My Father who is in Heaven* (see Matthew 7:21).

Thought for Today: The Lord is our strength and our shield.

Christ Revealed: In Asa's ridding the land of idols and sodomites (I Kings 15:11-14). Christ cleansed the Temple (Matt. 21:12-13; John 2:13-16). As Christians, we are the temples of God (I Cor. 6:19-20; II Cor. 6:16-17).

Word Studies: 14:3 **cracknels** means cakes; **cruse** means jug; 14:15 **groves** means pagan shrines; 15:17 **suffer** means allow.

Prayer Needs: Country: United Arab Emirates—2 million—on the eastern Arabian Peninsula • Pressure and hostility against Christians are increasing • 95% Muslim; 4% Christian.

APRIL 28: Read I Kings 16 — 18

Highlights: Evil kings of Israel: Elah, Baasha, Zimri, Omri, Ahab; Elijah's pronouncement of drought; Elijah fed by ravens and the widow of Zarephath; Elijah raises the widow's son; Elijah's contest with the prophets of Baal.

Verse for Today: *"And Elijah ... said unto Ahab, As the Lord God of Israel liveth, before whom I stand, there shall not be dew nor rain these years, but according to my word"* (I Kings 17:1).

T he prophet Elijah prophesied there would be a drought in the land because of the nation's sin. When it came, Elijah suffered along with the rest of the nation, but he trusted in God for his daily existence.

We should follow Elijah's example of praying and trusting the Lord for our needs. *The prayers of the righteous have a powerful effect. Elijah was only a man like ourselves, but he prayed earnestly that there would be no rain, and no rain fell* (see James 5:16-18).

The life of Elijah should encourage each of us to pray earnestly—and to keep on praying, not trusting in ourselves, but in the grace and promises of God. It is not enough merely to say a prayer—our thoughts and requests must be in harmony with His Word, and our desires must be from the heart.

Let us consider the prophets who spoke in the name of the Lord; they patiently endured suffering. We call them happy because they remained faithful (see James 5:10-11).

Thought for Today: Our attitude, words, and actions should be a testimony to others that we want our lives to be controlled by God.

Christ Portrayed: By Elijah, who provided flour and oil for the widow at Zarephath (I Kings 17:13). Christ is our Provider, the One who supplies all our needs according to His riches in glory (Phil. 4:19).

Word Studies: 16:13 **vanities** means idolatry; 16:33 **grove** means worship center for a Canaanite goddess; 17:9 **sustain** means feed; 17:16 **wasted not** means was not used up.

Prayer Needs: Country: Gabon—1 million—in west-central Africa • Religious freedom • 66% Roman Catholic; 30% Protestant; 3% animism and ancestor worship.

APRIL 29: Read I Kings 19 — 20

Highlights: Jezebel's threat against Elijah; Elijah's flight; the call of Elisha; Benhadad spared by Ahab.

Verse for Today: *" . . . he requested for himself that he might die; and said, It is enough; now, O Lord, take away my life . . . "* (I Kings 19:4).

T hat day on Mount Carmel, the great purpose for which Elijah lived seemed to have been accomplished. Baal's prophets were slain; Jehovah was exalted by one mighty miracle; and false worship was exposed.

Elijah fully expected this great victory to instill the fear of the Lord in the heart of the queen and encourage the king to bring about religious reform. Instead, Jezebel swore revenge and demanded that the prophet be put to death.

In despair, Elijah said: *"It is enough; now, O Lord, take away my life."* God did not punish or even rebuke Elijah for making such a request. But instead of answering Elijah's prayer for death, God gave him rest and food.

Elijah's greatest success was not in the display of fire on Mount Carmel, but in the strength he imparted to 7,000 people who confessed, *" . . . the Lord, he is the God"* (I Kings 18:39).

All of us have had times of disappointment and moments of hopelessness when it seemed that our highest expectations were met with ridicule. But we must look beyond appearances and remain faithful to the "still, small voice."

"And let us not be weary in well doing: for in due season we shall reap, if we faint not" (Galatians 6:9).

Thought for Today: God, our wise and loving Father, comes in our moments of weakness to restore and strengthen us.

Christ Portrayed: By the prophet who came to King Ahab (I Kings 20:13). Even when we as Christians have sinned, God's love to us in Christ is unchanged (Rom. 8:38-39); He is constantly expressing His love and revealing Jesus to us.

Word Studies: 19:6 **head** means pillow; 19:8 **the mount of God** refers to Mt. Sinai; 19:13 **wrapped** means covered; 19:14 **jealous** means zealous; 19:21 **instruments** means yokes; 20:11 **harness** means armor; 20:24 **rooms** means positions; 20:43 **heavy and displeased** means downhearted; sullen and vexed.

Prayer Needs: Country: East Germany—17 million—in north-central Europe ● 55% Protestant; 8% Roman Catholic.

APRIL 30: Read I Kings 21 — 22

Highlights: Ahab covets Naboth's vineyard; Jezebel arranges the murder of Naboth; doom of Ahab and Jezebel pronounced; Micaiah's prophecy of Ahab's death; Jehoshaphat and Ahab go to battle against Syria; Ahab's defeat and death.

Verses for Today: *"And Micaiah said, Behold . . . thou shalt go into an inner chamber to hide thyself. And the king of Israel said . . . Put this fellow in the prison . . . "* (I Kings 22:25-27).

Jehoshaphat, king of Judah, agreed to join Ahab, king of Israel, in attacking Syria. But Jehoshaphat was uneasy about making the attack, so he told Ahab, *Let us first seek counsel from the Lord* (see I Kings 22:5).

Ahab called 400 of his prophets, and they unanimously assured him of great success. But Jehoshaphat was still hesitant. Reluctantly, Ahab called in Micaiah, a godly prophet who had been imprisoned because of his faithfulness to God.

The messengers tried to persuade Micaiah to agree with Ahab's 400 prophets and thus gain the favor of the king. But Micaiah would not be intimidated. There were 400 "yes" votes to Micaiah's one "no" vote—a miserable minority, but the truth is not dependent upon the majority's vote.

When he foretold that Ahab would be killed, Micaiah was slapped and dragged back to prison. But God's presence—even in a dungeon—is worth far more than popular acceptance.

For it is pleasing in the sight of God, if from a sense of duty to God a man endures wrong, even suffering unjustly (see I Peter 2:19).

Thought for Today: God imparts His strength to those who remain faithful to Him.

Christ Portrayed: By Micaiah, who would say only what God instructed him to say (I Kings 22:14). Jesus very faithfully told others everything God told Him to say (John 8:28).

Word Studies: 21:5 **bread** means food; 21:25 **stirred up** means incited; 22:10 **void** means open; 22:11 **push** means gore; 22:16 **adjure** means command; 22:35 **stayed** means propped.

Prayer Needs: Country: Djibouti (formerly French Territory of Afars and Issas)—313,000—in eastern Africa ● Limited religious freedom ● 91% Muslim; 7% Roman Catholic; .75% Eastern Orthodox; about 300 Protestants.

PRAYERS IN THIS MONTH'S READING

II KINGS

Except for Saul, all the kings of Judah and Israel are recorded in the two books of Kings.

After the death of Solomon, 10 of the tribes revolted against his son Rehoboam and formed the Northern Kingdom, called Israel (sometimes referred to as Ephraim or Samaria). The rebellion was led by Jeroboam, who immediately established golden-calf worship centers at Dan and Beth-el to keep the people from worshiping in Jerusalem and reuniting with the other tribes.

The first 17 chapters of II Kings are devoted to the divided kingdom. Rehoboam was the first king of the Southern Kingdom, which was made up of the tribes of Judah and Benjamin, as well as the Levites who remained faithful to the God-appointed Temple worship in Jerusalem. (See I Kings 12:20-21.)

Prophets were prominent throughout the history of the kings. They exposed the nation's corruption, foretold God's judgment, and appealed to the people to return to Him. The most prominent prophet of I Kings is Elijah; in II Kings it is Elisha.

Nineteen kings ruled Israel during its 210-year history as a divided kingdom, but not one was a faithful worshiper of God.

In the ninth year of Hoshea, the last king of the northern tribes, Shalmaneser conquered Samaria. Most of the people were transported to various parts of the Assyrian empire, and all 10 tribes lost their identity (II Kings 17). The few remaining Israelites intermarried with other captives from foreign lands and became known as Samaritans. They were despised by the Jews (see John 4:9).

The tribes of Reuben and Gad and half the tribe of Manasseh had occupied territory on the eastern side of the Jordan River just outside the Promised Land and were the first to be defeated by the Assyrians (I Chronicles 5:25-26).

The smaller Southern Kingdom of Judah (II Kings 18—25) also had 19 kings. (This does not include the usurper, Queen Athaliah, or Gedaliah, who was appointed governor for two months—II Kings 11:1-16; 25:22-25.) It continued as a nation for approximately 136 years after Israel's destruction.

Nebuchadnezzar, king of Babylon, destroyed both Solomon's temple and Jerusalem. (Compare II Kings 25:3-13; Jeremiah 52:12-17.) The majority of the population was deported to Babylon. Those who were allowed to remain fled to Egypt, taking Jeremiah with them as a hostage.

MAY 1: Read II Kings 1 — 3

Highlights: Death of Ahaziah, king of Israel; Elijah taken up by a whirlwind; Elisha purifies Jericho's water; Elisha mocked by the children; defeat of the Moabites.

Verse for Today: *"And Ahaziah fell down through a lattice in his upper chamber that was in Samaria, and was sick: and he sent messengers, and said unto them, Go, inquire of Baal-zebub the god of Ekron whether I shall recover of this disease"* (II Kings 1:2).

A haziah, the king of Israel, was on the rooftop patio of his palace when he accidentally fell through a lattice opening to the marble floor below.

The king sent messengers to the idol Baal-zebub to ask whether or not he would recover. On the way, the messengers met Elijah, who told them that the king would soon die.

Ahaziah's servants returned and told the king what Elijah had said. Instead of turning to the Lord, Ahaziah expressed hatred for the prophet as his mother Jezebel had. He sent 50 soldiers to arrest Elijah and bring him into custody.

Ahaziah's unfaithfulness to God had hardened his heart, and he failed to see that the hand of God was in all that occurred—first in the death of his father, Ahab; then the prophesy of his mother Jezebel's violent death; and now his "accident." Because there was no repentence, Ahaziah died (see II Kings 1:17).

The providential circumstances of God have placed each of us exactly where we are at this moment; therefore, we should look for His message rather than blame the messenger He uses.

We may not be responsible for the circumstances in which we find ourselves, but we are responsible for the way we react to our circumstances. We can become angry with the people God brings into our lives, or we can yield to the Lord, who seeks to use our "accidents" to transform us into the likeness of Christ.

"For they verily for a few days chastened us after their own pleasure; but he for our profit, that we might be partakers of his holiness" (Hebrews 12:10).

Thought for Today: Even though we are not always conscious of His presence, the Lord is in every circumstance, and His grace is sufficient to meet every crisis, every need.

Christ Revealed: In the taking up of Elijah in the whirlwind and the dropping of the mantle—a symbol of God's presence and power that remains with His faithful servants (II Kings 2:8-15). This is a type of the ascension of the Lord Jesus Christ and the sending of the Holy Spirit to indwell the believers, giving them power to evangelize the world (Luke 24; Acts 1—2).

Word Studies: 1:8 **girdle of leather** means leather belt; 2:12 **the chariot of Israel, and the horsemen thereof** means the mighty defender of Israel; 2:24 **tare** means tore them to pieces; ripped up; 3:9 **fetched a compass** means made a circuit; 3:11 **which poured water on the hands** means personal servant; 3:27 **offered him** means offered him as a sacrifice to the god of Moab.

Prayer Needs: Country: Bermuda—58,000—a group of 360 small islands in the Atlantic; 580 miles east of North Carolina • Religious freedom • 66% Protestant; 19% Roman Catholic; 2% cults.

MAY 2: Read II Kings 4 — 5

Highlights: Widow's oil; Elisha and the Shunammite woman; Elisha's miracles for the prophets; Naaman cured of leprosy; Gehazi's leprosy.

Verse for Today: *"And it came to pass, when the king of Israel had read the letter, that he rent his clothes, and said, Am I God, to kill and to make alive, that this man doth send unto me to recover a man of his leprosy? wherefore consider, I pray you, and see how he seeketh a quarrel against me"* (II Kings 5:7).

W hen Jehoram (Joram), king of Israel, read the letter that the king of Syria (Aram) had sent him, requesting that he heal Naaman of his leprosy, King Jehoram jumped to the wrong conclusion. He assumed that Naaman, the powerful captain of the Syrian army, was seeking an excuse to declare war.

Like his brother Ahaziah, Jehoram failed to recognize God's hand in his circumstances. However, he did not consult Baalzebub, as his brother did (II Kings 1:2); neither did he attempt to destroy the prophet of God, as his mother Jezebel did (I Kings 19:1-2). Nevertheless, the king of Israel did not turn to God—even after Naaman was miraculously healed.

Pity the poor unbelievers who, like Jehoram, with all their fears and frustrations, believe that the conflicts which come into their lives are merely the arrangements of men who threaten to destroy them. How different are the "Elishas" who know the living God and know that He has arranged our conflicts, adversities, and distresses according to His own will! (See Ephesians 1:11.)

God's purpose is to bring us into closer fellowship with Himself by developing our trust in His guidance. In this way, He is able to perfect His plan for our lives.

"For consider him that endured such contradiction of sinners against himself, lest ye be wearied and faint in your minds" (Hebrews 12:3).

Thought for Today: It is not necessary to understand God's reason for our trials, but it is of utmost importance that we remain faithful to Him.

Christ Revealed: In the meal that took the poison out of the pot (II Kings 4:40-41). Meal, made of crushed corn, speaks of Christ, who was *pierced through for our transgressions, and crushed for our iniquities* (see Isa. 53:5).

Word Studies: 4:3 **not a few** means as many as you can; 4:6 **stayed** means ceased; 4:10 **candlestick** means oil lamp; lampstand; 4:27 **vexed** means distressed; 4:29 **Gird up thy loins** means fasten the loose, flowing garments with a belt in preparation for travel; 4:38 **seethe** means boil; 4:43 **servitor** means servant; 5:1 **Syria** means Aram; 5:10 **clean** means healed; 5:24 **tower** means a mound (a fortress); **bestowed** means hid.

Prayer Needs: **Country:** Iran—50 million—in southwestern Asia • Hostile to all Christian activity • 98% Muslim; .4% Christian.

MAY 3: Read II Kings 6 — 8

Highlights: The ax head made to float; Syrians (Arameans) attack Israel; famine in Samaria; Elisha's prophecy fulfilled; land restored to the Shunammite woman; Hazael, the new king of Syria; Jehoram's wicked reign over Judah; Ahaziah's reign over Judah.

Verse for Today: *"Then Elisha said, Hear ye the word of the Lord; Thus saith the Lord, Tomorrow about this time shall a measure of fine flour be sold for a shekel . . . in the gate of Samaria"* (II Kings 7:1).

S amaria, the luxurious fortress city, had been surrounded by Benhadad's powerful Syrian army for so long that the Israelites' food supply had been depleted. To keep from starving to death, they resorted to eating the most repulsive, defiling food (see II Kings 6:25). They even went so far as to eat human flesh, as one woman confessed, *We boiled my son and ate him* (see 6:29).

Because the Israelites had rejected the Word of God, they were helpless before the Syrians.

But God, in mercy, once again intervened, and the prophet Elisha confidently prophesied that food would be plentiful the next day. Since nothing can prevent the fulfillment of God's prophecies, *"A measure of fine flour was sold for a shekel, and two measures of barley for a shekel, according to the word of the Lord"* (7:16).

God has provided an abundance of spiritual food for all who will accept it.

" . . . Man shall not live by bread alone, but by every word that proceedeth out of the mouth of God" (Matthew 4:4).

Thought for Today: The answers to our prayers are sometimes postponed until we lose confidence in self-effort.

Christ Portrayed: By Elisha, who wept when he realized what Hazael would do to Israel and its people (II Kings 8:11-12). We are reminded of Jesus as He wept over Jerusalem (Matt. 23:37-38).

Word Studies: 6:31 **God do so and more also to me** means may God deal with me, be it ever so severely; 7:1 **measure** means about 1/4 bushel—about 10 lbs.; 7:5 **uttermost part** means border; 8:11 **settled his countenance** means fixed his gaze.

Prayer Needs: **Country:** Kuwait—2 million—in the northeastern corner of the Arabian Peninsula • Less religious freedom than other Gulf states • 95% Muslim; 4% Christian.

MAY 4: Read II Kings 9 — 10

Highlights: Jehu anointed king of Israel; Jehu kills Joram (Jehoram) and Ahaziah; Jezebel killed; Ahab's family killed; Baal worshipers executed.

Verses for Today: *" . . . Thus saith the Lord God of Israel, I have anointed thee king over the people of the Lord, even over Israel. And thou shalt smite the house of Ahab thy master, that I may avenge the blood of my servants the prophets. . . . For the whole house of Ahab shall perish . . . "* (II Kings 9:6-8).

A fter Ahab's death, his son, Ahaziah, reigned over Israel for two years, followed by the 12-year reign of Ahaziah's brother, Jehoram. All three of these kings of the Northern Kingdom had so zealously promoted idolatry in Israel that it spread into Judah and seriously weakened the true worship of Jehovah in Jerusalem.

During this serious spiritual decline, the Lord was preparing Jehu, the powerful captain-commander of the Northern Kingdom armies, as His instrument of judgment. God had revealed to Elijah that Jehu would become king over Israel (see I Kings 19:16). Perhaps as many as 20 years passed before God ordered Elisha to send a young prophet to anoint Jehu as Israel's king and the executioner of Jehoram and all the descendants of Ahab. What appeared to be a coincidence when Jehu met Jehoram (Joram) in the field of Naboth was actually the fulfillment of God's Word against Ahab, as foretold by Elijah (see 21:19-23).

The violent and untimely deaths of Jezebel, King Ahab, and King Jehoram confirm the limitation of earthly power. Once again, God confirms the infallibility of His Word.

" . . . the word of our God shall stand for ever" (Isaiah 40:8).

Thought for Today: Many people have died untimely deaths because of disobedience to God.

Christ Revealed: Through Jehu's destroying Baal worship (II Kings 10:25-28). Christ will one day destroy the false religions of the world (Rev. 14:10; compare 20:10).

Word Studies: 9:23 **treachery** means deceit; betrayal of trust; 9:30 **tired her head** means dressed or beautified her hair; 10:3 **Look even out the best and meetest** means select the best and most fit; 10:12 **shearing house** means place where wool is cut from sheep; 10:27 **draught house** means dung shed.

Prayer Needs: Country: Norway—4 million—in northern Europe • Religious freedom • 95% Protestant; .4% Roman Catholic.

MAY 5: Read II Kings 11 — 13

Highlights: Athaliah usurps the throne of Judah; David's royal line destroyed except for baby Joash; Athaliah's execution; Jehoash repairs the Temple; his death; evil reign of Jehoahaz; death of Elisha.

Verse for Today: *"And when Athaliah the mother of Ahaziah saw that her son was dead, she arose and destroyed all the seed royal"* (II Kings 11:1).

A bout eight years after the godly reign of Jehoshaphat, Athaliah seized control of the Southern Kingdom and reigned in Jerusalem, the city of David.

Athaliah's wicked six-year reign was the result of a compromise which Jehoshaphat had made years earlier when he arranged for his son, Jehoram, to marry Athaliah, daughter of the wicked, idol-worshiping Ahab and Jezebel.

Jehoshaphat had failed to foresee that the "unequal yoke" of his son's marriage to Athaliah would one day destroy all the influence for godliness that he had spent his life building.

The eventual destruction of Jerusalem and captivity of the chosen nation of Judah are easily traced to adopting the ways of unbelievers.

Many Christians are deceived and their usefulness to God destroyed because of close friendship with those who oppose the Lord.

"Be ye not unequally yoked together with unbelievers: for what fellowship hath righteousness with unrighteousness? and what communion hath light with darkness?" (II Corinthians 6:14)

Thought for Today: Like Jehoshaphat, some Christians today have discovered too late the danger of being unequally yoked with unbelievers.

Christ Portrayed: By Joash, who had to be hidden from those who wanted to kill him (II Kings 11:1-3). Mary and Joseph took Jesus to Egypt to hide from those who wanted to kill Him (Matt. 2:13).

Word Studies: 11:7 **two parts** means two divisions; 11:8 **compass** means surround; 11:6 **way** means gate; 12:5 **breaches** means broken places; 12:11 **laid it out** means paid it out; 13:6 **grove** means Asherah: the symbol of a Canaanite fertility goddess who was worshiped along with Baal (see also Judges 3:7; II Kings 23:6).

Prayer Needs: Country: Antigua and Barbuda—70,000—in the Leeward Islands of the eastern Caribbean • Religious freedom • 85% Protestant; 11% Roman Catholic; 2% Afro-American spiritist.

MAY 6:   Read II Kings 14 — 15

Highlights: Reigns of Amaziah, Azariah (Uzziah), and Jotham over Judah; reigns of Jeroboam, Zechariah, Shallum, Menahem, Pekahiah, and Pekah over Israel.

Verse for Today: *"He restored the coast of Israel from the entering of Hamath unto the sea of the plain, according to the word of the Lord God of Israel, which he spake by the hand of his servant Jonah, the son of Amittai, the prophet, which was of Gathhepher"* (II Kings 14:25).

K ing Jeroboam II (son of Jehoash) was very successful in all his battles and brought great prosperity to the nation, but this recognition did not lead him to worship God. Instead, he practiced all the sins of Jeroboam I.

Amos, Hosea, Joel, and Jonah all prophesied during his reign. However, none were successful in turning him toward God. *"He did that which was evil in the sight of the Lord"* (II Kings 14:24). Finally, God commanded Amos to go to Bethel and prophesy the destruction of the kingdom (Amos 7:9).

The Israelites seemed to believe that because they prospered, God approved of their idol worship. More and more, they placed their confidence in the supremacy of Baal worship rather than God.

Often, the Christian's greatest tests of loyalty and humility before God come during times of material blessing. While we are enjoying prosperity, we are usually less concerned about prayerfully seeking the Lord's guidance and will for our lives.

Many, like Jeroboam, boast of their material success, even though it was achieved at the cost of spiritual neglect. How tragic that some parents have left their children much material wealth, but have failed to emphasize the real spiritual wealth of the Word of God!

"For what is a man profited, if he shall gain the whole world, and lose his own soul? . . . " (Matthew 16:26).

Thought for Today: We forfeit God's best when we fail to keep His commandments.

Christ Revealed: When the Lord struck the king with leprosy and thrust him out from being king (II Kings 15:5-7). This pictures the time when Christ will cast out the unprofitable servant (Matt. 25:30).

Word Studies: 14:7 **Selah** means the rock city of Petra; 14:12 **put to the worse** means defeated; 14:25 **sea of the plain** means area as far south as the Dead Sea; 15:4 **Save** means except; 15:5 **a several house** means an isolated house; 15:20 **exacted** means took; 15:25 **in his room** means in his stead, place.

Prayer Needs: Country: South Yemen—2 million—on the southern part of the Arabian Peninsula · Gradual erosion of the strong position of Islam in favor of atheism · 92% Muslim; .1% Christian (all secret believers).

MAY 7: Read II Kings 16 — 17

Highlights: Ahaz defiles the Temple; fall of Samaria; captivity of Israel.

Verses for Today: *"In the ninth year of Hoshea the king of Assyria took Samaria [capital of the Northern Kingdom], and carried Israel away into Assyria. . . . They feared the Lord, and served their own gods . . . "* (II Kings 17:6,33).

H oshea paid tribute to the king of Assyria and pretended to be loyal to him, but he made a secret agreement with the king of Egypt, hoping to receive help from the Egyptians and free his nation from Assyrian control.

But Hoshea's clever schemes of double-dealing and double-mindedness revealed that his trust was not in God, but in himself. This kind of policy only temporarily seems to be successful. When the king of Assyria learned about Hoshea's agreement, he led in the battle that brought about the end of the Northern Kingdom. Egypt made no attempt to help Hoshea.

Hoshea was typical of the people of Israel, for they were attempting to serve two masters. They believed in Jehovah, the true God, but they also worshiped the gods of the heathens. What a warning against unfaithfulness to God!

Many today are making the same mistake Hoshea made. They have a certain amount of the fear of God—they are afraid to die—so they try to be religious, going to church and calling themselves Christians. But it is in name only.

"This people draweth nigh unto me with their mouth, and honoreth me with their lips; but their heart is far from me" (Matthew 15:8).

Thought for Today: Compromise is a characteristic of a double-minded person.

Christ Revealed: Through the initial brazen (bronze) altar (II Kings 16:10-15). The brazen altar is a type of the cross on which Christ, our whole burnt offering, offered Himself to God (Heb. 9:14).

Word Studies: 16:11 **against** means before; 16:13 **meat offering** means cereal grain offering made of fine flour (or unleavened bread), oil, and a portion of incense; 16:18 **turned he from** means he removed from; 17:11 **heathen** means nations.

Prayer Needs: Country: Peru—21 million—on the western coast of South America • Increased restrictions imposed against evangelism and conversion to Christ • 89% Roman Catholic; 4% Protestant.

MAY 8: Read II Kings 18 — 20

Highlights: Hezekiah's good reign; Assyria invades Judah; Hezekiah's prayer; his sickness; Hezekiah's display of wealth; his death.

Verses for Today: *" . . . Hezekiah . . . trusted in the Lord God of Israel; so that after him was none like him among all the kings of Judah, nor any that were before him. . . . And the Lord was with him . . . "* (II Kings 18:1,5,7).

T he Northern Kingdom had already been conquered by the Assyrians, and most of the people deported as slaves. Sennacherib, the Assyrian king, was determined then to conquer Judah, the Southern Kingdom; therefore, he surrounded Jerusalem with his seemingly invincible army. The chances for escape looked impossible; and to all human appearances, there was no hope. But King Hezekiah bypassed all his advisers and went immediately to the Temple and prayed. He then sent messengers to the prophet Isaiah. After that prayer, 185,000 Assyrian soldiers were destroyed by the angel of God. Furthermore, when Sennacherib returned to his palace in Nineveh, he was assassinated by two of his own sons (see II Kings 19:37; Isaiah 37:38).

We should never be fearful about our future, but we do need to pray and commit our needs to God. No matter how hopeless your situation may appear, just remember that when Hezekiah prayed, *"the Lord was with him,"* and He will be with you.

"Again I say unto you, That if two of you shall agree on earth as touching any thing that they shall ask, it shall be done for them of my Father which is in heaven" (Matthew 18:19).

Thought for Today: There is no substitute for prayer.

Christ Portrayed: By Hezekiah, who was leading Judah back to God (II Kings 19). Here we are reminded of Jesus' call, *Come to Me, and I will give you rest* (see Matt. 11:28).

Word Studies: 18:17 **Tartan** is the title of Assyria's commander; **Rabsaris** means the chief financial official; **Rabshakeh** means the chief officer; **fuller's field** means field where the laundering was done, possibly by trampling with the feet; 18:26 **Syrian** means Aramaic; 19:7 **blast** means spirit of bad fortune; 19:21 **daughter of Zion** means God's chosen people in Jerusalem; 20:3 **sore** means bitterly.

Prayer Needs: Country: Virgin Islands—125,000—a group of 89 islands in the West Indies, east of Puerto Rico • Religious freedom • 43% Protestant; 22% Roman Catholic.

MAY 9: Read II Kings 21 — 23:20

Highlights: Evil reigns of Manasseh and Amon; Josiah's good reign; Book of the Law discovered; idolatry destroyed.

Verses for Today: *" . . . I have found the book of the law in the house of the Lord.*

. . . So Hilkiah the priest . . . went unto Huldah the prophetess. . . . And she said unto them, Thus saith the Lord God of Israel . . . " (II Kings 22:8,14-15).

U nnoticed in the night of apostasy, the discovery of this Book was a confirmation of the indestructibility of the Divine written Word. In this instance, Huldah the prophetess acknowledged the authority of the Book which was discovered in the house of the Lord and announced that punishment would be imposed because Judah had abandoned Jehovah and had turned to other gods.

Though little is known of Huldah, there is sufficient evidence to indicate that she had great influence in Jerusalem. The high priest and the king recognized her remarkable prophetic gift and sought spiritual guidance from her.

There are only two other prophetesses mentioned in the Old Testament—Miriam (Exodus 15:20) and Deborah (Judges 4:4)—but neither of these seemed to have reached the spiritual elevation as that of Huldah. Miriam and Deborah sang sacred songs and aroused the enthusiasm of the people after great victories, but they did not prophesy like Huldah, with *"Thus saiith the Lord."*

God is no respecter of persons in the distribution of His precious gifts. His Word can be interpreted only by those who are led by the Holy Spirit. Just as the physician should be most competent to diagnose physical conditions, so the spiritual man or woman should be the authority in explaining spiritual things.

Many professing Christians do not bother to search for opportunities to serve the Lord. In fact, if someone comes to them, they look upon this as an intrusion instead of an opportunity to share God's Word and hope the person will soon depart.

"And he gave some, apostles; and some, prophets; and some, evangelists; and some, pastors and teachers; For the perfecting of the saints, for the work of the ministry, for the edifying of the body of Christ" (Ephesians 4:11-12).

Thought for Today: Christ is all-sufficient and will supply our every need to do His will.

Christ Revealed: Through the prophets (II Kings 21:10). *Long ago God spoke through His prophets . . . in these last days He speaks to us through His Son* (see Heb. 1:1-2).

Word Studies: 21:12 **both his ears shall tingle** means will be astonished; 22:4 **sum the silver** means count the money; 23:17 **title** means monument.

Prayer Needs: Country: Luxembourg—366,000—in western Europe • Religious freedom • 84% Roman Catholic; 2% Protestant; .1% Eastern Orthodox.

MAY 10: Read II Kings 23:21 — 25

Highlights: Passover restored; death of Josiah; Jehoahaz imprisoned; Jehoiakim conquered and controlled by Nebuchadnezzar; Jehoiachin captured by Nebuchadnezzar; Zedekiah's reign; fall of Jerusalem; captivity of Judah.

Verse for Today: *"And the king of Babylon smote them, and slew them at Riblah in the land of Hamath. So Judah was carried away out of their land"* (II Kings 25:21).

J ust 23 years after the death of godly Josiah, the Southern Kingdom of Judah surrendered to the control of Egypt. Because of the people's unfaithfulness and repeated disobedience to God's Word, the nation was reduced to ruin.

The last four kings were merely puppet-kings, appointed and controlled by Egypt and Babylon. Throughout their reigns, the nation experienced a series of conquests and deportations.

How pathetic the fall of Judah was, especially when we consider that the Northern Kingdom had also fallen about 135 years earlier! Together, Judah and the Northern Kingdom had once been Israel, one of the most powerful nations on earth. From a very small beginning, Israel reached a height of such imperial greatness that it commanded the admiration of the mightiest nations of its day. But, because of Solomon's idolatry, the nation became divided.

Later in the midst of Judah's decline, God raised up Jeremiah the prophet. If the people had followed his counsel, the outcome would have been much different. Jehoiachin, like Hezekiah, could have defied the invading forces. But the nation lost its power and the privilege of God's protection.

With an immense army, Nebuchadnezzar swept down upon the northern part of the country and surrounded Jerusalem. Eventually the city was reduced to starvation.

Zedekiah, with his wives, children, and guards, fled through an opening in the wall (Ezekiel 12:12); but they were captured in the plains of Jericho. Zedekiah was forced to witness the slaughter of his own family; then his eyes were put out, and he was carried in chains to Babylon. His agonizing ordeal fulfilled two prophecies that appeared to contradict each other: that Zedekiah would come to Babylon, but that he would not see it (Jeremiah 32:5; 34:21; Ezekiel 12:3; 17:20-21).

The destruction of the kingdom of Judah teaches us that the greatest nation on earth cannot survive if its people continually reject God and His righteousness. Wealth, vast armies, and nuclear protection are false security when a nation turns from God.

Some nations boast of their great military programs, but those who continually look to God and remain faithful to Him will be victorious (see Psalm 20:7-9).

Thought for Today: A nation's true success is dependent upon its faithfulness to God.

Christ Revealed: Through the Passover (II Kings 23:21-23). The Passover is a type of Christ, our Redeemer (see John 1:29; I Cor. 5:6-7; I Pet. 1:18-19).

Word Studies: 25:12 **husbandmen** means farmers; 25:27 **lift up the head** means show favor to; release.

Prayer Needs: Country: Zambia—7 million—in south-central Africa • Religious freedom • 30% Catholic; 25% Protestant; 24% ancestor worship, magic, and witchcraft; 19% cults.

I & II CHRONICLES _____

The books of I and II Samuel and I and II Kings provide the moral and political history of Israel and Judah; Chronicles presents the religious history of Judah.

The books of the Bible, from Genesis through II Kings, relate a succession of events from the creation of Adam to the time of Judah's captivity. But Chronicles is a review.

The book of I Chronicles opens with the largest genealogical list of names in the Bible and covers about 3,500 years of history (chapters 1—9). The genealogies are devoted to the families through whom God would carry out His plan of redemption. Beginning with Adam, they confirm the genealogy of Christ as recorded in the Gospels of Matthew and Luke. Many names are omitted, but those that were related to the prophecies of the promised Savior are recorded, including Zerubbabel, leader of the returning exiles (I Chronicles 3:19).

Saul's last battle and his death are mentioned in chapter 10; chapters 11—29 cover the reign of David, revealing a government that honors God. The book of I Chronicles ends with the death of David and the extension of the kingdom under Solomon.

The book of II Chronicles continues the history of David's line. It begins with the reign of Solomon, records the division of the kingdom under Rehoboam, and covers the history of the Southern Kingdom of Judah until the exile of the people to Babylon. The last verses contain Cyrus' proclamation, which allowed the Jews to return to Jerusalem.

The period of Solomon was the golden age of Israel. Much of the first nine chapters of II Chronicles tells of the construction of the Temple in Jerusalem on Mt. Moriah. It was built after the pattern of the Tabernacle (chapters 3—4). The work was completed in the eleventh year of Solomon's reign (chapter 5; compare I Kings 6:38) and consecrated to God in one of the great prayers of the Scriptures (chapter 6).

The remainder of II Chronicles tells of the kings of Judah, and the moral and spiritual decline of the nation. It ends with the fall of Jerusalem and the final destruction of the Temple (chapters 10—36).

This review of history not only emphasizes God's love for His people, but it also points out that when kings and people honored God, there was prosperity. But when they were unfaithful to the Lord, He withdrew His presence and defeat was inevitable.

MAY 11: Read I Chronicles 1 — 2

Highlights: Descendants of Adam, Noah, Abraham, Esau, Israel (Jacob), and Judah.

Verses for Today: *"Adam, Sheth, Enosh . . . Noah, Shem, Ham, and Japheth. . . . And the sons of Javan; Elishah, and Tarshish, Kittim, and Dodanim"* (I Chronicles 1;1,4,7).

To the casual observer, the long list of geneaologies in the book of I Chronicles may seem dry and uninteresting. But in reality, they point out the well-planned design of God down through the centuries, naming the descendants from Adam, the first man, to Christ, the second Adam.

Just as God personally decided who would be included in the genealogy of Christ, He is personally involved in every Christian's life, engineering every detail.

Things that happen to believers are not "accidents"; they are allowed by our Father, the master engineer. Although we don't understand many of the things God brings into our lives, we can rest assured that He has a purpose for them. May our heartfelt prayer be, "Lord, let me learn from this experience the lesson You are trying to teach me."

Trust in the Lord with all of your heart; don't depend on your own understanding. Look to Him in everything you do, and He will guide you (see Proverbs 3:5-6).

Thought for Today: There are no accidents with God.

Christ Revealed: By the first Adam (I Chronicles 1:1). Christ is the last Adam (I Cor. 15:45).

Prayer Needs: Country: Nigeria—109 million—in western Africa • Government permits all types of religious activity • 36% Muslim; 19% Protestant; 15% animist; 7% Roman Catholic.

MAY 12: Read I Chronicles 3 — 5

Highlights: Descendants of David, Solomon, Judah, Simeon, Reuben, and Gad.

Verses for Today: *"And Jabez was more honorable than his brethren. . . . And Jabez called on the God of Israel, saying, Oh that thou wouldest bless me indeed, and enlarge my coast, and that thine hand might be with me, and that thou wouldest keep me from evil. . . . And God granted him that which he requested"* (I Chronicles 4:9-10).

We know very little about Jabez except that he prayed for something besides worldly fame. He was *"more honorable than his brethren. . . . and God granted him that which he requested."*

Jabez found the joy that comes as one gives himself to God for His pleasure alone, seeking to be led in the path of God's choice. Accomplishments that bring eternal results are those that God initiates. Therefore, when we are faithfully serving Christ, we will neither murmur about anything nor be proud of our accomplishments. Furthermore, we should never be jealous of the advantages which other people have.

If our supreme desire is to gain God's blessing, there is no need to fear that we are being cheated. Our main goal in life should be to do the best we can with what we have. (See Philippians 4:11.) The only important thing is what we are in the eyes of God. Anything God wants us to do, He will help us do if we are willing to yield to His will for our lives.

God is a rewarder of those who diligently seek Him (see Hebrews 11:6).

Thought for Today: Those who entrust their all to God receive His best.

Christ Revealed: Through the genealogy of David (I Chronicles 3:1-24). Christ, the Son of God, was also from the line of David (Luke 3:23-31).

Prayer Needs: Country: Oman—1 million—on the southeastern coast of Arabia • Fewer restrictions on Christian activity than most of its neighbors • 97% Muslim; .5% Christian.

MAY 13: Read I Chronicles 6 — 7

Highlights: Descendants of Levi; Temple singers and keepers appointed; descendants of Aaron; cities of the Levites; genealogies continued.

Verse for Today: " . . . *And the number throughout the genealogy . . . was twenty and six thousand men"* (I Chronicles 7:40).

T he name of every individual, as well as the family and tribe to which he belonged, was carefully registered. There is a striking difference in the character of the men who are mentioned in these chapters. Some were devoted to their God-given responsibilities; others profaned their holy calling.

Aaron was a devoted priest, but his sons were hypocrites. Samuel was a godly judge, but his sons were evil. For years Abiathar was a high priest, but he later became a traitor to King David (see I Kings 1:5-7; 2:26-27). What a strange mixture of devout saints and sinful, undisciplined men! What a contrast between Heaven-born beginnings and forfeited opportunities!

The long, "uninteresting" list of names shows us that God does not look on mankind as a crowd of human beings who populate the world. In fact, He is so concerned about us that even the hairs of our heads are numbered by Him (see Matthew 10:30). He knows each of us by name; and either our names are written in the Lamb's Book of Life, or we will face the great white throne judgment.

"And I saw the dead, small and great, stand before God; and the books were opened: and another book was opened, which is the book of life: and the dead were judged out of those things which were written in the books, according to their works" (Revelation 20:12).

Thought for Today: Your name is recorded in the Book of Life when you receive Christ as your Savior.

Christ Revealed: In the cities of refuge (I Chronicles 6:57,67). For a person to have protection from the avenger of blood, he had to flee to a city of refuge. God provided His only begotten Son, Jesus Christ, to be our refuge from His judgment against sin. (Compare John 3:14-18; 10:24-30; Gal. 2:16; 3:1-13; Heb. 10:1-17; I John 2:2; Rev. 1:5). When, by faith in obedience to His Word, we come to Christ, He becomes our refuge.

Word Studies: 6:32 **waited on** means performed service in; 6:66 **the residue** means some; 6:74 **suburbs** means pasturelands; 7:24 **nether** means lower.

Prayer Needs: Country: Venezuela—18 million—on the northern coast of South America • Religious freedom • 94% Roman Catholic; 1% Protestant; 1% Indian pagan religions.

MAY 14: Read I Chronicles 8 — 10

Highlights: Descendants of Benjamin; priests and Levites in Jerusalem; genealogy of Saul; deaths of Saul and his sons.

Verse for Today: *"So Saul died for his transgression which he committed against the Lord, even against the word of the Lord, which he kept not, and also for asking counsel of one that had a familiar spirit, to inquire of it"* (I Chronicles 10:13).

G od had commanded Saul to *"utterly destroy"* all of the Amalekites and their possessions, but he spared King Agag and took home the choicest animals (I Samuel 15:3,9). His partial obedience was self-deceiving, for he proudly announced to Samuel, *"Blessed be thou of the Lord: I have performed the command-ment of the Lord"* (15:13). He obeyed the Lord only to the point that it pleased himself and the people.

As the years passed, Saul's rejection of God became more apparent—even ordering the execution of 45 *"priests of the Lord"* (I Samuel 22:17-18; compare 18:10-11; 24:17-20; 26:2-21; 28:15-16).

The night before his final battle with the Philistines on Mt. Gilboa, Saul hastily prayed (I Samuel 28:6). But he did not repent of his past sins nor wait for God to answer.

There is no evidence that Saul desired the Lord's will in his life. But we do read that he rushed through the night to the village of Endor to seek counsel from a spiritualist medium concerning the outcome of the battle. This exposed Saul's disloyalty as God's representative to enforce His Word that said: *"There shall not be found among you any one . . . that useth divination, or an observer of times, or an enchanter, or a witch, or a charmer, or a consulter with familiar spirits, or a wizard, or a necromancer. For all that do these things are an abomination unto the Lord"* (Deuteronomy 18:10-12).

Like Saul, many today have missed God's best for their lives and have created serious problems by patronizing those who practice sorcery, such as palm readers, fortune-tellers, spiritualists, astrologers, and other deceptive, evil advisors, rather than looking to God.

"But the fearful, and unbelieving, and the abominable, and murderers, and whoremongers, and sorcerers, and idolaters, and all liars, shall have their part in the lake which burneth with fire and brimstone: which is the second death" (Revelation 21:8).

Thought for Today: Faith comes to those who read God's Word.

Christ Revealed: By Jerusalem, which means "foundation of peace" (I Chronicles 9:3). Christ is the only foundation of peace between man and God (II Cor. 5:18; Eph. 2:14).

Word Studies: 8:29 **father** means founder; 8:33 **Eshbaal** means Ishbosheth; 9:23 **wards** means guards; 9:28 **bring them in and out by tale** means counted them when they brought them in and took them out; 10:2 **followed hard after** means closely pursued; 10:4 **uncircumcised** means godless Philistines.

Prayer Needs: Country: Russia (Soviet Union)—284 million—in northern Eurasia • Repression of unofficial churches and rigid control of registered denominations • 32% Eastern Orthodox; 11% Muslim; 2% Protestant; 2% Roman Catholic; 1% Jewish.

MAY 15: Read I Chronicles 11 — 13

Highlights: David made king over all Israel; David captures and then reigns in Jebus (Jerusalem); mighty men of David; David's army at Ziklag; his attempt to take the ark to Jerusalem; Uzza struck dead; ark of God taken to the house of Obed-edom.

Verse for Today: *"And moreover in time past, even when Saul was king, thou wast he that leddest out and broughtest in Israel: and the Lord thy God said unto thee, Thou shalt feed my people Israel, and thou shalt be ruler over my people Israel"* (I Chronicles 11:2).

W hile Saul was still king, David was anointed of God to reign over His people. David faced many years of trials and patient waiting before he began his promised reign.

After Saul's death, David was made king over the tribe of Judah at Hebron (II Samuel 2:4). But the 10 tribes of the Northern Kingdom did not accept him as king until after the death of Abner and Ishbosheth, Saul's son who was a puppet-king controlled by Abner (II Samuel 3:7-11).

David had learned, early in life, that God will take care of His people, and that human schemes are worthless without His blessings.

Once we recognize God's authority over our lives, we will patiently look to God for direction rather than forcefully take matters into our own hands.

"But they that wait upon the Lord shall renew their strength . . . "(Isaiah 40:31).

Thought for Today: We cannot build up ourselves by putting down someone else.

Christ Portrayed: By David, the anointed king (I Chronicles 11:3). Christ is the Anointed One who will reign as KING OF KINGS, AND LORD OF LORDS (see Revelation 19:16).

Word Studies: 11:16 **hold** means fortress; 12:1 **close** means concealed; 12:8 **separated themselves** means came to support; 12:17 **knit** means joined; 12:19 **fall to** means desert us and return to Saul.

Prayer Needs: Country: Egypt—52 million—in northeastern Africa • Christians are not permitted to evangelize Muslims • 82% Muslim; 16% Coptic; .6% Roman Catholic.

MAY 16: Read I Chronicles 14 — 16

Highlights: King Hiram's kindness to David; David's victories over the Philistines; the ark brought to Jerusalem; David's sacrifices and psalm of thanksgiving.

Verse for Today: *"And the fame of David went out into all lands; and the Lord brought the fear of him upon all nations"* (I Chronicles 14:17).

A fter David conquered the Jebusites, he established his capital in Jerusalem. Up to that time, the Israelites had never conquered the Jebusites.

The Philistines feared David's growing power, so they *"spread themselves in the valley"* near Bethlehem and prepared to attack Jerusalem (I Chronicles 14:9). David immediately *"inquired of God"* (14:10). He would not take his men into battle until he knew the will of God. Then he experienced a great victory.

The defeated Philistines then renewed their force with a second attack. But notice! Although the first battle was very successful, David did not assume to know God's will concerning the second attack. He *"inquired again of God"* (I Chronicles 14:14). This time God directed them in an altogether different way, and David gained another great victory.

The often-recorded phrase, *"David inquired of the Lord,"* was the key to his greatness. (See I Samuel 23:2,4; 30:8; II Samuel 2:1; 5:19,23; 21:1.)

Once we are awakened to the importance of prayer, Satan will seek to disrupt our prayers by such seemingly innocent things as an unexpected visitor or by calling to remembrance something important we forgot to do.

"Praying always with all prayer and supplication in the Spirit, and watching thereunto with all perseverance . . . " (Ephesians 6:18).

Thought for Today: The united prayers of Christians will put the enemy to flight.

Christ Revealed: Through David's fame and exaltation (I Chronicles 14:17). God has highly exalted Christ, our Redeemer, and has given Him a name above every name (Phil. 2:9).

Word Study: 14:13 **spread themselves abroad** means made a hostile invasion.

Prayer Needs: Country: Cuba—10 million—on the northern rim of the Caribbean • Strict government surveillance of all true Christian influence activities • 41% Roman Catholic; 2% various spiritists; 1% Protestant.

MAY 17: Read I Chronicles 17 — 20

Highlights: David forbidden to build the Temple; his prayer; David extends his kingdom; David defeats the Ammonites and Syrians (Arameans); Rabbah captured; war with the Philistines.

Verses for Today: "... *David said to Nathan the prophet, Lo, I dwell in a house of cedars, but the ark of the covenant of the Lord remaineth under curtains. Then Nathan said unto David, Do all that is in thine heart; for God is with thee*" (I Chronicles 17:1-2).

D avid had established true worship and brought the ark to Jerusalem, but he felt ashamed of the contrast between his luxurious house made of cedar and the old tent tabernacle of the Lord; therefore, he decided to build a temple for worship. This was his personal desire, but the Lord revealed His will, saying, *"Thou shalt not build me a house ... "* (I Chronicles 17:4). Upon hearing the will of God, David, in deep humility, said, *"Who am I ... that thou hast brought me hitherto?"* (17:16). And in adoration of the infinite wisdom of the incomparable God, David acknowledged, *"O Lord, there is none like thee ... "* (17:20).

Like David, those who please the Lord have learned that God is the only one who can say what is pleasing to Himself. To grumble about one's circumstances is to question *"the exceeding greatness of his power to us-ward who believe"* (Ephesians 1:19).

"O Lord, I know that the way of man is not in himself: it is not in man that walketh to direct his steps" (Jeremiah 10:23).

Thought for Today: What a privilege to trust God for guidance!

Christ Portrayed: By David, the great shepherd-king, symbolic of Christ in His human form (I Chronicles 17:7; compare Matt. 1:1-2; Rom. 1:3).

Word Studies: 17:1 **under curtains** means in the tent tabernacle; 17:6 **judges** means leaders; 17:7 **sheepcote** means a single entrance enclosure where the shepherd could protect his sheep at night; 18:4 **houghed** means hamstrung; crippled by cutting leg tendons; 19:4 **hard by** means near; 19:6 **odious** means detestable.

Prayer Needs: Country: Laos—4 million—in Southeast Asia • Great suppression of all Christian activities • 58% Buddhist; 33% belief in spirits and ancestor worship; 2% Christian; 1% Muslim.

MAY 18: Read I Chronicles 21 — 23

Highlights: David's sin in taking a military census; preparation for building the

Temple; David's instructions to Solomon; duties of the Levites.

Verses for Today: *"And Satan stood up against Israel, and provoked David to number Israel. And God was displeased with this thing; therefore he smote Israel"* (I Chronicles 21:1,7).

We could ask, why was it a sin to number the people? Did not the Lord command that a census be taken in the wilderness? (See Numbers 1:1-2.) Then, too, census-taking was customary with other kings in order that they might know what size army they would have in case of a war. In spite of our apparently logical reasoning, the Bible reveals that this decision was instigated by a supernatural enemy. Satan, the adversary, was permitted in some way to influence David to authorize the census. Yet, sin is man's own act; consequently a righteous God must administer judgment upon man's guilt.

Did David want to ascertain, and then boast of, his military strength? Did he momentarily lose sight of his source of strength? Did thoughts of pride and the praise of others become a means for Satan to provoke David's act of treason against God? Israel was God's people to number—not David's.

David's sin had the same root as the sin of Nebuchadnezzar, whom Jehovah taught by a crushing experience to *"honor the King of heaven, all whose works are truth, and his ways judgment: and those that walk in pride he is able to abase"* (Daniel 4:37).

David was not conscious that Satan was so near or so powerful in prompting sin. Be assured that wherever there is a ministry being done for Christ, Satan's strategy is to destroy it. This was true when Satan, in person, challenged the Lord in the wilderness temptation. Christ withstood him by quoting Scripture—then *"the devil left him"* (see Matthew 4:3-11).

Our Lord described Satan as the *"prince of this world,"* a *"murderer,"* the *"father of lies,"* who *"abode not in the truth"* (see John 8:44; 14:30), thus revealing the adversary as possessing the skill of a master mind, directing, with executive ability, his work *"in the children of disobedience"* (Ephesians 2:2).

Thought for Today: Satan will try to cause us to sin, but by God's grace we can resist him.

Christ Revealed: Through the Altar David built (I Chronicles 21:18). When we have sinned, the safest thing to do is to turn to Christ. Only through Him can the joy of our salvation be restored.

Word Studies: 21:15 **repented him of the evil** means had a change of plans due to man's repentance and intercession; 22:3 **without weight** means beyond calculation because it was more than could be weighed; 23:1 **old and full of days** means reached old age; 23:11 **reckoning** means group.

Prayer Needs: **Country:** Pakistan—105 million—in southern Asia • There is no freedom to convert Muslims to Christ. Pakistan is an Islamic republic • 97% Muslim; 2% Christian; 1% Hindu.

MAY 19: Read I Chronicles 24 — 26

Highlights: Work assignments given to the priests; offices of the singers; divisions of the porters (gatekeepers); treasurers and other officials chosen.

Verse for Today: " . . . *God blessed him [Obed-edom]"* (I Chronicles 26:5).

G od greatly blessed Obed-edom during the time the ark of the covenant was in his home.

Three months earlier, King David had planned to take the ark to Jerusalem and make Jerusalem the religious center of all Israel. The ark was placed on an ox cart driven by Uzzah and Ahio, who were to transport it from Kirjath-jearim to Jerusalem. Along the way, Uzzah was struck dead for touching the ark. David was displeased with God and refused to take the ark on to Jerusalem. It was taken instead to the home of Obed-edom. (II Samuel 6:1-11; I Chronicles 13:7-11.) Three months later, David was directed to have the ark transported to Jerusalem. This time he made sure it was transported in the way God had said (I Chronicles 15:2-3; Numbers 4:15; 7:9).

The ark was prominent in leading the Israelites through the wilderness (Numbers 10:33-36). Because it contained the Ten Commandments which God had given to Moses on Mt. Sinai, it was a symbol of the authority of God. When Obed-edom received the ark, he received more than God's Word; he received the very presence of God (see I Samuel 4:4; II Samuel 6:2).

Just as the ark brought God's blessing to the home of Obed-edom, so He will bless all who allow Christ—the Son of God—and His Word to rule their lives (see John 1:12).

Just before He ascended into Heaven, Jesus said, *All authority has been given unto Me in Heaven and in earth . . . go and teach all nations . . . to obey everything I have commanded* (see Matthew 28:18-20).

Thought for Today: The more our thoughts are occupied with Christ and His Word, the more we will realize His presence.

Christ Revealed: Through the Temple treasures (I Chronicles 26:20-28). In Christ are the treasures of wisdom, knowledge, and riches to supply all the believer's needs (Phil. 4:19).

Word Studies: 24:2 **executed the priest's office** means served as priests; 24:5 **divided by lot** means assignment by drawing lots (using specially marked stones, such as "yes" and "no," to determine God's will—see Prov. 16:33).

Prayer Needs: Country: Monaco—29,000—in southeastern France • No open evangelism permitted • 90% Roman Catholic; 7% Protestant; 1% Eastern Orthodox.

MAY 20: Read I Chronicles 27 — 29

Highlights: The officers of the kingdom; Solomon encouraged to build the Temple; David's gifts for the Temple; his thanksgiving and prayer; Solomon made king; David's death.

Verse for Today: *"Wherefore David blessed the Lord before all the congregation: and David said, Blessed be thou, Lord God of Israel our father, for ever and ever"* (I Chronicles 29:10).

D avid had grown old and knew his reign was nearing an end. But the nearer he came to the world of everlasting worship, the more he spoke the praise language of that world. His last recorded message to his kingdom was one of the greatest outbursts of worship found in the Old Testament. David adored the Lord

137

and proclaimed His unspeakable grandeur, *"Thine, O Lord, is the greatness, and the power, and the glory, and the victory, and the majesty . . . "* (I Chronicles 29:11).

Worship is not merely a ritual of singing, praying, or preaching. True worship is experienced within the heart of the worshiper. Every day, under every circumstance, we should give praise to the Lord. To grumble about our circumstances is to question His Word.

"To the praise of the glory of his grace, wherein he hath made us accepted in the beloved" (Ephesians 1:6).

Thought for Today: Let us freely offer our praise to God *continually*.

Christ Revealed: In the gold offered by David (I Chronicles 29:3-4). Gold represents Christ's warmth, preciousness, and great worth.

Word Studies: 27:2 **course** means division; 28:4 **liked** means chose; 28:7 **constant** means faithful; 28:14 **instruments** means vessels; articles; 29:1 **tender** means inexperienced; 29:3 **proper good** means personal treasure.

Prayer Needs: Country: Malaysia—16 million—in Southeast Asia • All Christian witness to Muslims is illegal • 49% Muslim; 39% Hindu, Buddhist, and Chinese religions; 4% Roman Catholic; 4% animism, magic, and head hunting; 3% Protestant.

MAY 21: Read II Chronicles 1 — 3

Highlights: Solomon's sacrifices; his dream of praying for wisdom; dimensions of and materials for the Temple.

Verse for Today: *"So Solomon, and all the congregation with him, went to the high place that was at Gibeon; for there was the tabernacle of the congregation of God, which Moses the servant of the Lord had made in the wilderness"* (II Chronicles 1:3).

S olomon, the last king of a united Israel, began his reign in humble submission, saying that he was but a "little child" compared to the Lord's greatness. The young king and all the congregation offered sacrifices and worshiped the Lord.

In that night the Lord appeared to Solomon in a dream saying, *"Ask what I shall give thee"* (II Chronicles 1:7). In response, the Lord assured him of wisdom—an answer to his father David's prayer (I Chronicles 22:12).

Worship always prepares the heart to recognize its need of God's wisdom and His willingness to give it.

All wisdom is to be found *" . . . in Christ Jesus, who of God is made unto us wisdom . . . "* (I Corinthians 1:30), by His own presence dwelling within the Christian.

Christ can impart wisdom in Christians only as He is allowed to have control of their hearts and lives. Self-sufficient people do not have the capacity to pray for the wisdom of God. They refuse to recognize their human helplessness and do not exercise faith.

" . . . the Spirit also helpeth our infirmities: for we know not what we should pray for as we ought: but the Spirit itself maketh intercession for us with groanings which cannot be uttered" (Romans 8:26).

Thought for Today: God is willing to give us His wisdom; are we willing to humbly seek it?

Christ Revealed: By the thousand burnt offerings of Solomon (II Chronicles 1:6). We can be thankful that the one offering of Christ has now done away with the many individual offerings (Rom. 6:10; Heb. 10:10-12,14).

Word Studies: 2:2 **told out** means counted; assigned; **hew** means cut; 2:7 **cunning** means skillful; **can skill to grave** means is skillful in engraving; 2:14 **find out every device** means execute any design.

Prayer Needs: Country: Bolivia—7 million—in South America • Religious freedom • 92% Roman Catholic; 3% Protestant; 3% Baha'i.

MAY 22: Read II Chronicles 4 — 6

Highlights: Furnishings of the Temple; the ark brought into the Temple; the cloud of the Lord fills the Temple; Solomon's prayer of dedication.

Verses for Today: *"Thus all the work that Solomon made for the house of the Lord was finished. . . . There was nothing in the ark save the two tables which Moses put therein at Horeb . . . "* (II Chronicles 5:1,10).

E leven months were needed to prepare for the dedication of the Temple and moving the ark to its final resting place within the Holy of Holies. For the first time in more than four hundred years, the priests were permitted to lift the ancient lid and see the contents of the ark.

The priests, the king, and the people all sang praises to God, and the Temple was filled with His presence in the form of a cloud as the Lord came to guide His people. The Israelites were so grateful that they *"were as one . . . in praising and thanking the Lord . . . "* (II Chronicles 5:13).

Jesus gave the assurance that after His resurrection, *"the Spirit of truth . . . will guide you"* (John 16:13). How much more we, His redeemed people, should praise God for His indwelling presence!

"Giving thanks always for all things unto God and the Father in the name of our Lord Jesus Christ" (Ephesians 5:20).

Thought for Today: Are we so busy expecting recognition and praise from others that we fail to praise Him?

Christ Revealed: In the ark (II Chronicles 5). The ark was a type of Christ; as such, it was a token of the presence of God. The Christian's body is the "temple" of the Holy Spirit. Without the indwelling Spirit, our lives would have no eternal value.

Word Studies: 4:2: **sea** means large basin; 4:22 **censers** means incense burners; 6:28 **dearth** means famine.

Prayer Needs: Country: Martinique—345,000—one of the Windward Islands in the West Indies • Religious freedom • 95% Roman Catholic; 4% Protestant .

MAY 23: Read II Chronicles 7 — 9

Highlights: Fire consumes Solomon's sacrifices; glory of the Lord fills the Temple; God appears a second time to Solomon; Solomon's activities; queen of Sheba visits Solomon; Solomon's riches and fame; his death.

Verse for Today: *"And when the queen of Sheba heard of the fame of Solomon, she came to prove Solomon with hard questions at Jerusalem . . . "* (II Chronicles 9:1).

S olomon attracted the attention of world leaders, including the queen of Sheba, who came to him with *"hard questions."* The Scriptures do not tell us what questions she may have asked Solomon concerning the Lord he worshiped, or how she could receive His blessing. But Solomon's profound wisdom caused her to exclaim, *"The one half of the greatness of thy wisdom was not told me"* (II Chronicles 9:6).

When a person comes to the King of all kings—the Lord Jesus Christ—he comes to One who has riches and wisdom far above anything Solomon had. The wonders of His grace are beyond compare.

"Let the word of Christ dwell in you richly in all wisdom . . . " (Colossians 3:16).

Thought for Today: Those who come to Christ will never be disappointed in Him.

Christ Revealed: Through the glory of Solomon's kingdom (II Chronicles 9:1-28). Even though Solomon had a rich and glorious kingdom, it cannot compare to Christ's coming kingdom.

Word Studies: 8:5 **nether** means lower; 8:16 **perfected** means completed; 9:1 **prove** means test; 9:14 **chapmen** means traders; 9:18 **stays** means armrests.

Prayer Needs: Country: Afghanistan—14 million—in central Asia • A capital offense for a Muslim to accept Christ as Savior • 99.3% Muslim; 11,000 Christians.

MAY 24: Read II Chronicles 10 — 13

Highlights: Rehoboam succeeds Solomon; revolt of the 10 tribes; Jeroboam becomes king of Israel; Rehoboam fortifies Judah; Jeroboam rejects the worship of God; Shishak's invasion; death of Rehoboam; Abijah becomes king of Judah; death of Jeroboam.

Verse for Today: *"And King Rehoboam took counsel with the old men that had stood before Solomon his father while he yet lived, saying, What counsel give ye me to return answer to this people?"* (II Chronicles 10:6).

W hen Rehoboam became king, the united kingdom still held its great influence in the world, but there is no mention of Rehoboam's beginning his reign with altar sacrifices and prayer for divine wisdom, nor do we read that Rehoboam was anointed of the Lord. Therefore, it is not surprising to read that *"he prepared not his heart to seek the Lord"* (II Chronicles 12:14). Where was the spiritual influence that had existed 40 years earlier when Solomon began to reign? Nowhere do we find Solomon admonishing his son to remain true to the Lord as David, his father, had done for him. Where were the Nathans or priests who were prominent in David's reign? It is evident that the advice of godly prophets and spiritual advisors was no longer wanted.

How empty it all sounds to read that Rehoboam, the shepherd of God's people, *"took counsel . . . with men . . . saying, What counsel give ye me?"*

"Except the Lord build the house, they labor in vain that build it: except the Lord keep the city, the watchman waketh but in vain" (Psalm 127:1).

Thought for Today: Without God, the most clever strategy of the wisest counselors is worthless.

Christ Revealed: Through the gold candlestick (lampstand) (II Chronicles 13:11). Jesus is *"the light of the world"* (John 9:5).

Word Studies: 10:10 **loins** means waist; 11:15 **devils** means he-goats or satyrs; 13:21 **waxed** means became.

Prayer Needs: Country: Czechoslovakia—16 million—in central Europe • Repression and persecution of Christians • 69% Catholic; 9% Protestant; .8% Eastern Orthodox.

MAY 25: Read II Chronicles 14 — 17

Highlights: King Asa's reforms; his covenant with God; his treaty with Syria; Asa rebuked by Hanani; Jehoshaphat succeeds Asa.

Verse for Today: *" ... The Lord is with you, while ye be with him; ... but if ye forsake him, he will forsake you"* (II Chronicles 15:2).

H aving learned that the Lord would be with him, Asa led the nation in a great revival. His faith was put to the test when he was confronted with an invading army almost twice as large as his army. But Asa prayed, *" ... help us, O Lord ...for we rest on thee, and in thy name we go against this multitude ... "* (II Chronicles 14:11), and the victory was overwhelming

As Asa's wealth and power increased, his dependence on God decreased. When the small army of Israelites invaded Judah, he hired Ben-hadad to fight the battle for him instead of praying. No longer could he say to God, *"We rest on thee."*

Temptation to rely on our clever manipulations is as real today as it was for Asa. *" ... thou hast left thy first love ... repent"* (Revelation 2:4-5).

Thought for Today: Unless our confidence is in God, we are powerless against the attacks of Satan.

Christ Revealed: Through the rest that God gave Judah (II Chronicles 14:7). Those who have the peace of Christ have rest indeed (John 14:27).

Word Studies: 14:9 **Ethiopian** means Cushite; 15:16 **mother** means grandmother; **stamped it** means crushed it; 16:14 **sepulchers** means tomb; 17:12 **castles** means strongholds.

Prayer Needs: Country: Comoros—415,000—in the Mozambique Channel of the Indian Ocean • Limited religious freedom • 99.7% Muslim; .2% Christian.

MAY 26: Read II Chronicles 18 — 20

Highlights: Jehoshaphat's alliance with Ahab; Ahab's false prophets; Micaiah's true prophecy; defeat of Jehoshaphat; death of Ahab; Jehu rebukes Jehoshaphat; Judah invaded by the Moabites.

Verse for Today: *"O our God, wilt thou not judge them? for we have no might against this great company that cometh against us; neither know we what to do: but our eyes are upon thee"* (II Chronicles 20:12).

S urrounded by the vast combined armies of Moab, Ammon, and Mount Seir, Jehoshaphat called for a nationwide prayer meeting and proclaimed a fast throughout Judah.

The king stood in the midst of a great congregation in Jerusalem and began to pray. He confessed, *"We have no might against this great company that cometh against us; neither know we what to do: but our eyes are upon thee."* God responded to their prayer by saying, *"Ye shall not need to fight in this battle"* (II Chronicles 20:17). Even before the battle was won, Jehoshaphat began praising the Lord for the victory (20:21).

Jehoshaphat was not closing his eyes to the impending disaster, nor did he seek help from other nations. He was trusting God's wisdom.

If we commit ourselves in prayer to God's care, He will use everything that comes into our lives for our eternal good. So we can rest assured that every unfair treatment, every unkind word, and every thoughtless deed that comes our way is ultimately for our good.

"In every thing give thanks: for this is the will of God in Christ Jesus concerning you" (I Thessalonians 5:18).

Thought for Today: We can praise God; the victory is His.

Christ Portrayed: By Micaiah, who told the truth even though it was unpopular with his listeners (II Chronicles 18:12-27). We are reminded of Christ when He spoke an unpopular truth to the Pharisees (Matt. 12:1-14).

Word Studies: 18:1 **joined affinity** means he allied himself with Ahab by arranging the marriage of his son to Ahab's daughter; 18:15 **adjure** means warn; command; 18:33 **harness** means armor.

Prayer Needs: Country: Maldives—196,000—400 miles southwest of Sri Lanka • Christian witnessing is banned • 99.9% Muslims; .1% Christian.

MAY 27: Read II Chronicles 21 — 24

Highlights: Jehoram's wicked reign; prophecy of Elijah; Ahaziah's reign and death; Athaliah's reign and death; Joash becomes king; Joash repairs the Temple; death of Jehoiada the priest; the nation of Judah turns to idolatry.

Verse for Today: *"And Jehoiada made a covenant between him, and between all the people, and between the king, that they should be the Lord's people"* (II Chronicles 23:16).

T he wife of Jehoiada the priest hid baby Joash, the only surviving descendant in the royal line of David, thus protecting him from being murdered by Athaliah. In the seventh year of Athaliah's reign, Jehoiada anointed Joash king and had Athaliah executed. During Joash's adolescent years, Jehoiada was really the leader of the nation. As high priest, he restored the nation to the laws of God, repaired the Temple, and destroyed Baal worship.

With the exception of Samuel, history records no priest equal to Jehoiada. Under his influence, the people strictly obeyed God's Law, and the nation once again prospered. But after Jehoiada's death, Joash soon drifted away from *"the house of the Lord...and wrath came upon Judah and Jerusalem..."* (II Chronicles 24:18).

Neglecting the Word of God can cause the truth we once lived by to become blurred or forgotten, and we gradually cease doing God's will. Spiritual stability and strength are achieved by those who are willing to sacrifice everything necessary to remain faithful to His will.

"...I count all things but loss for the excellency of the knowledge of Christ Jesus my Lord . . . That I may know him, and the power of his resurrection, and the fellowship of his sufferings, being made conformable unto his death" (Philippians 3:8,10).

Thought for Today: Neglecting the Bible has caused many to lose their sense of spiritual direction.

Christ Portrayed: By Joash, who had to be saved from death (II Chronicles 22:10-12). Christ was hidden from Herod, who wanted to kill Him (Matt. 2:13-14).

Word Studies: 21:19 **of sore diseases** means in severe agony; **no burning for him** means no public mourning; 22:9 **keep still** means maintain rule; 22:10 **seed royal** means royal family; children of the king; 23:14 **Have her forth of the ranges** means bring her forth from inside the house of the Lord out into the open; 24:22 **father** means foster father.

Prayer Needs: Country: Albania—3 million—in southeastern Europe • An avowed atheistic nation. All those known to be Christians have been killed, imprisoned, or are in hiding • 18% Muslim; 3% Eastern Orthodox; 2% Roman Catholic.

MAY 28: Read II Chronicles 25 — 27

Highlights: Amaziah reigns over Judah; war between Israel and Judah; Uzziah stricken with leprosy; Jotham's reign.

Verses for Today: *"Wherefore the anger of the Lord was kindled against Amaziah, and he sent unto him a prophet, which said unto him, Why has thou sought after the gods of the people, which could not deliver their own people out of thine hand? . . . I know that God hath determined to destroy thee, because thou hast done this, and hath not harkened unto my counsel"* (II Chronicles 25:15-16).

F ollowing the murder of his father, Joash, Amaziah became king over Judah (II Kings 12:21), *"and he did that which was right in the sight of the Lord, but not with a perfect heart"* (II Chronicles 25:2). He worshiped the Lord but permitted the people to offer *"sacrifice and burnt incense on the high places"* (II Kings 14:4). The mixed motives in his life eventually destroyed him. There was nothing wrong with his plan to go to war against Edom, but when he hired 100,000 men from Israel to help him, it revealed his "imperfect heart" to fully trust in the Lord who alone *"hath power to help, and to cast down"* (II Chronicles 25:8). Warned by a man of God, Amaziah dismissed the Israelites and conquered Edom, but again his "imperfect heart" was revealed when he brought back the gods of the Edomites and bowed down to them.

There were many good things about Amazia, for he did many things that were *"right in the sight of the Lord."* However, the mixtures in his life brought the judgment of God upon him. In chapter 2 of the book of Revelation, our Lord said of the church at Thyatira: *"I know thy works, and charity [love], and service, and faith, and thy patience, and thy works . . . [but] I have few things against thee, because thou sufferest that woman Jezebel . . . to teach and to seduce my servants."* The works of this good church were enumerated and praised, but then there was a mixture—an attitude of tolerance toward those with different convictions that led to impurity and false worship. And then He added, *"He that hath an ear, let him hear what the Spirit saith unto the churches"* (see Revelation 2:17-29).

Thought for Today: We should serve the Lord with a *"perfect heart"*—not one mixed with worldly interests.

Christ Revealed: Through the one hundred talents of silver (II Chronicles 27:5).

Silver is symbolic of redemption (Ex. 38:27—the sockets of the Tabernacle were made from the redemption money of the Israelites). *Christ redeemed us from the curse of the Law* (see Gal. 3:13).

Word Studies: 25:21 **saw one another in the face** means faced each other in battle; 26:10 **husbandry** means farm management; 26:23 **buried him . . . in the field of the burial which belonged to the kings** means he was not buried in the royal tombs.

Prayer Needs: Country: New Caledonia and Dependencies—150,000—located about 750 miles east of Australia • Religious freedom • 72% Roman Catholic; 18% Protestant; 4% Muslim.

MAY 29: Read II Chronicles 28 — 30

Highlights: Ahaz's reign; Hezekiah's reign; Temple worship restored; Passover reinstituted; confessions made to God.

Verse for Today: *"Now it is in mine heart to make a covenant with the Lord God of Israel, that his fierce wrath may turn away from us"* (II Chronicles 29:10).

In the first month of Hezekiah's reign, he began the greatest religious reforms in Judah's history and did *"that which was good and right and truth before the Lord his God"* (II Chronicles 31:20).

He restored worship in the Temple, removed idolatry, and proclaimed a national Passover that exceeded all Passover observances since the time of Solomon. He sent special letters to the Northern Kingdom of Israel, inviting them to keep this Passover. Hezekiah feared neither the reaction of King Hoshea of Israel nor the Assyrian kingdom that dominated them.

Many from the Northern Kingdom scoffed, but some of them participated in that great Passover feast. This is the only record in 210 years of all 10 tribes returning to Jerusalem to worship God.

The importance we place on Christ—our Passover Lamb (I Corinthians 5:7)—determines what we do with our time and effort. Christ's command is clear: *"As my Father hath sent me, even so send I you"* (John 20:21)—into homes, factories, offices, and to all nations.

"Go ye therefore, and teach all nations . . . to observe all things whatsoever I have commanded you . . . " (Matthew 28:19-20).

Thought for Today: Tell someone today what great things the Lord has done for you.

Christ Revealed: In the Passover (II Chronicles 30:1-5,15). Jesus Christ becomes our Passover Lamb (I Cor. 5:7) when we trust Him as the Lamb of God who takes away sin (John 1:29,34,36).

Word Studies: 28:3 **Hinnom** was later called Gehenna, which Jesus compared to the place of eternal punishment; 29:16 **all the uncleanness** means everything that was ceremonially unclean or impure; 29:24 **reconciliation** means sin offering; 29:34 **flay** means skin; 30:22 **comfortably** means encouragingly.

Prayer Needs: Country: Vanuatu—150,000—a group of 12 large islands southwest of the Solomons in the southwestern Pacific • Religious freedom • 78% Protestant; 17% Roman Catholic; 4% cargo cults.

MAY 30: Read II Chronicles 31 — 33

Highlights: Hezekiah destroys idols; firstfruits and tithes; Assyria invades Judah; Hezekiah's death; Manasseh's reign; Amon's reign.

Verse for Today: *"And when he was in affliction, he besought the Lord his God, and humbled himself greatly before the God of his fathers"* (II Chronicles 33:12).

Much of King Manasseh's life was spent doing away with the spiritual reformation which his father, Hezekiah, had brought about. Manasseh became a fanatical idolator, thus bringing his country to ruin. Because of this, God allowed the king of Assyria to defeat Manasseh and take him bound to Babylon.

During his captivity, Manasseh repented; and for the first time, it is recorded that Manasseh prayed (II Chronicles 33:12-13). God heard his prayer, forgave his sin, and restored him to his throne in Jerusalem. In his remaining years, he attempted to make amends for his evil ways and turn the nation back to God.

When Manasseh, a very wicked king, repented of his sins, he became an amazing example of God's forgiving love.

The most discouraged, defeated Christian has the assurance that God shows great mercy to all who humbly turn to Him.

" . . . let us cleanse ourselves from all filthiness of the flesh and spirit, perfecting holiness in the fear of God" (II Corinthians 7:1).

Thought for Today: God in His mercy has provided a way for even the vilest sinner to be saved.

Christ Revealed: In the tithe of oxen and sheep (II Chronicles 31:6). The ox typifies Christ as the patient and enduring Servant (compare I Cor. 9:9-10; Heb. 12:2-3). Sheep typify Christ in unresisting surrender to death on the cross (Isa. 53:7; Acts 8:32-35).

Word Studies: 31:14 **oblations** means offerings; gifts; 31:16 **courses** means assigned tasks; divisions; 32:17 **rail on** means belittle; denounce; 32:27 **pleasant jewels** means costly and attractive vessels; 33:11 **fetters** means chains.

Prayer Needs: Country: Japan—122 million—off the eastern coast of Asia • Religious freedom • 57% Buddhist; 27% Shintoist and other Eastern religions; 3% Christian.

MAY 31: Read II Chronicles 34 — 36

Highlights: Josiah's reign; book of the Law found; Josiah celebrates the Passover; Josiah killed in battle; reign and dethronement of Jehoahaz; reigns of Jehoiakim, Jehoiachin, and Zedekiah; fall of Jerusalem; captivity of Judah; decree of Cyrus to rebuild the Temple.

Verses for Today: *" . . . forbear thee from meddling with God, who is with me, that he destroy thee not. Nevertheless Josiah would not turn his face from him. . . . And the archers shot at king Josiah . . . and he died . . . "* (II Chronicles 35:21-24).

The highest honor ever given to a king was given to Josiah: *"Like unto him was there no king before him, that turned to the Lord with all his heart . . . "* (II Kings 23:25).

During the reign of Josiah, Pharaoh Neco of Egypt wanted to pass through Palestine with his armies to join the Assyrians in a war against Nebuchadnezzar,

145

king of Babylon. The Egyptian king urged Josiah not to interfere, saying, *"Forbear thee from meddling with God, who is with me, that he destroy thee not"* (II Chronicles 35:21).

On this occasion, there is no record that Josiah sought counsel from the Lord or asked the godly prophet Jeremiah for advice. Instead, he tried to keep the Egyptian king from passing through his country. As a result, he was fatally wounded. Just three months after his death, the kingdom of Judah lost its political independence.

Had someone failed to pray for the godly, 39-year-old king? Oh, how vital it is to pray for those in authority and for those who are effectively being used by God! Pause now to pray for your pastor, for other spiritual leaders, and for our nation's leaders, that God will protect and guide them.

"I exhort therefore, that, first of all, supplications, prayers, intercessions, and giving of thanks, be made for all men; for kings, and for all that are in authority . . . " (I Timothy 2:1-2).

Thought for Today: Have you prayed today for those in authority?

Christ Revealed: Through the messengers of God who were rejected by the people (II Chronicles 36:15-16; compare Isa. 53:3; Mark 9:12).

Word Studies: 35:8 **small cattle** means sheep; 35:13 **sod** means boiled; 36:3 **put him down** means dethroned him; **condemned** means taxed; fined; 36:10 **brother** means uncle; 36:15 **betimes** means early.

Prayer Needs: Country: Equatorial Guinea—340,000—in western Africa • Freedom for churches at this time • 71% Roman Catholic; 19% ancestral spirit worship and medicine men; 6% Protestant.

PRAYERS IN THIS MONTH'S READING

EZRA

Because of the sins of the Israelites, the prophet Jeremiah had foretold: *This whole land will be left in ruins, and its people will serve the king of Babylon seventy years. . . . For thus saith the Lord, After you have been captives for seventy years, I will visit you and keep My promise to bring you back home* (see Jeremiah 25:11; 29:10; compare II Chronicles 36:22-23; Ezra 1:1-3).

In fulfillment of prophecy, King Jehoiakim of Judah was conquered by Nebuchadnezzar, who began deporting the people to Babylon. Twenty years later, Jerusalem was defeated; the Temple was destroyed; and most of the Israelites who remained were taken to Babylon.

Eventually, the Medes and Persians, in a joint effort, conquered Babylon and made it part of the Persian Empire.

The book of Ezra tells of the small number of devout exiles who had the courage to return to Jerusalem after King Cyrus of Persia encouraged the Jews to *"build the house of the Lord God of Israel"* (1:3). The first expedition to Jerusalem (chapters 1—2), made up of 42,360 Jews and 7,337 servants (2:64-65), was led by Zerubbabel, the grandson of King Jeconiah (Jehoiachin) (I Chronicles 3:17-19).

Upon arriving in Jerusalem, they built an altar and observed the Feast of Booths (Tabernacles). In two years' time, they had completed only the foundation of the Temple (Ezra 3—4). During this time, they faced fierce opposition from the Samaritans, who finally succeeded in obtaining a decree to stop the work (4:21).

About 14 years later, through the preaching of God's Word as recorded in the books of Haggai and Zechariah, they once again *"began to build the house of God"* (5:1-2) and completed it in four years, in spite of intense opposition (chapters 5—6).

Between chapters 6 and 7, there is an interval of about 60 years. During this time the events recorded in the book of Esther took place, as well as the deaths of Zerubbabel and Haggai, and possibly Zechariah.

About 80 years after Zerubbabel's expedition, Ezra led about 1,800 Jewish men (plus women and children, totaling about 5,000 people) from the Persian capital to Jerusalem (chapters 7—8). When he arrived, he discovered that the Law of God was being neglected and that many of the Israelites had intermarried with people from heathen nations. Ezra immediately set about to correct these evils and went on to lead the people to a renewal of true worship (chapters 9—10).

JUNE 1: Read Ezra 1 — 2

Highlights: Cyrus' proclamation to rebuild the Temple; list of the Jews who returned from captivity.

Verses for Today: *"Thus saith Cyrus king of Persia, The Lord God of heaven*

... hath charged me to build him a house at Jerusalem, which is in Judah. Who is there among you of all his people? his God be with him, and let him go up to Jerusalem ... " (Ezra 1:2-3).

T he Lord *"stirred up the spirit"* of the famous Persian king, Cyrus, and caused him to make a decree that would allow the Israelites to return to Jerusalem and rebuild the Temple (see Ezra 1:1-3).

Most of the new generation of Israelites had no desire to leave Babylon—symbolic of the world's system of things—nor any vision to rebuild the Temple in the old, ruined city of Jerusalem more than 500 miles away. In fact, they were enjoying the luxuries, freedom, and prosperity of the new Persian Empire. Only a few whose hearts God had moved (1:5) were willing to hazard the long and difficult four-month journey on foot, sacrifice all the social and material pleasures in Babylon, and return with Zerubbabel to the place where they could truly worship God.

The majority of Christians today are involved with and motivated by worldly possessions and pleasures. Only a few seek to please the Lord above all else.

Just as an Israelite could not fulfill God's will for his life while remaining in Babylon, the Christian cannot please the Lord or experience true satisfaction until he turns his back on his "Babylons" and desires above all else to allow Christ to guide his life.

It is God who, in His kindness, works in you, making you willing and able to do His will (see Philippians 2:13).

Thought for Today: How much are *you* willing to give up to please the Lord?

Christ Portrayed: By Sheshbazzar, the prince (governor) of Judah (Ezra 1:8). Christ is both the Prince of Peace (Isa. 9:6) and the Lion of the tribe of Judah (Rev. 5:5).

Word Studies: 1:11 **Babylon** is the same as Chaldea (Dan. 5:30); 2:40 **Hodaviah** is also called Judah; 2:42 **porters** means gatekeepers; doorkeepers.

Prayer Needs: Country: Barbados—324,000—on the island farthest east in the West Indies • Religious freedom • 85% Protestant; 6% Roman Catholic; .1% Eastern Orthodox.

JUNE 2: Read Ezra 3 — 5

Highlights: Restoration of the altar and worship; rebuilding of the Temple begun; adversaries stop the work; work resumed; Tattenai writes to Darius.

Verses for Today: *" ... And all the people shouted with a great shout, when they praised the Lord, because the foundation of the house of the Lord was laid. But many of the priests ... who were ancient men, that had seen the first house ... wept with a loud voice ... "* (Ezra 3:11-12).

W hen Zerubbabel and the returning Jews left the pleasures and prosperity of Persia for the hardships of Jerusalem, they could have assumed that the first thing to do was build their own homes. But instead, they *"builded the altar of the God of Israel, to offer burnt offerings thereon, as it is written in the law of Moses ... "* (Ezra 3:2). The burnt offering sacrifices were not mere religious rituals, for these Jews had sacrificed everything in Persia in order to restore fellowship with God in Jerusalem.

This was only the beginning of a slow, day-by-day, difficult task of laying the foundation of the Temple, which brought fierce opposition.

Just deciding to serve the Lord and do His work does not guarantee a life of ease and freedom from problems. To the contrary! Once Satan sees that we have set our hearts on pleasing the Lord, he will use everything and everyone in his power to keep us from the task we have set out to accomplish. His purpose is to divert the attention of God's children from the Word of God and prayer—the Christian's weapons in the spiritual warfare against his attacks.

So let us purpose in our hearts to finish the work the Lord has called us to do. He has not called anyone else to do it for us.

" . . . *No man, having put his hand to the plough, and looking back, is fit for the kingdom of God"* (Luke 9:62).

Thought for Today: Each Christian is individually responsible for accomplishing what God has for him to do.

Christ Revealed: Through the huge stones used in building the Temple of God (Ezra 5:8). Christ is the Stone which the builders rejected, but He has become the chief Cornerstone (Psa. 118:22; Matt. 21:42).

Word Studies: 4:1 **adversaries** means enemies; 4:7 **Syrian** means Aramaic; 4:14 **certified** means informed; made known to.

Prayer Needs: Country: North Yemen—7 million—in southwestern Arabia • Attempts to convert Muslims to Christ are fiercely opposed • Approximately 100% Muslim.

JUNE 3:   Read Ezra 6 — 7

Highlights: Darius' decree to complete the Temple; dedication of the Temple; Passover restored; Ezra goes to Jerusalem; Artaxerxes' favorable commission to Ezra.

Verse for Today: *"And this house was finished on the third day of the month Adar . . . "* (Ezra 6:15).

T he building of the Temple had been at a standstill of 14 years, but once God's Word and authority were recognized, the people *"began to build the house of God"* (Ezra 5:2). What caused this revival? Their circumstances had not changed, and there was the same intense opposition and determination by the enemy to cause the work to cease. But this time, they were strengthened by the power of God's Word, and the enemy *"could not cause them to cease."* (Compare 4:4-5,23; 5:3-5.)

The key to their overcoming the opposition and gaining power to complete the Temple is clearly stated: *"They prospered through the prophesying of Haggai the prophet and Zechariah . . . "* (6:14).

God's work can only be sustained and strengthened through obedience to His Word, the foundation of our Christian life—one power that Satan cannot overcome. God's Word is the source of strength by which God's children cannot be defeated.

Many of God's people make little or no spiritual progress year after year, perhaps because they neglect, and consequently disobey, the Word of God!

" . . . *desire the sincere milk of the word, that ye may grow thereby"* (I Peter 2:2).

Thought for Today: Obedience is characteristic of a life of faith.

Christ Revealed: Through the Feast of Unleavened Bread (Ezra 6:22). Jesus said, *"I am the bread of life"* (John 6:35).

Prayer Needs: Country: Haiti—6 million—in the West Indies • Religious freedom • 75% Roman Catholic; 17% Protestant.

JUNE 4: Read Ezra 8 — 9

Highlights: Genealogy of Ezra's companions; Ezra proclaims a fast; treasures delivered to the priests; Ezra's prayer and confession.

Verses for Today: *" . . . I am ashamed . . . for we have forsaken thy commandments"* (Ezra 9:6,10).

E zra, the priest, not only prepared his own heart to seek the law of God, but he also wanted all of God's people to know God's will. His purpose for going to Jerusalem was *"to teach in Israel statutes and judgments"* (Ezra 7:10).

Four months after leaving Babylon, Ezra and his 1,800 followers completed the more than 500-mile journey and arrived in the Holy City.

Fifty-seven years before their arrival, Haggai and Zechariah had inspired the nation *"to seek the Lord God of Israel"* (6:21). But since that time, there had been no prophets to teach God's commandments to the new generation.

Ezra was heartbroken over the low moral and spiritual condition that prevailed among the inhabitants of Jerusalem. But when he read and taught the Scriptures to them, there was a great, sweeping revival (see Ezra 10:12-44).

Today the Holy Spirit indwells every believer, and we should pray that He will guide us *"into all truth"* (John 16:13).

"Thy word is a lamp unto my feet, and a light unto my path" (Psalm 119:105).

Thought for Today: Only the humble will yield to the Holy Spirit and follow His leading.

Christ Revealed: Through the burnt offerings (Ezra 8:35). The burnt offering typifies Christ as He offered Himself without spot to God, delighting to do His Father's will (see Heb. 10:10-12).

Word Studies: 8:21 **afflict** means to humble 9:3 **mantle** means robe; 9:12 **wealth** means welfare; prosperity.

Prayer Needs: Country: Channel Islands—140,000—off the northwestern coast of France • Religious freedom • 76% Protestant; 18% Roman Catholic; .2% Eastern Orthodox.

JUNE 5: Read Ezra 10

Highlight: Foreign wives and children.

Verse for Today: *"And Ezra the priest stood up, and said unto them, Ye have transgressed, and have taken strange wives, to increase the trespass of Israel"* (Ezra 10:10).

W hen Ezra and his followers arrived in Jerusalem, he was grief-stricken at the low moral and spiritual condition that had developed in such a brief period.

It had only been about 60 years since the preaching of God's Word by Haggai and Zechariah had inspired the nation to rebuild the house of God (Ezra 6:14-16).

Even some of the priests and rulers of the people had intermarried with the idol-worshiping Canaanites—one of the things that had previously led to their captivity. (See Deuteronomy 7:3-4.)

Ezra's great sorrow over their sins drove him to intense prayer, *"weeping and casting himself down"* (Ezra 10:1). As the Israelites were reminded of God's Word, the Lord brought conviction to their hearts. The people had to put away their heathen, idol-worshiping wives in order for *"the fierce wrath"* of God to be turned from them (10:14).

What heartbreak and tears are brought about because of disobedience to God! The price of sin is high—much higher than anyone suspects!

Those who sow wheat, reap wheat; but those who sow tares, never reap wheat. It is the law of nature. Those who sow to the flesh walk *"after the flesh"* (Romans 8:4). They have their hearts set on *"earthly things"* and make themselves available as *"instruments of unrighteousness"* (Romans 6:13; Philippians 3:19).

Only to the extent that our actions and motives are in harmony with God's Word can we expect Him to bless us.

When you admit your sins to God, He is ready and willing to forgive you of your sins, and through His Word, strengthen you to live to please Him.

"Be not deceived; God is not mocked: for whatsoever a man soweth, that shall he also reap" (Galatians 6:7).

Thought for Today: When we go against God's will, we cheat ourselves.

Christ Revealed: Through the ram (male sheep) offered for the offenses of the sons of the priests (Ezra 10:19). Christ offered Himself for the sins and offenses of mankind (Heb. 7:27).

Word Study: 10:18 **strange** means non-Jewish, foreign women.

Prayer Needs: Country: Greece—10 million—in southeastern Europe • Government restrictions on witnessing to others about Christ • 97% Greek Orthodox (2% are churchgoers); 2% Muslim; .4% Roman Catholic; .1% Protestant.

NEHEMIAH _____

Nehemiah, a Jew, held the honored position of cupbearer to Artaxerxes, king of the powerful Persian Empire.

About 14 years after Ezra led 1,800 Jewish men (plus women and children, totaling about 5,000 people) to Jerusalem, Nehemiah received a report of the spiritual and physical poverty that existed there. Heartbroken, Nehemiah mourned for several days, fasting and praying (1:4). The result was that the Persian king granted him a leave of absence, appointed him governor of Jerusalem, and gave him permission to rebuild the walls surrounding the city (chapters 1—2). For more than 100 years—since Nebuchadnezzar had invaded and destroyed the city—it had seemed impossible to restore the walls of Jerusalem (II Kings 25:8-11).

Nehemiah faced intense opposition from surrounding enemies of Jerusalem. Some of the leading citizens even refused to cooperate with him (Nehemiah 2:19; 3:5; 4:1-11). But with continued prayer and faith in God, Nehemiah led the people to complete the walls in a remarkably short time—just 52 days (chapters 3—7).

After the walls were completed, Ezra *"opened the book"* (8:5) and read the Scriptures from early morning until noon. The next day the leaders came to Ezra for more insight. This led to the celebration of the Feast of Tabernacles (Booths). *And Ezra read from the Book of the Law of God daily, from the first day to the last day. And they celebrated the feast seven days* (see 8:18). This resulted in much prayer, confession, fasting, and a renewed covenant with God (chapters 8—11). The walls were then dedicated by Ezra and Nehemiah (chapter 12).

Following this, Nehemiah continued as governor of Jerusalem and brought about reforms in several areas. Then there was an interval of about 12 years, during which Nehemiah probably returned to the Persian court.

During Nehemiah's absence from Jerusalem, many evils gained acceptance, such as Eliashib's alliance with Tobiah, failure of the people to support the Levites, breaking of the sabbath, and intermarriage with the heathen. However, when Nehemiah returned, he once again turned the nation from these evils and reestablished true worship (chapter 13).

JUNE 6: Read Nehemiah 1 — 3

Highlights: Nehemiah's prayer for Jerusalem; Nehemiah permitted to go to Jerusalem; Nehemiah inspects Jerusalem's walls; the builders of the walls.

Verses for Today: *"When Sanballat the Horonite, and Tobiah the servant, the Ammonite, heard of it, it grieved them exceedingly that there was come a man to seek the welfare of the children of Israel. . . . they laughed us to scorn, and despised us, and said, What is this thing that ye do? will ye rebel against the king? Then answered I them . . . The God of heaven, he will prosper us; therefore we his servants will arise and build: but ye have no portion, nor right, nor memorial, in Jerusalem"* (Nehemiah 2:10,19-20).

E xpressing mockery, Sanballat and his followers asked, *"What is this thing that ye do?"* The persecution then turned to slander: *"Will ye rebel against the king?"* Scoffing and implying evil motives have always been favorite tools of Satan to hinder the Lord's work.

Any ministry initiated of God will suffer satanic opposition. Ahab accused Elijah of troubling Israel (I Kings 18). Daniel was accused of disobedience and was consigned to the lion's den (Daniel 6). Christ was accused and executed as a malefactor (John 18).

Our Lord said, *"It is enough for the disciple that he be as his master, and the servant as his lord. If they have called the master of the house Beelzebub, how much more shall they call them of his household?"* (Matthew 10:25). It is not surprising to hear rumors of scandal and vicious ridicule against a man, ministry, or church that is effectively being used of God.

As the buildings of Jerusalem had many enemies, so the ministry of the gospel has many "formidable" enemies. How deliverance shall come we must leave to God who provides for the sparrow and will provide sufficient grace for His servants. Since *"the king's heart is in the hand of the Lord, as the rivers of water: he turneth it whithersoever he will"* (Proverbs 21:1), then you can be sure what God initiates, He completes.

"Commit thy way unto the Lord; trust also in him; and he shall bring it to pass" (Psalm 37:5).

Thought for Today: Be an expression of God's love, peace, and joy even when you face opposition.

Christ Revealed: Through Nehemiah's prayer for his people (Nehemiah 1:4-11). Christ also prayed for His own (John 17).

Word Studies: 1:1 **Chisleu** was about the same as our December, but covered some of November; 2:1 **Nisan** was about the same as our April.

Prayer Needs: Country: Seychelles—68,000—a group of islands in the Indian Ocean between Madagascar and India • Religious freedom • 89% Roman Catholic; 8% Protestant.

JUNE 7: Read Nehemiah 4 — 6

Highlights: Builders opposed and ridiculed; Nehemiah's prayer; weapons for the workers; evils corrected; plots of adversaries; walls completed.

Verse for Today: *" . . . our God shall fight for us"* (Nehemiah 4:20).

S anballat had done all he could through ridicule, trickery, and flattery. He finally resorted to openly accusing the Jews of rebelling against Persia. He made every effort to distract Nehemiah, asking often for an opportunity to discuss the situation. But his intentions were only to do evil, and Nehemiah replied: *" . . . I am doing a great work, so that I cannot come down: why should the work cease, whilst I leave it, and come down to you?"* (Nehemiah 6:3).

For more than 100 years it had seemed impossible to restore the walls, but in just 52 days, Nehemiah and his few organized workers rebuilt them. This seems incredible compared to the highly skilled laborers David used in building the first walls. This again reinforces our faith that *"With men this is impossible; but with God all things are possible"* (Matthew 19:26).

Nehemiah did not depend on *human* strategy, power, or ability. His eyes were upon the Lord as he said, *"The God of heaven, he will prosper us . . .* (Nehemiah 2:20). *"So the wall was finished . . . "* (6:15).

True obedience comes as a result of continual fellowship with God. The fellowship that Christ had with the Father was so complete and real that Christ lived in full dependence upon the Father, saying, *"The Son can do nothing of himself"* (John 5:19). This is what Nehemiah was acknowledging when he said, *"Our God shall fight for us."*

We can do all things through Christ who strengthens us (see Philippians 4:13).

Thought for Today: When we are weak in human strength, then we can rely on God's all-sufficient strength.

153

Christ Portrayed: By Nehemiah, who bought back the Jews who had been sold to the heathens as slaves (Nehemiah 5:8). Christ redeemed us when we were enslaved by sin (Rom. 7:14; I Pet. 1:18-19).

Word Studies: 5:3 **dearth** means famine; 5:7 **usury** means interest.

Prayer Needs: Country: Belgium—10 million—in northwestern Europe • Religious freedom • 88% Roman Catholic; 1% Muslim; .5% Protestant.

JUNE 8: Read Nehemiah 7 — 8

Highlights: Nehemiah's appointment of leaders; genealogy of returned exiles; Scriptures read and explained; the Feast of Tabernacles (Booths) observed.

Verses for Today: "... *For all the people wept, when they heard the words of the law. Then he said unto them ... neither be ye sorry; for the joy of the Lord is your strength*" (Nehemiah 8:9-10).

U nder the leadership of Zerubbabel, Ezra, and Nehemiah, the people had the privilege of restoring the altar, the Temple, and finally the gates and walls of Jerusalem. It appeared that everything had been completed. But God's ultimate purpose for His people was more than the restoration of buildings and city walls. These things were meaningless unless the people obeyed His Word.

All of the Law of God had not been read to the people since their return from Babylon. Without God's direction through His Word, all of their efforts would be in vain. Previous failures were a testimony of incomplete obedience to His Word.

When Ezra read from the book of the Law, explaining the Scriptures day after day, a marvelous revival took place. This was followed by great joy (Nehemiah 8: 1-12).

Once sin is confessed, God forgives and cleanses us from all unrighteousness. This is why Ezra told the people not to grieve any longer over past sins, saying, *"The joy of the Lord is your strength."* Since the Lord has accepted us, we can accept ourselves as well as others. This guilt-free conscience is one of the greatest blessings a Christian can possess—physically, mentally, emotionally, and spiritually.

"If we confess our sins, he is faithful and just to forgive us our sins, and to cleanse us from all unrighteousness" (I John 1:9).

Thought for Today: Confession of sin has no value unless we are willing to forsake the sin.

Christ Revealed: Through the register of names required for priestly service (Nehemiah 7:64). We must be sure our names are written in the Lamb's Book of Life and then make every effort to see that our loved ones and friends are also included (Rev. 20:12,15; see also Luke 10:17-20).

Prayer Needs: Country: Malta—362,000—about 60 miles south of Sicily • Religious freedom • 97% Roman Catholic; 2% Protestant.

JUNE 9: Read Nehemiah 9 — 10

Highlights: Fasting and confession of sins; the reading of the Law; confession of God's goodness; covenant to keep the Law.

Verse for Today: *"Thou gavest also thy good spirit to instruct them, and withheldest not thy manna from their mouth, and gavest them water for their thirst"* (Nehemiah 9:20).

L istening carefully as Ezra read to them from the Book of the Law, the Israelites realized they had not been living according to God's commandments. Humbly, the children of Israel *"assembled with fasting"* (Nehemiah 9:1), resulting in a spontaneous outpouring of confession, praise, and worship.

In reviewing the history of God's dealings with the Israelites in the wilderness, the priests revealed that God had provided His *"good spirit"* to instruct His people. This is a remarkable statement in the Old Testament, revealing the Holy Spirit teaching His people. (See also Isaiah 63:10.) The children of Israel in the wilderness could *see* the manna and *drink* of the miraculous flow of water in the desert, but there was little concern that God had given His Holy Spirit to instruct them.

One of the greatest needs in the Christian world today is for God's people to take a new look at the importance of having a right relationship with Him—a must, if the Holy Spirit is to teach and guide us.

" . . . we speak, not in the words which man's wisdom teacheth, but which the Holy Ghost teacheth . . . . " (I Corinthians 2:13).

Thought for Today: Only to the extent that we truly desire to please the Lord, will the Holy Spirit reveal His will.

Christ Revealed: As the Creator (Nehemiah 9:6). *For by Him all things were created* (see Col. 1:16).

Prayer Needs: Country: Turkey—53 million—in Asia Minor and southeastern Europe • Deep-seated official resistance to Christian witnessing • 99+% Muslim; .5% Christian.

JUNE 10: Read Nehemiah 11 — 12

Highlights: Residents of Jerusalem; priests and Levites with Zerubbabel; dedication of the walls; Temple offices restored.

Verse for Today: *"And the people blessed all the men, that willingly offered themselves to dwell at Jerusalem"* (Nehemiah 11:2).

J erusalem is the city that God chose as the center of sacrifice and worship. It is known as the city of God—the Holy City.

Before the return of the exiles, the buildings of Jerusalem were in ruins and the city was filled with rubbish—a testimony of Israel's disobedience to God's Word.

The completion and dedication of the walls surrounding this sacred place were made possible because ordinary people denied personal interests, left Babylon, and journeyed to Jerusalem. Even though they were not skilled in building walls, they willingly went to work and did the best they could.

After the walls were completed, only a few *"offered themselves"* to dwell inside the walls of Jerusalem, willing to sacrifice personal interests in order to strengthen the city of God.

Even today there are only a few who do not put a limit on how much they are "willing" to give of their lives—giving up personal benefits to serve the Lord.

"Because for the work of Christ he was nigh unto death, not regarding his life, to supply your lack of service toward me" (Philippians 2:30).

Thought for Today: No one who has willingly given up personal pleasures in order to do God's will has ever been cheated out of life's best.

Christ Revealed: Through the people as they blessed the men who volunteered to live in Jerusalem (Nehemiah 11:2). We are blessed when we abide in Christ and His words abide in us (John 15:7).

Word Study: 12:44 **that waited** means who served faithfully.

Prayer Needs: Country: Australia—16 million—an island continent between the Indian and Pacific Oceans • Religious freedom • 49% Protestant; 30% Roman Catholic; 3% Eastern Orthodox.

JUNE 11: Read Nehemiah 13

Highlights: Reading of the Law; separation from the heathen; tithes given; sabbath-breaking forbidden; mixed marriages condemned.

Verse for Today: *"Now it came to pass, when they had heard the law, that they separated from Israel all the mixed multitude"* (Nehemiah 13:3).

O ver the years, the Israelites had become slack in obeying God's commandments. But when the Word of God was read, they realized that a lot of changes in their lifestyle had to be made.

When Nehemiah returned to Jerusalem, he was shocked at the low moral and spiritual condition that existed in the nation. They were even allowing Tobiah—the very man who had tried to hinder the work many years earlier—to live in the house of God!

Nehemiah immediately threw Tobiah's things out of the house of God and ordered him to leave. As God's ordained leader, Nehemiah promptly set about to clean out the house of God and restore the Levites to the priesthood. No one could discourage him from doing what was right, for he knew where he stood with God and didn't care what anyone thought.

Most Christians who are truly concerned about getting the job done for Christ are not usually very popular with the world. However, there are many who seem to believe they can live like the world, act like the world, and talk like the world and still be a godly witness for Christ; but God is not interested in mixed multitudes. He cannot bless us as long as there is a mixture in our lives. If we are to be used as vessels to dispense His food—His Word—to the world, our lives must be clean—*"holy, acceptable unto God"* (Romans 12:1).

"Every man that hath this hope in him purifieth himself, even as he is pure" (I John 3:3).

Thought for Today: Fear of ridicule and loss of popularity keep many people from doing God's will.

Christ Revealed: Through Nehemiah's discovery that the Levites had not been receiving their tithes and were having to work in the fields (Nehemiah 13:10). We are reminded of Christ's words when He commissioned 70 of His followers: *Stay in that house, eating and drinking what they give you: for the laborer is worthy of his wages* (see Luke 10:7).

ESTHER

The book of Esther is the last of the historical books in the Old Testament. It comprises about 12 years' history of the Jews who remained in Persia after the 70 years of captivity. Most of these Jews were born in captivity and therefore had no loyalty to Jerusalem. They may not have realized the importance of the prophetic destiny of the Jewish race.

The events of this book probably occurred about 40 years after the Temple was rebuilt and about 30 years before the walls of Jersualem were rebuilt. Esther may have made it possible for Nehemiah to accomplish his work in Jerusalem.

The purpose of the book of Esther is to show the overruling power of the unseen God and His willingness to protect His people in answer to prayer—how He had the right person in the right place at the right time.

The events in this book did not happen by accident, for we see in Esther 4:16 that fasting—which would include prayer—had a part in bringing about God's plan.

JUNE 12: Read Esther 1 — 3

Highlights: Vashti removed as queen; Esther made queen; Mordecai saves the king's life; Haman's plan to destroy all the Jews.

Verse for Today: *"And the letters were sent by posts into all the king's provinces, to destroy, to kill, and to cause to perish, all Jews, both young and old, little children and women, in one day, even upon the thirteenth day of the twelfth month, which is the month Adar, and to take the spoil of them for a prey"* (Esther 3:13).

W hen the Persians defeated King Nebuchadnezzar and the Babylonian empire, all the Jews were urged to return to Jerusalem. They had lived in Babylon for 50 years, so most of them had never seen Jerusalem because they were descendants of those who had been taken to Babylon as captives. Since they were now free from Babylonian slavery, most of them preferred to remain in the friendly, prosperous atmosphere of the Persian kingdom rather than leave Babylon and return to Jerusalem, as God has said they should.

Perhaps another 50 years had passed before Haman's decree to destroy all the Jews.

It is no surprise then that in the book of Esther there is no direct mention of God, prayer, or the Scriptures. When we refuse to obey God's Word, our prayers and Bible reading become mere ritual, and God seems far removed from our daily experiences.

" . . . Come out of her, my people, that ye be not partakers of her sins. . . . Standing afar off for the fear of her torment, saying, Alas, alas, that great city Babylon . . . for in one hour is thy judgment come" (Revelation 18:4,10).

157

Thought for Today: When we are obedient to God's Word, our Bible reading becomes a sweet time of fellowship with Him.

Christ Revealed: Through Esther's name, which means "star." Jesus is also called the bright and morning star (Rev. 22:16).

Word Study: 3:15 **posts** means special messengers.

Prayer Needs: Country: United States—243 million—in North America • Religious freedom • 51% Protestant; 22% Roman Catholic; 4% cults; 3% Jewish; 2% Eastern Orthodox; 1% Muslim; 17% other religions.

JUNE 13: Read Esther 4 — 7

Highlights: Fasting among the Jews; Esther's banquet for Haman and the king; Haman forced to honor Mordecai; Haman executed.

Verse for Today: *" . . . and so will I go in unto the king, which is not according to the law: and if I perish, I perish"* (Esther 4:16).

H aman had issued a decree to have all Jews executed (Esther 3:9-13). When this was made known, Mordecai and Queen Esther (both Jews) prayed and fasted. Mordecai told Esther that she must go to the king and ask him to spare her people.

The risk was real, for the king had a law that said no one could enter his presence unless he called for them. To make Esther's situation even more serious, she had not been called to see the king for 30 days. If the king had lost interest in Esther, how could she hope to influence him for the condemned Jewish race?

With the words, *"If I perish, I perish,"* Queen Esther stood in the inner court of the king's palace, waiting to see if she would face life or death from the monarch who ruled the Persian Empire. She was willing to give up everything—even her own life, if necessary—for what she knew to be the will of God for her people.

Not only did the king accept her, but he also offered her *"half of the kingdom"* (5:3,6; 7:2). Esther could have clutched her prize, considering it far too precious to risk losing by mentioning her request to the king. But saving the lives of her people meant more to her than riches.

The attitude of most people is to firmly hold on to their rights and possessions. But the way to gain the most for our lives, our children, or our spouses is to commit them to God. By clutching anything too tightly, we can squeeze the life out of it. Both love and life are choked, strangled, and smothered by selfishness and jealousy.

"For whosoever will save his life shall lose it; but whosoever shall lose his life for my sake and the gospel's, the same shall save it" (Mark 8:35).

Thought for Today: God never asks us to do anything He doesn't supply the strength to accomplish.

Christ Revealed: In the honor shown to Mordecai as he was led through the streets (Esther 6:10-11). Jesus was greatly honored in His triumphal entry into Jerusalem (Matt. 21:8-9).

Prayer Needs: Country: Nicaragua—3 million—in Central America • Limited religious freedom is being repressed • 95% Roman Catholic; 5% Protestant.

Highlights: Esther's plea to reverse Haman's decree; enemies of the Jews destroyed; Feast of Purim instituted; Mordecai promoted to great honor.

Verses for Today: *"Because Haman ... the enemy of all the Jews, had devised against the Jews to destroy them, and had cast Pur, that is, the lot, to consume them, and to destroy them ... wherefore they called these days Purim after the name of Pur"* (Esther 9:24,26).

H aman appeared to be invincible, and his decree to execute all the Jews seemed final. The law had been established, and the decree had been approved by the Persian king; and under the law of the Medes and Persians, a decree could not be altered.

Haman's astrologers *"had cast Pur"* (meaning, "had cast lots") to determine the most favorable time for the execution of all Jews. Haman's "lucky day" fell on the thirteenth day of the last month. The divine principle which Haman did not realize was, *"The lot is cast into the lap; but the whole disposing thereof is of the Lord"* (Proverbs 16:33).

The determined day of execution, known as Purim, was turned from death to deliverance, and the Jews have celebrated it each year for centuries.

The Feast of Purim is a testimony to the fact that what seems to be chance and good luck is really the work of the Almighty Controller of world affairs.

How tragic that in later years when Christ, their Messiah, came to bring them a far greater deliverance, they failed to recognize Him!

The judgment of death has passed upon all men, for all have sinned. By accepting Christ as our Savior, we receive deliverance from sin and death, and are granted eternal life.

"For God so loved the world, that he gave his only begotten Son ... that the world through him might be saved" (John 3:16-17).

Thought for Today: No sin works more deceitfully than the sin of pride.

Christ Revealed: By Mordecai's exaltation from servant to a position of honor and glory (Esther 8:2,15). Christ came to earth as a servant and was exalted to the right hand of God (Phil. 2:7-9; Mark 16:19).

Word Study: 9:19 **portions** means gifts of food.

Prayer Needs: Country: Scotland—6 million—north of England and part of the United Kingdom • Religious freedom • 73% Protestant; 16% Roman Catholic.

JOB

This book opens with a brief history about a man named Job. He was godly and very prosperous—*the greatest man among all the people of the East. . . . he was blameless and upright* (see 1:3; 2:3). In the first two chapters, we read of Satan's accusations against Job and the incredible ordeal God permitted Job to experience.

In the book of Job, we see the reasonings of God, Satan, Job, his wife, his three friends, and Elihu. As you read through each chapter, carefully distinguish between the wisdom of Job and the well-meaning, but inaccurate and misleading, arguments of Job's friends (chapters 3—37). God highly complimented Job for having spoken the truth. God said Job's friends had not spoken the truth about Him the way His servant Job had (see 42:7; compare 1:1,8).

The speeches of Job's friends reveal the fallacy of human reasoning unless it is guided by the Scriptures.

In the final chapters (38—42), God reveals His wisdom and once again acknowledges Job's righteousness.

The book of Job clearly reveals that it is not important for us to know why we suffer, but it is important that we maintain a steadfast trust in God.

Through the fierce trials and sufferings of Job, his faith, love, and loyalty to God were strengthened; and he was brought to a deeper revelation of God's wisdom. Although God never revealed to Job the reason for his tragedies, Job believed that God, who created all things, was in control of all things.

JUNE 15:   Read Job 1 — 4

Highlights: Job's wealth and godliness; Satan permitted to afflict Job; condemnation by Job's wife; Job visited by his three friends; Job tells of his misery and despair; Eliphaz rebukes Job.

Verse for Today: *"Again there was a day when the sons of God came to present themselves before the Lord, and Satan came also among them to present himself before the Lord"* (Job 2:1).

We are startled to find Satan in the presence of the Lord. (See Job 1:6-12; 2: 1-7.) He was there to slander and accuse *"a perfect and an upright man, one that feareth God, and escheweth evil"* (see Job 1:1,8; 2:3).

Satan, *"the accuser of our brethren"* (Revelation 12:10), later used Job's "friends" to talk down, belittle, and discourage him.

Who can understand the heartache and sorrow of Job—the servant of the Lord who was stripped of family, possessions, and health? This suffering was not a misfortune or bad luck; nor was it punishment from God, as Job's friends supposed. All of Job's sufferings were the attacks of Satan, but God allowed them in order to bring Job into a closer relationship with Himself.

Spiritual victories do not just happen; they are dependent upon one's faith in God. Apart from the indwelling power of His Word, all efforts to live a victorious Christian life are doomed to failure.

"Wherefore take unto you the whole armor of God . . . and the sword of the Spirit, which is the word of God" (Ephesians 6:13,17).

Thought for Today: To remain faithful in the midst of trials, we must develop a love for God's Word and a confident faith in Him.

Christ Revealed: In the conversation between Satan and the Lord (Job 1:8-12), we can see the meaning of Christ's statement to Peter: *" . . . Satan hath desired to have you, that he may sift you as wheat"* (Luke 22:31).

Word Studies: 1:1 **eschewed** means shunned; 1:9 **nought** means nothing; 1:20 **rent** means tore; **mantle** means robe; 3:24 **roarings** means groanings.

Prayer Needs: Country: Tunisia—8 million—in North Africa • An Islamic state—no open ministry for Christ is permitted; strict surveillance of all Christian activities • 99+% Muslim; .3% Christian.

JUNE 16: Read Job 5 — 8

Highlights: Eliphaz' rebuke of Job continued; Job's response; Job reproaches his friends; Bildad's theory of Job's affliction.

Verses for Today: *"But Job answered and said, Oh that my grief were thoroughly weighed, and my calamity laid in the balances together! . . . For the arrows of the Almighty are within me, the poison whereof drinketh up my spirit: the terrors of God do set themselves in array against me"* (Job 6:1-2,4).

A fter one full week of silent contemplation about Job's suffering, Eliphaz, the eldest of his four friends, was first to speak. His many years of observation led him to believe that all suffering was the result of sin. Therefore, he said to Job, *"I have seen, they that plow iniquity, and sow wickedness, reap the same"* (Job 4:8). Eliphaz tried to convince Job that he should confess his sin.

Bildad and Zophar agreed with Eliphaz' opinion. Ignoring the insinuation of being a hypocrite, Job appealed for a more complete assessment of his character, saying, *"Oh that my grief were thoroughly weighed."*

Job felt the bitter sting of condemnation from Eliphaz; but even worse, it seemed that he had been struck down by *"the arrows of the Almighty."*

The experiences of Job make it easier to remain faithful, regardless of adverse circumstances. We learn through Job's suffering that God not only is in complete control but is working out His perfect will in and through us. This gives meaning to the statement: *"For unto you it is given in the behalf of Christ, not only to believe on him, but also to suffer for his sake"* (Philippians 1:29).

It should not surprise us then, if we are misunderstood or face sorrows and suffering.

"Beloved, think it not strange concerning the fiery trial which is to try you, as though some strange thing happened unto you: But rejoice, inasmuch as ye are partakers of Christ's sufferings" (I Peter 4:12-13)

Thought for Today: God never forsakes one of His children.

Christ Revealed: Through Job's sorrowful condition (Job 7:1-6). Christ was known as *"a man of sorrows, and acquainted with grief"* (Isa. 53:3).

Word Studies: 7:21 **sleep in the dust** means be dead in the grave; 8:5 **seek . . . betimes** means inquire of God early, with earnestness, painstakingly.

Prayer Needs: Country: Somalia—8 million—on the Horn of Africa • Islam is officially favored and all other religions opposed • 99.8% Muslim; .1% Christian.

JUNE 17: Read Job 9 — 12

Highlights: Job acknowledges God's justice; his weariness of life; Zophar's accusation; Job's affirmation of faith in God's wisdom and omnipotence.

161

Verses for Today: *"Then answered Zophar the Naamathite, and said ... Should thy lies make men hold their peace? And when thou mockest, shall no man make thee ashamed? For thou hast said, My doctrine is pure, and I am clean in thine eyes. But oh that God would speak, and open his lips against thee"* (Job 11:1,3-5).

Z ophar was misled by the same false opinion expressed by his companions that severe sufferings prove gross sins. As is often the case, this legalistic religious "comforter" became a critic. He proceeded to reprove and denounce Job as a vain and lying, self-righteous pretender.

Zophar went on to say, *"Oh that God would speak, and open his lips against thee!"* God did open His lips and speak, but it was against these critics. He emphatically said, *"My wrath is kindled against thee ... for ye have not spoken of me the thing that is right"* (Job 42:7). This reveals that the counsel and conclusions of this man and his friends were merely human reasoning and not of God. We need to recognize God's estimate of these three men and what they had to say.

Here we see that people who express unkind criticism of Christians do Satan's work. We are cautioned not to impose added suffering to those who need our comfort. Religious, judgmental critics of Christians often misunderstand God's method of dealing with His disciples.

It is not easy to pray for one's "comforters" as Job did. But nothing shows more accurately what we are than the way we react to the critics who misjudge us.

"But I say unto you, Love your enemies, bless them that curse you, do good to them that hate you, and pray for them which despitefully use you, and persecute you" (Matthew 5:44).

Thought for Today: Be careful how you react to those who are unkind to you.

Christ Portrayed: Through the daysman (mediator) (Job 9:32-33). Christ is the *"one mediator between God and men"* (I Tim. 2:5).

Word Study: 11:6 **exacteth** means demands.

Prayer Needs: Country: Portugal—10 million—in western Europe • Limited religious freedom • 90% Roman Catholic; .8% Protestant.

JUNE 18: Read Job 13 — 16

Highlights: Job's defense of his integrity; his desire to die; Eliphaz' intensified condemnation; Job's complaint of God's dealing.

Verses for Today: *"Though he slay me, yet will I trust in him: but I will maintain mine own ways before him ... How many are mine iniquities and sins? make me to know my transgression and my sin?"* (Job 13:15,23).

Z ophar, a highly-opinionated man, convinced (by mere outward circumstances) that Job was guilty of great sin, since tragedy had struck in every area of Job's life. His conclusions led him to say, *"Should thy lies make men hold their peace? ...Know therefore that God exacteth of thee less than thine iniquity deserveth"* (Job 11:3,6).

Satan instigated the criticisms by Job's wife and his "devoted" friends in order to substantiate his satanic accusation that Job would curse God if he were put to the test of death—that he would give up everything, even his faith in God, in order to save his own life. But each accusation only deepened Job's faith and love for God until he could say, *"Though he slay me, yet will I trust in him."* This was the turning point in Job's testing.

To be conformed to Christ's death, we must be willing to give up everything dear—even life itself, if necessary—for the privilege of pleasing Him.

"For I reckon that the sufferings of this present time are not worthy to be compared with the glory which shall be revealed in us" (Romans 8:18).

Thought for Today: When our heart does not condemn us, we have confidence that God will hear and answer our prayers.

Christ Revealed: In the smiting of Job (Job 16:10). Christ also was smitten by those who ridiculed Him (Matt. 27:29-44; see also Psa. 22:7; 109:25; Isa. 53).

Word Studies: 15:4 **restrainest** means hinders; 15:25 **strengtheneth** means conducts proudly; 15:27 **collops of fat** means folds of fat flesh; 15:30 **depart** means escape; 16:12 **broken me assunder** (figuratively speaking) means thoroughly crushed me, so that I am heartbroken; 16:13 **reins** means heart and mind—the center of emotions; **poureth out my gall** means leaves me no hope of life.

Prayer Needs: Country: Nepal—18 million—a mountain-ringed Himalayan state between Tibet and India • Limited religious freedom • 89% Hindu; 7% Buddhist; 3% Muslim; .3% Protestant.

JUNE 19: Read Job 17 — 20

Highlights: Job's appeal to God; Bildad's cruel accusation; Job's reaffirmation of faith in a living Redeemer; Zophar's reference to Job as a wicked man.

Verse for Today: *"For I know that my Redeemer liveth, and that he shall stand at the latter day upon the earth"* (Job 19:25).

B ildad's second speech was the most critical of all, saying that Job's sufferings exposed him as a sinful hypocrite who was trapped by his own evils (Job 18:8). He concluded by saying of Job, *"Surely such are the dwellings of the wicked, and this is the place of him that knoweth not God"* (18:21).

These staggering accusations from Job's friends must have been a bitter blow. But his suffering and continuous harassment drove him closer to his Lord. He could look beyond his suffering and say, *"I know that my Redeemer liveth."*

This magnificent revelation was uttered by Job when he had no one who cared; and by all outward observation, it appeared that God did not exist. However, Job could bear the intense suffering and unjust reproaches because he was living in the expectation of the glorious appearing of his Redeemer.

We, too, can endure many trials and be victorious as we look to Jesus, our living Redeemer. He is always faithful.

" . . . I know whom I have believed, and am persuaded that he is able to keep that which I have committed unto him . . . " (II Timothy 1:12).

Thought for Today: When all else fails, we are aware of the everlasting arms of our heavenly Father.

Christ Revealed: As the Redeemer (Job 19:25). Christ, our Redeemer, has bought us with His own blood on the cross (Rev. 5:9).

Word Studies: 17:1 **breath** means spirit; 19:14 **familiar** means intimate; 19:17 **strange** means repulsive; 19:19 **inward** means close.

Prayer Needs: Country: Austria—8 million—in central Europe • Religious freedom • 88% Roman Catholic; 6% Protestant.

JUNE 20: Read Job 21 — 24

Highlights: Job declares that wicked men sometimes prosper; Eliphaz accuses Job of sin; Job's desire to plead before God.

Verses for Today: *"My foot hath held his steps, his way have I kept, and not declined. Neither have I gone back from the commandment of his lips; I have esteemed the words of his mouth more than my necessary food"* (Job 23:11-12).

I n a final attempt to convince Job that he was a hypocrite, Eliphaz said: *"Acquaint now thyself with him, and be at peace . . . "* (Job 22:21). Eliphaz reasoned that wicked men are miserable. And since Job was very miserable, he must be a very wicked man.

But Job reasoned that since God was faithful to His Word, He therefore would be faithful to His servant. That is why Job said God's Word was more precious to him than his *"necessary food."*

In every generation there are faithful Christians who are satisfied with nothing less than reading God's Word and seeking to understand His will in order to walk in His ways. In the midst of confusion and suffering, His Word is their source of true strength.

" . . . It is written, Man shall not live by bread alone, but by every word that proceedeth out of the mouth of God" (Matthew 4:4).

Thought for Today: As we receive strength from God's Word on a day-to-day basis, we can be faithful to Him in times of testing.

Christ Revealed: Through Job's faithfulness to God through his suffering (Job 23:10) *" . . . Christ also suffered for us, leaving us an example . . . "* (I Pet. 2:21).

Word Studies: 21:2 **consolations** means comfort; 21:3 **suffer** means allow; 21:8 **seed** means children; 21:10 **gendereth** means breeds.

Prayer Needs: Country: Cape Verde—344,000—15 islands in the Atlantic Ocean, 390 miles off the coast of Africa • Religious freedom • 91% Roman Catholic; 3% Protestant.

JUNE 21: Read Job 25 — 29

Highlights: Bildad's answer; Job's reproof of Bildad; Job's praise to God; Job's truthfulness; source of wisdom; recalling past wealth.

Verses for Today: *"But where shall wisdom be found? And where is the place of understanding? . . . Behold, the fear of the Lord, that is wisdom; and to depart from evil is understanding"* (Job 28:12,28).

I n the midst of all the false insinuations and accusations, Job's faith in the Lord was the source of his strength. His spiritual insight was not swayed by the opinions of his critics. Job let it be known that he was not as concerned about knowing the "reason" for his suffering as he was in having a right relationship with God, who knows all things.

164

When we meet the Lord in person, the mystery of suffering will be fully understood. We will see that God in His wisdom had some eternal purpose for allowing it.

Human "knowledge" of our ever-changing world is very limited and continually being revised, enlarged, and discarded. Apart from God, man has no final answers to life's problems and knows nothing concerning eternity. Spiritual truth can only be understood by those who have been born again by His Spirit. *"The world by wisdom knew not God"* (I Corinthians 1:21), but the knowledge of His will is within the reach of every believer.

Strange as it may seem to a skeptical world, God's wisdom can only be found as we obey His Word—*" . . . a good understanding have all they that do his commandments . . . "* (Psalm 111:10).

Those who leave Christ—the Living Word—out of their lives never discover true wisdom and understanding. They miss the greatest discovery of life—Christ, who is Truth. *In Him are hidden all the treasures of wisdom and knowledge* (see Colossians 2:3).

Thought for Today: The depth of our faith is revealed by the way we react to our sorrows and sufferings.

Christ Revealed: Through Job's compassion for others (Job 29:15-16). Christ had compassion on the multitudes of people who needed help (Matt. 14:14; 15:30-39).

Word Study: 28:1 **a vein** means a mine.

Prayer Needs: Country: Republic of China (Taiwan)—20 million—77 islands off the southeastern coast of Red China • Religious freedom • 47% Chinese folk-religionist; 44% Buddhist; 4% Protestant; 1% Roman Catholic.

JUNE 22: Read Job 30 — 33

Highlights: Job's proclamation of integrity; Elihu's accusations.

Verses for Today: *"They abhor me . . . and spare not to spit in my face. . . . I cry unto thee, and thou dost not hear me . . . "* (Job 30:10,20).

There seemed to be no end to the anguish which Job suffered—even contempt from those who spit in his face as he cried out in prayer. And as far as he could determine, God was not hearing his prayers—*"Thou regardest me not"* (Job 30:20).

One of the most difficult trials for a Christian is to pray, and continue praying, without any apparent sign that God has heard. But the effectiveness of our prayers cannot be judged by immediate results. There are many reasons for delay. Some-times, God does not grant our requests because he wants to provide something better. At other times, He withholds material benefits in order to impart spiritual enlightenment and understanding. The very fact that our requests are sometimes granted and sometimes denied is proof in itself that we are cared for by a God of love, whose ways are governed by His wisdom and always for our best.

" . . . how unsearchable are his judgments, and his ways past finding out! For who hath known the mind of the Lord? or who hath been his counselor?" (Romans 11:33-34).

Thought for Today: God gives more grace as the burdens become greater.

Christ Revealed: Through the ridicule and affliction which Job suffered (Job 30:10-11). Christ was afflicted and spit upon (Mark 15:15-20; see also Isa. 50:6; 53:2-5; Matt. 27:26; John 19:1-5).

Word Studies: 30:3 **solitary** means left with nothing but dry and barren ground; 30:4 **mallows** are plants of the salt marsh; 30:29 **dragons** means jackals or wolves; 31:40 **cockle** means weeds; 33:13 **strive** means contend.

Prayer Needs: Country: Bahamas—239,000—in the northern portion of the West Indies • Religious freedom • 56% Protestant; 13% Roman Catholic; 1% Afro-American spiritist.

JUNE 23: Read Job 34 — 37

Highlight: Elihu continues accusations.

Verses for Today: *"My desire is that Job may be tried unto the end. . . . he addeth rebellion unto his sin. . . . therefore doth Job open his mouth in vain; he multiplieth words without knowledge"* (Job 34:36-37; 35:16).

T he youngest man, Elihu, did not speak until the three friends had ended their complaints, criticism, and condemnation of Job.

He agreed that the *experience* of Eliphaz, the *traditional views* of Bildad, and the *good judgment* of Zophar were all in vain.

Elihu was angry with Job's three friends because they had accused Job, yet were unable to answer Job. Elihu was also angry at Job because he felt Job was a self-righteous sinner (see Job: 34:7-8). Therefore, Elihu believed that he alone could act as God's priest to intercede on Job's behalf.

We are often prone to criticize and condemn another's actions when we simply do not know what God is doing or how He is working in the heart of someone with whom we do not agree. But judging another person is a serious sin (see James 3:1). It robs us of our joy in the Lord and instills a root of bitterness.

"Who art thou that judgest another man's servant? to his own master he standeth or falleth. Yea, he shall be holden up: for God is able to make him stand" (Romans 14:4).

Thought for Today: Enjoying fellowship with God is dependent upon one's attitude toward others.

Christ Revealed: As the One whose *"eyes are upon the ways of man"* (Job 34:21). *"For the eyes of the Lord are over the righteous, and his ears are open unto their prayers . . . "* (I Pet. 3:12).

Word Study: 36:33 **The noise thereof showeth concerning it, the cattle also concerning the vapor** means His thunder announces the coming storm; even the cattle make known its approach.

Prayer Needs: Country: Guyana—766,000—on the northeastern coast of South America • The government is becoming increasingly Marxist, radical, and atheistic • 36% Hindu; 28% Protestant; 10% Roman Catholic; 9% Muslim.

JUNE 24: Read Job 38 — 40

Highlights: Elihu's speech interrupted by God; God's challenge to Job; man's weakness and ignorance; Job humbled.

Verse for Today: *"Canst thou bind the sweet influences of Pleiades, or loose the bands of Orion?"* (Job 38:31).

G od challenged Job to consider the limitations of his wisdom compared to the wisdom of God, who created the vast constellations and planets that are spread throughout the heavens. Neither the wisest astronomer nor the most spiritual person can explain or change one star in the marvelous array of the stars of Pleiades—one of the most beautiful clusters of stars visible to the naked eye. The only true explanation of the arrangement of the world is that which is recorded in the Bible as happening on the fourth day of Creation (Genesis 1:14-19).

God's questions to Job reveal how man is totally inadequate to comprehend His wisdom. This mighty God who created the universe is our Lord. He cares for us, listens to our prayers, and helps us with our needs! This should cause us to bow before Him in adoration and praise.

"Ah Lord God! behold, thou hast made the heaven and the earth by thy great power and stretched out arm, and there is nothing too hard for thee" (Jeremiah 32:17).

Thought for Today: The vastness of the universe reveals God's unlimited resources and matchless wisdom.

Christ Revealed: As the One who *"laid the foundations of the earth"* (Job 38:4). By Christ, God *"made the worlds"* (Heb. 1:1-2; see also John 1:1-3).

Word Study: 39:9 unicorn means wild ox.

Prayer Needs: Country: Malawi—8 million—in southeastern Africa • Religious freedom • 34% Protestant; 23% Roman Catholic; 16% Muslim; 16% animist; 4% cults.

JUNE 25: Read Job 41 — 42

Highlights: God's great power reviewed; Job's submission to God; his prayer for his friends; God blesses Job.

Verse for Today: *"So the Lord blessed the latter end of Job more than his beginning . . . "* (Job 42:12).

F rom all outward appearances, it seemed that Job's four friends were enjoying God's favor and that God was displeased only with Job.

Job's friends fully expected God's approval on their efforts to convince Job how wrong he was. Eliphaz must have been astounded to hear the voice from Heaven say, *I am angry with you and your two friends because you did not speak of Me what is right, the way My servant Job did* (see Job: 42:7). On the other hand, Job must have been equally surprised to hear that God was pleased with him, for immediately preceding the voice from Heaven, Job had said, *I am ashamed of myself for what I have said, and I repent in dust and ashes* (see 42:6).

Although Job recognized his inadequacies, he had a sincere desire to please the Lord.

Job could have become proud when he saw that God was coming to his defense. But instead, he prayed for his friends who had so greatly misjudged him. Because of Job's humble, submissive spirit, God gave him even greater blessings and possessions than he had enjoyed before all his trials and sufferings.

Truly, our Lord is able to do so much more than we can ever imagine (see Ephesians 3:20).

Thought for Today: God is often most pleased with us when we are least pleased with ourselves.

Christ Revealed: Through Job's praying for his "friends" (Job 42:10). We are reminded of Christ's command: *Pray for those who mistreat you* (see Luke 6:28).

Word Studies: 41:11 **prevented** means preceded; came before; 41:17 **sundered** means separated; 42:6 **abhor** means despise.

Prayer Needs: Country: Iraq—17 million—in southern Asia • Surveillance and harassment of non-Muslims • 96% Muslim; 3% Christian.

PSALMS

The book of Psalms is composed of 150 poems, most of which are prayer-praise songs to God. The Hebrew word for *psalms* means "praises," a term that reflects much of the book's content.

The Holy Spirit is the Author who moved King David to write over 70 Psalms. Other writers include Moses, Solomon, Asaph, Ethan, and the sons of Korah. The writers of about 50 Psalms are not identified.

The psalmists' thoughts often wander from feelings of utter failure to feelings of delight, but usually conclude by expressing praise and gratitude to God. Throughout the Psalms, the Holy Spirit brings to light the fact that every complaint reveals a lack of faith in God and His promises.

The Psalms make a clear-cut distinction between sin and righteousness. The words "righteous" and "righteousness" are used more than 130 times. The words "sin," "iniquity," and "evil" occur more than 90 times.

The Psalms of judgment upon the evildoer reveal what sin really is—rebellion against God. These Psalms are the words of people who have identified themselves with God in hating sin.

When the Spirit of God directed the psalmists to speak of vengeance or judgment upon the evildoer, the psalmists were not referring to personal revenge; they were making known the will of God concerning all injustices. These Psalms are a revelation by the Spirit of God that sin will inevitably be punished. The same truth is revealed in the New Testament—*"Be not deceived; God is not mocked: for whatsoever a man soweth, that shall he also reap"* (Galatians 6:7).

The Psalms prepare us to pray and meditate, and offer guidance in expressing our gratitude and praise. Some of the Psalms, such as Psalm 51, teach us how to confess sin and express our yearning for forgiveness. Others, such as Psalm 23, teach us that we should be content with God's personal care over us.

Many Psalms refer to the Messiah—His birth, life, betrayal, crucifixion, resurrection, and ascension. Jesus Himself revealed that the Psalms spoke of Him: " . . . *all things must be fulfilled, which were written in the law of*

Moses, and in the prophets, and in the psalms, concerning me" (Luke 24:44). Consequently, those who read only the New Testament limit their knowledge of Christ, since the Holy Spirit speaks of Christ throughout the Old Testament as well. (See John 5:39.)

The New Testament encourages us to "sing the Psalms" (see Colossians 3:16).

The Psalms are quoted or referred to about 100 times in the New Testament—more than any other book of the Old Testament, with the possible exception of Isaiah.

JUNE 26: Read Psalms 1 — 9

Highlights: The blessed and the ungodly; David's prayers of confidence and trust in God; prayer for protection, mercy, and deliverance; psalms of God's glory and praise for His justice.

Verse for Today: *"Blessed is the man that walketh not in the counsel of the ungodly . . . "* (Psalm 1:1).

A blessed person is one who possesses the happiness produced by experiencing God's favor. He is content with God's guidance, regardless of outward circumstances.

The secret to having a blessed life is to refuse to walk *"in the counsel of the ungodly."* But a mere worldly goodness will not ensure true blessedness. Therefore, the psalmist revealed the all-inclusive secret of true happiness: *"But his delight is in the law of the Lord"* (Psalm 1:2). What a contrast this happiness is to the superficial, empty happiness the world offers!

As we meditate day and night upon God's Word for the purpose of doing His will, our lives take on new meaning.

"This book of the law shall not depart out of thy mouth; but thou shalt meditate therein day and night ... for then thou shalt make thy way prosperous, and then thou shalt have good success" (Joshua 1:8).

Thought for Today: Only to the extent that we love God will we enjoy obeying His Word.

Christ Revealed: As the Son of God (Psalm 2:7). *"For God so loved the world, that he gave his only begotten Son, that whosoever believeth in him should not perish, but have everlasting life"* (John 3:16; see also Acts 13:33; Heb. 1:5).

Word Studies: 2:2 **Anointed** means Christ; 5:6 **leasing** means lies; deceitfully.

Prayer Needs: Country: Mauritius—1 million—500 miles east of Madagascar • Limited religious freedom • 50% Hindu; 27% Roman Catholic; 17% Muslim; 5% Protestant.

JUNE 27: Read Psalms 10 — 17

Highlights: A prayer for judgment upon the wicked; David's desire for justice; the foolishness of men; those who shall dwell with God; prayer for protection.

Verse for Today: *"In the Lord I put my trust: how say ye to my soul, Flee as a bird to your mountain?"* (Psalm 11:1).

D avid's friends advised him to flee to the mountainous parts of the land of Judah in order to avoid the danger which was threatening him. He refused to retreat from the scene of conflict. Nor would he resort to revenge against Saul. God seemed to have deserted David, but he did not allow his circumstances to weaken his faith. Even though he was a victim of great personal danger, his faith was unshaken; he stood his ground and trusted in God.

There is absolute assurance that in due time the Christian will triumph (Psalm 11:7). All of God's people may expect to be severely tested. Let us reject the advice of those who would have us *flee like a bird to the mountains* and retreat or withdraw from our convictions because of opposition. The voice of logic will always first ask, not what is right, but what is safe.

"And fear not them which kill the body, but are not able to kill the soul: but rather fear him which is able to destroy both soul and body in hell" (Matthew 10:28).

Thought for Today: Knowing God's Word enables us to face our difficulties, realizing He is in control.

Christ Revealed: In the prophecy, *"For thou wilt not leave my soul in hell; neither wilt thou suffer thine Holy One to see corruption"* (Psalm 16:10). This foretells the resurrection of our Lord Jesus Christ (see Acts 2:25-27; 13:35-39).

Word Studies: 10:13 **contemn** means spurn; despise; 11:3 **foundations** means principles of society based on the Word of God.

Prayer Needs: Country: Tibet—population unknown—in eastern Asia • The Chinese government is still committed to promoting atheism, while at the same time, officially permitting Lamaism (a form of Buddhism) • No religious statistics are available, but at one time all were Lamaists. Lamaism was all but exterminated by Chinese invaders in the 1950s, but it is now permitted under strict control.

JUNE 28: Read Psalms 18 — 22

Highlights: Thanksgiving for deliverance; creation and covenants of God; a prayer for God's people; praise for victory; cry of anguish and song of praise.

Verses for Today: *"Now know I that the Lord saveth his anointed; he will hear him from his holy heaven with the saving strength of his right hand. Some trust in chariots, and some in horses: but we will remember the name of the Lord our God. They are brought down and fallen: but we are risen, and stand upright"* (Psalm 20:6-8).

P rayer has always turned apparent defeat into victory for God's obedient servants. The "armies" of those who trust in "chariots and horses" and rely on vast resources often seem secure and invincible. But the people of God who pray and trust in His unseen presence will always rise up triumphantly while the unbeliever will be brought down. Prayer will deliver, but pride will defeat.

If David could pray and then testify how God delivered him from Saul and all his armies, how much more we can pray and trust that God will answer our prayers because of Jesus Christ, our Intercessor!

The repeated reminder by Christ to pray proves that He knows our hearts—He knows how doubt and distrust toward God are natural to us and how easily we are inclined to repeat our prayers without expecting an answer. (See John 14:13-

14; 15:7; 16:23-24; I John 3:21-22; 5:14-15.)

Before Jehoshaphat entered into battle with the vast armies of the Moabites and Ammonites, he prayed, then appointed singers to praise the Lord for the answer. He obtained an easy victory (II Chronicles 20:20-22).

"Ask, and it shall be given you; seek, and ye shall find; knock, and it shall be opened unto you: For every one that asketh receiveth; and he that seeketh findeth; and to him that knocketh it shall be opened" (Matthew 7:7-8).

Thought for Today: Have you remembered to praise and thank the Lord for the victories in your life today?

Christ Revealed: As the One who was forsaken by God (Psalm 22:1). *"My God, my God, why hast thou forsaken me?"* (Matt. 27:46; Mark 15:34).

Word Studies: 18:14 **discomfited them** means cause them to panic, thus creating confusion; 18:26 **froward** (first use) means evil; **froward** (second use) means unfavorable; 18:45 **close places** means caves or strongholds; 22:5 **confounded** means put to shame; 22:17 **tell** means count.

Prayer Needs: Country: South Africa—34 million—on the southern tip of the African continent • Religious freedom • 67% Protestant; 20% animism, magic, and ancestor worship; 10% Roman Catholic; 3% Asian religions.

JUNE 29: Read Psalms 23 — 30

Highlights: David's confidence in the Great Shepherd; the King of glory; a prayer for guidance and protection; David's love for God's house; his prayer for God's help; adoration of God's mighty power; thanksgiving for deliverance.

Verses for Today: *"The Lord is my shepherd; I shall not want. . . . He restoreth my soul: he leadeth me in the paths of righteousness for his name's sake"* (Psalm 23:1,3).

D avid, the old shepherd-king, looked upon himself as nothing more than a sheep that had to be led by the Great Shepherd in the paths of righteousness.

No other livestock requires so much attention as sheep. Left alone, sheep follow the same trails until those trails become ruts. A sheep can be so engrossed in following its own eating path that it becomes separated from the flock and is lost.

We, by nature, are like sheep, blindly and habitually following the same paths that we have seen ruin the lives of others, or becoming so wrapped up in our own affairs that we lose our way.

There is something almost terrifying about the destructive self-willed determination of those who are not willing to be led *"in the paths of righteousness"*—actually going their own way, knowing that "path" has taken others straight into trouble.

How many times have we prayed, "Lord, lead me in the paths of righteousness," while in our day-by-day conduct, we still refuse to deny ourselves, to give up our "rights," or to yield our own interests to the interests of others?

If we truly want God's will, we will follow the Great Shepherd.

"Then said Jesus unto his disciples, If any man will come after me, let him deny himself, and take up his cross, and follow me" (Matthew 16:24).

Thought for Today: The tender voice of our Good Shepherd is still calling, *"Come unto me."*

171

Christ Revealed: As our Shepherd (Psalm 23). Christ is the Good Shepherd who *"giveth his life for the sheep"* (John 10:11).

Word Studies: 23:1 **want** means lack anything; 28:3 **mischief** means malice; evil.

Prayer Needs: Country: Burkina Faso (formerly Upper Volta)—9 million—in western Africa • Religious freedom • 47% Muslim; 39% belief in false gods, idolatry, and heathenism; 12% Roman Catholic; 2% Protestant.

JUNE 30:   Read Psalms 31 — 35

Highlights: David's trust in God; blessedness of forgiveness; praise to the Lord for His creation; the Lord hears the righteous; David's prayer for safety.

Verse for Today: *"I acknowledged my sin unto thee, and mine iniquity have I not hid. I said, I will confess my transgressions unto the Lord; and thou forgavest the iniquity of my sin"* (Psalm 32:5).

W hen Nathan the prophet confronted David with his iniquity, he confessed his sin and his need for mercy and forgiveness. And the Lord forgave David—not only for his sins, but also for the iniquity of his sin.

"Iniquity" means more than rejecting God's Word—more than mere failure or weakness. It means turning aside from what we know is right by twisting the truth to satisfy our personal desire. The inevitable result of iniquity is always misery and unhappiness. There can be no lasting peace and joy until sin is sincerely confessed and forsaken.

"Be not deceived; God is not mocked: for whatsoever a man soweth, that shall he also reap" (Galatians 6:7).

Thought for Today: To continue in sin is to choose a life of misery and emptiness.

Christ Revealed: In the prophecy, *"He keepeth all his bones: not one of them is broken"* (Psalm 34:20; compare John 19:36).

Word Studies: 31:4 **privily** means secretly; 32:2 **guile** means deceit.

Prayer Needs: Country: Jamaica—3 million—in the West Indies • Religious freedom • 78% Protestant; 10% Roman Catholic; 7% Afro-American spiritist.

PRAYERS IN THIS MONTH'S READING

172

NOTE: There are many prayers in Psalms, but space does not permit us to list each prayer separately.

JULY 1: Read Psalms 36 — 39

Highlights: David's confidence in God; destruction of the wicked; the prayer of a penitent heart; brevity of life.

Verses for Today: *"For with thee is the fountain of life: in thy light shall we see light. O continue thy loving-kindness unto them . . . "* (Psalm 36:9-10).

T he loving-kindness of our Heavenly Father was manifested by the gift He gave to the world—the gift of *"his only begotten Son . . . "* (John 3:16).

Jesus revealed God's marvelous love: *"For God . . . hath shined in our hearts, to give the light of the knowledge of the glory of God in the face of Jesus Christ"* (II Corinthians 4:6). He is the Source of life and light to all who accept Him as their Savior.

Just as our earthly existence is dependent upon the *sun* to maintain physical life,we are dependent upon the *Son* of God to maintain spiritual life. The "light" of human wisdom or effort can never produce assurance that one is saved and at peace with God.

We are totally dependent upon the light of God's Word to receive His loving-kindness, for " . . . *thy words giveth light; it giveth understanding unto the simple"* (Psalm 119:130).

When a person neglects God's Word, he rejects the Source of life and light—Christ—the Light of the world. (See John 1:1-14.)

"Then spake Jesus again unto them, saying, I am the light of the world: he that followeth me shall not walk in darkness, but . . . if ye believe not that I am he, ye shall die in your sins" (John 8:12,24).

Thought for Today: When we read God's Word, it provides light for life's pathway.

Christ Revealed: As the Fountain of life and the true Light (Psalm 36:8-9). Not only is Jesus the *Fountain* of life, but He is also the *Source* of the river of living water (compare John 4:10,14; Rev. 22:1).

Word Studies: 36:11 **remove me** means drive me away; 37:9 **cut off** means destroyed; 37:26 **seed** means descendants; 37:28 **judgment** means justice; 38:8 **roared** means groaned.

173

Prayer Needs: Country: Spain—39 million—in southwestern Europe • Limited religious freedom • 94% Roman Catholic; .5% Protestant.

JULY 2: Read Psalms 40 — 45

Highlights: Praise for answered prayer; treachery of David's enemies; his longing for God's presence; a prayer for deliverance from present troubles; a psalm of the king.

Verses for Today: *"My tears have been my meat day and night, while they continually say unto me, Where is thy God? . . . I shall yet praise him for the help of his countenance"* (Psalm 42:3,5).

B ecause of King Saul's jealousy, David had been forced to leave Jerusalem—the city of God—and stay in hiding for years.

Through difficult and trying events, God allowed David to face circumstances which he did not understand. From all outward appearances, it seemed that his life was being wasted—that God did not care.

But David's suffering was God's way of deepening his spiritual life. God had placed him exactly where he was in order to develop the characteristics that made David a man after God's own heart.

To become frustrated over our circumstances is a natural tendency. But whether our apparent dilemmas are caused by our own shortcomings, by Satan, or whether they are arranged of the Lord, God can use them to His advantage—and to ours— if we allow Him time to do so. We don't have to understand *why* we are having struggles. God wants us to accept our trials as His way of developing our faith.

"In every thing give thanks: for this is the will of God in Christ Jesus concerning you" (I Thessalonians 5:18).

Thought for Today: God's grace is sufficient to sustain us in every situation— regardless of its severity or duration.

Christ Revealed: As the One who will do God's will (Psalm 40:6-8; compare John 4:34; Heb. 10:7,9). As Deity and One who loves righteousness (Psalm 45:6-7; compare 33:5; Isa. 9:6-7; Heb. 1:8-9).

Word Studies: 40:12 **compassed** means surrounded; 41:3 **languishing** means sickness; **make all his bed** means restore him; 42:1 **hart** means deer; **panteth after** means longs for; 44:20 **stretched out our hands** means worshiped; 45:1 **inditing** means overflowing with; 45:4 **terrible** means awesome; fearful; wonderful; 45:13 **within** means within the palace.

Prayer Needs: Country: Thailand—54 million—in Southeast Asia • Limited freedom of religion, Buddhism is the state religion • 92% Buddhist; 4% Muslim; 2% Chinese folk-religionist; 1% Christian.

JULY 3: Read Psalms 46 — 51

Highlights: The psalmist's confidence and praise; deception of worldly wealth; a prayer for mercy and forgiveness.

Verses for Today: *"Have mercy upon me, O God, according to thy lovingkindness: according unto the multitude of thy tender mercies blot out my transgressions....For I acknowledge my transgressions: and my sin is ever before*

174

me. . . . Create in me a clean heart, O God; and renew a right spirit within me" (Psalm 51:1,3,10).

David was capable of the highest spiritual triumphs as noted in the Psalms he wrote. But in the midst of all his victories, he selfishly took for himself Bathsheba, the beautiful wife of Uriah. Kings from any other nation could have done this without any thought of blame. Although David was Jehovah's anointed shepherd king, he was guilty without any possible means of evading the judgment of God.

The fearless prophet Nathan went to David and denounced the king's selfish act. Oh, the destructive power of even one sin! David was convicted and prayed for mercy: *"Create in me a clean heart, O God; and renew a right spirit."*

No child of God should look upon sin as merely a mistake or failure to obey God. "Sin" is far more than "missing the mark" of God's high calling; it is cooperating with Satan—the supreme enemy of God and of righteousness, the destroyer of all that is good.

"It is a fearful thing to fall into the hands of the living God" (Hebrews 10:31).

Thought for Today: God does not overlook our sins because of our position.

Christ Revealed: As the One who redeemed us from sin with His own precious blood (Psalm 49:8-9,15; compare I Pet. 1:18-19).

Word Study: 49:10 **brutish** means senseless.

Prayer Needs: Country: West Germany—61 million—in north-central Europe • Religious freedom • 46% Protestant; 43% Roman Catholic; 2% Muslim.

JULY 4: Read Psalms 52 — 59

Highlights: Tendency of corrupt tongue; foolishness of atheism; a prayer for protection; a cry against deceitful friends; the psalmist's trust in God; prayers for deliverance.

Verse for Today: *"Consume them in wrath, consume them, that they may not be: and let them know that God ruleth in Jacob unto the ends of the earth . . . "* (Psalm 59:13).

Some of the Psalms express anger against enemies and evildoers. This may seem hard to understand, but they explain the judgment of God against all who do evil.

These inspired words of God express His abhorrence of sin.

The authoritative reaction against sin found in the Psalms of judgment is also found in the New Testament where Paul said, *"Alexander the coppersmith did me much evil: the Lord reward him according to his works"* (II Timothy 4:14).

The psalmist's motive, as well as the Apostle Paul's, had nothing to do with personal jealousy, spite, or hatred. Both of these men were anointed of God to express His hatred against sin.

The Christian's attitude toward sin must be in harmony with God's Word—recognizing sin as God views it.

"In flaming fire taking vengeance on them that know not God, and that obey not the gospel of our Lord Jesus Christ: Who shall be punished with everlasting

175

destruction from the presence of the Lord, and from the glory of his power" (II Thessalonians 1:8-9).

Thought for Today: Rebellion against God is *"exceeding sinful"* (see Romans 7:13).

Christ Revealed: As the One who saves those who call upon Him (Psalm 55:16-17). *"For whosoever shall call upon the name of the Lord shall be saved"* (Rom. 10:13).

Word Studies: 55:4 **sore** means grievously; 55:9 **divide their tongues** means bring confusion; 56:5 **wrest** means distort; 56:8 **tellest** means has taken account of; 59:10 **prevent** means precede.

Prayer Needs: Country: Sierra Leone—4 million—in western Africa • Increasing restrictions on Christian work in some areas • 50% belief in river spirits, medicine men, and witchcraft; 39% Muslim; 7% Protestant; 2% Roman Catholic.

JULY 5: Read Psalms 60 — 66

Highlights: David's prayer for deliverance from his enemies; his confidence in God's promises; David's exhortation to praise God for His goodness.

Verses for Today: *"Hear my cry, O God; attend unto my prayer. From the end of the earth will I cry unto thee, when my heart is overwhelmed. Lead me to the rock that is higher than I"* (Psalm 61:1-2).

K ing Saul had forced David to retreat to the country east of the Jordan River. It was not part of the Promised Land, and the psalmist felt exiled from God's presence in this foreign country. Although that desolate location seemed like *"the end of the earth,"* he still prayed. In the midst of his dilemma, he could say with perfect confidence, *"So will I sing praise unto thy name . . . "* (Psalm 61:8).

Every person has burdens, and each one often thinks his own are the heaviest. The Lord never promised to take away our burdens, but He did promise *"My grace is sufficient"* (II Cor. 12:9).

When some burden seems too heavy to bear or a problem seems too severe to face, just remember that all these are appointed by the Lord in love as gracious necessities in developing your spiritual life. *"And we know that all things [must] work together for good . . . "* (Romans 8:28). This promise should dispel every trace of doubt or impatience and instill confidence that God in His wisdom truly cares.

The child of God never needs to fear. His chief concern should be to please Christ and bring honor to His name.

" . . . Most gladly therefore will I rather glory in my infirmities, that the power of Christ may rest upon me. . . . for when I am weak, then am I strong" (II Corinthians 12:9-10).

Thought for Today: As we daily read God's Word, our confidence in the Lord's power and protection will be increased.

Christ Revealed: As the Rock—the unmovable, eternal, unchanging Savior (Psalm 61:2; 62:2,6-7). Jesus is the Rock of our salvation (I Cor. 10:4).

Word Studies: 60:6 **mete out** means measure, divide, and portion out; 64:2 **insurrection** means violence; 65:8 **tokens** means evidence of Your presence; 66:12 **a wealthy place** means a favorable situation; a place of abundance.

Prayer Needs: Country: New Zealand—3 million—two large islands southeast of Australia • Religious freedom • 51% Protestant; 16% Roman Catholic; 3% cults.

JULY 6: Read Psalms 67 — 71

Highlights: God's blessing upon His people; His judgment upon enemies; David's affliction; prayer of thanksgiving.

Verse for Today: *"God setteth the solitary in families: he bringeth out those which are bound with chains: but the rebellious dwell in a dry land"* (Psalm 68:6).

C hristianity is often misunderstood by the unbelieving world as a gloomy, uninteresting existence. But just the opposite is true—it is those who rebel against God that *"dwell in a dry land."* The brightest prospects of sinful enjoyment eventually leave their victims empty and wretched. But those who trust in God *"shall be abundantly satisfied . . . "* (Psalms 36:8). Even the trying experiences of life are often blessings in disguise.

So regardless of external circumstances, the Christian's ultimate future is radiant, beautiful, and inviting as he looks forward to meeting his Savior, Jesus Christ.

"Let us therefore come boldly unto the throne of grace, that we may obtain mercy, and find grace to help in time of need" (Hebrews 4:16).

Thought for Today: Our life is like a raging sea until we turn to the Lord, who is able to bring about sweet peace.

Christ Revealed: As the One who led captivity captive (Psalm 68:18). When Christ rose from the dead, He broke the captive power of Satan (Gal. 5:1).

Prayer Needs: Country: Yugoslavia—23 million—on the Balkan Peninsula • Virtually no freedom to preach the gospel • 40% Eastern Orthodox; 31% Roman Catholic; 10% Muslim; 1% Protestant.

JULY 7: Read Psalms 72 — 77

Highlights: David's prayer for Solomon; mystery of the prosperity of the wicked; the wicked and the proud rebuked; God's majesty praised.

Verses for Today: *"Give the king thy judgments, O God, and thy righteousness unto the king's son. . . . He shall redeem their soul from deceit and violence: and precious shall their blood be in his sight"* (Psalm 72:1,14).

T his Psalm is a prayer that the king might rule as God Himself would rule. It is a prayer for a just government where the rights of all are equal—for the widows, the aged, the orphans, and the handicapped.

Achieving prosperity, safety, equality, and justice for all persons has never existed—not even with King David. And the complexity of our modern world has led to even greater complications. As time goes on, our Lord has foretold that *"evil men and seducers shall wax worse and worse"* (II Timothy 3:13).

But the child of God is patiently waiting for that day when the King of kings shall reign in perfect righteousness for all.

"And I heard a great voice out of heaven saying, Behold, the tabernacle of God is with men, and he will dwell with them, and they shall be his people, and

God himself shall be with them, and be their God. And God shall wipe away all tears from their eyes; and there shall be no more death, neither sorrow, nor crying, neither shall there be any more pain: for the former things are passed away. And he that sat upon the throne said, Behold, I make all things new" (Revelation 21:3-5).

Thought for Today: Are you setting your hope in things of this world or on the precious promises of God's Word?

Christ Revealed: As the righteous Judge: *"He shall . . . break in pieces the oppressor"* (Psalm 72:4). Psalm 75:8 describes the judgment of God upon those who refuse to accept the salvation so freely offered by Jesus, the Lamb of God (John 1:29,34-36). They must face *"the wrath of the Lamb"* (Rev. 6:15-17; compare II Thess. 1:8-9).

Word Studies: 72:10 **Seba (Sheba)** is present-day Ethiopia; 73:10 **waters of a full cup** means fruit of prosperity; 74:4 **roar** means threaten; 74:13 **dragons** means whales or large sea animals; 75:10 **horns** means strength; 77:2 **my sore ran** means my heart ached, and I stretched out my hand.

Prayer Needs: Country: Denmark—5 million—in northern Europe • Religious freedom • 92% Protestant; 1% Muslim; .5% Roman Catholic; .5% cults; .1% Jewish.

JULY 8: Read Psalms 78 — 80

Highlights: God's long-suffering toward Israel; His judgment against disobedience; a prayer for the destruction of heathen enemies; a prayer for mercy and restoration.

Verses for Today: *"For he established . . . a law in Israel, which he commanded our fathers, that they should . . . declare them to their children: that they might set their hope in God, and not forget the works of God, but keep his commandments"* (Psalm 78:5-7).

T he responsibility of teaching God's Word to children rests upon the parents. Yet, this is a great weakness in many Christian families.

"I do not intend to interfere with my child's religion," said one parent. "When he becomes old enough, I want him to choose his own religion." But the same parent was doing everything possible to encourage his child to eat the right food in order to maintain good health, and to choose a career that would best ensure financial security. It seems strange that it was only in eternal matters that the parent refused to give direction.

Far too many parents plan and work, preparing their children for the few short years of life, but their relationship with Christ is ignored.

"And that from a child thou hast known the holy scriptures, which are able to make thee wise unto salvation through faith which is in Christ Jesus" (II Timothy 3:15).

Thought for Today: Daily Bible reading and prayer in the home will bless and strengthen any family.

Christ Revealed: As the true Shepherd (Psalm 80:1). Jesus Christ is the Good Shepherd, the Door of the sheepfold. He alone is the way to Heaven. *" . . . I am the door . . . I am the good shepherd . . . I am the way, the truth, and the life: no man cometh unto the Father, but by me"* (John 10:7,11; 14:6).

Word Studies: 78:15 **clave** means split; 78:61 **his strength ... and his glory** means the ark of the covenant (compare I Samuel 4:21-22); 80:13 **waste** means eat.

Prayer Needs: Country: Cameroon—10 million—in west-central Africa • Pressure on Christians from authorities and Muslims • 28% Roman Catholic; 23% Muslim; 18% animism, divination, and animal sacrifices; 14% Protestant.

JULY 9: Read Psalms 81 — 87

Highlights: God's goodness and Israel's waywardness; blessedness of living in God's presence; David's desire to walk in truth; the goodness and power of God.

Verses for Today: *"For a day in thy courts is better than a thousand. ... no good thing will he withhold from them that walk uprightly"* (Psalm 84:10-11).

D avid was always aware of the presence of God. Nothing—the rebellion of his sons, betrayal by his best friend, or the disloyalty of the people—could separate him from God's presence. With this assurance, he could say, *"No good thing will he withhold."* God would not permit him to miss out on, or be deprived of, any good thing.

Oh, that more of God's children would enjoy the presence of God! A day in the Lord's presence is better than a thousand days anywhere else.

Most of us want to tell God what we think is best for us instead of being content to let Him lead us one day at a time. Waiting patiently on the Lord not only tests our faith, but also strengthens it. Most of our mistakes are the result of our impatience and failure to recognize His presence.

Do you doubt God's day-by-day guidance for the future? If you do, then think back over the years. No child of God can do so without a feeling of grateful praise and thankfulness for His mercies. He has been with you all the way.

"Commit thy way unto the Lord; trust also in him; and he shall bring it to pass" (Psalm 37:5).

Thought for Today: God's grace is available for you today. Rest in His love.

Christ Revealed: Psalm 82:8 may be taken as a prayer for the hastening of the coming of Christ, the Judge of the earth (John 5:22).

Word Studies: 83:2 **lifted up the head** means exalted themselves; 84:4 **still** means always; throughout life.

Prayer Needs: Country: Bhutan—2 million—in the eastern Himalayas of central Asia • Public worship, evangelism, and proselytization by any religion other than the state religion of Buddhism are illegal • 70% Buddhist; 24% Hindu; 5% Muslim; .1% Christian.

JULY 10: Read Psalms 88 — 91

Highlights: A cry for deliverance from death; the psalmist's praise for God's covenant and His promises; the frailty and brevity of human life; protection for the faithful.

Verses for Today: *"He that dwelleth in the secret place of the Most High shall abide under the shadow of the Almighty. I will say of the Lord, He is my refuge and my fortress: my God; in him will I trust"* (Psalm 91:1-2).

David's life was filled with dangers, but he regarded God as a *"refuge"* and a *"fortress."* The godly recognize the need of a refuge during bodily pain, mental perplexities, sorrows, and struggles.

The very nature of trials and testings involves the idea of possible failure. Bodily pain can result in bitterness ... mental perplexities can lead to unbelief ... and many trials end in defeat. But Christians recognize their need for a "refuge and a fortress." Our adversary, the devil, goes about *"as a roaring lion ... seeking whom he may devour"* (I Peter 5:8).

Christians are hated by the world. Powerful forces and seductive influences are brought to bear upon us to lead us astray. The spirit and principles of the world system—many of its practices, amusements, and much of its literature—are opposed to the interests and lifestyle of the Christian.

Moreover, there are *"fleshly lusts which war against the soul"* (I Peter 2:11). However, the Christian who is victorious has *"no confidence in the flesh"* (Philippians 3:3), but *dwells in the secret place*—in prayer and meditation in God's Word and relies upon the Most High for wisdom and strength.

What is there to fear when one trusts in *"the Most High?"*

"The Lord knoweth how to deliver the godly out of temptations, and to reserve the unjust unto the day of judgment to be punished" (II Peter 2:9).

Thought for Today: Think back on your life and recognize how the Lord has cared for you along the way.

Christ Revealed: In Psalm 89:27, we see Christ, the firstborn of the Father who will be the most exalted King of the earth (see Isa. 9:6-7).

Word Studies: 88:4 **pit** means grave; 89:14 **habitation** means the basis; foundation; 89:41 **spoil** means plunder and rob; 91:3 **noisome pestilence** means deadly epidemic or plague; 91:13 **dragon** means serpent.

Prayer Needs: Country: Trinidad and Tobago—1 million—two islands seven miles off the coast of Venezuela• Religious freedom • 34% Protestant; 29% Roman Catholic; 25% Hindu; 7% Muslim.

JULY 11: Read Psalms 92 — 100

Highlights: Praise for the loving-kindness of the Lord; appeal for justice; a call to sing, worship, and praise.

Verses for Today: *"O come, let us sing unto the Lord: let us make a joyful noise to the rock of our salvation. Let us come before his presence with thanksgiving. ... O come, let us worship and bow down: let us kneel before the Lord our maker. For he is our God; and we are the people of his pasture, and the sheep of his hand. Today if ye will hear his voice, harden not your heart ... "* (Psalm 95:1-2, 6-8).

One of the reasons many Christians make such a little impression on the world is their melancholy attitude. Their general mood is the reflection of a funeral rather than a celebration of Christ, our risen Lord.

A singing, joyful attitude is evidence of those who are in submission to God. This begins when we *"come before his presence with thanksgiving"* because of who He is—*"the Lord our maker. For he is God."* Consider the insult of our daily conduct when our attitude is critical, dull, or unhappy.

The psalmist calls, *"O come, let us worship and bow down."* God is more than an impersonal Creator: *"He is our [Shepherd] God; and we are the people [sheep] of his pasture."* It is not the nature of sheep to fear the changes and chances of life or to question the leadership of the shepherd.

Thus, the psalmist's praise foretells the coming of our Lord who said, *"I am the good shepherd, and know my sheep, and am known of mine"* (John 10:14).

Thought for Today: Is your attitude today a reflection of God's love toward you?

Christ Revealed: As the Creator—*"it is he that hath made us"* (Psalm 100:3; compare John 1:3; Col. 1:16; Rev. 4:11).

Prayer Needs: Country: Wales—3 million—in western Britain • Religious freedom • 82% Protestant; 18% Roman Catholic.

JULY 12: Read Psalms 101 — 105

Highlights: Personal commitment to the Lord's ways; a cry in distress; gratefulness to God for His mercy; His mighty power; God's providence over Israel.

Verses for Today: *"Moreover he called for a famine upon the land. . . . He sent a man before them, even Joseph, who was sold for a servant: whose feet they hurt with fetters: he was laid in iron . . . the word of the Lord tried him"* (Psalm 105:16-19).

G od brought about a famine in the days of Jacob which forced him to send his sons to Egypt to buy food. (See Psalm 105:6-16.) There they discovered that Joseph, whom they had sold as a slave years earlier, was a great ruler in Egypt. Although their treatment of Joseph had been evil, God *"meant it unto good"* (Genesis 50:20).

For many years, Joseph may not have understood his unfortunate series of circumstances as *"the word of the Lord tried him."* But this incident of God's guidance reveals the merit of trusting Him—even though we do not understand what is happening. (See Proverbs 3:5-6.)

God often withholds the understanding of His will in order to develop our faith, confidence, and trust in Him.

"For all the promises of God in him are yea, and in him Amen, unto the glory of God by us" (II Corinthians 1:20).

Thought for Today: God often overrules our wishes and plans in order to accomplish His purpose.

Christ Revealed: As the One who *"forgiveth all thine iniquities; who healeth all thy diseases"* (Psalm 103:3). Forgiveness of sin and God's healing power describe the ministry of our Lord, who was sent *"to preach deliverance to the captives, and recovering of sight to the blind, to set at liberty them that are bruised, to preach the acceptable year of the Lord"* (Luke 4:18-19).

Word Studies: 101:4 **not know** means have nothing to do with; 101:5 **privily** means secretly.

Prayer Needs: Country: Zimbabwe (formerly Rhodesia)—9 million—in south-central Africa • Limited religious freedom • 43% Protestant; 38% animism, mediums, and spirit-possession cults; 16% Catholic.

JULY 13: Read Psalms 106 — 107

Highlights: Israel's wilderness rebellion; God's great mercies to Israel; exhortation to praise God for His goodness.

Verses for Today: *"He sent his word, and healed them, and delivered them from their destructions. Oh that men would praise the Lord for his goodness, and for his wonderful works to the children of men!"* (Psalm 107:20-21).

T he psalmist could have said, "The Lord delivered them." Instead, he specifically said, *"He sent his word, and healed them."* This simply means that God's Word is the means by which He has chosen to supply and satisfy every need. Furthermore, there is no other reliable source of counsel for the inner emotional conflicts that seek to control our minds. Experience proves that people are prone to view their weaknesses in the light of their abilities and thus do not recognize the greatness of God's gift—His Word. But throughout the Bible we are taught the absolute necessity of relying on God's Word for every problem and in every situation—without exception.

Yes, God's Word does give direction to solve any problem that confronts us. And the Word by which the heavens were made is the same Word by which God *"is able to do exceeding abundantly above all that we ask or think, according to the power that worketh in us"* (Ephesians 3:20; compare Psalm 33:6).

Through daily Bible reading, we obtain the power that helps us have faith to trust God to fulfill His promises.

"For the word of God is quick, and powerful, and sharper than any two-edged sword, piercing even to the dividing asunder of soul and spirit, and of the joints and marrow, and is a discerner of the thoughts and intents of the heart" (Hebrews 4:12).

Thought for Today: How much of the Word do you make available for God to use in your life?

Christ Revealed: As the One who *"maketh the storm a calm"* (Psalm 107:29). When Jesus calmed the storm, His disciples exclaimed: *"What manner of man is this, that even the winds and the sea obey him!"* (Matt. 8:27). In all our stormy troubles, Jesus offers us great peace (John 14:27).

Word Studies: 106:19 **Horeb** is Sinai; 106:30 **stayed** means ceased; 107:11 **contemned** means spurned; despised.

Prayer Needs: Country: Swaziland—700,000—in southern Africa • Religious freedom • 67% Protestant; 19% animism, spirit-possession cults, and divination; 11% Roman Catholic; 2% Baha'i.

JULY 14: Read Psalms 108 — 118

Highlights: David's praise to God for His sovereignty over nations; prayer for judgment upon the wicked; exhortation to trust in God—not idols; praise for deliverance from death.

Verse for Today: *"Praise ye the Lord. Blessed is the man that feareth the Lord, that delighteth greatly in his commandments"* (Psalm 112:1).

A reverential fear of God creates a love for Him that will inspire us to delight in His commandments. It is an attitude of awe and reverence toward God.

Godly fear deepens our sense of humility and leads us to see how unworthy we are of His love.

The words "the fear of God" characterized the prophets of the Old Testament. This fear of God is the foundation of the more abundant life of the New Testament. It is one of the great promises foretold by the prophet Jeremiah: *"And I will make an everlasting covenant with them . . . but I will put my fear in their hearts, that they shall not depart from me"* (Jeremiah 32:40).

A New Testament example of this is found in Acts 9:31: *"Then had the churches rest . . . and were edified; and walking in the fear of the Lord, and in the comfort of the Holy Ghost, were multiplied."*

A holy fear of God is the result of walking *"in thy truth"* (Psalm 86:11)—not being afraid of God, for the Holy Spirit reveals Him as our loving Father, desiring only our good.

This reverence of God is an essential part of the life of a Christian who is pleasing to God.

" . . . let us have grace, whereby we may serve God acceptably with reverence and godly fear" (Hebrews 12:28).

Thought for Today: Fears vanish as we trust God.

Christ Revealed: Christ quoted Psalm 118:22—*"The stone which the builders refused . . . "* to the chief priests and Pharisees when they rejected Him (Matt. 21: 42-45).

Word Studies: 111:7 **verity and judgment** means absolute truth and justice; faithful and right; 112:9 **horn** here symbolizes esteem; strength; 118:22 **the head stone of the corner** means Israel has become the most important nation of all.

Prayer Needs: Country: Algeria—23 million—in North Africa • Authorities have virtually ended all open mission work • 99% Muslim; .9% Christian.

JULY 15: Read Psalm 119

Highlights: The greatness, power, and perfection of God's Word.

Verses for Today: *"With my whole heart have I sought thee. . . . Righteous art thou, O Lord. . . . Thy testimonies . . . are righteous and very faithful"* (Psalm 119:10,137-138).

More than 170 times in Psalm 119 preeminence is given to the Scriptures with such terms as "law," "lamp," "testimonies," etc. Since Christ and the testimonies of Scriptures are one and the same (John 1:1), the *"Righteous . . . Lord"* becomes central in this Psalm. Everything else is incidental to His preeminence.

"Righteous art thou, O Lord" was also the message of Jeremiah who foretold: *"He shall be called, THE LORD OUR RIGHTEOUSNESS"* (Jeremiah 23:6).

Your concern for understanding of all the Scriptures is in direct relationship to your love for Christ.

Our spiritual stature can be measured by the amount of time we give to reading the Scriptures. We cannot expect the Lord to impart further revelation of Himself or His will until we delight with our *"whole heart"* to live what He has already made clear to us.

The psalmist declared how precious God's Word was to him by saying it *"is better*

183

unto me than thousands of gold and silver" (Psalm 119:72). It is then that His Word *"giveth light; it giveth understanding"* (119:130).

The psalmist's love for God's Word was like that of the merchant in the Lord's parable: *"Who, when he had found one pearl of great price, went and sold all that he had, and bought it"* (Matthew 13:46).

"Blessed are they which do hunger and thirst after righteousness . . . " (Matthew 5:6).

Thought for Today: Your spiritual growth is dependent on the amount of time you spend with the Lord in reading His Word.

Christ Portrayed: By the psalmist, who delighted in God's commandments (Psalm 119:47). Christ said, *"For I came down from heaven, not to do mine own will, but the will of him that sent me"* (John 6:38).

Word Studies: 119:25 **quicken thou me** means nourish me; renew my life; 119:28 **melteth** means weeping and weary because of grief; 119:80 **sound** means blameless; 119:147 **prevented** means arose before.

Prayer Needs: Country: Bahrain—464,000—11 islands in the Persian Gulf near Saudi Arabia • No evangelical work is allowed among the Bahraini people • 95% Muslim; 4% Christian.

JULY 16: Read Psalms 120 — 131

Highlights: Prayer for deliverance from lying lips; God's sustaining power; prayer for Jerusalem; blessings of trusting in God.

Verses for Today: *"I wait for the Lord, my soul doth wait, and in his word do I hope. My soul waiteth for the Lord more than they that watch for the morning: I say, more than they that watch for the morning"* (Psalm 130:5-6).

T here is an unusual emphasis in the repetition, *"I say, more than they that watch for the morning."* It shows the importance of waiting upon the Lord—looking to Him to supply our every need.

The watchmen on the walls of Jerusalem were obligated to stay awake because of their responsibility to alert others in case an enemy were to attack the city.

With far more concern than that of a watchman, the psalmist urged the Israelites to place their full confidence and trust in God—*"Let Israel hope in the Lord . . . "* (Psalm 130:7).

It is a natural tendency to depend upon one's own strength or the strength of others, as the Israelites did when they sought help from Egypt. But those who value the Lord's blessing live in the confidence that He will fulfill His Word.

"Rest in the Lord, and wait patiently for him: fret not thyself because of him who prospereth in his way, because of the man who bringeth wicked devices to pass" (Psalm 37:7).

Thought for Today: Happy Christians are those who can commit everything to Christ, knowing He can choose for us better than we can choose for ourselves.

Christ Revealed: As our Protector—the One who *"shall preserve thy going out and thy coming in . . . "* (Psalm 121:8). *" . . . by me if any man enter in, he shall be saved, and shall go in and out, and find pasture"* (John 10:9).

Prayer Needs: Country: Western Samoa—175,000—in the South Pacific • Religious freedom • 68% Protestant; 21% Roman Catholic; 9% cults; 2% Baha'i.

JULY 17: Read Psalms 132 — 138

Highlights: A prayer for God's blessing; joy of unity; exhortation to praise the Lord; God's enduring mercy; mourning of the exiles in Babylon; God's Word magnified.

Verse for Today: *"Behold, how good and how pleasant it is for brethren to dwell together in unity!"* (Psalm 133:1).

T he Israelites went to Jerusalem at least three times a year to worship, singing this Psalm as they went.

There were many types of people on the road to Jerusalem, but they all had one thing in common—they were on their way to the city of God to worship Jehovah.

Surely those who are members of the family of God should live in peace with one another. This pleasant harmony is the peace of God that is dependent upon our harmony with others.

All believers in Christ—regardless of nationality, education, or wealth—are redeemed by the same Savior, love the same Master, and are looking forward to living together with Christ in the same Eternal City.

Surely the prayer of Christ is a strength to all of us: *"...Holy Father, keep through thine own name those whom thou hast given me, that they may be one, as we are"* (John 17:11).

Since all Christians experience similar trials, temptations, and sorrows, we are to encourage one another in love.

"...keep the unity of the Spirit in the bond of peace" (Ephesians 4:3).

Thought for Today: The unity of believers can be compared to a great orchestra—many instruments and yet beautiful harmony.

Christ Revealed: As the descendant of David who would sit upon the throne (Psalm 132:11; compare Luke 1:32; Acts 2:30).

Word Studies: 132:6 **Ephratah** was the district in which Bethlehem was located; 135:4 **his peculiar treasure** means God's treasured people to be carefully protected (see Exodus 19:5-6); 137:5 **her cunning** means skill upon the harp.

Prayer Needs: Country: Nauru (formerly Pleasant Island)—9,000—in the central Pacific • Religious freedom • 57% Protestant; 24% Roman Catholic; 10% Buddhist and Chinese folk-religionist.

JULY 18: Read Psalms 139 — 143

Highlights: The all-seeing providence of God; David's prayer for deliverance from Saul; comfort in prayer; prayer for mercy in judgment.

Verses for Today: *"O Lord, thou hast searched me, and known me. Thou knowest my downsitting and mine uprising; thou understandest my thought afar off"* (Psalm 139:1-2).

T he psalmist knew that everything in his life was an open book to God. Loneliness lost its power, and fears had little control over him, for he knew that God was with him and that God cared.

God is so concerned about you that nothing in your life is too insignificant for His attention. Morning, noon, and night, He observes your every thought, your secret desires, and your real needs. God is present at all times.

An awareness of His presence during times of unexpected temptations should enable us to control our attitudes, our words, and our conduct. Allow the Holy Spirit to continue to change you into the image of Christ by making *His will* your will.

"Being confident of this very thing, that he which hath begun a good work in you will perform it until the day of Jesus Christ" (Philippians 1:6).

Thought for Today: God is as near as a prayer.

Christ Revealed: As our Deliverer (Psalm 143:11). *"The Lord knoweth how to deliver the godly out of temptations . . . "* (II Pet. 2:9).

Word Studies: 139:13 **reins** means heart and mind as the inner self; 141:7 **Our bones are scattered** means overwhelming destruction is contemplated; 141:9 **gins** means traps.

Prayer Needs: Country: Costa Rica—3 million—in Central America • Religious freedom is increasing • 90% Roman Catholic; 6% Protestant.

JULY 19:   Read Psalms 144 — 150

Highlights: David's praise for God's mercy and goodness; benefits of trusting in God; all creation to praise the Lord; triumph in the God of Israel.

Verses for Today: *"Put not your trust in princes, nor in the son of man, in whom there is no help. . . . Happy is he that hath the God of Jacob for his help, whose hope is in the Lord his God"* (Psalm 146:3,5).

I n situations that baffle us, we are prone to place our faith and confidence in the wisdom and abilities of men. Even our closest friends may fail us at times. But if our *"hope is in the Lord,"* we should begin each day by seeking Him—having fellowship with Him through prayer and Bible reading. Then, by having our hope in the Lord and not in others, there will be no need for disappointment.

When we are not putting any confidence in the flesh, our faith is greatly strengthened. As we wholeheartedly turn from the world, read God's Word, and pray, He will always meet our needs.

When we are seeking advancement at work, by human nature we tend to cater to the influential ones who can promote us. However, the psalmist declared that no one, regardless of how powerful, is able to advance us to a desired position unless it is God's will. So let us humbly seek to please the Lord who will *exalt us in due time* (see I Peter 5:6).

" . . . Cursed be the man that trusteth in man . . . " (Jeremiah 17:5). The Lord reveals that man's lasting eternal values are found only in *"the God of Jacob."*

"And again, The Lord knoweth the thoughts of the wise, that they are vain. Therefore let no man glory in men . . . " (I Corinthians 3:20-21).

Thought for Today: Trusting in the Lord's unsearchable ways is better than hoping in man's predictable ways.

Christ Revealed: As the One who gives sight to the blind (Psalm 146:8). Christ gave sight to the man who was born blind (John 9:1-41).

186

Word Studies: 144:13 **garners** means grain storehouses; 148:7 **dragons** means large sea animals.

Prayer Needs: Country: San Marino—23,000—inside north-central Italy • Religious freedom • 95% Roman Catholic; 5% atheist.

PROVERBS

The book of Proverbs is a collection of moral and spiritual teachings in the form of sayings and proverbs.

Almost every subject dealing with our relationships with others, as well as with God, is covered—morality, family relations, business dealings, common sense, good manners, and a host of others.

The word "wisdom" occurs about 50 times in Proverbs. This book of practical wisdom divides mankind into two classes—wise and foolish—and exposes a series of pitfalls that defeat many people on life's pathway.

The word "wisdom" is a term describing the godly person; the ungodly are referred to as "fools."

The truly wise person recognizes that *"the fear of the Lord is the beginning of knowledge"* (Proverbs 1:7).

In contrast to the book of Proverbs, the word "wisdom" in the book of Ecclesiastes primarily speaks of human learning or worldly knowledge, which is considered vanity—meaningless (Ecclesiastes 2:12-15).

JULY 20: Read Proverbs 1 — 3

Highlights: Fear of God—the beginning of wisdom; necessity of searching for wisdom; importance of trusting in the Lord.

Verses for Today: *"Wisdom crieth without; she uttereth her voice in the streets. ...Because I have called, and ye refused; I have stretched out my hand, and no man regarded; but ye have set at nought all my counsel, and would none of my reproof: I also will laugh at your calamity; I will mock when your fear cometh; when your fear cometh as desolation, and your destruction cometh as a whirlwind; when distress and anguish cometh upon you. Then shall they call upon me, but I will not answer; they shall seek me early, but they shall not find me: for that they hated knowledge, and did not choose the fear of the Lord"* (Proverbs 1:20,24-29).

Y ou have the freedom to ignore God's Word; but if you do, a day will come when His words of wisdom will mock your misery.

Do not misunderstand; this Scripture does not say that God Himself will laugh when you are terrified—it is *His Words of wisdom* that will haunt you. This was also made clear by our Lord, who said, *"He that rejecteth me, and receiveth not my words, hath one that judgeth him: the word that I have spoken, the same shall judge him in the last day"* (John 12:48).

What could be worse for a person than to remember throughout eternity that he refused to read and heed the Word of God. Oh, how terrifying to think of the lost who will cry out in torment, "I am in hell," remembering that the Lord was *"not willing that any should perish, but that all should come to repentance"* (II Peter 3:9).

All who are lost shall remember that it was because *"they hated knowledge, and did not choose the fear of the Lord"* (Proverbs 1:29). So shall it be for all eternity.

Thought for Today: Read God's Word with willingness and desire to accept His wisdom and reproof.

Christ Revealed: As the wisdom of God (Proverbs 1:20). Christ *"is made unto us wisdom"* (I Cor. 1:30).

Word Studies: 1:18 **privily** means secretly; 1:21 **concourse** means public affairs; 1:22 **simple** means foolish; 2:7 **buckler** means shield; 3:8 **marrow** means strength.

Prayer Needs: Country: El Salvador—5 million—in Central America • Churches outside the state religion (Catholicism) are free to operate, though sometimes with official obstruction • 96% Roman Catholic; 3% Protestant.

JULY 21: Read Proverbs 4 — 7

Highlights: The power of wisdom to protect from evil; seven most hated sins; necessity of keeping God's commandments.

Verses for Today: *"These six things doth the Lord hate; yea, seven are an abomination unto him: a proud look, a lying tongue, and hands that shed innocent blood, a heart that deviseth wicked imaginations, feet that be swift in running to mischief, a false witness that speaketh lies, and he that soweth discord among brethren"* (Proverbs 6:16-19).

T he first of these seven most hated sins is a proud look. It precedes the other six sins that are abominable to God. It was pride that caused Eve to believe Satan and eat the forbidden fruit (see Genesis 3:5-6). Three—perhaps four—of these sins are directly caused by an evil tongue.

Because of the tongue, the effectiveness of many Christians is seriously hindered. Instead of showing the love of Christ, their careless talk has destroyed their usefulness.

The blessed Christian is a peace-maker whose words are an overflow of the Spirit-filled life.

"A good man out of the good treasure of the heart bringeth forth good things: and an evil man out of the evil treasure bringeth forth evil things. . . . and by thy words thou shalt be condemned" (Matthew 12:35,37).

Thought for Today: Our speech often exposes our inner thoughts.

Christ Portrayed: By the teacher of wisdom (Proverbs 4:11; see also 4:7). Christ is the Teacher *"in whom are hid all the treasures of wisdom and knowledge"* (Col. 2:3).

Word Studies: 5:6 **movable** means unstable; 5:19 **ravished** means delighted; 6:1 **surety** means guarantee; 7:2 **as the apple of thine eye** means as something as precious as one's eye, to be guarded with special care.

Prayer Needs: Country: Brazil—147 million—in South America • Religious freedom • 87% Roman Catholic; 7% Protestant; 4% various forms of spiritism.

JULY 22: Read Proverbs 8 — 11

Highlights: Benefits of wisdom; wise and foolish contrasted.

188

Verse for Today: *"The liberal soul shall be made fat: and he that watereth shall be watered also himself"* (Proverbs 11:25).

O ne of our greatest privileges as a Christian is to cooperate with God. Some people say, "I believe God can do it," but they make no effort to cooperate with the Lord in fulfilling His will. *"... faith without works is dead ... "* (James 2:26).

When we use our time and money to share God's Truth with those who desire His will, He sees to it that we gain much—*"The liberal soul shall be made fat."*

These great promises of God can only become a reality when we give in the right spirit. Whether we give money, kind words, or prayer, everything depends upon our motive. If you give expecting to receive as much in return, that is exchange. If you give in order to receive more, that is covetousness. If you give expecting thanks, that is vanity. If you give to be seen, that is vainglory. If you give to cover ulterior motives, it is bribery. If you give from a heart of compassion, it is love.

Those who give with the right motive are always receiving and always have more to give.

" ... freely ye have received, freely give" (Matthew 10:8).

Thought for Today: What motivates your giving?

Christ Revealed: As being with the Father *"when he prepared the heavens"* (see Proverbs 8:27-31). *"Thou, Lord, in the beginning hast laid the foundation of the earth; and the heavens are the works of thine hands"* (Heb. 1:10).

Word Studies: 9:15 **passengers** means those who pass by; 10:9 **surely** means safely.

Prayer Needs: Country: Guam—125,000—in the western Pacific, the most southerly of the Marianas • Religious freedom • 79% Roman Catholic; 17% Protestant.

JULY 23: Read Proverbs 12 — 15

Highlights: Moral virtues; the pitfalls of evil.

Verse for Today: *"Lying lips are abomination to the Lord: but they that deal truly are his delight"* (Proverbs 12:22).

C hrist exposed the fact that all lies originate from Satan (see John 8:44). It was Satan who lied to Eve and brought death into the world.

A lying tongue can destroy the effectiveness of another person's life. Just one conversation can do irreparable damage. Although *"a lying tongue is but for a moment"* (Proverbs 12:19), its effects can last a lifetime and maybe for generations.

A vicious lie can strip a man of his good name and destroy his character. But sincere, thoughtful words help heal the wounded spirit that has been crushed by a slandering tongue.

The tongue that is controlled by the Holy Spirit becomes an instrument of imparting His life to others.

"For he that will love life, and see good days, let him refrain his tongue from evil, and his lips that they speak no guile" (I Peter 3:10).

Thought for Today: Guard your tongue; speak only those things that build up another.

Christ Revealed: As One who hates lying (Proverbs 12:22). *" ... all liars, shall have*

189

Word Studies: 12:16 **presently known** means quickly and openly seen; 13:24 **betimes** means diligently; 15:17 **stalled** means fattened.

Prayer Needs: Country: Papua New Guinea—4 million—in the southwestern Pacific • Growing pressure to limit the activities of missions and churches • 64% Protestant; 33% Roman Catholic; 2% ancestor worship, belief in spirits, and witchcraft.

JULY 24: Read Proverbs 16 — 19

Highlight: The values of pleasing the Lord and choosing wisdom.

Verses for Today: *"The preparations of the heart in man, and the answer of the tongue, is from the Lord. . . . By mercy and truth iniquity is purged: and by the fear of the Lord men depart from evil"* (Proverbs 16:1,6).

W hen the earth was *"without form, and void; and darkness was upon the face of the deep"* (Genesis 1:2), the earth was not "prepared" to receive seed. There was a need of preparation before it was fit to produce *"herb yielding seed after his kind"* (1:12).

Man's heart, in its fallen condition, is like the earth before the *"Spirit of God moved upon the face of the waters"* (Genesis 1:2). The spiritual heart needs preparation before *"the answer of the tongue, is from the Lord."*

The judgment day of Christ may reveal that the damage done by loose talk far exceeded that done in any other way. Once words have escaped the lips, they cannot be recovered. They go on and on, from mouth to ear, and ear to mouth, spreading damage as they go. One can repent and be forgiven, but no one can retrieve what has been released. The careless words of the tongue release a destructive force that never ends.

Many careless words we have uttered in the past were "idle words," but they are no longer "idle"; they are very busy working great damage.

When *"by mercy and truth iniquity is purged,"* the tongue can have a moral and spiritual healing influence. It speaks peace to the troubled conscience and soothes the anguish of the afflicted. It subdues the passions of anger and heals divisions. When the tongue makes known God's saving power, it imparts eternal life to the lost and dying.

"Not that which goeth into the mouth defileth a man; but that which cometh out of the mouth, this defileth a man" (Matthew 15:11).

Thought for Today: Let us always be alert and separate ourselves from all associations that would involve us in careless talk lest we jeopardize our God-given usefulness to Him.

Christ Revealed: As the One who punishes the proud (Proverbs 16:5). *"For whosoever exalteth himself shall be abased; and he that humbleth himself shall be exalted"* (Luke 14:11).

As the *"friend that sticketh closer than a brother"* (Proverbs 18:24). Jesus is our Friend (John 15:14-15) and will never leave us or forsake us (Heb. 13:5).

Word Studies: 16:2 **spirits** means motives; 19:18 **and let not thy soul spare for his crying** means if you do not discipline your child, you will ruin his life.

Prayer Needs: Country: North Korea—22 million—in northeastern Asia • Violent oppression against Christianity • 39% Buddhism, Confucianism, and other Korean religions; 1% Christian.

JULY 25: Read Proverbs 20 — 22

Highlights: Deception of wine; sovereignty of God over the kings of the earth; moral virtues rewarded.

Verse for Today: *"Train up a child in the way he should go: and when he is old, he will not depart from it"* (Proverbs 22:6).

O bedience is the key to pleasing God. It is the parents' responsibility to teach their children to be obedient. *"Correct thy son, and he shall give thee rest; yea, he shall give delight unto thy soul"* (Proverbs 29:17).

Some parents do not correct their children when they do wrong. But the blessing of discipline far exceeds the pain, as expressed by the psalmist when he said, *"Before I was afflicted I went astray: but now have I kept thy word"* (Psalm 119:67).

The cruelest injustice parents can do to their children is to fail to discipline them. To love is to chasten, but *"he that spareth his rod hateth his son . . . "* (Proverbs 13;24). How contrary to the popular way of thinking! How deceptive is the philosophy of many parents who say they love their children too much to discipline them!

Discipline should be firm, but still manifest the gracious love of Christ. The parents' failure to discipline their children shows a lack of concern for their ultimate destiny.

"Children, obey your parents in the Lord: for this is right. Honor thy father and mother; which is the first commandment with promise; that it may be well with thee, and thou mayest live long on the earth" (Ephesians 6:1-3).

Thought for Today: With the same love our heavenly Father disciplines us, we must discipline our children.

Christ Revealed: As the One who can say, *I am clean and without sin* (see Proverbs 20:9; compare Heb. 4:15).

Word Study: 22:29 **mean** means of no importance.

Prayer Needs: Country: Italy—57 million—in southern Europe • Religious freedom • 81% Roman Catholic; .4% Protestant; .1% Eastern Orthodox.

JULY 26: Read Proverbs 23 — 26

Highlights: Moral, ethical, and spiritual teachings; comparisons, warnings, and instructions.

Verses for Today: *"I went by the field of the slothful, and . . . it was all grown over with thorns . . . "* (Proverbs 24:30-31).

A slothful person is a lazy person. Because of this characteristic, he does not provide for his family or respond to opportunities to serve the Lord. Instead, he buries his talent and soon loses what he thought he possessed. (See Luke 8:18.)

In Proverbs 6:6, such a person is called a sluggard and is advised to observe the ant to see how it works, storing up food for the long winter months.

Slothfulness destroys character and discourages others who have to assume the responsibilities the slothful person shirks. *"He also that is slothful in his work is brother to him that is a great waster"* (Proverbs 18:9).

The Christian who is *"redeeming the time"* (Ephesians 5:16) looks for opportunities to be useful. He will volunteer his services, for he realizes that he has no assurance of being able to serve his Lord tomorrow and he wants to take advantage of every opportunity.

" . . . we commanded you, that if any would not work, neither should he eat" (II Thessalonians 3:10).

Thought for Today: A slothful person forfeits the privilege of being the person God wants him to be.

Christ Revealed: As the One who rewards those who repay evil with good (Proverbs 25:21-22). *"If thine enemy hunger, feed him; if he thirst, give him drink . . . "* (Rom. 12:20). Jesus said *"Love your enemies"* (Matt. 5:44; Luke 6:27,35).

Word Studies: 24:26 **kiss his lips** means a fair and just answer is as assuring and pleasant as a kiss on the lips; 25:9 **discover not a secret to another** means do not betray another man's confidence.

Prayer Needs: Country: Brunei—250,000—on the northern coast of Borneo • Limited religious freedom • 66% Muslim; 19% Chinese religions; 6% animist; 4% Protestant; 4% Roman Catholic.

JULY 27: Read Proverbs 27 — 31

Highlights: Comparisons, warnings, and instructions; Agur's confession of his faith; the words of King Lemuel; praise of a good wife.

Verses for Today: *"There be . . . things which are too wonderful for me . . . which I know not: The way of an eagle in the air . . . "* (Proverbs 30:18-19).

I f we could ask the eagle if it is afraid of the law of gravity, it would reply, "I have never heard of gravity; I know nothing of its law. I fly because it is my nature to fly."

Not only does the eagle have the power of flight, but it has the ability to overcome the law of gravity. Yet gravity remains. Once life is gone from the eagle, we are reminded at once of the law of gravity. But while the eagle lives, it overcomes gravity by the very nature of its life.

The unconverted are sinners in rebellion against God because it is their nature to be so.

Sinners are children of Adam in that they are like him—inwardly sinful. The saved are the children of the "second Adam" in that they possess Christ's nature. *"For as by one man's disobedience many were made sinners, so by the obedience of one shall many be made righteous"* (Romans 5:19, see also I Corinthians 15:22,45).

The miracle of conversion is that it makes our lives Christ-conscious and Christ-centered. There is an overwhelming desire to read and meditate upon His Word—what He has to say—and bring others to a saving knowledge of His love. These are the natural, joyous impulses in the heart of the child of God.

"For the law of the Spirit of life in Christ Jesus hath made me free from the law of sin and death" (Romans 8:2).

Thought for Today: Christ is not just the world's Savior in the sweet by and by, but here and now.

Christ Revealed: As the Son of God (Proverbs 30:4). *"This is my beloved Son, in whom I am well pleased"* (Matthew 3:17).

Word Studies: 27:16 **Whosoever hideth her hideth the wind, and the ointment of his right hand, which bewrayeth itself** means restraining her is like attempting to hold the wind or grasp oil with the hand (and she slips through his fingers); 31:10 **virtuous woman** means far more than having good moral character. It also includes the traits of courage and faith.

Prayer Needs: Country: Tuvalu (formerly Ellice Islands)—8,000—nine islands in the southwestern Pacific • Religious freedom • 92% Protestant; 5% Baha'i; 2% Roman Catholic.

ECCLESIASTES _____

In the book of Ecclesiastes, there is no mention of prayer, thankfulness, or praise to God.

This book reveals the emptiness of living for any other purpose than to please the Lord. It is a confession of pessimism from Solomon, who was famous for his wisdom (1:16), had unlimited opportunities for earthly pleasure (2:3), and was blessed with great wealth (2:8).

Even though the word "God" is mentioned 40 times in Ecclesiastes, without exception, it is the Hebrew word "elohim." This word for God was used by believers, but it was also used by unbelievers and idolaters in referring to their false gods and idols.

Throughout the book, the name Jehovah, by which our Father is known by His people in covenant relationship with Him, is not mentioned once.

JULY 28: Read Ecclesiastes 1 — 4

Highlights: The vanity (emptiness) of living for pleasure and material gain; a reason for everything; varied proverbs of wisdom.

Verses for Today: *"And I gave my heart to seek and search out by wisdom concerning all things that are done under heaven . . . behold, all is vanity and vexation of spirit"* (Ecclesiastes 1:13-14).

K ing Solomon spoke with inexcusable discontent when he said, *"I gave my heart to seek and search out . . . all things."* He concluded that he knew all that was to be known, but he chose to ignore the Word of God.

Solomon had the remarkable privilege of having the Lord appear to him, saying, *"If thou wilt walk before me . . . in integrity of heart . . . I will establish . . . thy kingdom upon Israel for ever . . . "* (I Kings 9:4-5). But the "wisest" man on earth tried to substitute his knowledge for God's wisdom (see I Kings 11:9-10.)

The pleasure-seeking Solomon began life with high hopes, but later he became cynical and pessimistic, saying, *"Therefore I hated life . . . for all is vanity and vexation of spirit"* (Ecclesiastes 2:17).

Solomon's life is a testimony to the fact that no one can be satisfied with mere worldly knowledge. He was unable to escape the reality that God has instilled within each person a hunger that can only be satisfied by Christ—the Bread of life.

"...I am the bread of life: he that cometh to me shall never hunger; and he that believeth on me shall never thirst" (John 6:35).

Thought for Today: Worldly possessions and worldly pleasures are no substitute for the One Person to whom we owe our supreme devotion—the Lord Jesus Christ.

Christ Revealed: In Ecclesiastes 2:11, *"Then I looked on all the works that my hands had wrought, and on the labor that I have labored to do: and, behold, all was vanity and vexation of spirit, and there was no profit under the sun,"* we are reminded of Christ's words: *"For what is a man profited, if he shall gain the whole world, and lose his own soul? or what shall a man give in exchange for his soul?"* (Matt. 16:26).

Word Studies: 1:17 **madness and folly** means the opposite of true wisdom—he pursued worldly wisdom as well as vice and wickedness; **vexation of spirit** means very unsatisfying.

Prayer Needs: **Country:** Vatican City—800—in Rome, Italy Religious freedom • Approximately 100% Roman Catholic.

JULY 29: Read Ecclesiastes 5 — 8

Highlights: Caution against hasty vows; the emptiness of riches; wisdom and goodness upheld; respect for rulers.

Verses for Today: *"And so I saw the wicked buried, who had come and gone from the place of the holy, and they were forgotten in the city where they had so done: this is also vanity. Because sentence against an evil work is not executed speedily, therefore the heart of the sons of men is fully set in them to do evil"* (Ecclesiastes 8:10-11).

I t would seem as if God did not hear the groanings of the innocent or see the hypocrisy of the evildoers who actually attended the sanctuary of God, *"the place of the holy."* This hypocrisy was allowed to continue—God did not interfere to bring His judgment upon them.

It often appears that Divine justice has been suspended as we observe the chaotic condition of world affairs. Furthermore, the oppression of the defenseless and the prosperity of the wicked is a source of perplexity.

Not only during life but even in death itself, the wicked are often praised and "buried" with all the recognition of their popularity. Yet, with all the advantages of these external appearances which are carried on even to the grave, they fail to deceive God.

While the course of life seems to run smoothly, the sinner begins to imagine that God is indifferent to human conduct, and God, after all, can be ignored. Even Christians, ignorant of God's Word, are staggered by the delay of Divine justice to inflict penalty for the wicked sins of mankind. But the judgment which God's law attaches to sin is certain and with eternal consequences.

"For if the word spoken by angels was steadfast, and every transgression and disobedience received a just recompense of reward; How shall we escape, if we neglect so great salvation" (Hebrews 2:2-3).

Thought for Today: Do not envy prosperity of evildoers—it is only temporary.

Christ Revealed: As the One who expects us to keep our vows (Ecclesiastes 5:4). *"But let your communication be, Yea, yea; Nay, nay: for whatsoever is more than these cometh of evil"* (Matt. 5:37).

Word Study: 5:6 **the angel** means the priest whose duty it was to collect what had been vowed.

Prayer Needs: Country: Cambodia—7 million—in Southeast Asia • Churches have suffered under Communism • 88% Buddhist; 3% animism and spirit worship; 2% Muslim; .6% Christian.

JULY 30: Read Ecclesiastes 9 — 12

Highlights: Struggles of the righteous and the wicked; wisdom better than strength; the wise versus the foolish; the Creator to be remembered.

Verses for Today: *"Let us hear the conclusion of the whole matter: Fear God, and keep his commandments: for this is the whole duty of man. For God shall bring every work into judgment, with every secret thing, whether it be good, or whether it be evil"* (Ecclesiastes 12:13-14).

S olomon lived to please himself, seeking to satisfy everything his heart desired. He not only forfeited his opportunities to exalt the great name of Jehovah, but he miserably confessed that *life came to mean nothing to him* (see Ecclesiastes 2:17). Solomon ended the book with regret, knowing that he must face God, who *"shall bring every work into judgment."*

Although Solomon knew that God was angry with him because he *"did evil in the sight of the Lord,"* we have no record that Solomon repented or asked God to forgive him for leading the nation of Israel into idolatry (see I Kings 11:4-11).

King Solomon is an example of those who have great abilities and have achieved great things, but whose desire for pleasure robbed them of the joy of fulfilling God's will for their lives.

There are many things we can do that are good and worthwhile that are not sinful. But, like Solomon, we can become so involved in "good" activities that our hearts are turned from the things of God. Ultimately, we not only dishonor the Lord, but we lose out on eternal rewards because we missed His best for our lives.

"And that which fell among thorns are they, which, when they have heard, go forth, and are choked with cares and riches and pleasures of this life, and bring no fruit to perfection" (Luke 8:14).

Thought for Today: To obey the Lord Jesus Christ should be the primary desire of our hearts.

Christ Revealed: In the statement, *"For God shall bring every work into judgment . . ."* (Ecclesiastes 12:14). *" . . . true and righteous are his judgments . . . "* (Rev. 19:2).

Word Studies: 10:14 **is full of words** means talks as though he knows everything about which he knows nothing; 10:15 **he knoweth not how to go to the city** means he is ignorant concerning the most obvious matters; 12:11 **goads** means rods with iron spikes, or sharpened at the ends, used in driving oxen (see Judges 3:31; I Sam. 13:21; Acts 9:5); **The words of the wise are as goads** means words of wisdom are as goads because they rouse into action, restrain from error, impel to right—the sting and pain which they inflict are for our good and are not to be resented; **and as nails fastened by the masters of assemblies, which are given from one shepherd** means wise men allow words of truth (verse 10) to penetrate deeply, no longer floating loosely about, but secured with other truths, providing a certain unity of purpose for one's life.

Prayer Needs: Country: Jordan—3 million—in southwestern Asia • Considerable tolerance of the few Christians in Jordan • 93% Muslim; 5% Christian.

SONG OF SOLOMON

The Jews believed that the Song of Solomon—often called Song of Songs—expressed the love relationship between God and His chosen people—the king representing God, and the bride representing the people of Israel.

Others believe that the purpose of this book is to teach the sacredness and beauty of the married-love relationship that should exist between a man and woman, which God Himself ordained.

Many Christians believe the book is symbolic of the great love between Christ and His people—the king representing Christ, and the bride representing His Church.

"The voice of my beloved! Behold, he cometh . . . " (2:8) was the desire of the shepherdess-maid. She waited for the hour when her king—*"the chiefest among ten thousand"* (5:10), the man she loved—would return.

Even as the shepherdess-maid longed to see her beloved, so the Church now waits for the return of her unseen Savior.

No matter how poverty-stricken a Christian may be, he is rich, for he can say, *"I am my beloved's, and his desire is toward me"* (7:10). The King of kings left His throne in glory to come to earth to demonstrate His love for undeserving sinners. And all who love Him will rejoice when He returns.

JULY 31: Read Song of Solomon 1 — 8

Highlight: Virtues of married love—symbolic of Christ's love for the Church.
Verse for Today: *"The Song of songs, which is Solomon's"* (Song of Solomon 1:1).

K ing Solomon owned a vineyard in the area of Ephraim (Song of Solomon 8:11).

His tenant family had a daughter whose brothers seemingly despised her. They made her work long hard hours, taking care of the vineyard as well as the sheep. She worked in the hot sun all day and became sunburned and quite tanned, and said, *"Mine own vineyard have I not kept,"* meaning that she had no opportunity to take care of herself (1:6).

One day as she was caring for the sheep, she looked up and saw a stranger-shepherd. Embarrassed, she said, *"Look not upon me, because I am black, because the sun hath looked upon me"* (1:6). But to him, she was altogether lovely: *"Behold, thou art fair, my love"* (1:15).

Little by little, that friendship grew into love, and finally this shepherd had won the heart of the despised daughter. When she asked him where he fed his flock, he was evasive (1:7). But before her beloved went away, he told her that he would return and said to her, *"Rise up, my love, my fair one, and come away"* (2:10). She trusted that some day he would come back for her.

So she thought of that day when she would be his bride. Sometimes she dreamed of him but awakened only to find that he was not there (3:1).

One day a long procession of the king's *"valiant men"* and Solomon himself stopped just outside the vineyard (3:7). To the amazement of the Shulamite daughter, the royal guard announced that the king had arrived for her. As she approached and looked into his face, she was surprised to learn that he was the stranger-shepherd who had won her heart. She said, *"I am my beloved's, and his desire is toward me"* (7:10).

From Genesis to Revelation, we have the story of the Shepherd-King who came from Heaven's highest glory down into this dark world that He might win a bride for Himself. And then He went away, but He said, *"I will come again, and receive you unto myself"* (John 14:3). And so His bride is expectantly waiting for the royal announcement: *"Behold, the bridegroom cometh . . . "* (Matthew 25:6).

Thought for Today: Are you ready for the Lord's return?

Christ Revealed: As *"the chiefest among ten thousand"* (Song of Solomon 5:10). Jesus is the *"KING OF KINGS, AND LORD OF LORDS"* (Rev. 19:16).

Word Studies: 1:12 **spikenard** means perfume; 1:14 **camphire** means flowers; 2:5 **sick of love** means lovesick; 2:12 **turtle** means turtledove; 2:24 **comely** means lovely; 5:4 **bowels** means heart; 6:6 **barren** means childless.

Prayer Needs: Country: Dominican Republic—7 million—in the West Indies, occupying the eastern two-thirds of the island of Hispaniola • Religious freedom • 96% Roman Catholic (one-half of which are spiritists); 2% Protestant; 1% Afro-American spiritist.

PRAYERS IN THIS MONTH'S READING

David — for forgiveness after his sin
with Bathsheba .... Psalm 51

David — for help when the Philistines took
him in Gath .... Psalm 56

Psalmist — for help in his old age .... Psalm 71

David — for guidance; to be taught God's ways .... Psalm 86

Moses — concerning God's eternity,
and man's brevity of life .... Psalm 90

Psalmist — prayer of the afflicted
when he is overwhelmed .... Psalm 102

Psalmist — concerning God's Word .... Psalm 119

David — for help when in trouble .... Psalm 142

Agur — for honesty and moderation
in his life .... Proverbs 30:7-9

NOTE: There are many prayers in Psalms, but space does not permit us to list each prayer separately.

ISAIAH

The book of Isaiah was written by the prophet Isaiah, who lived in Jerusalem, the capital of Judah. His ministry continued for 50 to 60 years through the reigns of Uzziah, Jotham, Ahaz, Hezekiah, and possibly Manasseh.

This was an age of prosperity, and only a few people in the kingdom of Judah remained faithful to Jehovah.

The sister kingdom of Israel, under Jeroboam II, also enjoyed prosperity; but it was even more corrupt than Judah—socially, politically, and morally.

In the beginning of Isaiah's ministry, Assyria dominated the world. During the lifetime of Isaiah, Assyria attacked Samaria, capital of the Northern Kingdom, and defeated the ten-tribed kingdom of Israel, as Isaiah had prophesied (9:8—10:4). The Israelites were taken as captives to Assyrian territories east of the Tigris River.

Israel had forsaken *all the commandments of the Lord their God, and made themselves two golden images; idols cast in the shape of two calves.* Because of this, the prophet foretold that they would be destroyed (see II Kings 17:16,18).

Isaiah's burden was to keep the small kingdom of Judah from a similar destruction by turning them back to the Lord.

The first chapter in Isaiah is a summary of his entire message. It exposes the sinfulness of Judah and Jerusalem (1:3-8), expresses the Lord's loving appeals for them to repent (1:16-19), and points out the certainty of coming judgment (1:24-25,29-31). He appealed to them to walk in the light of God's Word (2:5). But the nation of Judah was indifferent and continued in mere formality of worship, thus despising their covenant relationship with God.

The phrase *"the Holy One of Israel"* (1:4) is used 30 times in this book. It was this Holy One that the nation had rejected.

Isaiah foretold that, because of its sins, the nation of Judah would be destroyed by the Babylonians. But he also gave messages of comfort and hope for those who would remain faithful.

Many of the prophecies of salvation reach beyond the kingdom of Judah to all mankind. The invitation to accept this salvation is extended to everyone in chapter 55.

Isaiah also foretold that the Messiah would be born of a virgin (7:14) and that He would sit on David's throne and rule the world in righteousness and truth.

Jesus quoted Isaiah 61:1-2 as referring to Himself (see Luke 4:17-21).

The New Testament quotes more prophecies from Isaiah than from any other Old Testament book.

AUGUST 1: Read Isaiah 1 — 4

Highlights: The nation's sin; Isaiah's exhortation for repentance; coming of Christ's kingdom; Jerusalem's glorious future.

Verse for Today: *"The ox knoweth his owner, and the ass his master's crib: but Israel doth not know, my people doth not consider"* (Isaiah 1:3).

D uring Isaiah's ministry, the ten-tribed nation of Israel was defeated by Assyria. Isaiah's burden was to call the remaining small nation of Judah back to the Lord: *"... make you clean, put away the evil of your doings from before mine eyes; cease to do evil"* (Isaiah 1:16); *"O house of Jacob, come ye, and let us walk in the light of the Lord"* (2:5). The nation had *"provoked the Holy One of Israel unto anger"* by placing their faith in false gods (see 1:4).

Even though God had chosen them to be His people, delivered them from Egyptian slavery, taken them through the wilderness journeys, and given them the Promised Land, they did not remain faithful to Him. Consequently, the prophet Isaiah looked far beyond their sins and God's imminent judgment to a glorious future when God's people would be established in peace.

We look forward to that day when the King of kings shall reign—when *"the Lord alone shall be exalted"* (2:17).

"Having therefore these promises dearly beloved, let us cleanse ourselves from all filthiness of the flesh and spirit, perfecting holiness in the fear of God" (II Corinthians 7:1).

Thought for Today: Continued disobedience blinds one's eyes to the will of God.

Christ Revealed: As the One who will judge the nations (Isaiah 2:2-4; compare Micah 4:1-3). Our Lord is a righteous Judge who will reward those who obey His Word and look for His return (Rom. 6:17-18; II Tim. 4:1-8).
"The branch of the Lord" (Isaiah 4:2) refers to Christ Himself as the descendant of David.

Word Studies: 1:25 **purely** means thoroughly; 1:31 **as tow** means as an object to be set on fire; **the maker of it** means his work; 2:9 **mean** means common; 2:11 **lofty** means proud; 2:15 **fenced** means fortified; 3:3 **artificer** means craftsman; 3:16 **mincing** means tripping; 3:18 **bravery** means beauty; **cauls** means netting for the hair; 3:20 **tablets** means perfume boxes; 3:22 **wimples** means a woman's veil; headpiece; **crisping pins** means handbags; 3:23 **glasses** means mirrors; 3:24 **rent** means rope; **a stomacher** means rich dress clothes; 4:6 **covert** means shelter.

Prayer Needs: Country: Canada—26 million—in North America • Religious freedom • 47% Roman Catholic; 37% Protestant; 3% Eastern Orthodox; 2% cults; 1% Jewish.

AUGUST 2: Read Isaiah 5 — 9

Highlights: God's judgment upon sinners; Isaiah's vision of God's holiness; his message for King Ahaz; Christ's birth and kingdom foretold.

Verses for Today: *"In the year that king Uzziah died I saw also the Lord sitting upon a throne.... Holy, holy, holy, is the Lord of hosts: the whole earth is full of his glory"* (Isaiah 6:1,3).

D uring the reign of King Uzziah (also called Azariah), the nation of Judah reached its greatest power and prosperity since the death of Solomon.

At the height of his popularity, he ignored the priests, entered the Temple to worship God, and burned incense (symbolic of prayer) on the altar—a ceremony that was to be performed only by priests. God said that Uzziah's *"heart was lifted up to his destruction: for he transgressed against the Lord his God."* Therefore, the Lord struck him with leprosy. (See II Chronicles 26:16-21.)

Although he was a king, he did not have the right to ignore the fact that sinful man can only worship God through an intercessor.

After Uzziah's death, Isaiah beheld another King, *"... high and lifted up"* (Isaiah 6:1)—the King whose name *"shall be called Wonderful, Counselor, The mighty God, The everlasting Father, The Prince of Peace"* (9:6)—The One who today intercedes before God for sinful man.

No matter how good and important we may think we are, we are unworthy to approach a holy god—except through our High Priest, the Lord Jesus Christ, who *"ever liveth to make intercession"* for us (Hebrews 7:25).

"Who is he that condemneth? It is Christ that died, yea rather, that is risen again, who is even at the right hand of God, who also maketh intercession for us" (Romans 8:34).

Thought for Today: Self-righteous people assume they are "good enough" without the Savior.

Christ Revealed: As Immanuel, the Son of a virgin (Isaiah 7:14). Other prophecies concerning Christ are found in Isaiah 8:14; 9:2,6-7. Isaiah 9:6 reveals that a Child shall be born; a Son shall be given (crucifixion); and the government shall be upon His shoulders (His Second Coming) (Rev. 19:11-21; see also Matt. 1:21-25; 4:13-16; Luke 1:26-33; I Tim. 3:16).

Word Studies: 6:1 **train** means robe; 7:6 **vex** means attack; terrify; **make a breach** means force an entrance; 7:14 **Immanuel** means God with us; 7:16 **abhorrest** means hate; 7:23 **silverlings** means shekels of silver; 7:25 **lesser cattle** means sheep; 8:3 **the prophetess** means my wife; 8:19 **peep** means whisper; 8:21 **hardly bestead** means sorely distressed; 9:8 **lighted** means come to be known; 9:9 **stoutness** means arrogance.

Prayer Needs: Country: French Guiana—92,000—on the northeastern coast of South America • Religious freedom • 87% Roman Catholic; 4% Protestant; 1% animism; 1% Muslim; 1% Chinese religions.

AUGUST 3: Read Isaiah 10 — 14

Highlights: Assyria to be broken; promise of Israel's restoration; Christ, the Branch; thanksgiving for God's mercies; Babylon's doom predicted; Israel to be preserved.

Verses for Today: *"Behold, God is my salvation. . . . Therefore with joy shall ye draw water out of the wells of salvation. . . . Praise the Lord, call upon his name, declare his doings among the people . . . "* (Isaiah 12:2-4).

S alvation and fellowship with God are the great themes of the Bible. All who trust in His Word—the Living Water of salvation—have experienced satisfaction beyond compare. It then becomes their greatest joy to lead others to the well-spring of eternal life.

All the wells of salvation are in Christ. Every believer receives the priceless, satisfying "water" from Christ alone. The wells of salvation are revealed in His Word. (See John 3:3-5; 7:37-38; 15:3.)

"And the Spirit and the bride say, Come. And let him that heareth say, Come. And let him that is athirst come. And whosoever will, let him take the water of life freely" (Revelation 22:17).

Thought for Today: Our Lord's wells of life-giving water are overflowing and inexhaustible.

Christ Revealed: As the descendant of Jesse, King David's father (Isaiah 11:1). Isaiah 11 reveals Christ's earthly rule of righteousness (Matt. 25:31-46; Rev. 20—21).

Word Studies: 10:4 **under** means among; 10:20 **stay** means rely; 10:22 **consumption** means destruction; 10:28 **carriages** means baggage; 10:33 **lop** means cut off; 11:5 **reins** means waist; 11:8 **cockatrice's** means viper's; 11:10 **an ensign** means a standard; 13:4 **mustereth** means calls together; 13:21 **satyrs** means demons in the shape of goats (See also 34:14. According to Rev. 18:2, the ruins of Babylon later became the *"habitation of devils."*); 14:8 **feller** means tree cutter; 14:11 **viols** means musical instruments, such as harps or lyres; 14:23 **bittern** means hedgehog; **besom** means broom; 14:28 **burden** means mournful, inspired prophecy.

Prayer Needs: Country: Iceland—245,000—at the northern end of the Atlantic • Religious freedom • 94% Protestant; 6% Roman Catholic.

AUGUST 4: Read Isaiah 15 — 21

Highlights: Moab's ruin foretold; Syria and Israel threatened; God's judgments; Egypt to worship the Lord; captivity of Egypt foretold.

Verses for Today: *" . . . He calleth to me out of Seir [Edom], Watchman, what of the night? Watchman, what of the night? The watchman said, The morning cometh, and also the night . . . "* (Isaiah 21:11-12).

E dom's watchman had an unfavorable report. There was nothing to look forward to except a long and dark **night** of Babylonian captivity.

The Edomites descended from Abraham and Isaac and were treated as brethren by Israel at the time they came out of Egypt. But as the Edomites then returned evil for good (Numbers 20:14-21), they lost all hope of God's future blessings. The inevitable result is, *"Whoso rewardeth evil for good, evil shall not depart from his house"* (Proverbs 17:13).

We see ourselves surrounded by the **night** of unbelief and sin, which is moral and spiritual **night**: *"Men love darkness rather than light"* (see John 3:19).

But Christians have a glorious **light** within them to comprehend God's will in this evil world. Every earnest Christian is a watchman, longing for the Advent of the new **morning**.

Christians become discouraged over many things—materialism exalted by popular atheistic teachers; abounding luxury of the wicked; violence and cruelty defiling our society. But looking beyond these, we read in God's Word of a new day—the coming of the King of kings—and we know that the **morning** will soon come.

"And, behold, I come quickly; and my reward is with me" (Revelation 22:12).

Thought for Today: Be vigilant and ever prepared for the return of Jesus Christ.

Christ Revealed: As the One who will sit on the throne of David (Isaiah 16:5; compare Luke 1:32-33) and as the Savior (Isaiah 19:20).

Word Studies: 16:3 **bewray** means betray; 16:5 **hasting righteousness** means speeds the cause of righteousness; 16:14 **contemned** means despised; 17:11 **a heap** means a ruin; 18:7 **peeled** means to make bald or bare of all its comeliness; 19:8 **angle** means line and hook; 20:1 **Tartan** means the commander-in-chief; 21:7 **chariot** means wagon; 21:8 **he cried, a lion** means a watchman shouted like a lion (compare Rev. 10:3); **ward** means guard post; 21:14 **prevented with their bread him that fled** means gave food necessary to save them from starvation.

Prayer Needs: Country: Morocco—23 million—on the northwestern coast of Africa • Government very hostile to Christians and missions • 99+% Muslim; .5% Christian.

AUGUST 5: Read Isaiah 22 — 26

Highlights: Prophecy about Jerusalem; Tyre to be destroyed; God's judgment upon the earth; Isaiah glorifies God; God's dominion over Judah; praise to the Lord.

Verse for Today: *"O Lord our God, other lords besides thee have had dominion over us; but by thee only will we make mention of thy name"* (Isaiah 26:13).

B ecause of the sins of God's chosen people—led by their own evil, idolatrous kings—they were defeated again and again.

Isaiah confessed how other nations had ruled over them, each one attempting to force the faithful minority to accept their pagan worship.

God's people in every generation have faced enemies of God who seek to force them to accept pagan ways. Evil influences, motivated by Satan, are constantly seeking to corrupt those who are loyal to Christ.

The true worshiper of God can say with Isaiah, *"Other lords besides thee have had dominion over us; but by thee only will we make mention of thy name."* Christ is to be Lord of our lives; it is never acceptable to God for us to compromise our loyalty to Him.

"Neither yield ye your members as instruments of unrighteousness unto sin: but yield yourselves unto God, as those that are alive from the dead, and your members as instruments of righteousness unto God. For sin shall not have dominion over you: for ye are not under the law, but under grace" (Romans 6:13-14).

Thought for Today: Trials have helped many people come to know God's will for their lives.

Christ Revealed: As the One who holds *"the key of the house of David"* (Isaiah 22:22). Christ is holy and true and *"hath the key of David."* It is He *"that openeth, and no man shutteth; and shutteth, and no man openeth"* (Rev. 3:7).

Word Studies: 22:24 **flagons** means bottles or jars; 23:8 **traffickers** means merchants; 23:10 **strength** means ability to resist; 23:11 **the merchant city** means Canaan; 23:13 **raised up** means overthrew; 24:6 **desolate** means guilty; 24:8 **tabrets** means tambourines; 24:19 **clean dissolved** means split open; 26:7 **weigh** means direct or prepare; 26:12 **ordain** means establish.

Prayer Needs: Country: Kenya—22 million—in eastern Africa • Religious freedom • 46% Protestant; 27% Roman Catholic; 17% belief in mystical powers; 6% Muslim; 1% Eastern Orthodox.

AUGUST 6: Read Isaiah 27 — 31

Highlights: Assurance of Israel's deliverance; judgment of Ephraim; Jerusalem warned; Israel's hypocritical worship exposed; Israel rebuked for its alliance with Egypt; future hope assured.

Verse for Today: *"For the Egyptians shall help in vain, and to no purpose: therefore have I cried concerning this, Their strength is to sit still"* (Isaiah 30:7).

T he Israelites were under the special guardianship of God, who had wrought many deliverances for them. Yet, when the Assyrians threatened to invade their nation, they turned to Egypt—the very people who had once so cruelly oppressed their forefathers. To ensure Egyptian alliance, they sent Egypt a large sum of money.

It was in rebuke of such lack of faith in God that the prophet said *"sit still"*—don't panic, but rely on God to help. Today, the believer in Christ is often tempted to sin in a very similar way.

To *"sit still"* doesn't mean we are to remain idle and use none of our God-given abilities. If we are to receive God's blessings on our efforts, we must, in a sense, *"sit still"*—place our whole dependence on God and not on our own plans.

"It is good that a man should both hope and quietly wait for the salvation of the Lord" (Lamentations 3:26).

Thought for Today: When it seems there is no hope, is it because we are relying on human strength instead of God's strength?

Christ Revealed: As *"a tried stone, a precious corner stone, a sure foundation"* (Isaiah 28:16). Jesus Himself became the chief cornerstone (Matt. 21: 42-46; Acts 4:10-12; Rom. 9:29-33; Eph. 2:8-22; I Pet. 2:6-8).

Word Studies: 27:12 **beat off** means to handpick His "harvest," separating the true Israelites from the apostate Israelites—like separating grains of wheat from their husks; 28:4 **hasty fruit** means first ripe fig; 29:1 **Ariel** means Jerusalem; 29:3 **mount** means military post; 29:9 **wonder** means wait; 30:6 **bunches** means humps; 30:24 **ear** means plow; **clean provender** means good fodder; 31:3 **holpen** means helped.

Prayer Needs: Country: Liechtenstein—27,000—in western Europe • Religious freedom • 87% Roman Catholic; 12% Protestant.

AUGUST 7: Read Isaiah 32 — 37

Highlights: Righteous King foretold; women of Jerusalem warned; judgment upon nations; Jerusalem threatened; Hezekiah's prayer; destruction of the Assyrians.

Verses for Today: *"Now it came to pass in the fourteenth year of king Hezekiah, that Sennacherib king of Assyria came up against all the defenced cities of Judah, and took them. . . . Thus saith the king [of Assyria], Let not Hezekiah deceive you . . . Neither let Hezekiah make you trust in the Lord, saying, The Lord will surely deliver us: this city shall not be delivered into the hand of the king of Assyria"* (Isaiah 36:1,14-15).

J ust eight years after he invaded and destroyed the Northern Kingdom, Sennacherib, king of Assyria, attacked Judah. (Compare II Kings 18:13-17 and

II Chronicles 32:1-8.) It was during this crisis that King Hezekiah trusted in God and told his nation, " ... *with us is the Lord our God ...* " (II Chronicles 32:8).

Hezekiah sought to lead his people to trust in God as their only hope of survival against Assyria. When he read the letter which the Assyrian ambassador had brought from Sennacherib, Hezekiah *"went up into the house of the Lord, and spread it before the Lord. And Hezekiah prayed ..."* (II Kings 19:14-15).

The prayer was short but sincere, and the angel of the Lord destroyed 185,000 soldiers in Sennacherib's army.

If we truly live in fellowship with God, we will look to Him in prayer—not merely when we are in trouble, but for all things.

" ... *in everything by prayer and supplication with thanksgiving let your requests be made known unto God"* (Philippians 4:6).

Thought for Today: You can depend on God's promises; they cannot fail.

Christ Revealed: As the unmovable Rock (Isaiah 32:2). Christ is always available to provide "rest"—comfort and security—to all who put their trust in Him rather than in human strength. *"The Lord is my rock, and my fortress. ... who is a rock save our God?"* (Psa. 18:2,31; see also Matt. 11:28-30).

As the King who will bring judgement upon the earth (Isaiah 33:17; 34:4-5). In that day, Christians will see the King in His power and great glory, but the lost will face His fiery indignation (Matt. 24:30; II Pet. 3:10).

Word Studies: 32:3 **tempest** means storm; 32:5 **churl** means crafty; 33:23 **tacklings** means hoisting ropes; 34:7 **unicorns** means wild oxen; 34:11 **cormorant** means pelican; 36:2 **Rabshakeh** means chief officer; 36:11 **Syrian** means Aramaic.

Prayer Needs: Country: Central African Republic—3 million—in the center of the African continent • Religious freedom • 51% Protestant; 34% Roman Catholic; 10% animist; 3% Muslim.

AUGUST 8: Read Isaiah 38 — 42

Highlights: Hezekiah's life lengthened; Babylonian captivity foretold; comfort for God's people; God's assurance to Israel; song of praise to the Lord; Israel's suffering a result of sin.

Verses for Today: *"Comfort ye, comfort ye my people, saith your God ... The voice of him that crieth in the wilderness, Prepare ye the way of the Lord, make straight in the desert a highway for our God ... The grass withereth, the flower fadeth: but the word of our God shall stand for ever"* (Isaiah 40:1,3,8).

W hen certain men asked John the Baptist if he were the Messiah, he quoted the words, *"I am the voice of one crying in the wilderness, Make straight the way of the Lord, as said the prophet Isaiah"* (John 1:23).

Although there does not seem to be any comfort in the words *"All flesh is as grass, and ... the grass withereth, the flower fadeth"* (Isaiah 40:7-8), they illustrate a basic principle. Until we see our utter helplessness, we will never turn to Christ for salvation. If we think we are good enough, we will never seek the Savior.

A sense of total desolation is needed to bring us to dependence upon Him. We can never know Him as Savior until we come to the end of our own resources, repent of our sins, and trust in His love.

Pride and self-righteousness loom like a mountain and are in opposition to salvation through God's mercy and grace.

"And they said, Believe on the Lord Jesus Christ, and thou shalt be saved, and thy house" (Acts 16:31).

Thought for Today: Don't be deceived by trusting in anything or anyone but the Lord Jesus Christ for your eternal salvation.

Christ Revealed: As the Creator (Isaiah 40:28; compare John 1:1-3); as a Shepherd (Isaiah 40:11; compare John 10:11); as Redeemer (Isaiah 41:14).

Word Studies: 38:13 **reckoned** means composed my soul; 40:2 **comfortably** means kindly; 40:12 **span** means nine inches.

Prayer Needs: Country: Colombia—31 million—in southwestern South America • Missionaries are under great pressure • 96% Roman Catholic; 1% Protestant; 1% Indian tribal religions.

AUGUST 9: Read Isaiah 43 — 46

Highlights: God's care for Israel; folly of idolatry; Jerusalem and the Temple to be rebuilt; God's purpose for Cyrus; the power of the Lord and the weakness of idols.

Verses for Today: *"Thus saith the Lord ... I am the Lord ... that saith to Jerusalem, Thou shalt be inhabited; and to the cities of Judah, Ye shall be built, and I will raise up the decayed places thereof ... that saith of Cyrus, He is my shepherd, and shall perform all my pleasure ... "* (Isaiah 44:24-28).

O nly the Spirit of God could have given Isaiah such amazing details about a man named Cyrus 130 years before he was born.

When Isaiah foretold, *"I [God] will raise up the decayed places thereof,"* there were no *"decayed places"* to be raised up. The Temple was still standing; the walls were in perfect condition; and the nation was still enjoying freedom. Furthermore, it did not seem likely that a world conqueror would release the Jews and then urge them to return to Jerusalem to rebuild the Temple for *"the God of heaven"* (Nehemiah 1:4). No prophecy seemed more unlikely to be fulfilled. Yet, all these things happened exactly as Isaiah had foretold.

The prophet's message reveals our lack of foresight and our need to trust the Lord for whatever lies ahead. We dare not doubt God's loving concern or His almighty power to keep His promises. His Word should give us confidence that every detail of our lives is ordained by God.

"Heaven and earth shall pass away, but my words shall not pass away" (Matthew 24:35).

Thought for Today: God is not limited; He will keep His Word—in His time.

Christ Revealed: As the Redeemer (Isaiah 43:1; 44:22-24). Through His death on the cross, Christ has redeemed all who will trust Him as Savior (I Cor. 6:20; I Pet. 1:18-19).

Word Studies: 43:13 **let it** means prevent it from happening; change it; 44:9 **delectable** means desirable; 46:4 **hoar hairs** means gray hairs.

Prayer Needs: Country: Niger—7 million—in west-central Africa • Christian evangelism is limited • 89% Muslim; 10% animism; .4% Christian.

AUGUST 10: Read Isaiah 47 — 51

Highlights: Judgment on Babylon; Christ, a Light to the Gentiles; restoration of Israel; the suffering of the Lord's Servant; words of comfort to the faithful.

Verse for Today: *"Who is among you that feareth the Lord, that obeyeth the voice of his servant, that walketh in darkness, and hath no light? let him trust in the name of the Lord, and stay upon his God"* (Isaiah 50:10).

T he captives and afflicted servants of God are often overwhelmed with calamities (Isaiah 49:14). We naturally expect judgment upon the ungodly or perhaps even the backslider. But we think it strange when seemingly bad things happen to the most sincere Christians—those *"that feareth the Lord, that obeyeth the voice of his servant!"*

When hope after hope is shattered, plan after plan is crushed, and a succession of trials take place—each darker and more painful than before—then with Jeremiah you may say, *"I am the man that hath seen affliction by the rod of his wrath. He hath led me, and brought me into darkness, but not into light."* When darkness continued and answers to prayer seemed to be withheld, Jeremiah knew there was but one safe decision: *"It is good that a man should both hope and quietly wait for the salvation of the Lord"* (Lamentations 3:1-2,26).

Wait upon Him in earnest, fervent, persevering prayer. Continue in prayer just as the man did in our Lord's parable who did not have a loaf of bread in the house but went to his friend at midnight and continued to plead (Luke 11:5-8). The answers come to those who actively ask, seek, and knock, to those who do not remain passively content.

All servants of God know what it is to feel as if the light they expected had turned to darkness. Our Lord felt it when He uttered the cry, *"My God, my God, why hast thou forsaken me?"* (Matthew 27:46). But the cry of the forsaken Savior was followed by the words, *"Father, into thy hands I commend my spirit . . . "* (Luke 23:46).

"Even unto this present hour we both hunger, and thirst, and are naked, and are buffeted, and have no certain dwelling place; And labor, working with our own hands: being reviled, we bless; being persecuted, we suffer it" (I Corinthians 4:11-12).

Thought for Today: Remember that God never forsakes His children (see Matthew 28:20).

Christ Revealed: As the *"light"* of the nations (Isaiah 49:6) to bring the light of God's salvation to all the nations of the earth (Luke 2:32; Acts 13:47).

Prayer Needs: Country: Romania—23 million—in southeastern Europe • Persecution of Romanian churches is more severe than in most European countries • 70% Eastern Orthodox; 7% Protestant; 6% Roman Catholic; 1% Muslim.

AUGUST 11: Read Isaiah 52 — 57

Highlights: Christ to bear our grief, suffering, and sin; the Lord's everlasting love for Israel; everyone a sinner; a call to faith and repentance.

Verse for Today: *"All we like sheep have gone astray; we have turned every one to his own way; and the Lord hath laid on him the iniquity of us all"* (Isaiah 53:6).

S heep wandering without a shepherd are easy prey to wild beasts and enemies. Furthermore, the wandering sheep are likely to perish for lack of pasture; they are unable to provide for themselves or find their way back from where they strayed.

"All we ... have gone astray." All of us are guilty; all need the Savior Shepherd. Surely Jesus Christ deserves the name of the Good Shepherd, who freely laid down His life to restore His sheep. Praise the Good Shepherd for His tender mercy.

Jesus Christ is the *"man of sorrows and acquainted with grief"* and *"the Lord hath laid on him the iniquity of us all."* The full meaning of His crucifixion is indescribable. No one can fully express the suffering and sorrows that Jesus Christ endured for our sins. (See Isaiah 53:3-6.)

God's judgment on sin was expressed in the Garden of Eden: *" ... in the day that thou eatest thereof thou shalt surely die"* (Genesis 2:17). Christ felt that punishment until He *yielded His life unto the Father* (see Matthew 27:50).

Think of the astounding mass of sin that must have been laid on Christ (John 1:29; I John 2:2)—all the sins against God—open sins, hidden sins of the heart, sins against the Father, sins against the Son, sins against the Holy Ghost, sins against all the revealed Word of God. The sins of all mankind were laid upon Him!

Oh, why are so few affected by God's redeeming love!

"That in the ages to come he might show the exceeding riches of his grace in his kindness toward us through Christ Jesus" (Ephesians 2:7).

Thought for Today: How slow we are to express gratefulness for the amazing love of our Lord.

Christ Revealed: As the One who was rejected by His own people (Isaiah 53:3; compare Luke 23:18; John 1:11); remained silent when He was falsely accused (Isaiah 53:7; Mark 15:4-5); was buried with the rich (Isaiah 53:9; Matt. 27:57-60); and was crucified with sinners (Isaiah 53:12; Mark 15:27-28).

Word Studies: 52:1 **uncircumcised** means heathen; 52:10 **made bare his holy arm** means revealed His power; 52:15 **sprinkle** means startle with astonishment (from utter amazement that One who had been so utterly rejected would be so highly exalted); 57:13 **companies** means collection of idols.

Prayer Needs: **Country:** Switzerland—7 million—in central Europe • Religious freedom • 53% Roman Catholic; 41% Protestant.

AUGUST 12: Read Isaiah 58 — 63

Highlights: A description of true fasting; sin, confession, and redemption; future glory of Jerusalem; the day of vengeance; God's loving-kindness to Israel.

Verse for Today: *"But they rebelled, and vexed his holy Spirit: therefore he was turned to be their enemy, and he fought against them"* (Isaiah 63:10).

W hen recalling Israel's failure, Isaiah reminded the nation that each time they complained, they were rebelling against God, which in turn *"vexed his holy Spirit."*

The children of Israel complained against God and Moses ten specific times *and did not hearken to His voice* (see Numbers 14:22). Unbelief resulted in 38 wasted years of wandering in the wilderness.

But even with all of God's provisions to the children of Israel in the desert, the kingdom of Judah failed to relate God's miraculous provisions in the past to their present needs. The great kingdom so richly blessed of God was as guilty of unbelief as were the children of Israel in the desert, for *"they rebelled, and vexed his holy Spirit."*

Interruption in personal plans causes many to complain because they believe they deserve better. Grumbling about our circumstances does *"vex his holy Spirit,"* and we forfeit His blessings.

Far too often we fail to see the seriousness of discontentment. We are actually questioning the wisdom and ability of our loving Heavenly Father to guide us. Satan has the victory when we complain about what God hasn't done.

"And grieve not the holy Spirit of God . . . " (Ephesians 4:30).

Thought for Today: Graciously submit to God's arrangements, and under no circumstances grieve the Holy Spirit.

Christ Revealed: As the One anointed *"to preach good tidings"* (Isaiah 61:1-2). Jesus preached this passage to the rulers of the synagogue (Luke 4:16-22), stopping in the middle of the sentence, thus showing that although He fulfilled the first part, the second part—the day of judgment—was yet to be fulfilled. Christ heals the brokenhearted (Isaiah 61:1; Psa. 147:3) and frees us by His truth (John 8:32-36).

Word Studies: 58:4 **debate** means contention; quarreling; 58:11 **fat** means strong; 60:2 **gross** means thick; dense; 60:6 **dromedaries** means young camels; 60:17 **exactors** means oppressors; taskmasters; civil officers; 62:4 **Beulah** means married; 63:15 **the sounding of thy bowels** means the stirring of your heart.

Prayer Needs: Country: Togo—3 million—in western Africa • Limited religious freedom • 41% belief in false gods and voodoo; 32% Roman Catholic; 19% Muslim; 8% Protestant.

AUGUST 13: Read Isaiah 64 — 66

Highlights: Our righteousness as filthy rags; prayer for God's presence; New Jerusalem; promises of inward contentment.

Verses for Today: *"Oh that thou wouldest rend the heavens, that thou wouldest come down, that the mountains might flow down at thy presence. . . . For since the beginning of the world men have not heard, nor perceived by the ear, neither hath the eye seen, O God, beside thee, what he hath prepared for him that waiteth for him"* (Isaiah 64:1,4).

I t may seem that our relationship with the Lord is hindered by what appear to be huge, insurmountable problems. Some of these "mountains" are the result of active opposition from Satan and can be overcome *"because greater is he that is in you, than he that is in the world"* (I John 4:4).

Then, there are mountains of sin and self-interest that sever every connection with divine power. These must be broken down to enjoy God's presence.

But other mountains of hindrance actually arise from our lack of faithfulness in praying. We cannot be effective in our Christian life unless we are effective in prayer. When we *"do those things that are pleasing in his sight"* (I John 3:22), we can pray and fully expect God to remove every mountain, every difficulty.

" . . . Eye hath not seen, nor ear heard, neither have entered into the heart of man,

the things which God hath prepared for them that love him" (I Corinthians 2:9).

Thought for Today: Self-seeking and sin break our communion with the Lord and keep us from receiving true peace, joy, and wisdom.

Christ Revealed: As the Creator of new heavens and a new earth (Isaiah 65:17; 66:22; compare II Pet. 3:13).

As the One whose glory will be declared among the nations (Isaiah 66:18-19; Rev. 5:12-13).

Prayer Needs: Country: Transkei—3 million—on the southeastern coast of South Africa • Religious freedom • 65% Protestant; 26% belief in false gods, ancestor worship, and magical practices; 6% Roman Catholic.

JEREMIAH

There is an interval of about 70 years between the books of Isaiah and Jeremiah. During Isaiah's time, Assyria destroyed the ten-tribed nation of Israel. But as the years passed, Assyria's empire weakened considerably and Babylon gradually gained supremacy.

Jeremiah was born about 75 years after the Assyrians had defeated the Northern Kingdom of Israel. He prophesied during the last part of the kingdom of Judah's history. Jeremiah's ministry continued throughout the reigns of Josiah, Jehoiakim, Jehoiachin, Zedekiah, and Gedaliah. During this time, the Babylonians defeated two great empires—Assyria and Egypt.

The prophet Jeremiah pleaded with the nation of Judah to repent of its sins and serve the Lord, but the people refused. Eventually Nebuchadnezzar, the Babylonian king, attacked Jerusalem, as foretold by the prophet.

After a siege of about 18 months, the city was defeated, the walls and Temple were destroyed, and many people were taken captive to Babylon.

Nebuchadnezzar left Jeremiah and the poor people in Jerusalem and appointed Gedaliah as the Jewish puppet-governor of Jerusalem. After only two months, Gedaliah was assassinated. Fearing Nebuchadnezzar's retaliation, the few people who remained in Judah fled to Egypt, taking Jeremiah as a hostage.

The last record we have of the aged prophet Jeremiah, he was preaching against the Jewish women worshiping *"the queen of heaven"* (44:15-30).

Although Jeremiah lived to see his prophecy against Jerusalem come true, he also foretold that Babylon would sink to rise no more (51:64), and that the people of Judah would return and the nation would be restored.

AUGUST 14: Read Jeremiah 1 — 3

Highlights: Jeremiah's call; his message to sinful Judah; present apostasy, resulting in idolatry; Judah entreated to repent.

Verses for Today: *" . . . my people have changed their glory for that which doth not profit. Be astonished, O ye heavens, at this. . . . For my people have committed two evils; they have forsaken me the fountain of living waters, and hewed them out* *cisterns, broken cisterns, that can hold no water"* (Jeremiah 2:11-13).

I n the desert climate of Palestine, water was the first necessity of human existence. Men fought and died over wells. No man in his right mind would exchange an artesian well, where there was a great supply of water, for some man-made, broken cistern, and hope for water to sustain his life. We would consider such a person foolish indeed.

But the Israelites were even more foolish. They were the only people in the world who had received a revelation of the one true God and His will—the only source of the Water of life. Yet, they deserted Him for man-made, lifeless gods—broken cisterns that cannot sustain life. What an astounding example of ingratitude!

This is symbolic of those who reject the Bible as the Fountain of living water. In place of the Bible, many have turned to substitutes written by men. But compared to the Word of God, they are little more than *"cisterns, that can hold no water."* Many writings of men may be helpful in life, but they should not be used as a substitute for Bible study.

"Whosoever drinketh of the water that I shall give him shall never thirst; but the water that I shall give him shall be in him a well of water springing up into everlasting life" (John 4:14).

Thought for Today: God's Word reveals the difference between truth and error.

Christ Revealed: As the Fountain of living waters (Jeremiah 2:13). Jesus is the only Fountain that can satisfy the thirsty soul (John 4:1-26).

Word Studies: 2:22 **nitre** means lye; strong soap; 2:31 **lords** means independent; 3:2 **been lain with** means acted like a prostitute; 3:10 **feignedly** means falsely; 3:16 **visit** means miss.

Prayer Needs: Country: Vietnam—64 million—in Southeast Asia • Very strict control of Christians in the North; the South has been more lenient, but is getting tighter • 65% Buddhist and Buddhist sects; 7% Roman Catholic; 4% belief in evil spirits and ancestor worship; .4% Protestant.

AUGUST 15: Read Jeremiah 4 — 6

Highlights: God's call to Israel; Jeremiah's lamentations for Judah; spiritual and civil corruption; destruction of Judah.

Verses for Today: *"The prophets prophesy falsely, and the priests bear rule by their means; and my people love to have it so. . . . behold, the word of the Lord is unto them a reproach; they have no delight in it"* (Jeremiah 5:31; 6:10).

I t was deplorable and unthinkable that the kingdom of Judah had *"no delight"* in the *"word of the Lord."*

When those who call themselves Christians live day after day without reading the Word of God—year after year without ever reading the Bible through—it is quite apparent that they also *"have no delight in it."*

Turning away from God's message is a trend toward apostasy, but reading and upholding every word of God as pure and true and vital for our well being is a mark of sonship (see Proverbs 30:5). A true Christian delights in His Word: *"More to be desired are they than gold . . . "* (Psalm 19:10).

The trend in our secular society is a moving away from the *"word of the Lord."*

The Thessalonian Christians were taught that the day of the Lord would not come until there is a falling away (literally, "the apostasy") and the man of sin is revealed (see II Thessalonians 2:1-3).

Many who call themselves Christians will forsake the Lord as Demas did (II Timothy 4:10) and as is foretold in the book of Jude.

"For there are certain men crept in unawares, who were before of old ordained to this condemnation, ungodly men, turning the grace of our God into lasciviousness, and denying the only Lord God, and our Lord Jesus Christ" (Jude 1:4).

Thought for Today: As we spend more time reading God's Word, His ways will become our ways, His thoughts will become our thoughts.

Christ Revealed: God would have pardoned Jerusalem for one righteous person (Jeremiah 5:1). God is very willing to forgive those who come to Him with repentant hearts (I John 1:9).

Word Studies: 4:13 **he** means the enemy (foretelling the destruction of Jerusalem by the Chaldeans); 4:19 **bowels** means soul; **I am pained at my very heart** means I am in anguish; 4:22 **sottish** means stupid; 4:30 **rentest thy face with painting** means paint your eyelids to enhance charm in order to attract favor of the enemy; 6:22 **sides** means remote areas.

Prayer Needs: Country: American Samoa—38,000—six small islands between Hawaii and New Zealand • Religious freedom • 64% Protestant; 17% Roman Catholic; 13% cults.

AUGUST 16: Read Jeremiah 7 — 10

Highlights: Jeremiah's plea for repentance; punishment for Judah's rebellion; Jeremiah's mourning over the sins of his people; God and the idols.

Verse for Today: *"Is this house, which is called by my name, become a den of robbers in your eyes? Behold, even I have seen it, saith the Lord"* (Jeremiah 7:11).

J ehoiakim (Josiah's son) was an evil ruler (see II Kings 23:36-37). He despised Jeremiah's prophecies against his cruel oppression of the people—especially the prophecies against perverted Temple worship. Jeremiah had accused the king of making the Temple of God *"a den of robbers."*

Our Lord used this Scripture hundreds of years later when He entered the courts of the Temple with a whip made of small cords and drove out the money changers, saying, *My Temple shall be called the house of prayer; but you have made it a place for thieves* (see Matthew 21:13; see also Isaiah 56:7).

Although the people still offered sacrifices to Jehovah, they also worshiped other gods. Through Jeremiah, God had made it clear that no amount of sacrifices could take the place of obedience, saying, *Obey My Word* (see Jeremiah 7:23).

Many people overlook the importance of cleansing themselves *from all that pollutes the flesh and spirit* (see II Corinthians 7:1). They fail to see there are no substitutes for a sincere desire to please the Lord (see II Corinthians 7:11).

Pursue righteousness, faith, love, and peace, together with those whose prayers go up to the Lord from a clean heart (see II Timothy 2:22).

Thought for Today: Religious activity is never a substitute for godly living.

Christ Revealed: As the One who demanded a cleansed Temple and undefiled

211

worshipers (Jeremiah 7:1-11). Christ quoted from these verses in Matthew 21:13 and Mark 11:17. (See also I Cor. 6:19-20.)

Word Studies: 7:33 **fray** means frighten; 8:14 **water of gall** means bitter afflictions; 10:22 **noise of the bruit** means sound of a rumor.

Prayer Needs: Country: Argentina—31 million—in southern South America • Much religious intolerance • 87% Roman Catholic; 6% Protestant; • 2% Jewish.

AUGUST 17: Read Jeremiah 11 — 14

Highlights: Jeremiah's proclamation of God's covenant; plot against Jeremiah; Jeremiah's complaint and God's answer; lesson from the marred linen girdle (belt); lesson from the filled bottles; message of the famine.

Verse for Today: *"This evil people, which refuse to hear my words, which walk in the imagination of their heart, and walk after other gods, to serve them, and to worship them, shall even be as this girdle, which is good for nothing"* (Jeremiah 13:10).

I t seems strange indeed that God would lead His chosen prophet to travel nearly 250 miles to the Euphrates River, bury a girdle there until it was rotten, and then wear the worthless garment back to Jerusalem to tell Judah of her national condition and spiritual value before the Lord.

They were His people, a kingdom who had access to Him above all other nations. To them were committed the Scriptures—the only Guide to true worship. But it had to be written of them, *"good for nothing."*

Jeremiah's journey may have seemed a waste of time and effort, but his unquestioned obedience was evidence of his willingness to fulfill God's will. When a person will not hear God, he puts self before God—forsaking true, he follows the false.

God's commandments are often, according to human reasoning, not essential. His instructions often involve much effort and inconvenience that we would prefer to avoid.

Many would have said: "Why go to the Euphrates? Why wear a rotten girdle? What will people think? Why me, Lord?" But those who desire to obey God willingly surrender all of self to please Him. They are not burdened with the responsibility of life's decisions because they understand that their lives belong to the Lord.

"And he that sent me is with me: the Father hath not left me alone; for I do always those things that please him" (John 8:29).

Thought for Today: Are you willingly serving the Lord?

Christ Revealed: As the Hope and Savior of His people (Jeremiah 14:8-9). Neither Jews nor Gentiles will have peace until they accept Christ, the King of peace, as Savior (Luke 21:24-27).

Word Studies: 12:13 **revenues** means harvest; 13:1 **girdle** means waistband; belt; 13:9 **mar** means ruin; 13:10 **girdle** means wide sash; linen belt; 13:22 **skirts discovered . . . heels made bare** means fine clothes torn off as you are driven into exile, barefoot and with violence (compare Nahum 3:5); 14:4 **chapt** means dried up, parched because of repeated droughts (compare Lev. 26:3-20; Deut. 11:17; 28:23).

Prayer Needs: Country: Botswana—1 million—in southern Africa • Limited religious freedom because of local chiefs • 49% animist; 21% Protestant; 4% Roman Catholic.

AUGUST 18: Read Jeremiah 15 — 18

Highlights: Jeremiah's prayer; signs of coming captivity; regulations concerning the sabbath; lesson from the potter; God's absolute power over nations.

Verses for Today: *"Then I went down to the potter's house . . . and the vessel that he made of clay was marred in the hand of the potter: so he made it again another vessel, as seemed good to the potter to make it. . . . O house of Israel [Judah], cannot I do with you as this potter? . . . "* (Jeremiah 18:3-4,6).

T he potter was not satisfied with the first vessel he made—perhaps because the clay was not the right texture to make the shape he had in mind—so he reshaped it.

This is the story of God's chosen people. God is the Potter; Israel (the remnant of Judah) the clay; history the wheel—slowly turning as God, the Master Potter, changes and shapes His chosen vessels. As a nation, Israel resisted the will of God and was miserably marred by sin. Therefore, the *"vessel"*—Israel—was broken by Babylon, and the people were taken into captivity.

After 70 years in exile, God made of the *"clay"* yet another *"vessel"* as the Jews returned to Jerusalem to rebuild the Temple.

God wants our will to be as submissive to His will as clay is in the potter's hands—*"as seemed good to the potter to make it."*

Every Christian is like an earthen vessel, and God—the Master Potter—has a plan for each of our lives as a vessel to honor Him.

"For it is God which worketh in you both to will and to do of his good pleasure" (Philippians 2:13).

Thought for Today: It is for God's glory that we were created.

Christ Revealed: Jeremiah said, *" . . . thy word was unto me the joy and rejoicing of mine heart . . . "* (Jeremiah 15:16). Jesus said, *" . . . the words that I speak unto you, they are spirit, and they are life"* (John 6:63).

As the One who searches the heart of man and rewards him accordingly (Jeremiah 17:10; Psa. 139:23-24; Rev. 2:23).

Word Studies: 15:9 **given up the ghost** means died; breathed out her last breath; expired; 15:12 **Shall iron break . . . steel?** means just as man is unable to break iron, the Jewish people will be unable to break the cruel power of the north; 15:20 **I will make thee unto this people a fenced brazen wall . . . they shall not prevail against thee** means I will make you as a fenced brazen wall which the storm batters and beats violently upon but cannot shake; 16:7 **tear themselves** means prepare food; 17:10 **try the reins** means test the mind; 18:15 **in a way not cast up** means on unmarked paths, not on a highway.

Prayer Needs: Country: Burundi—5 million—in east-central Africa • Losing religious freedom • 51% Roman Catholic; 12% animist; 11% Protestant; 1% Muslim.

AUGUST 19: Read Jeremiah 19 — 22

Highlights: Jeremiah imprisoned; Jeremiah smitten by Pashur; Jeremiah's grief expressed to God; the destruction of Jerusalem foretold; the way of life and the way of death.

Verse for Today: *"Inquire, I pray thee, of the Lord for us; for Nebuchadnezzar*

213

king of Babylon maketh war against us . . . " (Jeremiah 21:2).

K ing Zedekiah was afraid the Babylonians would soon destroy the little nation of Judah. Therefore, he sent Zephaniah and Pashur (not the same man who had earlier beaten the prophet Jeremiah and *"put him in the stocks"*—Jeremiah 20:2; compare 20:1 with 21:1) to ask Jeremiah to pray, hoping perhaps the Lord would bless them *"according to all his wondrous works"* (21:2).

The king's inquiry sounded spiritual, but there was no indication that he desired to worship God as the true King of Israel.

Jeremiah told the messengers to tell Zedekiah that God would not fight for him, but would fight against him. Furthermore, he said that King Zedekiah and his people would be defeated in battle and taken as slaves by Nebuchadnezzar.

Many would-be believers today are making the same mistake as King Zedekiah. They have gone to the right source for information, and have called upon the right God, but they are not truly seeking the Lord's will. They merely want God to agree with what they want to do.

"Your faith should not stand in the wisdom of men, but in the power of God" (I Corinthians 2:5).

Thought for Today: When praying for God to bless your plans, be willing to pray, "Not my will, but Yours be done."

Christ Revealed: As the One who speaks judgment upon evildoers and those who do not obey His Word (Jeremiah 19:15; compare Matt. 7:26-27).

Word Studies: 19:3 **his ears shall tingle** means he will be utterly stunned by the news of it (compare II Kings 21:12); 19:9 **straitness** means confinement; disability; anguish; distress; 20:10 **halting** means fall; 22:24 **signet** means ring.

Prayer Needs: Country: Chad—5 million—in north-central Africa • Limited religious freedom • 35% Muslim; 31% animist; 11% Protestant; 5% Roman Catholic.

AUGUST 20: Read Jeremiah 23 — 25

Highlights: Future restoration foretold; Christ's rule promised; the lying prophets; restoration foreshown by good and bad figs; God's judgment on the nations; destruction of Babylon foretold.

Verses for Today: *"Behold, the days come, saith the Lord, that I will raise unto David a righteous Branch, and a King shall reign and prosper, and shall execute judgment and justice in the earth. . . . and this is his name whereby he shall be called, THE LORD OUR RIGHTEOUSNESS"* (Jeremiah 23:5-6).

T he Israelites, God's chosen people, had once been a powerful nation among the kingdoms of the earth. But because of their disregard for God's commandments, the prophet Jeremiah announced the terrifying news that the nation of Judah would soon face God's judgment. Yet, he gave them a ray of hope beyond the judgment when he foretold of the coming Messiah—a *"righteous Branch,"* the King of righteousness, the Savior—who could deliver God's people from bondage.

In man, there is no righteousness, for *"all have sinned"* (Romans 3:23). But Christ is *"THE LORD OUR RIGHTEOUSNESS."* When we accept Him as our Savior and Lord, His life—His righteousness—flows through us. Therefore, we stand justified before God—not upon our own merits, but upon the righteousness of Christ. As God looks upon us, He sees Christ's righteousness in us, and we are acceptable to Him.

Many Christians are weak and worldly because they do not understand this. They believe that it took Christ, the Righteous One, to save them, but they do not recognize that His indwelling Holy Spirit can empower them to live holy, righteous lives through the Word of God.

" . . . *I count all things but loss . . . that I may win Christ, and be found in him, not having mine own righteousness, which is of the law, but that which is through the faith of Christ, the righteousness which is of God by faith*" (Philippians 3:8-9).

Thought for Today: Our righteousness is Christ in us—*"THE LORD OUR RIGHTEOUSNESS."*

Christ Revealed: As *"THE LORD OUR RIGHTEOUSNESS"* (Jeremiah 23:5-6; see also I Cor. 1:30; II Cor. 5:21).

Word Studies: 23:10 **swearing** means the curse; 24:2 **naughty** means poor.

Prayer Needs: Country: Mainland China—1,064 million—in eastern Asia • Limited religious freedom • 18% Chinese folk-religionist; 6% Buddhist; 2% Muslim; number of Christians unknown but growing.

AUGUST 21: Read Jeremiah 26 — 28

Highlights: Jeremiah's arrest; Judah's subjection to Nebuchadnezzar foretold; Hananiah's false prophecy; his death.

Verse for Today: *"Then spake the priests and the prophets unto the princes and to all the people, saying, This man is worthy to die; for he hath prophesied against this city, as ye have heard with your ears"* (Jeremiah 26:11).

F or more than nine years, all of Jeremiah's fervent appeals for King Zedekiah to heed God's Word had been in vain. Urijah also *"prophesied against this city . . . according to all the words of Jeremiah"* (Jeremiah 26:20). These prophecies infuriated the king, and he sought the death of both men.

The prophet Urijah escaped into Egypt but was taken into custody, brought before King Jehoiakim, and executed. But Jeremiah did not flee; he persisted in pleading with the king: *"Why will ye die, thou and thy people, by the sword, and the famine, and by the pestilence, as the Lord hath spoken against the nation. . . . Hearken not to the words of your prophets . . . "* (27:13,16).

Jeremiah would rather have died than be silent about God's judgment upon His nation. What became of Jeremiah was wholly unimportant compared to his hope that the people of Judah would repent and turn to the Lord.

It is this same Spirit that led the Apostle Paul to say, *"I am ready not to be bound only, but also to die at Jerusalem. . . . I could wish that myself were accursed from Christ for my brethren . . . "* (Acts 21:13; Romans 9:13). And it is the same self-sacrificing Spirit that leads Christians to willingly reject self-interests that interfere with what we know would please Him.

The Christian must gently instruct those who oppose him in the hope that God will bring them to repentance and lead them to the knowledge of the truth (see II Timothy 2:25).

215

Thought for Today: Your boldness to speak out for Christ helps others escape the deceptions of secular influence.

Christ Portrayed: By Jeremiah, who was falsely accused by the priests and false prophets (Jeremiah 26:8-9). Our Lord was threatened and falsely accused on many occasions as His teachings did not agree with the teachings of the religious rulers of His day (John 8:48,59).

Word Study: 26:14 **meet** means right.

Prayer Needs: Country: Congo—2 million—in west-central Africa • Limited religious freedom but government hostility has lessened • 41% Roman Catholic; 20% fetishism and belief in ancestral spirits; 17% Protestant; 9% cults.

AUGUST 22: Read Jeremiah 29 — 31

Highlights: Letter to captives in Babylon; Jews' deliverance foretold; full restoration of all things foretold.

Verse for Today: *"For I am with thee, saith the Lord, to save thee: though I make a full end of all nations whither I have scattered thee, yet will I not make a full end of thee: but I will correct thee in measure, and will not leave thee altogether unpunished"* (Jeremiah 30:11).

T he prophets repeatedly foretold that the Jews would be scattered throughout the world, yet would not be totally destroyed by their conquerors. They would remain a distinct people. On the other hand, God declared that He would destroy their conquerors.

This unusual prophetic truth has been fulfilled. The mighty world kingdoms of Babylon and Assyria have vanished. Nothing remains except ruins—evidence of their once-magnificent grandeur.

Although the small Jewish nation was also destroyed and her people taken as slaves and scattered throughout the world, they have continued to exist as a distinct people for centuries.

In our generation, the Jews have fulfilled a portion of still another prophecy by returning to Jerusalem and once again becoming a nation. (Compare Isaiah 11:11-16; Jeremiah 16:14-15; Ezekiel 36:24; 37:11-12,14,21.)

It is a fact that God has a purpose for His people—not only for Jewish people, but also for all who repent of their sins and receive Christ as their Savior.

We can rest assured, dear Christian friend, that our faith is founded upon the unchanging, eternal Word of God.

The word of prophecy has been confirmed. We will do well to pay attention to it because it is like a lamp shining in a gloomy place until the day dawns and the light of the morning star shines in our hearts (see II Peter 1:19).

Thought for Today: Every sincere reader of the Bible can clearly see that it is the inspired Word of God.

Christ Revealed: As the One who forgives sin (Jeremiah 31:34). *"But that ye may know that the Son of man hath power on earth to forgive sins, (then saith he to the sick of the palsy,) Arise, take up thy bed, and go unto thine house"* (Matt. 9:6; compare John 8:10-11).

Word Studies: 31:14 **satiate** means satisfy fully; 31:21 **high heaps** means guideposts.

Prayer Needs: Country: Ecuador—10 million—in South America, crossed by the equator • Religious freedom • 91% Roman Catholic; 3% Protestant.

AUGUST 23: Read Jeremiah 32 — 33

Highlights: Jeremiah's imprisonment; Jeremiah buys a field at Anathoth; glorious return promised to the captives; Christ, the Branch of righteousness, promised.

Verses for Today: *"Ah Lord God! behold ... Thou showest loving-kindness unto thousands, and recompensest the iniquity ... to give every one according to his ways, according to the fruit of his doings"* (Jeremiah 32:17-19).

J eremiah said almost the same words as David who wrote, *"How excellent is thy loving-kindness, O God! Therefore the children of men put their trust under the shadow of thy wings"* (Psalm 36:7).

In the midst of suffering and final defeat, the prophet Jeremiah proclaimed that God, in loving-kindness, was waiting to bless the nation of Judah if they would turn from their sins. But they would not heed his warning.

Whether we are accepted or rejected, we should faithfully remind others how important it is to read all of God's Word and how He bestows His loving-kindness upon all who put their trust in Him.

Every adverse circumstance that confronts us is an opportunity to express His loving-kindness—a privilege to bless and pray for those who offend us. In the words of the psalmist we can say, *"It is a good thing ... to show forth [talk about] thy loving-kindness ... "* (Psalm 92:1-2).

When the Christian yields himself to the influence and guidance of the Holy Spirit, there will be no room in the heart for jealousy, bitterness, or hatred.

"A new commandment I give unto you, That ye love one another; as I have loved you ... " (John 13:34).

Thought for Today: All who reject God's Word will one day be judged by the very Word they have rejected.

Christ Revealed: As the Branch of David (Jeremiah 23:5; 33:15). Christ is the Messiah, *" ... made of the seed of David according to the flesh"* (Rom. 1:3).

Word Study: 32:44 **subscribe evidences** means sign deeds.

Prayer Needs: Country: Finland—5 million—in northern Europe • Religious freedom • 91% Protestant; 1% Eastern Orthodox; 1% Roman Catholic.

AUGUST 24: Read Jeremiah 34 — 36

Highlights: Jeremiah's warning to Zedekiah; obedience of the Rechabites; scroll read by Jehudi and destroyed by King Jehoiakim.

Verses for Today: *"So the king sent Jehudi to fetch the roll.... And it came to pass, that when Jehudi had read three or four leaves, he cut it with the penknife, and cast it into the fire ... "* (Jeremiah 36:21,23).

T hrough the prophet Jeremiah, God foretold that the king of Babylon would again come and destroy the kingdom of Judah, leaving neither man nor beast. When Jehudi read the prophecy to King Jehoiakim, the king should have humbly

217

turned to God. But instead, Jehoiakim destroyed the scroll by cutting it with a penknife and casting it into the fire. Unknowingly, he sealed his own death by willfully rejecting and destroying the Word of God (Jeremiah 36:29-30).

There have been thousands since Jehoiakim who have attempted to destroy the Word of God by burning Bibles and killing Christians. Their names have been forgotten, but God's Word continues to remain the most sought-after book year after year.

"Heaven and earth shall pass away: but my words shall not pass away" (Luke 21:33).

Thought for Today: Those who get counsel from the Lord through His Word will not be deceived.

Christ Revealed: As the One who desires liberty for those in bondage (Jeremiah 34:13-16; compare Isa. 61:1). Jesus said, *"The Spirit of the Lord is upon me . . . to set at liberty . . . "* (Luke 4:18-19; compare II Cor. 3:17).

Prayer Needs: Country: Guinea—7 million—on the Atlantic coast of western Africa • Freedom for nationals, but strict limitations on missionaries • 71% Muslim; 28% animist; 1% Christian.

AUGUST 25: Read Jeremiah 37 — 40

Highlights: Jeremiah imprisoned in a dungeon; his counsel rejected; Jerusalem destroyed; Jeremiah set free; Ishmael's plan to assassinate Gedaliah.

Verse for Today: *"Then Zedekiah the king sent, and took him out; and the king asked him secretly in his house, and said, Is there any word from the Lord? And Jeremiah said, There is: for, said he, thou shalt be delivered into the hand of the king of Babylon"* (Jeremiah 37:17).

D uring the last year of Zedekiah's reign, the world-conquering armies of Nebuchadnezzar had surrounded Jerusalem. Fearful of the outcome, Zedekiah secretly removed Jeremiah from prison and asked, *"Is there any word from the Lord?"* He had appealed to the prophet to intercede in prayer once before when the king of Babylon's army first approached, but Zedekiah did not repent of his sins and seek the Lord (chapter 21). Jeremiah would not pray; instead, he said, *"Thus saith the Lord; Deceive not yourselves"* (Jeremiah 37:9).

Because Zedekiah did not seek the Lord, his downfall was inevitable. Pitiful as it may seem, Israel's last king, Zedekiah, was captured in Jericho (39:5)—the same area where Joshua had won the first victory in entering the Promised Land.

This blinded and imprisoned king (39:7) is an example of what happens spiritually to anyone who fails to follow the will of God.

"In whom the god of this world hath blinded the minds of them which believe not . . . " (II Corinthians 4:4).

Thought for Today: A person who rejects the Lord and His Word is working toward his own destruction.

Christ Portrayed: By Jeremiah, who stood as a faithful witness to God's revealed will (Jeremiah 38:2-9), even when religious leaders hated him and tried to put him to death (compare Matt. 26:59).

Word Studies: 37:12 **separate himself thence** means receive his portion there; 37:16

218

cabins means cells; 38:12 **cast clouts** means wornout clothes; 39:3 **Rabsaris** means the chief financial official.

Prayer Needs: Country: Guadeloupe—336,000—in the Leeward Islands of the West Indies • Religious freedom • 94% Roman Catholic; 2% Protestant.

AUGUST 26: Read Jeremiah 41 — 44

Highlights: Gedaliah's assassination; Jeremiah taken to Egypt; desolation of Judah because of idolatry.

Verses for Today: " . . . and all the captains of the forces, took . . . Jeremiah the prophet. . . . So they came into the land of Egypt . . . " (Jeremiah 43:5-7).

A fter Nebuchadnezzar defeated Zedekiah, he made Gedaliah governor over the few who remained in Judah—"of the poor of the land" (Jeremiah 40:7). About two months later, because of his loyalty to Babylon, Gedaliah was assassinated by Ishmael.

The Jewish people expected Nebuchadnezzar to retaliate, so they fled to Egypt, forcing the prophet Jeremiah to go with them.

Nothing could have been more distressing to Jeremiah than finally being forced into Egypt as a prisoner. There he watched the people sink further into sin and idolatry. Rejecting the true God, they worshiped the Egyptian false goddess, the queen of heaven (44:15-19).

Some would assume that surely the great prophet Jeremiah deserved better treatment for his loyalty to God than to be forced to Egypt. But Jeremiah was not looking for an easy life; he was living to please his God.

Like Jeremiah, we will not experience true joy until we learn to sacrifice our interests to do the Lord's will.

"But what things were gain to me, those I counted loss for Christ" (Philippians 3:7).

Thought for Today: The person who rejects God's Word is walking in darkness that ends in defeat.

Christ Revealed: By *"my servants the prophets"* (Jeremiah 44:4; compare Acts 3: 20-21).

Word Studies: 41:14 **cast about** means deserted; 42:20 **dissembled in your hearts** means only deceived yourselves; erred in your hearts.

Prayer Needs: Country: Greenland—54,000—northeast of Canada • Religious freedom • 98% Protestant; .1% Roman Catholic.

AUGUST 27: Read Jeremiah 45 — 48

Highlights: Jeremiah's message to Baruch; judgment against Egypt, Philistia, and Moab.

Verses for Today: *"Thus saith the Lord, the God of Israel, unto thee, O Baruch; Thou didst say, Woe is me now! for the Lord hath added grief to my sorrow; I fainted in my sighing, and I find no rest. . . . And seekest thou great things for thyself? Seek them not . . . "* (Jeremiah 45:2-3,5).

T he greatest moment in Baruch's life came when he wrote *"all the words of the Lord"* (Jeremiah 36:4) at Jeremiah's dictation.

As national security became more critical, a fast was proclaimed in Jerusalem. At that time, Baruch had the privilege of reading all of Jeremiah's prophecies to the multitude assembled at the Temple. When King Johoiakim heard the news, he issued an order for the arrest of both Baruch and Jeremiah, but the Lord *"hid them"* (36:26).

Baruch became discouraged in the midst of such strong opposition. Perhaps it was godly sorrow over the rejection of the Word of God. When the faithful Christian is hated or slandered, he should remember that the servant can be no greater than his Lord.

Christ was continually rejected. There was no room for Him in the inn at His birth; He had no place among the notable people in His life; and He was crucified by those He came to save.

" . . . Christ also suffered for us, leaving us an example, that ye should follow his steps" (I Peter 2:21).

Thought for Today: It is far better to be poor and despised in this life and have our Lord's approval than to seek great things for ourselves or approval from the world.

Christ Revealed: As the One who corrects His people (Jeremiah 46:28). *"For whom the Lord loveth he chasteneth . . . "* (Heb. 12:6).

Word Studies: 46:4 **furbish** means polish; **brigandines** means armor; 46:11 **daughter** means people; 48:6 **heath** means destitute and forsaken person; 48:10 **deceitfully** means negligently; half-heartedly; 48:19 **espy** means watch; 48:28 **hole's mouth** means mouth or opening of a pit.

Prayer Needs: Country: Ivory Coast—11 million—in western Africa • Religious freedom • 40% animist; 25% Muslim; 10% Roman Catholic; 5% Protestant.

AUGUST 28: Read Jeremiah 49 — 50

Highlights: Judgments against Ammon, Edom, Damascus, Kedar, Hazor, Elam, and Babylon foretold; redemption of Israel promised.

Verses for Today: *"Therefore thus saith the Lord of hosts, the God of Israel; Behold, I will punish the king of Babylon and his land. . . . And I will bring Israel again to his habitation . . . and his soul shall be satisfied . . . "* (Jeremiah 50:18-19).

B abylon's defeat was foretold to strengthen the Israelites' faith in God and to reassure them that He had not forgotten His covenant promise to their forefathers. It was also given to encourage them to return to Jerusalem. Surely this would keep them from participating in Babylon's idol worship.

As foretold by the prophets, the Medes and the Persians successfully defeated Babylon, and Cyrus urged the Jews to return to Jerusalem and rebuild the Temple.

Their faith in the prophetic message is symbolic of the backslider who returns to God—freed from the power of sin and restored to fellowship with Him.

"If the Son therefore shall make you free, ye shall be free indeed" (John 8:36).

Thought for Today: God will hear the cry of any repentant sinner.

Christ Revealed: As the Redeemer (Jeremiah 50:34). *"Blessed be the Lord God of Israel; for he hath visited and redeemed his people"* (Luke 1:68).

220

Word Studies: 49:8 **dwell deep** means hide in deeply concealed hiding places; 50:12 **hindermost** means last; 50:31 **visit** means punish; 50:36 **shall dote** means will become fools.

Prayer Needs: Country: Indonesia—180 million—five large and 13,662 lesser islands in Southeast Asia • Growing pressure from Muslim leaders to limit advances of Christianity by not renewing many of the missionaries' permits to stay in the country • 44% Muslim; 35% Islamic mixtures; 10% Protestant; 4% animist; 4% Roman Catholic; 2% Hindu; 1% Buddhist.

AUGUST 29: Read Jeremiah 51 — 52

Highlights: Judgment of Babylon; fall of Jerusalem; captivity of Judah.

Verse for Today: *"And thou shalt say, Thus shall Babylon sink, and shall not rise from the evil that I will bring upon her: and they shall be weary . . . "* (Jeremiah 51:64).

T he great Babylon—*"the land of the Chaldeans"* (Jeremiah 24:5; 25:12)—was enjoying her greatest power when God declared that she would be *like a desert forever*—that she would *sink to rise no more* (see 51:62,64).

Under the rule of Nebuchadnezzar, who ruled much of the known world at that time, Babylon seemed unconquerable. (See Daniel 2:37-38.) But Babylon's splendor and gigantic world empire did not keep God from bringing about her defeat at the end of the Israelites' 70 years of Babylonian capitivity. The great Babylonian Empire fell the night Belshazzar saw the handwriting on the wall (Daniel 5). To this day, ancient Babylon is uninhabited, as foretold (see Jeremiah 51:61-62).

The world, as we know it, is a system, as well as a planet. Babylon represents the world system which has many attractive things such as *physical desires, things people see and want, and all the glamour of this whole world system* (see I John 2:16). These things can occupy our time and keep us from accomplishing what we should for the Lord.

Behind all the worldly activities is a satanic system that seeks to control the world and defeat and destroy the work of God. We are living in a world that does not know God and hates Christ (see John 15:18; I Corinthians 1:21). We are warned not to become captivated and controlled by the things of the world.

Do not adopt the customs of this world, but let God transform you inwardly by a complete change of your mind and attitude (see Romans 12:2).

Thought for Today: As Christians, we must live in the world; but we don't have to live by its standards.

Christ Revealed: As the Creator (Jeremiah 51:15). *"For by him were all things created . . . "* (Col. 1:16).

Word Study: 52:22 **chapiter** means upper part, a capital which goes on top of a column or pillar.

Prayer Needs: Country: Liberia—2 million—in West Africa • Religious freedom • 41% ancestor worship and witchcraft; 21% Muslim; 13% Protestant; 2% Roman Catholic.

LAMENTATIONS

Jeremiah lived in Jerusalem and saw his prophecies fulfilled. Jerusalem was first subjected to the horrors of starvation (2:19; 4:10); then the Babylonian armies marched in and ravaged the Holy City, destroying the Temple. Outside Jerusalem, Jeremiah wept.

The book of Lamentations is a message of deep sorrow over the destruction of the kingdom he had tried so hard to save.

Jeremiah knew the inevitable consequences of the people's disobedience—*the Lord has made Israel suffer because of her many sins* (see 1:5). The City of God had become as evil as Sodom (4:6; compare Luke 12:47-48).

Knowing that God is merciful, Jeremiah appealed to Him in prayer. However, he was unable to prevent the people of Judah from turning from God or to lead them back to worshiping Him. Although the book of Lamentations shows that the God of love and righteousness must also be the God of judgment on sin, there is a note of trust in God and hope for the future.

AUGUST 30: Read Lamentations 1 — 2

Highlight: Jeremiah's lamentation over Jerusalem's misery.

Verse for Today: *"Her gates are sunk into the ground; he hath destroyed and broken her bars: her king and her princes are among the Gentiles: the law is no more; her prophets also find no vision from the Lord"* (Lamentations 2:9).

Jerusalem—that great and glorious city of God—was in ruins. The emptiness and anguish that swept over the people at their terrible loss was pitifully expressed by the grief-stricken prophet. The destruction of the Temple with its holy of holies, the mercy seat, and the ark of the covenant with the original Law of Moses is evidence of the awful consequences of sin.

Jeremiah first expressed sorrow over the loss of all the precious material things in the city of God. But then his sorrow turned to the still greater calamity—the loss of God's presence and protection. In fact, the religious worship was all empty pretense, and her prophets could *"find no vision from the Lord."*

If we give less than our best—only our spare time and spare money—it is possible that our worship is empty. Our faith and trust in God are strengthened as we appropriate the Word of God in our lives.

"My people are destroyed for lack of knowledge: because thou hast rejected knowledge, I will also reject thee, that thou shalt be no priest to me: seeing thou hast forgotten the law of thy God, I will also forget thy children" (Hosea 4:6).

Thought for Today: God's written Word is accepted through the eyes of faith.

Christ Revealed: By Jeremiah's sorrow over Jerusalem at her fall (Lamentations 1:12-22). Jesus expressed His sorrow for Jerusalem's failure to come to Him (Matt. 23:37; Luke 13:34).

Prayer Needs: Country: Mexico—82 million—in North America • Limited religious freedom • 88% Roman Catholic; 4% Protestant; .1% Eastern Orthodox.

AUGUST 31: Read Lamentations 3 — 5

Highlights: God's mercy; punishment of Zion; the faithful grieve over their disaster and confess their sins.

Verses for Today: *"I am the man that hath seen affliction by the rod of his wrath. He hath led me, and brought me into darkness, but not into light"* (Lamentations 3:1-2).

T he old prophet Jeremiah had walked with God through one adversity after another. *"He hath led me, and brought me into darkness."* But he had assurance that the God he represented was able to guide him through the darkness.

Jeremiah experienced the sad memories of a thankless ministry to which he had given his life, but he had no regrets for his faithfulness.

Even though a Christian may be "in darkness," it need not lead to despair. It should draw him closer to God. Often God does not reveal Himself in these times of darkness because He is teaching us to walk by faith, not by sight. Be prepared for times of darkness when you just can't understand what God is doing in your life.

"Fear none of those things which thou shalt suffer . . . be thou faithful unto death, and I will give thee a crown of life" (Revelation 2:10).

Thought for Today: God's Word gives assurance that His hand is guiding us, whether we are walking with Him in darkness or in light.

Christ Revealed: As a merciful Savior (Lamentations 3:22). *"For I will be merciful to their unrighteousness, and their sins and their iniquities will I remember no more"* (Heb. 8:12).

Word Studies: 4:10 **pitiful** means compassionate; **sodden** means boiled.

Prayer Needs: Country: Mauritania—2 million—in western Africa • An Islamic state with no mission work allowed • 99+% Muslim; .5% Roman Catholic; there are no known native Mauritanian believers.

PRAYERS IN THIS MONTH'S READING

EZEKIEL

Ezekiel was among the second group of captives taken to Babylon when Nebuchadnezzar returned to Palestine and removed Jehoiachin, puppet-king of Judah. Nebuchadnezzar appointed Zedekiah (third son of Josiah) to govern Palestine for him. (See II Kings 24:10-17; I Chronicles 3:15.)

About 10 years after Zedekiah's appointment, he rebelled against Nebuchadnezzar, who then attacked Jerusalem, broke down its walls, and destroyed the Temple (II Kings 24:18—25:21; II Chronicles 36:11-21).

The prophet Jeremiah was still in Jerusalem, where he had been prophesying for about 35 years. Daniel, who had been taken to Babylon about nine years earlier than Ezekiel, now held a prominent position in the Babylonian Empire. He was mentioned by Ezekiel three times (Ezekiel 14:14,20; 28:3).

Ezekiel's message pointed out the approaching destruction and judgment caused by the sin of idolatry. He communicated God's message through symbols, allegories, and visions—the same methods used by Daniel and later by John in the book of Revelation.

The purpose of his symbolic actions—such as his silent grief over the death of his wife (24:15-24) and his lying on the ground (4:4-6)—was to gain the attention of the people. All these things revealed a yielded life of obedience to God. Indeed, he was a powerful communicator who was driven by an overwhelming sense of obligation to warn that Jerusalem would be destroyed unless the people repented. However, the hearts of the people were already hardened in idolatry.

After Jerusalem's fall in 586 B.C., Ezekiel then began a message of hope, consolation, and reconstruction. His emphasis shifted to comforting the exiled Hebrews. Just as forcefully as he had prophesied God's judgment, he foretold that the Israelites would be restored to their own land—a prophecy we have seen fulfilled in our generation in a very thrilling manner.

God's purpose in the remarkable fulfillment of prophecy concerning the restoration of the nation of Israel is that all mankind *"shall know that I am the Lord"*—a phrase which occurs more than 60 times in the book of Ezekiel.

In conclusion, Ezekiel foretold the coming of the New Jerusalem and its Temple, where God Himself will dwell with His people.

SEPTEMBER 1: Read Ezekiel 1 — 4

Highlights: Ezekiel's vision of God's administration; his call; warning of judgment.

Verses for Today: *"...I send thee ... to a rebellious nation ... And thou shalt speak my words unto them ... Be not thou rebellious like that rebellious house: open thy mouth, and eat that I give thee"* (Ezekiel 2:3,7-8).

G od spoke to Ezekiel, saying, *"Speak my words,"* but told him he would not be appreciated, and the people would not accept his message. They were a *"rebellious nation."*

The servant of God should not be concerned about *success*—only *faithfulness*. In serving the Lord, there is so much that is rewarding, even though there are disappointments.

Perhaps we have accepted a task in the name of the Lord only to have felt unappreciated. But God allows every discouragement that we might place our faith in Him—and not in ourselves.

It is impossible for us to know *"what is the exceeding greatness of his power to usward who believe"* (Ephesians 1:19) until we have stood in the midst of the work which the Master has given and have seen the futility of our own strength.

"Nay, in all these things we are more than conquerors through him that loved us" (Romans 8:37).

Thought for Today: When our lives are in harmony with His Word, we will recognize that God is working through us to accomplish His eternal purposes.

Christ Revealed: In *"the likeness as the appearance of a man"* who sat upon the throne (Ezekiel 1:26-28). The description is that of the pre-incarnate Christ, who alone is worthy to receive glory and honor and power (Rev. 4:3-11).

Word Studies: 1:4 **infolding itself** means flashing continually; 1:20 **up over against** means close beside; 2:4 **impudent** means stubborn; 3:9 **an adamant** means a stone; 3:14 **heat** means anger; 4:16 **care** means anxiety.

Prayer Needs: Country: Netherlands Antilles—182,000—a Dutch-speaking territory in the Caribbean area • Religious freedom • 80% Roman Catholic; 8% Protestant.

SEPTEMBER 2: Read Ezekiel 5 — 9

Highlights: Famine, pestilence, and sword; remnant to be spared; vision of the glory of God; vision of slaying in Jerusalem.

Verses for Today: *"And the word of the Lord came unto me, saying ... your altars shall be desolate, and your images shall be broken: and I will cast down your slain* *men before your idols. . . . Yet will I leave a remnant, that ye may have some that shall escape the sword among the nations, when ye shall be scattered through the countries"* (Ezekiel 6:1,4,8).

W hen the Israelites first entered Canaan, God provided an abundance of material blessings. As the people lived in obedience to His Word, the land was fruitful, their flocks multiplied, and no enemy was able to invade the nation. However, the blessings were withdrawn as they ignored God's Word, turned to idols, and lived to please themselves.

But God did not forget His promise to Abraham and his descendants. Ezekiel foretold that Jerusalem would be rebuilt and Israel would realize that Jehovah had dealt with them—not according to their evil ways, but according to His lovingkindness. They would be restored to their land after they repented of their evil ways.

A remnant of faithful believers has always *feared the Lord, and thought upon his name* (see Malachi 3:16). Even in a godless society, believers find opportunities to meet for mutual fellowship to honor His Word.

"Even so then at this present time also there is a remnant according to the election of grace" (Romans 11:5).

Thought for Today: Restoration is always available to those who repent.

Christ Portrayed: By the man clothed in linen (Ezekiel 9:2-11), who represents Christ as Mediator, saving His people from the flaming sword of vengeance. *"For there is one God, and one mediator between God and men, the man Christ Jesus"* (I Tim. 2:5).

Word Studies: 8:12 **imagery** means perverse imagination; 8:14 **Tammuz** means a Babylonian idol.

Prayer Needs: Country: Philippines—62 million—in Southeast Asia • Religious persecution in some areas • 64% Roman Catholic; 11% Protestant; 8% indigenous Catholic; 8% Muslim; 7% cults.

SEPTEMBER 3: Read Ezekiel 10 — 13

Highlights: Glory of the Lord leaving the Temple; judgment upon lying leaders; the promise of Israel's restoration and renewal; captivity near; false prophets condemned.

Verse for Today: *"Thus saith the Lord . . . I know the things that come into your mind, every one of them"* (Ezekiel 11:5).

G od exposed the plans of Israel's 25 princes, who were national leaders and advisers. Believing their clever strategy would insure their national security against Nebuchadnezzar, they ignored God's command, through the prophet Ezekiel, to cooperate with Nebuchadnezzar. Instead, they placed their confidence in their secret defense alliance with Egypt. This was in opposition to the will of God and brought about the final destruction of the Holy City, Jerusalem.

How foolish to believe that their own thoughts and plans could be successful when they ignored God's Word.

No thought is so small or so clever that God does not take notice, for He knows *"the things that come into your mind."* We can hide nothing from Him.

Do not think that foolish or evil thoughts are insignificant, or that they can do no harm as long as they remain unexpressed. Your thoughts mold your mind and character, *for as a person thinks in his heart, so he is* (see Proverbs 23:7). Oh, how often we need to pray, *"Cleanse thou me from secret faults"* (Psalm 19:12)!

"Casting down imaginations, and every high thing that exalteth itself against the knowledge of God, and bringing into captivity every thought to the obedience of Christ" (II Corinthians 10:5).

Thought for Today: It is impossible to please the Lord if we are thinking wrong thoughts.

Christ Revealed: As the One who gives a new spirit (Ezekiel 11:19). This promise is fulfilled when one accepts Jesus as Savior (Gal. 4:4-7).

Word Study: 13:18 **women that sew pillows to all armholes** means false prophetesses who sew magic charms on divining garments and fasten protective charms to their wrists.

Prayer Needs: Country: Saudi Arabia—15 million—on the Arabian Peninsula in southwestern Asia • Christian worship services for foreign personnel are tolerated, but those who seek to convert Muslims to Christianity face persecution • 99% Muslim; 1% Christian.

SEPTEMBER 4: Read Ezekiel 14 — 16

Highlights: Judgment pronounced upon elders of Israel and Jerusalem; parable of the vine; promises of future blessings under the new covenant.

Verse for Today: *"Thou hast also taken thy fair jewels of my gold and of my silver, which I had given thee, and madest to thyself images of men, and didst commit whoredom with them"* (Ezekiel 16:17).

G od made Israel to prosper above all nations. He drew them out of slavery and gave them royal dignity, great power, and wealth. His blessings should have encouraged them to be a holy people who would teach the world to worship the one true God—but they turned to idols. Disobedience kept them from fulfilling their purpose as God's chosen people. (See Isaiah 5; Jeremiah 2:21; Hosea 10; Revelation 14:18.)

We, too, are a chosen generation and are *"kings and priests unto God"* (Revelation 1:6). All Christians should desire to *show forth the praises of him who hath called us out of darkness into his marvelous light* (see I Peter 2:9).

The important thing for you and for me is to be diligent students of the Word, not reading into the Bible, not trying to interpret from our background, but humbly beseeching God to speak to us and to guide us in His holy will.

Of course, if you have never taken Christ into your life, the Bible is a closed Book to you. It cannot be understood unless you really know the Author. To know the Author you must be born again, that is, born from above by believing on Christ. You need a spiritual rebirth. This is a miracle of God. You cannot achieve it. You cannot obtain it. You can only receive it by faith by believing on Christ, the Son of the Living God.

"Thus saith the Lord, Let not the wise man glory in his wisdom, neither let the mighty man glory in his might, let not the rich man glory in his riches: But let him that glorieth glory in this, that he understandeth and knoweth me, that I am the Lord . . . " (Jeremiah 9:23-24).

227

Thought for Today: If our hearts are truly set on doing the Lord's will, we will give much attention to the study of *all* His Word.

Christ Revealed: In the everlasting covenant (Ezekiel 16:60-63). Jesus is the same yesterday, today, and forever (Heb. 13:8).

Word Studies: 14:15 **noisome** means wild; 15:4 **meet** means useful; 16:4 **supple** means cleanse; 16:30 **imperious** means arrogant, haughty, presumptuous; 16:31 **eminent place** means pagan shrine; 16:43 **fretted** means angered.

Prayer Needs: Country: Bulgaria—9 million—in southeastern Europe • Severe limitation and control of all religious groups • 62% Eastern Orthodox; 10% Muslim; .75% Roman Catholic; .5% Protestant.

SEPTEMBER 5: Read Ezekiel 17 — 19

Highlights: Parable of the eagles; judgment upon bad conduct and blessings for good conduct; lamentation (words of sorrow) over the leaders of Israel.

Verse for Today: *"Yet saith the house of Israel, The way of the Lord is not equal [fair or just]. O house of Israel, are not my ways equal? are not your ways unequal?"* (Ezekiel 18:29).

D uring the final days of Jerusalem, the people of Judah endured much suffering before they were taken as slaves to Babylon. Consequently, they were bitter and accused God of being unjust in allowing them to be disgraced and defeated by the Babylonians.

Why didn't God keep them from slavery? Surely they were not as evil as Nebuchadnezzar and his cruel heathen armies. Why would God permit the wicked Babylonians to prosper and control the earth?

Because the Israelites refused to turn from their sins, God could not bless or protect them. Nebuchadnezzar became His instrument for executing judgment upon them, destroying Jerusalem and taking the people captive. Then, as foretold by Jeremiah, God's judgment fell upon the Babylonians (Jeremiah 50:1-3).

The ways of the Lord are always perfect. His ways will seem unfair only to those who live in rebellion against what is truly right.

God does not suggest, He demands, that everyone repent and turn from sin (Ezekiel 18:30).

Just as the idols had to be removed from the Temple, known sin must not remain in the Christian life. *"How shall we, that are dead to sin, live any longer therein?"* (Romans 6:2).

God, in wisdom and love, desires that everyone turn from sin and enjoy His protection and provisions.

"The Lord is . . . not willing that any should perish, but that all should come to repentance" (II Peter 3:9).

Thought for Today: The highest calling of God in Christ Jesus is that we may know Him and make Him known to others.

Christ Revealed: As the One whose forgiveness provided life (Ezekiel 18:20-22). *God made Christ—who knew no sin—to be sin for us, that we might be made the righteousness of God* (see II Cor. 5:21).

Word Study: 18:8 **usury** means interest.

228

Prayer Needs: Country: Andorra—48,000—in the eastern Pyrenees between France and Spain • Religious freedom • 88% Roman Catholic; .2% Protestant.

SEPTEMBER 6: Read Ezekiel 20 — 21

Highlights: God's refusal to be consulted by the elders; the history of rebellious Israel; the Israelites defeated by Babylon and scattered among the heathen.

Verse for Today: *"But the house of Israel rebelled against me in the wilderness: they walked not in my statutes, and they despised my judgments . . . "* (Ezekiel 20:13).

T hrough the prophet Ezekiel, God declared that the real reason for Israel's failure was because *"they walked not in my statutes, and they despised my judgments"* (compare Ezekiel 20:11,18,21). Morally, they had sunk to the corrupt conduct of the heathen nations around them. Because they disregarded His Word and did as they pleased, God could not bless them. He cannot bless evil.

On three occasions the elders went to Ezekiel *"to inquire of the Lord,"* presumably to seek God's will (8:1; 14:1; 20:1). On the first occasion, Ezekiel exposed their sins and foretold Jerusalem's doom because of idolatry. At the second meeting, God revealed to Ezekiel that the elders were not sincere and did not have a desire to do His will. The third time, Ezekiel told them that the destruction of Jerusalem and the nation was certain.

To *"inquire of the Lord"* without a sincere desire to please Him and to obey His Word is just as foolish for Christians today as it was for the Israelites then.

God is indeed long-suffering, and He extends forgiving mercy to every sinner who repents and turns to Christ as Savior and Lord.

"Before I was afflicted I went astray: but now have I kept thy word" (Psalm 119:67)

Thought for Today: In loving-kindness, God chastens His people when they sin in order to bring them back into fellowship with Him.

Christ Revealed: As the One who will gather His people from all nations and *"will purge out"* the false from the true (Ezekiel 20:34-38; compare Matt. 3:12; 25:32).

Word Studies: 20:5 **lifted up mine hand** means promised; 20:6 **espied** means searched out; 20:24 **were after** means lusted after; 20:40 **oblations** means gifts; 21:9 **furbished** means polished; 21:31 **brutish** means cruel.

Prayer Needs: Country: Ethiopia—47 million—in eastern Africa • Enemies of Christianity hostile toward the Church • 41% Eastern Orthodox; 35% Muslim; 10% Protestant; 10% animist; .7% Roman Catholic.

SEPTEMBER 7: Read Ezekiel 22 — 24

Highlights: Sins of Israel enumerated; abominations of the two sisters; parable of the boiling pot; the death of Ezekiel's wife.

Verses for Today: *"Again in the ninth year, in the tenth month, in the tenth day of the month, the word of the Lord came unto me, saying . . . the king of Babylon set himself against Jerusalem this same day"* (Ezekiel 24:1-2).

E zekiel foretold that Nebuchadnezzar, king of Babylon, would soon destroy Jerusalem. The siege and capture were pictured as a caldron (large kettle) set over a fire. The caldron represented the nation, and pieces of flesh inside the caldron represented its people, who would be consumed.

Despite all the optimistic forecasts made by false prophets who had said that the families already taken into captivity would soon be set free, the time of destruction for the kingdom of Judah had finally come. The people recognized too late that Ezekiel's prophecies were true. The final sentence of destruction was carried out upon the people of Judah because they had turned from God and were worshiping idols.

When people or possessions keep us from living to please the Lord, these persons or things become our idols.

"He that loveth father or mother more than me is not worthy of me: and he that loveth son or daughter more than me is not worthy of me. And he that taketh not his cross, and followeth after me, is not worthy of me" (Matthew 10:37-38).

Thought for Today: The more we see things from God's point of view, the more we will see how *"exceeding sinful"* sin really is (Romans 7:13).

Christ Revealed: In the denunciation of Israel's false prophets (Ezekiel 22:25-28). Compare these denunciations with those Christ spoke against the scribes and Pharisees (Matt. 23:13-36).

Word Studies: 22:5 **vexed** means confused; 23:16 **doted upon** means lusted after; 24:17 **tire** means turban.

Prayer Needs: Country: Ghana—14 million—in western Africa • The government permits freedom to churches and missionaries that do not get involved in politics • 31% belief in spirits and witches; 22% Protestant; 17% Muslim; 11% Roman Catholic.

SEPTEMBER 8: Read Ezekiel 25 — 28

Highlights: Gentile nations judged; judgment on Tyre's king and the fate of Satan who inspired him; future regathering of Israel.

Verses for Today: *" . . . Behold, I am against thee, O Tyrus. . . . I will make thee like the top of a rock . . . thou shalt be built no more . . . "* (Ezekiel 26:3,14).

T he island fortress of Tyre, including its coastal territorial possessions, was one of the greatest trading centers of its time.

Tyre gained control of world commerce when Jerusalem, her greatest competitor, was destroyed. Because of their rejoicing over the fall of God's people, God told Ezekiel to prophesy that Tyre would be completely destroyed.

Surrounded by water and protected by her great fleet of Phoenician ships, Tyre seemed like the most secure place on earth. But the time came when Ezekiel's prophecy was fulfilled.

Alexander the Great besieged Tyre, tore down the walls and other buildings on the mainland, and literally built a rock road to the island fortress, thus fulfilling Ezekiel's amazing prophecy: *"I will make thee like the top of a rock: thou shalt be a place to spread nets upon; thou shalt be built no more . . . "* (Ezekiel 26:14).

Why haven't the "atheists" rebuilt this once-great seaport? There are no laws that say they can't do it! But the One who inspired Ezekiel to prophesy said it shall never be rebuilt. Every hour of every day, ancient Tyre is a testimony of the reliability of the Bible.

God also wants our lives to be a testimony to the truth of His Word in our everyday experiences.

"Thy word is true from the beginning: and every one of thy righteous judgments endureth for ever" (Psalm 119:160).

Thought for Today: God will always keep the promises in His Word.

Christ Revealed: As the One who will execute judgment upon Satan (Ezekiel 28:14-17; see also Rev. 20).

Word Studies: 25:5 **couching place** means resting place; 26:17 **haunt it** means dwell there; 27:25 **did sing of thee in thy market** means were the carriers for your merchandise.

Prayer Needs: Country: Senegal—7 million—in western Africa • Religious freedom • 92% Muslim; 4% animism and ancestor worship; 3% Roman Catholic; .1% Protestant.

SEPTEMBER 9: Read Ezekiel 29 — 32

Highlights: Egypt's defeat by Babylon foretold; Assyria's fall—a warning to Egypt; lamentation (great sorrow) over Egypt's fall.

Verses for Today: *"And I will make the land of Egypt desolate ... and her cities among the cities that are laid waste shall be desolate forty years.... At the end of forty years will I ... cause them to return.... It shall be the basest of the kingdoms ... "* (Ezekiel 29:12-15).

F or centuries, Egypt, a magnificent world power, had been famous for her commerce, art, literature, science, and military might. Observing world politics, it would have been impossible for anyone to foresee that Egypt would be defeated and then rebuilt in 40 years. Even more amazing was the added prophecy that Egypt would never regain world superiority but would remain as one of *"the basest of the kingdoms."*

This prophecy is a striking contrast to the prophecies that Tyre, Assyria, and Babylon would never be rebuilt.

In all the Bible, not one prophecy has ever failed to be fulfilled. The prophecy concerning Egypt's defeat and rebuilding seemed so unlikely to be fulfilled, yet it has been. God will fulfill all His promises. God's Word is settled in Heaven, forever (see Psalm 119:89). How reassuring then to read God's promises to Christians and know they will all be fulfilled.

"Heaven and earth shall pass away: but my words shall not pass away" (Luke 21:33).

Thought for Today: During the tests of all the ages, God's Word remains unchanged ... and sure.

Christ Revealed: Through the prophets by the *"word of the Lord"* (Ezekiel 29:1). *"God, who ... spake in time past unto the fathers by the prophets, Hath in these last days spoken unto us by his Son ... "* (Heb. 1:1-2).

Word Studies: 29:6 **staff of reed** means weak support; 30:2 **Woe worth the day**

means a day of terror is coming; 30:21 **roller** means bandage.

Prayer Needs: Country: Gibraltar—29,000—on the southern coast of Spain • Religious freedom • 72% Roman Catholic; 9% Muslim; 8% Protestant; 2% Jewish; 1% Hindu.

SEPTEMBER 10: Read Ezekiel 33 — 36

Highlights: Jerusalem's destruction; the justice of God's dealings; reproof of the faithless shepherds; God's punishment of Edom; restoration of Israel foretold.

Verses for Today: " ... *Woe be to the shepherds of Israel that do feed themselves! should not the shepherds feed the flocks? ... Therefore will I save my flock. ... And I will set up one shepherd over them* ... " (Ezekiel 34:2,22-23).

G od expressed His anger against Israel's religious leaders because they were more concerned in protecting their own interests than they were in warning the people to turn from their evil ways and worship the Lord. Consequently, the nation was like a shepherdless flock and eventually was taken into slavery by the Babylonians.

Ezekiel foretold of a Shepherd who would truly love and care for His sheep—the Messiah, King of kings.

Jesus identified Himself as Israel's Shepherd who would lay down (give) His life for His sheep (John 10:11-15).

Our Savior did not give His life as a martyr for truth or as a moral example of self-sacrifice; He, of His own free will, gave His life for lost, sinful people. Jesus Christ died on the cross for our sins so that we might have eternal life.

Jesus said: *"I am the good shepherd, and know my sheep, and am known of mine. As the Father knoweth me, even so know I the Father: and I lay down my life for the sheep"* (John 10:14-15).

Thought for Today: If the Good Shepherd had not died as our substitute, we could not have eternal life with Him.

Christ Revealed: As the Shepherd (Ezekiel 34:23). Jesus said, *"I am the good shepherd, and know my sheep, and am known of mine"* (John 10:14).

Word Studies: 34:14 **fat** means rich; 34:17 **cattle** means sheep.

Prayer Needs: Country: Grenada—85,000—the southernmost of the Windward Islands • Religious freedom • 61% Roman Catholic; 31% Protestant.

SEPTEMBER 11: Read Ezekiel 37 — 39

Highlights: Valley of dry bones; prophecy against Gog; vision of restored Israel.

Verse for Today: *"Then he said unto me, Son of man, these bones are the whole house of Israel: behold, they say, Our bones are dried, and our hope is lost: we are cut off for our parts"* (Ezekiel 37:11).

I n Ezekiel's vision, he saw a valley full of scattered bones. These bones represented the Israelites who were in Babylonian captivity and had lost all hope of ever again becoming a nation. They said, *"Our bones are dried, and our hope is lost."* The majority of these exiled Jews were also dead in the sense that sin had destroyed their faith in the promises of God.

Just as God was the only One who could restore life to the dry bones, He was also the only One who could restore the Israelite nation to life (Ezekiel 37:13-14). Israel, as a nation, was made to live again, and the Israelites' return to Jerusalem is also foretold in the book of Nehemiah.

All mankind is as spiritually dead as the dry bones until they are made alive—born again *"of the Spirit"* (John 3:5). We then have the privilege of being led by His Spirit. It is not by our effort or any human insight, but by God's Spirit, that we see things of eternal significance accomplished.

Christ will return in great glory to reward His faithful children.

"And, behold, I come quickly; and my reward is with me, to give every man according as his work shall be" (Revelation 22:12).

Thought for Today: Every believer can be assured that God can transform even the most hopeless situation. His Word has the answer for every need.

Christ Revealed: As the One who made possible the resurrection from the grave (Ezekiel 37:12; see also John 11:25; I Thess. 4:16).

Word Studies: 39:6 **carelessly** means securely; 39:14 **sever out** means set apart; **passengers** means those passing by.

Prayer Needs: Country: Lebanon—3 million—in the Middle East • Limited religious freedom • 67% Muslim; 19% Roman Catholic; 10% Eastern Orthodox; 1% Protestant.

SEPTEMBER 12: Read Ezekiel 40 — 42

Highlight: Vision of future Temple.

Verse for Today: *"Afterward he brought me to the temple . . . "* (Ezekiel 41:1).

T hese three chapters describe a future Temple, the priests, and their duties. Once completed, the glory of the Lord will return and truly make this Temple magnificent. The presence of God as a brilliant cloud, which was in the Holy of Holies of the Tabernacle as well as Solomon's Temple, will once again be in their midst.

Ezekiel previously had seen this same "cloud" linger, then slowly move from the Temple to the Mount of Olives, and disappear. The people had no true interest in being led of God. The glory of this Temple is emphasized by the statement: *"The Lord is there"* (Ezekiel 48:35; see also 43:5).

The Christian is likened to the temple of God—for we are the Lord's dwelling place. His Holy Spirit desires to control our will.

There are two ways for Christians to receive direction: one, by human reasoning; the other, by His Word as the Holy Spirit enlightens and gives understanding. The natural mind can only make decisions based on limited knowledge in any given situation. But the Holy Spirit may lead in a much different way at times because all things are known to God. *"Trust in the Lord with all thine heart; and lean not unto thine own understanding. In all thy ways acknowledge him, and he shall direct thy paths"* (Proverbs 3:5-6).

It is also vital that we pray before making decisions. As we pray, we should have an attitude of *"not my will, but thine, be done"* (Luke 22:42). If we are intent on our own ways, we will miss the leading of the Holy Spirit.

You are the temple of God, and the Spirit of God dwells in you (see I Corinthians 3:16).

Thought for Today: If you are willing to submit to God, He will take care of the outcome.

Christ Revealed: In the exactness of instruction for the Temple (Ezekiel 40). Just as our Lord took great care in giving details for the Temple, He has given directions for His people—who are the temple of God (I Cor. 6:19-20; II Cor. 6:16-17).

Word Studies: 40:23 **over against** means opposite; 41:12 **separate place** means Temple yard.

Prayer Needs: Country: Panama—2 million—in southern Central America • Religious freedom • 78% Roman Catholic; 12% Protestant; 5% Muslim; .1% Eastern Orthodox.

SEPTEMBER 13: Read Ezekiel 43 — 45

Highlights: Vision of God's glory filling the Temple; ordinances for the priests; land for the sanctuary and city described.

Verses for Today: *"So the spirit took me up . . . and, behold, the glory of the Lord filled the house. And I heard him speaking unto me out of the house; and the man stood by me"* (Ezekiel 43:5-6).

A t the time Ezekiel prophesied, Israel's worship was not according to God's Word. They were observing religious rituals, but their hearts were not devoted to God. Consequently, the elders in authority did not desire the presence of the Lord nor recognize the importance of the Word of God.

But the Spirit of God lead Ezekiel to behold *"the glory of the Lord"* and *hear Him speaking.* The unaided intellect of *"the natural man receiveth not the things of the Spirit of God"* (I Corinthians 2:14).

Nothing so effectually hinders our hearing God's voice as getting advice from unsaved, worldly-minded counselors. Too often, Christians are influenced by the views of people rather than by God through daily reading His Word. If we are to discern God's will, we must allow the Holy Spirit to speak to us through His Word.

"It is the spirit that quickeneth; the flesh profiteth nothing: the words that I speak unto you, they are spirit, and they are life" (John 6:63).

Thought for Today: When our hearts are full of loving obedience to His Word, we will serve God acceptably.

Christ Revealed: As the *"glory of the Lord"* (Ezekiel 43:4). Jesus is *"the brightness"* of God's glory (Heb. 1:3).

Word Studies: 43:20 **settle** means ledge; 44:22 **put away** means divorced; 44:25 **come at** means go near; 45:14 **the cor** means a measure of things both dry and liquid; 45:20 **simple** means simpleminded.

Prayer Needs: Country: South Korea—42 million—in northeastern Asia • Religious freedom • 33% Buddhist; 24% Protestant; 22% Confucianism and other eastern religions; 4% Roman Catholic.

SEPTEMBER 14: Read Ezekiel 46 — 48

Highlights: Worship of the prince; the river from the Temple; boundaries and divisions of the land; the gates of Jerusalem.

Verses for Today: *"Afterward he brought me again unto the door of the house; and, behold, waters issued out from under the threshold. . . . Then said he unto me, These waters issue out toward the east country, and go down into the desert, and go into the sea: which being brought forth into the sea, the waters shall be healed"* (Ezekiel 47:1,8).

In a vision Ezekiel saw the waters of life flowing into the Dead Sea, bringing forth life-giving water. Where there once had been death and desolation, great schools of fish could now be seen. Everywhere the river flowed, it brought life (Ezekiel 47:9).

God has a pure river of life for His redeemed ones. All the blessings of life come through Christ, who is the source of the Water of life. It begins with a small stream from Christ the Fountainhead, and continues to increase in depth and preciousness as we walk after the Spirit in the light of His Word. All who accept Him as Savior shall have *"rivers of living water"* flowing from them (John 7:37-38).

" . . . whosoever will, let him take the water of life freely" (Revelation 22:17).

Thought for Today: Fellowship with Christ brings a fullness of life that overflows with blessings for others.

Christ Revealed: In the river of living waters and the name of the city—*"The Lord is there"* (Ezekiel 47:1-12; 48:35; see also Rev. 21—22).

Word Studies: 46:22 **of one measure** means the same size; 48:28 **the river** means a ravine or valley that is dry except during the rainy season.

Prayer Needs: Country: Rwanda—7 million—in central Africa • Religious freedom • 40% Roman Catholic; 21% Protestant; 14% belief in false gods, ancestor worship, and spirit-possession cults; 9% Muslim.

DANIEL

Daniel, a God-fearing Jew of royal lineage, was among the first Jewish captives taken to Babylon after Nebuchadnezzar seized control of Jerusalem around 605 B.C. (1:1-7). At the time, Daniel was probably in his late teens or early twenties. Daniel's ministry covered the entire 70-year period of Judah's exile in Babylon. He served as an official in the courts of both Babylon and Persia.

The book of Daniel was written during a time when the Jews were suffering because of persecution and oppression.

The first section (chapters 1—6) tells about Daniel and some of his fellow exiles who, through their faith and obedience to God, triumphed over their enemies. Although he was surrounded by wickedness in the great city of Babylon, far from home, Daniel remained true to God. In fact, Daniel is one of the few individuals in Scripture about whom no sin is recorded. Ezekiel

235

compared Daniel's righteous life to the lives of Noah and Job (Ezekiel 14:14,20).

The second section (chapters 7—12) records Daniel's visions. Daniel revealed that the empires of Babylon, Persia, Greece, and Rome would rise and fall. He also foretold the victory of God's people.

The book of Daniel reveals God's intervention in the affairs of governments, as well as individuals. He is in control.

Daniel's visions foretold the time that the Messiah's work would begin. Christ's kingdom is depicted as a stone *"cut out . . . without hands"*—without human involvement or power, a kingdom which shall never be destroyed and which will bring to an end all other kingdoms (2:44-45).

Daniel provides vital information about the last days of Israel and the earth. He also reveals the superiority and sovereignty of God over all creation, including world governments.

Jesus quoted often from the book of Daniel and spoke of him as *"Daniel the prophet,"* meaning "one through whom divine revelation was given" (Matthew 24:15; Mark 13:14).

SEPTEMBER 15: Read Daniel 1 — 3

Highlights: Daniel and his friends confronted with the king's food; Nebuchadnezzar's dream and its interpretation; fiery furnace proven harmless to three Jews.

Verse for Today: *"But Daniel purposed in his heart that he would not defile himself with the portion of the king's meat . . . "* (Daniel 1:8).

D aniel was blessed of God with unusual wisdom. And soon after his captivity, he and other selected Israelite captives were given a special three-year training course in the language and customs of their new country.

Nebuchadnezzar's purpose for this specialized training may have been to use these young leaders to influence the other captives to become loyal to their new country and thus weaken their loyalty to God.

One of the requirements of these "privileged" men was to eat the same kind of food the king ate. But Daniel and his three friends would not eat the "defiled" food. It probably was not prepared according to God's Levitical standards. As a result, God honored these men with healthier bodies and clearer minds than any of the others.

God will also bless our loyalty and obedience to Him.

Although it may seem difficult at times, God expects His people to remain true to godly principles in every situation.

"There is therefore now no condemnation to them which are in Christ Jesus . . . who walk not after the flesh, but after the Spirit" (Romans 8:1,4).

Thought for Today: Always remain true to God and His Word—regardless of your circumstances.

Christ Revealed: As the *"stone that smote the image"* (Daniel 2:35). The Stone was none other than Jesus Christ (Acts 4:11; Eph. 2:20; I Pet. 2:4-8).

236

Word Studies: 1:10 **liking** means in appearance; 1:12 **pulse** means vegetable diet; 2:31 **terrible** means magnificent; awesome; frightening; 3:19 **the form of his visage was changed** means his facial expression was changed to antagonism; **wont** means usually; 3:21 **hosen** means undergarments; 3:28 **changed** means violated.

Prayer Needs: Country: Tanzania—24 million—in eastern Africa • Churches are expected to help implement Marxist policy • 33% Muslim; 19% Roman Catholic; 19% animist; 15% Protestant.

SEPTEMBER 16: Read Daniel 4 — 6

Highlights: Nebuchadnezzar's dream and Daniel's interpretation of it; fulfillment of the dream; Belshazzar's feast; handwriting on the wall and Daniel's interpretation of it; its fulfillment; Daniel cast into the lions' den.

Verse for Today: *"Belshazzar the king made a great feast to a thousand of his lords, and drank wine before the thousand"* (Daniel 5:1).

T he 70 years of Jewish exile were nearing an end at the time Belshazzar was enjoying this great party. In his drunken condition, he ordered his servants to bring him the holy vessels that Nebuchadnezzar had taken from Solomon's Temple many years earlier and to fill the vessels with wine. As his guests drank, they hilariously *"praised the gods of gold, and of silver . . . "* (Daniel 5:4).

But God had no trouble getting the arrogant king's attention through the miraculous handwriting on the wall. In his hour of crisis, the proud king panicked, and his *"knees smote one against another"* (5:6). In fear, he cried for his astrologers and soothsayers, but they were unable to interpret the message.

The actions of the God-rejecting Belshazzar find their parallel in the lives of many today who disregard attending church and desecrate the Lord's day. Unless our nation heeds the lessons of history, a similar calamity may also suddenly come upon us.

"God resisteth the proud, and giveth grace to the humble" (I Peter 5:5).

Thought for Today: Pride is the root of much sin in our lives.

Christ Revealed: Through the sending of an angel to *"shut the lions' mouths"* (Daniel 6:22). The Lord sent an angel to deliver Peter (Acts 12:11).

Word Studies: 4:37 **abase** means humble; 5:5 **candlestick** means lamp.

Prayer Needs: Country: Syria—11 million—in southwestern Asia • Limited religious freedom for Christians • 90% Muslim; 4% Eastern Orthodox; 2% Roman Catholic; .25% Protestant.

SEPTEMBER 17: Read Daniel 7 — 9

Highlights: Daniel's vision of the beasts; vision of Christ's kingdom; vision of the ram and goat; Daniel's prayer for his people; vision of 70 weeks.

Verses for Today: *"Daniel spake and said, I saw in my vision by night, and, behold, the four winds of the heaven strove upon the great sea. And four great beasts came up from the sea, diverse one from another"* (Daniel 7:2-3).

The great sea, driven by opposing winds, represents the confusion and contention that exist in the world. And from this tempestuous situation arise four savage beasts, depicting the history of the world from the time of Daniel to the kingdom of Christ.

Fifty years before Daniel's vision, these same four great kingdoms were revealed to the worldly-minded Nebuchadnezzar, but from a far different point of view (Daniel 2).

Nebuchadnezzar had viewed a great and glorious giant figure, representing succeeding world empires that would exist until the end of time. But to the prophet, the kingdoms of this world appeared as savage beasts that were controlled by the impulses of selfish ambition, cruelty, and strife. Daniel saw humanity as it is when it rejects Christ—degraded by its sinful nature and enslaved by Satan.

There are many dazzling "giants" in our day—many "good" things to buy and places to go. These "giants" seek to lure us away from God's purpose for our lives. Actually, the dazzling giants are beasts that can steal our time and destroy our testimony if we yield to them.

Eternal treasures can only be gained as we desire, more than anything else, to be guided by God's Word and Spirit.

"Love not the world, neither the things that are in the world. If any man love the world, the love of the Father is not in him. For all that is in the world, the lust of the flesh, and the lust of the eyes, and the pride of life, is not of the Father, but is of the world" (I John 2:15-16).

Thought for Today: To some people, worldly popularity and power appear as a dazzling giant prize to be gained at any price.

Christ Revealed: As the *"Son of man"* (Daniel 7:13-14). This vision was confirmed by our Lord Jesus Christ as He spoke of the last days. *"... and they shall see the Son of man coming in the clouds of heaven with power and great glory"* (Matt. 24:30).

Word Studies: 7:28 **cogitations** means thoughts; 8:7 **choler** means anger.

Prayer Needs: Country: Sudan—24 million—at the eastern end of the Sahara Desert • Limited religious freedom • 74% Muslim; 15% king worship, spirit-possession cults, and ancestral spirit worship; 5% Roman Catholic; 3% Protestant.

SEPTEMBER 18: Read Daniel 10 — 12

Highlights: Heavenly messenger detained; prophecy of kingdoms from David to Antichrist; the Great Tribulation.

Verse for Today: *"I ate no pleasant bread, neither came flesh nor wine in my mouth, neither did I anoint myself at all, till three whole weeks were fulfilled"* (Daniel 10:3).

In the first year of his reign, Cyrus, king of Persia, issued a proclamation to encourage the Jews to return to Jerusalem (Ezra 1). Only a few, about 50,000 Israelites, responded and went with Zerubbabel to help rebuild the Temple.

Opposition eventually persuaded King Artaxerxes to force the Israelites to stop reconstruction (Ezra 4).

Daniel became distressed when he learned of the difficulties his people were facing. After three weeks of fasting and praying, God revealed to Daniel that evil powers had, for a time, kept his prayer from being answered.

There is a constant warfare taking place in the unseen spirit world. It is vital that we recognize the power of prayer and how much God is expecting and depending on us to pray for those who are doing His work.

We, like Daniel, should realize that there is a life beyond what meets the physical eye and our natural resources.

"He that overcometh shall inherit all things; and I will be his God, and he shall be my son" (Revelation 21:7).

Thought for Today: Our faith makes victorious Christian living a reality everyday (see I John 5:4-5).

Christ Revealed: As the One *"that liveth for ever"* (Daniel 12:7). Christ always has been and always will be (Rev. 4:8).

Word Studies: 10:3 **pleasant bread** means tasty food; 11:15 **most fenced** means best fortified; 11:24 **forecast his devices** means devise plans; 11:34 **holpen** means helped.

Prayer Needs: Country: St. Kitts-Nevis—55,000—in the Leeward Islands of the West Indies • Religious freedom • 74% Protestant; 7% Roman Catholic.

HOSEA

While Hosea was proclaiming his message to the Northern Kingdom of Israel, the prophets Micah, Amos, and Isaiah were in the Kingdom of Judah.

Israel was experiencing great prosperity. However, her golden calf worship centers, erected many years earlier in the cities of Bethel and Dan, had turned the people far from God. As time passed, the immoral and pagan worship of Baal and Ashtoreth eventually spread throughout their culture (II Kings 12:28-32; see also Hosea 10:5-6; 13:2).

Instead of remaining faithful, Israel had broken her covenant relationship with God—as an unfaithful wife who had many lovers (2:7-13).

Even though Israel was guilty of spiritual adultery in her idol worship, God still loved these people (2:8,16; 11:8-9; 14:4). The prophet pleaded with Israel to repent so that God in His mercy could restore His protection and blessings upon them (10:12; 12:6; 14:1).

The unique thing about Hosea's message is that he had experienced sorrow and humiliation through his wife's unfaithfulness; and because of his forgiving love toward her, he could express God's compassion to the people.

Hosea is referred to several times in the New Testament (compare 6:6 with Matthew 9:13 and 12:7; 10:8 with Revelation 6:16).

SEPTEMBER 19: Read Hosea 1 — 6

Highlights: Israel compared to an unfaithful wife; judgment upon adulterous Israel; Jehovah's withdrawal from His people; repentance urged.

Verse for Today: *"Hear the word of the Lord, ye children of Israel: for the Lord* *hath a controversy with the inhabitants of the land, because there is no truth, nor mercy, nor knowledge of God in the land"* (Hosea 4:1).

G od called the Israelites to be His chosen people, comparing their relationship to a marriage—they were to Him as a wife; He to them as a husband (Isaiah 54:5). Therefore, Israel's forsaking God and turning to the idols of heathen nations was compared to a woman's leaving her faithful husband and living with other men.

God was charging Israel with rejecting His love (compare Micah 6:2-5; Jeremiah 2).

When Hosea said there was no *"knowledge of God,"* he did not mean that people were ignorant of the existence of God or His Word, but that the Israelites were showing no concern about doing His will.

There was no knowledge of God like that which the Apostle John wrote about when he said, *"And this is life eternal, that they might know thee the only true God, and Jesus Christ, whom thou hast sent"* (John 17:3). This kind of knowledge is more than mental—it is spiritual, something made real by the Spirit of God. This is the result of not only hearing His Word, but also believing and acting upon it.

"And why call ye me, Lord, Lord, and do not the things which I say?" (Luke 6:46).

Thought for Today: A successful Christian life can only be lived on the basis of continued obedience to God's revealed Word.

Christ Revealed: Through Hosea's love for his unworthy, sinful wife (Hosea 3: 1-5). Our Lord Jesus not only loved us while we were yet in sin, but He also died the death of shame for us on Calvary so that all He had might be ours (see Rom. 8:32; II Pet. 1:3). *"I will betroth thee unto me for ever"* (Hosea 2:19).

Word Studies: 4:12 **staff** means diviner's wand; 5:15 **early** means earnestly.

Prayer Needs: Country: St. Helena—8,500—in the southern Atlantic about 1,200 miles west of Angola, Africa • Religious freedom • 95% Protestant; 3% cults; .75% Roman Catholic.

SEPTEMBER 20: Read Hosea 7 — 14

Highlights: Israel's sin rebuked and captivity foretold; Israel's ruin and ultimate blessing.

Verse for Today: *"I will heal their backsliding, I will love them . . . "* (Hosea 14:4).

T he former warnings of judgment are now changed to a message of love. This did not mean that God had changed His mind; it meant that, even though a holy God must judge His people, His love still reaches out to them. He called for Israel to repent, return to Him, and reject the idols which drew them away, saying, *"O Israel, return unto the Lord thy God; for thou hast fallen by thine iniquity"* (Hosea 14:1).

In the past, they had turned to the powerful nations of Egypt and Assyria for help. This led to the Israelites' accepting their idols (4:17; 8:4; 11:2; 13:2; Isaiah 42:17; 44:17).

Every person worships something—and often many things. Objects of worship might be a person, material possessions, a wooden image, or God Himself. When anyone rejects Christ as Savior and Lord of his life, allowing other things or people to take the place of Christ in his life, then these things or people become idols.

"No man can serve two masters: for either he will hate the one, and love the other; or else he will hold to the one, and despise the other. Ye cannot serve God and mammon" (Matthew 6:24).

Thought for Today: Sin and submission to God's Word do not go together!

Christ Revealed: In the son who was called out of Egypt (Hosea 11:1). This prophecy is twofold: one is a historical reference pertaining to Israel (see Ex. 4:22-23); and the other is prophetic, looking to Christ's sojourn in Egypt (Matt. 2:15).

Prayer Needs: Country: Uganda—16 million—in eastern Africa • Religious freedom • 51% Roman Catholic; 30% Protestant; 10% animist; 7% Muslim.

JOEL

The prophet Joel's message to the Southern Kingdom of Judah grew out of a national calamity. An invasion of locusts swept through the country, devouring the crops and stripping every leaf from the trees. This was followed by a severe famine. Joel spoke of God's judgment as an illustration of the result of a nation's spiritual fruitlessness. The people needed revival in light of the coming *"day of the Lord"* (1:15; 2:1,11,31; 3:14).

The locusts were described in terms of an army—soldiers, horses, and chariots—symbolic of the enemies that God would allow to invade Israel because of her sins (2:4-7).

The prophet also foretold of a future day when God would pour out His Spirit *"upon all flesh."* Both Peter at Pentecost (Acts 2:21) and Paul to the Romans (Romans 10:13) quoted Joel: *" . . . whosoever shall call on the name of the Lord shall be delivered"* (2:32).

We are living in the *"last days"* that began on the day of Pentecost, and God's Spirit is being poured out. This means that anyone can receive Christ as Savior and Lord and be filled with His Spirit (see Acts 2:38; John 7:37-38; Ephesians 5:18).

SEPTEMBER 21: Read Joel 1 — 3

Highlights: Plague of locusts; Joel's warnings and call to repentance; future day of the Lord; outpouring of the Holy Spirit; restoration of Israel; judgment on nations.

Verse for Today: *"And it shall come to pass afterward, that I will pour out my spirit upon all flesh; and your sons and your daughters shall prophesy, your old men shall dream dreams, your young men shall see visions"* (Joel 2:28).

O n the day of Pentecost, after the Christians in the Upper Room were all filled with the Holy Spirit, the Apostle Peter said, *"This is that which was spoken by the prophet Joel"* (Acts 2:16).

Peter later said, *"Whereby are given unto us exceeding great and precious promises: that by these ye might be partakers of the divine nature, having escaped the corruption that is in the world through lust"* (II Peter 1:4).

241

Here, the two natures of life are contrasted: the Adamic nature, which we received at birth and which has brought about all *"the corruption that is in the world,"* and the spiritual nature, which we receive when we accept Christ as Savior.

The contrast between life in Adam, before we were saved, and life in Christ, from the moment we accepted Him as our Savior, is the difference between being children of darkness and children of light; the spirit of error (Satan) and the Spirit of truth (I John 4:6).

But spiritual birth is only the beginning of our Christian life; we are to *"be filled with the Spirit"* (Ephesians 5:18). Then, led by the Spirit of God, we should determine to let the indwelling Christ take full control of our lives at all times.

"This I say then, Walk in the Spirit, and you shall not fulfill the lust of the flesh. For the flesh lusts against the Spirit, and the Spirit against the flesh: and these are contrary the one to the other . . . " (Galatians 5:16-17).

Thought for Today: The Holy Spirit, through the Word of God, empowers the believer to do the will of God.

Christ Revealed: As the One who will *"pour out"* His Spirit upon all flesh (Joel 2:28)—fulfilled (in part) on the day of Pentecost (Acts 2:16-17).

Word Studies: 1:7 **barked** means chewed off the bark; 1:12 **languisheth** means waste away; 2:6 **all faces shall gather blackness** means their faces will turn pale with terror; 2:20 **hinder part** means rear guard; **ill savor** means foul smell.

Prayer Needs: Country: Benin (formerly Dahomey)—5 million—in western Africa • Some hostility toward Christians • 59% animism and voodoo; 17% Muslim; 16% Roman Catholic; 3% Protestant.

AMOS

Amos, the "farmer preacher," was a herdsman and a dresser of sycamore-fig trees near the small mountain village of Tekoa, located about 12 miles south of Jerusalem in the kingdom of Judah. However, his preaching was directed to the Northern Kingdom of Israel (1:1; 3:9; 7:7-15).

During this time, Uzziah was king of Judah, and Jeroboam II was king of Israel. Both kingdoms were enjoying prosperity (II Chronicles 26; II Kings 14:25). But Amos exposed the religious and social evils of that period (2:4-8; 3:13—4:5) and foretold the destruction of the Northern Kingdom (see 5:1-3).

Nothing looked less likely to be fulfilled than the warnings of this herdsman. But less than 40 years later, the Northern Kingdom of Israel was invaded and destroyed by the Assyrians.

Amos also foretold the greatness of the kingdom of the coming Messiah (9:11-15).

SEPTEMBER 22: Read Amos 1 — 5

Highlights: Judgments pronounced on Judah, Israel, and surrounding nations; Jehovah's sorrow over Israel's future captivity.

Verse for Today: *"They hate him that rebuketh in the gate, and they abhor him that speaketh uprightly"* (Amos 5:10).

T he prophecy of Amos seems to have been proclaimed *"in the gate"* at Bethel, one of the religious centers of the Israelites, about 30 years before they were defeated by the Assyrians.

"The gate" was a well-known center of business where the elders judged the people (compare Jeremiah 17:19; 19:2). It was at this place of business that the Lord spoke through Amos, saying, *"For I know . . . your mighty sins."* Amos appealed to them to *"seek good, and not evil, that you may live"* (Amos 5:12,14). But his message from God was unwelcomed and ignored.

Christians are often criticized when they speak out against sin.

"He that rejecteth me, and receiveth not my words, hath one that judgeth him: the word that I have spoken, the same shall judge him in the last day" (John 12:48).

Thought for Today: It is only through the power of God's Word that we will seek good and not evil.

Christ Revealed: As the Creator (Amos 5:8; see also Rev. 4:11).

Word Studies: 3:5 **gin** means trap; 4:1 **kine of Bashan** were the finest cattle, raised in the best pasturelands—but here, it is used figuratively in referring to self-gratifying, sensual, influential women; **masters** means husbands; 4:3 **breaches** means breaks in the wall; 5:21 **smell** means delight; 5:23 **viols** means harps.

Prayer Needs: **Country:** Chile—13 million—on the southwestern coast of South America • Religious freedom • 63% Roman Catholic; 23% Protestant.

OBADIAH _____

Obadiah, the shortest book in the Old Testament, warns of the certainty of God's just judgment on all who oppose Him and His people. Obadiah also highlights the ultimate establishment of God's kingdom.

The prophet Obadiah foretold the final destruction of the Edomites who were the descendants of Esau and should have shown brotherly concern for Judah. However, they were cruel and aided Nebuchadnezzar in destroying Jerusalem (verse 10). Within four years after Jerusalem was defeated, the Edomites were also defeated.

Unlike the prophecy against the Edomites, who were to be destroyed and never again to be a nation, Obadiah foretold that the nation of Judah would recover and *"possess their possessions."* (See verses 15-17.)

It is generally assumed that Obadiah prophesied during the reign of either Jehoram or Zedekiah, the last king of Judah.

SEPTEMBER 23: Read Amos 6 — Obadiah 1

Highlights: Woe pronounced upon sin; the grasshoppers; fire; plumbline; basket of summer fruit; famine of God's Word; certainty of Israel's being scattered and Edom's being destroyed.

Verse for Today: *"And the Lord said unto me, Amos, what seest thou? And I said,*

A plumbline. Then said the Lord, Behold, I will set a plumbline in the midst of my people Israel: I will not again pass by them any more" (Amos 7:8).

A plumbline is a line with a weight at one end. The mason (a craftsman who builds with stone or brick) uses a plumbline to make sure the walls are exactly vertical or upright as he lays the stones one upon another.

The Lord stood upon a wall with a plumbline in His hand. His purpose for standing on the wall was not to build it, but to announce its destruction. The wall had become so hopelessly off-center that destruction was the only solution (Amos 7:7-9).

The wall was a symbol of separation of the kingdom of Israel from the world, and His prophets were the "plumbline"—proclaiming the message of Truth.

God's Word is our plumbline. It must be our guide to make sure our thoughts and ways are upright in God's sight. Just as a mason uses a plumbline to make sure the wall is truly upright, we as Christians must be just as precise in applying Bible truths to our lives, as if Christ Himself held the plumbline of His Word to measure the correctness of our lives.

"Not every one that saith unto me, Lord, Lord, shall enter into the kingdom of heaven; but he that doeth the will of my Father which is in heaven" (Matthew 7:21).

Thought for Today: God's Word is the only reliable "plumbline" for our lives, for it reveals God's viewpoint to us.

Christ Revealed: As the Plumbline (Amos 7:7-8). Christ walks in the midst of His people, exposing the good and the bad, the true and the false (Rev. 2 and 3).

Word Studies: Amos 6:13 **horns by our own strength** means military strength to conquer any enemy (see Deut. 33:17; I Kings 22:11). Obadiah 1:21 **saviors** means deliverers.

Prayer Needs: Country: Suriname—390,000—on the northeastern coast of South America • Very limited religious freedom • 27% Hindu; 22% Roman Catholic; 20% Protestant; 20% Muslim; 6% witchcraft and spirit worship.

JONAH

Jonah lived during the prosperous but evil reign of King Jeroboam II and was a prominent prophet in Israel. He had foretold the great military success of King Jeroboam II over the Syrians (II Kings 14:25).

The book of Jonah is the historic account of the prophet Jonah's mission to the people of Nineveh—Israel's great enemy—to announce its destruction. At first Jonah willfully failed to comply with God's command. But after a series of dramatic events, Jonah reluctantly obeyed. However, he was unhappy when the king and the people of Nineveh repented and God's judgment was prevented.

This book portrays God as a God of love and mercy, One who would forgive and save even the enemies of His people if they would repent, rather than punish and destroy them.

Jesus contrasted the repentance of the heathen people of Nineveh, who had so little knowledge of God's righteous judgment, with the hardness of the Israelites, who possessed so much knowledge of God's Word and His ways.

The people of Nineveh repented at the preaching of Jonah, but most of the people refused to repent at the preaching of Jesus.

Jonah is a type of the resurrection of Christ—*"As Jonah was three days and three nights in the whale's belly; so shall the Son of man be three days and three nights in the heart of the earth"* (Matthew 12:39-41; compare Luke 11:29-32).

God's judgment is sure—whether we have little or much knowledge of His Word. Everyone who does not receive Christ as Savior and Lord will be eternally lost.

We have the privilege of having God's Word available to us. With that privilege comes the great responsibility to share it with others.

SEPTEMBER 24: Read Jonah 1 — 4

Highlights: Jonah commissioned; his effort to avoid God's will; Jonah swallowed by a great fish; prayer of Jonah; second commission; Nineveh repents; Jonah's displeasure.

Verses for Today: *"Now the word of the Lord came unto Jonah . . . saying, Arise, go to Nineveh, that great city, and cry against it . . . But Jonah rose up to flee . . . from the presence of the Lord, and went down to Joppa; and he found a ship going to Tarshish: so he paid the fare thereof, and went down into it . . . "* (Jonah 1:1-3).

J onah was unwilling to be a foreign missionary to Nineveh, that great capital city of the cruel and ruthless Assyrian enemy. He mistakenly thought he could choose his own city in which to serve God, ignore the Lord's revealed will for his life, and bring about a change in the mind of God.

It must have seemed like an answer to prayer when Jonah discovered that a ship was sailing to Tarshish on the exact day he arrived in Joppa. But while Jonah was discovering such satisfying answers to prayer, there was a lot of "going down" that is recorded: he went *"down to Joppa"*; *"down into the . . . ship"*; and finally, *"down to the bottoms of the mountains"* (Jonah 1:3—2:6).

For a while, circumstances seemed to favor Jonah's plan and gave him such peace of mind that he was soon *"fast asleep"* on the ship (1:5).

However, favorable circumstances in avoiding God's will never lead to a satisfactory end. Jonah thought he was leaving his troubles behind, but such "good luck" always ends in "deep water." Often we are more persistent in planning our own ruin than in seeking to do God's will.

When Jonah *"paid the fare,"* he did not realize the high price he was paying for self-satisfaction. One may boast of acting for God and talk of having His approval, but if self is satisfied instead of Christ, the steps will always be down, down, down.

God loved this unsettled prophet too much to permit him to prosper in his self-centered ways. *"For whom the Lord loveth he chasteneth, and scourgeth every son whom he receiveth"* (Hebrews 12:6).

Thought for Today: Ask the Lord to keep you from doing your will if it conflicts with His will for your life.

Christ Revealed: In Jonah (1:7—2:10). Jesus used this as an illustration to tell of His death, burial, and resurrection when the Pharisees demanded a sign from Him as to who He was (Matt. 12:39-40; see also I Cor. 15:4).

Prayer Needs: Country: Dominica—94,000—in the British West Indies • Religious freedom • 75% Roman Catholic; 12% Protestant.

MICAH

Micah and Isaiah prophesied in Judah during the time of King Hezekiah's reformation (Isaiah 1:1; Jeremiah 26:18).

Micah was faithful *"to declare unto Jacob his transgression, and to Israel his sin"* (3:8). His prophecy was intended to bring Israel and Judah to repentance and avoid God's judgment.

This book closes with a declaration of the ultimate fulfillment of God's covenant blessing to Abraham (7:20).

SEPTEMBER 25: Read Micah 1 — 7

Highlights: Impending judgment against Israel and Judah; future deliverance of a remnant; birth of Christ foretold; the Lord's judgment and mercy.

Verse for Today: *"But thou Bethlehem Ephratah, though thou be little among the thousands of Judah, yet out of thee shall he come forth unto me that is to be ruler in Israel; whose goings forth have been from of old, from everlasting"* (Micah 5:2).

T he birthplace of our Savior was foretold by Micah 700 years before Jesus was born. Micah was the only prophet who specifically said that Christ would be born in Bethlehem.

Since 19 of Judah's 20 kings were born in the royal city of Jerusalem, it seemed unlikely that the Messiah-King would be born in Bethlehem.

All the circumstances surrounding the birth of Jesus made it seem unlikely that this prophecy could be fulfilled. Mary, Jesus' mother, and Joseph were living in Nazareth, about 90 miles from Bethlehem. But because of a decree concerning taxation which Caesar Augustus made in Rome, Mary, who could have stayed in Nazareth, traveled with Joseph to Bethlehem, where Jesus—the Messiah—was born (Luke 2:1-7).

The size of Bethlehem is also significant—*"little among the thousands of Judah."* Christ is always "born" among the "little ones"—in hearts humble enough to confess sin and acknowledge Him as Lord. Bethlehem was an insignificant place until the Lord Jesus was born there.

Your life may seem insignificant. But when you receive Christ as your Savior and are born of the Spirit, your body becomes a temple of the living God and that makes you very important to Him. What makes our lives significant is the One who lives in us and expresses Himself through us.

"What? know ye not that your body is the temple of the Holy Ghost which is in you, which ye have of God, and ye are not your own?" (I Corinthians 6:19).

Thought for Today: True satisfaction can only be found in Christ.

Christ Revealed: As the coming Ruler from Bethlehem Ephratah (Micah 5:2; see also Matt. 2:5-6).

Word Studies: 1:6 **discover** means lay bare; 1:7 **hires** means earnings; 1:8 **dragons** means jackals; 1:14 **lie** means deception; 1:16 **poll thee** means cut off your hair; 2:8 **pass by securely** means walk along peaceably (see also Psalm 120:7); 2:13 **The breaker** means a leader who overcomes all obstacles that would oppose Israel's return from captivity; 6:9 **hear ye the rod** means pay attention to the ruler.

Prayer Needs: Country: Mali—9 million—in West Africa • Religious freedom despite Muslim majority • 81% Muslim; 17% animism and spirit worship; 2% Christian.

NAHUM & HABAKKUK _____

Nahum foretold the destruction of Nineveh, the powerful capital of Assyria. But unlike the people of Nineveh in Jonah's day more than 100 years earlier, there was no sign of repentance.

Within 50 years after Nahum's prophecy, the mighty world empire of Assyria—the nation that had destroyed the Northern Kingdom of Israel—was conquered by the Babylonians. As foretold by Nahum, Assyria never again rose to power.

Habakkuk prophesied in Judah probably during the reign of King Jehoiakim. Unlike his godly father Josiah, Jehoiakim *"did that which was evil in the sight of the Lord"* (II Kings 23:37). Habakkuk cried out against the moral corruption that prevailed. He foretold that God would allow the wicked Babylonians to bring judgment upon His people.

Although they were to expect destructive days ahead, God told Habakkuk that the just shall live by faith in God and have confidence that He is doing what is right.

The just shall live by faith has been called the watchword of the Christian church (see Habakkuk 2:4; Romans 1:17; Hebrews 10:38).

Habakkuk, like anyone else, had to live by faith.

Our loving and all-wise God knows what is best, and we must accept every situation by faith.

The book of Habakkuk gives encouragement that ultimately righteousness and justice will triumph.

SEPTEMBER 26: Read Nahum 1 — Habakkuk 3

Highlights: Prophecy and fulfillment of Nineveh's destruction; vision of coming woes; Habakkuk's prayer.

Verse for Today: *"O Lord, how long shall I cry, and thou wilt not hear! even cry out unto thee of violence, and thou wilt not save!"* (Habakkuk 1:2).

In sympathy for his fellow-sufferers the prophet Habakkuk cried for help as if he himself needed it. He prayed, Why is it, Lord, that violence, strife and contention abound; the Law is ignored; the righteous are oppressed; the evil man reigns; and I am helpless to stop it?

247

In the midst of the horrifying Chaldean invasion of their country—the Promised Land—the prophet Habakkuk declared, *"The just shall live by his faith"* (Habakkuk 2:4).

Thousands of Christians who have been wrongly accused, tortured, or put to death have asked the same question: Why is this happening?

We seldom know why God allows these things to happen, but one of the greatest encouragements to faith is the assurance that our all-wise and loving heavenly Father cares for His people. When God has not answered your prayers and defeat seems inevitable, declare with the prophet, *"The just shall live by his faith."*

The Apostle Paul—who *"suffered the loss of all things"*—proclaimed, *"The just shall live by faith"* (Philippians 3:8; Romans 1:17). And today, all over the world, Christians express confident trust in a caring Father—regardless of their circumstances.

"Now the just shall live by faith . . . " (Hebrews 10:38).

Thought for Today: There are problems to which no one but God has the full answer. Just trust Him.

Christ Revealed: As the One whom even the sea obeys (Nahum 1:4; see also Matt. 8:26-27).

Word Studies: Nahum 1:5 **burned** means upheaved; 2:7 **Huzzab** (meaning, set firm) is the name given to Nineveh, the queen of nations; **tabering** means beating; 3:19 **bruit** means report. Habakkuk 2:6 **him that ladeth himself with thick clay** means all of the massive accumulation of wealth will be of no more benefit to Nebuchadnezzar than if it were a massive load of clay.

Prayer Needs: Country: Qatar—316,000—in southwestern Asia • Muslim conversion to Christ is forbidden, but expatriate Christians are allowed to meet informally • 92% Muslim; 4% Protestant; 2% Roman Catholic; 1% Hindu; .5% Eastern Orthodox.

ZEPHANIAH

Zephaniah, the great-great grandson of King Hezekiah, was a prophet during the early part of the reign of Josiah. In all probability, he greatly influenced young King Josiah.

Zephaniah foretold the fall of Jerusalem about 20 years before it took place (1:4-13). He warned that because of all her sins, the Lord would bring judgment on Judah and that a devastating invasion from the north would come in the near future. He foretold that the people of Judah would be punished for worshiping idols and that the surrounding wicked nations would also be punished (1:1—2:15). God revealed not only that Jerusalem was doomed to destruction, but that, in time, the city would be restored (3:1-20).

Zephaniah prophesied that Christ would return in power and glory. This future time, known as *"the great day of the Lord,"* is referred to at least 20 times in these three chapters.

Zephaniah, Nahum, and Jeremiah probably prophesied during the same time. They were among the last prophets before the captivity.

HAGGAI & ZECHARIAH

Both Haggai and Zechariah were probably born in Babylon during the exile and went to Jerusalem some time after King Cyrus gave the decree to rebuild the Temple.

The work on the Temple foundation began immediately after the first exiles arrived in Jerusalem. After the foundation was laid, the Israelites faced intense opposition from the Samaritans, who succeeded in getting the king of Persia to stop the work (Ezra 4:23).

About 15 years later, Haggai and Zechariah began preaching in Jerusalem.

Haggai appealed to those who were selfishly preoccupied with building their own dwelling places rather than with building the Lord's house. Haggai exhorted them to put God first.

Zechariah joined Haggai in encouraging the Jews to rebuild the Temple. Writing about the coming of Zion's King, Zechariah told of the expected Messiah and the final judgment.

Through preaching the Word of God, they turned the feeble nation from an attitude of indifference to one of new zeal for completing the Temple (Ezra 6:14).

SEPTEMBER 27: Read Zephaniah 1 — Haggai 2

Highlights: The day of the Lord's judgment; future destruction of the Gentile nations; the people urged to rebuild the Temple; unfaithfulness reproved.

Verse for Today: *"Ye have sown much, and bring in little ... he that earneth wages earneth wages to put it into a bag with holes"* (Haggai 1:6).

T he Israelites who went to Jerusalem because of Cyrus' decree set up the altar, established daily worship, and rebuilt the foundation of the second Temple. But their enthusiasm soon faded, and the persistent opposition by the Samaritan enemies caused the construction to cease. It seemed incredible that 14 years passed and nothing more was accomplished. But they continued to hope for better times and less opposition.

Haggai gave *five* messages, urging the people to put God first in their lives. Upon hearing the words of the Lord, they began at once to build the Temple; and it was completed in just four years.

Similar excuses may be made today for not doing the Lord's work. It is hearing the Word of God that renews our love and determination to put the Lord first in our lives.

"But seek ye first the kingdom of God, and his righteousness; and all these things shall be added unto you" (Matthew 6:33).

Thought for Today: Accepting what someone else says about the Bible may not be good enough; we must read it for ourselves to be sure.

Christ Revealed: As *"the king of Israel, even the Lord"* (Zephaniah 3:15; see also John 18:33-37).

Word Studies: Zephaniah 1:7 **bid** means consecrated; 1:9 **leap on the threshold** means violently and suddenly rush into houses to confiscate property of the helpless; 1:14 **hasteth greatly** means coming quickly; 2:3 **wrought** means kept; 2:14 **bittern** means porcupine.

Prayer Needs: Country: Solomon Islands—300,000—in the southwestern Pacific • Religious freedom • 66% Protestant; 17% Roman Catholic; 4% spirit worship, ancestor worship, and sorcery; 3% cargo cults.

SEPTEMBER 28: Read Zechariah 1 — 7

Highlights: A call to return to the Lord; Zechariah's visions; warnings of Jehovah's displeasure; Joshua resisted by Satan; visions of the golden lampstand, the flying scroll, four chariots; condemnation of insincere fasting; disobedience resulting in captivity.

Verses for Today: *"Then he answered and spake unto me, saying, This is the word of the Lord unto Zerubbabel, saying, Not by might, nor by power, but by my spirit, saith the Lord of hosts. Who art thou, O great mountain? before Zerubbabel thou shalt become a plain . . . "* (Zechariah 4:6-7).

T he foundation of the Temple lay desolate for 14 years. This was evidence of the lack of faith among the Israelites who had returned from Babylonian captivity. Then God raised up the prophets Haggai and Zechariah (Ezra 5:1) to proclaim His Word and to challenge them to finish rebuilding the Temple (Haggai 1:3-11). This time they ignored the threats of their enemies, *"and the elders of the Jews builded, and they prospered through the prophesying of Haggai the prophet and Zechariah . . . "* (Ezra 6:14).

The word *"mountain"* is a symbol of the obstacles and evil powers of the opposition that often face Christians. (Note Isaiah 40:4; 49:11.) But all the mountain-like problems can be overcome by faith when Christians put Christ and His Word first in their lives.

Haggai and Zechariah proclaimed God's Word—the source of power through which any work of God is accomplished. It is *"not by might, nor by power,"* but by the Holy Spirit that His Word is made effective in our lives.

Jesus said, *"It is the spirit that quickeneth; the flesh profiteth nothing: the words that I speak unto you, they are spirit, and they are life"* (John 6:63).

Thought for Today: God's Spirit can perfect His strength in the weakest believer.

Christ Revealed: As *"my servant the Branch"* (Zechariah 3:8). Christ was brought forth into the world in the fullness of time, and *"took upon him the form of a servant"* (Phil. 2:7; see also Gal. 4:4).

Word Study: 1:21 **fray** means terrify.

Prayer Needs: Country: Tonga—99,000—in the southwestern Pacific • Religious freedom • 55% Protestant; 22% Mormon; 14% Roman Catholic.

SEPTEMBER 29: Read Zechariah 8 — 14

Highlights: Restoration of Jerusalem promised; judgment on neighboring nations; Zion's future King and Jerusalem's future deliverance.

Verse for Today: *"Rejoice greatly, O daughter of Zion; shout, O daughter of Jerusalem: behold, thy King cometh unto thee: he is just, and having salvation; lowly, and riding upon an ass, and upon a colt the foal of an ass"* (Zechariah 9:9).

Z echariah's prophetic message was far more than words of comfort and encouragement to the returned exiles. It was a message of hope, foretelling of the coming King of kings when *"many nations shall be joined to the Lord"* (Zechariah 2:11).

This prophecy was fulfilled in part when Jesus entered Jerusalem, *"sitting upon an ass"* (Matthew 21:1-11). This was His formal presentation as King. But the cry "Hosanna" was soon changed to "Crucify Him!" Yes, Christ died for our sins, was buried, and rose from the grave. After 40 days, He was carried *"into heaven itself, now to appear in the presence of God for us"* (Hebrews 9:24).

But Zechariah also foretold of a time when the King will return, *"and the Lord shall be king over all the earth"* (Zechariah 14:9).

Christians have the wonderful privilege of living after the fulfillment of our Lord's earthly ministry and in the expectation of His soon return to be *"king over all the earth."* And all who have confessed Christ as their Savior will then reign with Him.

It is wonderful to know the forgiveness of sins and have the assurance of soon being with our king.

Jesus said, *"If I go and prepare a place for you, I will come again, and receive you unto myself; that where I am, there ye may be also"* (John 14:3).

Thought for Today: If the Lord were to come today, would you rejoice to see Him face to face?

Christ Revealed: As King (Zechariah 9:9; see Mark 11:7-11; John 12:12-19). He was to be sold for 30 pieces of silver (Zech. 11:12; Matt. 26:15); His side, hands, and feet were to be pierced (Zech. 12:10; John 19:34; 20:27); and Christ, the Great Shepherd, was to be smitten and His disciples scattered (Zech. 13:7; Matt. 26:31,56).

Word Studies: 14:2 **rifled** means robbed; 14:8 **former** means eastern (Dead Sea); **hinder** means western (Mediterranean Sea); 14:21 **seethe** means boil.

Prayer Needs: Country: Mongolia—2 million—in east-central Asia • Christianity is strongly suppressed • 29% shamanist; 2% Buddhist; 2% Muslim; .2% Christian.

MALACHI _____

Malachi may have prophesied 100 years after Zerubbabel had led the exiles back to Jerusalem—possibly about the time of Ezra and Nehemiah. His message was to the descendants of the Israelites that returned to Jerusalem from Babylonian captivity. The people had lost the zeal and dedication to God that existed when the Temple was being rebuilt under the preaching of Haggai and Zechariah.

Malachi's desire was to renew their relationship with God. His message points out the sins that separated them from God's love and blessings. This godly prophet appealed first to Israel to return to the Lord who loved them (chapter 1); then he appealed to the priests, pointing out their sins (chapter

2). In chapter 3, he foretold of a future time when *"the messenger of the covenant"*—Christ, the Messiah (3:1-3)—would appear. Finally, he foretold *"the coming of the great and dreadful day of the Lord"* (4:5), when *"all that do wickedly"* will be destroyed and all who have lived to please the Lord will be rewarded (4:1-2).

SEPTEMBER 30: Read Malachi 1 — 4

Highlights: The Lord's love for Jacob; the sins of the priests; Israel's unfaithfulness rebuked; the day of the Lord and final judgment.

Verses for Today: *"And I will come near to you to judgment; and I will be a swift witness against the sorcerers. . . . For I am the Lord, I change not . . . "* (Malachi 3:5-6).

The Israelites who had returned to Jerusalem and rebuilt the city walls and the Temple were dead. Their descendants had lost sight of their high calling and the purpose for their existence. Many had developed an attitude of religious formality and indifference toward God. This easily opened the door to toleration of evil, including witchcraft and sorcery. Although God strongly and clearly warned against all forms of sorcery, the people had become insensitive to His Word.

Any attempt to gain guidance or information about the future through occult powers—including communication with the dead, Ouija boards, fortune-tellers, horoscopes, and astrology—is an insult to God, who desires to guide and control our lives. (See Leviticus 19:26-31; 20:6; Deuteronomy 18:9-14; Isaiah 8:16-20; 44:25; Jeremiah 14:13-16; 27:8-11; Ezekiel 13:6-9,23.)

The Christian's life is a walk by faith—trusting the Holy Spirit to give understanding and guidance from the Word of God—the only reliable source of truth. The Christian should look to God and trust Him for what lies ahead.

"Trust in the Lord with all thine heart; and lean not unto thine own understanding. In all thy ways acknowledge him, and he shall direct thy paths" (Proverbs 3: 5-6).

Thought for Today: To be led by God's Word is to be led by truth.

Christ Revealed: As *"the messenger of the covenant"* (Malachi 3:1; see also Heb. 9:11-15).

Word Study: 3:13 **stout** means arrogant.

Prayer Needs: Country: Uruguay—3 million—on the southeastern coast of South America • Religious freedom • 60% Roman Catholic; 2% Protestant; 2% Jewish; .7% Orthodox Christian.

PRAYERS IN THIS MONTH'S READING

Ezekiel — for the remnant of Israel .... Ezekiel 9:8; 11:13
Daniel — thanks and praise to God .... Daniel 2:23
Daniel — for restoration of Jerusalem .... Daniel 9:4-19
Hosea — how Israel should pray .... Hosea 6:1-3; 14:2
Joel — help from locust plague and drought .... Joel 1:19-20

252

MATTHEW

Each of the four Gospels portrays the life of Christ from a different point of view.

The Gospel of Matthew was written by a Jew named Matthew. He was a tax collector for the Roman government before he became an apostle.

Matthew reveals Jesus as the Son of David—heir to Israel's throne—and as King of the Jews. Jesus was the fulfillment of all prophecies made to Israel concerning the Messiah-King.

Matthew quotes almost every book in the Old Testament. He uses more than 60 quotations, representative of the entire Old Testament—the Law, the prophets, and the Psalms—and establishes beyond all possible doubt, to a sincere inquirer, that Jesus is the Christ, the promised Messiah, King of kings, and the Savior.

The genealogy of Jesus is traced through Joseph—the legal (although not the actual) father of Jesus—to David, then to Abraham, as evidence that He fulfilled the prophecies of the covenants God made with Abraham and David (Genesis 12:1-3; II Samuel 7:8-17).

Matthew also records 23 miracles proving Messiahship and 30 parables. Throughout the Gospel of Matthew the kingdom of Heaven is prominent.

More of what Jesus said is recorded in Matthew than in the other Gospels because Jesus is presented as the great Teacher. But more significantly, the words of a king are authoritative and of utmost importance. Of the four Gospels, only Matthew tells of the Wise Men inquiring, *Where is the Child that was born to be King of the Jews?* (see Matthew 2:2).

OCTOBER 1: Read Matthew 1 — 4

Highlights: Ancestors of Jesus Christ; His birth; the visit of the Wise Men; flight into Egypt; return to Nazareth; the ministry of John the Baptist; baptism of Jesus; temptation by Satan; first apostles called.

Verses for Today: *" . . . behold, there came wise men from the east to Jerusalem, Saying, Where is he that is born King of the Jews? for we have seen his star in the east, and are come to worship him"* (Matthew 2:1-2).

G uided by a star, the Gentile Wise Men made the long journey from the East (possibly Persia, about 800 miles away) to worship the promised Messiah-King. They probably were familiar with the book of Daniel and other prophecies concerning the birth of the Messiah. They sacrificed many weeks of time and money traveling to Bethlehem to worship Him.

The chief priests and scribes who lived in Jerusalem knew the Scriptures concerning the Messiah's birth in Bethlehem just six miles away, but they did not present gifts to the newborn King (Matthew 2:4-6; compare Micah 5:2).

Many people who hear about Christ react as Herod did, who *"was troubled"* (Matthew 2:3) about any recognition given to Jesus. Others, like the chief priests and scribes, are satisfied in merely knowing the historical facts.

Those who are willing to sacrifice personal pleasure and all else for the privilege of giving their best to Christ are in the minority. True "wise men" still seek Jesus.

"For as many as are led by the Spirit of God, they are the sons of God" (Romans 8:14).

Thought for Today: It takes more than human reasoning for someone to willingly sacrifice time and treasure to the Lord; it takes genuine love and dedication.

Word Studies: 1:18 **birth of Jesus Christ was on this wise** means these are the facts concerning the birth of Jesus Christ; **espoused** means engaged; **she was found with child of the Holy Ghost** means while she was still a virgin, she became pregnant through the power of the Holy Spirit; 1:19 **privily** means secretly; 2:6 **rule** means govern; shepherd; 2:16 **mocked of** means disobeyed and outwitted by; **coasts** means districts; vicinities; 2:22 **parts** means districts; 3:4 **raiment** means clothes; 3:8 **fruits meet for repentance** means a life that proves your change of heart; 3:12 **garner** means barn; 3:15 **Suffer** means permit; allow; 3:16 **straightway** means immediately; 4:24 **divers** means various.

Cross References: For **Matthew 1:23:** See Isa. 7:14. **Matt. 2:6:** See Mic. 5:2. **Matt. 2:15:** See Hos. 11:1. **Matt. 2:18:** See Jer. 31:15. **Matt. 3:3:** See Isa. 40:3. **Matt. 4:4:** See Deut. 8:3. **Matt. 4:6:** See Psa. 91:11-12. **Matt. 4:7:** See Deut. 6:16. **Matt. 4:10:** See Deut. 6:13. **Matt. 4:15-16:** See Isa. 9:1-2.

Prayer Needs: Country: Bangladesh (formerly East Pakistan)—107 million—in southern Asia • Present religious freedom may become limited • 87% Muslim; 12% Hindu; .4% Christian.

OCTOBER 2: Read Matthew 5 — 6

Highlights: Sermon on the Mount; the Beatitudes; believers likened to salt and light; Jesus' teaching on the Law, divorce, oaths, giving to the needy, prayer, fasting, serving one Master.

Verse for Today: *"Blessed are the poor in spirit; for theirs is the kingdom of heaven"* (Matthew 5:3).

E ach Beatitude is given in the order in which the Christian life progresses, and each is essential to the next one. *"Blessed are the poor in spirit"* is the first Beatitude and the foundation of all others.

Recognizing one's spiritual poverty is the first step in the growth of a Christian. The worldly-minded would say, "Blessed are the rich, the wise, the influential, the great." But those who are *"poor in spirit"* feel their own littleness, their own sinfulness in the presence of a Most Holy God. They recognize that without Christ, they have nothing, are nothing, can do nothing, and have need of all things. Jesus said, *You can do nothing without Me* (see John 15:5).

"Poor in spirit" has no reference to financial poverty, for there is as much pride

254

and independence among the poor as there is among the rich.

The world—both the rich and the poor—admires an independent, self-sufficient person. Many books appeal to one's ego as they tell how to be "successful," but few teach that we must renounce our attitudes of self-confidence, self-sufficiency, and self-importance before Christ can manifest His life in and through us. Jesus, our perfect example, is gentle and humble, and He said, *Learn from Me* (see Matthew 11:29).

It is not until we recognize our destitute spiritual condition that we will mourn over our emptiness and unworthiness. Then our will can be broken, preparing us to submit to Christ.

Let Christ Jesus be your example of humility. He stripped Himself of all His glory and became a servant, humbling Himself and obediently dying on the cross (see Philippians 2:5-8).

Thought for Today: The poor in spirit will not be easily offended, and they are careful not to offend others.

Word Studies: 5:3 **the poor in spirit** means those who recognize how spiritually destitute they are apart from Christ; 5:13 **savor** means quality; usefulness; 5:18 **one jot or one tittle** means smallest letter or the dot of an "i"; 5:21 **kill** means murder; 5:22 **Raca** (a word of utter contempt) means you empty-headed, good-for-nothing person; 5:23 **aught** means anything; 5:26 **farthing** means fraction of a penny; 5:31 **put away** means divorce; 5:32 **saving** means except; 5:33 **forswear thyself** means break your vows; 5:47 **salute** means greet; 6:1 **alms** means good deeds to the poor and needy; 6:7 **vain** means meaningless; 6:22 **if therefore thine eye be single** means if you have a singleness of purpose; 6:24 **mammon** means material things; 6:25 **Take no thought** means do not worry; 6:27 **cubit** means 18 inches; **stature** means height.

Cross References: For **Matthew 5:21:** See Ex. 20:13; Deut. 5:17. **Matt. 5:27:** See Ex. 20:14; Deut. 5:18. **Matt. 5:31:** See Deut. 24:1. **Matt. 5:33:** See Num. 30:2; Deut. 23:21. **Matt. 5:38:** See Ex. 21:24; Lev. 24:20; Deut. 19:21. **Matt. 5:43:** See Lev. 19:18.

Prayer Needs: Country: Fiji—728,000—in the southwestern Pacific • Religious freedom • 41% Hindu; 40% Protestant; 9% Roman Catholic; 8% Muslim.

OCTOBER 3: Read Matthew 7 — 9

Highlights: Conclusion of the Sermon on the Mount; preaching and miracles; call of Matthew.

Verse for Today: *"Judge not . . . "* (Matthew 7:1).

J udging the motives of others is a serious offense, for it invades the office of God Himself—*"Who art thou that judgest another man's servant?"* (Romans 14:4).

One who is quick to look for faults in others is usually not as concerned about his own sins as he should be; for at whatever point a person condemns others, he automatically condemns himself (see Romans 2:1).

Criticizing or judging another is seldom, if ever, done with justice or fairness; it often comes from a spirit of revenge or self-righteousness. The good a person does is usually overlooked, and the attention is placed on a weakness or failure that does not necessarily reveal the true character of the person.

The Bible says, *"Judge not according to the appearance, but judge righteous judgment"* (John 7:24).

We must, at all times, guard against saying or implying anything that would be harmful to another's reputation.

"Who art thou that judgest another man's servant? to his own master he standeth or falleth. Yea, he shall be holden up: for God is able to make him stand" (Romans 14:4).

Thought for Today: As we think on things which are true, honest, just, pure, lovely, and of good report, we will not be as likely to think evil of others, or to criticize them.

Word Studies: 7:2 **measure ye mete** means severity you judge others; 7:5 **mote** means speck; 7:13 **strait** means narrow; 8:6 **sick of the palsy** means paralyzed; 9:9 **receipt of custom** means tax collector's office; 9:10 **at meat** means eating.

Cross References: For **Matthew 7:23:** See Psa. 6:8. **Matt. 8:4:** See Lev. 13:49. **Matt. 8:17:** See Isa. 53:4. **Matt. 9:13:** See Hos. 6:6.

Prayer Needs: Country: Guinea-Bissau (formerly Portuguese Guinea)—930,000—on the western coast of Africa • Religious freedom • 51% animist; 42% Muslim; 6% Roman Catholic; .7% Protestant.

OCTOBER 4: Read Matthew 10 — 11

Highlights: Mission of the 12 apostles; John the Baptist's questions; judgment on unrepentant cities; the great invitation.

Verse for Today: *" . . . learn of me; for I am meek and lowly in heart: and ye shall find rest unto your souls"* (Matthew 11:29).

N o one word is capable of fully expressing the meaning of meekness. The meek are humble; yet, meekness is more than humility. Gentleness is also a characteristic of the meek: *"I . . . beseech you by the meekness and gentleness of Christ . . . "* (II Corinthians 10:1).

The meek submit themselves to God's Word and yield to His direction. They accept His correction, knowing that *"whom the Lord loveth he chasteneth . . . "* (Hebrews 12:6).

True meekness does not mean weakness, compromise, or lack of boldness. It is an expression of the love of Christ which patiently bears insults and injuries and does not have a harsh, critical spirit or an attitude of vengeance. We need to express the long-suffering and mercy that the Lord has shown to us—a spirit of gentleness, humility, and patience.

"But the wisdom that is from above is first pure, then peaceable, gentle, and easy to be entreated, full of mercy and good fruits, without partiality, and without hypocrisy" (James 3:17).

Thought for Today: The meek are gentle toward others.

Word Studies: 10:35 **set . . . at variance** means bring division; 11:20 **upbraid** means scold; pronounce judgment upon.

Cross References: For **Matthew 10:11, 35-36:** See. Mic. 7:6. **Matt. 11:5:** See Isa. 35:5; 61:1. **Matt. 11:10:** See Mal. 3:1. **Matt. 11:23:** See Ezek. 26:20; 31:14; 32:18,24. **Matt. 11:29:** See Jer. 6:16.

Prayer Needs: Country: Lesotho—2 million—within the east-central part of the Republic of South Africa • Limited religious freedom • 43% Roman Catholic; 30% Protestant; 6% ancestor worship, divination, and spirit-possession cults.

OCTOBER 5: Read Matthew 12

Highlights: Jesus, Lord of the sabbath; controversy with the Pharisees; unpardonable sin; Christ's death and resurrection foretold; His true kin.

Verse for Today: *"For as Jonah was three days and three nights in the whale's belly; so shall the Son of man be three days and three nights in the heart of the earth"* (Matthew 12:40).

C hrist, who knew the truth about all things, quoted from the book of Jonah as the very Word of God and declared unhesitatingly that Jonah had been in the belly of the great fish.

The Lord not only acknowledged the validity of Jonah's experience, but He also used it as a prophecy of His own death, burial, and resurrection.

The people of Nineveh believed the prophet Jonah and repented, but the people of Israel in Jesus' day would not repent—even though Jesus was far greater than Jonah.

The ministry of Christ was saturated with the words of the Old Testament. He revealed how *"all the Scriptures"* speak of Him, thus removing any doubt as to whether the Old Testament is the Word of God.

"Beginning at Moses and all the prophets, he expounded unto them in all the scriptures the things concerning himself" (Luke 24:27).

Thought for Today: How foolish are those who question the Scriptures!

Word Studies: 12:1 **corn** means grain-fields; 12:29 **spoil his goods** means take away his possessions; 12:40 **whale's** means huge fish's; 12:44 **garnished** means put in order.

Cross References: For **Matthew 12:7:** See Hos. 6:6. **Matt. 12:18-21:** See Isa. 42:1-4. **Matt. 12:40:** See Jonah 1:17.

Prayer Needs: Country: Puerto Rico—4 million—smallest island of the Greater Antilles • Religious freedom • 66% Roman Catholic; 27% Protestant.

OCTOBER 6: Read Matthew 13 — 14

Highlights: Jesus' parables; execution of John the Baptist; feeding of 5,000; Jesus walking on the water.

Verse for Today: *"But Jesus said unto them, They need not depart; give ye them to eat"* (Matthew 14:16).

J esus was moved with compassion to feed a *"multitude"* (Matthew 14:14). But the disciples could not see a way to feed so many people, so they said, *"Send the multitude away"* (14:15).

But Jesus did not send them away. Instead, He accepted five loaves and two fishes offered by a young boy. (See John 6:9.) This amount seemed insignificant compared to the vast multitude, but Jesus blessed the boy's gift and told the disciples to distribute the food to the people. Even though they could not understand how the multitude could be fed, they obeyed the Lord, and thousands of people ate until they were filled.

Our Lord acts according to the same principle today. He can use anyone who is willing to obey His Word. And He has given us the privilege of being *"laborers together with God"* (I Corinthians 3:9). Even though we are only able to give a little, God can multiply it to meet the need in any situation!

Like the disciples, it is possible to be overwhelmed by the great numbers of spiritually hungry people in the world. But God has blessed His Word and given us the responsibility to distribute what we can of the Bread of life to the starving multitudes. How thankful we can be that God's blessings are not given according to our strength, but according to our faith in Him and His Word. God always blesses obedience—even when we are weak.

"He that hath my commandments, and keepeth them, he it is that loveth me: and he that loveth me shall be loved of my Father, and I will love him, and will manifest myself to him" (John 14:21).

Thought for Today: Our faith is strengthened as we obey God's Word—the *source* of faith.

Word Studies: 13:15 **is waxed gross** means has become calloused; **be converted** means be turned to God; 13:21 **by and by he is offended** means his enthusiasm fades; he gives up and quits; 13:25 **tares** means weeds resembling wheat; 13:33 **leaven** means yeast or fermented dough; 13:41 **them which do iniquity** means those who do evil; wrongdoers; 14:8 **charger** means platter; 14:22 **constrained** means directed, urged.

Cross References: For **Matthew 13:14-15:** See Isa. 6:9-10. **Matt. 13:32:** See Psa. 104:12; Ezek. 17:23; 31:6; Dan. 4:12. **Matt. 13:35:** See Psa. 78:2. **Matt. 13:41:** See Zeph. 1:3. **Matt. 13:43:** See Dan. 12:3.

Prayer Needs: Country: Sweden—8 million—in northern Europe • Religious freedom • 66% Protestant; 2% Roman Catholic; .7% Eastern Orthodox.

OCTOBER 7: Read Matthew 15 — 17

Highlights: Scribes and Pharisees rebuked; 4,000 fed; the leaven; Peter's confession; transfiguration; the disciples' unbelief; temple tax from a fish.

Verses for Today: *"Ye hypocrites . . . This people draweth nigh unto me with their mouth, and honoreth me with their lips; but their heart is far from me. But in vain they do worship me . . . "* (Matthew 15:7-9).

T he scribes and Pharisees rigidly practiced all external religious formalities and proclaimed their belief in the Scriptures as the Word of God. But the majority would not accept Jesus as the fulfillment of the Scriptures concerning Christ, the Messiah. (See John 1:41; 4:25.) For a scribe or Pharisee to accept Christ as Savior would mean losing his position of authority, as well as the honor and praise he received from the people. He probably would experience the loss of social, political, and economic advantages (John 12:42-43). Therefore, their worship was not truly from the heart. Jesus called them hypocrites, saying their hearts were far from Him.

Like the Pharisees, the worship of many is not truly from the heart because of their desire to be popular or to hold some important position. The true worshiper not only has repented of his sins and believed that Christ died for his sins but also allows the Word of God—through the indwelling Holy Spirit—to transform his thoughts and actions. His decisions are based on the principle, "What would Jesus have me do?"

May our desire be Jesus' desire—not to seek our own will but the will of the Father (see John 5:30).

Thought for Today: Our worship is in vain unless we truly desire to obey God's Word.

Word Studies: 15:4 **die the death** means be put to death; 15:17 **is cast out into the draught** means passes from the body and is eliminated; 15:26 **bread** means necessities of life; 16:6 **leaven** means corrupt teaching; 16:18 **gates of hell** means all the powers of hell; 16:23 **thou savorest not** means you are not setting your mind on; 17:1 **apart** means separately; privately; 17:25 **prevented him** means spoke to him first.

Cross References: For **Matthew 15:4**: See Ex. 20:12; 21:17; Lev. 20:9; Deut. 5:16. **Matt. 15:8-9:** See Isa. 29:13. **Matt. 16:27:** See Psa. 62:12; Prov. 24:12.

Prayer Needs: Country: Mozambique—15 million—on the eastern coast of Africa • Christians are harassed and churches have been closed by the government • 60% worship of false gods, ancestral spirits, and some witchcraft; 13% Roman Catholic; 13% Muslim; 6% Protestant.

OCTOBER 8: Read Matthew 18 — 20

Highlights: A child and humility; parable of the lost sheep; importance of forgiveness; marriage and divorce; rich young ruler; workers in the vineyard; two blind men healed.

Verses for Today: " . . . *what good thing shall I do, that I may have eternal life? . . . what lack I yet?*" (Matthew 19:16,20).

A wealthy religious leader came running to Jesus and knelt before Him, asking the most important question that could ever be asked—*what could he do to inherit eternal life* (see Mark 10:17). He greatly desired assurance of salvation. But all of his good works and keeping of the commandments left him unsatisfied. He was still asking, *What else do I need to do?*

Perhaps he thought he was ready to make any sacrifice or do anything for God. But when Jesus said, *Go and sell your possessions and give the money to the poor, then come back and follow Me, the young man went away sad, because he was very rich* (see Matthew 19:21-22). By telling him to sell his possessions, Jesus was pointing out that his real problem was covetousness. His wealth was his god, and he needed to face that fact. Sad to say, he loved his money more than he loved Jesus, and he chose to give up eternal life rather than repent of his covetousness and accept Christ as Savior.

The fact that riches are deceitful is not often recognized until a person is confronted with the decision either to do God's will—which may mean losing friends, employment, security, and wealth—or hold on to material things.

Today, rich and poor alike must decide whether their desire to please the Lord is greater than their desire for material and physical satisfactions.

Jesus not only will forgive a repentant sinner of greed for material possessions, defiling lusts, deceitful pride, and self-righteousness, but He also can give strength to overcome the temptation of these things.

God can be depended on, and He will not allow you to be tested more than you can stand. But when you are tested, He will also make a way out so that you can come through the temptation victoriously (see I Corinthians 10:13).

Thought for Today: It is better to live for the Lord and enjoy the peace of God than it is to live to please self and end up in hell.

Word Studies: 18:28 **a hundred pence** equals about four months' wages. However, the **ten thousand talents** in verse 24 represents a debt 600,000 times greater; 19:23 **That a rich man shall hardly enter into the kingdom of heaven** means the rich have difficulty loving and trusting Christ instead of their riches (see Matthew 13:22; Mark 4:19; 10:24); 20:3 **third hour** means 9:00 a.m.; 20:10 **and** means but; 20:15 **Is thine eye evil . . . ?** means are you envious, do you begrudge my being generous?; 20:26 **minister** means servant.

Cross References: For **Matthew 18:16:** See Deut. 19:15. **Matt. 19:4:** See Gen. 1:27; 5:2. **Matt. 19:5:** See Gen. 2:24. **Matt. 19:7:** See Deut. 24:1. **Matt. 19:18:** See Ex. 20:13-16; Deut. 5:17-20. **Matt. 19:19:** See Ex. 20:12; Lev. 19:18; Deut. 5:16.

Prayer Needs: Country: Angola—8 million—in west-central Africa • Christianity is gradually being driven underground by Communism • 70% Roman Catholic; 22% Protestant; 8% belief in ancestor spirits, witches, and medicine men.

OCTOBER 9: Read Matthew 21 — 22

Highlights: Jesus' triumphal entry; Temple cleansed; fig tree cursed; authority of Jesus questioned; more parables; paying taxes to Caesar; the greatest commandment.

Verses for Today: *"All this was done, that it might be fulfilled which was spoken by the prophet . . . Tell ye the daughter of Zion, Behold, thy King cometh unto thee, meek, and sitting upon an ass, and a colt the foal of an ass"* (Matthew 21:4-5).

More than 500 years before this event, the prophet Zechariah had foretold that the King of kings would one day appear, *"riding upon an ass"* (Zechariah 9:9).

The garments of the disciples and the branches which the multitude spread out for Jesus could not compare to the extravagant splendor with which other kings would have made their royal entries into Jerusalem! Nothing could be less pretentious than this memorable event that fulfilled prophecy.

Jesus said, *" . . . learn of me; for I am meek and lowly in heart . . . "* (Matthew 11:29). The proud and self-willed never recognize that humility and meekness are essential principles of true greatness. But true greatness in our Christian lives comes by putting aside the false pride of self-importance and yielding our will to the control of God.

True humility and meekness are not qualities we can produce; they are characteristics of Christ that He is able to express through us as we surrender ourselves to His indwelling Spirit (II Corinthians 4:10-11).

"But the meek shall inherit the earth; and shall delight themselves in the abundance of peace" (Psalm 37:11).

Thought for Today: True humility before God will always result in a demonstration of that humility before men.

Word Studies: 21:2 **over against you** means in front of, opposite you; 21:8 **strawed** means spread; 21:33 **husbandmen** means tenant farmers; 22:6 **remnant** means others; 22:20 **superscription** means inscription; 22:25 **issue** means children.

Cross References: For **Matthew 21:5:** See Isa. 62:11; Zech. 9:9. **Matt. 21:9:** See Psa. 118:26. **Matt. 21:13:** See Isa. 56:7; Jer. 7:11. **Matt. 21:16:** See Psa. 8:2. **Matt. 21:33:** See Psa. 80:8; Isa. 5:1-2. **Matt. 21:42:** See Psa. 118:22-23. **Matt. 22:24:** See Deut. 25:5. **Matt. 22:32:** See Ex. 3:6. **Matt. 22:37:** See Deut. 6:5. **Matt. 22:39:** See Lev. 19:18. **Matt. 22:44:** See Psa. 110:1.

Prayer Needs: Country: St. Lucia—152,000—in the eastern Caribbean • Religious freedom • 83% Roman Catholic; 13% Protestant; 2% spirit worship.

OCTOBER 10: Read Matthew 23 — 24

Highlights: Hypocrisy denounced; destruction of the Temple foretold; signs of Christ's return.

Verses for Today: *"Ye blind guides, which strain at a gnat, and swallow a camel. . . . Woe unto you, scribes and Pharisees, hypocrites! for ye are like unto whited sepulchers, which indeed appear beautiful outward, but are within full of dead men's bones, and of all uncleanness"* (Matthew 23:24,27).

O f the three prominent "denominations" that existed at the time of Christ—the Pharisees, Sadducees, and Essenes—the Pharisees were the largest and most influential.

The scribes were a special group of educators whose opinions were accepted concerning the meaning of any doctrine or teaching of the Scriptures. Most of them were members of the Pharisee organization.

The scribes and Pharisees lived in strict obedience to the external demands of the Scriptures, but were equally strict in observing their religious traditions not taught in the Scriptures. They became very indignant and hostile toward anyone who did not accept their rules and regulations. They bitterly opposed Jesus because of His refusal to practice their traditions and because of His claim to be the Messiah (John 9:16,22).

Do we, like the scribes and Pharisees, tend to put ourselves on a self-righteous pedestal and condemn those who do not accept our standards?

The Lord has shown us what is good. What He requires of us is this: to do what is just, to love mercy, and to live in humble fellowship with our God (see Micah 6:8).

Thought for Today: God is more concerned about the inward condition of the heart than with the outward keeping of rules and regulations.

Word Studies: 23:5 **phylacteries** means small boxes containing Scripture texts worn for religious purposes; 23:6 **uppermost rooms** means best places; places of honor; 23:15 **compass** means travel about, making a great effort; **proselyte** means convert; 24:19 **them that give suck** means mothers with nursing babies; 24:45 **meat in due season** means food at the proper time.

Cross References: For **Matthew 23:39:** See Psa. 118:26. **Matt. 24:15:** See Dan. 9:27; 11:31; 12:11. **Matt. 24:29:** See Isa. 13:10; 24:23; 34:4; Ezek. 32:7; Joel 2:10, 31; 3:15. **Matt. 24:30:** See Dan. 7:13. **Matt. 24:31:** See Deut. 4:32; Isa. 27:13; Dan. 7:2; Zech. 2:6. **Matt. 24:38:** See Gen. 7:7.

Prayer Needs: Country: France—56 million—in western Europe • Religious freedom • 74% Roman Catholic; 5% Muslim; 2% Protestant; 1% Jewish.

OCTOBER 11: Read Matthew 25 — 26

Highlights: Parable of 10 virgins; parable of talents; judgment of the nations; plot to kill Jesus; Jesus anointed at Bethany; Lord's Supper; Christ's agony and prayer; Judas' betrayal; Jesus on trial; Peter's denial.

Verse for Today: " . . . *Inasmuch as ye have done it unto one of the least of these my brethren, ye have done it unto me*" (Matthew 25:40).

T here should come a time in every Christian's spiritual growth when material possessions, personal advantage, and popularity are seen for their true worth. If they are used for personal pleasure, they are worthless in the light of eternal values; if they are used to enlarge the family of God, they may become anointed tools of the Lord.

It is the indwelling love of God that makes the Christian willing to give of himself to win a lost world to Christ. And as we do, it is as though we are giving to Christ Himself.

A spiritual law in God's kingdom is that we reap what we sow. So whatever we give of God's love, we receive back. The return may not be immediate, but it will always be *"in due season"* (see Galatians 6:7-9). It is also true that the more of God's loving-kindness we share with others, the greater our capacity becomes to receive His love.

We know that we have passed from death into life because we love our fellow Christians. Whoever does not love is still under the power of death. . . . If a person sees another in need, yet closes his heart against him, how can he claim that the love of God is in him? (See I John 3:14,17.)

Thought for Today: Christian growth is evident as we help others discover spiritual values.

Word Studies: 25:27 **usury** means interest; 26:4 **subtilty** means trickery; 26:7 **box** means vase; 26:15 **they covenanted with him** means they bargained and paid him; 26:27 **Drink ye all of it** means all of you drink from it; 26:43 **heavy** means sleepy; 26:47 **staves** means clubs; 26:63 **I adjure thee** means I command you, as if under oath before God; 26:73 **thy speech bewrayeth [betrayeth] thee** means your Galilean accent gives you away.

Cross References: For **Matthew 26:31:** See Zech. 13:7. **Matt. 26:64:** See Psa. 110:1; Dan. 7:13.

Prayer Needs: Country: St. Vincent and the Grenadines—131,000—in the Lesser Antilles of the eastern Caribbean • Religious freedom • 50% Protestant; 17% Roman Catholic; 2% spiritist.

OCTOBER 12: Read Matthew 27 — 28

Highlights: Judas' suicide; Jesus before Pilate; Jesus' crucifixion, burial, and resurrection; Great Commission.

Verse for Today: *"He is not here: for he is risen, as he said. Come, see the place where the Lord lay"* (Matthew 28:6).

B efore Mary Magdalene and the others arrived at the tomb, the angel of the Lord had rolled back the stone from the entrance. The triumphant resurrection of

Jesus Christ had already taken place when the angel announced to the astounded women, *"He is risen, as he said."*

An empty tomb would have been sad news indeed if this had been all the women were told. But the exciting news was that Jesus had risen triumphantly from the grave (Romans 1:4).

Christians rejoice in the cross of Christ, for it was there that He paid the price for our redemption. But we rejoice even more in the resurrection of Christ, for it assures us of our heavenly home with Him. We have the assurance that *"the dead shall be raised incorruptible, and we shall be changed"* (I Corinthians 15:52). This is the great and glorious hope of every Christian, the comfort at the graveside of a loved one, the victory that removes the sting of death, and the anticipation that we, too, shall be like Him.

It is wonderful to know we have been forgiven of all our sins and have the assurance of soon being with Christ. But until that time, we can praise Him that we have been set free from the power of sin (Romans 6:10-11). We can live in that deliverance by faith.

" ... with the Lord there is mercy, and with him is plenteous redemption" (Psalm 130:7).

Thought for Today: Jesus willingly died for you; are you willing to live for Him?

Word Studies: 27:15 **wont to release** means in the habit of setting free; 27:16 **notable** means notorious; 27:24 **tumult** means riot; 27:44 **cast the same in his teeth** means heaped insults on Him in the same way; 27:64 **sure** means secure; well guarded; 28:19 **baptizing** means immersing, as in Romans 6:4.

Cross References: For Matthew **27:9-10:** See Zech. 11:12-13. **Matt. 27:34:** See Psa. 69:21. **Matt. 27:35:** See Psa. 22:18. **Matt. 27:39:** See Job 16:4; Psa. 22:7; 109:25; Lam. 2:15. **Matt. 27:43:** See Psa. 22:8. **Matt. 27:46:** See Psa. 22:1.

Prayer Needs: Country: Anguilla—7,000—part of the British West Indies • Religious freedom • 97% Protestant; 2% Roman Catholic.

MARK _____

Mark presents Jesus as a servant, the perfect workman of God, and highlights His life of service to others.

No one is concerned about the genealogy of a servant, so the Gospel of Mark says nothing about the ancestry of Jesus. In fact, there is no mention of angels announcing His birth, of Wise Men seeking a King or giving Him costly gifts, or of His amazing wisdom expressed to the learned doctors of the Law when He was only 12 years old.

Since servants are not recognized for what they say, but for what they do, Mark leaves out the great Sermon on the Mount and most of Jesus' parables.

The urgent mission of Jesus as the Servant of God is revealed in such words as "straightway," "immediately," "at once," and "soon"—which are used more than 40 times.

In Mark, the hands of Jesus are also prominent, revealing the acts and duties of a servant. When the Lord healed Peter's mother-in-law, He *"took her by the hand, and lifted her up"* (1:31). At Bethany, He took the blind man *"by the hand"* and afterward laid *"his hands upon him"* (8:23). In healing the deaf and dumb man, He put His fingers in the man's ears (7:33).

Mark also portrays Jesus as the Christ who gave His life and rose from the dead so that all repentant sinners who receive Him as their personal Savior can inherit eternal life.

At the close of the book, Christ's disciples are urged to take His place on earth; He continues to serve through them. Jesus commissioned them: *"Go into all the world, and preach the gospel to every creature. He that believeth and is baptized shall be saved; but he that believeth not shall be damned"* (16:15-16).

OCTOBER 13: Read Mark 1 — 3

Highlights: Ministry of John the Baptist; baptism and temptation of Jesus; His Galilean ministry; twelve apostles chosen; the unpardonable sin.

Verse for Today: *"And in the morning, rising up a great while before the day, he went out, and departed into a solitary place, and there prayed"* (Mark 1:35).

O ur Lord had just endured a long, difficult day and was now facing another equally trying day. After having slept for only a few hours, He arose very early in the morning to pray.

Prayer was an important part of Jesus' life. He habitually devoted the early morning hours to prayer to His Father, seeking guidance and strength for each day. The many hours in prayer made it possible for Him to say, *I do nothing on My own, but I say exactly what the Father has instructed Me to say* (see John 8:28).

Jesus' life was much like ours—surrounded by opportunities for service and pressed by great needs. However, unlike Him, most of us give little time to prayer. Too often, we are so busy we don't take time to pray, but we still hope everything will turn out all right. This is not faith; it is foolishness.

When we neglect our time in prayer with the Lord, our efforts will always be less effective and far more likely to be hindered by Satan's deceptions. If we follow our Lord's example, we will spend much more time in prayer.

Even though we may be surrounded by difficult circumstances or great responsibilities, the Lord enables us to overcome them when we pray.

Christians should always pray and never become discouraged (see Luke 18:1).

Thought for Today: The greater the outward pressures, the more time we must give to unhurried prayer.

Word Studies: 1:7 **latchet** means sandal strap; 1:26 **torn him** means thrown him into convulsions; 1:30 **anon** means at once or soon; immediately; 1:43 **straitly charged** means sternly warned; 21:15 **publicans** means tax collectors; 2:19 **children of the bridechamber** means wedding guests; 2:26 **showbread** means bread that had been consecrated for the worship service.

Cross References: For Mark 1:2: See Mal. 3:1. **Mark 1:3:** See Isa. 40:3.

Prayer Needs: **Country:** Cyprus—684,000—in the Middle East • No open evangelism or conversion to Christ • 75% Greek Orthodox; 19% Muslim; 1% Protestant; 1% Roman Catholic.

OCTOBER 14: Read Mark 4 — 5

Highlights: Jesus' parables; storm stilled; legion of demons cast out; Jairus' daughter raised.

Verse for Today: *"And they come to Jesus, and see him that was possessed with the devil, and had the legion, sitting, and clothed, and in his right mind; and they were afraid"* (Mark 5:15).

R estless, naked, and raging, this demon-possessed man had been dwelling among the tombs, the burial places of the dead. He was controlled by Satan until Jesus set him free.

When Jesus cast out the demons from this man, He permitted them to enter a herd of pigs. The demons in turn caused the pigs to run violently into the sea and drown. This illustrates how Satan seeks to destroy whomever he can.

At the sight of Christ, this demon-possessed man ran to Jesus and bowed down before Him, and his life was transformed. Prior to meeting Jesus, he was symbolic of every unsaved person who, in some way, is under the control and mastery of Satan and his evil forces.

People sometimes think that a single individual doesn't count very much, but God and the devil both know that is not true. The devil thought it worthwhile to let a whole legion of demons take possession of one man; Christ considered this man so precious that He was willing to be rejected by an entire city in order to deliver the man from Satan's stronghold. As a result of his encounter with Jesus, the man was changed—*"sitting, and clothed, and in his right mind."* He then became a witness to others. Because of his testimony, many people came to Jesus (see 5:20; 6:53-56).

A transformation takes place when we respond to Christ!

The new life we have is not one that was passed down to us from our parents, for the life they gave us will fade away. This new life will last forever, for it comes from Christ (see I Peter 1:23).

Thought for Today: It is not *what* a person possesses that is important, but *who* possesses him.

Word Studies: 4:31 **less than all the seeds** means the smallest of all seeds; 5:26 **was nothing bettered** means was no better; 5:30 **virtue** means healing power.

Cross Reference: For **Mark 4:12:** See Isa. 6:9-10.

Prayer Needs: Country: Paraguay—5 million—in southern South America • Religious freedom • 96% Roman Catholic; 2% Protestant.

OCTOBER 15: Read Mark 6 — 7

Highlights: Twelve apostles sent out; John the Baptist beheaded; 5,000 fed; Jesus walks on water; His rebuke of the Pharisees; faith of the Syrophoenician woman.

Verse for Today: *"Howbeit in vain do they worship me, teaching for doctrines the commandments of men"* (Mark 7:7).

J esus rebuked the Pharisees and the scribes for their hypocrisy. They placed greater importance on their own traditions than they did on the commandments of God. Some of the commandments God gave Moses taught the need for purifying the heart from worldly desires and sinful ambitions. But instead of realizing the importance of their hearts being right with God, the Pharisees substituted many of their own doctrines.

No one today goes by the name of scribe or Pharisee, but many have departed from the revealed Word of God by substituting their own rules. Outwardly they are religious, but inwardly their hearts are not right with God.

"Woe unto you ... hypocrites! for ye pay tithe ... and have omitted the weightier matters of the law, judgment, mercy, and faith: these ought ye to have done, and not to leave the other undone" (Matthew 23:23).

Thought for Today: Our daily actions, attitudes, and conversations will express the thoughts of our hearts.

Word Studies: 6:8 **scrip** means travel bag for provisions; 6:20 **observed him** means kept him safe (under guard); 6:21 **chief estates** means his most important men; 6:33 **outwent them** means got there ahead of those in the boat; 7:19 **purging** means making clean; 7:27 **meet** means proper.

Cross References: For **Mark 7:6-7:** See Isa. 29:13. **Mark 7:10:** See Ex. 20:12; 21:17; Lev. 20:9; Deut. 5:16.

Prayer Needs: Country: Netherlands—15 million—in northwestern Europe • Religious freedom • 39% Roman Catholic; 29% Protestant; 2% Muslim.

OCTOBER 16: Read Mark 8 — 9

Highlights: Feeding of the 4,000; leaven explained; healing of a blind man; Peter's confession of faith; death and resurrection foretold; transfiguration; inability of disciples to cast out a demon; dispute over who should be the greatest; warning of hell.

Verses for Today: *" ... and he was transfigured before them.... and a voice came out of the cloud, saying, This is my beloved Son: hear him"* (Mark 9:2,7).

O ur Lord came into the world and *"look upon him the form of a servant, and was made in the likeness of men"* (Philippians 2:7). But at His transfiguration, Jesus appeared as the glorious eternal Son of God.

The Holy Spirit directed Matthew to write, *"His face did shine as the sun"* (Matthew 17:2). Luke was inspired to write, *"The fashion of his countenance was altered, and his raiment was white and glistering"* (Luke 9:29), meaning He radiated with the matchless glory of His deity.

Moses represented the Law, and Elijah, the prophets; both foretold of the coming Messiah-King (see Luke 24:44).

Moses and Elijah were great men of God, but Christ is far superior to the greatest men on earth. All other leaders fade into insignificance when Jesus becomes Lord of our lives.

"Seek ye the Lord while he may be found, call ye upon him while he is near" (Isaiah 55:6).

Thought for Today: The worship that is due Christ cannot be shared with man.

Word Studies: 8:22 **besought** means begged; 9:3 **fuller** means launderer; 9:12 **set at nought** means rejected; 9:13 **listed** means desired; 9:18 **teareth him** means throws him into violent convulsions; **pineth away** means becomes rigid, motionless; 9:30 **would not** means did not want; 9:43 **maimed** means crippled.

Cross References: For Mark 8:18: See Ezek. 12:2. Mark 9:44,46,48: See Isa. 66:24.

Prayer Needs: Country: Cook Islands—18,000—several islands in the South Pacific, between Tonga and Tahiti • Religious freedom • 70% Protestant; 11% Roman Catholic; 6% cults; 1% Baha'i.

OCTOBER 17: Read Mark 10 — 11

Highlights: Jesus on divorce; children blessed; rich young ruler; request of James and John; blind Bartimeus healed; triumphal entry; cleansing the Temple; lesson from the withered fig tree; Jesus' authority questioned.

Verse for Today: *"And when ye stand praying, forgive, if ye have aught against any: that your Father also which is in heaven may forgive you your trespasses"* (Mark 11:25).

T he spirit of forgiveness may not seem very important, especially when we feel that someone has wronged us. But it is vital to a right relationship with Christ. Having an unforgiving spirit is of Satan, and it keeps a person from receiving forgiveness from God. (See Matthew 18:32-35.) It is Satan who is our real enemy— not others, for they, too, may be struggling against his attacks and need our compassionate love.

Just as Christ paid the price for forgiveness of our sins by His death on the cross, we must also, from the heart, forgive all who have wronged us. This does not mean merely saying, "I forgive you," and then continuing to have ill will toward that person, cutting off all communication and avoiding all opportunities for reconciliation. If our forgiveness is truly an expression of Christ's love, the result should be a restored friendship.

"But if ye do not forgive, neither will your Father which is in heaven forgive your trespasses" (Mark 11:26).

Thought for Today: A person can become a slave to the one he hates by allowing bitter thoughts about that person to dominate his mind.

Word Study: 10:42 accounted to rule means considered rulers.

Cross References: For Mark 10:6: See Gen. 1:27; 5:2. Mark 10:7-8: See Gen. 2:24. Mark 10:19: See Ex. 20:12-16; Deut. 5:16-20. Mark 11:9: See Psa. 118: 26. Mark 11:17: See Isa. 56:7; Jer. 7:11.

Prayer Needs: Country: Northern Ireland—2 million—on the second largest of the British Isles • Religious freedom • 63% Protestant; 36% Roman Catholic.

OCTOBER 18: Read Mark 12 — 13

Highlights: Wicked tenant farmers; paying taxes to Caesar; question about the resurrection; greatest commandment; widow's offering; signs of the end.

Verse for Today: *"And Jesus answering said unto them, Render to Caesar the things that are Caesar's, and to God the things that are God's...."* (Mark 12:17).

T he Pharisees were strict religious leaders of Israel; they deeply resented the excessive taxes they had to pay the Roman government. The Herodians were worldly and irreligious, but they urged submission to the Roman government. The book of Matthew tells us that these two opposite-thinking groups of people plotted together in an effort to trap Jesus (22:15-17). They asked Him, *"Is it lawful to give tribute to Caesar, or not?"* (Mark 12:14). If He said no, the Herodian party would accuse Him of conspiracy against the Roman government. If He said yes, the Pharisees would say that He could not be the Messiah of Israel because He taught subjection to a Gentile government.

Our Lord, in His wisdom, told them to give to Caesar what belonged to him. But the rest of His comment came as a stinging rebuke of their hypocrisy when He told them to render to God *"the things that are God's."*

As Christians faithfully render to God the things that are His, the Word of God can be more effectively proclaimed throughout the world.

"Give unto the Lord the glory due unto his name; worship the Lord in the beauty of holiness" (Psalm 29:2).

Thought for Today: Have you prayed today for those who are in authority over you? (See I Timothy 2:2.)

Word Studies: 12:1 **let** means rented; 12:17 **Render** means pay; 12:19 **seed** means children; 12:34 **durst** means dared; 12:41 **over against** means opposite; 12:42 **mites** means little copper coins. A mite had the least value of any coin.

Cross References: For **Mark 12:1:** See Isa. 5:2. **Mark 12:10-11:** See Psa. 118:22-23. **Mark 12:19:** See Deut. 25:5. **Mark 12:26:** See Ex. 3:6. **Mark 12:29:** See Deut. 6:4. **Mark 12:30:** See Deut. 6:5. **Mark 12:31:** See Lev. 19:18. **Mark 12:32:** See Deut. 4:35. **Mark 12:33:** See Deut. 6:5. **Mark 12:36:** See Psa. 110:1. **Mark 13:14:** See Dan. 9:27; 11:31; 12:11. **Mark 13:24:** See Isa. 13:10. **Mark 13:26:** See Dan. 7:13. **Mark 13:27:** See Deut. 30:4; Zech. 2:6.

Prayer Needs: Country: England—57 million—in the British Isles • Religious freedom • 48% Protestant; 9% Roman Catholic.

OCTOBER 19: Read Mark 14 — 16

Highlights: Plot against Jesus; Jesus anointed at Bethany; His last Passover; Lord's Supper instituted; prayer in Gethsemane; betrayal and arrest of Jesus; Peter's denial; Jesus before Pilate; Christ's crucifixion, burial, resurrection, and ascension.

Verse for Today: *"And it was the third hour, and they crucified him"* (Mark 15:25).

T hink of these words! The Son of God was crucified! God *"spared not his own Son, but delivered him up for us all . . . "* (Romans 8:32).

Through His death on the cross, Jesus paid the penalty for all who repent of their sins and receive Him as Lord and Savior. Our sins merit death, but our substitute, the Lord Jesus Christ, bore our sins *"in his own body on the tree, that we, being dead to sins, should live unto righteousness"* (I Peter 2:24).

Jesus was raised from the dead by the power of God. As Christians, we have the privilege of being identified with Him in death and resurrection—*"buried with him by baptism into death: that like as Christ was raised up from the dead by the glory of the Father, even so we also should walk in newness of life"* (Romans 6:4).

"All we like sheep have gone astray; we have turned every one to his own way; and the Lord hath laid on him the iniquity of us all" (Isaiah 53:6).

Thought for Today: Jesus' death on the cross brought victory over the power of sin so that we might have forgiveness of sin and enjoy eternal life.

Word Studies: 14:3 **ointment** means perfume; 14:31 **vehemently** means insistently;

14:43 **staves** means clubs; 14:44 **token** means signal; 14:65 **buffet him** means hit Him with their fists; 15:15 **scourged** means whipped.

Cross References: For **Mark 14:27:** See Zech. 13:7. **Mark 14:62:** See Psa. 110:1; Dan. 7:13. **Mark 15:24:** See Psa. 22:18. **Mark 15:28:** See Isa. 53:12. **Mark 15:29:** See Psa. 22:8. **Mark 15:34:** See Psa. 22:1. **Mark 16:19:** See Psa. 110:1.

Prayer Needs: Country: Libya—4 million—in North Africa • No form of Christian witness to Libyans is permitted • 98% Muslim; 2% Christian.

LUKE

Luke addressed his book to a Gentile named Theophilus, giving special attention to the humanity of the Savior and presenting Him as the perfect man. Luke was a Greek physician and missionary companion to the Apostle Paul.

Tracing Jesus' genealogy back 4,000 years to Adam, the first man, Luke establishes Jesus as the Son of man who understands man's weaknesses and has compassion for his needs (see also Isaiah 53:3). The phrase "Son of man" is mentioned at least 26 times in Luke.

More details of the human characteristics of Jesus are given in this Gospel. It tells us about Jesus' parents; the birth of His cousin, John the Baptist; and Mary and Joseph's journey to Bethlehem, where Jesus was born and placed in a manger (Luke 1:5—2:7).

Events not found in the other Gospels are the annunciation of Christ by the angels; Simeon's holding Baby Jesus in his arms; the genealogy of Christ through Mary; Jesus' conversation with the teachers in the Temple at the age of 12; His increasing *"in wisdom and stature, and in favor with God and man"*; the story of the prodigal son; the rich man and Lazarus; the story of the Good Samaritan; and additional events of Jesus' final journey to Jerusalem.

Luke reveals Jesus' human dependence upon the Father in prayer (3:21; 5:16; 6:12; 9:29; 10:21; 11:1; 22:17,19; 23:46).

Luke makes it unquestionably clear that Jesus' purpose for leaving Heaven and being born in human flesh was *to seek and to save the lost* (see 19:10).

OCTOBER 20: Read Luke 1

Highlights: Virgin birth of Jesus foretold; Mary's visit to Elisabeth; Mary's praise; birth of John the Baptist.

Verses for Today: *"To give knowledge of salvation unto his people by the remission of their sins, through the tender mercy of our God ... "* (Luke 1:77-78).

F ive times we are reminded of the mercy of God in providing a way to redeem mankind from sin (Luke 1:50,54,58,72,78).

God's *"tender mercy"* means more than His willingness to forgive. It means that, with compassion, he accepts us.

The whole plan of salvation was based on mercy. Because of the sin of Adam and Eve in the Garden of Eden, fellowship between God and man was broken. But our heavenly Father looked down upon mankind—dead in trespasses and sin, helpless, and hopelessly lost—and in tender mercy, sent His only begotten Son into the world to *"save his people from their sins"* (Matthew 1:21-25).

Being saved from sin means being reconciled and restored to God—brought back into fellowship with Him. Oh, how we should rejoice and praise our wonderful heavenly Father! His tender mercy has made it possible for everyone who will *"call upon the name of the Lord"* to be saved (Romans 10:13).

"For his great love wherewith he loved us, even when we were dead in sins, hath quickened us together with Christ, (by grace ye are saved)" (Ephesians 2:4-5).

Thought for Today: Since the Lord has shown mercy to us—we should also show mercy to others.

Word Studies: 1:40 **saluted** means greeted; embraced; 1:46 **magnify** means praise; 1:54 **holpen** means come to the help of.

Cross References: For **Luke 1:17:** See Mal. 4:6. **Luke 1:50:** See Psa. 103:17. **Luke 1:53:** See Psa. 107:9. **Luke 1:71:** See Psa. 106:10. **Luke 1:76:** See Mal. 3:1. **Luke 1:79:** See Isa. 9:1-2; 59:8.

Prayer Needs: Country: Ireland—4 million—on the second largest of the British Isles • Religious freedom • 93% Roman Catholic; 4% Protestant; .1% Eastern Orthodox.

OCTOBER 21: Read Luke 2 — 3

Highlights: Birth of Jesus; shepherds' adoration; Simeon's and Anna's prophecies; return to Nazareth; Jesus among the teachers; ministry of John the Baptist; baptism of Jesus; genealogy of Jesus through Mary.

Verse for Today: *"For unto you is born this day in the city of David a Savior, which is Christ the Lord"* (Luke 2:11).

T he birth of Jesus is probably the most familiar event in history. And the vital truths about His birth are so essential to eternal life that they require our utmost attention.

Thousands of people think of the birth of Christ only as a delightful Christmas story. They reject the historical accuracy of the Word of God which says Jesus is the virgin-born, only begotten Son of God. Yes, the Babe in Bethlehem's manger was the Son of God; He became a man in order that He might bear our sins in His own body on the cross and thereby make it possible for every repentant sinner to have eternal life.

That Christ should come to earth to redeem mankind from the curse of sin is indeed tidings of great joy!

Seven hundred years before Jesus was born, Isaiah the prophet foretold His birth, saying, *A son is given to us. He will be called Wonderful, Counselor, Mighty God, Eternal Father of everlasting life, Prince of peace* (see Isaiah 9:6).

Thought for Today: The certainty that God's Word will be fulfilled is the foundation of our faith.

Word Studies: 2:46 **doctors** means teachers; 3:1 **tetrarch** means ruler.

Prayer Needs: **Country:** The Gambia—760,000—in West Africa • Religious freedom • 87% Muslim; 10% animism and ancestral spirit worship; 2% Roman Catholic; .7% Protestant.

OCTOBER 22: Read Luke 4 — 5

Highlights: Temptation of Jesus; His teachings; healings; miraculous catch of fish; other miracles; call of Matthew; Jesus questioned by the scribes and Pharisees.

Verse for Today: *"And when they had brought their ships to land, they forsook all, and followed him"* (Luke 5:11).

I n answer to Christ's call, Peter and Andrew immediately *"forsook all"*—a profitable business, valuable property, and friends—and launched out, not knowing how their needs would be met. What wonderful faith—just to trust the Lord Jesus Christ! Everything else seemed insignificant compared to the call to reach those who needed a Savior.

God so arranged His plan of salvation that He works through human beings to carry out His ministry *"to seek and to save"* lost sinners (Luke 19:10). Thus we become *"workers together with him"* (II Corinthians 6:1). What a privilege and an honor!

When Christ becomes the most important person in our lives, no sacrifice will seem too great to reach those who have not received Him as their Savior. Those we can witness to today may be gone tomorrow, and our opportunities to share His love with them will be gone forever.

The call to service is urgent. Every minute of the day, more than 100 people die and go to a Christless eternity. Whatever we do to reach the unsaved, we must do now!

"The fruit of the righteous is a tree of life; and he that winneth souls is wise" (Proverbs 11:30).

Thought for Today: Every Christian has a responsibility to participate in the work of God.

Word Studies: 4:29 **brow** meand edge; 5:9 **draught** means catch; 5:31 **whole** means well; healthy; 5:36 **rent** means tear.

Cross References: For **Luke 4:4:** See Deut. 8:3. **Luke 4:8:** See Deut. 6:13. **Luke 4:10-11:** See Psa. 91:11-12. **Luke 4:12:** See Deut. 6:16. **Luke 4:18-19:** See Isa. 61:1-2. **Luke 5:14:** See Lev. 13:49.

Prayer Needs: **Country:** Macao—438,000—on a small peninsula on the southern coast of China • Religious freedom • 66% Chinese religions; 11% Roman Catholic; 1% Protestant.

OCTOBER 23: Read Luke 6 — 7

Highlights: Jesus and the sabbath; 12 apostles chosen; Sermon on the Mount; healing and miracles; John the Baptist's questions; Jesus anointed.

Verses for Today: *"And why beholdest thou the mote that is in thy brother's eye, but perceivest not the beam that is in thine own eye? . . . Thou hypocrite, cast out* *first the beam out of thine own eye, and then shalt thou see clearly to pull out the mote that is in thy brother's eye"* (Luke 6:41-42).

It is impossible for us to be among people without observing their conduct; but this is not the thing Jesus spoke against. Rather, it was the attitude of condemning and criticizing the shortcomings, faults, and preferences of others who do not agree with us.

Jesus did not say that the mote did not exist; it is very real. But because we cannot know another person's heart and it is impossible to know all the facts and circumstances, we are commanded not to criticize, find fault, or judge (see John 7:24).

Criticism of others is often the result of one of two evils: a spirit of self-righteousness to build one's own image or esteem before others, or a devilish desire to slander and destroy another. It is this *"beam"* of self-righteousness and failure to express God's mercy and love that Jesus spoke of when He said, *First take the beam out of your own eye.*

Christ's words should convict us of our self-righteousness in judging others and cause us to make a determined effort to avoid the evil of criticism.

Let us not speak evil or slander anyone, but be considerate and gentle, showing meekness and courtesy to all (see Titus 3:2).

Thought for Today: It is unjust to criticize anyone—even those whose efforts fall short of what we expect.

Word Studies: 6:11 **communed** means plotted; planned; discussed; 6:29 **smiteth** means hits; strikes; 7:4 **besought him instantly** means pleaded with Him earnestly; 7:14 **bier** means an open coffin—a simple, flat board; 7:25 **are gorgeously appareled** means are dressed in expensive clothes (generally worn by kings or officials).

Cross References: For **Luke 7:22:** See Isa. 61:1. **Luke 7:27:** Mal. 3:1.

Prayer Needs: Country: Israel—5 million—in the Middle East • Witnessing to Jews about Christ the Messiah is actively discouraged • 88% Jewish; 8% Muslim; 2% Christian.

OCTOBER 24: Read Luke 8 — 9

Highlights: Jesus' teaching; more miracles; 12 apostles sent forth; 5,000 fed; Peter's confession; transfiguration; healing of the boy with an evil spirit; the Samaritans' refusal to receive Jesus; tests of discipleship.

Verses for Today: *" . . . a certain man said unto him, Lord, I will follow thee whithersoever thou goest. And Jesus said unto him, Foxes have holes, and birds of the air have nests; but the Son of man hath not where to lay his head"* (Luke 9: 57-58).

The spiritual sincerity of this would-be disciple was put to the test as Jesus pointed out that he would have to face many hardships in order to follow Him.

When Jesus said, *"The Son of man hath not where to lay his head,"* He was saying that He was not attached to any earthly possessions. The foxes and the birds had a place of protection, but Jesus' life was exposed to suffering, humiliation, and self-denial.

The cost of discipleship has kept many people from following the Lord, for they are not willing to deny themselves the pleasures and interests that conflict with doing God's will. But those who are willing to live for Him know that the rewards for discipleship far exceed earthly pleasures.

"For even Christ pleased not himself; but, as it is written, The reproaches of them that reproached thee fell on me" (Romans 15:3).

Thought for Today: Worldly ambitions fade into insignificance as we come to know the Lord through His Word.

Word Studies: 8:44 **stanched** means stopped; 9:3 **staves** means staffs; walking sticks; 9:29 **glistering** means shining with the brilliance of lightning.

Cross Reference: For **Luke 8:10:** See Isa. 6:9.

Prayer Needs: **Country:** Guatemala—9 million—in Central America • Religious freedom • 93% Roman Catholic; 5% Protestant.

OCTOBER 25: Read Luke 10 — 11

Highlights: Seventy sent out; Good Samaritan; Martha and Mary; Pharisees denounced.

Verse for Today: *"But a certain Samaritan, as he journeyed, came where he was: and when he saw him, he had compassion on him"* (Luke 10:33).

I n reply to the lawyer's question—*"And who is my neighbor?"*—Jesus gave this touching parable of a destitute sufferer who had been beaten, robbed, and left *"half dead"* (see Luke 10:29-37).

The priest and the Levite should have been first to show compassion to this helpless man, but they both avoided him. Each of them could have justified his cruel indifference, using the excuse that he was on his way to serve God in the Temple and did not have the time or could not risk becoming defiled. For all they knew, the unconscious man could have been dead! Touching a dead body would have made them ceremonially unclean (see Numbers 19:11-19).

The priest and the Levite both knew that the Law taught, *"Thou shalt not see thy brother's ass or his ox fall down by the way, and hide thyself from them: thou shalt surely help him to lift them up again"* (Deuteronomy 22:4).

Christ is that good Samaritan who came from Heaven and saw lost mankind, lying helpless in the road of this world, stripped of spiritual life, and left physically dying. Jesus bound up our wounds, poured within us the oil of the Holy Spirit, cleansed us by His blood, and lifted us up.

" . . . the Lord hath laid on him the iniquity of us all" (Isaiah 53:6).

Thought for Today: It is one thing to serve God, but quite another thing to show compassion to those who are less fortunate than we are.

Word Studies: 10:6 **if the son of peace be there** means if they are willing to receive you graciously; 10:40 **cumbered about** means distressed by; distracted with; 10:41 **careful** means frustrated; upset; worried; 11:53 **urge him vehemently** means fiercely attempt to provoke the Lord to say something that would give them a reason to make accusations against Him.

Cross References: For **Luke 10:27:** See Deut. 6:5; Lev. 19:18. **Luke 10:28:** See Lev. 18:5.

Prayer Needs: **Country:** Hong Kong—6 million—at the mouth of the Canton River in China • Religious freedom • 66% Buddhist and other Chinese religions; 7% Protestant; 5% Roman Catholic.

OCTOBER 26: Read Luke 12 — 13

Highlights: Warnings against greed and hypocrisy; more parables, healings, and teachings.

Verses for Today: *" ... Take no thought for your life, what ye shall eat; neither for the body, what ye shall put on. The life is more than meat, and the body is more than raiment. ... But rather seek ye the kingdom of God; and all these things shall be added unto you"* (Luke 12:22-23,31).

J esus was assuring His people of His care for them. There was no need for them to worry about their daily needs; for just as He clothes the lilies of the field and cares for the birds (Luke 12:6-7,24-28), He will also supply the needs of those who put Him first in their lives.

Our Lord's message is in contrast to the world's determined effort to accumulate "things" as a means of security for the future. The Christian is to *seek first the kingdom of God and His righteousness*—then the Lord will take care of the necessities of life (see Matthew 6:24-34). This does not mean that we are to sit back and do nothing. It means that we are to seek the things of God with all our hearts. Doing the will of God should be the most important desire of our hearts—even as an outstanding athlete has only one desire—to win.

" ... There is no man that hath left house, or brethren, or sisters, or father, or mother, or wife, or children, or lands, for my sake, and the gospel's, But he shall receive a hundredfold now in this time, houses, and brethren, and sisters, and mothers, and children, and lands, with persecutions; and in the world to come eternal life" (Mark 10:29-30).

Thought for Today: If we are truly concerned about God's interests, He will take care of ours.

Word Studies: 12:50 **straitened** means pressed with anguish; distressed; burdened; 13:8 **dung it** means put manure on the soil; 13:11 **had a spirit of infirmity** means had suffered under some spirit that disabled her.

Cross References: For **Luke 13:27:** See Psa. 6:8. **Luke 13:35:** See Psa. 118:26.

Prayer Needs: Country: Hungary—11 million—in east-central Europe • 61% Roman Catholic; 24% Protestant.

OCTOBER 27: Read Luke 14 — 16

Highlights: Humility; more parables; prodigal son; rich man and Lazarus.

Verses for Today: *" ... the younger son ... took his journey into a far country, and there wasted his substance. ... and he began to be in want. ... and no man gave unto him. And when he came to himself, he said, ... I perish with hunger! I will arise and go to my father, and will say unto him, Father, I have sinned against heaven, and before thee"* (Luke 15:13-18).

T his self-centered prodigal son insisted on being free from his father's authority and any responsibility to him.

We ordinarily think of the word "prodigal" as meaning a wanderer, but it has quite a different meaning. A prodigal is a waster; he *"wasted"* his father's substance. Eventually, he became destitute; but rather than confess his sin and ask his father's forgiveness, he struggled with a sense of emptiness and the shame of a wasted life. Finally he came to his senses and returned to his father.

This is the story of the human race. It is human nature to be self-willed and self-sufficient—seeking to be independent from God's authority, living to satisfy self.

Just as the prodigal son discovered that his father's compassion and love were far greater than he had realized, every repentant sinner will discover that the Heavenly Father—in love and compassion—is waiting to transform the wasted lives of all who come to Him.

God loved us so much, that even though we were spiritually dead, undeserving, and doomed sinners, He made it possible for us to receive forgiveness through Christ Jesus, who paid the penalty for our sins (see Ephesians 2:4-7).

Thought for Today: Have you wandered away from God? Turn back to the Father; He is lovingly waiting to welcome you home.

Word Studies: 14:10 **worship** means honor; 14:32 **an ambassage** means representatives; 15:16 **would fain** means longed to; 16:11 **mammon** means riches; 16:14 **derided** means ridiculed.

Prayer Needs: Country: Belize—168,000—on the east-ern coast of Central America • Religious freedom • 54% Roman Catholic; 26% Protestant.

OCTOBER 28: Read Luke 17 — 18

Highlights: Jesus' teaching on forgiveness; 10 lepers; Christ's second coming foretold; more parables; children blessed; rich young ruler; Christ's death and resurrection foretold; healing of a blind beggar.

Verse for Today: *"And he spake a parable unto them to this end, that men ought always to pray, and not to faint"* (Luke 18:1).

J esus told the story of a judge who would not carry out justice for a poor widow; nevertheless, she went to him day after day, pleading for protection from her adversary (Luke 18:3-5). Because of her persistence, the judge granted her request.

This parable should teach us that we have an adversary—the devil—who makes every attempt to keep us from gaining our rightful inheritance and receiving answers to prayer.

The parable of the destitute widow is an encouragement for Christians to continue taking their requests to God in prayer, even when it seems that He does not hear or answer.

God is not as the unjust judge, for He is more interested in our prayers being answered than we are.

If an unjust judge would respond to the request of a widow he did not know, certainly we can depend upon God—our Heavenly Judge—to grant the requests of His own children who call upon Him. God is faithful and never fails.

"For every one that asketh receiveth; and he that seeketh findeth; and to him that knocketh it shall be opened" (Matthew 7:8).

Thought for Today: We can thank God that He always gives His best when it is best for us.

Word Studies: 17:9 **trow** means think; 17:20 **with observation** means in such a manner that we can visibly observe it; 18:1 **faint** means give up; 18:3 **Avenge** means protect; 18:12 **possess** means acquire; gain; 18:30 **manifold more** means many times as much.

Cross Reference: For **Luke 18:20:** See Ex. 20:12-16; Deut. 5:16-20.

Prayer Needs: Country: Honduras—5 million—in Central America • Religious freedom • 86% Roman Catholic; 10% Protestant.

OCTOBER 29: Read Luke 19 — 20

Highlights: Jesus and Zaccheus; triumphal entry; cleansing of the Temple; parable of the wicked tenants; paying taxes to Caesar; questions concerning the resurrection; Jesus' authority.

Verses for Today: *"And Jesus entered and passed through Jericho. And, behold, there was a man named Zaccheus . . . And he sought to see Jesus who he was; and could not for the press, because he was little of stature"* (Luke 19:1-3).

J ericho, located about 20 miles from Jerusalem, was a pleasant, popular place to live, for it was the city of palm trees. It was here that Zaccheus, a Jew, worked as chief tax collector.

The tax collectors were greatly disliked because they were thought to be dishonest as well as disloyal to the Jewish community because they worked for the Roman government. Consequently, they were unwelcome in the synagogues.

Zaccheus *"was chief among the publicans [tax collectors], and he was rich"* (Luke 19:2). However, buried beneath his shrewd, questionable business dealings was a deep dissatisfaction with himself. He desperately longed for something that money could not satisfy. This outcast was a lost sinner and he knew it.

It was the love which Christ had for a world of outcasts that made Him willing to die on the cross to save us from our sins.

"For the Son of man is come to seek and to save that which was lost" (Luke 19:10).

Thought for Today: Our greatest satisfaction comes through living for the Lord.

Word Studies: 19:2 **publicans** means tax collectors; 19:12 **nobleman** means one in charge of vast holdings, such as a kingdom; 19:13 **Occupy** means manage my business; 19:21 **austere** means severe; stern; 20:20 **feign themselves** means pretend to be.

Cross References: For **Luke 19:38:** See Psa. 118:26. **Luke 19:46:** See Isa. 56:7; Jer. 7:11. **Luke 20:17:** See Psa. 118:22. **Luke 20:28:** See Deut. 25:5. **Luke 20:37:** See Ex. 3:6. **Luke 20:42-43:** See Psa. 110:1.

Prayer Needs: Country: Madagascar—11 million—an island in the Indian Ocean off the coast of Mozambique • Increasingly anti-Christian • 43% witchcraft, ancestor worship, and some astrology; 21% Protestant; 21% Roman Catholic; 2% Muslim.

OCTOBER 30: Read Luke 21 — 22

Highlights: The widow's offering; signs of the end; plot against Jesus; last Passover; the Lord's Supper; Jesus' arrest; Peter's denial.

Verses for Today: *"And he took bread, and gave thanks, and brake it, and gave it unto them, saying, This is my body which is given for you: this do in remembrance* *of me. Likewise also the cup after supper, saying, This cup is the new testament in my blood, which is shed for you"* (Luke 22:19-20).

T he annual Passover was the most sacred feast of the Jewish religious year. It commemorated the Israelites' deliverance from bondage in Egypt.

When Jesus, the Messiah, gave Himself as the Lamb of God, He fulfilled the true meaning of the Passover. Any observance of the Passover after that time would have been meaningless. (Compare Exodus 12:7; I Corinthians 5:7.)

As the sacrifice of the Passover lamb was necessary for the Israelites to have deliverance from Egyptian bondage, so Christ, *"the Lamb of God,"* was sacrificed to deliver us from the bondage of sin (John 1:29). Through His death, Christ *"redeemed us from the curse of the law"* (Galatians 3:13) and established a new covenant with His redeemed people, saying, *"This cup is the new testament in my blood, which is shed for you."*

This New Testament covenant is the assurance that our Redeemer will return. The redeemed of God look forward to His coming when we will enter into His actual presence.

" . . . he is the mediator of a better covenant, which was established upon better promises" (Hebrews 8:6).

Thought for Today: Have you been to Jesus for His cleansing power? Are you washed in the blood of the Lamb?

Word Studies: 21:4 **penury** means poverty; 21:13 **And it shall turn to you for a testimony** means this will give you an opportunity to tell the Good News; 21:19 **patience** means steadfastness; 21:34 **overcharged with surfeiting** means overcome by self-indulgence; 22:15 **With desire I have desired** means I have looked forward to this hour with intense desire.

Cross References: For Luke 21:27: See Dan. 7:13. **Luke 22:37:** See Isa. 53:12. **Luke 22:69:** See Psa. 110:1.

Prayer Needs: Country: Zaire—32 million—in south-central Africa • Limited religious freedom • 42% Roman Catholic; 28% Protestant; 12% magical practices, ancestor worship, and witchcraft; 1% Muslim.

OCTOBER 31: Read Luke 23 — 24

Highlights: Jesus before Pilate and Herod; His crucifixion and resurrection; ministry of the risen Christ; His commission; His ascension.

Verses for Today: *"And he said unto Jesus, Lord, remember me when thou comest into thy kingdom. And Jesus said unto him, Verily I say unto thee, Today shalt thou be with me in paradise"* (Luke 23:42-43).

B etween the crosses of the two thieves stood the cross of Christ. Although the arrangement may have appeared to be the outcome of Roman hatred, there was a divine purpose behind the wrath of man. Jesus came to identify Himself with sinners; He had lived among them, and it was necessary that He should die among them, thus fulfilling the Scripture, *" . . . he was numbered with the transgressors"* (Isaiah 53:12).

On one cross was a hardened criminal who defied and cursed the Savior. On the other cross was a man who also, at first, blasphemed Christ. Then, in the presence of the angry chief priests, scribes, and a skeptical crowd, he turned to Christ and cried out for mercy, saying, *"Lord, remember me when thou comest into thy kingdom."* There is no reason to doubt that this thief had been a wicked sinner, but he turned to Christ and was saved.

The world today is made up of two kinds of people—those who continue to reject the Lord and those who accept Him as their Savior. For one there is the certainty of eternal damnation; for the other the promise of everlasting life (see Romans 6:23; John 5:24). Like Matthew the publican, Mary Magdalene, and this criminal, God's mercy is sufficient for all.

"For the preaching of the cross is to them that perish foolishness; but unto us which are saved it is the power of God" (I Corinthians 1:18).

Thought for Today: God gives mercy to those who ask.

Word Studies: 23:5 **Jewry** means the Judean land, a region of Palestine; 23:15 **unto him** means by Him; 23:16 **chastise** means whip; 23:19 **sedition** means riot; 23:32 **malefactors** means criminals; 24:13 **threescore furlongs** means about seven miles; 24:27 **expounded** means explained; 24:29 **far spent** means almost over.

Cross References: For **Luke 23:30:** See Hos. 10:8. **Luke 23:34:** See Psa. 22:18. **Luke 23:46:** See Psa. 31:5.

Prayer Needs: Country: Sao Tome and Principe—114,000—two larger and several smaller islands in the Gulf of Guinea, 125 miles off the western coast of Africa • Religious freedom is fairly new • 83% Roman Catholic; 3% Protestant; 2% animist.

PRAYERS TO GOD

Jesus — The Lord's Prayer .... Matt. 6:9-13; Luke 11:2-4
Jesus — of praise .... Matt. 11:25-26; Luke 10:21
Jesus — in Gethsemane .... Matt. 26:39,42;
Mark 14:36; Luke 22:42
Jesus — on the cross .... Matt. 27:46; Mark 15:34
Simeon — of praise upon holding Baby Jesus .... Luke 2:29-32
Pharisee — of self-praise .... Luke 18:11-12
Publican — for God's mercy .... Luke 18:13
Jesus — forgiveness for His enemies .... Luke 23:34
Jesus — last cry from the cross .... Luke 23:46

PRAYERS TO THE LORD WHILE ON EARTH

Leper — for cleansing .... Matt. 8:2; Mark 1:40; Luke 5:12
Centurion — for his servant .... Matt. 8:5-13
Disciples — to be saved
from the storm .... Matt. 8:25; Mark 4:38; Luke 8:24
Jairus — for his daughter .... Matt. 9:18; Mark 5:23
Two blind men — for sight .... Matt. 9:27-28; 20:30-34

JOHN

The Gospel of John introduces Jesus as the preexistent, eternal Word who became a man: *When all things began, the Word already existed; He was with God. In fact, He was God Himself* (see 1:1). Consequently, John does not present Jesus as the descendant of David the king, as Matthew did, or trace His genealogy back to Adam, as Luke did; John portrays Jesus in His deity as the Son of God.

In the Gospel of John, Jesus claims equality with God the Father (see 5:19-29):

1. In working (verse 19)
2. In knowing *"all things"* (verse 20)
3. In receiving honor (verse 23)
4. In regenerating from *"death unto life"* (verses 24-25)
5. In self-existence (verse 26)
6. In judging (verses 22,27)
7. In resurrecting *"whom he will"* (verses 21,28-29).

Christ added, *"Before Abraham was, I am"* (8:58), showing that He is the eternal *"I AM"* as revealed in the Old Testament (Exodus 3:14). This was further clarified when He spoke of *"the glory"* which He had with the Father *"before the world was"* (John 17:5).

The book of John is a Gospel of love (3:16), revealing Christ not only as God, but also as the Bread of life that forever satisfies the hungry soul (6:35, 41,48,51). Jesus not only points the way to God's love; He is *"the way, the truth, and the life"* (14:6).

Christ is *"full of grace and truth"*—full of grace to redeem man, and the source of truth to reveal God (1:14). Furthermore, He is the Light of the world, illuminating the darkness of sin on the earth (8:12); He is the Good Shepherd who cares for His sheep (10:11,14); and He is the resurrection life that conquers death and gives eternal life (11:25-26).

The Gospel of John was written *that you might believe that Jesus is the promised Savior, the Son of God; and that believing in Him you may have eternal life* (see 20:31).

NOVEMBER 1: Read John 1 — 3

Highlights: Deity of Christ; ministry of John the Baptist; Jesus announced as the Lamb of God; first miracle in Cana; cleansing of the Temple; Nicodemus and the new birth; John the Baptist's testimony of Jesus.

Verses for Today: *And as Moses lifted up the serpent in the wilderness, even so must the Son of man be lifted up: that whosoever believeth in him should not perish, but have eternal life"* (John 3:14-15).

D uring Israel's wilderness wanderings, the people complained against God and Moses. Because of their sinful rebellion, the Lord sent poisonous snakes and many Israelites died (Numbers 21:5-6).

When the people confessed their sins, Moses prayed for them. In answer to his prayer, the Lord directed him to make a snake of brass (bronze) and lift it up on a pole. All who would obey the Lord's command to look at the brass snake were healed (Numbers 21:8-9).

The poisonous snakes were a type of the deadly, destructive power of that old serpent, the devil, who tempted Adam and Eve to sin. When they yielded to his suggestion, Adam and Eve not only sinned, but also experienced spiritual death. Because of this, all mankind has inherited a sinful nature (see Romans 5:12).

Just as brass in the Bible is symbolic of judgment, the brass serpent was symbolic of God's judgment on sin. This symbolic judgment was made real when Christ, the sinless Son of God, came to earth *with a nature and body resembling our sinful nature and body* (see Romans 8:3) and was lifted up on the cross to die for the sins of the world. Such drastic judgment was necessary because all mankind has sinned (Romans 3:23; 6:23). But Christ became sin for us so that *we, through union with Him, might have the righteousness of God* (see II Corinthians 5:21).

The bitten Israelites could live only as they trusted in God's provision of the uplifted snake. Likewise, mankind can have eternal life only by obediently trusting in the crucified, risen Christ as personal Savior.

Whoever believes in the Son is not condemned; but whoever does not believe is already under condemnation (see John 3:18).

Thought for Today: Only Jesus can forgive sin and restore us to fellowship with the Father.

Word Studies: 1:1 **the Word** means Jesus Christ; 1:4 **the life** means Christ; **the light of men** means Christ; 1:5 **in darkness** means among the unbelieving world; **and the darkness comprehended it not** means the unbelieving world has not desired to understand Christ or to be receptive to Him; 1:11 **his own** means His own people, the Jews; 1:28 **Betha-bara** means Bethany; 1:47 **guile** means dishonesty; 2:6 **firkin** means a liquid measure of about 10 gallons; 2:15 **scourge** means whip; 3:3 **Verily, verily, I say unto thee** means I most solemnly tell you the truth; 3:20 **reproved** means exposed; 3:25 **purifying** means religious washing.

Cross References: For **John 1:23:** See Isa. 40:3. **John 2:17:** See Psa. 69:9.

Prayer Needs: Country: Burma—39 million—in Southeast Asia • Limited religious freedom • 87% Buddhist; 5% Protestant; 4% Muslim; 3% spirit worship, Hindu, and other Asian religions; 1% Roman Catholic.

NOVEMBER 2: Read John 4 — 5

Highlights: Jesus and the Samaritan woman; miracles of healing; Jesus' answers to the Jews.

Verses for Today: *"Jesus answered and said unto her, Whosoever drinketh of this water shall thirst again: But whosoever drinketh of the water that I shall give him shall never thirst; but the water that I shall give him shall be in him a well of water springing up into everlasting life"* (John 4:13-14).

W eary from His long journey from Judea to Samaria, Christ sat down to rest at Jacob's Well while the disciples went to the village to buy food. While He was there, a woman of Samaria came to draw water from the well. She must have been surprised when Jesus asked her for a drink of water. Ordinarily, a Jew would not even travel through Samaria, much less stop and talk to a Samaritan.

The Samaritan woman reached the turning point in her life when Christ revealed Himself as the fulfillment of her great spiritual need, for she had a thirst that neither her religion nor the world could satisfy. She said to Jesus, *"Sir, give me this water, that I thirst not ... "* (John 4:15).

The person who drinks from the wells of the world will thirst again. But the living presence of the Savior continually satisfies all who repent of their sins and trust in Him as Savior.

There are thirsty souls all around us, looking for satisfaction. As we let Christ's love flow out from us, others will be drawn to His Spirit in us. The real purpose for our existence is for Jesus Christ to live in and through us.

"Blessed are they which do hunger and thirst after righteousness: for they shall be filled" (Matthew 5:6).

Thought for Today: Temporal "satisfactions" may "quench our thirst" momentarily, but they will never truly satisfy.

Word Studies: 4:6 **sixth hour** probably means noon; 5:3 **impotent folk** means invalids; 5:21 **quickeneth them** means gives them life.

Prayer Needs: Country: Djibouti (formerly French Territory of Afars and Issas)— 313,000—in eastern Africa • Limited religious freedom • 91% Muslim; 7% Roman Catholic; .75% Eastern Orthodox; about 300 Protestants.

NOVEMBER 3: Read John 6 — 8

Highlights: Feeding 5,000; Jesus walking on the sea; Jesus, the Bread of life; Jesus at the Feast of Tabernacles; Jesus forgives an adulteress; Jesus, the Light of the world; Abraham's true descendants.

Verse for Today: *" ... I am the light of the world: he that followeth me shall not walk in darkness, but shall have the light of life"* (John 8:12).

T he unbelieving world has chosen the darkness of sin because *"the god of this world hath blinded the minds of them which believe not ... "* (II Corinthians

4:4). But all who have accepted Christ as Savior have passed from spiritual death to life. No longer do they love the *"darkness,"* but they desire the *"light"*—instruction and insight on the Scriptures. To Christians, the Word of God is *"a lamp unto [their] feet, and a light unto [their] path"* (Psalm 119:105).

Merely knowing that Christ is the Light of the world, or just believing that the Bible is the inspired Word of God, does not give enlightenment. The Christian receives light by reading the Bible, praying, and allowing the Holy Spirit to guide his life (see John 16:13).

We may read a Bible verse many times and not see its full meaning. Then, on the next reading, we may receive new light that will enrich our lives.

And the key to receiving more light on the Scriptures is to live according to what light the Holy Spirit has already given us.

"If we say that we have fellowship with him, and walk in darkness, we lie, and do not the truth: but if we walk in the light, as he is in the light, we have fellowship one with another, and the blood of Jesus Christ his Son cleanseth us from all sin" (I John 1:6-7).

Thought for Today: To know what is right and not live accordingly is sin.

Word Studies: 6:46 **save he** means except Jesus; 6:52 **strove** means had an angry dispute; argued; 7:1 **Jewry** means Judea, a region of Palestine; 8:34 **the servant** means a slave; 8:58 **Before Abraham was, I am** means I was in existence before Abraham was born.

Cross References: For **John 6:31:** See Psa. 78:24. **John 6:45:** See Isa. 54:13.

Prayer Needs: Country: East Germany—17 million—in north-central Europe • 55% Protestant; 8% Roman Catholic.

NOVEMBER 4: Read John 9 — 10

Highlights: Healing of the man born blind; Jesus, the Good Shepherd; the Jews' unbelief.

Verse for Today: *"I am the good shepherd: the good shepherd giveth his life for the sheep"* (John 10:11).

Our Lord, the Great Shepherd of the sheep, is also *"the Lamb of God"* who gave His life for His sheep—for everyone who would accept Him as Savior (see John 1:29; Hebrews 13:20).

Christ did not give His life as a martyr for the truth or as a moral example of self-sacrifice; He died so that we might receive a new nature. Our Lord compared this new nature to the nature of a lamb.

Sheep are gentle. Christians also are to be *gentle, easy to get along with, submissive, and kind* (see James 3:17).

Lambs are harmless; they do not bite, fight, or kill. Even children can approach a lamb without fear of being attacked or bitten. Likewise, Christians are warned of satanic opposition that is likened to wolves that attack sheep; yet, we are to be *"harmless as doves"* (Matthew 10:16).

Even old sheep are known for their tendency to wander. When they are placed in a fenced pasture, they often find openings and get out—each one following the other with no thought to where they are going.

Isaiah declared that we, like sheep, have gone astray (Isaiah 53:6), having a tendency to follow the crowd or go our own way instead of following the Lord's way. But if we are to enjoy the "good pasture," we must follow the Good Shepherd and read His Word daily with a desire to be in His will.

Jesus said, *"My sheep hear my voice, and I know them, and they follow me"* (John 10:27).

Thought for Today: Christians, like sheep, need to stay close to the Shepherd in order to be protected from the dangers of the world.

Word Study: 9:28 **reviled** means verbally abused.

Cross Reference: For **John 10: 34:** See Psa. 82:6.

Prayer Needs: Country: French Polynesia—186,000—in the south-central Pacific • Religious freedom, but Christianity opposed because of animistic beliefs • 45% Protestant; 39% Roman Catholic; 8% cults.

NOVEMBER 5: Read John 11 — 12

Highlights: Raising of Lazarus; the Pharisees' plot to kill Jesus; Mary's anointing of Jesus' feet; triumphal entry; Jesus' answer to the Greeks.

Verses for Today: *"Jesus said unto her, I am the resurrection, and the life: he that believeth in me, though he were dead, yet shall he live: and whosoever liveth and believeth in me shall never die . . . "* (John 11:25-26).

L azarus had been dead four days. When Jesus told the people to take away the stone that sealed the tomb, Lazarus' sister Martha objected, believing that his body would already be decaying in the grave. But when Christ said, *Lazarus, come out!* (see John 11:43), Lazarus heard the Lord's voice and obeyed.

Physical death illustrates the condition of all who have not accepted Christ as Savior. They are *spiritually dead because of disobedience and sin* (see Ephesians 2:1)—just as separated from God as Lazarus was separated from his loved ones here on earth.

It is only through Christ that we can have eternal life, for He conquered death through His own resurrection. Because of this, every Christian has within him the indwelling resurrection life of Christ—a power over which Satan is unable to prevail.

The day will come when *"all that are in the graves shall hear his voice, and shall come forth . . . "* The Christian will come forth to eternal life and the unsaved to eternal damnation (see John 5:24-29). Both saint and sinner need to understand clearly that life is *not* over with death!

"Verily, verily, I say unto you, He that heareth my word, and believeth on him that sent me, hath everlasting life, and shall not come into condemnation; but is passed from death unto life" (John 5:24).

Thought for Today: We should live in such a way that others can see Christ living in us.

Word Studies: 11:47 **What do we?** means what shall we do now?; 12:6 **bare what was put therein** means stole what was put in the treasury box he carried; 12:7 **against the day** means for the day.

Cross References: For **John 12:13:** See Psa. 118:26. **John 12:15:** See Zech. 9:9. **John 12:38:** See Isa. 53:1. **John 12:40:** See Isa. 6:9-10.

Prayer Needs: Country: Faeroe Islands—47,000—a group of islands in the Atlantic Ocean, north of Scotland • Religious freedom • 99% Protestant; .1% Roman Catholic.

NOVEMBER 6: Read John 13 — 16

Highlights: Jesus washes the disciples' feet; Jesus foretells His betrayal; commandment of love; Peter's denial foretold; Jesus foretells His death and second coming; Holy Spirit promised.

Verses for Today: *"And when he is come, he will reprove the world of sin, and of righteousness, and of judgment. . . . he will guide you into all truth . . . "* (John 16:8,13).

B efore Jesus returned to the Father, He promised to send the Holy Spirit to be a Comforter and Counselor—the One called alongside to help. Jesus promised, *"I will send him"* (see John 14:16-18; 15:26; 16:7-11).

No matter what the circumstances, the Holy Spirit is able to impart peace to the hearts of Christians. He comforts those who are sick, those who have lost loved ones, and those who are experiencing trials.

Furthermore, the Holy Spirit makes our prayers effective, *" . . . for we know not what we should pray for as we ought: but the Spirit itself maketh intercession for us . . . "* (Romans 8:26).

Most important, the indwelling Holy Spirit imparts spiritual insight into the Word of God, guiding Christians *"into all truth."* But the Holy Spirit can only guide us into all truth as we read all His truth—the Bible.

As we read the Bible, the Holy Spirit causes us to see the dangers of *"sin . . . and of judgment"* and brings conviction to our hearts. As we yield to His leading, He continues to work in our hearts the things that are pleasing to the Lord.

"Grieve not the holy Spirit of God, whereby ye are sealed unto the day of redemption" (Ephesians 4:30).

Thought for Today: Oh, how much we need to become more aware of the ministry of the Holy Spirit!

Word Studies: 13:30 **sop** means piece of bread; 14:8 **sufficeth** means will satisfy; 15:2 **purgeth** means prunes; 15:22 **cloak** means excuse; 16:7 **expedient** means to your advantage.

Cross References: For John 13:18: See Psa. 41:9. **John 15:25:** See Psa. 35:19; 69:4.

Prayer Needs: Country: Gabon—1 million—in west-central Africa • Religious freedom • 66% Roman Catholic; 30% Protestant; 3% animism and ancestor worship.

NOVEMBER 7: Read John 17 — 18

Highlights: Jesus' prayer of intercession; His betrayal and arrest; Peter's denial; Jesus condemned and Barabbas released.

Verse for Today: *" . . . Holy Father, keep through thine own name those whom thou hast given me, that they may be one, as we are"* (John 17:11).

O ur relationship with Christ unites us with all Christians. While we wait for our Lord's return, let us daily pray the Master's prayer—that we may be one.

284

Beginning with ourselves, let us determine that His prayer will be answered in our attitude toward other believers. A spirit of unity should be evident in our own homes and with those we enjoy being with, as well as with those who may not believe or worship Christ exactly as we do.

God sometimes brings people into our lives who are difficult to love—those who try our patience or are unkind to us—in order that we might have an opportunity to express His love to them. We are to respond to these "difficult" people with an attitude of gentleness, patience, and humility (Ephesians 4:2).

As the love of Christ controls us, we are enabled to serve one another, to share one another's burdens, and to love the unlovely. And perhaps when they see our Christlike love, they will desire to be more loving.

How wonderful and pleasant it is for God's people to live together in harmony! (see Psalm 133:1).

Thought for Today: We receive the joy of the Lord as we share His love with others.

Word Studies: 17:15 **the evil** means Satan, the evil one; 18:1 **the brook Cedron** means the Kidron Valley; 18:2 **resorted thither** means met there; 18:30 **a malefactor** means a criminal.

Prayer Needs: Country: Zambia—7 million—in south-central Africa • Religious freedom • 30% Roman Catholic; 25% Protestant; 24% ancestor worship, magic, and witchcraft; 19% cults.

NOVEMBER 8: Read John 19 — 21

Highlights: Christ's crucifixion, burial, and resurrection; His appearance to His disciples; Peter's allegiance to Christ reaffirmed.

Verse for Today: *"Then said Jesus to them . . . as my Father hath sent me, even so send I you"* (John 20:21).

J esus linked His disciples with Himself in His great mission when He said, *"As my Father hath sent me, even so send I you."*

The supreme purpose for Christ's coming into the world was *"that the world through him might be saved"* (John 3:17). This was also the message of Luke, who wrote that Christ came into the world *"to seek and to save that which was lost"* (Luke 19:10). In Mark, Jesus said that he came to call *"sinners to repentance"* (Mark 2:17). In Matthew, the angels said that Jesus would *"save his people from their sins"* (Matthew 1:21).

Christ depends on and works through us—His disciples—to communicate the message of His redeeming love. His words *"even so send I you"* proclaim that Christians are not to expect the unsaved to go out looking for someone to tell them how to be saved; Christians are to go to them. It is our responsibility to tell others of His salvation.

"Ye have not chosen me, but I have chosen you, and ordained you, that ye should go and bring forth fruit, and that your fruit should remain . . . " (John 15:16).

Thought for Today: Every Christian has a personal "world" to which he is responsible for showing and telling of God's saving power.

Word Studies: 19:29 **hyssop** means a hyssop branch; 19:41 **sepulcher** means tomb;

20:14 **she turned herself back** means she turned around; 21:7 **girt** means put on.

Cross References: For **John 19:24:** See Psa. 22:18. **John 19:36:** See Ex. 12:46; Psa. 34:20. **John 19:37:** See Zech. 12:10.

Prayer Needs: Country: Virgin Islands—125,000—a group of 89 islands in the West Indies, east of Puerto Rico • Religious freedom • 43% Protestant; 22% Roman Catholic.

ACTS

The book of Acts is a continuation of the Gospel of Luke and covers about 30 years—from the ascension of Christ to the imprisonment of Paul in Rome.

Luke, the author, was known as the *"beloved physician"* (Colossians 4:14) and was a companion of the Apostle Paul.

Acts records the disciples' obedience in staying in Jerusalem to wait for the fulfillment of the Father's promise—the Holy Spirit (Acts 1:4)—and in being His witnesses to the farthest part of the earth (1:8).

The Holy Spirit, who is the mighty spiritual power within the believer, is mentioned or referred to more than 30 times as filling, guiding, and sustaining the Christian. There are also more than 30 references to "the Word" in relation to Christians and their witnessing. Jesus, as the Living Word, is prominent throughout the book of Acts. (See 2:41; 4:4,29,31; 6:2,4,7; 8:4, 14,25; 10:36-37,44; 11:1,16; 12:24; 13:7,44,46,48-49; 14:3,25; 15:7,35-36; 16:6,32; 17:11,13; 18:11; 19:10,20; 20:32.)

The first 12 chapters focus on the Apostle Peter and the church in Jerusalem. Beginning with the death of Stephen, there was intense persecution against Christianity. Saul of Tarsus was one of the leaders of this persecution. But after he was converted, he dedicated his life to worldwide evangelism and became known as the Apostle Paul. Paul made his headquarters in Antioch, a Gentile city which became the center of world evangelism. It was in Antioch that Christ's followers were first called Christians (11:26).

The events of Paul's three missionary journeys are described in Acts 13 through 21:19.

The principles of church growth and true Christian success as revealed in the book of Acts still apply today.

NOVEMBER 9: Read Acts 1 — 3

Highlights: Ascension of Christ; promise of the Lord's return; Matthias chosen to replace Judas; coming of the Holy Spirit at Pentecost; Peter's sermon; unity of the believers; healing of a lame man at the Temple gate.

Verse for Today: *"And it shall come to pass, that whosoever shall call on the name of the Lord shall be saved"* (Acts 2:21).

J ust before He was taken up into Heaven, the Lord emphasized the responsibility of every Christian to carry the gospel *"unto the uttermost part of the earth"*

(Acts 1:8). The early Christians knew that all hope for eternal life rested in Christ alone, and they worked together to make this truth known to the rest of the world.

Godly men were appointed to take care of the people's physical needs so the spiritual leaders could give themselves *"continually to prayer, and to the ministry of the word"* (Acts 6:4).

Christ has given every Christian a personal responsibility to be a witness for Him: "Ye shall be witnesses unto me." And the early Christians set the example: *"Daily in the temple, and in every house, they ceased not to teach and preach Jesus Christ"* (Acts 5:42).

The Christian's faith and hope rest in Christ and His Word. And if we love the Lord, we will accept our responsibility to be *"doers of the word, and not hearers only"* (James 1:22).

" . . . ye shall be witnesses unto me . . . unto the uttermost part of the earth" (Acts 1:8).

Thought for Today: Everyone can do something to help others come to know the Lord.

Word Studies: 1:1 **former treatise** means the book of Luke; 1:12 **a sabbath day's journey** means a little over one-half mile; 2:23 **determinate counsel** means God's own plan; 2:27 **wilt not leave my soul in hell** means will not abandon My soul to the place of death; 2:40 **untoward** means wicked; 3:17 **wot** means know.

Cross References: For Acts **1:20:** See Psa. 69:25; 109:8. **Acts 2:17-21:** See Joel 2:28-32. **Acts 2:25-28:** See Psa. 16:8-11. **Acts 2:34-35:** See Psa. 110:1. **Acts 3:22-23:** See Deut. 18:18-19. **Acts 3:25:** See Gen. 12:3; 22:18.

Prayer Needs: **Country:** Venezuela—18 million—on the northern coast of South America • Religious freedom • 94% Roman Catholic; 1% Protestant; 1% Indian pagan religions.

NOVEMBER 10: Read Acts 4 — 6

Highlights: Peter and John imprisoned; believers share their possessions; Ananias and Sapphira; persecution of the Apostles; Gamaliel's advice; seven helpers chosen; Stephen's arrest.

Verse for Today: *"And now, Lord, behold their threatenings: and grant unto thy servants, that with all boldness they may speak thy word"* (Acts 4:29).

P eter and John had been ordinary fishermen, committed to taking the Good News of salvation to others. As they witnessed about their faith in Christ, many people were saved!

When the officials in Jerusalem commanded Peter and John to stop preaching about Jesus, they did not ask God to punish their persecutors; neither did they stop witnessing (Acts 4:17-20). Instead, they met with other Christians and joined together in prayer for courage and opportunities to continue proclaiming God's Word (4:24,29).

As you continue your journey through the book of Acts, you'll find that other prayers were also answered. This should give encouragement to every Christian that God hears and answers *our* prayers.

When we are faced with problems, we often do everything but pray. How often we limit God's ability to answer prayer because we depend on our own efforts instead of turning to Him in prayer!

We are to pray about all things, thanking God for everything He brings into our lives; for this is the will of God in Christ Jesus concerning us (see I Thessalonians 5:17-18).

Thought for Today: Nothing is impossible when you put your trust in God.

Word Studies: 4:3 **hold** means jail; prison; 4:17 **straitly threaten** means sternly warn; 5:2 **being privy to it** means helped plan the deception; 5:6 **wound him up** means wrapped up his corpse for burial; 5:12 **wrought** means performed; 5:13 **durst** means dared; 5:16 **vexed** means afflicted; 5:17 **indignation** means jealousy; 5:30 **slew and hanged on a tree** means put to death by nailing Him to a cross; 6:11 **suborned** means bribed; persuaded; influenced.

Cross References: For **Acts 4:11:** See Psa. 118:22. **Acts 4:25-26:** See Psa. 2:1-2.

Prayer Needs: **Country:** United Arab Emirates—2 million—on the eastern Arabian Peninsula • Pressure and hostility against Christians are increasing • 95% Muslim; 4% Christian.

NOVEMBER 11: Read Acts 7 — 8

Highlights: Stephen's speech; his martyrdom; Saul's persecution of Christians; the gospel preached in Samaria; Simon, the sorcerer; Philip and the Ethiopian.

Verse for Today: *"And Saul was consenting unto his [Stephen's] death. And at that time there was a great persecution against the church which was at Jerusalem; and they were all scattered abroad throughout the regions of Judea and Samaria, except the apostles"* (Acts 8:1).

T he stoning of Stephen marked the beginning of *"great persecution against the church,"* and Christians were *"scattered abroad."* But rather than defeating the churches, it resulted in the first missionary movement.

Philip, one of the seven deacons in Jerusalem, traveled a short distance north to Samaria, where many people believed and were baptized as a result of his preaching (Acts 8:12). What had at first seemed a disaster to the early Christians turned out to be a fulfillment of the Lord's words, *"Ye shall be witnesses unto me ... in Samaria, and unto the uttermost part of the earth"* (Acts 1:8).

To see only Satan in all our misfortunes and suffering is a serious mistake. God often uses persecution and difficulty to bring about the fulfillment of His will.

God is in control. Even though at times Satan deceives us or it appears that someone has kept us from God's best, if we look beyond our circumstances we will see that *"all things work together for good to them that love God"* (Romans 8:28).

"For our light affliction, which is but for a moment, worketh for us a far more exceeding and eternal weight of glory" (II Corinthians 4:17).

Thought for Today: You can never know God's peace until you have encountered some of life's storms.

Word Studies: 7:6 **sojourn** means dwell temporarily (as aliens); 7:11 **dearth** means famine; 7:19 **subtilly** means treacherously; **fathers** means forefathers; **cast out their young children, to the end they might not live** means forced them to expose where they were hiding the babies so they could be put to death; 7:20 **exceeding fair** means very special to God; 7:38 **lively oracles** means living words; 7:45 **Jesus** means Joshua;

7:54 **gnashed on him** means ground their teeth at him in rage; 8:2 **lamentation** means great weeping and loud mourning; 8:3 **haling** means dragging off; 8:9 **used sorcery ... great one** means used mysterious religious practices to lead people to believe he had supernatural powers.

Cross References: For Acts 7:3: See Gen. 12:1. **Acts 7:27-28:** See Ex. 2:14. **Acts 7:32:** See Ex. 3:6. **Acts 7:33-34:** See Ex. 3:5,7-8,10. **Acts 7:37:** See Deut. 18:15. **Acts 7:40:** See Ex. 32:1. **Acts 7:42-43:** See Amos 5:25-27. **Acts 7:49-50:** See Isa. 66:1-2. **Acts 8:32-33:** See Isa. 53:7-8.

Prayer Needs: Country: Sri Lanka (formerly Ceylon)—17 million—an island in the Indian Ocean off the southeastern tip of India • Religious freedom officially, but Buddhism is actively promoted by the government • 67% Buddhist; 15% Hindu; 8% Roman Catholic; 7% Muslim; .75% Protestant.

NOVEMBER 12: Read Acts 9 — 10

Highlights: Conversion of Saul; Dorcas raised from the dead; visions of Peter and Cornelius; Gentiles receive the Holy Spirit.

Verse for Today: *"And he trembling and astonished said, Lord, what wilt thou have me to do? And the Lord said unto him, Arise, and go into the city, and it shall be told thee what thou must do"* (Acts 9:6).

S aul of Tarsus was born a Roman citizen (Acts 16:37-38; 22:25-29) and received his theological training under one of the greatest rabbinical teachers of the first century—Gamaliel (22:3). In addition, Saul had great influence among both Jewish and Roman authorities of his day. Because of all this, it is assumed that he was a man of great wealth.

From the time of his conversion, Saul was convinced that the whole world must hear that Jesus was the Christ, the Messiah-Savior. Saul later became known as the Apostle Paul—the apostle who wrote, *"I have suffered the loss of all things, and do count them but dung ... that I may know him, and the power of his resurrection"* (Philippians 3:8,10).

Paul had a steadfast determination to do the will of his Lord—whatever the cost.

Many Christians would like to be greatly used by God, even as Paul was, but few are willing to pay the price—to deny themselves and take up the cross and follow Jesus (Luke 9:23).

Each of us must decide whether we will live to please self or surrender our self-achievements, self-pleasures, and material goals to do God's will.

As we yield ourselves to the Lord and His Word, Christ will live His life through us. This is the secret to having the power to live a victorious Christian life.

" ... be thou faithful unto death, and I will give thee a crown of life" (Revelation 2:10).

Thought for Today: When our desires are in accordance with God's Word, we can be sure of gaining His best.

Word Studies: 9:26 **assayed to join** means tried to associate himself with; 9:43 **tanner** means one who makes leather from animal hides; 10:1 **centurion** means captain; **band** means army unit; 10:3 **evidently** means visibly; distinctly; 10:11 **knit at** means suspended by; 10:14 **common** means unholy; 10:29 **without gainsaying**

means promptly; without hesitation; 10:43 **remission** means forgiveness; deliverance; 10:46 **magnify** means praising.

Prayer Needs: Country: Singapore—3 million—in Southeast Asia • Religious freedom • 54% Chinese religions; 17% Muslim; 5% Protestant; 4% Roman Catholic.

NOVEMBER 13: Read Acts 11 — 13

Highlights: Peter's report to the church at Jerusalem; death of James; Peter's imprisonment and deliverance; death of Herod; Paul's first missionary journey.

Verses for Today: *"As they ministered to the Lord, and fasted, the Holy Ghost said, Separate me Barnabas and Saul for the work whereunto I have called them. . . . they came to Perga in Pamphylia: and John departing from them returned to Jerusalem"* (Acts 13:2,13).

Paul and Barnabas had chosen John Mark as their "minister"—meaning their helper (Acts 13:5). Perhaps he worked—as Epaphroditus did (Philippians 2:25-30)—to help earn their support so Paul and Barnabas could devote themselves more fully to preaching the Word of God in countries where the people had never heard that Jesus died for their sins.

But John Mark *"departed from them from Pamphylia, and went not with them to the work"* (Acts 15:38). He quit and returned home before the missionary journey was completed.

Still today, God calls helpers to every ministry. It is often necessary for them to work long, hard hours, usually without receiving recognition for their labors. Others are called to support missionary ministries (Romans 12:6-8). Their part in the ministry is just as important as the work of those who are called to be spiritual leaders.

Like young John Mark, many people give up and go back to an easier way of life. Perhaps they are unwilling to deny themselves of personal comforts, not realizing they are cheating themselves of spiritual achievements and God's best blessings. But don't give up on quitters—they may change, as John Mark did. Paul later said, *He can be a help to me in the ministry* (see II Timothy 4:11).

Even Jesus did not come to earth to be waited on, but to minister to others and to give His life for them (see Mark 10:45).

Thought for Today: Every Christian can be a helper in ministering the Word of God to others.

Word Studies: 12:4 **four quaternions** means four squads of four soldiers each; **Easter** means Passover; 12:15 **mad** means insane; out of your mind; 12:21 **an oration** means a speech; 13:17 **a high arm** means wondrous power; 13:18 **suffered** means patiently endured; 13:43 **proselytes** means Gentile converts to Judaism.

Cross References: For Acts 13:22: See Psa. 89:20. **Acts 13:33:** See Psa. 2:7. **Acts 13:34:** See Isa. 55:3. **Acts 13:35:** See Psa. 16:10. **Acts 13:41:** See Hab. 1:5. **Acts 13:47:** See Isa. 49:6.

Prayer Needs: Country: Russia (Soviet Union)—284 million—in northern Eurasia • Repression of unofficial churches and rigid control of registered denominations • 32% Eastern Orthodox; 11% Muslim; 2% Protestant; 2% Roman Catholic; 1% Jewish.

NOVEMBER 14: Read Acts 14 — 16

Highlights: Paul and Barnabas at Iconium; the stoning of Paul at Lystra; his return to Antioch; Paul's second missionary journey with Silas; Paul's Macedonian vision; conversion of Lydia; conversion of the Philippian jailer.

Verses for Today: *"Now when they had gone throughout Phrygia and the region of Galatia, and were forbidden of the Holy Ghost to preach the word in Asia, after they were come to Mysia, they assayed to go into Bithynia: but the Spirit suffered them not"* (Acts 16:6-7).

T he Apostle Paul had planned to preach in the great cities of Asia Minor—now part of western Turkey—but the Spirit of God prevented him from carrying out his plans.

Paul could have become discouraged, but he recognized that the "forbidding" was done by the Lord, who was instructing and guiding him. (See Acts 8:29; 10:19-20; 11:12; 13:2,4.)

When *our* well-laid plans are shattered, there is a tendency to blame people or circumstances for the hindrances and disappointments, when actually it is God's way of redirecting our lives in order to accomplish His will.

God often works through ordinary, everyday circumstances to reveal what He wants us to do. But it is always in harmony with His Word. Furthermore, His indwelling Holy Spirit will confer His peace upon all who wait on Him. Whatever spiritual understanding we may receive is made possible by the Holy Spirit. (See I Corinthians 2:9-14; Ephesians 1:17; I John 2:20.) Further direction from God is dependent upon our yielding to the direction He has already given.

We have the assurance from Christ that He, the Spirit of truth, will guide us into all truth (see John 16:13).

Thought for Today: Failure to be guided into all truth is the result of not reading all the truth.

Word Studies: 14:2 **made their minds evil affected against** means turned them against; 14:6 **were ware of it** means learned about it; 15:2 **dissension and disputation** means serious disagreement and debate; 15:10 **yoke** means burden; 15:24 **subverting your souls** means causing you to doubt or be confused; 15:30 **epistle** means letter; 15:32 **confirmed** means strengthened; 16:7 **assayed** means attempted; 16:13 **wont** means supposed; 16:35 **sergeants** means officers; 16:37 **privily** means secretly.

Cross Reference: For **Acts 15:16-17:** See Amos 9:11-12.

Prayer Needs: Country: Peru—21 million—on the western coast of South America • Increased restrictions imposed against evangelism and conversion to Christ • 89% Roman Catholic; 4% Protestant.

NOVEMBER 15: Read Acts 17 — 19

Highlights: Jewish opposition; Paul and Silas in Berea; Paul's sermon from Mars' Hill; Paul at Corinth; Priscilla and Aquila; beginning of Paul's third missionary journey; Paul at Ephesus; uproar of the silversmiths.

Verses for Today: *"After these things Paul departed from Athens, and came to Corinth; and found a certain Jew named Aquila . . . with his wife Priscilla. . . . And* *because he was of the same craft, he abode with them, and wrought: for by their occupation they were tentmakers"* (Acts 18:1-3).

Although Aquila and Priscilla faced unjust humiliation when they were forced to leave Rome because of their Jewish nationality, God was directing their lives. They moved to Corinth, where they established their business. Soon they met the Apostle Paul, who had moved to Corinth after his discouraging meetings in Athens. Through their fellowship with him, they became dedicated Christians.

After some time, Priscilla and Aquila gave up their business in Corinth to assist Paul in his journeys (Acts 18:18). Later they returned to Rome, where they *"laid down their own necks"*—ready to risk all for Christ—when they opened their house as a place of worship in a hostile country (Romans 16:3-4). .

The ministry of the early Church was effective because of ordinary Christians, like Priscilla and Aquila, who believed that world evangelism was the most important thing in life. They were willing to serve in any capacity to help those who had been called to preach and teach His Word.

Priscilla and Aquila could have become resentful when they were forced to leave home. But instead, through trusting God during their bitter disappointments, they received a deeper revelation of His love. Having passed that test, they could have allowed financial security in Corinth to keep them from full-time service for Christ; but their hearts were set on eternal values.

God always arranges circumstances in our lives—not only to test the sincerity of our calling, but also to make us more effective in His service.

"For we are laborers together with God" (I Corinthians 3:9).

Thought for Today: In our flesh, we may not always agree with God's way of accomplishing His will through us, but we will find peace as we submit to His will.

Word Studies: 17:3 **alleging** means giving evidence by quoting Scriptures; 17:4 **consorted** means joined; 17:5 **lewd** means evil; 17:19 **Areopagus** is the name of the court or council which met on Mars' Hill; 19:9 **divers** means some; 19:13 **exorcists** means Jews who claimed they could drive out evil spirits; 19:19 **used curious arts** means practiced magic; 19:27 **be set at nought** means lose its reputation; 19:31 **adventure himself** means risk his life by entering; 19:35 **appeased** means quieted; 19:37 **robbers of churches** means destroyers of temples; 19:38 **implead** means bring charges against.

Prayer Needs: Country: Oman—1 million—on the southeastern coast of Arabia • Fewer restrictions on Christian activity than most of its neighbors • 97% Muslim; .5% Christian.

NOVEMBER 16: Read Acts 20 — 22

Highlights: Paul visits Macedonia and Greece; raising of Eutychus from death; Paul's message to the Ephesian elders; Paul seized in the Temple at Jerusalem; Paul's personal testimony.

Verses for Today: *" . . . and the people ran together: and they took Paul, and . . . went about to kill him . . . "* (Acts 21:30-31).

Immediately after he arrived in Jerusalem, the Apostle Paul faced serious opposition. His enemies created a riot that resulted in his being brutally beaten by an angry mob.

Throughout Paul's Christian life, he was persecuted, mobbed, and opposed. He was cruelly beaten many times; once, he was stoned and left for dead.

Many Christians turned against him. In fact, at one time in his ministry, Paul said, *"No man stood with me, but all men forsook me"* (II Timothy 4:16). But an even more crushing blow was to hear that some Christians, who had received spiritual insight on the Scriptures under his teaching, were questioning his integrity and his calling of God. (See II Corinthians 10:10; 11:6,23,31; 12:12; 13:3,6.)

Paul faced what seemed to be impossible problems, but he knew he was in the will of God. He was willing to serve the Lord—regardless of the loneliness, sorrow, disappointments, suffering, and humiliation he had to face.

Paul took seriously the Lord's words, *"If any man will come after me, let him deny himself, and take up his cross daily, and follow me"* (Luke 9:23).

Bearing a cross does not necessarily mean being a martyr. The cross that Jesus meant was one of daily denying ourselves of pleasures, privileges, and even necessities in order to help others come to know Him—choosing to do His will at any cost.

"For even hereunto were ye called: because Christ also suffered for us, leaving us an example, that ye should follow his steps" (I Peter 2:21).

Thought for Today: Our willingness to die daily to self-interests will determine how much we really want to follow in the Master's footsteps.

Word Studies: 20:2 **exhortation** means encouraging words; 20:3 **abode** means stayed; 20:37 **wept sore** means cried very much; 21:3 **unlade her burdens** means unload its cargo; 21:11 **girdle** means belt; 21:15 **took up our carriages** means packed our baggage; 21:39 **no mean city** means a very important city; 22:24 **scourging** means whipping.

Prayer Needs: Country: Norway—4 million—in northern Europe • Religious freedom • 95% Protestant; .4% Roman Catholic.

NOVEMBER 17: Read Acts 23 — 25

Highlights: Paul before the religious rulers; Jews vow to kill Paul; Paul sent to Felix; Paul before Festus; his appeal to Caesar.

Verse for Today: *"But this I confess unto thee, that after the way which they call heresy, so worship I the God of my fathers, believing all things which are written in the law and in the prophets"* (Acts 24:14).

P aul was tried before three great rulers. As he faithfully testified how Jesus fulfilled all the Scriptures as Messiah, each of his judges had a different reaction: Felix the governor trembled; Festus seemed unconcerned; and, for whatever the king may have meant, Agrippa said, "You almost persuade me to become a Christian" (see Acts 26:28). But as far as we know, none of them received Christ as their Lord and Savior. Little did they realize that it was not Paul who was on trial, but they themselves were on trial before the court of Heaven because they were rejecting the Savior.

It has often been said that it doesn't make any difference what a person believes as long as he is sincere. But what a deception this statement is, for our eternal destiny depends upon what we believe! God has provided only one way for salvation, and that is through the death of His Son on the cross of Calvary: *"Neither is there salvation in any other . . . "* (Acts 4:12).

The wrath of God remains on all who refuse to believe that Christ died for their sins (John 3:36). What a person believes has tremendous eternal significance. Each person must decide either to receive Christ as Lord and Savior or to reject Him and be eternally lost. The King of kings cannot be ignored.

"Jesus saith unto him, I am the way, the truth, and the life: no man cometh unto the Father, but by me" (John 14:6).

Thought for Today: Christ gave His all for us; let's allow Him to live His life through us.

Word Studies: 23:3 **whited wall** means hypocrite; 24:2 **Seeing . . . by thy providence** means because of your wise judgment, wrongs are corrected and this nation enjoys improved living conditions; 24:4 **clemency** means accustomed fairness; 24:18 **tumult** means riot; disorderly disturbance; 24:26 **communed** means talked things over; 25:16 **license** means opportunity.

Cross Reference: For Acts 23:5: See Ex. 22:28.

Prayer Needs: Country: Monaco—29,000—in southeastern France • No open evangelism permitted • 90% Roman Catholic; 7% Protestant; 1% Eastern Orthodox.

NOVEMBER 18: Read Acts 26 — 28

Highlights: Paul's defense before King Agrippa; his voyage to Rome; storm at sea; shipwreck at Melita (Malta); Paul at Rome.

Verses for Today: *" . . . Festus said with a loud voice, Paul, thou art beside thyself; much learning doth make thee mad. . . . Then Agrippa said unto Paul, Almost thou persuadest me to be a Christian"* (Acts 26:24,28).

W hen Saul (Paul) of Tarsus was threatening believers and having them arrested, his friends thought he was wise. But when he confessed his faith in Jesus— the risen Savior—Festus, the Roman governor of Judea, told him he had lost his mind.

Paul's two famous, powerful listeners, Festus and King Agrippa, refused Paul's message but, in reality, they were refusing the Word of Almighty God.

Regardless who Paul was speaking to, he faithfully witnessed for Christ, confirming that Jesus was the Messiah who had died to save sinners.

When King Agrippa heard Paul's message, he was not persuaded to become a Christian, but he could not deny anything Paul had said. His heart was touched and his mind enlightened; but he put off accepting Jesus as Savior and Lord.

Whether or not King Agrippa's words were spoken sarcastically, as some people think, is not important; the outcome was still the same—he rejected Christ.

Like King Agrippa and Felix, the former governor to whom Paul was first taken (Acts 23:24—24:27), countless thousands of people have been "almost" persuaded to accept Christ as their Savior; but they waited for "a more convenient time" to turn from their sins. Oh, how many have gone to a Christless eternity because they "almost" accepted Christ as Savior, but they waited until it was too late!

" . . . behold, now is the accepted time; behold, now is the day of salvation" (II Corinthians 6:2).

Thought for Today: There is no guarantee that you can accept Christ tomorrow—or that you will even have a tomorrow.

Word Studies: 26:7 **instantly** means earnestly; 27:10 **lading** means cargo; something carried; freight; 27:30 **under color** means pretending; 27:40 **hoised** means hoisted; raised; 28:1 **they** means we; 28:13 **fetched a compass** means made a circuit, following the coast; 28:16 **suffered** means permitted; 28:27 **be converted** means turn to God.

Cross Reference: For **Acts 28:26-27:** See Isa. 6:9-10.

Prayer Needs: Country: Malaysia—16 million—in Southeast Asia • All Christian witness to Muslims is illegal • 49% Muslim;39% Hindu, Buddhist, and Chinese religions; 4% Roman Catholic; 4% animism, magic, and some headhunting; 3% Protestant.

ROMANS _____

The theme of Romans can be summed up in one verse: *" . . . the gospel . . . is the power of God unto salvation to every one that believeth . . . "* (1:16).

Salvation is progressively explained, chapter by chapter. The first three chapters establish the truth that all mankind has sinned—that not one person is without sin (see 3:9-10). Even after a person has made every possible effort to earn salvation, the Word of God still says, *No one can be made right in God's sight by merely doing what the Law requires* (see 3:20).

A righteous God provided a way for any person to be forgiven of all his sins—a plan that was fulfilled through the sacrificial death and resurrection of Jesus, the perfect Son of God. But to be saved, a person must believe what the Word of God says and personally receive Jesus Christ as Lord and Savior. Then His indwelling Holy Spirit enables the Christian to know and live according to the will of God.

A proper attitude of gratitude will lead a Christian to be transformed inwardly (12:1-2), to be kind and helpful to weaker Christians (chapter 14), and to make every effort to maintain harmony with a Christlike spirit (15:1-13).

NOVEMBER 19: Read Romans 1 — 3

Highlights: Paul's desire to visit the Christians in Rome; judging others; the Jew and the Law; both Jews and Gentiles under condemnation; righteousness through faith.

Verses for Today: *"For the wrath of God is revealed from heaven against all ungodliness and unrighteousness of men, who hold the truth in unrighteousness. . . . Who changed the truth of God into a lie, and worshiped and served the creature more than the Creator. . . . For this cause God gave them up unto vile affections . . . "* (Romans 1:18,25-26).

T he judgment of God is on all sexual sins. And the sexual perversion that is gaining social acceptance today is the same sin that brought God's judgment upon the cities of Sodom and Gomorrah during the time of Abraham and Lot.

Because the people of Sodom and Gomorrah participated in perverted sex orgies—especially the sin of sodomy (homosexuality)—God sent fire from Heaven and destroyed them (Genesis 19; Jude 1:7).

"Gays" and so-called bisexuals are often looked upon merely as people who are "different" and unable to help being the way they are. But God calls their perversion shameful, vile passions—men lusting for other men, and women lusting for other women. *Even the women turned against God's natural plan for them and indulged in sex acts with each other. In the same way the men gave up natural sexual relations with women and were swept into lustful passion for each other. Men did shameful things with each other, and as a result they brought upon themselves the inevitable punishment of their own perverseness* (see Romans 1:26-27).

These immoral passions are simply an expression of an evil nature that has chosen to fulfill the lusts of the flesh and reject the Word of God as the guide for moral standards.

There will be no victory over sexual perversion until it is seen for what it really is—a vile sin—and not a sickness or a way of life. But those who forsake and turn from their sin can receive forgiveness and deliverance as they trust God.

"And they that are Christ's have crucified the flesh with the affections and lusts" (Galatians 5:24).

Thought for Today: God's concern has always been that man turn from his sins and enjoy His protection and provisions.

Word Studies: 1:13 **let** means hindered; 1:21 **vain** means misguided; idolatrous; morally wicked; 1:27 **recompense ... meet** means due penalty; 1:29 **debate** means strife; contention.

Cross References: For **Romans 1:17:** See Hab. 2:4. **Rom. 2:24:** See Isa. 52:5. **Rom. 3:4:** See Psa. 51:4. **Rom. 3:10:** See Psa. 14:1. **Rom 3:11:** See Psa. 14:2. **Rom. 3:12:** See Psa. 14:3. **Rom. 3:13:** See Psa. 5:9; 140:3. **Rom. 3:14:** See Psa. 10:7. **Rom. 3:15:** See Isa. 59:7. **Rom. 3:16-17:** See Isa. 59:7-8. **Rom. 3:18:** See Psa. 36:1.

Prayer Needs: Country: Laos—4 million—in Southeast Asia • Great suppression of all Christian activities • 58% Buddhist; 33% belief in spirits and ancestor worship; 2% Christian; 1% Muslim.

NOVEMBER 20: Read Romans 4 — 7

Highlights: Faith and righteousness through Jesus Christ; sin through Adam; salvation through Christ; freedom from the power of sin; Christians under grace, not law; conflict of the flesh with the spiritual nature.

Verses for Today: *"Likewise reckon ye also yourselves to be dead indeed unto sin. . . . yield yourselves unto God . . . as instruments of righteousness unto God"* (Romans 6:11,13).

A s children of God, we are responsible to *"reckon"*—to accept as a fact—that sin is no longer our master and that we are *"dead indeed"* to the old life of sin. This doesn't mean we are not *able* to sin, but that we are able *not* to sin.

God sees the believer as no longer in Adam, but in Christ—the Head of a new creation. *When anyone is in union with Christ, he is a new being* (see II Corinthians 5:17). But to *enjoy* this wonderful relationship with Christ, one must yield his will to the indwelling Holy Spirit.

Defeat is always the result of unbelief—a failure to trust in God's Word and act on the fact that the Holy Spirit in us is greater than the power of Satan (I John 4:4).

God has placed the responsibility on us to yield our lives to Him *to be used for righteous purposes*—not in our own strength, but in the power of the indwelling Spirit, for *we have been brought from death to life* (see Romans 6:13). His life in us makes the difference. The decision is ours!

Our old self has died with Christ on His cross in order that the power of the sinful nature might be destroyed; therefore, we should no longer be the slaves of sin (see Romans 6:6).

Thought for Today: When we see ourselves for what we really are, we will bow in grateful humility for God's great love to us.

Word Studies: 4:13 **seed** means descendants; 5:11 **atonement** means reconciliation; 5:14 **similitude** means likeness; 6:17 **God be thanked, that ye were the servants of sin** means thank God that, although you once chose to be slaves of sin; 7:8 **concupiscence** means evil desires of lust; covetousness.

Cross References: For **Romans 4:3:** See Gen. 15:6. **Rom. 4:7-8:** See Psa. 32:1-2. **Rom. 4:17:** See Gen. 17:5. **Rom. 4:18:** See Gen. 15:5. **Rom. 7:7:** See Ex. 20:17.

Prayer Needs: **Country:** Iran—50 million—in southwestern Asia • Hostile to all Christian activity • 98% Muslim; .4% Christian.

NOVEMBER 21: Read Romans 8 — 10

Highlights: The new law of life in the Spirit; suffering versus future glory; children of the flesh; children of the promise; Israel's failure because of unbelief; a means of mercy to Gentiles.

Verses for Today: *"That the righteousness of the law might be fulfilled in us, who walk not after the flesh, but after the Spirit. . . . Because the carnal mind is enmity against God . . . "* (Romans 8:4,7).

B ecause of the sin of Adam and Eve in the Garden of Eden, all mankind inherited a sinful nature (Romans 5:12-19). But when a person receives Christ as his personal Savior, he receives the nature of God, which enables him to be controlled by the Spirit of God. Because of this, Christians should no longer live according to their old way of life (6:4-14).

A person may imitate a true Christian in many ways, such as joining a church, attending worship services, giving generously, or even attempting to keep the Ten Commandments, as the rich young ruler did (see Matthew 19:16-22; Luke 18:18-23). But until Christ becomes one's personal Savior, he is still unsaved and at *"enmity against God."*

Repentance had a prominent place in the teachings of Jesus (Matthew 11:20-21; 12:41; Mark 1:15; Luke 5:32; 10:13; 11:32; 13:3,5; 15:7,10; 16:30; 17:3-4; 24:47).

Genuine faith in Christ is inseparably linked to repentance. The Holy Spirit directed Paul to summarize his ministry in these words: *"Testifying both to the Jews, and also to the Greeks, repentance toward God, and faith toward our Lord Jesus Christ"* (Acts 20:21).

Sin destroyed mankind's relationship to God. Therefore, sin must be confessed and forsaken. Through the convicting and illuminating power of the Holy Spirit, we are led to see the terribleness of sin. Only when a person sees himself as a lost sinner in rebellion against God will there be genuine repentance.

Repentance means more than being sorry for our sins; it even means more than confessing our guilt. Repentance means turning from sin to God (Proverbs 28:13; I John 1:9). Genuine repentance allows no room for any unconfessed, "secret" sin.

"Or despisest thou the riches of his goodness and forbearance and long-suffering; not knowing that the goodness of God leadeth thee to repentance?" (Romans 2:4).

Thought for Today: Without the transforming power of the Holy Spirit—as revealed in the Word of God—no one can ever be saved.

Cross References: For **Romans 8:36:** See Psa. 44:22. **Rom. 9:7:** See Gen. 21:12. **Rom. 9:9:** See Gen. 18:10. **Rom. 9:12:** See Gen. 25:23. **Rom. 9:13:** See Mal. 1:2-3. **Rom. 9:15:** See Ex. 33:19. **Rom. 9:17:** See Ex. 9:16. **Rom. 9:25:** See Hos. 2:23. **Rom. 9:26:** See Hos. 1:10. **Rom. 9:27-28:** See Isa. 10:22-23. **Rom. 9:29:** See Isa. 1:9. **Rom. 9:33:** See Isa. 28:16. **Rom. 10:5:** See Lev. 18:5. **Rom. 10:6-7:** See Deut. 30:12-13. **Rom. 10:8:** See Deut. 30:14. **Rom. 10:11:** See Isa. 28:16. **Rom. 10:13:** See Joel 2:32. **Rom. 10:15:** See Isa. 52:7. **Rom. 10:16:** See Isa. 53:1. **Rom. 10:18:** See Psa. 19:4. **Rom. 10:19:** See Deut. 32:21. **Rom. 10:20:** See Isa. 65:1. **Rom. 10:21:** See Isa. 65:2.

Prayer Needs: Country: India—800 million—in southern Asia • Religious freedom, but increasing harassment and persecution of Christians by religious radicals • 78% Hindu; 12% Muslim; 4% Christian; 2% Sikhs.

NOVEMBER 22: Read Romans 11 — 13

Highlights: The remnant of Israel; warning to Gentiles; Israel still to be saved; duties of a Christian; believers' attitude toward civil government; Christians to walk in love.

Verse for Today: *"I beseech you therefore, brethren, by the mercies of God, that ye present your bodies a living sacrifice, holy, acceptable unto God, which is your reasonable service"* (Romans 12:1).

The book of Romans first describes the guilty condition of man without Christ—completely corrupt and deserving of eternal death. Then it reveals God's wonderful and perfect salvation through the precious blood of Jesus and His finished work on the cross.

Christianity is a new life—a new beginning. As Christ lives in and through us, He transforms our lives to be like His.

Therefore, it is only "reasonable" that we present our bodies to Him—to accomplish His perfect will. It is not enough that we do the right things; our inner desire must also be to please Him.

Often Christians fail to live victoriously, not realizing that His Spirit—the indwelling Living Word—is the source of all spiritual power.

As we prayerfully read the Bible with a desire to do His will, His Word becomes our spiritual food—our very life. Just as physical food is assimilated into our bodies to provide physical strength, so the indwelling Spirit strengthens our spiritual lives through His Word. Then, and only then, can we truly accomplish His purposes.

"And be not conformed to this world: but be ye transformed by the renewing of

your mind, that ye may prove what is that good, and acceptable, and perfect will of God" (Romans 12:2).

Thought for Today: As we are controlled by the indwelling Holy Spirit, we become pleasing to God.

Word Studies: 11:14 **emulation** means jealousy; 11:23 **graft** means implant; 12:8 **with simplicity** means generously; without self-seeking; with liberality; 12:9 **dissimulation** means hypocrisy; 13:1 **soul** means person; 13:9 **kill** means murder.

Cross References: For **Romans 11:3:** See I Kings 19:10,14. **Rom. 11:4:** See I Kings 19:18. **Rom. 11:8:** See Isa. 29:10. **Rom. 11:9-10:** See Psa. 69:22. **Rom. 11: 26-27:** See Isa. 59:20-21. **Rom. 11:34:** See Isa. 40:13. **Rom. 11:35:** See Job 41:11. **Rom. 12:19:** See Deut. 32:35. **Rom. 12:20:** See Prov. 25:21-22. **Rom. 13:9:** See Ex. 20:13-17; Lev. 19:18.

Prayer Needs: Country: Egypt—52 million—in northeastern Africa • Christians are not permitted to evangelize Muslims • 82% Muslim; 16% Coptic; .6% Protestant; .6% Roman Catholic.

NOVEMBER 23: Read Romans 14 — 16

Highlights: Law of love concerning doubtful things; Jewish and Gentile believers share the same salvation; Paul's desire to visit Rome; personal greetings.

Verses for Today: *"We then that are strong ought to bear the infirmities of the weak, and not to please ourselves. Let every one of us please his neighbor for his good to edification. For even Christ pleased not himself . . . "* (Romans 15:1-3).

E ven Christ, the Son of God, *"pleased not himself."* It was for the sake of others that He came into the world, lived, prayed, wept, and died. And it is for others that He will come again. How opposite this is to the self-centered philosophy of the world that says, "Every man for himself!"

Those who allow Christ to be Lord of their lives will show concern for others—not only for a weak brother or sister in Christ, but for the brokenhearted and fallen. We can be a blessing just by being understanding, or having a listening ear, and praying with those who truly need comfort and encouragement. Our desire should be to live for the glory of God and to see souls saved and strengthened through the Word of God.

We should thank and praise the Lord for the privilege of bearing the burdens of others and helping them learn more about Christ and His will for their lives!

"Now the God of patience and consolation grant you to be likeminded one toward another according to Christ Jesus: that ye may with one mind and one mouth glorify God, even the Father of our Lord Jesus Christ. Wherefore receive ye one another, as Christ also received us to the glory of God" (Romans 15:5-7).

Thought for Today: Giving—not getting—is the key to *being* a blessing as well as *receiving* a blessing.

Word Studies: 16:2 **succorer** means helper; 16:23 **chamberlain** means treasurer.

Cross References: For **Romans 14:11:** See Isa. 45:23. **Rom. 15:3:** See Psa. 69:9. **Rom. 15:9:** See Psa. 18:49. **Rom. 15:10:** See Deut. 32:43. **Rom. 15:11:** See Psa. 117:1. **Rom. 15:12:** See Isa. 11:1,10. **Rom. 15:21:** See Isa. 52:15.

Prayer Needs: Country: Cuba—10 million—on the northern rim of the Caribbean

• Strict government surveillance of all true Christian activities • 41% Roman Catholic; 2% various spiritists; 1% Protestant.

I & II CORINTHIANS _____

Corinth was the capital of the Roman province of Achaia. This seaport community was one of the most prominent cities in Greece, having an estimated population of 400,000 or more.

Paul stayed in Corinth for more than a year and a half on his second missionary journey. During that time, Priscilla and Aquila helped him establish a church. Silas and Timothy also helped Paul in the ministry. After Paul left Corinth, Apollos became a leader there. (See Acts 18:1-28; I Corinthians 3:5-6.)

Paul's purpose for writing the first letter to the church at Corinth was to correct problems that existed among its members. The church was divided (1:10—4:21), and some of its members were involved in sins that greatly hindered the spiritual life of the church (5:1-13).

The finest definition of love ever written is recorded in chapter 13, and the best explanation of the resurrection of Christ, as well as the believer, is given in chapter 15.

Soon after Paul had written I Corinthians, he almost lost his life in the great riot at Ephesus (see Acts 19). Paul left Ephesus and went to Macedonia on his way to Corinth. At Macedonia, in the midst of many anxieties and sufferings, he met with Titus, who was returning from Corinth with word that Paul's letter to the Corinthian church had accomplished much good. Paul gave Titus another letter to the Corinthian church and indicated that he himself planned to go to Corinth soon.

The major theme of the book of II Corinthians is the ministry of reconciliation. Christians have the responsibility to make every effort to bring about peaceable solutions to their family problems, as well as personal conflicts with others. This book also shows the importance of sharing one's resources with the needy.

In II Corinthians, Paul commended the church for correcting its moral problems. He pointed out the necessity to resolve divisions within the church and the importance of a generous offering for the church in Jerusalem.

NOVEMBER 24: Read I Corinthians 1 — 4

Highlights: The grace and faithfulness of God; church problems at Corinth; God's power and wisdom; Jesus, the only Foundation; Christians, the temples of God; authority of the apostles.

Verses for Today: *"Who then is Paul, and who is Apollos, but ministers by whom ye believed, even as the Lord gave to every man? I have planted, Apollos watered;*

but God gave the increase.... Now he that planteth and he that watereth are one ... " (I Corinthians 3:5-6,8).

T he church at Corinth was divided over who was the most important spiritual leader. Some preferred Paul; others, Apollos or Peter; still others were saying, "I am of Christ."

Peter, Paul, and Apollos were only servants of Christ, chosen by God and enabled by Him to serve His people—no one man possessing all knowledge and abilities. Therefore, all praise should have gone to God, the Giver of all gifts, for He has *"set the members every one of them in the body, as it hath pleased him"* (I Corinthians 12:18).

A Christian should consider himself neither more nor less important than others when it comes to gifts or abilities that God has bestowed for it takes every Christian to make up the Body of Christ.

A body has many parts with different functions, but each part and each function is necessary for the strength and usefulness of the whole. For *"... what hast thou that thou didst not receive? now if thou didst receive it, why dost thou glory, as if thou hadst not received it?"* (4:7).

The true worth of any church or gospel ministry is dependent upon God. Apart from His blessing, the most earnest and well-performed service will be ineffective and fruitless.

"Let the peace of God rule in your hearts ... and be ye thankful" (Colossians 3:15).

Thought for Today: We should not boast—or complain—about the gifts or abilities that God has bestowed on us or on others.

Word Studies: 1:21 **the foolishness of preaching** means the foolishness, as unbelievers consider it, of the message of salvation; 2:6 **perfect** means spiritually mature; 4:4 **For I know nothing by myself; yet am I not hereby justified** means my conscience is clear of all intentional unfaithfulness, but even that isn't final proof that I haven't fallen short of God's best; 4:5 **counsels** means motives; 4:11 **buffeted** means mistreated.

Cross References: For **I Corinthians 1:19:** See Isa. 29:14. **I Cor. 1:31:** See Jer. 9:24. **I Cor. 2:16:** See Isa. 40:13. **I Cor. 3:19:** See Job 5:13. **I Cor. 3:20:** See Psa. 94:11.

Prayer Needs: Country: Bermuda—58,000—a group of 360 small islands in the Atlantic, 580 miles east of North Carolina • Religious freedom • 66% Protestant; 19% Roman Catholic; 2% cults.

NOVEMBER 25: Read I Corinthians 5 — 9

Highlights: Immorality and other sins condemned; guidelines for marriage and Christian conduct.

Verses for Today: *"... Be not deceived: neither fornicators, nor idolaters, nor adulterers, nor effeminate, nor abusers of themselves with mankind... shall inherit the kingdom of God"* (I Corinthians 6:9-10).

T he rejection of God's moral standards is the very thing that has caused the "sexual revolution" and moral chaos of our day.

The Word of God teaches that the wicked—including adulterers and fornicators—will not *"inherit the kingdom of God."*

Many times in the Scriptures, we are warned about God's judgment against fornication or adultery. (See Exodus 20:14,17; Leviticus 18:20; 20:10-12; 21:9; Deuteronomy 22:13-21; Matthew 5:32; 19:9; Mark 10:11-12; John 8:3-5; Romans 7:2-3; 13:14; I Corinthians 5:9-11; 6:9—7:17,39; Ephesians 5:3-6; Colossians 3:5-6; I Thessalonians 4:3-7; I Timothy 1:9-10; II Timothy 2:22; Hebrews 13:4; I Peter 2:11; Revelation 21:8; 22:15.)

The Ten Commandments make it unmistakably clear, *"Thou shalt not commit adultery"* (Exodus 20:14).

And in our Lord's Sermon on the Mount, Jesus warned that sexual sins start with the eyes and in the heart, saying, *" . . . whosoever looketh on a woman to lust after her hath committed adultery with her already in his heart"* (Matthew 5:28).

One thing is absolutely sure—God's judgment upon sexual sins remains unchanged. Therefore, it is of utmost importance that our conduct concerning sex be based on the inspired, infallible written Word of God.

God is love, but He is also a God of justice.

Where there is recognition of sin and genuine repentance—forsaking and turning from sin—God will fully forgive the sinner. Then His Word can give power to live a victorious life.

"If we confess our sins, he is faithful and just to forgive us our sins, and to cleanse us from all unrighteousness" (I John 1:9).

Thought for Today: To reject the Bible as the standard for one's life is to reject God Himself.

Word Studies: 7:5 **Defraud ye not one the other** means do not rob or cheat each other of marital rights; 7:12 **put her away** means divorce her; 7:32 **without carefulness** means free from anxieties; 8:10 **emboldened** means tempted to violate his convictions; 9:9 **corn** means grain; 9:17 **dispensation** means stewardship.

Cross References: For **I Corinthians 6:16:** See Gen. 2:24. **I Cor. 9:9:** See Deut. 25:4.

Prayer Needs: Country: Antigua and Barbuda—70,000—in the Leeward Islands of the eastern Caribbean • Religious freedom • 85% Protestant; 11% Roman Catholic; 2% Afro-American spiritist.

NOVEMBER 26: Read I Corinthians 10 — 13

Highlights: Guidelines for worship; the Lord's Supper; spiritual gifts; charity (love), the greatest gift.

Verse for Today: *"And now abideth faith, hope, charity, these three; but the greatest of these is charity"* (I Corinthians 13:13).

T he biblical meaning of the word *charity* is "love in action." It is true affection for God as well as others. This love is the result of a spiritual new birth—*"We know that we have passed from death unto life, because we love the brethren . . . "* (I John 3:14). For the Bible equates one who hates his brother to a murderer, in whom eternal life is not found (see 3:15). Love should be characteristic of a Christian because God is love.

Jesus said, *"By this shall all men know that ye are my disciples, if ye have love one to another"* (John 13:35). Our love toward others is more important to the Lord than all our talents, knowledge, service, or sacrificial giving.

As Christians, let us search our hearts for the reason we are serving the Lord. Is it for self-recognition or because of love for Christ? Love is a guideline for measuring our attitudes and actions.

Love will not envy the rich or covet their possessions. It is free from suspicion and evil imagination. It forgives the inconsiderate actions of others—even if the offense is repeated seven times in a day (Luke 17:4). Love does not boast or seek recognition (I Corinthians 13:4-5).

Love does not insist on its own rights; it prompts us to promote the welfare of others (I Corinthians 10:24,33). Love will return good for evil as we recognize our indebtedness to God for His love toward us (Romans 5:8; 12:20-21).

"My little children, let us not love in word, neither in tongue; but in deed and in truth" (I John 3:18).

Thought for Today: When you love the Lord with all your heart, love for others will be a natural overflow.

Word Studies: 10:24 **another's wealth** means what is best for others; 10:25 **shambles** means meat market; 11:19 **heresies** means doctrinal errors that are a willful departure from truth; 12:25 **schism** means division; 13:1 **charity** means love; 13:4 **vaunteth not itself** means is not boastful; 13:5 **Doth not behave itself unseemly** means is not indecent (implying shame—compare Romans 1:27); 13:12 **through a glass, darkly** means as if we were looking in a mirror that gives only a dim view of spiritual things.

Cross References: For **I Corinthians 10:7:** See Ex. 32:6. **I Cor. 10:26:** See Psa. 24:1.

Prayer Needs: Country: Nigeria—109 million—in western Africa • Government permits all types of religious activity • 36% Muslim; 19% Protestant; 15% animist; 7% Roman Catholic.

NOVEMBER 27:   Read I Corinthians 14 — 16

Highlights: Gifts in the church; the resurrection of Christ; collection for the saints in Jerusalem; Paul's future plans.

Verses for Today: *"In a moment, in the twinkling of an eye, at the last trump: for the trumpet shall sound, and the dead shall be raised incorruptible, and we shall be changed. . . . thanks be to God, which giveth us the victory through our Lord Jesus Christ"* (I Corinthians 15:52,57).

I t is a triumphant fact that Christ rose from the dead! This gives us assurance of the day when *"all that are in the graves shall hear his voice, And shall come forth; they that have done good, unto the resurrection of life; and they that have done evil, unto the resurrection of damnation"* (John 5:28-29).

The supreme purpose for living is to prepare ourselves and others for eternity. For the Christian, physical death is a transition into the actual presence of Christ. But this victory over death is only for those who have personally believed in and received Christ as their Lord and Savior.

When Christ returns, all Christians shall be changed *"like unto his glorious body, according to the working whereby he is able even to subdue all things unto himself"* (Philippians 3:21; see also I Corinthians 15:51-55).

"He that believeth on him is not condemned: but he that believeth not is

condemned already, because he hath not believed in the name of the only begotten Son of God" (John 3:18).

Thought for Today: Because Christ died and rose again, we can live for all eternity with Him. What precious assurance!

Word Studies: 14:10 **signification** means meaning; 14:20 **in malice be ye children** means be as harmless as a baby; 14:27 **by course** means in turn; 15:20 **slept** means have died; 15:33 **evil communications corrupt good manners** means evil companions or associations ruin or defile good character; 15:38 **his own body** means just the kind of form He wants it to have; 15:40 **celestial** means heavenly; **terrestrial** means earthly; 16:13 **stand fast in the faith** means remain true to the Lord; **quit you** means be courageous; 16:22 **Anathema** means accursed; **Maranatha** means Our Lord, come!

Cross References: For I Corinthians 14:21: See Isa. 28:11-12. I Cor. 15:25: See Psa. 110:1. I Cor. 15:27: See Psa. 8:6. I Cor. 15:32: See Isa. 22:13. I Cor. 15:45: See Gen. 2:7. I Cor. 15:54: See Isa. 25:8. I Cor. 15:55: See Hos. 13:14.

Prayer Needs: Country: Pakistan—105 million—in southern Asia • There is no freedom to convert Muslims to Christ. Pakistan is an Islamic republic • 97% Muslim; 2% Christian; 1% Hindu.

NOVEMBER 28: Read II Corinthians 1 — 4

Highlights: Forgiving those who have repented of sin; Lordship of Christ; suffering of Christians.

Verse for Today: *"Who comforteth us in all our tribulation, that we may be able to comfort them which are in any trouble, by the comfort wherewith we ourselves are comforted of God"* (II Corinthians 1:4).

T rials and troubles in one form or another are a necessary part of every Christian's spiritual growth (Acts 14:22; I Peter 1:6-7; 4:12-13). Christ was always conscious of His purpose for coming to earth—to die on the cross to pay the penalty for the sins of the world. Just as it was necessary for Him to die, we, too, must be willing partakers of His sufferings.

On the basis of forgiveness of sins, Christ imparts to us His very life, which sustains us in suffering. We then, by faith, can bear all suffering and every trial with confident peace that God has privileged us with the opportunity to manifest the characteristics of the resurrected Christ (II Corinthians 4:10).

We can face trials and suffering with the assurance that our Lord has never made a mistake and that He lovingly cares for all His people. God imparts a comfort that only He can give. This comfort of the Holy Spirit has a twofold effect: our burdens are lifted, and we also become qualified to comfort others *"by the comfort wherewith we ourselves are comforted of God."*

"But rejoice, inasmuch as ye are partakers of Christ's sufferings; that, when his glory shall be revealed, ye may be glad also with exceeding joy" (I Peter 4:13).

Thought for Today: God's comfort to us enables us to comfort others.

Word Studies: 2:14 **savor** means fragrance; 2:17 **which corrupt the word of God** means who preach the gospel for personal gain; 3:1 **epistles** means a written message; 3:10 **For even that which was made glorious had no glory in this respect, by reason of the glory that excelleth** means for what was glorious (the Law given to Moses) has no glory now in comparison to the surpassing glory of Jesus Christ.

Cross References: For **II Corinthians 3:13:** See Ex. 34:33. **II Cor. 4:13:** See Psa. 116:10.

Prayer Needs: Country: South Yemen—2 million—on the southern part of the Arabian Peninsula • Gradual erosion of the strong position of Islam in favor of atheism • 92% Muslim; .1% Christian (all secret believers).

NOVEMBER 29: Read II Corinthians 5 — 8

Highlights: Living by faith; ministry of reconciliation; believers not to be unequally joined with unbelievers; Paul's summary of the ministry; the grace of giving.

Verses for Today: *"For the love of Christ constraineth us ... God was in Christ, reconciling the world unto himself, not imputing their trespasses unto them; and hath committed unto us the word of reconciliation"* (II Corinthians 5:14,19).

W hen a person becomes a Christian, he receives a spiritual nature—God's divine nature. This nature enables the Christian to have a change of attitude from self-interest and hostility toward God and others when things do not go his way, to one of love for others and a desire to please the Lord. *If we love one another, God actually does live within us, and His love is made perfect in us* (see I John 4:12).

Reconciliation began with God, who loved the world so much *"that he gave his only begotten Son"* so that sinners could be restored to fellowship with Him. (See John 3:16.) The ministry of reconciliation is a sacred trust that *"constraineth us"*—urges us to serve Christ—because of His great love.

As we yield to His constraining power, we will have a desire to share the wonderful news of His marvelous love so that others can be reconciled to God. The love of Christ should so control our lives that our greatest desire will be to accomplish His will. Every decision made in life should be based on what would please Him most.

Loving God means doing what His Word tells us to do (see I John 5:3).

Thought for Today: It is only by the grace of God that we *are* anything or can *do* anything of eternal value.

Word Studies: 5:21 **For he hath made him to be sin for us, who knew no sin** means Christ was without sin, but He bore our sins; 6:11 **our heart is enlarged** means we love you with all our heart; 6:12 **Ye are not straitened in us** means our love toward you is not restricted; **bowels** means affections; 7:10 **not to be repented of** means and without regret; 8:1 **we do you to wit of the grace of God** means we want you to know what God's grace has accomplished; 8:8 **forwardness** means eagerness.

Cross References: For **II Corinthians 6:2:** See Isa. 49:8. **II Cor. 6:16:** See Lev. 26:11-12. **II Cor. 6:17:** See Isa. 52:11. **II Cor. 8:15:** See Ex. 16:18.

Prayer Needs: Country: Luxembourg—366,000—in western Europe • Religious freedom • 84% Roman Catholic; 2% Protestant; .1% Eastern Orthodox.

NOVEMBER 30: Read II Corinthians 9 — 13

Highlights: Offering for the church at Jerusalem; Paul's spiritual authority; warning against false teachers; Paul's suffering as an apostle; his thorn in the flesh; his plans to visit Corinth.

Verses for Today: *"But this I say, He which soweth sparingly shall reap also sparingly; and he which soweth bountifully shall reap also bountifully. Every man according as he purposeth in his heart, so let him give; not grudgingly, or of necessity: for God loveth a cheerful giver"* (II Corinthians 9:6-7).

C hrist not only spoke of the terrible consequences of being unfaithful stewards, but He also told of the blessings of being faithful in our stewardship responsibilities (Luke 12:42-46).

God has given each of us certain possessions—whether they are in the form of money, property, or other belongings. What we do with those possessions can make the difference of eternal life or death to someone.

Have you ever thought about what it means for a person to die without having been saved? The neighbor next door? A friend? Someone in your own home who is lost and on the way to hell? Surely each person deserves the right to hear, at least once, that *"Christ Jesus came into the world to save sinners"* (I Timothy 1:15).

The Lord has given each of us the privilege and responsibility of reaching our neighbors and loved ones, as well as people throughout the world. Assuming that someone else will tell them about Jesus does not relieve us of our responsibility. God will bless every effort we make to help others read His Word.

Stewardship is a part of everyday life with which most of us are familiar. Banks are entrusted with money that belongs to other people, and trustees are appointed to take care of the estates of others.

For Christians, being good stewards means wisely using everything the Lord has entrusted to us—our time, talents, and money. Everything we possess belongs to the Lord—even we ourselves.

The Lord gave Himself as an example of the principle of Christian giving: *" . . . though he was rich, yet for your sakes he became poor, that ye through his poverty might be rich"* (II Corinthians 8:9).

We should not give grudgingly or merely from a sense of duty, for *"God loveth a cheerful giver"* —one who finds satisfaction in giving. And He expects us to be generous with the possessions He has entrusted to us. Only then will we discover the blessing of giving.

"It is more blessed to give than to receive" (Acts 20:35).

Thought for Today: Our willingness to give reveals the condition of our hearts.

Word Studies: 9:15 **his unspeakable gift** means the gospel of Christ—a gift too wonderful for words; 11:3 **simplicity** means sincere, single-minded dedication; 12:20 **swellings** means pride; arrogance; haughtiness; 13:6 **we are not reprobates** means we are genuine Christians.

Cross References: For **II Corinthians 9:9:** See Psa. 112:9. **II Cor. 10:17:** See Jer. 9:24. **II Cor. 13:1:** See Deut. 19:15.

Prayer Needs: **Country:** Kuwait—2 million—in the northeastern corner of the Arabian Peninsula • Less religious freedom than other Gulf States • 95% Muslim; 4% Christian.

PRAYERS IN THIS MONTH'S READING

GALATIANS

This book was written to expose the difference between true Christianity and being religious.

Doing good works—no matter how good they are—can never make a person a Christian. But a Christian is empowered by the indwelling Spirit of God to allow Christ to be Lord of his life, to keep His commandments, and to do good works.

Galatians reaffirms that our salvation is dependent upon Christ alone. We cannot be saved apart from Jesus Christ—even if we were able to keep every commandment—*"for by the works of the law shall no flesh be justified"* (2:16).

To illustrate this fact, this book points out that just as Abraham was declared righteous and inherited the promises of God by faith, so those who trust Christ as their Savior are declared righteous and given a perfect relationship with God. Galatians also makes it clear that *our Lord Jesus Christ gave Himself for our sins, that He might deliver us from this present evil world* (see Galatians 1:3-4).

Although God is a loving God, He is also a holy God. Perfect justice, as well as the Law, demands, *All who sin will die* (see Ezekiel 18:20). The New Testament is equally clear that *"all have sinned"* and *"the wages of sin is death"* (Romans 3:23; 6:23).

Because of the sin of Adam and Eve in the Garden of Eden, all mankind inherited a sinful nature that separates us from God, the Source of life (Romans 5:12; Isaiah 59:2). But all who repent of their sins and receive Jesus Christ as their Savior are no longer spiritually dead in trespasses and sins. We can stand before God forgiven (Ephesians 2:4-7; Colossians 2:13; compare John 3:36).

Galatians reveals that Christ *redeemed us from the curse of the Law by taking the curse on Himself* (see Galatians 3:13).

No one but Jesus can say that his obedience for a lifetime has been perfect —no one. Because Jesus was the perfect Son of God who never once sinned (II Corinthians 5:21), He could take our place as the sinner's substitute.

DECEMBER 1: Read Galatians 1 — 3

Highlights: Only one gospel; Paul's rebuke of Peter; justification by faith, not Law; the Law, our guide to Christ.

Verses for Today: *"Grace be to you and peace from God the Father, and from our Lord Jesus Christ. Who gave himself for our sins, that he might deliver us from this present evil world ... "* (Galatians 1:3-4).

A lthough God is a loving God, He is also a holy God. Perfect justice, as well as the Law, demands, *All who sin will die* (see Ezekiel 18:20).

Because of the sin of Adam and Eve in the Garden of Eden, all mankind inherited a sinful nature that separates us from God, the Source of life (Romans 5:12; Isaiah 59:2). But all who believe in the Son of God and receive Jesus Christ as their Savior are no longer spiritually dead in trespasses and sins. We can stand before God forgiven (Ephesians 2:4-7; Colossians 2:13; compare John 3:36).

The Book of Galatians reveals that Christ *redeemed us from the curse of the Law by taking the curse on Himself* (see Galatians 3:13).

No one but Jesus can say that his obedience for a lifetime has been without sin—no one. Because Jesus was the perfect Son of God who never once sinned (II Corinthians 5:21), He could take our place. As the sinner's substitute, Jesus willingly and lovingly gave Himself to die on the cross for our sins.

Salvation is the result of God's grace—through our faith in Jesus—not our own efforts but God's gift, so that it will be impossible for anyone to boast about it (see Ephesians 2:8-9). If it had been possible for anyone to be good enough to attain salvation, there would have been no need for Jesus to die.

If you have repented of your sins and received this gift of salvation, serve Him gladly and faithfully. If you have not, do so today!

Whoever does not obey everything written in the Law is under God's curse! Now, it is clear indeed, the Law cannot make a man acceptable to God, because the Scriptures say, Only the person who is right with God through faith shall live (see Galatians 3:10-11).

Thought for Today: How can we help but love Him who gave Himself for us!

Word Studies: 1:11 **certify you** means declare unto you; 1:13 **conversation** means manner of life; 2:13 **dissimulation** means insincerity; 3:3 **made perfect** means being perfected.

Cross References: For **Galatians 3:6:** See Gen. 15:6. **Gal. 3:8:** See Gen. 12:3. **Gal. 3:10:** See Deut. 27:26. **Gal. 3:11:** See Hab. 2:4. **Gal. 3:12:** See Lev. 18:5. **Gal. 3:13:** See Deut. 21:23.

Prayer Needs: Country: Barbados—324,000—on the island farthest east in the West Indies • Religious freedom • 85% Protestant; 6% Roman Catholic; .1% Eastern Orthodox.

DECEMBER 2: Read Galatians 4 — 6

Highlights: Allegory of Hagar and Sarah; liberty of the gospel; fruit of the Spirit.

Verses for Today: *"For all the law is fulfilled in one word, even in this; Thou shalt love thy neighbor as thyself. But if ye bite and devour one another, take heed that ye be not consumed one of another"* (Galatians 5:14-15).

L ove should be the guiding principle for every Christian in every decision. Christians are commanded to love all people.

But we are especially to have harmonious love for other Christians (John 13:35) because we are all a part of each other as the Body of Christ—as closely knit together with one another as hands and feet are to the physical body—*members one of another, united together in the Body of Christ* (see Ephesians 4:25). Christ is the Head of this Body, and *"we are members of his body"* (5:30). No part can be severed from the Body without hindering the whole because all the parts are dependent on each other.

We dare not ignore our responsibility to love other Christians *with all our hearts* (see I Peter 1:22)—even those we feel do not deserve our love. Expressing the love of Christ enables us to overcome divisions and bitterness and restore the unity of the Spirit; it is absolutely essential in order for us to be in a right relationship to Christ.

God hates divisions. Whether we are right or have been offended is of little consequence; we are responsible to God for making every attempt to bring the weaker or offended brother or sister back into fellowship. God has left no room for exceptions—not even one.

If someone is caught in any kind of wrongdoing, those of you who are spiritual should make every effort to restore that person to a right relationship to Christ in a spirit of gentleness (see Galatians 6:1).

Thought for Today: Perhaps the failure we see in another person's life is only a reflection of the hidden sin of self-righteousness in our own hearts.

Word Studies: 4:24 **gendereth to** means is destined for; 6:6 **communicate unto him that teacheth in all good things** means meet the financial needs of their spiritual leaders.

Cross References: For **Galatians 4:27:** See Isa. 54:1. **Gal. 4:30:** See Gen. 21:10. **Gal 5:14:** See Lev. 19:18.

Prayer Needs: Country: Channel Islands—140,000—off the northwestern coast of France • Religious freedom • 76% Protestant; 18% Roman Catholic; .2% Eastern Orthodox.

EPHESIANS

The book of Ephesians reveals the "exceeding greatness" of true spiritual power and wisdom, which are part of every Christian's inheritance. This power raised Jesus from the dead and gave Him dominion over everything, including the Church.

All Christians are spiritually united into one Body as members of this Church, of which Christ is the Head (2:16; 5:23).

Through the indwelling Spirit, Christians are empowered by God's Word to be victorious in each of the four major areas of life: (1) *in the church*, to maintain unity (1:22-23; 4:13,16,32); (2) *in society*, to practice Christian principles (4:22—5:21); (3) *in the home*, to manifest love (5:22—6:4); and (4) *in the world*, to resist Satan and the powers of darkness (6:10-18).

Ephesians is a book of practical Christian living, giving guidance for believers. We not only have the promise of a home in Heaven, but we also have a purpose for living—to glorify the Lord through accomplishing His purpose for our lives.

DECEMBER 3: Read Ephesians 1 — 3

Highlights: Spiritual blessings in Christ; prayers of Paul; unity of believers; Paul's mission to the Gentiles.

Verse for Today: *"For through him we both have access by one Spirit unto the Father"* (Ephesians 2:18).

In Old Testament times, God provided a way, through the high priest, for His people to offer prayer to Him. Only the high priest was allowed to enter into the presence of God in the Holy of Holies to offer prayer on behalf of the worshipers.

Before Christ, the Gentiles did not have a covenant relationship with God. But in Christ, Jews and Gentiles alike who have received Christ as Lord and Savior are united in "one Spirit" with all the family of God.

The Good News is that Jesus *"is able also to save them to the uttermost that come unto God by him, seeing he ever liveth to make intercession for them"* (Hebrews 7:25). Christ has made it possible for each of us to come to God in prayer at any time.

Satan does not want us to pray, so he often seeks to divert our attention just when we start to pray—possibly by reminding us of something we need to do, making us feel that we are too busy to pray, or hindering in some other way.

But we dare not let Satan get the victory in our prayer life. This sacred privilege is a great responsibility. Failure to pray is not merely negligence; it is also sin!

"Let us therefore come boldly unto the throne of grace, that we may obtain mercy, and find grace to help in time of need" (Hebrews 4:16).

Thought for Today: No one can conquer evil apart from prayer.

Word Studies: 1:8 **prudence** means practical insight; 1:10 **dispensation** means administration; 1:14 **earnest** means pledge; 2:13 **sometimes** means formerly (not "occasionally"); 3:2 **dispensation** means special work.

Prayer Needs: Country: Greece—10 million—in southeastern Europe • Government restrictions on witnessing to others about Christ • 97% Greek Orthodox (2% are churchgoers); 1% Muslim; .4% Roman Catholic; .1% Protestant.

DECEMBER 4: Read Ephesians 4 — 6

Highlights: Exhortations to unity, holiness, love; marriage, symbolic of the Church; duties of children and slaves.

Verses for Today: *"Speaking to yourselves in psalms and hymns and spiritual* *songs, singing and making melody in your heart to the Lord . . . Submitting yourselves one to another in the fear of God"* (Ephesians 5:19,21).

E very Christian is a representative of the Lord Jesus Christ. The indwelling Holy Spirit makes it possible for us to respond in love toward others. God's love is made known through us by the Holy Spirit (Romans 5:5).

The Holy Spirit dwells within every Christian, and the life of each member of the family of God should reflect His love. *"Beloved, let us love one another: for love is of God; and every one that loveth is born of God, and knoweth God"* (I John 4:7).

Our submission to God will be manifested through our submission *"one to another in the fear of God."* God's love is a unifying power. Our greatest usefulness comes through cooperating with God and with other Christians—endeavoring to win a lost world to Christ.

"And be ye kind one to another, tenderhearted, forgiving one another, even as God for Christ's sake hath forgiven you" (Ephesians 4:32).

Thought for Today: Those who give to others for Christ's sake will receive His blessing.

Word Studies: 4:13 **perfect** means spiritually mature; 4:14 **sleight** means craftiness; 6:11 **wiles** means strategies; 6:14 **girt about** means encircled; 6:16 **the wicked** means Satan, the wicked one (see also II Thess. 3:3; 1 John 5:18).

Cross References: For **Ephesians 4:8:** See Psa. 68:18. **Eph. 4:25:** See Zech. 8:16. **Eph. 4:26:** See Psa. 4:4. **Eph. 5:31:** See Gen. 2:24. **Eph. 6:2-3:** See Ex. 20:12; Deut. 5:16.

Prayer Needs: Country: Malta—362,000—group of islands in the Mediterranean • Religious freedom • 97% Roman Catholic; 2% Protestant.

PHILIPPIANS _____

When Paul wrote this "thank you" letter, he was in prison enduring bitter hardships—not because he had committed any crime, but because of his love and his loyalty to Christ (1:7,12-16). But whatever the outcome, he knew that his imprisonment encouraged others to be faithful (1:14). He viewed every circumstance in his life with the confidence that he belonged to Christ and was in God's care.

Although Paul had been imprisoned for preaching the gospel, he never once mentioned that he was a prisoner of the Roman government; he was a prisoner of Jesus Christ. (See Ephesians 3:1; 4:1; II Timothy 1:8; Philemon 1:1,9.)

Paul was very aggressive in sharing the gospel with the guards and those around him. It is no surprise to read that there were Christians even in the emperor's palace (Philippians 4:22).

A spirit of joy permeates the entire book of Philippians; we can have inner peace in Christ regardless of our external circumstances.

Christ was uppermost in Paul's life; He is mentioned about 38 times in this short book. Consequently, such words as "joy" and "rejoice" are used frequently. When Christ becomes pre-eminent in our lives, we experience contentment each day.

The key thought is in Philippians 4:4: *"Rejoice in the Lord always: and again I say, Rejoice."*

DECEMBER 5: Read Philippians 1 — 4

Highlights: Exhortation to faithfulness; Christ's humiliation and exaltation; the peace and joy of knowing Christ.

Verses for Today: *"For it is God which worketh in you both to will and to do of his good pleasure. Do all things without murmurings and disputings"* (Philippians 2:13-14).

P hilippians is a triumphant letter from the Apostle Paul to the Christians living in Philippi. It is filled with *joy* and *rejoicing*, which are mentioned about 17 times in these four chapters.

Why all the rejoicing? Did Paul receive an award or special recognition? Were great crowds gathering to hear him preach? No! For quite some time Paul had been in prison for preaching the gospel. But he still praised the Lord because something far more precious than material possessions controlled him—he knew that God was in control and that his present circumstances were for *God's good pleasure*.

It is through difficult experiences that the Christian can exercise faith in God and find pleasure in what pleases Him. This must come from within by the power of the Spirit. God works *in* us before He works *through* us, and He uses the Word, the Spirit, and prayer (I Thessalonians 2:13; Ephesians 3:20).

To express discontentment because of an adverse situation is an insult to our Lord's judgment, for it questions His love and wisdom.

Oh, what satisfaction comes through enjoying the Lord in all circumstances—disappointments or delights—knowing that God can and will make all things work together for good in accomplishing His will!

Now there are varieties of gifts, but the same Spirit. . . . And there are varieties of effects, but it is the same God who achieves His purposes through them all (see I Corinthians 12:4,6).

Thought for Today: Christ wants us to be an expression of Himself.

Word Studies: 1:28 **an evident token of perdition** means a clear sign of their impending destruction; 2:3 **vainglory** means boasting; self-conceit; 3:2 **the concision** means false circumcision; 3:20 **conversation** (from a different Greek word than the one used in Galatians 1:13) means citizenship; 4:5 **moderation** means patience; 4:18 **I have all** means I have all I need.

Prayer Needs: Country: Australia—16 million—an island continent between the Indian and Pacific Oceans • Religious freedom • 49% Protestant; 30% Roman Catholic; 3% Eastern Orthodox.

COLOSSIANS _____

The supremacy of Christ over His people—the Church—is the theme of this book. The Church is compared to the physical body that is subject to the control of the head. As Christians, we are the Body of Christ and are to be subject to Him, the Head, in all things.

A personal relationship with Christ produces within the Christian a desire to obey Him—to please Him and to live for Him. Christ is our life, and we are *"complete in him"* (2:10).

This book points out that the Christian life does not mean resting one's salvation upon obedience to a set of rules; rather, it means trusting Christ and allowing Him to work in and through our lives. Our hope of eternal life is based on Christ alone—not on ourselves.

A key thought is *"that in all things he might have the pre-eminence"* (1:18).

DECEMBER 6: Read Colossians 1 — 4

Highlights: The supremacy of Christ; reconciliation in Christ; warning against false teaching; the new life in Christ; Christian virtues.

Verses for Today: *"For this cause we . . . pray . . . that ye might be filled with the knowledge of his will in all wisdom and spiritual understanding . . . strengthened with all might, according to his glorious power, unto all patience and long-suffering with joyfulness; Giving thanks unto the Father"* (Colossians 1:9,11-12).

T o grasp the importance of this prayer, notice how many times the word "all" is used: *"all wisdom . . . all might . . . all patience."*

God desires that we be led by *"the knowledge of his will in all wisdom"* and strengthened with *"his glorious power."* Two keys to accomplishing this are prayer and the Word of God. As we read all of His Word with a desire to please Him in all things, we will be strengthened with *"his glorious power."* There is no limit to the divine wisdom, strength, and endurance that is made available to every Christian!

The *"exceeding great and precious"* promises of God are given to those who pray specifically and persistently (II Peter 1:4).

"And whatsoever we ask, we receive of him, because we keep his commandments, and do those things that are pleasing in his sight" (I John 3:22).

Thought for Today: The prayers of the upright are the Lord's delight.

Word Studies: 1:13 **translated** means transferred; bought; 2:19 **bands** means that which binds firmly together; 3:5 **concupiscence** means evil desire; lust; 4:16 **epistle** means letter, message.

Prayer Needs: Country: Republic of China (Taiwan)—20 million—77 islands off the southeastern coast of Red China • Religious freedom • 47% Chinese folk-religionist; 44% Buddhist; 4% Protestant; 1% Roman Catholic.

I & II THESSALONIANS _____

The Apostle Paul was led to Thessalonica, a leading city in Macedonia, on his second missionary journey (see Acts 17:1-9). Although he met with violent opposition, some Jews and also many Greeks were won to Christ, and a faithful church was established.

Thessalonica, located at the northwest corner of the Aegean Sea, is still a prosperous Greek city.

The purpose of I and II Thessalonians is to prepare us for Christ's return so that our *whole spirit and soul and body will be blameless when our Lord Jesus Christ returns* (see I Thessalonians 5:23).

In II Thessalonians, Paul points out that before Christ returns, evil and wickedness will become more intense under the leadership of a mysterious person, known as the wicked one, who will be in opposition to Christ (see II Thessalonians 2:3-4).

Christians are urged to remain faithful during times of suffering or persecution, while patiently waiting for Christ's return.

His return is the major theme of these two short letters and is referred to more than twenty times in just eight chapters.

DECEMBER 7: Read I Thessalonians 1 — 5

Highlights: Paul's preaching; his appeal for purity; the coming of the Lord.

Verses for Today: *"And the Lord make you to increase and abound in love one toward another, and toward all men, even as we do toward you: To the end he may stablish your hearts unblamable in holiness before God, even our Father, at the coming of our Lord Jesus Christ with all his saints"* (I Thessalonians 3:12-13).

A mong the words of comfort to His disciples was the Savior's promise that He would come again and receive them unto Himself (John 14:1-3). This is the confident expectation of every Christian. Christ's return to earth will be the greatest event ever to take place since His ascension when *"a cloud received him out of their sight"* (Acts 1:9). Christians should be eagerly awaiting His return.

Let us beware of becoming involved in worldly activities that rob us of our spiritual usefulness and preparedness. Faithfully watch and wait for the triumphant return of our Redeemer, *"the author and finisher of our faith"* (Hebrews 12:2).

"For the Lord himself shall descend from heaven with a shout, with the voice of the archangel, and with the trump of God: and the dead in Christ shall rise first: Then we which are alive and remain shall be caught up together with them in the clouds, to meet the Lord in the air: and so shall we ever be with the Lord" (I Thessalonians 4:16-17).

Thought for Today: The Lord is returning for those who have made themselves ready (see Revelation 19:7).

Word Studies: 2:2 **entreated** means insulted; 2:9 **chargeable** means an expense; 3:8 **fast** means firm; 4:4 **possess his vessel** means control his own body; 4:15 **prevent** means precede; 5:14 **unruly** means the loafers; the disorderly; the insubordinate; 5:22 **all appearance** means every kind.

Prayer Needs: Country: Scotland—6 million—north of England and part of the United Kingdom • Religious freedom • 73% Protestant; 16% Roman Catholic .

314

Highlights: Encouragement in persecution; instruction concerning the day of the Lord; commandment to work.

Verse for Today: *"And to you who are troubled rest with us, when the Lord Jesus shall be revealed from heaven with his mighty angels"* (II Thessalonians 1:7).

T he second coming of Christ is mentioned 318 times in the 260 chapters of the New Testament. His second coming is the predominant theme in these two short letters to the Thessalonians and is referred to more than twenty times.

Christ's first coming was sudden, and He surprised the religious leaders of His time; but His second coming will be an even greater surprise to most people. *" . . . the day of the Lord so cometh as a thief in the night"* (I Thessalonians 5:2), but it will be good news to all who love Him and mourn over the chaos and suffering of a world that is ruined by sin.

Bible-reading Christians are earnestly awaiting this blessed event. As the bride prepares for her bridegroom, so those who sincerely anticipate His return will prepare themselves for this great and wonderful day: *"And every man that hath this hope in him purifieth himself, even as he is pure"* (I John 3:3).

Although we do not know the exact day or hour of our Lord's return, the time is drawing near *"when he shall come to be glorified in his saints, and to be admired in all them that believe (because our testimony among you was believed) in that day"* (II Thessalonians 1:10).

"Watch therefore, for ye know neither the day nor the hour wherein the Son of man cometh" (Matthew 25:13).

Thought for Today: Jesus is coming soon! Are you ready to meet Him?

Word Studies: 1:3 **meet** means proper; duty; 2:17 **stablish** means strengthen; 3:7 **disorderly** means irresponsibly; undisciplined.

Prayer Needs: Country: Austria—8 million—in central Europe • Religious freedom • 88% Roman Catholic; 6% Protestant.

I & II TIMOTHY

In writing the first letter to Timothy, the Apostle Paul, under the inspiration of God, points out the necessity of right doctrine in order to worship and live to please the Lord.

He emphasizes the importance of godly leadership—of elders and deacons being men whose lives are consistent with the Word of God. He also points out certain qualifications which they must meet (3:1-13).

Paul challenges Timothy to be a good servant of Jesus Christ (4:6), to remain loyal to Christ and His authoritative Word (6:3-4), and to *"fight the good fight of faith"* (6:12). God had entrusted the gospel to Paul (1:11), and Paul was faithful to pass it along to Timothy (1:18-19; 6:20).

The book of II Timothy points out the all-sufficiency of the Scriptures—through the indwelling Holy Spirit—to reveal the answers to all of life's problems. Because of this, it shows the importance of thoroughly studying all the Bible.

Think of it! The Bible *is profitable for instruction in righteousness: that every Christian may be thoroughly furnished unto all good works*—fully equipped and prepared to accomplish the purpose for which God created us (see 3:16-17).

These two letters point out that believing God's Word as the ultimate authority is the only effective safeguard against believing false doctrine—against living a life that is a mixture of truth and error.

DECEMBER 9: Read I Timothy 1 — 6

Highlights: Warning against false doctrine; thankfulness for mercy; qualifications of church leaders; instructions about widows and the elderly; the good fight of faith.

Verses for Today: *"I exhort therefore, that, first of all, supplications, prayers, intercessions, and giving of thanks, be made for all men; For kings, and for all that are in authority; that we may lead a quiet and peaceable life in all godliness and honesty"* (I Timothy 2:1-2).

T his world would be a wonderful place to live if all the rulers, kings, and presidents were Christians who were concerned with administering justice for everyone—rich and poor alike. To the contrary, the majority of the people in the world are ruled by ungodly men.

Although there is no mention in the Bible of the cruel Roman ruler Nero, it appears that at the time Paul wrote the book of I Timothy, Nero was persecuting Christians and even having them put to death. Yet, Paul emphasized the importance of Christians praying for those who were in authority over them.

As we pray for world leaders, we can be sure our prayers will have an effect upon the actions of rulers—whether they are godly or evil. But equally important, prayer will produce in the one who prays *"a quiet and peaceable life in all godliness."*

Let every Christian submit to the governing authorities. No authority exists without God's permission, and the existing authorities have been put there by God (see Romans 13:1).

Thought for Today: The peace of God can rule our hearts—regardless of outward circumstances.

Word Studies: 1:5 **faith unfeigned** means a genuine, sincere faith; 1:6 **vain jangling** means purposeless talk and arguing; 1:10 **menstealers** means people who are enslaving and controlling others for their own evil purposes; 2:7 **verity** means truth; 2:9 **shamefacedness** means freedom from vanity; decency of behavior; 2:12 **usurp** means claim; 3:1 **bishop** means spiritual overseer; 3:2 **vigilant** means self-controlled; 3:8 **of filthy lucre** means for gain; 3:13 **purchase to themselves a good degree** means acquire an excellent standing for themselves; 4:14 **presbytery** means board of elders; 5:3 **widows indeed** means truly widowed—alone and without support; 5:11 **wax wanton** means allow their passions to draw them away from Christ; 5:18 **that treadeth out the corn** means while he is threshing grain; 6:4 **questions** means controversies; 6:5 **supposing that gain is godliness** means assuming that godliness is a means to financial gain.

Cross Reference: For **Timothy 5:18:** See Deut. 25:4.

Prayer Needs: **Country:** South Africa—34 million—on the southern tip of the African continent • Religious freedom • 67% Protestant; 20% animism, magic, and ancestor worship; 10% Roman Catholic; 3% Asian religions.

DECEMBER 10: Read II Timothy 1 — 4

Highlights: Exhortations to Timothy; the coming apostasy; steadfastness in the Scriptures; the charge to preach.

Verse for Today: *"Thou therefore endure hardness, as a good soldier of Jesus Christ"* (II Timothy 2:3).

T he ministry of Paul was marked by much suffering that demanded great endurance (II Corinthians 11:22-28). He was in Roman prisons many times, but through it all, he never considered himself the prisoner of anyone other than Jesus (see Philemon 1:1).

Paul knew that the end of his life was near, and he was deeply concerned that Timothy, his "son in the faith," be prepared to carry on the work of the Lord as a good soldier of Jesus Christ. He urged him to *"endure hardness"* (hardships and sufferings) and told him the secret of his success by urging him: *"Study to show thyself approved unto God, a workman that needeth not to be ashamed, rightly dividing the word of truth"* (II Timothy 2:15).

Paul emphasized that *all* Scripture is necessary for a Christian to be fully prepared to do the work of God.

Timothy, as well as Christians today, is exhorted to be fully equipped with the Word of God (3:16-17) and be willing to witness *"in season, out of season"* (4:2)—when it is convenient, as well as when it seems inconvenient.

"A good soldier of Jesus Christ" obeys our Lord's orders. He knows that Christ is concerned for his welfare and will not leave him alone in any situation.

"But continue thou in the things which thou hast learned and hast been assured of, knowing of whom thou hast learned them; And that from a child thou hast known the holy scriptures, which are able to make thee wise unto salvation through faith which is in Christ Jesus" (II Timothy 3:14-15).

Thought for Today: The *will* of God does not lead where the *grace* of God cannot protect.

Word Studies: 2:4 **entangleth himself** means becomes involved; 2:5 **strive for masteries** means compete as an athlete; 2:17 **canker** means cancer; 2:23 **gender** means produce; 3:3 **incontinent** means without self-control; 4:15 **be thou ware** means be aware; be on guard.

Cross Reference: For II Timothy 2:19: See Num. 16:5.

Prayer Needs: Country: Tibet—population unknown—in eastern Asia • The Chinese government is still committed to promoting atheism, while at the same time officially permitting Lamaism (a form of Buddhism) • No religious statistics are available, but at one time all were Lamaists. Lamaism was all but exterminated by Chinese invaders in the 1950s, but it is now permitted under strict control.

TITUS _____

Titus emphasizes moral and spiritual guidelines for church leaders. They must be blameless in their personal lives and true to the Word (1:6-9).

This book warns that *there are many undisciplined people who deceive others with their nonsense. They teach things they should not teach, and all with the shameful motive of making money. They openly claim to know the Lord, but by their actions they deny Him* (see 1:10-11).

The importance of acceptable Christian service is emphasized many times in Titus. We should be examples of good behavior (2:7), eager to do good (2:14), obedient to those in authority (3:1), and spend what time we can providing for the needs of others (3:8,14).

The key thought in Titus is that Christ *gave Himself for us, that He might redeem us from all sin and purify unto Himself a special group of people who are not only zealous to do good works but also to live godly lives* (see 2:14).

PHILEMON

Philemon, a convert of Paul, was probably a wealthy person in Colossae.

Onesimus, a slave who belonged to Philemon, had run away to Rome and had met the Apostle Paul. Paul sent him back to his master with this beautiful letter, urging Philemon to forgive the runaway slave and receive him back—not only as a Christian brother, but as he would receive Paul himself.

As Paul was willing to pay the price for disobedient Onesimus, so Christ paid the price on the cross for us. This emphasizes that forgiving love should bring about reconciliation.

The key thought is that Christ has joined every Christian to Himself and thus created a spiritual brotherhood that will cause both master and slave to recognize that they are one in Christ.

DECEMBER 11: Read Titus—Philemon

Highlights: Qualifications of church officers; warning against false teachers; Christian conduct; Paul's appeal for Onesimus.

Verses for Today: *"Put them in mind to be subject to principalities and powers, to obey magistrates, to be ready to every good work, To speak evil of no man, to be no brawlers, but gentle, showing all meekness unto all men"* (Titus 3:1-2).

U nder the inspiration of God, the Apostle Peter emphasized the responsibility of Christians to be law-abiding citizens: *"Submit yourselves to every ordinance of man for the Lord's sake: whether it be to the king, as supreme; Or unto governors, as unto them that are sent by him for the punishment of evildoers, and for the praise of them that do well"* (I Peter 2:13-14).

Does this Scripture mean we should submit passively to corrupt governments or be unfaithful to God's Word if evil forces demand it? Of course not!

When Peter and the other apostles were commanded by religious authorities not to tell others that Jesus was the Messiah-Savior of the world, they responded as faithful Christians, saying, *"We ought to obey God rather than men"* (Acts 5:29).

But early Christians never reacted with hatred against those who attempted to silence them. Christians should faithfully declare the truth—even when it could mean imprisonment or death. No one is ever justified in responding with force or violence. It is Satan who instigates violence and rioting.

"For so is the will of God, that with well doing ye may put to silence the ignorance of foolish men" (I Peter 2:15).

Thought for Today: Peace comes to those who joyfully submit to God and His Word.

Word Studies: Titus 1:1 **servant** means slave; bond servant; 1:7 **no striker** means not quarrelsome; not a bully; 1:9 **gainsayers** means those who contradict and oppose; 1:11 **subvert whole houses, teaching things which they ought not** means mislead whole families by false teaching; **lucre** means money; 2:10 **purloining** means stealing; pilfering; embezzling; 2:14 **peculiar people** means a people for His own special possession; Philemon 1:8 **enjoin** means give directions; 1:12 **mine own bowels** means my very heart.

Prayer Needs: Country: Bahamas—239,000—in the northern portion of the West Indies • Religious freedom • 56% Protestant; 13% Roman Catholic; 1% Afro-American spiritist.

HEBREWS _____

The superiority of Christ is the theme of this book. He is presented as far superior to the prophets, the priests, Moses, the Law, and even angels.

Christ cleansed us from our sins by His blood, and He now sits at the right hand of God as our High Priest who *lives forever to intercede in prayer* for us (see 7:25).

The first covenant of God, centered upon the Ten Commandments, was written on tablets of stone; but Christ's covenant is to be written upon our hearts (8:10). The old covenant was temporary, but Christ's covenant is eternal (13:20). For believers to worship God under the old covenant, it was necessary for the blood of many animals to be offered daily. But the new covenant required only one sacrifice—Christ's own blood (see 10:1-29).

The word "better" is one of the key words in the book of Hebrews—we have a better hope (7:19), a better covenant (8:6), better promises (8:6), and a better possession (10:34).

This book shows that the source of power to live the victorious Christian life is Jesus Christ. He is the Living Word of God, who is all-wise and all-knowing. *He upholds all things by the word of His power* (see 1:3).

Let us approach God's throne of grace with assurance, that we may receive mercy for our failures and find grace to help us when we need it (see 4:16).

DECEMBER 12: Read Hebrews 1 — 4

Highlights: Why Christ assumed a human body; Christ's superioritity to angels and to Moses; Christ's work of salvation; danger of unbelief; a rest for God's people; Christ, our High Priest.

Verses for Today: *"There remaineth therefore a rest to the people of God. For he that is entered into his rest, he also hath ceased from his own works, as God did from his"* (Hebrews 4:9-10).

C hrist's rest is not a rest from work, but a rest while working. It is not the rest of inactivity, but of inward contentment and peace of mind. This is a result of allowing our thoughts, actions, and reactions to be pleasing to Him. With this rest, the day-by-day activities of our lives are neither frustrating nor boring.

But many have never entered into God's rest. They rely upon their own clever strategies to accomplish their goals and become angry or resentful when their plans fail or when someone opposes them. They have no *"rest"*—no resting from self-effort; consequently, they cheat themselves of enjoying His peace. They do not experience the joy of letting Christ express Himself through them.

It is impossible to experience God's rest while maintaining an attitude of dissatisfaction or criticism toward another. Even if we are right and can "justify" our opinions, it is a serious offense against God to hold bitterness toward someone. Satan loves to turn our attention from Christ to self, thus destroying the peace of God in our lives.

So then, let us seek those things that make for peace (see Romans 14:19).

Thought for Today: We must determine whether we will let Christ, the Prince of peace, rule our hearts, or insist on having things our way and suffer the consequences of frustration and despair.

Word Studies: 2:17 **behooved** means was necessary for; 4:8 **Jesus** means Joshua; 4:12 **quick** means living.

Cross References: For **Hebrews 1:5:** See Psa. 2:7; II Sam. 7:14. **Heb. 1:6:** See Psa. 97:7. **Heb. 1:7:** See Psa. 104:4. **Heb. 1:8-9:** See Psa. 45:6-7. **Heb. 1:10-12:** See Psa. 102:25-27. **Heb. 1:13:** See Psa. 110:1. **Heb. 2:6-8:** See Psa. 8:4-6. **Heb. 2:12:** See Psa. 22:22. **Heb. 2:13:** See Isa. 8:18. **Heb. 3:7-11:** See Psa. 95:7-11. **Heb. 4:3:** See Psa. 95:11. **Heb. 4:4:** See Gen. 2:2.

Prayer Needs: **Country:** Haiti—6 million—in the West Indies • Religious freedom • 75% Roman Catholic; 17% Protestant.

DECEMBER 13: Read Hebrews 5 — 7

Highlights: Christ, the High Priest; priestly order of Melchizedek; Aaronic priesthood inferior to Christ's priesthood.

Verse for Today: *"And no man taketh this honor unto himself, but he that is called of God, as was Aaron"* (Hebrews 5:4).

E very year on the day of Atonement, God directed Aaron to offer a sacrifice as an atonement—first for his own sins and then for the sins of his family. Only then was he qualified to make an atonement for the sins of the people (Leviticus 16:11-16).

By contrast, on *the* great day of Atonement, Christ—the Lamb of God—offered Himself once and for all as a sacrifice and was crucified. Through His death, He made atonement for the sins of all who would believe in Him.

Because Jesus is the sinless Son of God, there was no need for Him to make a sin offering for Himself as Aaron did.

How assuring to know that anytime, day or night, we can come to God, confess our sins, and receive His gracious mercy through Jesus, our High Priest!

"If we confess our sins, he is faithful and just to forgive us our sins, and to cleanse us from all unrighteousness: (I John 1:9).

Thought for Today: No sin is so great God's mercy cannot forgive.

Word Study: 6:17 **immutability** means unchangeableness.

Cross References: For **Hebrews 5:5:** See Psa. 2:7. **Heb. 5:6:** See Psa. 110:4. **Heb. 6:14:** See Gen. 22:17.

Prayer Needs: Country: Jamaica—3 million—in the West Indies • Religious freedom • 78% Protestant; 10% Roman Catholic; 7% Afro-American spiritist .

DECEMBER 14: Read Hebrews 8 — 10

Highlights: The new covenant; the perfect sacrifice of Christ compared to the inferior sacrifices under the Law; an appeal to be steadfast in our faith.

Verses for Today: *" ... I will put my laws into their mind, and write them in their hearts: and I will be to them a God, and they shall be to me a people ... for all shall know me, from the least to the greatest"* (Hebrews 8:10-11).

F ellowship with God became possible in a new way through His covenant: *I will put my laws into their minds and write them on their hearts.*

God greatly desires to have fellowship with mankind—to have us know Him in a very personal way.

When a person turns to Christ as Savior, he receives a new nature, making it possible for him to *"serve the living God"* (Hebrews 9:14). We have the privilege of living in the presence of the Most High every moment of every day, in every circumstance, *by a new way, a living way* that imparts a heartfelt desire to please the Lord (see 10:20).

We do not have a High Priest who cannot sympathize with our weaknesses, but One who has been tempted just as we are, yet He never sinned (see Hebrews 4:15).

Thought for Today: God created man with a heart so unique that nothing less than fellowship with God can really satisfy him.

Word Studies: 9:2 **candlestick** means lampstand; 10:33 **gazingstock** means object of ridicule; 10:36 **patience** means steadfast endurance—a trust that all is in His hands; 10:39 **perdition** means destruction.

Cross References: For **Hebrews 8:5:** See Ex. 25:40. **Heb. 8:8-12:** See Jer. 31:31-34. **Heb. 9:20:** See Ex. 24:8. **Heb. 10:5-7:** See Psa. 40:6-8. **Heb. 10:12-13:** See Psa. 110:1. **Heb. 10:16-17:** See Jer. 31:33-34. **Heb. 10:30:** See Deut. 32:35-36. **Heb. 10:37-38:** See Hab. 2:3-4.

Prayer Needs: Country: Nepal—18 million—a mountain-ringed Himalayan state between Tibet and India • Limited religious freedom • 89% Hindu; 7% Buddhist; 3% Muslim; .3% Protestant.

DECEMBER 15: Read Hebrews 11 — 13

Highlights: Worthy fruits of faith, patience, godliness; warning against disobedience; service well-pleasing to God.

Verses for Today: *"By faith Abraham, when he was called to go out into a place which he should after receive for an inheritance, obeyed; and he went out, not knowing whither he went. By faith he sojourned in the land of promise, as in a strange country, dwelling in tabernacles [tents] . . . For he looked for a city . . . whose builder and maker is God"* (Hebrews 11:8-10).

A braham is the father of the faithful (see Romans 4:11). In obedience to God and His Word, he left family, friends, and the security of his own country to live in tents as a homeless stranger in the land of promise (see Genesis 12:1; Acts 7:2-4).

Abraham *"was called to go out into a place which he should after receive for an inheritance."* Although there were many disappointments, there is no record he ever complained that he had been cheated or given less than God's best.

Many people feel that it is not possible to leave the security of one's home, country, friends, or family and still be happy and content. But the example of Abraham illustrates the great secret of faith in our God to guide us through the ordinary experiences of life—where we should live, what our occupation should be, and whom we will have as friends.

We may experience many disappointments before we recognize that God is leading us to see beyond life's unsatisfying, false rewards.

God seldom fulfills His promises in ways we would expect. But as our faith in God grows, we will be less concerned over earthly possessions and pleasures, and our thoughts will be more and more occupied with that heavenly city *"whose builder and maker is God."*

"He is a rewarder of them that diligently seek him" (Hebrews 11:6).

Thought for Today: To fulfill God's purpose, we obey His Word by faith.

Word Studies: 11:13 **embraced them** means by faith, saw it all awaiting them; 11:29 **assaying** means attempting; 13:9 **divers** means various.

Cross References: For **Hebrews 11:18:** See Gen. 21:12. **Heb. 12:5-6:** See Prov. 3:11-12. **Heb. 12:12:** See Isa. 35:3. **Heb. 12:26:** See Hag. 2:6. **Heb. 13:5:** See Josh. 1:5. **Heb. 13:6:** See Psa. 118:6.

Prayer Needs: Country: Burkina Faso (formerly Upper Volta)—8 million—in western Africa • Religious freedom • 47% Muslim; 39% belief in false gods, idolatry, and heathenism; 12% Roman Catholic; 2% Protestant.

JAMES

The book of James is a guide to Christian living and conduct. It presents a series of practical tests whereby we may recognize the genuineness of our faith. True faith not only produces visible works of Christian service in obedience to the Scriptures, but it also enables us to endure trials and remain faithful to God and His Word.

James gives advice on subjects such as wealth and poverty, showing favoritism, temptation, controlling the tongue, anger, pride, humility, patience, boasting, sickness, and prayer.

In the first and last chapters, James urges Christians to pray (1:5-8; 5:13-18). He illustrates the great power of prayer by reminding us of Elijah—just an ordinary person who believed that God could and would answer his prayer.

God is the source of all true wisdom. When we become aware of this fact, we will read His Word with meekness and then pray for understanding and His direction—that God's Holy Spirit will work through us to make us *"doers of the word, and not hearers only"* (1:22).

DECEMBER 16: Read James 1 — 5

Highlights: Christians to rejoice in trials; heeding God's Word; faith that works; dangers of the tongue; worldliness and pride; warning to the rich; the power of prayer.

Verses for Today: *"Is any among you afflicted? let him pray. . . . The effectual fervent prayer of a righteous man availeth much"* (James 5:13,16).

A s Christians, it is of utmost importance that we listen to what God is saying as we read the Bible, for it is through His Word that we learn what wonderful resources are available to us.

All of us are "afflicted" at times. Afflictions are the distresses, burdens, and problems of life. Every affliction we face presents the opportunity, as well as the responsibility, to pray and trust God for the solution.

But too often we allow people or wrong attitudes to keep us from praying. Furthermore, when we fail to pray and wait for direction from God, our efforts often become fruitless because we are substituting our own plans for God's will.

Our prayer lives should express our desire for God to work in us and fulfill His will through us.

Prayer is God's way of releasing His power to accomplish His will. Just as praying Christians release God's power, prayerless Christians are a hindrance to accomplishing His will.

"If ye abide in me, and my words abide in you, ye shall ask what ye will, and it shall be done unto you" (John 15:7).

Thought for Today: It is not only sinful things that blight our lives, but anything that we allow to take the place of prayer or Bible reading.

Word Studies: 1:21 **superfluity of** means excessive; 1:27 **visit** means look after the needs of; 2:11 **kill** means murder; 3:2 **in many things we offend all** means we all make mistakes, fall short of God's best, and offend others; 3:4 **listeth** means chooses; 5:3 **cankered** means rusted through; 5:11 **pitiful** means full of compassion; 5:16 **effectual** means unceasing; intense; unwavering.

Cross References: For **James 2:8:** See Lev. 19:18. **James 2:11:** See Ex. 20:13-14. **James 2:23:** See Gen. 15:6. **James 4:6:** See Prov. 3:34.

Prayer Needs: Country: Cape Verde—344,000—15 islands in the Atlantic Ocean, 390 miles off the coast of Africa • Religious freedom • 91% Roman Catholic; 3% Protestant.

I & II PETER

The purpose of I Peter is to encourage Christians to depend on God to answer prayer, sustain and strengthen them, and meet their needs in the midst of suffering (5:10). Since the days of the early Church when great persecution forced believers to leave Jerusalem (see Acts 8:1), Christians have been subjected to all kinds of suffering.

During times of suffering, the assurance of the Lord's presence and the expectation that He will soon return become *"more precious"* to Christians than ever before (1:7).

In II Peter the true knowledge of our Lord is contrasted with false knowledge. The work of false teachers and the immorality that results from such teaching is also exposed (3:3-8,17-18).

DECEMBER 17: Read I Peter 1 — 2

Highlights: Call to Christian dedication; proper use of Christian liberty; the example of Christ's suffering.

Verses for Today: *"Wherefore gird up the loins of your mind . . . not fashioning yourselves according to the former lusts in your ignorance: But as he which hath called you is holy, so be ye holy in all manner of conversation"* (I Peter 1:13-15).

In Bible times, girding up the loins of the body meant tucking up the long garments with a sash-like belt to prepare for physical work. If people let their clothing hang loosely, it would greatly hinder their ability to work or run.

Christians, too, are commanded to *"gird up the loins"* of their minds in preparation for service to God. This can only be done by reading His Word and praying that the indwelling Holy Spirit will strengthen us to live according to His Word.

At the time we accepted Christ as our Savior, the Holy Spirit came to live within us and brought about a miraculous change that we call the new birth or being born again. No longer should we live by those desires we had before we received Christ. We are called to a life of separation from the defiling things of the world. Christians can be holy through yielding control of our lives to the Holy Spirit. We can do what is pleasing to our Lord.

We are prone to let our minds follow the "fashion" of the world and have an attitude of indifference to the Lord's will in reaching a lost world unless we set aside a time for prayer and reading through His Word. It is so important that we do what we can to influence others for Christ.

"Stand therefore, having your loins girt about with truth, and having on the breastplate of righteousness" (Ephesians 6:14).

Thought for Today: If the world cannot see a difference between the life of a Christian and that of an unbeliever, then the Christian is not serving the Lord effectively.

Word Studies: 1:1 **strangers** means exiles; 1:17 **sojourning** means temporarily residing; 2:2 **sincere** means pure; without a mixture; 2:4 **disallowed** means rejected; 2:19 **thankworthy** means approved; 2:24 **stripes** means wounds.

Cross References: For **I Peter 1:16:** See Lev. 11:44. **I Pet. 1:24-25:** See Isa. 40:

6-8. **I Pet. 2:6:** See Isa. 28:16. **I Pet. 2:7:** See Psa. 118:22. **I Pet. 2:22:** See Isa. 53:9. **I Pet. 2:24:** See Isa. 53:4-5.

Prayer Needs: Country: Iraq—17 million—in southern Asia • Surveillance and harassment of non-Muslims • 96% Muslim; 3% Christian.

DECEMBER 18: Read I Peter 3 — 5

Highlights: Duties of husbands and wives; suffering and reward; duty of elders.

Verses for Today: *"But and if ye suffer for righteousness' sake, happy are ye: and be not afraid of their terror, neither be troubled.... Forasmuch then as Christ hath suffered for us in the flesh, arm yourselves likewise with the same mind ... "* (I Peter 3:14; 4:1).

C hrist gives spiritual strength to believers that they may be victorious over suffering as He was when He was on earth.

When Jesus told His disciples that *He must go to Jerusalem, suffer much, and be put to death*, Peter did not realize that suffering was God's will. This is why Peter rebuked the Lord, saying *This must never happen to You* (see Matthew 16:21-22).

But through the years, Peter learned that all of us at times may experience humiliation and suffering and have to go without certain personal enjoyments because of our stand for Christ. *This is the life to which we have been called, for Christ Himself suffered for us* (see I Peter 2:21).

Our reaction to suffering or trials depends on our faith in the sovereignty of God. When we realize that all things work together for good and that we are actually strengthened through these trials, we will praise the Lord. Our suffering ought not make us angry or bitter and lead us to sin. *When Christ was insulted, He did not retaliate; when He suffered, He made no threats. Instead, He entrusted Himself to God, the righteous Judge* (see 2:23).

"But the God of all grace, who hath called us unto his eternal glory by Christ Jesus, after that ye have suffered a while, make you perfect, stablish, strengthen, settle you" (I Peter 5:10).

Thought for Today: Christ always provides the needed strength to those who remain faithful to Him in times of testing.

Word Studies: 3:11 **eschew** means avoid; turn from; **ensue** means pursue; go after; 3:20 **were saved by water** means were saved from the water by entering the ark; 4:15 **busybody** means meddler.

Cross References: For **I Peter 3:10-12:** See Psa. 34:12-16. **I Pet. 5:5:** See Prov. 3:34.

Prayer Needs: Country: Mauritius—1 million—500 miles east of Madagascar • Limited religious freedom • 50% Hindu; 27% Roman Catholic; 17% Muslim; 5% Protestant.

DECEMBER 19: Read II Peter 1 — 3

Highlights: God's manifold graces; false teachers; the certainty of Christ's coming.

Verses for Today: *" ... what manner of persons ought ye to be in all holy conversation and godliness, Looking for ... the coming of the day of God ... ?"* (II Peter 3:11-12).

As Christians, our greatest desire should be to please Christ and glorify Him—not only in the way we think, act, and talk, but also in helping others prepare to meet the Lord.

There is a real danger in becoming so involved with material, personal, or social demands that our daily lives do not glorify Christ. Even though we may not be committing any particular sin, our time, conduct, and thoughts can be wasted on "good things" that keep us from God's best.

As Christians, we need to avoid the things that are not in harmony with God's eternal purpose and calling. Out of a grateful heart to the Lord for our salvation, we should seek opportunities to serve Him, giving freely of ourselves so that the same saving gospel may be spread throughout the world.

So let us humbly and diligently walk before God with our lives dedicated to Him, dying to self-exaltation and avoiding things that waste our time.

"Whereby are given unto us exceeding great and precious promises: that by these ye might be partakers of the divine nature, having escaped the corruption that is in the world through lust" (II Peter 1:4).

Thought for Today: Those who continually yield to worldly influences will stand ashamed before the Lord.

Word Study: 2:7 **filthy conversation** means immoral conduct.

Cross Reference: For **II Peter 2:22:** See Prov. 26:11.

Prayer Needs: Country: North Yemen—7 million—in southwestern Arabia • Attempts to convert Muslims to Christ are fiercely opposed • Approximately 100% Muslim.

I JOHN

The book of I John encourages Christians to live in fellowship with the Lord and with others.

The word "love," in its various forms, appears more than 40 times in the five short chapters of I John.

Love is the distinguishing characteristic of a Christian. Love for others and our love for God are inseparably linked together. If a person says he loves God but hates another person, he is only deceiving himself. The Scriptures say that *anyone who keeps on hating his brother is a murderer, and you know that a murderer does not have eternal life in him* (see 3:15).

God's indwelling love causes a remarkable, two-fold change in the lives of Christians: a desire to please God, and a love for others—regardless of their attitudes and actions toward us (3:10-11,14; 4:7,11-12,19-20).

The book of I John also warns against following false teaching that would keep us from true fellowship with God and His Son.

In these days when religious deception abounds, it is important that we study the tests John provides to carefully examine our convictions as well as our lives.

DECEMBER 20: Read I John 1 — 3

Highlights: Tests of fellowship with God; reality of and remedy for sin; danger of antichrists; loving one another.

Verses for Today: *" . . . whosoever doeth not righteousness is not of God, neither he that loveth not his brother. For this is the message that ye heard from the beginning, that we should love one another. Not as Cain, who was of that wicked one, and slew his brother. And wherefore slew he him? Because his own works were evil, and his brother's righteous"* (I John 3:10-12).

Cain was a religious person—one who built an altar and offered a sacrifice to God. But he became jealous because God blessed his brother Abel. God warned Cain to repent of his jealousy, saying, *If you do what is right, then you will be accepted; if you desire to offer an acceptable sacrifice, you must have a right attitude toward your brother.* But Cain disregarded God's warning, and his hatred led to murder. (See Genesis 4:7-8.)

To become jealous, resentful, or hateful over someone else's blessings, promotions, or recognition is a sin. Hatred is one of the *"works of the flesh."* Love is a *"fruit of the Spirit."* (See Galatians 5:19-26.)

We know that we have left death and have come over into life because we love our fellow Christians. Whoever does not love them is still under the power of death (see I John 3:14).

Thought for Today: Those who continue to harbor hatred always do more damage to themselves than they do to those they hate.

Prayer Needs: Country: Tunisia—8 million—in North Africa • An Islamic state—no open ministry for Christ permitted; strict surveillance of all Christian activities • 99+% Muslim; .3% Christian.

DECEMBER 21: Read I John 4 — 5

Highlights: How to test the spirits; an appeal to brotherly love; the witness of the Spirit.

Verse for Today: *"Beloved, if God so loved us, we ought also to love one another"* (I John 4:11).

Men have written millions of books on every conceivable subject. In contrast, God has given only one Book throughout all the history of mankind; and each word is important—*"All scripture is given by inspiration of God, and is profitable . . . "* (II Timothy 3:16).

A rule to remember concerning the importance of what God has said is this: When God says something once, it is important; but when He says it more than once, we must give it utmost consideration. In I John 4, love is referred to more than 25 times. In view of this, let's consider the seriousness of our responsibility as stewards of God's love.

The very nature of God is love, and if we have received His nature, we have love for other Christians (I John 4:7).

It is not enough merely to know of God's love; we must manifest His love and long-suffering in our daily encounters with others. Expressing the nature of God's love should be more important to us than insisting on our rights.

The sincerity of our love can be measured by the kindness that we show to others.

"If a man say, I love God, and hateth his brother, he is a liar: for he that loveth not his brother whom he hath seen, how can he love God whom he hath not seen?" (I John 4:20).

Thought for Today: The very nature of love compels us to give of ourselves for the sake of others.

Word Study: 5:18 **he that is begotten of God keepeth himself** means Jesus, who was born of God, carefully watches over and protects the child of God.

Prayer Needs: **Country:** Somalia—8 million—on the Horn of Africa • Islam is officially favored and all other religions opposed • 99.8% Muslim; .1% Christian.

II & III JOHN, JUDE _____

The book of II John emphasizes the importance of teaching the truth of the Word of God. The word "truth" is used several times in the first four verses. John urges believers to examine their opinions, beliefs, and motives to make sure they are living according to the truth of God's Word.

The book also warns against false teachers and appeals to readers to continue to love each other, *living in the truth as the Father commanded us* (see verse 4).

In III John, we are introduced to three people: Demetrius, a pleasant Christian whom John praises; Gaius, a generous helper in the Lord's work; and Diotrephes, a proud, demanding man with exceptional abilities, but who is a hindrance to the ministry of God's Word. These men are examples of many today—either helping or hindering the ministry of Christ.

The book of Jude reveals the fearful consequences of believing false doctrines. The purpose of this letter, as stated in verses 3 and 4, is to expose the nature and conduct of false teachers. These godless people (verse 4) are denounced and their inevitable fate made known—*"Woe unto them! . . . to whom is reserved the blackness of darkness for ever"* (verses 11,13).

Although Jude speaks of judgment, he carefully points out that the true believer is kept in Christ (verse 1) and will be presented *faultless before His glorious presence* (see verse 24).

DECEMBER 22: Read II & III John, Jude

Highlights: The commandment of love; a warning against deceivers; rebuke to Diotrephes; judgment on false teachers.

Verse for Today: *"For many deceivers are entered into the world, who confess not that Jesus Christ is come in the flesh. This is a deceiver and an anti-christ"* (II John 1:7).

G od warns us to beware of false teachers who come as "angels of light"—having some Bible truth in their religion and basing their beliefs on *part* of the

Scriptures. Even Satan can quote Scripture. (See Matthew 4:5-6.)

The false teachers can be identified by their answer to the question, "Who is Jesus Christ?" They refuse to accept both His deity and humanity.

There are many religions today that are deceiving multitudes who will be eternally lost. Their false teachers are posing as "angels of light" but they are "wolves in sheep's clothing" (Matthew 7:15), motivated by Satan to deceive those who do not know the Scriptures.

We are to prayerfully question and carefully examine the doctrines of every preacher and teacher according to God's Word in order to ascertain if they are actually led by the Spirit of God. (See I John 4:1.)

"For there shall arise false Christs, and false prophets, and shall show great signs and wonders; insomuch that, if it were possible, they shall deceive the very elect" (Matthew 24:24).

Thought for Today: God's Word is able to keep you from being deceived.

Word Studies: III John 1:10 **prating against** means unjustly accusing; Jude 1:4 **turning the grace of God into lasciviousness** means using God's grace as an excuse to justify indulging in immorality; 1:19 **separate themselves** means cause divisions.

Prayer Needs: **Country:** Poland—38 million—in eastern Europe • Religious freedom • 87% Roman Catholic; 1% Eastern Orthodox; .5% Protestant.

REVELATION

This is the only book of prophecy in the New Testament. More than 300 symbolic terms describe the historic events concerning Christ and His Church. His glorious and eternal reign is the outstanding theme. All of God's promises will be fulfilled, and every judgment will come to pass.

Many Christians become so involved in trying to understand all the symbols, mysteries, and judgments that they fail to see that the book of Revelation is the unveiling of the Person, Jesus Christ, who is the center of everything. He is revealed as the *"Alpha and Omega, the first and the last"* (1:11); *"a Lamb as it had been slain"* (5:6); *"the first begotten of the dead"* (1:5; see also 1:18; 2:8).

It is the Revelation of Christ's final triumph over all evil. It gives assurance that the Lord rules and uses all the activities of men and all the calamities of nature to accomplish His purposes.

So remember the promise, *"Blessed is he that readeth, and they that hear the words of this prophecy, and keep those things which are written therein: for the time is at hand"* (1:3).

The last words of Christ in His Revelation are: *"Surely I come"*; and the response of every believer who is prepared to meet Him will be, *"Even so, come, Lord Jesus"* (22:20).

DECEMBER 23: Read Revelation 1 — 2

Highlights: Greetings to the seven churches; a vision of the Son of man; His messages to the churches.

Verses for Today: *"I know thy works and tribulation, and poverty, (but thou art rich). . . . be thou faithful unto death, and I will give thee a crown of life"* (Revelation 2:9-10).

T he Christians at Smyrna faced great tribulation—not merely small tests of faith, but intense trials.

Jesus did not tell the church at Smyrna what we would like to hear—"Be faithful and I will reward you and show the world how it pays to be a Christian." Instead, He observed their suffering and said, *"Thou art rich,"* and then went on to say, *"Be thou faithful unto death."*

The Christians who remained faithful to Christ were also told to *"fear none of those things"* which they were to suffer (Revelation 2:10). There is at least one important reason why God allows persecution—trials enable us to become more like Him—*"All that will live godly in Christ Jesus shall suffer persecution"* (II Timothy 3:12; compare I Peter 4:12-19).

The safeguard against defeat is to be strengthened in the Word daily. Then when we face tribulation because of our faith, we will be able to remain faithful.

"Yet if any man suffer as a Christian, let him not be ashamed; but let him glorify God on this behalf" (I Peter 4:16).

Thought for Today: Our present burdens may sometimes seem heavy, but the Lord enables us to bear them.

Word Studies: 1:8 **Alpha and Omega** are the first and last letters of the Greek alphabet. Christ is saying that He is everything—A to Z; 1:13 **girt** means wrapped; **paps** means chest; 2:19 **charity** means love; 2:23 **reins** means mind—the center of one's emotions.

Cross References: For **Revelation 1:7:** See Dan. 7:13. **Rev. 2:27-28:** See Psa. 2:8-9.

Prayer Needs: Country: Belgium—10 million—in northwestern Europe • Religious freedom • 88% Roman Catholic; 1% Muslim; .5% Protestant.

DECEMBER 24: Read Revelation 3 — 5

Highlights: Our Lord's messages to the churches at Sardis and Philadelphia; disapproval of the church at Laodicea; the sealed book; the Lion and the Lamb.

Verses for Today: *"And to the angel of the church in Philadelphia write; These things saith he that is holy, he that is true, he that hath the key of David, he that openeth, and no man shutteth; and shutteth, and no man openeth; I know thy works: behold, I have set before thee an open door, and no man can shut it: for thou hast a little strength, and hast kept my word, and hast not denied my name"* (Revelation 3:7-8).

T he church in Philadelphia probably seemed weak and insignificant as far as the world was concerned; their number was small and they had only *"a little strength."* But notice! That small group of Christians in Philadelphia was not dependent upon their *"little strength"*; their faith was in Christ, who had opened a door that no one—not even the synagogue of Satan—was able to close.

Our Lord still opens doors, regardless of how great opposition may be or how impossible our situation may seem. God works through those who, like the people in Philadelphia, recognize the insufficiency of their strength to accomplish His work.

Today God has opened a door to evangelize the world. It is an open door which God in His grace has entrusted to us. We must not let Him down.

" . . . *Most gladly therefore will I rather glory in my infirmities, that the power of Christ may rest upon me. Therefore I take pleasure in infirmities, in reproaches, in necessities, in persecutions, in distresses for Christ's sake: for when I am weak, then am I strong"* (II Corinthians 12:9-10).

Thought for Today: A Christian can lay up treasures in Heaven which no earthly power can destroy.

Word Study: 3:20 **sup** means provide spiritual food and fellowship.

Cross Reference: For **Revelation 4:8:** See Isa. 6:3.

Prayer Needs: Country: Guyana—766,000—on the northeastern coast of South America • The government is becoming increasingly Marxist, radical, and atheistic • 36% Hindu; 28% Protestant; 10% Roman Catholic; 9% Muslim.

DECEMBER 25: Read Revelation 6 — 8

Highlights: The seven seals; 144,000 sealed; the numberless multitude; four trumpets sounded.

Verse for Today: *"Blessing [Praise], and glory, and wisdom, and thanksgiving, and honor, and power, and might, be unto our God for ever and ever. Amen"* (Revelation 7:12).

T hese seven words of praise should cause every Christian to join with the angels of Heaven in ceaseless worship of God—now and for eternity.

Heaven echoes with "praise" and ceaseless adoration by the angels and living creatures that surround the throne of God.

"Glory" describes the splendor of His being. *"Wisdom"* reveals the supremacy of His knowledge that becomes available to us through His Word (I Corinthians 1:30; Colossians 2:3).

"Thanksgiving" is a natural expression of our gratitude to the Lord who alone is worthy of the highest *"honor"* (see I Thessalonians 5:18).

"Power" points out the supremacy of our God over all evil forces. *"Might"* emphasizes His unlimited strength to perform His promises to all who call upon Him.

The concluding *"Amen"* expresses the full support and agreement of the innumerable host of people who stand before the throne. Praise God! We, too, can be included with that innumerable host!

" . . . *Praise our God, all ye his servants, and ye that fear him, both small and great"* (Revelation 19:5).

Thought for Today: Praise to the Lord comes from a heart that is experiencing His power in daily living.

Word Studies: 6:13 **untimely** means green; unripe; 6:15 **bondman** means slave.

Prayer Needs: Country: United States—243 million—in North America • Religious freedom • 51% Protestant; 22% Roman Catholic; 17% other religions; 4% cults; 3% Jewish; 2% Eastern Orthodox; 1% Muslim.

DECEMBER 26: Read Revelation 9 — 11

Highlights: Fifth and sixth trumpets; the angel and the little scroll; the two witnesses; the seventh trumpet.

Verses for Today: *"And I will give power unto my two witnesses. . . . And when they shall have finished their testimony, the beast that ascendeth out of the bottomless pit shall make war against them, and shall overcome them, and kill them"* (Revelation 11:3,7).

T hese two witnesses will be called by the Lord to face the fierce opposition of those who hate God. Furthermore, God will empower them to fulfill their calling, and they will be invincible until they *"have finished their testimony."* Then and only then will these witnesses of Christ be martyred in the city *"where also our Lord was crucified"* (Revelation 11:8).

Their dead bodies will be left in the street. Those who will have opposed the servants of God will be so happy over the deaths of the two witnesses that they will declare a celebration and will refuse to allow them to be buried.

Satan works through other people—both believers and unbelievers—to oppose us and the work we are doing for Christ. But as *"ambassadors for Christ"* (II Corinthians 5:20), we have a commission to be His faithful witnesses.

Jesus said, *" . . . ye shall be witnesses unto me"* (Acts 1:8). We, too, are called to live—or die—as faithful witnesses for Christ. His Word must and will be preached *"in all the world for a witness unto all nations; and then shall the end come"* (Matthew 24:14).

The message of God's Divine love cannot be defeated:*"Therefore, my beloved brethren, be steadfast, unmovable, always abounding in the work of the Lord, for as much as ye know that your labor is not in vain in the Lord"* (I Corinthians 15:58).

Thought for Today: Our work for the Lord cannot end until He allows it.

Word Studies: 9:11 **Apollyon** means a destroyer, Satan; 10:6 **there should be time no longer** means there will be no more delay.

Cross Reference: For **Revelation 10:6**: See Neh. 9:6.

Prayer Needs: **Country:** Malawi—8 million—in southeastern Africa • Religious freedom • 34% Protestant; 23% Roman Catholic; 16% Muslim; 16% animist; 4% cults.

DECEMBER 27: Read Revelation 12 — 13

Highlights: The sun-clad woman; the dragon; a baby boy; the blood of the Lamb; the beasts.

Verses for Today: *"And there appeared . . . a woman clothed with the sun. . . . And there appeared another wonder . . . a great red dragon, having seven heads and ten horns, and seven crowns upon his heads. . . . And I heard a loud voice saying . . . the accuser of our brethren is cast down. . . . And they overcame him by the blood of the Lamb, and by the word of their testimony; and they loved not their lives unto the death"* (Revelation 12:1,3,10-11).

S atan is "the dragon"—the perpetual enemy of Christ. He is as determined to destroy the work of Christ now as he was to have Pharaoh kill all the Hebrew

332

male children during the time of Moses and to have Herod slaughter all the babies in Bethlehem in an effort to kill Christ.

The seven heads, ten horns, and crowns of the dragon indicate the great influence and the many forms of Satan's malicious, evil activities in working through people to oppose the work of Christ.

But these verses assure us that Christ and His followers in every generation will overcome Satan *"by the blood of the Lamb, and by the word of their testimony."* Satan and his host of demons continually seek to destroy the likeness of Christ in every Christian, but we need not fear. We, too, can overcome Satan by the blood of the Lamb and by faithfully speaking the truth of God's Word. *The Spirit in us is greater than he [Satan] that is in the world* (see I John 4:4).

We are assured of final triumph over all evil. That is the day for which we are praying!

" . . . Now is come salvation, and strength, and the kingdom of our God, and the power of his Christ: for the accuser of our brethren is cast down, which accused them before our God day and night" (Revelation 12:10).

Thought for Today: Satan thrives on the ignorance of saints concerning himself. God's Word reveals his tactics.

Word Studies: 12:1 **wonder** means sign; 12:6 **threescore** means 60; 12:17 **wroth** means furious.

Prayer Needs: Country: Nicaragua—3 million—in Central America • Limited religious freedom • 95% Roman Catholic; 5% Protestant.

DECEMBER 28: Read Revelation 14 — 16

Highlights: The Lamb; messages of the angels; harvest of the earth; preparation for the seven vials (bowls) of wrath.

Verse for Today: *"And they sing the song of Moses the servant of God, and the song of the Lamb"* (Revelation 15:3).

M oses led the Israelites victoriously through the Red Sea—free from Egyptian bondage. Pharaoh's army was destroyed in the sea as they pursued the Israelites.

Pharaoh is a type of Satan who influences unbelievers in an attempt to hinder God's followers from being faithful to Him.

Filled with praise to God, the Israelites sang the song of Moses in gratitude for their merciful deliverance from death (see Exodus 15).

Thousands of years have passed since that time, but the same song will be sung by Christians who choose to die rather than deny their faith in Christ. They will also stand beside a sea—not the Red Sea, but a *sea of glass mixed with fire*—symbolic of the fiery trials they suffered on earth (see Revelation 15:2). But the rejoicing martyrs will have no regrets over past sufferings. Instead, they will adore and praise God, saying, *Lord God Almighty, wonderful are Your works; King of nations, how just and true are Your ways!* (see 15:3).

Christians may not be delivered from death, but they will be with the Lord and see God's wisdom and loving-kindness in allowing them to become martyrs for His sake; and *"sing the song of Moses . . . and the song of the Lamb."*

The rewards God has in store for His people far exceed any sacrifice we could ever make in faithfully serving Him.

The suffering or death that we as Christians may encounter because of our faith in Christ seems insignificant compared to the glorious, eternal future our Lord has prepared for us.

The things that God has prepared for those who love Him are beyond anything we have seen or heard—even greater than anything we could ever imagine (see I Corinthians 2:9).

Thought for Today: Everything we do that has eternal value is the result of Christ, who lives within our hearts.

Word Studies: 14:5 **no guile** means no lie; 15:6 **girded** means wrapped; 15:7 **vials** means bowls.

Cross References: For **Revelation 15:4:** See Psa. 86:9; Isa. 66:23.

Prayer Needs: Country: Portugal—10 million—in western Europe • Limited religious freedom • 90% Roman Catholic; .75% Protestant.

DECEMBER 29: Read Revelation 17 — 18

Highlights: Babylon, the mother of abominations; the doom of Babylon predicted; fall of Babylon.

Verse for Today: *"And upon her forehead was a name written, MYSTERY, BABYLON THE GREAT, THE MOTHER OF HARLOTS AND ABOMINATIONS OF THE EARTH"* (Revelation 17:5).

O ld Testament Babylon, originally called Babel, was the city where human government openly defied God (Genesis 11:1-9).

Centuries later, Babylon became the most magnificent capital city of the ancient world. During that time, the Israelites were taken into captivity by the Babylonians.

Babylon is symbolic of political, social, and economic systems that attempt to deceive, hinder, and enslave Christians.

The harlot in alliance with the beast is called Babylon—a city. She pretends to represent God's Church; but she is a deceiver, attempting to corrupt Christianity. To the unbelieving world, she is a *"mystery"* because the unsaved cannot discern the difference between true Christians and the counterfeit church, with all its worldly splendor and power.

The false church is not concerned in reaching a lost world with the Word of God—the message that Christ Jesus came into this world to save sinners. It is governed by humanistic principles, social issues, and material things.

In these false churches, God's Word has been set aside, and lifeless formalism—and often good works—has taken its place.

It is by reading God's Word with a desire to know the truth that we are protected against deception.

As Christians, we must not participate in the evil things the world has to offer (see Revelation 18:4).

Thought for Today: To reach our intended destination, it is not enough merely to be traveling; we must be on the right road. It is possible to be religious, but eternally lost.

Word Studies: 17:8 **perdition** means destruction; 18:12 **thyine** means scented wood.

Cross References: For **Revelation 18:7:** See Isa. 47:7-8; Zeph. 2:15.

Prayer Needs: Country: Seychelles—68,000—a group of islands in the Indian Ocean between Madagascar and India • Religious freedom • 89% Roman Catholic; 8% Protestant.

DECEMBER 30: Read Revelation 19 — 20

Highlights: Marriage supper of the Lamb; rider on the white horse; Satan bound for a thousand years; the doom of Satan; great white throne judgment.

Verses for Today: *"And I saw an angel come down from heaven, having the key of the bottomless pit and a great chain in his hand. And he laid hold on the dragon, that old serpent, which is the Devil, and Satan, and bound him a thousand years"* (Revelation 20:1-2).

There are many things in the Word of God that we do not clearly understand. But one thing is clear: There is a devil—*"that old serpent,"* called Satan.

Satan is behind all evil, seeking to destroy the work of God and all that is good (see I Peter 5:8). He is a deceiver and will attempt to ensnare every Christian. But we have an indwelling Power that enables us to be overcomers (see I John 4:4).

Jesus defeated Satan by the very Word that we have in our hands today—the Bible. (See Matthew 4:4,7,10.)

We, too, can defeat the evil forces that surround us through the power of the Word of God.

"Wherefore take the whole armor of God, that ye may be able to withstand in the evil day. . . . And take . . . the sword of the Spirit, which is the word of God" (Ephesians 6:13,17).

Thought for Today: Satan is a deceiver and distorts the facts, but the Word of God is a revealer of truth.

Word Studies: 19:6 **omnipotent** means all-powerful; 19:13 **vesture** means robe; 20:9 **compassed** means surrounded.

Cross References: For **Revelation 19:2:** See Psa. 19:9; Deut. 32:43; II Kings 9:7. **Rev. 19:3:** See Isa. 34:10.

Prayer Needs: Country: Turkey—53 million—in Asia Minor and southeastern Europe • Deep-seated official resistance to Christian witnessing • 99+% Muslim; .5% Christian.

DECEMBER 31: Read Revelation 21 — 22

Highlights: The new Heaven and the new earth; the heavenly Jerusalem; Christ's coming.

Verse for Today: *"But the fearful, and unbelieving, and the abominable, and murderers, and whoremongers, and sorcerers, and idolaters, and all liars, shall have their part in the lake which burneth with fire and brimstone: which is the second death"* (Revelation 21:8).

Note the characteristics of the unsaved, beginning with *"the fearful"*—the coward who will not confess Christ, for fear of what others might say or do (Matthew 10:32-33; Romans 10:9).

The *"unbelieving"* may be morally good, but they are still lost sinners to be cast into *"the lake which burneth with fire."*

How solemn is the warning concerning *"all liars,"* those who are morally corrupt—including whoremongers, fornicators, and homosexuals—and those dealing in the various forms of witchcraft, spiritualism, and idolatry! All will be cast into the lake of fire. (See Deuteronomy 18:10-12; Ephesians 5:3,5; Colossians 3:5-6; Hebrews 13:4.)

As wicked as these sins are, God is willing to forgive anyone—even the vilest sinner. His love reaches out to every repentant sinner who turns from his sins to Christ.

If you haven't yet received Christ as your personal Savior, do it now. Believe that Jesus died to save you and ask God to forgive you of your sins. You will never be good enough; you must trust Him to save you.

"And every man that hath this hope in him purifieth himself, even as he is pure" (I John 3:3).

Thought for Today: For the Christian, death is but a stepping-stone to everlasting life.

Prayer Needs: Country: American Samoa—38,000—six small islands between Hawaii and New Zealand • Religious freedom • 64% Protestant; 17% Roman Catholic; 13% cults.

INTERCESSORY PRAYERS
IN THIS MONTH'S READING

Paul — for the Ephesians .... Ephesians 1:15-19; 3:14-19

Paul — righteousness for the Philippians .... Philippians 1:9-11

Paul and Timothy — for the Colossians .... Colossians 1:9-14

Epaphras — for the Colossians .... Colossians 4:12

Paul, Silas, and Timothy —
  thanksgiving, unity .... I Thessalonians 1:2-3; 3:9-13

Paul — devotion and purity .... I Thessalonians 5:23

Paul, Silas, and Timothy — worthiness .... II Thessalonians 1:11-12

Paul — comfort, direction,
  benediction .... II Thessalonians 2:16-17; 3:5,16

Paul — mercy for Onesiphorus .... II Timothy 1:16-18

Paul — for Philemon .... Philemon 1:4-7

Paul — perfecting of Christians .... Hebrews 13:20-21

When You Pray
Luke 11:1-4

Prayer is so simple that even a child can pray. However, the apostles never asked Jesus to teach them to preach or teach, but there was something about Jesus' praying that led them to say: *"Lord, teach us to pray"* [11:1].

"Our Father which art in heaven"

We cannot pray to God as *"Our Father"* without first having a right relationship with Him [see Hebrews 4:14,16; 10:19-23; 11:6]. The unconverted are not children of God, but *"children of this world"* ... *"children of wrath"* ... and *"children of disobedience"* [Luke 16:8; Ephesians 2:3; 5:6].

Jesus told Nicodemus, a "good" religious man, *"Except a man be born again, he cannot see the kingdom of God"* [John 3:3]. And He said to the very religious Pharisees: *"You are the children of your father the devil"* [see John 8:44].

Until we are actually born into the family of God, we do not possess God's nature, are not a part of God's family, and therefore do not have the rights and privileges of a child of God. How different for all who repent of their sins and receive Christ as Savior. We become His child, a joint-heir with Jesus Christ, adopted into the family of God: *"Whereby we cry, Abba, Father"* [Romans 8:15,17].The Lord Jesus Christ made this relationship possible. He was crucified -- took our place, dying on the cross for our sins.

Through Jesus we learn that God loves us, saying: *"How much more shall your Father which is in heaven give good things to them that ask him?"* [Matthew 7:11].

Whenever prayer is offered to impress or inform people, it loses its true meaning. It is also true that we cannot live in disobedience to Him and expect answers to our prayers. Only by reading all His Word do we know all our Heavenly Father's commands. *"Beloved, if our heart condemn us not, then have we confidence toward God. And whatsoever we ask, we receive of him, because we keep his commandments, and do those things that are pleasing in his sight"* [I John 3:21-22; see also 5:14].

"Hallowed be thy name"

We must recognize our Father as the Almighty Creator and Controller of all the universe. Added to that, even His name is *"hallowed"* -- sacred and holy.

The name of God should never be used in trivial conversation, nor in bitterness or anger, but only in holy, reverent prayer and praise. We dare not speak the name of the Lord in vain, saying: "Oh, Lord this" or "Oh, my God";

or refer to Him as "the man upstairs." Jesus said: *"Every idle word that men shall speak, they shall give account thereof in the day of judgment"* [Matthew 12:36]. On this point we can see why some "prayers" go unanswered.

An important principle and key to effective prayer is a desire to honor and glorify God. *"For of him, and through him, and to him, are all things: to whom be glory for ever. Amen"* [Romans 11:36]. This is illustrated in the Scriptures when Moses prayed that God would not destroy Israel in the wilderness, even though they deserved to be destroyed! Moses' chief concern was not for Israel, but for God's honor among the heathen nations. [See Exodus 32:11-13.]

Sincere Christians, recognizing their faults and failures, often do not have faith in their personal relationships with God to get answers to their prayers. They mistakenly think that God would be more impressed if some "more important" person would pray for them. But God is a loving Father who delights in the prayers of all His children. So, we should *"come boldly unto the throne of grace"* -- placing full confidence in Christ, the perfect mediator between us and God the Father [Hebrews 4:16; 13:6].

Every Christian's prayers are of great importance in accomplishing the Lord's purposes. We all have a mandate from our King: *"As my Father hath sent me, even so send I you"* [John 20:21]. He has committed His will to be worked out through His children who will exercise their responsibility to release the power of God through prayer. God has chosen to accomplish His work in and through us *"both to will and to do of his good pleasure"* [Philippians 2:13].

"Thy kingdom come"

When we pray: *"Thy kingdom come,"* we are not praying that God will get control of things. Some have imagined that the natural laws of the universe, as well as Satan, are outside of God's control. But God rules over everything, and nothing takes place outside His permissive will.

When Jesus said: *"Thy kingdom come in earth,"* He wanted us to see that we who have already received the King into our lives are a part of His kingdom now. Jesus said: *"For, behold, the kingdom of God is within you"* [Luke 17:21]. In the parable of the Sower and the Seed, Jesus referred to the good seed as children of the kingdom [Matthew 13:38-41].

If we sincerely pray: *"Thy kingdom come,"* we will take seriously our Lord's command: *"Go . . . teach all nations . . . Teaching them to observe all things"* [Matthew 28:19-20]. We must have a real concern that people in every nation of the world have God's Word and through-the-Bible teaching literature to help them *"observe all things."*

"Thy will be done, as in heaven, so in earth"

Neglect in reading the Bible is one of the major reasons that so many prayers go unanswered. It is foolish presumption to think we know His will without reading all His Word: *"He that turneth away his ear from hearing the law, even his prayer shall be an abomination"* [Proverbs 28:9].

If we sincerely desire our prayers to be answered, we will read all His Word with a desire -- without reservation -- to be all that He would have us be, as well as do all that He would have us do, then His indwelling Holy Spirit enlightens our minds and stirs our hearts to pray according to His will. He did not inspire one unimportant chapter. No guide on earth can compare to the Bible because it is our prayer manual whereby we can obtain the answers for every real need.

"Give us day by day our daily bread"

The word *"bread"* as used in this prayer [also Matthew 6:9-13] is the same word used by our Lord when he was tempted by Satan after fasting for 40 days. He quoted Old Testament Scripture, saying: *"Man shall not live by bread alone, but by every word that proceedeth out of the mouth of God"* [Matthew 4:4, see Deuteronomy 8:3]. *"Daily bread"* goes beyond asking for physical food; it is a prayer for spiritual food -- even *"the true bread of God which cometh down from heaven; and giveth life unto the world"* [see John 6:32-33]. Jesus used this word to let us know that our Father is vitally concerned about all our needs -- spiritual, material, and physical [see Philippians 4:19]. This does not mean that we can expect every material thing we want, but need to be thankful for His provisions: *"Having food and raiment let us be therewith content"* [I Timothy 6:8].

We can memorize a menu, but we will not receive nourishment until we actually eat the food. The same is true with our spiritual lives. We need spiritual bread daily to nourish the inner life -- the real person -- or we will suffer from malnutrition. Only His daily Bread can strengthen us to overcome the enemies of jealousy, greed, hate, and lust. *"Wherefore laying aside all malice, and all guile, and hypocrisies, and envies, and all evil speakings, As newborn babes, desire the sincere milk of the word, that you may grow thereby"* [I Peter 2:1-2].

"Forgive us our sins; for we also forgive every one that is indebted to us"

There are two ways that the term "forgiveness" is used in the Bible. First, all who come to Christ for salvation and trust in Him have all their sins forgiven -- *"Having forgiven you all trespasses"* [Colossians 2:13]. But we also need forgiveness from day to day to maintain fellowship with our Heavenly Father [see I John 1:8-9].

There is another essential principle of forgiveness -- *"If you forgive not men their trespasses, neither will your Father forgive your trespasses"*

[Matthew 6:15; see also 18:21-22; Mark 11:25-26].

We are to forgive others with the same spirit that we expect our Heavenly Father to forgive us. It means more than saying, "I forgive you" -- then avoiding that person. We surely would not want that separation to happen in our relationship with God.

"And lead us not into temptation; but deliver us from evil"

Temptations come to all of us. Even Jesus was tempted by Satan during His 40-day fast, but he defeated him by quoting Scripture [see Matthew 4:3-10]. Jesus is our example on how to overcome every temptation. Prayer and His Word are the two weapons of our warfare to keep temptation from deceiving and defeating us. To qualify for His provision, we must also heed His warnings: *"Abstain from all appearance of evil."* ... *"Flee also youthful lusts."* ... *"Abstain from fleshly lusts, which war against the soul"* [I Thessalonians 5:22; II Timothy 2:22; I Peter 2:11].

"Lead us not into temptation" teaches that we need His leading at all times, not merely when we are aware that we need help. And *"deliver us from evil"* reminds us of our weakness and need for daily deliverance from the evil one. Satan *"seeks whom he may devour"* [see I Peter 5:8], and he never ceases in his efforts to lead us astray.

But we can be *"more than conquerors"* [Romans 8:37] over all the enemy's temptations. For *"there hath no temptation taken you but such as is common to man: but God is faithful, who will not suffer you to be tempted above that you are able; but will ... make a way to escape, that you may be able to bear it"* [I Corinthians 10:13].

"For thine is the kingdom, and the power, and the glory, for ever. Amen" [Matthew 6:13]

We should not hesitate in retaining these words in our prayers. For these words express a truth that is in perfect harmony with all Scripture: *"Thine, O Lord, is the greatness, and the power, and the glory, and the victory, and the majesty: for all that is in the heaven and in the earth is thine; thine is the kingdom, O Lord, and thou art exalted as head above all"* [I Chronicles 29:11].

There are no accidents and no agencies outside God's control. Each of the phrases in this prayer reveals the formula Jesus gave us to make our prayers acceptable. As we pray to bring honor to His name, we are assured of His answers to all our prayers. *"For of him, and through him, and to him, are all things: to whom be glory for ever. Amen"* [Romans 11:36].

The Guide to Life

This brief summary of the value of God's Word to meet all of life's needs and prepare us for eternity should convince everyone to set aside more time for reading through all the Bible.

The Guide to eternal life

"Wherefore lay apart all filthiness and superfluity of naughtiness, and receive with meekness the engrafted word, which is able to save your souls. But be doers of the word, and not hearers only" [James 1:21-22];

"Being born again, not of corruptible seed, but of incorruptible, by the word of God, which lives and abides for ever" [I Peter 1:23];

"Of his own will begat he us with the word of truth" [James 1:18].

Prepares us to live according to His will

"All scripture is given by inspiration of God, and is profitable for doctrine, for reproof, for correction, for instruction in righteousness: That the man of God may be perfect, throughly furnished unto all good works" [II Timothy 3:16-17].

The guide to success

"This book of the law shall not depart out of your mouth; but you shall meditate therein day and night, that you may observe to do according to all that is written therein: for then you shall make your way prosperous, and then you shall have good success" [Joshua 1:8];

"Keep the charge of the Lord your God, to walk in his ways, to keep his statutes, and his commandments, and his judgments, and his testimonies, as it is written in the law of Moses, that you may prosper [do wisely]" [I Kings 2:3];

"All scripture . . . is profitable" [II Timothy 3:16].

Qualifications for Answered Prayer

"Whatsoever we ask, we receive of him, because we keep his commandments, and do those things that are pleasing in his sight" [I John 3:22];

"He that turns away his ear from hearing the law, even his prayer shall be an abomination [disgusting and revolting]" [Proverbs 28:9].

Approves

"Study to show yourself approved unto God, a workman that needs not to be ashamed, rightly dividing the word of truth" [II Timothy 2:15].

Comforts

"But the Comforter, which is the Holy Spirit . . . he shall teach you" [John 14:26];

"Wherefore comfort one another with these words" [I Thessalonians 4:18].

Produces faith

"Faith comes by hearing, and hearing by the word of God" [Romans 10:17].

Strengthens our spiritual and moral life

"Thy word have I hid in my heart, that I might not sin against you" [Psalm 119:11];

"Strengthen me according unto your word" [Psalm 119:28].

Perfects God's Love

"Whoso keeps his word, in him verily is the love of God perfected: hereby know we that we are in him" [I John 2:5];

"Seeing you have purified your souls in obeying the truth through the Spirit unto unfeigned love of the brethren" [I Peter 1:22].

Instills peace

"Great peace have they which love your law: and nothing shall offend them" [Psalm 119:165];

"These things I have spoken unto you, that in me you might have peace. In the world you shall have tribulation: but be of good cheer; I have overcome the world" [John 16:33].

Imparts joy

"These things have I spoken unto you, that my joy might remain in you, and that your joy might be full" [John 15:11];

"Your words were found, and I did eat them; and your word was unto me the joy and rejoicing of my heart" [Jeremiah 15:16].

Will judge us

"He that rejects me, and receives not my words, has one that judges him: the word that I have spoken, the same shall judge him in the last day" [John 12:48].

Sustains through suffering

"Unless your law had been my delights, I should then have perished in my affliction" [Psalm 119:92]

God's Word will prosper

"So shall my word be that goes forth out of my mouth: it shall not return unto

me void, but it shall accomplish that which I please, and it shall prosper in the thing whereto I sent it" [Isaiah 55:11];

"Blessed is the man ... [whose] delight is in the law of the Lord; and in his law does he meditate day and night ... and whatsoever he does shall prosper" [Psalm 1:1-3].

Provides Spiritual food

"Laying aside all malice, and all guile, and hypocrisies, and envies, and all evil speakings, As newborn babes, desire the sincere milk of the word, that you may grow thereby" [I Peter 2:1-2];

"Your words were found, and I did eat them; and your word was unto me the joy and rejoicing of my heart" [Jeremiah 15:16];

"It is written, Man shall not live by bread alone, but by every word that proceeds out of the mouth of God" [Matthew 4:4];

"Neither have I gone back from the commandment of his lips; I have esteemed the words of his mouth more than my necessary food" [Job 23:12].

The water to cleanse

"You are clean through the word which I have spoken unto you" [John 15:3];

"Wherewithal shall a young man cleanse his way? by taking heed thereto according to your word" [Psalm 119:9].

Imparts ability to discern

"The entrance of your words gives light; it gives understanding" [Psalm 119:130];

"The natural man receives not the things of the Spirit of God: for they are foolishness unto him: neither can he know them, because they are spiritually discerned" [I Corinthians 2:14];

"But strong meat belongs to them that are of full age, even those who by reason of use have their senses exercised to discern both good and evil" [Hebrews 5:14].

The sword to proclaim and defend

"And take the helmet of salvation, and the sword of the Spirit, which is the word of God" [Ephesians 6:17].

The fire to inspire

"Then I said, I will not make mention of him, nor speak any more in his name. But his word was in my heart as a burning fire shut up in my bones, and I was weary with forbearing, and I could not stay" [Jeremiah 20:9].

The hammer to break

"Is not my word like as a fire? says the Lord; and like a hammer that breaks the rock in pieces?" [Jeremiah 23:29]

The mirror to reveal

"For if any be a hearer of the word, and not a doer, he is like unto a man beholding his natural face in a glass: For he beholds himself . . . and straightway forgets what manner of man he was" [James 1:23].

The light to guide

"Your word is a lamp unto my feet, and a light unto my path" [Psalm 119:105].

The gold to treasure

"More to be desired are they than gold, yea, than much fine gold: sweeter also than honey and the honeycomb" [Psalm 19:10].

Indestructible

"Heaven and earth shall pass away, but my words shall not pass away" [Matthew 24:35];

"Your word is true from the beginning: and every one of your righteous judgments endure for ever" [Psalm 119:160];

"The word of the Lord endures for ever" [I Peter 1:25].

NO TIME . . .

"No time, no time to study
To meditate and pray,

And yet much time for doing
In a fleshly, worldly way;

No time for things eternal,
But much for things of earth;

The things important set aside
For things of little worth.

Some things, 'tis true, are needful,
But first things must come first;

And what displaces God's own Word
Of God it shall be cursed.."

M.E.H.